ARCHAEOLOGY OF FORMATIVE ECUADOR

This volume is dedicated to these five pioneers of
the archaeology of Formative Ecuador.

Donald W. Lathrap

Clifford Evans

Carlos Zevallos Menéndez

Emilio Estrada

Betty J. Meggers

ARCHAEOLOGY OF FORMATIVE ECUADOR

A Symposium at Dumbarton Oaks
7 and 8 October 1995

J. Scott Raymond and Richard L. Burger, *Editors*

Jeffrey Quilter
General Editor

Dumbarton Oaks Research Library and Collection
Washington, D.C.

A cataloging-in-publication record for this book is available from
the Library of Congress.
ISBN 0-88402-292-7

Contents

Contents

Preface

S tudents in introductory classes in New World Archaeology invariably learn of the precocious cultures of the Ecuadorian coast. They learn that the great coastal desert that stretches northwards from Chile and continues through Peru ends in southern Ecuador and is succeeded by beaches backed by tropical forest. They learn that along those palm-fringed shores, into Colombia, are found the earliest New World ceramic traditions. They learn of the controversy of where and how pottery came into the lives of coastal people more than 5,000 years ago. Students also commonly learn of the fascinating tradition of Valdivia clay figurines and the similarities between Valdivia ceramics and the carved gourds found at Huaca Prieta, Peru. They also may be told of the stylistic affinities between Chorrera symbolism and those of Cupisnique and Chavín as in evidence on beautifully crafted ceramic vessels.

Students are taught of how Ecuador's location in relation to northern tropical waters and the Humboldt Current, to the south, placed it in an advantageous position. The red-rimmed, spiny oyster, *Spondylus princeps*, is found in the warm ocean off the Ecuadorian coast but not in Peruvian waters. Thus, ancient Ecuadorians were in a position to provide their southern neighbors with spondylus, the very food of the gods more valued than gold. The combination of environmental factors and the ideology of preciosity associated with these molluscs led to a cultural dynamic of interchange among the peoples of much of western South and Central America that lasted for hundreds of years.

Those professors with interests in environmental issues may spend more time discussing the rich biodiversity of Ecuador. Cold and warm currents were both present off the coast and the abundance of different maritime resources was matched by environmental richness on the land. Ecuador partakes of the same vertical stacking of environmental zones, with their different resources, along the sides of the Andes as occurs in other western South American nations. With tropical forest on both sides of the mountains, early humans were able to exploit a wide variety of resources relatively quickly and without the constricting effects of coastal deserts. This distinct environmental setting may have been crucial in the rapid development of early Ecuadorian cultures. And so, the student also may learn of the early adoption of maize and other domestic plants in Ecuador.

Unfortunately, unless the professor in question is a North Andean specialist, the topics mentioned above are about all these students are likely to learn of ancient Ecuador beyond its role, at the end of prehistory, in the dynastic struggles of the last Inka emperors. Ecuador, like its northern neighbors in the Intermediate Area, lies in the shadows of the pyramids and other monumental constructions cast by the Andean civilizations to the south and Mesoamerican cultures to the north. This is unfortunate, for the prehistory of ancient Ecuador is rich and fascinating and the amount of new information we have learned regarding it, especially in the last two decades, is great.

No single symposium or volume of the length or size to which resources commonly are devoted could do justice to the amount of information now available on Ecuadorian prehistory. This volume and the symposium on which it was based were devoted, therefore, to the archaeology of Formative Ecuador in order to bring new information on one of the most important periods of the region's past to the attention of New World scholars. While the volume includes two chapters on ideology and iconography, the focus is distinctly archaeological, with an emphasis on the fundamentals of archaeological science, including settlement patterns, subsistence, health, and ceramic variability. So too, there is extensive coverage of issues of chronology.

The editors and I decided to supplement the volume with four appendices in order to provide current perspectives on all the regions of Ecuador as an aid to future research. One of the great advances in our understanding of the Formative period in the northern Andes is a growing awareness and appreciation for extensive and intensive settlement throughout the region at an early time. How people in those different regions interacted with one another and the consequences of those interactions remain to be more fully investigated. Recognition of the role of volcanism and other environmental factors are now entering into the evaluations of such dynamics to a much greater degree and with the potential for much greater chronological control than ever before. The volume then is both a summary of work to date and a chart for future action. It reflects how far we have advanced and how far we have yet to go. Moreover, it is the hope of the authors and editors that this volume will serve a useful role as a reference for the great amount of work on the Ecuadorian Formative that remains to be done.

Jeffrey Quilter
Director of Studies
Dumbarton Oaks

Introduction

J. SCOTT RAYMOND
UNIVERSITY OF CALGARY

RICHARD L. BURGER
YALE UNIVERISTY

For many decades, the archaeology of the Peruvian highlands and coastal desert has outshone Ecuadorian archaeology. The earliest evidence of complex societies, monumental architecture, and associated art and iconography in the western hemisphere came from Peru. This "nuclear area" was also credited as one of the world's hearths of plant and animal domestication and as a center of technological innovation in metallurgy, hydraulic agriculture and other fields. Understandably, most archaeologists have been attracted to Peru, with its rich, easily accessible archaeological record.

In recent decades, however, a growing number of archaeologists have turned their attention to Ecuador. Civil strife in Peru during the 1980s and 1990s by the Sendero Luminoso and the Tupac Amaru revolutionary groups reinforced this trend. The tremendous amount of new data and the new interpretations coming from the work there are casting a different light on Ecuadorian prehistory and on the role of Ecuadorian culture played in the development of Andean civilizations. It has been a multinational effort, with investigators from Ecuador, the United States, Canada, Great Britain, France, Spain, and Germany. The most exciting field research has focused on the Formative period in Ecuador, raising questions about the early social, technological, economic, religious, and political development in the Andes.

This volume derives from the Dumbarton Oaks Symposium on the Archaeology of Formative Ecuador. The stimulus for organizing this conference was the perception that while investigations on the Ecuadorian Formative had been advancing significantly, the results were known only to a small group of specialists involved directly in the research. In contrast to Peru, no general synthesis on Ecuadorian prehistory had been written since 1966, and much of the recent research has appeared only in Ecuadorian publications not easily accessible to the broader archaeological community. The organizers of the symposium saw an opportunity to remedy this situation and to synthesize the progress of the last two decades. Thus participants focused on specific aspects of the Ecuadorian Formative in order to ensure broad coverage of the subject. Among the contributors are several investigators who have been actively involved in this research for the past two decades. Their research, however, was built on a foundation of fieldwork and synthesis carried out from the 1950s to the early 1970s. Hence, this volume is dedicated to Emilio Estrada, Clifford Evans, Donald W. Lathrap, Betty J. Meggers, and Carlos Zevallos Menéndez, who were responsible for much of the earlier research that stimulated debate and piqued general interest about the Ecuadorian Formative.

Although it was Geoffrey Bushnell who first *excavated* and published Valdivia ceramics, it was Emilio Estrada who first *recognized* that the pottery style belonged to the Early Formative, and it was his joint research with Betty Meggers and Clifford Evans that first established its great antiquity (late fourth millenium B.C.). The fact that pottery in Ecuador predated the earliest known pottery in Peru by more than 1,000 years was startling news at the time and was not accepted with equanimity by most archaeologists, nor was the assertion of Meggers, Evans, and Estrada (1965) that the ceramic technology was brought to Ecuador from Japan. Meggers, Evans, and Estrada were also responsible for raising the consciousness among archaeologists about other Formative Ecuadorian cultures, notably Machalilla and Chorrera. Meggers's 1966 book *Ecuador* made Ecuadorian archaeology accessible to the general public, students, and professionals for the first time in an easily read form and called attention to the precocious development of ceramic technology.

Carlos Zevallos Menéndez carried out his research on the Formative independently from Meggers, Evans, and Estrada. He is widely known because his excavations revealed that Valdivians were farmers, cultivating maize among other crops. Donald Lathrap, who saw Valdivia as a product of demographic expansion from the neotropical floodplains, was attracted to Zevallos's agrarian view of Valdivia and rejected the Japanese origin hypothesis. The appearance of early pottery production in Ecuador and, by extension, the emergence of early agriculture excited Lathrap because of his broader research agenda on the history and potential of the tropical forest for human development, and his conviction that these environments had been underestimated and misinterpreted by prehistorians and ethnographers.

The debate among these protagonists was heated and sometimes acrimonious. It did, however, attract the interest of other archaeologists, and it stimulated a new generation of archaeologists to focus their own research on issues raised by the debate, as well as to define additional sets of research questions worthy of investigation. Now the debate is less heated. The verbal exchanges are more measured. But the issues debated are no less important and no less exciting.

Although we have chosen to honor five individuals for their pioneering research on the Ecuadorian Formative, there are several others worthy of mention as well. In the mid-1960s, Edward Lanning fielded a research project on the Santa Elena peninsula and brought a team of graduate students to the area. Among the important contributions of Lanning's project was the confirmation of the early dating of Valdivia and a refined seriation of the ceramics, which established the eight-phase chronology used by the authors of this volume. Lanning's concern with chronological precision grew out of his training in Peruvian archaeology garnered from John Rowe. His pioneering research on the Preceramic cultures of the Peruvian central coast in collaboration with Thomas Patterson likewise led him to initiate research on the Preceramic cultures of Ecuador's coast. Although Lanning never fully published his Ecuadorian investigations, his seminal research eventually resulted in the definition of the Las Vegas culture. Also, regional surveys by Lanning's team showed that Valdivia sites were to be found in the river valleys and not just along the coast and in coastal lagoons.

Olaf Holm, late director of the Museo Antropológico del Banco Central del Ecuador in Guayaquil, must also be mentioned. Holm collaborated with Zevallos in the excavation of San Pablo, an important Valdivia site. More importantly, over many years, he provided encouragement and support to several generations of archaeologists carrying out research on the Ecuadorian Formative. We invited Holm to the symposium, but unfortunately, because of failing health, he was unable to participate or submit a paper.

Another pioneer was the late Donald Collier, who in the 1940s, assisted by John Murra, carried out investigations at Cerro Narrío and other sites in the highlands that later proved to be of Formative age. In his later years, Collier, like Holm, played a critical role in supporting and encouraging the Formative research of others.

The late Presley Norton, among those encouraged by Collier, had an intense interest in Formative archaeology. With his former wife, Leonor Pérez, he amassed a significant private collection of Formative ceramics, which Collier brought to the Field Museum in Chicago for exhibition. It formed the basis for the richly illustrated and evocative book, *Ancient Ecuador: Culture, Clay and Cre-*

ativity by Lathrap, Collier, and Chandra (1975). Norton also discovered and was the first to excavate the site of Loma Alta, which demonstrated that Valdivia settlements were present deep in the coastal valleys far from the earliest known manifestations of the ceramic style along the shoreline.

Henning Bischof's excavations at the Valdivia typesite, established the existence of a pre-Valdivia, Preceramic occupation on the Ecuadorian coast. Additionally, his discovery of distinctive ceramics, San Pedro, raised the possibility that there was a ceramic industry contemporary with, or earlier than, the early Valdivia ceramics. His investigations of other Formative sites on the Ecuadorian coast are also noteworthy, as is his description and seriation of Engoroy ceramics.

The late Pedro Porras carried out excavations at several Formative sites. These included the Valdivia site of El Encanto on La Puná Island, the Machalilla site of La Ponga in the Valdivia valley, and the site of Cotocollao on the outskirts of Quito. Father Porras was an energetic fieldworker who always published the results of his excavations.

There are many individuals actively engaged in the archaeology of the Ecuadorian Formative who did not present papers at the symposium but whose research has contributed significantly to the chapters in this volume. Notable among these are Stephen Athens, Laurie Beckwith, Jonathan Damp, Evan Engwall, Terence Grieder, Jean Guffroy, Judy Kreid, Ronald Lippi, Collin McEwan, Michael Muse, Patricia Netherly, Dolores Piperno, Arthur Rostoker, John Staller, David Stemper, and Marcello Villaba. Betsy Hill, Eugene McDougal, and Allison Paulsen, although no longer actively involved in fieldwork, should also be recognized for their significant contributions, as should late archaeologists Francisco Huerta Rendon, Emil Peterson, and Julio Viteri.

Conversely, Ernesto Salazar did present a paper on Formative occupations in the Ecuadorian Oriente but chose not to submit a chapter for this volume. We are grateful to him for his contribution to the symposium and look forward to the results of his research once it is further developed.

Those who read all of the chapters herein will note that there is variation in the terminology for the subdivisions of the Formative chronology and in the correlation of the absolute and relative chronologies. Such discrepancies and disagreements reflect the uneven record of the Formative among the different regions of Ecuador and the lack of consensus on matters chronological. We chose not to enforce a single standard terminology and correlation. Instead, we have added four appendices, which summarize and evaluate the Formative period radiocarbon dates for each region of Ecuador. These supplementary contributions should clarify the regional chronologies and their relationships.

In closing, we wish to express our thanks to Elizabeth Hill Boone, the Director of Pre-Columbian Studies at Dumbarton Oaks at the time of conference planning, for encouraging us to organize a symposium on the Ecuadorian Formative and for her advice and help. We also thank Jeffrey Quilter, Director of Pre-Columbian Studies, for his contributions to making the symposium a success. We thank him as well for the help, advice, and patience he showed as we labored to turn this manuscript into published form.

A Reassessment of the Ecuadorian Formative

JORGE G. MARCOS

ESCUELA SUPERIOR POLITÉCNICA DEL LITORAL

THE CONCEPT OF FORMATIVE

It was James Ford who established the basic concept and definition of the New World Formative. He noted that the definition of the Formative by Gordon Willey and Philip Phillips (1958: 144–45) was identical to what Gordon Childe had called Early Neolithic. Ford wrote:

> "Formative" has come into use to denote what in the Old World would be called early or initial Neolithic. Neolithic would be a perfectly good name, but Americanists have been very reluctant to commit themselves to any terminology that would seem to imply Old World relationships.

> Willey and Phillips (1958, p. 144) have defined the Formative stage "by the presence of maize and/or manioc agriculture and by the successful socioeconomic integration of such agriculture into a well-established sedentary village life." This is a parallel to Childe's definition for the beginning of the Old World Neolithic as a point in which man became a food producer rather than a predator. (1969: 4–5)

But in the "nuclear area" of ancient America sedentism, agriculture, polished stone tools, and ceramics did not simultaneously occur as expected. "Both in the Mexican highlands and the Peruvian coast, agriculture was practiced many centuries before such commonly accepted Formative traits as ceramics and polished stone tools came on the scene" (Ford 1969: 5). Ford also pointed out that although small New World Formative settlements seem to have been sedentary, they might not have represented "well-established village life," meaning that "the population explosion had not started." Besides, it was assumed by Ford and others that New World early ceramics were not being made by agricultural people at all but were manufactured and spread by coastal groups who subsisted mainly on shellfish. Archaeological investigations on Ecuadorian Formative sites during the last two decades have completely upset this conceptual "apple cart," however.

Continuing his critical analysis of the Formative on a continental scale, Ford points out that the marriage of agriculture and ceramics occurred at different times in different parts of the New World. For these reasons, he suggests that the Formative be defined more loosely as

> the 3,000 years (or less in some regions), during which the elements of ceramics, ground stone tools, handmade figurines, and manioc and maize agriculture were being diffused and welded into the socioeconomic life [of peoples from Peru to the northeastern United States, and that at the onset of these changes] all these people had an Archaic economy and technology; at its end they possessed the essential elements for achieving civilization. (Ford 1969: 5)

Although we may agree with Ford's proposal in more general terms, we ought to consider that most archaeologists working in the New World during his era, had a different idea of the actual development reached by the societies classified as having an Archaic economy or possessing the essential elements for achieving civilization. Notably, our present knowledge of Formative societies is based on data unavailable to Ford in 1969.

Many archaeologists felt that the Formative concept should utilize a tripartite division, following the classic concept in Mesoamerican archaeology: Early, Middle, and Late Formative. But Ford noticed that, while this division might be useful for Mesoamerica, it would not hold true and is inappropriate for the entire American Formative. From the data available to him in the mid-1960s, he found that a more useful division would be a bipartite division based on the Colonial Formative and the Theocratic Formative.

The Colonial Formative (3000–1200 B.C.) was "a period in which ceramics were being distributed over the Americas, apparently by the establishment of sea-borne colonies. [The Theocratic Formative (1200-400 B.C.), on the other hand,] is rather sharply defined by the first appearance of mound structures and other appurtenances of organized politico-religious control" (Ford 1969: 5). The two most salient examples of the Theocratic Formative were the Olmec in Mesoamerica and Chavín in the Central Andes. Although at the time the Ecuadorian Chorrera ceramic style compared favorably with Olmec and Chavín, no contemporary evidence was available for Chorrera mounds or other types of structures that might have suggested a form of "organized politico-religious control." Therefore, the bipartite division for the Formative suggested by Ford was translated into Early Formative and Late Formative in Ecuador (Fig. 1) (Meggers 1966: 34–66; Zevallos and Holm 1960).

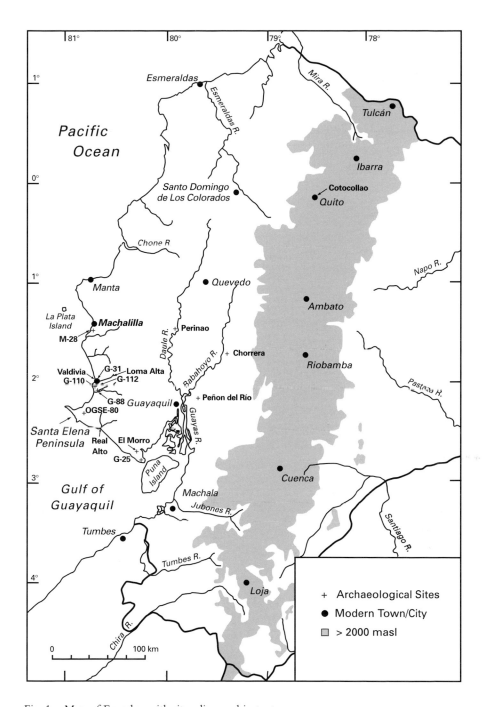

Fig. 1   Map of Ecuador with sites discussed in text.

9

DEFINITION OF THE ECUADORIAN FORMATIVE

In defining the Ecuadorian Formative, Meggers, Evans, and Estrada (1965: 9–14) considered the environmental characteristics of the southern Ecuadorian coast. They focused on the area between Machalilla and Tumbes as a well-defined environmental zone, very different from those of the Pacific littoral of Colombia and the northern coast of Ecuador, which range from yearround tropical rains in Colombia to heavy seasonal monsoons in northern Ecuador and are quite distinct from the Peruvian desert coast south of Piura. They point out that the Caribbean coast of Colombia is in certain aspects similar to the Guayas coast; not only is its vegetation xerophytic, but its shore is also in a similar stage of development, offering active mangrove flats as well as old dried-up bays. They also point out the seasonal alternation between rain and drought. Finally, they argue that Early Formative sites appear only on the Caribbean coast of Colombia and on the coast of southern Manabí and Guayas provinces in Ecuador.

Meggers et al. (1965: 107–109) suggested that although Valdivia ceramics exhibit considerable changes through time, they are sufficiently distinctive from other pottery phases in the area to build a sequence for the earliest known ceramics in the New World. To characterize the Valdivia phase without benefit of sufficient evidence, they tried to reconstruct intrasite settlement patterns, house construction, and patterns of subsistence at the type-site (G-31), Palmar Norte (G-88), and Punta Arenas (G-25). They based this reconstruction on their notion that the main subsistence resources of Valdivia were acquired by collecting in the littoral, with some marginal deer hunting. They inferred that terrestrial plant food sources also must have been exploited because of the practices among recent food-gathering groups and on comparative evidence found at sites of the Preceramic period of the adjacent dry coast of Peru.

It was Emilio Estrada (1958: 21) who wrote that Valdivia appeared to be related to other Ceramic cultures older than 1850 B.C., in Mesoamerica, the Amazon delta, and Peru. He also noted that the type-site covered an area of about two hectares on the hillside, overlooking the present village and a luxurious river valley with water, even during dry periods. He notes that a great number of agricultural products were presently grown toward the interior of the Valdivia River valley and that the valley was largely populated during the Chorrera, Guangala, and later periods. Estrada assumed that Valdivia was pre-agricultural, although a variety of data, including depictions of ceramics, supported the belief that later cultures were agricultural. Lacking a survey of the Valdivia valley but aware that Chorrera had been found by Bushnell (1951) at the Engoroy site on the Santa Elena peninsula and by Huerta Rendon (Estrada

1958) in the Guayas basin, Estrada suggested that all Early Formative sites would be close to the seashore and ancient mangrove stands, whereas Chorrera sites might be anywhere on the Ecuadorian coastal plain. He suggested that archaeologists should look for Valdivia occupations along the coast, where evidence of ancient bays existed, and he pointed to the hillsides of the coastal *cordilleras* that bordered such bays as the likely location of most Valdivia sites. He also suggested the possibility of Valdivia sites in the Guayas and the Salado River deltas, deep within the Gulf of Guayaquil. Meggers et al. (1965: 5–14) and Meggers (1966: 34–54) also concluded that Early Formative sites in Ecuador would only be along the coast.

In fact, regions between the southeastern United States and northwestern South America were thought to have the only significant Early Formative occupations. Because all early ceramic sites, especially those with fiber-temper pottery, had been found at the seashore or close to mangrove stands. But, regional surveys in the interior valleys later revealed that Early Formative period sites also began to appear inland, at great distance from the shore (Damp 1988: 45–55; Marcos 1988: 75–77; Raymond 1989, 1993).

To define the Machalilla phase of the Early Formative period, Meggers et al. (1965: 110–146) used the same methodology for defining the Valdivia phase. The sites studied were the Machalilla cemetery (M-28), La Cabuya (G-110), and Ayangue Bay (G-112). They integrated ceramic-type seriation, the evaluation of settlement patterns, the possible environmental setting at the time, as well as any evidence that suggested forms and means of production. Unfortunately, they failed to complete their monograph on Late Formative Chorrera.

It may be argued that the evidence Meggers et al. considered was not enough to determine the life styles of Formative societies in coastal Ecuador. It is important, however, to take into consideration that their effort to integrate ceramic changes with an evaluation of settlement patterns, environmental reconstruction, and the economic indicators operating on Formative societies was a contribution toward focusing research in the right direction. It is precisely these geographical and social considerations that must be reexamined today, in the light of present knowledge, in order to explain what constituted Ecuadorian Formative societies.

REASSESSING THE FORMATIVE CHRONOLOGY

To reassess the Formative chronology of Ecuador, we should review the definition of the Archaic and Formative stages according to Willey and Phillips (1958: 104–181). It is important to determine in which way the Vegas, Valdivia, and Machalilla archaeological complexes, unknown to them in 1958, conform to their definition of the Formative. To do this, it is necessary to take into consideration Meggers et al.'s interpretation of the Early Formative phases of Ecuador and contrast their notions with the original theoretical framework. Then a reassessment of new data available for Vegas, Valdivia, Machalilla, and Chorrera (in light of the original definition of Archaic and Formative periods of development) can serve as a working framework for the coastal Formative. Afterwards, a sequence for the whole Formative of Ecuador can be offered.

The Archaic

Willey and Phillips (1958: 104–139) defined the *Archaic* as "the stage of migratory hunting and gathering cultures continuing into the environmental conditions approximating those of the present." They suggested that the large Pleistocene mammals became extinct by the beginning of the altithermal period and that their disappearance produced a shift in the food procurement patterns of the lithic-stage peoples. Now humans had to depend on smaller and more varied fauna and on gathering.

According to Willey and Phillips, examples of Archaic sites in Mesoamerica, Central America, and the Andes are the Nogales phase in Tamaulipas, Cerro Mangote in Panama, and Huaca Prieta in the Chicama valley of the Peruvian north coast.

In 1964, Edward P. Lanning led a team of students from Columbia University on a survey of the Santa Elena peninsula in Ecuador. They located several Preceramic sites and test excavated one on the Vegas River. It is now the most thoroughly studied Archaic settlement of coastal Ecuador (OGSE-80), thanks to excavations by Karen Stothert (1985, 1988) and physical analyses of burials by Douglas Ubelaker (1988: 105–132), faunal remains by Thomas Chase (1988:71-178) and Elizabeth Wing (1988: 179–185), and plant remains by Dolores Piperno (1988: 203–224).

The Vegas complex conforms to Willey and Phillips's general definition for the Archaic. The faunal remains indicate a dependence on small and varied fauna, such as "lobo" (*Dusicyon sechurae*), reptiles, rodents, and the small bush deer (*Mazama* sp.), catfish, crabs, and estuarine shell species such as *Anadara tuberculosa*, among other diverse fauna. There was an apparent importance on gathering mangrove shellfish and some plant foods, and there are indications that some domesticates were grown in household gardens. According to Willey and Phillips, it was in this stage that sites began to yield large numbers of stone implements and utensils assumed to be connected with the preparation of "wild" vegetable foods. Vegas is one site where this hypothesis seems to hold true because of numerous stone implements, such as mortars and pestles—*manos* and *metates*—as well as partially polished chipped stone axes and adzes. Shell utensils, including ladles, scoops, hoes, and pickaxes, probably were employed in the collection, preparation, and consumption of wild, managed, or domesticated food. Remnants of plants, such as the bottle gourd (*Lagenaria siceraria*) and phytoliths of corn (*Zea mays*), confirm the experimental handling of plant domesticates and suggest the possibility of initial horticulture at dooryard gardens.

The initial cultivation of corn probably took place around 6000 B.C.[1] on the Santa Elena peninsula and at around 4300 B.C.[2] at Lake Ayauchi in the southeastern Oriente of Ecuador (Pearsall 1995: 127–128; Piperno 1988: 203–224, 1990, 1995). Thus, it seems that Archaic-period populations were engaged in an early but long-term process of experimentation in plant domestication.

There are estimates that place the original size of the Vegas site midden (OGSE-80) at 1.25 hectares (13,000 m²), reduced by erosion to 2,250 m², not allowing for an evaluation of possible settlement size at any given time (Stothert 1985: 614). The long period of occupation of the site also makes it difficult to estimate the size of the Archaic communities who populated OGSE-80.[3] In Stothert's words (1985: 631): "The Vegas social groups were small, but the local community probably had relations with similar peoples across a wider region. Preceramic refuse has been found near Morro and the Guayas estuary about 75 km from Site 80" (Spath 1980).

At Real Alto, halfway between Vegas and El Morro, evidence of a terminal Archaic occupation appears to underlie the Valdivia phase 1a occupation of the site. House floors at structures 58, 59, 60 and 61 found close to the intersection between trenches A and C, did not have any associated sherds, and the only material culture on them was Vegas-like, plus some sandstone spindle whorls. Two radiocarbon assays from that area, GX 5267 and ISGS 448, suggest, once calibrated, a period dating anywhere between cal 4800 and 4000 B.C. which could represent a Terminal Archaic underlying the Valdivia phase 1a occupation,[4] which dates between cal 3900 and 3500 B.C.

Henning Bischof and Julio Viteri Gamboa (1972) presented evidence for a Preceramic occupation at the type-site, underlying a deposit that contained

[1] Dates have been calibrated from original ¹⁴C assays, 7000 BP.
[2] Radiocarbon assays measure to 5300 BP.
[3] However, the Vegas occupation could have been between the 15 to 20 people allotted by MacNeish (1964) to macrobands, or around 10 to 100 people, as in Blanton's (1972) definition of *hamlet*.
[4] Damp discarded a third date, GX 5269 (6195 BP), which calibrates to 5322–4901 B.C. at 68.3%. However, its lower range may date the same occupation.

pottery sherds distinct from the Valdivia ceramics found in the overlying strata; they named this complex San Pedro. However at Real Alto, Damp (1988) suggested that the San Pedro Ceramic could be associated with Valdivia Phase 2 ceramics. This ongoing debate can only be solved by further excavations at Valdivia and Real Alto.

The Early Formative

Interdisciplinary research at Real Alto (OGSECh-12) and Loma Alta (OGSEMa-182) further shows that although the initial Valdivia nonceramic component is similar to Vegas, village size, early ceramics and an increase in identifiable agricultural remnants speak for a society with a sedentary village life. Willey and Phillips (1958: 146) define the Formative by "the presence of agriculture, or any other subsistence economy of comparable effectiveness, and by the successful integration of such an economy into well-established, sedentary village life."

Of the nearly 100 Valdivia sites known today, most are neither near the sea nor old mangrove salt flats[5]; they all present indications of a "well-established sedentary village life." The earliest Valdivia sites, like Loma Alta, Perinao, Punta Concepción and Punta Tintina, are found both inland and on the coast: Loma Alta, on the inner Valdivia River valley; Perinao, on the Daule River on upper Guayas basin; and Punta Concepción and Punta Tintina on bluffs overlooking the sea. Three basic pottery vessel shapes were used during Valdivia Phase 1 of the eight-phase Valdivia sequence proposed by Betsy Hill (1975).

> We are dealing with societies of a certain minimal complexity and stability whose population sizes and gross groupings have been made possible by specific food economies, but, since these are preponderantly agricultural, we are also dealing with a historical phenomenon— the diffusion or diffusions, of native American agriculture. Pottery-making, weaving, stone carving and a specialized ceremonial architecture are usually associated with these American Formative cultures. (Willey and Phillips 1958: 146)

Around the time of Phase 2b of the Valdivia sequence, major long-term occupation sites like Real Alto began to show a more complex intrasite settlement pattern. There is a change from the *U*-shaped elliptical village of Phases 1a and 1b, populated by 150 to 250 inhabitants, to a rectangular preurban cen-

---

[5] The most important mangrove-oriented sites in Ecuador are El Encanto (Porras 1973) and La Emerenciana (Staller n.d.). However, further research is needed to establish if their inhabitants produced or acquired the Valdivia ceramics found in these shell midden.

ter, with a central plaza exhibiting four mounds topped by politico-religious structures. The population during Phase 3 increased from about 1,250 to 1,800. Charred plant remains and phytoliths point to agricultural practices involving plants like *achira*, jack bean, runner bean, cotton, peppers, and corn (Zevallos 1971; Zevallos et al. 1977). By Valdivia Phase 3, 30 different pottery vessel shapes had been identified.

> These elements are not linked to American agriculture through any inner causality, and some of them are often found in contexts that are non-agricultural. Seldom, however, are American agricultural societies lacking in all of them. There are insufficient data as yet to establish the relative chronological appearances of these trait complexes in various New World areas, but it is unlikely that they exploded concurrently in one locality to effect a sudden and sweeping cultural revolution. Their significance is less one of origins than of function. It is a practical certainty that the origins of Formative stage cultures will be found to be extremely complex and diverse—the gradual assemblage of elements over considerable periods of time and over wide areas to produce cumulative and patterned results. (Willey and Phillips 1958: 146)

Inland earliest Valdivia. In Ecuador, it is undoubtedly easier to find archaeological sites on the coastal plain, especially in the area between the coastal cordilleras and the sea, than further inland. There, most exposed surfaces date from the tertiary, with a narrow and thin quaternary deposit at valley bottoms. South of the equator in Peru, ground cover is thinner. It allows for less difficult and more successful surveys. Whereas north of the equator and in the Guayas basin, the deep quaternary alluvium deposited by meandering tropical rivers has tended to bury most Formative sites. The thick tropical forest cover and/or plantations make archaeological survey in the area a challenging and problematic proposition (DeBoer 1996; Marcos 1988; Stahl n.d., 1995).

In 1991 and 1992,[6] coastal surveys of pipeline right-of-ways were conducted from Manta to La Libertad, from La Libertad to Pascuales north of Guayaquil, and from there to Quevedo, and to Santo Domingo de Los Colorados. Another right-of-way was established from Santo Domingo to Esmeraldas (see Fig. 1). In these surveys site distribution consistently showed that all Early and Middle Formative sites occurred along valley bottomlands, whereas Late Formative sites were also located on the bluff, up to 40 m above the valley bottom.

[6] Contract between Escuela Superior Politécnica del Litoral and Petrocomercial, 1990–1991.

Excavations at (a) Perinao in the Colimes de Balzar area of the Guayas basin, (b) at Loma Alta, 12 km deep in the Valdivia river drainage, and (c) Real Alto 3.5 km from the seashore but overlooking the floodplain of the Río Verde demonstrate the inland orientation of the earliest Valdivia people (Lathrap, Marcos, and Zeidler 1977; Norton 1982; Raymond, Marcos, and Lathrap 1980). It is important to point out that coastal groups that subsisted mainly on shellfish occupied none of these sites. Furthermore, the on-site changes in settlement pattern displayed throughout Real Alto's history, clearly speak for a well-established village life, the development of urban lifestyles, and the rise of civilization at the end of the Early Formative period (Marcos 1993; Zeidler 1991).

The rise of civilization during the Early Formative of Ecuador was also characterized by the establishment of trade networks. Kleppinger, Kuhn, and Thomas (1977) have shown that at Real Alto, coca chewing was a ritual activity since Valdivia Phase 3. Spinning and weaving were an established practice by Valdivia Phase 6 (Marcos 1973), and the presence of *murices* associated with spindle whorls suggests the use of dyes since that period (Marcos 1995). *Mogote* incised and punctate sherds, associated with Valdivia Phase 7 ceramics and obsidian blades in the northeast sector of Real Alto, have been shown to be quite similar in paste and decoration to Early Cotocollao incised and punctate ceramics in Quito. Furthermore, the associated obsidian blades have been determined to come from the source at Quiscatola in the Valley of Quito (Marcos, Álvarez, and Bigazzi 1988). To these and other trade items, we must add the Valdivia occupation of La Plata Island as evidence for open-sea navigation at least from Valdivia Phase 3 (Marcos and Norton 1981, 1984).

Early Formative settlement patterns. In Ecuador, Early Formative settlers maintained a strategy common to early farming societies the world over: occupation of the best lands for agriculture. These are the rich alluvial deposits of river floodplains. Many of the regional surveys in coastal Ecuador show that sites are found in a dendritic pattern of settlement, along riverine systems and their floodplains. Depending on the width of the valley and the floodplain, Formative farmers settled on the bottomlands, the surrounding bluffs, and, in a few cases, hillsides. Formative settlements varied in size. While some size differences appear to have temporal implications, a good number seemed to correspond to a hierarchical scheme (Alvarez, Tobar, and Marcos 1992; Raymond 1993; Schwarz and Raymond 1996; Tobar n.d.; Zeidler 1986).

It was evident that during the first period of occupation, Real Alto was a small, circular to elliptical hamlet, approximately 150 m in diameter. This intrasite settlement pattern lasted approximately 1,400 years, covering Valdivia Phases 1a to 2a (cal 4400–3000 B.C.). Its 50 to 60 inhabitants apparently lived in 12 to 15 small, single-family huts. These were elliptical and were constructed possibly of bent poles and thatched with palm fronds or straw. The archaeological material culture and the biological data from this period suggest an endogamic community with a restricted mode of exchange in the area. To complete the similarity with ethnographic circular villages, the men might have slept in a larger (8 x 6 m) central, and more substantial wooden pole structure, with daubed walls and a thatched roof (Damp 1988; Marcos 1993: 22).

During the second period, which lasted some 600 years (cal 3000–2400 B.C.), there were important changes in the intrasite settlement patterns and community development. During Valdivia Phases 2b and 3, a major change took place in Real Alto. The circular hamlet gave way to a rectangular settlement with a central plaza. It covered approximately 16 hectares, with 90 to 100 residential structures, for approximately 600 to 1,100 inhabitants. In the plaza, four mounds topped by public buildings, looked down on the open space. The two largest mounds, A (or fiesta-house mound) and B (or charnel house mound), faced each other in the northern third of the open plaza. Mounds A and B and the space between them formed the ceremonial precinct. The two smaller mounds, C on the northeast sector of the plaza, and D on the southwestern side, appear to have been designated for meetings and ceremonies by the initiated few in each of the village halves. Real Alto can be classified as a *regional center* in Parsons–Blanton terminology (Blanton 1972).[7]

The size and substance of the village houses also changed (Álvarez 1989) from the smaller single-family huts described above to elliptical solid structures, with upright post walls, covered with daub, and topped by large thatched roofs. These structures were between 10 m and 12 m on the longer axis and between 7 m and 9 m on the shorter one, and were apparently occupied by extended families (Zeidler n.d.: 73–99). The substantial increment in population and other biological evidence suggest an increase in social and economic interaction at the regional level.

The third period corresponded to the 600 years that elapsed between Valdivia Phases 4 and 7 (2400–1800 B.C.) when part of the on-site population moved from a central location at Real Alto to 5 satellite *hamlets*, or "daughter" communities, along the Río Verde and Río Real. Each of these communities con-

---

[7] According to its size, Real Alto is between large nucleated village and secondary regional center in Parsons–Blanton site typologies. If Damp's hypothesis that the Centinela site is Real Alto's mother community is correct (Damp 1988: 48), then Centinela (OGSEh-019) could be classified as a primary regional center.

sisted of five to ten houses with 40 to 100 inhabitants. At Real Alto, as in the daughter communities, house size remained roughly the same as in the previous period. In the north of Real Alto, no houses were built, but a large number of bell-shaped storage pits were constructed. The number of residential structures for this period is estimated to number between 60 to 80, with some 500 to 1,000 inhabitants.

Real Alto at this time exhibited an intrasite and a regional settlement pattern that could classify it as a *large dispersed village*, or as a *regional center* in Parsons–Blanton site typology. Craft specialization by *barrios* and evidence of elite control of production could explain the building of a series of bell-shaped storage pits in the north segment and the alienation of polished stone adzes and axes within civic–ceremonial structures topping mound B during this period.

During Valdivia Phases 8a and 8b (1800–1450 B.C.) major regional centers appeared in deep inland valleys, including San Isidro, in the province of Manabí and San Lorenzo del Mate, in Guayas province, and near the coast at La Emerenciana, in El Oro (Staller n.d.). During this period, the great changes that led to the consolidation of the Formative process were crystallized.

The Real Alto settlement pattern and sociopolitical organization suggested by Zeidler (1991, n.d.: 255–258) conforms nicely with the changes in forms of production (Marcos 1993: 19–26) and with proposed stages of Valdivia colonization and site evolution for the Azucar/Zapotal/Río Verde drainage, referred to as the Chanduy valley (Damp 1988: 50–52).

The original notion that all Early Formative sites were small hamlets close to the sea or ancient mangrove stands does not hold up in the face of the information presented above. Consequently, a new site-typology and settlement pattern definition are needed to characterize Formative societies.

The Middle Formative

Many authors have begun to use a tripartite chronological division (Beckwith n.d.: 469; Lippi n.d.a; Marcos 1986; Schwarz and Raymond 1996; Zeidler 1994: 205) of the Ecuadorian Formative, adding a Middle Formative period to the former two-period scheme referred to above. Each period, of course, must be defined broadly if it is to be used meaningfully to align Formative societies chronologically outside the original southwestern Ecuadorian chronological scheme. The broad dispersal of the Machalilla style in coastal Ecuador and its patent influence on ceramic styles of other areas of Ecuador may justify the use of the term *Machalilla* to identify a Middle Formative period ranging between cal 1400 and 850 B.C.

Lippi (n.d.a) has argued convincingly that the Machalilla style developed out of the Valdivia style. Nowhere is this more explicit than in the Valdivia 8b ceramics of El Oro province (see below), where a Valdivia–Machalilla transitional style can be identified (Staller n.d.).

Although archaeological surveys in several areas of Ecuador have provided information about different forms of regional settlement pattern during the Formative and later periods, little information on intrasite settlement exists for sites of the Middle and Late Formative. At the Middle Formative site of Cotocollao, for instance, where excavations were conducted over a long period of time, salvage archaeology constraints did not permit a very full exposure of the lacustrine Formative village mode of settlement. Post molds in some excavation units could be interpreted as evidence of a combined part palafittic/ part on-shore settlement typical of lacustrine Neolithic villages (see Villalba 1988: 63, figs. 34, 35).

The earliest macrofossil evidence for corn dates to the Middle Formative (Lippi, Bird, and Stemper 1984). Earlier evidence, during the Preceramic at Las Vegas (Piperno 1988) and Valdivia (Pearsall 1988), consists of microfossil remains identified through phytolith analysis. The initial presence of charred corn in Middle Formative sites and in larger quantities during the Late Formative (Pearsall 1980) reflects, most likely, the success and expansion of intensive agriculture. Possibly by then, most corn was dried before processing, whereas during the Preceramic and the Early Formative, the smaller quantities grown may have been consumed green.

The Late Formative

G.H.S. Bushnell (1951) excavated for the first time what we know today as Late Formative ceramics in the Santa Elena peninsula. The single-component site was located on the Engoroy hill in La Libertad. Bushnell also defined Guangala and Manteño cultures, but because he did not find these components stratified, he placed Engoroy late in the sequence between Guangala and Manteño. It was not until Estrada (1958) published similar material from an excavation conducted by Evans and Meggers (1957, 1982 [1971]; Evans, 1957) at the Hacienda Chorrera that the proper identification of Engoroy–Chorrera as a Late Formative phase was recognized.

Today, we must add to the study of Engoroy and Chorrera sites, and/or ceramics, the work of Aleto (n.d.), Beckwith (n.d.: 470), Bischof (1982 [1971]), Paulsen and McDougle (n.d.), Simmons (1970), and Zedeño (n.d.). However, as Beckwith points out, "Perhaps one of the most pressing needs in research on the ceramics of the Late Formative period of southwestern Ecuador is the publication of ceramic material from the Guayas basin, in particular the material from the type site of La Chorrera."

Chorrera and Peñon del Río, so far, provide the only information available on the Formative occupation of the lower Guayas basin. The excavations conducted at Hacienda Perinao and La Cadena–Quevedo (under the auspices of the Liechtenstein Foundation) give a glimpse of what appears to have been a continuous Formative occupation in the upper Guayas basin. The available evidence shows that it may have begun in the earlier Valdivia phases (Porras 1983; Raymond et al. 1980; Reindel 1995). A Valdivia 2a occupation at Hacienda Perinao was covered by an overburden of 8.5 m of stratified alluvium and human occupation deposits, which make it a site worth excavating in detail. At La Cadena, Machalilla and Chorrera deposits overlay Valdivia 6,7, and 8 occupation layers, and all were surmounted by mounds constructed during the Regional Developmental and Integration periods.

FORMATIVE CERAMICS

Originally, Early Formative ceramics from Ecuador were viewed as exotic, conforming to the notion of a Colonial Formative proposed by Ford (1969: 5). Hypotheses for the *Jomon* (Japanese) origin of Valdivia ceramics and for a possible Mexican origin of the Machalilla style (although the Mexican affiliation of Machalilla ceramics presents problems) were presented by Meggers et al.:

> Reconstruction of the origin, interrelations and ramifications of the Valdivia and Machalilla Phases has moved us beyond the boundaries of available evidence into the realm of hypothesis. Although we hope that some of the interpretations will be confirmed by future work, others will undoubtedly be altered. If calling attention to the potential importance of Colombia and Central America in the origin and dissemination of certain South American cultural complexes serves to stimulate fieldwork in these areas, our efforts will have been well spent regardless of whether or not the hypotheses are upheld. (1965: 157–158)

Donald Lathrap, on the other hand, proposed a different source of origin for the Early Formative ceramics of Ecuador. He stated that Puerto Hormiga and Valdivia ceramics showed substantial differences so that neither the earliest Colombian nor the earliest Ecuadorian pottery could be antecedents of the other. He suggested that an earlier focus of indigenous ceramic development should lie somewhere between Manaus and the mouth of the Amazon (Lathrap 1970). Roosevelt's (1995) discovery of pottery dating, possibly, to the sixth millennium B.C. at the site of Taperinha near Santarem seems to support Lathrap's hypothesis. Stylistic comparisons between Early Formative ceramics, however, should be treated with caution, for their similarity might come from the skeuomorph representation of antecedent containers.

Most Early Valdivia vessels seem to be skeuomorphs of gourd, basket, and possibly rawhide containers. These gave an initial imprint to the Valdivia style, which developed locally into a more complex style in later phases. As noted above, Lippi (n.d.b) argued that the Machalilla pottery style developed from Valdivia, and the Valdivia–Machalilla transitional ceramic complex found by Staller around La Emerenciana clinched the argument. The development of the Engoroy and Chorrera ceramics from Machalilla has been well argued by Beckwith (n.d.: 469).

Ceramic analysis of Real Alto and San Lorenzo del Mate potsherds have shown that since Phase 1b, Valdivia potters were selecting clays and manipulating ceramic fabric according to their intended use (Álvarez 1995a,b, 1996; Álvarez, Marcos, and Spinolo 1995). In recent analyses Valdivia 1b sherds were segregated into three classes according to their function, judging from context: vessel shape, surface treatment, and surface finish parameters. For the manufacture of cooking pots and for liquid storage vessels, there was a selection for the feldspars-rich clays that occur naturally in the area. These clays are found in pockets on some of the bluffs in the valleys of the Santa Elena peninsula. Fired between 800 and 900 °C, they produce strong, durable utilitarian wares. However, the fabric used in cooking-pot manufacture contained a larger quantity of quartz than did the fabrics of liquid containers, quartz being predominant over feldspars. This uncommon combination does not seem to occur naturally in the peninsula, or it is rare, suggesting that the fabric was manipulated by the addition of quartz-rich sands commonly found in river bottoms. Natural or not, in selecting for a quartz-rich fabric the thermal shock resistance of cooking vessels was greatly increased (Bronitsky and Hamer 1986; Rice 1987; cf. Rye 1981). The fabric used for serving and ceremonial wares was the more common naturally decanted clay found throughout the area. These clays contained only small and fine-fraction clay minerals with a lesser proportion of feldspars and quartz. These vessels were fired at low temperatures never reaching above 650 °C.

In terminal Valdivia phases and later in the Formative sequence, these differences became more clear-cut. Valdivia 8 potters never fired the fancy "baroque" ceremonial and fiesta wares beyond 600 °C. Cooking pots contained larger proportions of quartz to feldspars than those found in the paste of vessels designated to contain liquids.

Further refinements in the ceramic technology occurred in the Middle and

Late Formative, particularly in the manufacture of fancy prestige wares. Vessel walls became notably thinner. The use of burnishing to achieve smooth shiny surfaces was refined and became more common. Line painting using slip pigments was added to the repertoire of decorative techniques. Iridescent painting, first developed during the Early Formative, was refined during the Middle Formative and became a distinctive decorative characteristic of fancy pottery during the Late Formative.

CONCLUSIONS

From this synthesis of the Formative, it becomes clear that our knowledge of the social history and lifestyles of Valdivia culture has been greatly advanced through interdisciplinary research at Loma Alta, Real Alto, and environs. Investigations at San Isidro (Manabí), San Lorenzo del Mate and Anllulla (Guayas), La Emerenciana (El Oro) (Jadán 1986; Marcos and Alvarez 1989; Staller 1994; Zeidler and Pearsall 1994) have likewise enriched our understanding of the terminal Valdivia phase and of the Valdivia–Machalilla transition. Archaeological research in the Guayas basin[8] has not only shown the widespread distribution of Valdivia 8, but the depth of the Valdivia historical process in the area (Raymond et al. 1980). The appearance of a few Valdivia 8 sherds at R-53 on the lower drainage of Estero de Mafa, up river from Borbón, in Esmeraldas (DeBoer 1996: 68–70) demonstrates the need of further Formative research there, as well as in the Guayas basin.

Our increasing knowledge of Valdivia customs shows that newer and more profound investigations are still required to reconstruct the Early Formative historical process fully. There are more than 100 Valdivia sites known from coastal Ecuador that should be excavated, not to mention the need for detailed studies of other Ecuadorian Formative societies.

The knowledge of Machalilla, its chronological position, its ceramic style, and its distribution has been augmented by Bischof (1975b), Lippi (n.d.b), Paulsen and McDougle (n.d.), and Zeidler (1986). Museum collections without exact provenance give a wider view of the Machalilla style than what is evident from archaeological research. A good example of this can be seen in an exhibit catalogue of the Field Museum of Natural History on ancient Ecuador (Lathrap et al. 1975: 32–34, 41, 82–86).

This tendency is exacerbated during the Late Formative period. Recent archaeological research (Bischof 1975b; Marcos 1982; Evans and Meggers, 1982;

---

[8] See Peñón del Río (Marcos 1987), Milagro (Gonzalez de Merino n.d.), and La Cadena-Quevedo (Reindel 1995).

López y Sebastián and Caillavet 1979; Zedeño, n.d.; Zevallos 1965/66) has provided excellent information on Chorrera ceramics and the Engoroy and Tachina variants. However, materials from good archaeological contexts do not compare with the great number of Late Formative vessel and figurine shapes and finishes found in Ecuadorian national museums and museums abroad (Cummins this volume).

This problem is the result of misconceptions and flawed policies in Ecuadorian archaeology:

1. A generalized concept that "national heritage" (*patrimonio nacional*) is represented by portable art and monuments, rather than the historical data encapsulated in archaeological activity areas and contexts within archaeological sites.

2. Few archaeologists, on the other hand, have directed their interests to the excavation of cemetery and ceremonial sites, instead focusing on archaeological middens. Although it is important to construct local chronologies and, through interdisciplinary research, discover forms of production and reconstruct lifestyles, it is wrong to leave the excavation of ceremonial paraphernalia and grave goods to those who supply collectors and museums. This neglects an important aspect of archaeological material culture and leaves it out of contextual archaeological analysis.

3. This has been exacerbated by a national museum policy that has directed most funds to the acquisition of archaeological material culture rather than research. This policy, directed supposedly to maintaining Ecuadorian national heritage at home, has resulted in the support of illegal excavations and destruction of archaeological sites.

Here we can only mention these problems to explain some causes of our uneven knowledge of the Ecuadorian Formative, especially for the long period during which research on the Formative focused mostly on the coast. A welcome initiative by the Central Bank Archaeological Museum in Cotocollao has served to reconstruct the early social history of the Quito valley (Villalba 1988). I applaud that and other indications that state-supported field research in Ecuador is heading in a new direction.

Jorge G. Marcos

Acknowledgments   My thanks go to Richard Burger and J. Scott Raymond for their advice and suggestions in editing this essay. However, as to the concepts and errors expressed herein, they are completely mine.

BIBLIOGRAPHY

ALETO, THOMA
    n.d.   A View of the Ecuadorian Late Formative and Regional Developmental Periods from the Gulf of Guayaquil. Paper presented at the 52nd Annual Meeting of the Society for American Archaeology, Toronto, 1987.

ÁLVAREZ, AURELIO
    1995a   Áreas fuente. In *Primer encuentro de investigadores de la costa ecuatoriana en Europa* (A. Álvarez, S. G. Álvarez, C. Fauría, and J. G. Marcos, eds.): 299–336. Ediciones Abya-Yala, Quito.
    1995b   La cerámica arqueológica del Ecuador. *In Cultura y medio ambiente en el área andina septentrional* (Mercedes Guinea Bueno, Jean-François Bouchard, and Jorge G. Marcos, eds.): 434–481. Ediciones Abya-Yala, Quito.
    1996   Materiales cerámicos: Producción, dispersión y clasificación. Un ejemplo: La cerámica precolombina de Real Alto (Ecuador). In *Ciencia y tecnología de recursos naturales y medio ambiente* (P. Lapuente Ma., ed.): 191–210. Excelentísimo Ayuntamiento de Castellón, Actividades Culturales 1996. Castellón, Spain.

ALVAREZ AURELIO, JORGE G. MARCOS, AND GIORGIO SPINOLO
    1995   The Early Formative Pottery from the Santa Elena Peninsula in Southwest Ecuador. *Studies on Ancient Ceramics: Proceedings of the European Meeting on Ancient Ceramics* (M. Vendrell-Saz, T. Pradell, J. Molera, and M. García, eds.): 99–107. Catalunya, Department of Culture, Barcelona.

ALVAREZ, RITA, OSWALDO TOBAR, AND JORGE G. MARCOS
    1992   Informe del estudio del impacto ambiental, mitigación del impacto a los testimonios arqueológicos, históricos, y socioculturales en el trazado de los oleoductos Manta-La Libertad-Pascuales (Guayaquil)—Santo Domingo de Los Colorados. Convenio Petrocomercial 1991. Escuela Superior Politécnica del Litoral, Guayaquil.

ALVAREZ, SILVIA G.
    1989   *Tecnología prehispanica, naturaleza y organización cooperativa en la cuenca de Guayas.* Coleción Peñon del Río, Centro de Estudios Arqueológicos y Antropólogicos/ Escuela Superior Politécnica del Litoral, Guayaquil.

BECKWITH, LAURIE A.
    n.d.   Late Formative Period Ceramics from Southwestern Ecuador. Ph.D. dissertation, Department of Archaeology, University of Calgary, Calgary, Alberta, 1997.

BISCHOF, HENNING
    1975a   La Fase Engoroy—Períodos, cronología y relaciones. In *Estudios sobre la arqueología del Ecuador* (U. Oberem, ed.): 11–37. Bonner Amerikanistesche Studien, Bonn.
    1975b   El Machalilla Temprano y algunos sitios cercanos a Valdivia (Ecuador). In *Estudios sobre la arqueología del Ecuador* (U. Oberem, ed.): 39–67. Bonner Amerikanistische Studien, Bonn.

Jorge G. Marcos

1982   La Fase Engoroy—Períodos, cronología, y relaciones. In *Primer Simposio de Correlaciones Antropológicas Andino-Mesoamericano,* 25–31 de julio 1971 Salinas, Ecuador, (Jorge G. Marcos and Presley Norton, eds.): 135–176. Escuela Superior Politécnica del Litoral, Guayaquil.

BISCHOF, HENNING, AND JULIO VITERI GAMBOA
1972   Pre-Valdivia Occupation on the Southwest Coast of Ecuador. *American Antiquity* 37(4): 548–551.

BLANTON, RICHARD E.
1972   *Prehispanic Settlement Patterns of the Ixtapalapa Peninsula Region, Mexico.* Occasional Papers in Anthropology 6. Pennsylvania State University, University Park.

BRONITSKY, GORDON, AND ROBERT HAMER
1986   Experiments in Ceramic Technology: The Effects of Various Tempering Materials on Impact and Thermal-Shock Resistance. *American Antiquity* 1: 89–101.

BUSHNELL, GEOFFREY H. S.
1951   *The Archaeology of the Santa Elena Peninsula in South-west Ecuador.* Cambridge University Press, Cambridge.

CHASE, THOMAS (IN COLLABORATION WITH E. WING)
1988   Restos faúnicos. In *La prehistoria temprana de la Península de Santa Elena, Ecuador: Cultura Las Vegas.* Miscelanea Antropológica Ecuatoriana, Serie Monográfica 10 (K. E. Stothert, ed.): 171–178. Banco Central del Ecuador, Guayaquil.

DAMP, JONATHAN E.
1988   *La primera ocupación Valdivia de Real Alto: Patrones económicos, arquitectónicos e ideológicos.* Biblioteca Ecuatoriana de Arqueología 3. Escuela Superior Politécnica del Litoral/Corporación Editora Nacional, Quito.

DeBOER, WARREN E.
1996   *Traces behind the Esmeraldas Shore, Prehistory of the Santiago–Cayapas Region, Ecuador.* University of Alabama Press, Tuscaloosa.

ESTRADA, EMILIO
1958   *Las Culturas pre-clásicas, formativas o arcaicas del Ecuador.* Museo Victor Emilio Estrada, Guayaquil.

EVANS, CLIFFORD
1957   Los periodos Tejar y Chorrera de la provincia del Guayas. *Cuadernos de historia y arqueología, Guayaquil, Ecuador* 7(21): 243–245. Casa de la Cultura Ecuatoriana, Nucleo del Guayas.

EVANS, CLIFFORD, AND BETTY J. MEGGERS
1957   Formative Period Cultures in the Guayas Basin, Coastal Ecuador. *American Antiquity* 22: 235–247.
1966   Mesoamerica and Ecuador. In *Handbook of Middle American Indians* (Robert Wauchope, Gordon F. Ekholm, and Gordon R. Willey, eds.), vol. 4: 243–264. University of Texas Press, Austin.
1982   Técnicas decorativas diagnósticas y variantes regionales Chorrera: An análisis preliminar. In *Primer Simposio de Correlaciones Antropológicas Andino-Mesoamericano,* 25–31 de julio, Salinas, Ecuador (J. G. Marcos and P. Norton, eds.): 121–134. Escuela Superior Politécnica del Litoral, Guayaquil.

FORD, JAMES A.
  1969   *A Comparison of Formative Cultures in the Americas: Diffusion or the Psychic Unity of Man?* Smithsonian Contributions to Anthropology 11, Washington, D.C.

GONZÁLEZ DE MERINO, JUANA
  n.d.   Botellas Valdivia fálicas en Milagro, Ecuador. Manuscript in possession of the author, 1984.

HILL, BETSY
  1975   A New Chronology of the Valdivia Ceramic Complex from the Coastal Zone of Guayas Province, Ecuador. *Ñawpa Pacha* 10/12: 1–39.

JADÁN, MARY
  n.d.   La cerámica del Complejo Piquigua (Fase 8) de la cultura Valdivia en San Isidro, norte de Manabí: Un análisis modal. Tésis licenciatura, Centro de Estudios Arqueológicos y Antropológicos, Escuela Superior Politécnica del Litoral, Guayaquil, 1986.

KLEPPINGER, LINDA, J. K. KUHN, AND J. THOMAS JR.
  1977   Prehistoric Dental Calculus: Biological Evidence for Coca in Early Coastal Ecuador. *Nature* 260: 507.

LATHRAP, DONALD W.
  1970   *The Upper Amazon.* Praeger, New York.

LATHRAP, DONALD W., DONALD COLLIER, AND HELEN CHANDRA
  1975   *Ancient Ecuador: Culture, Clay and Creativity, 3000–300 B.C.* Field Museum of Natural History, Chicago.

LATHRAP, DONALD W., JORGE G. MARCOS, JAMES A. ZEIDLER
  1977   Real Alto, an Ancient Ceremonial Center. *Archaeology* 30(1): 2–13.

LIPPI, RONALD D.
  n.d.a   La Ponga and the Machalilla Phase of Coastal Ecuador. Unpublished Ph.D. dissertation, Department of Anthropology, University of Wisconsin–Madison, 1983.
  n.d.b   Report on Excavations at Río Perdido (OGCh-20), Guayas, Ecuador, with Emphasis on the Ceramic Chronology. Master's thesis, Department of Anthropology, University of Wisconsin–Madison, 1980.

LIPPI, RONALD D., ROBERT M. BIRD, AND DAVID M. STEMPER
  1984   Maize Recovered at La Ponga, an Early Ecuadorian Site. *American Antiquity* 49: 118–124.

LÓPEZ Y SEBASTIÁN, LORENZO E., AND CHANTAL CAILLAVET
  1979   La Fase Tachina en el contexto cultural del Horizonte Chorrera. *Actes du XLII Congres International des Américanistes (1976):* IX-A: 199–215. Société des Américanistes, Paris.

MACNEISH, RICHARD S.
  1964   Ancient Mesoamerican Civilization. *Science* 143: 531–537.

MARCOS, JORGE G.
  1973   Tejidos hechos en telar en un contexto Valdivia Tardio. *Cuadernos de historia y arqueología* 40: 163–183.
  1982   Los Morros. In *Primer Simposio de Correlaciones Antropológicas Andino-*

Mesoamericano, 25–31 de julio, Salinas, Ecuador (J. G. Marcos and P. Norton, eds.): 177–210. Escuela Superior Politécnica de Litoral, Guayaquil.

1986   Breve Prehistoria del Ecuador. In *Arqueología de la costa ecuatoriana: Nuevos enfoques* (J. G. Marcos, ed.). Biblioteca Ecuatoriana de Arqueología 1: 25–50. Escuela Superior Politécnica del Litoral, Guayaquil.

1987   Los campos elevados de la Cuenca del Guayas, Ecuador: El proyecto Peñon del Río. In *Pre-Hispanic Agricultural Fields in the Andean Region* (W. Denevan, K. Mathewson, and G. Knapp, eds.): 217–224. BAR International Series 359 (II). British Archaeological Reports, Oxford.

1988   *Real Alto: La historia de un centro ceremonial Valdivia*. Biblioteca Ecuatoriana de Arqueología 4 y 5. Escuela Superior Politécnica del Litoral/Corporación Editora Nacional, Guayaquil.

1993   La arqueología como ciencia histórica y la problemática de la arqueología ecuatorial: Los agro-alfareros Valdivia de Real Alto, en el antiguo Ecuador, un modelo para la "revolución neolítica en el Nuevo Mundo." *Gaceta Arqueológica Andina* 7: 23.

1995   El mullo y el pututo: La articulación de la ideología y el trafico a larga distancia en el formación del estado Huancavilca. In *Primer encuentro de investigadores de la costa ecuatoriana en Europa* (A. Álvarez, S. G. Álvarez, C. Fauría, and J. G. Marcos, eds.): 97–142. Ediciones Abya-Yala, Quito.

MARCOS, JORGE G., AURELIO ÁLVAREZ, AND GIULIO BIGAZZI
1988   El tráfico a distancia temprano entre la hoya de Quito y la península de Santa Elena: Las evidencias de Real Alto. Simposio ARQ-13. In *Intercambio y comercio en los Andes: La interacción tierras altas-tierras bajas desde una perspectiva arqueológica y etnohistórica* (Fernando Cardenas-Arroyo, Tamara Bray, and Carl K. Langebaek, eds.). Cuarenta y noveno Congreso Internacional de Americanistas, Bogotá.

MARCOS, JORGE, AND SILVIA G. ÁLVAREZ
1989   Proyecto San Lorenzo del Mate. Convenio del Banco Central con Fundación Pedro Vicente Maldonado, Informe final. Fundación Pedro Vicente Maldonado, Guayaquil.

MARCOS, JORGE G., AND ADAM MICHZYNSKI
1996   Good Dates and Bad Dates in Ecuador; Radiocarbon Samples and Archaeological Excavation: A Commentary Based on the "Valdivia Absolute Chronology." Proceedings of the Third Latin American Congress of the University of Varsovia, Varsovia and Biskupin-Wenecja. Andean Archaeological Mission of the Institute of Archaeology, Warsaw University.

MARCOS, JORGE G., AND PRESLEY NORTON
1981   Interpretación sobre la arqueología de la Isla de La Plata. *Miscelanea Antropológica Ecuatoriana* 1: 136–154.

MEGGERS, BETTY J.
1966   *Ecuador*. Praeger, New York.

MEGGERS, BETTY J., CLIFFORD EVANS, AND EMILIO ESTRADA
1965   *The Early Formative Period of Coastal Ecuador: The Valdivia and Machalilla Phases*. Smithsonian Contributions to Anthropology 1. Smithsonian Institution Press, Washington, D.C.

NORTON, PRESLEY
    1982   Preliminary Observations on Loma Alta, an Early Valdivia Midden in Guayas Province, Ecuador. In *Primer Simposio de Correlaciones Antropológicas Andino-Mesoamericano*, 25–31 de julio, Salinas, Ecuador (J. G. Marcos and P. Norton, eds.): 101–120. Escuela Superior Politécnica del Litoral, Guayaquil.

PARSONS, JAMES J., AND ROY SCHLEMON
    1987   Mapping and Dating the Prehistoric Raised Fields of the Guayas Basin, Ecuador. Symposium on the Pre-Hipanic Agricultural Fields in the Andean Region, pt. 2. (W. Denevan, K. Mathewson, and G. Knapp, eds.). In *Proceedings of the Congreso Internacional de Americanistas, Bogotá, 1985*. BAR International Series 359(2): 217–224. British Archaeological Reports, Oxford.

PAULSEN, ALLISON C., AND EUGENE J. McDOUGLE
    n.d.   The Machalilla and Engoroy Occupations of the Santa Elena Peninsula in South Coastal Ecuador. Paper presented at the 39th Annual Meeting of the Society for American Archaeology, Washington, D.C., 1974.

PEARSALL, DEBORAH M.
    1980   Analysis of an Archaeological Maize Kernel Cache from Manabí Province, Ecuador. *Economic Botany* 34(4): 344–351.
    1988   *La producción de alimentos en Real Alto*. In Biblioteca Ecuatorina de Arqueología 3, Escuela Superior Politécnica del Litoral/Corporación Editora Nacional, Guayaquil.
    1995   "Doing" Paleoethnobotany in the Tropical Lowlands: Adaptation and Innovation in Methodology. In *Archaeology in the Lowland American Tropics. Current Analytical Methods and Their Applications* (Peter W. Stahl, ed.): 113–129. Cambridge University Press, Cambridge.

PIPERNO, DOLORES R.
    1988   Primer informe sobre los fitolitos de las plantas del sitio OGSE-80 y la evidencia de cultivo del maíz en el Ecuador. In *La prehistoria temprana de la península de Santa Elena, Ecuador: Cultura Las Vegas*. Miscelanea Antropológica Ecuatoriana, Serie Monográfica 10 (K. E. Stothert, ed.): 203–214. Banco Central del Ecuador, Guayaquil.
    1990   Aboriginal Agriculture and Land Usage in the Amazon Basin, Ecuador. *Journal of Archaeological Science* 17: 665–677.
    1995   Plant Microfossils and Their Application in New World Tropics. In *Archaeology in the Lowland American Tropics. Current Analytical Methods and Their Applications* (Peter W. Stahl, ed.): 130–153. Cambridge University Press, Cambridge.

PORRAS, PEDRO I.
    1973   *El Encanto—La Puná. Un sitio insular de la cultura Valdivia asociado a un conchero anular*. Catholic University, Quito.
    1983   *Arqueología: Palenque, Los Ríos. La Ponga, Guayas*. Catholic University, Quito.

RAYMOND, J. SCOTT
    1993   Ceremonialism in the Early Formative of Ecuador. In *El Mundo ceremonial andino* (L. Millones and Y. Onuki, eds.): 25–43. Senri Ethnological Studies 37. National Museum of Ethnology, Osaka.
    1995   From Potsherds to Pots: A First Step in Constructing Cultural Context from Tropical Forest Archaeology. In *Archaeology in the Lowland American Tropics:*

Current Analytical Methods and Recent Applications (Peter W. Stahl, ed.): 224–242. Cambridge University Press, Cambridge.

n.d.   Early Formative Societies in the Tropical Lowlands of Western Ecuador: A View from the Valdivia Valley. Paper presented at the Circum-Pacific Prehistory Conference, Seattle, 1989.

RAYMOND, J. SCOTT, JORGE G. MARCOS, AND DONALD W. LATHRAP

1980   Evidence of Early Formative Settlement in the Guayas Basin, Ecuador. *Current Anthropology* 21(5): 700–701.

REINDEL, MARKUS

1995   Das archaeologische Projekt La Cadena, Ecuador. Untersuchungen zur Kulturgeschichte des Guayasbeckens im Kustengebiet Ecuadors. Beitrage zur Allgemeinen und Vergleichenden Archaologie, Band 15: 259–307. Verlag Philipp von Zabern, Mainz am Rhein.

RICE, PRUDENCE M.

1987   *Pottery Analysis: A Source Book.* University of Chicago Press, Chicago.

ROOSEVELT, ANNA C.

1995   Early Pottery in Amazonia: Twenty Years of Obscurity. In *The Emergence of Pottery: Technology and Innovation in Ancient Societies* (William K. Barnett and John Hoopes, eds.): 115–131. Smithsonian Institution Press, Washington, D.C.

RYE, OWEN S.

1981   *Pottery Technology: Principles and Reconstruction.* Taraxacum, Washington, D.C.

SCHWARZ, FREDERICK, AND J. SCOTT RAYMOND

1996   Formative Settlement Patterns in the Valdivia Valley, Southwest Coastal Ecuador. *Journal of Field Archaeology* 23(2): 205–224.

SIMMONS, MICHAEL P.

1970   *The Ceramic Sequence from La Carolina, Santa Elena Peninsula, Ecuador.* Ph.D. dissertation, University of Arizona, University Microfilms International, Ann Arbor, Mich.

SPATH, CARL D.

1980   *The El Encanto Focus: A Post-Pleistocene Maritime Adaptation to the Expanding Littoral Resources.* Ph.D. dissertation, University of Illinois at Urbana–Champaign, University Microfilms International, Ann Arbor.

STAHL, PETER W.

1995   Differential Preservation Histories Affecting the Mammalian Zooarchaeological Record from the Forested Neotropical Lowlands. In *Archaeology in the Lowland American Tropics: Current Analytical Methods and Their Applications* (Peter W. Stahl, ed.): 154–179. Cambridge University Press, Cambridge.

n.d.   Encountering Paradise Lost: The Archaeological Recovery of Ancient Biodiversity in the Lowlands of Western Ecuador. Paper presented at the 91st Annual Meeting of the American Anthropological Association, San Francisco, 1992.

STALLER, JOHN E.

n.d.   Late Valdivia Occupation in Southern Coastal El Oro Province, Ecuador: Excavations at the Early Formative Period (3500–1500 B.C.) Site of La Emerenciana. Unpublished Ph.D. dissertation, Department of Anthropology, Southern Methodist University, Dallas, 1994.

STOTHERT, KAREN E.
    1985   The Preceramic Las Vegas Culture of Coastal Ecuador. *American Antiquity* 50: 613–637.
    1988   *La prehistoria temprana de la península de Santa Elena, Ecuador: Cultura Las Vegas.* Miscelanea Antropológica Ecuatoriana, Serie Monográfica 10. Banco Central del Ecuador, Guayaquil.

TOBAR ABRIL, OSWALDO
    n.d.   La morfología fluvial como fundamento para la prospección arqueológica probabilística. Tésis de licenciatura, Centro de Estudios Arqueológicos y Antropológicos, Escuela Superior Politécnica del Litoral, Guayaquil, 1988.

UBELAKER, DOUGLAS H.
    1988   Restos de esqueletos humanos del sitio OGSE-80. In *La prehistoria temprana de la península de Santa Elena, Ecuador: Cultura Las Vegas.* Miscelanea Antropológica Ecuatoriana, Serie Monográfica 10 (Karen Stothert, ed.): 105–132. Banco Central del Ecuador, Guayaquil.

VILLALBA, MARCELO
    1988   *Cotocollao: Una aldea formativa del valle de Quito.* Miscelanea Antropológica Ecuatoriana, Serie Monográfica 2. Museos del Banco Central del Ecuador, Quito.

WILLEY, GORDON R., AND PHILIP PHILLIPS
    1958   *Method and Theory in American Archaeology.* University of Chicago Press, Chicago.

WING, ELIZABETH S.
    1988   Dusicyon sechurae, en contextos arqueológicos tempranos. In *La prehistoria temprana de la península de Santa Elena, Ecuador: Cultura Las Vegas.* Miscelanea Antropológica Ecuatoriana, Serie Monográfica 10 (K. E. Stothert, ed.): 179–185. Banco Central del Ecuador, Guayaquil.

ZEDEÑO, MARÍA NIEVES
    n.d.   Análisis de cerámica Chorrera del sitio Peñón del Río. Tésis de licenciatura, Escuela de Arqueología, Escuela Superior Politécnica del Litoral, Guayaquil, 1994.

ZEIDLER, JAMES A.
    1986   La evolución local de asentamientos Formativos en el litoral ecuatoriano: El caso de Real Alto (OGSECh-012). In *La arqueología de la costa ecuatoriana: Nuevos enfoques* (J. G. Marcos, ed.): 86–127. Corporación Editora Nacional, Quito.
    1991   Maritime Exchange in the Early Formative Period of Coastal Ecuador: Geopolitical Origins of Uneven Development. *Research in Economic Anthropology* 13: 247–268.
    n.d.   Social Space in Valdivia Society: Community Patterning and Domestic Structure at Real Alto, 3000–2000 B.C. Unpublished Ph.D. dissertation, Department of Anthropology, University of Illinois at Urbana-Champaign.

ZEIDLER, JAMES A., AND DEBORAH M. PEARSALL (EDS.)
    1989   *Regional Archaeology in Northern Manabí, Ecuador,* vol. 1. *Environment, Cultural Chronology, and Prehistoric Subsistence in the Jama River Valley.* University of Pittsburgh, Pittsburgh, and Ediciones Libri Mundi, Quito.

Jorge G. Marcos

ZEVALLOS MENÉNDEZ, CARLOS
1965–66   Informe preliminar sobre el cementerio Chorrera, Bahía de Santa Elena, Ecuador. *Revista del Museo Nacional* (Peru) 34: 20–27.
1971   *La agricultura en el Formativo Temprano del Ecuador.* Editorial Casa de la Cultura Ecuatoriana, Guayaquil.

ZEVALLOS, CARLOS, WALTON GALINAT, DONALD W. LATHRAP, EARL LENG, JORGE MARCOS, AND KATHLEEN KLUMPP
1977   The San Pablo Corn Kernel and Its Friends. *Science* 196: 385–389.

ZEVALLOS MENÉNDEZ, CARLOS, AND OLAF HOLM
1960   *Excavaciones arqueológicas en San Pablo: Informe preliminar.* Editorial Casa de la Cultura Ecuatoriana, Guayaquil.

Social Formations in the Western Lowlands of Ecuador during the Early Formative

A t the time of the Spanish Conquest of the Andean region, Ecuador comprised a number of regional polities commonly referred to as *chiefdoms*, some of which, mainly highland chiefdoms, had been loosely incorporated into the Inka empire. The early historic and ethnohistoric sources indicate that the power structures of these polities were based on wealth and hierarchy, sustained by limited political centralization, long-distance trade, and access to resources (material and ideological) restricted to the elite, and elite control over communication with the supernatural. The foundations of this complexity in the western lowlands go back 5,000 years to the Formative, a period of economic development and demographic expansion over the whole of the lowland region and of emerging social, possibly economic, differentiation among local populations.

The Andes to the east and the Pacific Ocean to the west and north border the western lowlands of Ecuador (Fig. 1). The huge Guayas basin, which discharges into the Gulf of Guayaquil, drains the interior of the lowlands to the south, and the Esmeraldas River and tributaries drain the northern part of the lowlands. A series of low mountain ranges rise along the coastal margin, and a series of small valleys descend from these mountains to the sea. A combination of cool ocean currents and prevailing southerly winds creates arid conditions along the southern and central coastal regions. Precipitation increases dramatically, however, toward the interior and northern parts of the lowlands. Cactus and other xerophytic vegetation characterize the southwestern corner of the lowlands and areas immediately along the coast, but the valleys, mountains, and the interior alluvial lowlands are covered with tropical rainforest.

The record of early settlement in the western lowlands of Ecuador is uneven. In the Santa Elena region, the record goes back to the early Holocene, and only there and in immediately neighboring regions to the north and east

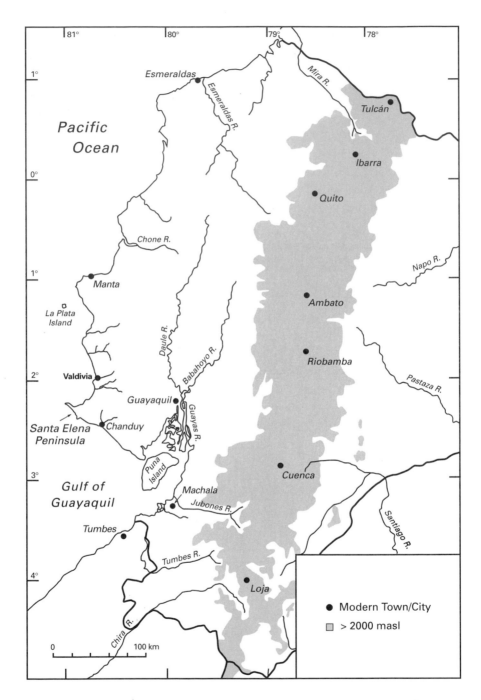

Fig. 1   Map of Ecuador.

does the record encompass the earliest manifestations of pottery and sedentary communities ca. 3000 B.C.[1] Not for another millennium is there evidence of human occupation in the northern or southern parts of the Pacific lowlands of Ecuador. Although the possibility that this record reflects a real temporal pattern of demographic expansion cannot be ruled out, it seems much more likely that it is a product of the combined effects of where archaeologists have chosen to carry out research and of environmental, geological, and eustatic conditions that have affected the visible survival of archeological sites (Raymond, Marcos, and Lathrap 1980). Periodic volcanic eruptions in the neighboring Andes, for example, spewed ash over huge areas of the lowlands, displacing populations and obscuring earlier evidence of settlement (Zeidler and Isaacson this volume). The southwestern part of Ecuador was further from the source of such eruptions and less affected than other regions. The drier conditions of the region also meant that archaeological sites were less subject to the destructive effects of erosion and sedimentation.

The archaeological sequence in southwestern Ecuador begins with the Preceramic culture known as Vegas, which dates roughly from 8000 to 4600 B.C. Vegas is followed by Valdivia, which marks the beginning of pottery making and a change toward increased sedentism. Valdivia began around 3000 B.C. and endured as a distinctive ceramic style for more than 1,500 years. The Valdivia style evolved into Machalilla, which in turn evolved into Chorrera (Marcos this volume). Ceramics are ubiquitous on the archaeological sites, and their stylistic changes serve as important chronological markers.

BACKGROUND

Just as the Viru valley for many years was the peephole through which Peruvian prehistory was viewed, so the Santa Elena region has been the vantage point from which the Ecuadorian Formative has been interpreted. Although there has been a concerted effort to counter the narrow regional bias of the peninsula through research in the Guayas basin (Raymond, Marcos, and Lathrap 1980), in the valleys of the southern El Oro province (Netherly n.d.; Staller n.d.a), in the northern valleys of Manabí (Zeidler and Pearsall 1994) and in the wet lowlands of Esmeraldas (DeBoer 1996), the sequence from Santa Elena and the neighboring Valdivia and Chanduy valleys (Fig. 1) still serve as the principal framework for organizing, understanding, and explaining the Formative societies, particularly during the earliest phases. Although I recognize the inherent weakness of this bias, I have not been able to escape it in any substantial way.

---

[1] All dates in this chapter are uncalibrated.

Valdivia, the precocious pottery-bearing Early Formative culture, has held center stage in Ecuadorian research since its remarkable antiquity was discovered in the 1950s (Estrada 1956; Estrada, Evans, and Meggers 1959). More than three decades ago, Meggers, Evans, and Estrada (1965) argued that the precocity of Valdivia's ceramic technology could be explained as a trans-Pacific introduction from Japan, brought to the shores of Ecuador by Jomon fishermen swept across the ocean by storms and currents. They conceptualized Valdivia as a foreign-born, littoral culture:

> Between 3200 and 1500 B.C. sedentary life on the Ecuadorian coast appears to have been restricted to the margin of the sea, which provided a localized food supply that could not be equaled inland until after the development of agriculture. (Meggers 1966: 51)

Building on the model of Meggers et al. (1965), Ford (1969) saw Valdivia as the first in a chain of maritime cultures stretching from the shores of Ecuador to the estuaries of the southeastern United States and giving rise to Formative societies in the respective regions of colonization. Several archaeologists, however, expressed skepticism about the possible transoceanic origin of Valdivia and its purported catalytic role in New World prehistory. The most vocal of the skeptics, Donald Lathrap, saw Valdivia as a product of Tropical Forest Culture, which he identified with large sedentary communities, efficient agriculture, decorated ceramics, and extensive trade. The immediate source of Valdivia, then, according to Lathrap, was not from across the sea but more probably from the floodplains of the neighboring Guayas basin (Lathrap 1967, 1970, 1973b; Lathrap Collier, and Chandra 1975). From this line of reasoning, two expectations arise: (a) an earlier manifestation of Valdivia in the Guayas basin than on the coast or in the coastal valleys and (b) larger communities with, perhaps, greater sociopolitical complexity along the broad floodplains of the Guayas (Raymond et al. 1980).

Lanning (1967, n.d.), while not denying long-distance contact for Valdivia within the western South American region, focused on local cultural development in the Santa Elena region and together with his students explored the local antecedents.[2] Lanning doubted the predominance of a maritime orientation of the Valdivia economy, as did Zevallos (Zevallos and Holm 1960a,b), and research carried out during the late 1960s and early 1970s confirmed that early Valdivia settlements were to be found a considerable distance inland (Hill 1975; Norton 1982).

---

[2] Karen Stothert, almost single-handedly, has carried on investigations of the earliest settlement of the Santa Elena region, establishing a credible sequence for the Preceramic occupation extending back to the Early Holocene. My discussion of the Vegas culture below is based almost entirely on evidence recovered from her survey and excavations (Stothert 1985, 1988).

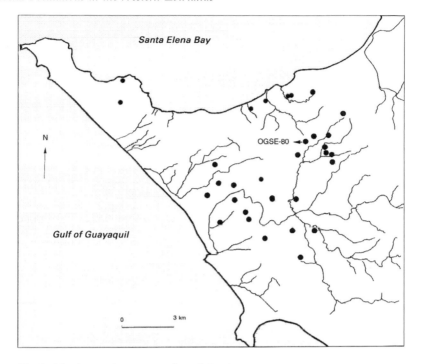

Fig. 2 The Santa Elena peninsula and the distribution of Las Vegas sites.

The debate that ensued about the origins of Valdivia and its economic base inspired a generation of research in lowland Ecuador. Investigations of the past two decades have yielded much data on settlement patterns, the relative sizes of settlements, densities, plans, houses and households, ceremonial constructions, ritual activities, and funerary customs, all of which allow inferences and speculations about the society and its cultural context. The speculations of today are more firmly anchored in evidence than they were in the 1960s, but we are still far from being able to submit them to a full empirical test.

PRECERAMIC ANTECEDENTS: LAS VEGAS

I begin with the early- to mid-Holocene culture known as *Vegas,* partly because of its continuities with early Valdivia, but mainly because of the contrasts that highlight social and economic changes marking the beginning of sedentary communities in Ecuador.

Vegas is represented by more than 30 sites, all of which are restricted to the Santa Elena peninsula (Fig. 2). Sites are situated near a variety of potential resource localities, including bays, estuaries, open sea, riverbeds, ravines, and low interior hills. Sites vary in size and artifact density but are generally small with dense scatters of lithics. A notable exception to this pattern is OGSE-80, which covers an area of about 2,200 m² and preserves a history of occupation from about 8000 to 4600 B.C. Despite the proximity of the sea and estuaries, the Vegas sites have relatively low densities of shell in comparison with later sites of coastal fishing populations. There are high proportions of terrestrial mammal bones and fish bones from a variety of near and off-shore species. Preserved botanical remains are nearly nonexistent, but a broad range of wild plants was probably eaten. *Algarrobo* (*Prosopis,* also known as *mesquite* and *carob*) was abundant in the region, judging from carbonized wood remains, and the nutritious seeds may have been an important staple. After 6000 B.C., phytoliths in the deposits attest the probable cultivation of maize (Pearsall 1988, 1999; Pearsall and Piperno 1990; Piperno 1988; Stothert 1985, 1988).

The Vegas settlement pattern raises important questions about sedentism and nucleation of population in what seems to have been an economy of coastal collectors who practiced some horticulture. None of the sites is separated by more than 6 km, meaning that any one of the resource localities could have been exploited daily from one location. Stothert (1988: 236), who excavated the large site OGSE-80, found no hiatus in settlement and suggests that it was occupied continuously over the approximate 4,000-year span. The Santa Elena peninsula, however, is an area of marked seasonal variation in precipitation and is known to experience droughts lasting several years. The modern populations adapt to these droughts by temporarily moving to the interior valleys. It seems probable, then, that the Vegas populations had flexible demographic habits that enabled them to adjust to both seasonal and long-term variations in the environment.

The Vegas pattern is reminiscent of one recently recorded by Meehan (1982) for present-day littoral collectors in Arnhem Land, Australia. Meehan describes four communities of collectors who vary significantly in their degree of mobility. All exhibit high mobility in their daily collecting cycle, traveling as much as 20 km per day, usually making lunchtime camps near their resources, but returning to a homebase each night. Some shift their homebases frequently, others infrequently, exhibiting a high degree of sedentism. Communities get together for prolonged periods—up to six months—bringing together more than 100 people to practice rituals, among the most important of which are funerary rites.

The Arnhem Land societies demonstrate that there can be considerable demographic variability among groups of collectors exploiting similar environments with similar technologies. The variability may be induced by subtle differences in resource patterning, differences in preferred collecting strategies among the groups or simply because of intergroup social variability. The cause is not clear. The relict camp patterns of the Arnhem Land collectors, however, are similar and bear close resemblance to the Vegas site pattern. One relatively large site is associated with a number of small sites, all within a few kilometers of each other; the small sites in turn are adjacent to probable food-collecting localities. In such a scenario, OGSE-80 can plausibly be interpreted as a homebase or base camp to which collectors returned at the end of each day. There is evidence, however, to suggest that it was a site of sacred activities as well.

OGSE-80 is the only Vegas site with human skeletal remains. Stothert's excavations uncovered 192 buried skeletons with distinct gender and age-based patterns of orientation. Some of the burials are associated with grave goods such as shell spoons, shell ornaments, polished stone axes, red ochre, and round stones. OGSE-80, then, may have functioned as a kind of ceremonial center, a sacred location, which, like the large Arnhem Land camps, brought the community together to participate in sacred rituals. Whether groups gathered there on a daily basis or just periodically (i.e., whether it was a base camp as well as a ceremonial center) cannot be determined from the evidence recovered so far. Funerary rites seem to have been a principal ritual in the Vegas community, just as they are at the Arnhem Land camps, and it seems reasonable to speculate that such rituals associated the living members of the community with a community of ancestors.

A small structure which was discovered by Stothert (1988: 50–54), no more than 1.5 m across, was likely used for sleeping or as temporary protection from inclement weather. It is consistent with shelters used by mobile populations around the world and could be built or taken down quickly. The association of a buried female with the structure, however, and other clusterings of burials in patterns indicative of other structures suggest that shelters or houses may have played a symbolic role associated with particular individuals or social groups of the community.

The evidence is more suggestive than definitive. The Vegas settlement pattern, however, together with the features revealed at OGSE-80, indicates that the groups occupying the Santa Elena peninsula during the early to mid-Holocene shared a sense of community and that, although there may have been a high degree of mobility, they also shared a sense of belonging to a specific geographical location. The continuity of that relationship was symbolically reinforced through periodic funerary events. Furthermore, I suggest that shelters, flimsy as they may have been, were laden with social value and played a symbolic role.

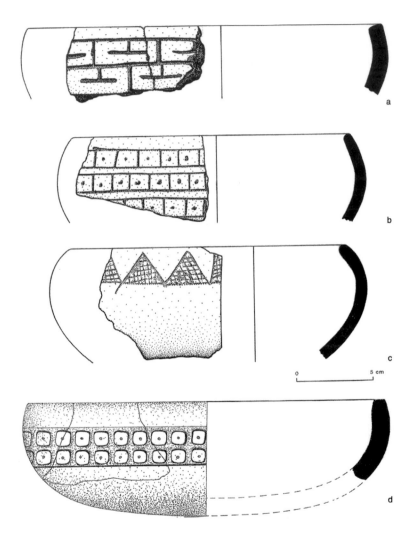

Fig. 3 Examples of Early Valdivia ceramics from Loma Alta (a, b, c) and Real Alto (d). Drawings by Cathy Ringer Driver (a, b, c) and Anjan Raymond-Bhatt (d).

EARLY FORMATIVE

Early Valdivia

With the appearance of Valdivia ceramics (Fig. 3) between 3500 and 3000 B.C., there is a dramatic shift in settlement patterns, which probably relates to economic, social, and demographic changes. The focus of settlement is now in the valleys, and the corner of the Santa Elena peninsula formerly occupied by Vegas populations bears only slight evidence of settlement (Fig. 4). The drama of this shift, however, may be exaggerated. It is not believable that prior to 3500 B.C. occupation of western Ecuador was confined to one little arid corner, or that the Vegas community was a population isolate. There is some evidence (Spath n.d.) of Preceramic collecting/fishing populations in the estuary of the Guayas River, and indications of buried Preceramic components in sites to the west of Real Alto (Kreid n.d.) and at the Valdivia type site (Bischof and Viteri Gamboa 1972), but otherwise, no evidence of early- to mid-Holocene occupation has been discovered in the western lowlands of Ecuador. It is probable that many Preceramic coastal settlements were drowned by rising sea levels

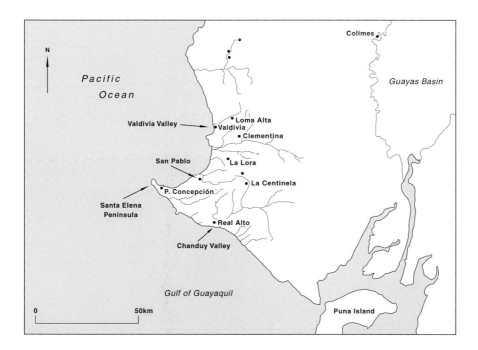

Fig. 4   Southwestern Ecuador and the distribution of Early Valdivia sites.

prior to 5,000 years ago, but explaining the absence of evidence from the coastal hills and valleys is more problematic, particularly for those areas, like the Valdivia valley, which have been thoroughly surveyed. We can assume, I think, that these interior regions were occupied but that preferred settlement locations were different from those of Early Valdivia, and perhaps because of their smaller size and locations, pre-Valdivia sites were more vulnerable to erosion and burial.

A pattern of settlement along the edge of the valley bottom is consistently repeated for early Valdivia sites. Although some sites are situated near the sea, such as Valdivia and Real Alto, they are also situated near large expanses of self-irrigating floodplain. The lone exception, Punta Concepción, is perched on a cliff above the sea and is also exceptional in having a comparatively shallow midden and a low density of pottery. In the valleys surveyed between Chanduy in the south and Valdivia in the north, five of eight major sites with Early Valdivia occupations are situated from 10 to 20 km from the sea, and all but one of these is on high ground adjoining a broad alluvial plain. Only one Early Valdivia site (near Colimes) has yet been discovered in the broad alluvial region of the Guayas basin (Raymond et al. 1980). That site was buried under 7.5 m of sedimentary deposit (Fig. 5), and other than a small excavation which revealed a burnt floor and burnt post-molds from what may have been a structure (Fig. 6), the site remains uninvestigated. Redeposited ceramics indicate that other sites exist as well; however, discovery and excavation of sites in the huge floodplain is problematic and expensive.

Early Valdivia sites are 4 to 10 times larger than the largest of the Vegas sites, and small sites, associated with specialized collecting and processing activities, are unknown for Early Valdivia (Raymond 1993). The sites are at least 10 km distant from one another and/or are situated within separate valley systems. They exhibit a distinctive settlement plan with the domestic area surrounding a vacant central arena, and for many of the sites, which are situated on low hills, the boundary of the settlement is physically set apart from the surrounding landscape (Figs. 7, 8). Although lithic flakes and debitage are abundant on Valdivia sites, as they were on Vegas sites, Valdivia sites are also laden with high densities of broken pottery.

These are key differences and undoubtedly reflect demographic changes that correspond to changes in the frequency of population movement and in social and economic organization. From the first, archaeologists interpreted Valdivia sites as sedentary settlements, an interpretation fostered by the size of the sites and the high densities of pottery, and reinforced by the growing consensus that agriculture was a mainstay of the economy. While I am in agreement that the settlements were largely sedentary, I argue for further review,

Fig. 5   Early Valdivia site at Colimes in the Guayas basin, underlying 7.5 m of sediment.

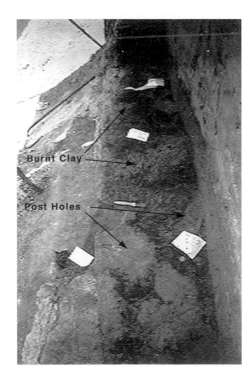

Fig. 6   Post holes and charred floor from a possible Early Valdivia structure at Colimes. Photograph by Jorge Marcos.

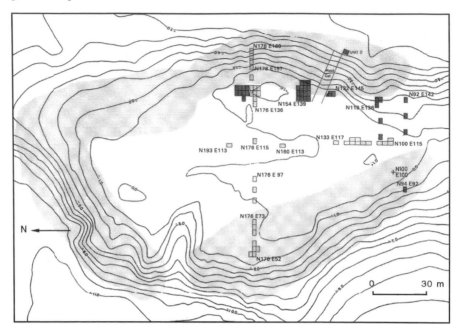

Fig. 7   Loma Alta: Shaded area shows approximate distribution of midden.

especially in regard to the Early Valdivia settlements.

The spacing between the Early Valdivia sites and their positioning within the landscape suggest that the settlements were associated with specific geographical domains, which could plausibly be interpreted to mean that they were politically and economically independent communities. As Stahl (n.d.a) has shown, however, the faunal remains from Loma Alta, a midvalley settlement, come from a wide variety of habitats, including sea, estuary, valley, forest, and hills. Stable isotope measurements on human skeletons also indicate some dependence on seafood, while indicating that the bulk of the protein came from terrestrial forest animals (van der Merwe, Lee-Thorp, and Raymond 1993). It follows that there was some economic interdependence among communities, especially between those situated near the seaside and the up-valley settlements. Alternatively, communities may have shared access to resources, with task groups, probably mainly composed of adult males, traveling to distant locales (e.g., Punta Concepción) to hunt or fish. In the latter case, however, we would expect to find evidence of small short-term camps, like those reported for Vegas, but no camps have been discovered. Also, the presence of seafood remains at inland sites is indicative of the sedentary character of the settlements, with foods being brought from nonlocal sources to the village.

Relations among communities probably extended beyond economic inter-dependence and may have included connubial exchanges, intercommunity cer-emonial occasions and sharing of esoteric knowledge. Membership in the communities may also have been fluid, with social units occasionally moving

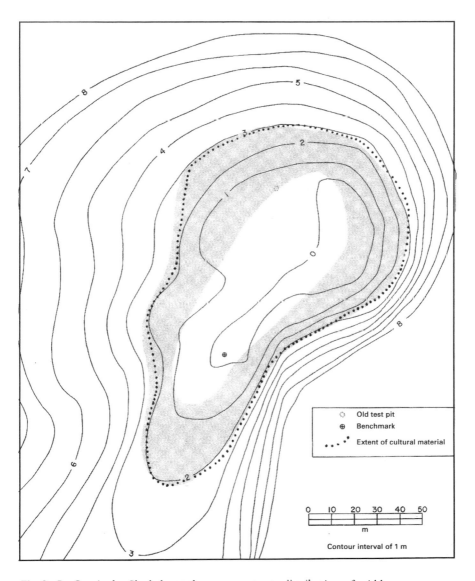

Fig. 8   La Centinela. Shaded area shows approximate distribution of midden.

from one community to another. None of these possibilities is testable with the current data. The high degree of standardization of Valdivia pottery (Hill 1975; Marcos n.d.; Meggers 1965; Raymond 1993), which persists through time over a rather large region, however, suggests a high frequency of social interaction among communities and a shared notion of cultural identity (Fig. 9). Ritualized exchange of local products, including foodstuffs, widely recorded among indigenous populations in the Amazon (see Chernela 1993; Hugh-Jones 1995; Lathrap 1973a; Roth 1924) may explain the occasional occurrence of seafood at the inland settlements.

Using a structured analogical argument, Zeidler (n.d.a) cogently compared the Middle Valdivia pattern of settlement at Real Alto with that of ethnographically recorded Gê-Bororo villages of the Amazon basin, and several other archaeologists have noted the general similarity that exists between the apparent oval arrangement of Valdivia settlements and the plans of Central Brazilian native villages (Damp n.d.; Lathrap et al. 1975; Raymond 1993; Stahl n.d.b). Among the Gê-Bororo, the village plan defines social groupings and symbolically maps out relations among them. The consistent repetition of this pattern in Valdivia settlements at the very least indicates the importance of spatially structuring the social world and is suggestive of the social–symbolic function of Gê-Bororo villages. Social units (e.g., individuals or families) may have been able to move from one settlement to another with the confidence that community relations would be mapped by their position within the arc of the domestic perimeter.

The concept of concentric dualism is widespread among South American societies and is physically structured in social space among a majority of Amazonian cultures (Carsten and Hugh-Jones 1995; Lévi-Strauss 1963; Nimuendaju 1946). Whether a settlement consists of a nucleated arrangement of small houses or one large round house, the same principles apply. The center of the house or settlement is opposed to the peripheral domestic space, and the settlement as a

Fig. 9   A standard set of Early Valdivia ceramic vessels. Drawing by Peter Mathews.

whole is opposed to the peripheral forest or natural space. The Valdivia settlements fit this set of oppositions precisely, although we cannot be certain that they were conceived in that way. Continuing, however, with these comparisons there are further correspondences. The central space of the house or settlement functions as a stage or arena for communal activities. It is here that visitors are welcomed, that ritual dances and other community ceremonies take place, and here that members of the community congregate in the evenings to talk and plan. Personal and political rivalries are acted out in the central spaces. The space is cleaned and kept clear of domestic garbage, in part to symbolically emphasize its sacred quality as opposed to the profane domestic space surrounding it. Again, the central spaces of Early Valdivia settlements, notably Loma Alta and La Centinela (Figs. 7, 8), were kept almost spotlessly clean, with the broken pottery and other refuse limited to the domestic periphery. Although they were built on a much grander scale, the ceremonial/administrative centers built by the Inka state exhibit the same principles, with the *ushnu*, or throne of the emperor, situated in the sacred, central plaza (see Morris and Thompson 1985 for a discussion of this pattern).

Funerary rites were an important part of ritual life at Valdivia settlements, just as they were in the Vegas culture, and the association of burials with houses is a material remnant of a community connection with the ancestors (Fig. 10). Further evidence of ritual is the occurrence of small stone figurines (Fig. 11). These are unprecedented in Vegas but occur in high frequency at Early Valdivia sites. They are ubiquitous throughout the midden, suggesting that they were either objects of household ritual or were removed from the central arena as part of the ritual cleansing of that space. Their high prevalence and the fact that the figurines are usually broken, possibly defaced, not only indicate that they were not curated icons but also suggest that they participated in frequent cyclical ceremonies (Di Capua 1994; Lundberg n.d.; Raymond 1993; Stahl 1986).

Pottery, in addition to food storage, cooking, and serving roles, probably also functioned significantly in community rituals. Damp (1982), Lathrap et al. (1975), and Stahl (1985) have perceptively suggested that red, polished, incised bowls were likely used for ritual drinking. The high degree of standardization of these vessels (Fig. 9) among the different Early Valdivia assemblages shows that a visitor would have no trouble distinguishing which vessels were for drinking.

Small, nucleated settlements, then, seem to characterize the early evidence of sedentism in Ecuador. The layouts of these settlements, enclosing both the secular and sacred space, seem to emphasize the separateness, the autonomy of the community. In fact, it seems probable that there was a good deal of mutual dependence among communities—economic, social, and ritual. Although there

Fig. 10   An Early Valdivia burial from Loma Alta. Photograph by Lisa Valkenier.

30 mm

Fig. 11 Examples of Early Valdivia stone figurines from Loma Alta. Photograph by Gerald Newlands.

may have been the ideal of a closed community there was probably a fair degree of mobility for individuals and perhaps kin groups who wanted to move from one settlement to another. There are no indications in the material remains such as grave goods or house size of social or political inequalities; the spatial structuring of the domestic area, however, holds the potential of symbolically encoding inequalities among households.

Middle and Late Valdivia

At both Loma Alta and Real Alto, the two sites for which detailed settlement data are recorded, the area of the settlements seem to have gradually expanded throughout Early Valdivia, beginning at about one hectare and expanding to nearly three hectares by the end of Phase 2. At about 2500 B.C. at the beginning of the Middle Valdivia period, both settlements changed dramatically but quite differently. Loma Alta was reduced to a small hamlet-sized settlement and remained so throughout the rest of the Early and Middle Formative. The

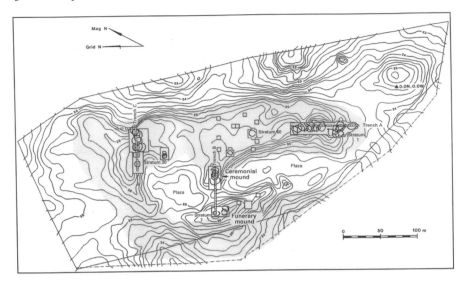

Fig. 12   Real Alto: Shaded area shows residential area during Middle Valdivia.

concentric settlement plan was apparently abandoned.

In contrast, Real Alto grew to more than four times its earlier size during Middle Valdivia, eventually embracing an area of nearly 12.5 hectares. Damp (n.d.), Marcos (n.d.), and Zeidler (n.d.b) have documented the transformation of the settlement (Fig. 12). The oval settlement plan of Early Valdivia was transformed into a rectangular arrangement of houses, with an opening at the southern end. The enlarged central arena was divided into two parts, a small inner plaza and a larger outer plaza. The division was created by mounds that extended opposite each other into the central arena from the surrounding residential area, leaving a small gap for access between the two plazas. Marcos (n.d., 1988) has discriminated seven mound-building or renewal episodes and has found evidence of ceremonial structures built atop the mounds. In the residential areas, houses were built over the ruins and refuse of earlier houses, but the central plazas were kept clean so that over time the residential area became elevated, giving the impression of a sunken plaza.

Together with the overall growth in size of the settlement, there was a change in the size and permanence of houses (Zeidler n.d.b). Early Valdivia houses, as evidenced at Loma Alta and Real Alto (Damp 1984), were only slightly larger than the Vegas shelters and no less flimsy. The Middle Valdivia houses at Real Alto, however, are substantial structures with floor areas three to five times those of Early Valdivia (Fig. 13). Zeidler (n.d.b) estimated that there may have

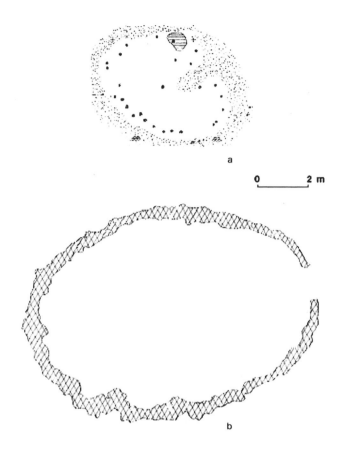

Fig. 13 Comparison of an Early Valdivia structure (a) (after Damp 1984) and a Middle Valdivia structure (b) (after Zeidler n.d.a).

been 8 to 10 residents, on average, of each house. He has also demonstrated that there is a clustering pattern among houses, suggesting that there were social groupings within the settlement. There is also a bimodal pattern in the size distribution of houses.

It seems that an increase in social complexity accompanied the punctuated growth of Real Alto. Zeidler (1988) has argued cogently that the higher local population density fostered ranking of social relations and was expressed through social competition and intensification of prestige structures. The analogy with Gê-Bororo communities is strengthened, with the residential clusters of Real

Alto paralleling the "clan" residences of the Amazonian societies. Residential groups, represented by a house or a group of houses and stressing both consanguineal and affinal ties have been shown to be a more powerful analytical unit than either lineage or clan for understanding Amazonian societies such as the Kayapó or Bororo (Carsten and Hugh-Jones 1995). Just as the settlement symbolically represents the community, the "house," which may be a single dwelling or a cluster of dwellings, is the fundamental sociosymbolic unit, structuring socioeconomic relations within and between settlements and, as a cultural concept, defining social relations within the community. In both North and South America, among diverse ethnolinguistic groups, terms for *house* and *settlement* are used interchangeably, and both the layout of villages and of ceremonial centers are conceived as big houses (Carsten and Hugh-Jones 1995; DeBoer 1997; Moore 1996; Swanton 1931: 10-11). The power and prestige of community leaders are often represented by house size and symbolic representations on the outside and/or the inside of the house.

Marcos, Lathrap, and Zeidler (1976: 4) remarked on the physical similarity between the large oval houses at Real Alto with an opening at one end and the overall plan of the settlement with a southern opening. As mentioned above, Loma Alta, during the Early Valdivia period of occupation, had a similar settlement plan, and surficial evidence from other sites indicates that this plan was characteristic of the larger Valdivia settlements (Raymond 1993). Symbolically, then, the concept of "house" may have distinguished the local community within a region and identified and structured relations among socioresidential units within a community. The variability in house size, as noted by Zeidler (1988), and the relative distance from the sacred center of the community may well have denoted rank and privilege among house leaders.

Unfortunately, there are no other excavated Middle Valdivia sites with which to compare Real Alto in any detail. San Pablo, near the coast north of Santa Elena, is the only known site that may compare in size (Fig. 14), but, because of severe looting, details of its settlement plan may never be known. La Centinela, situated inland in the same valley as Real Alto (Fig. 4) and comparable in size or possibly larger than Real Alto during Early Valdivia, is dwarfed by Real Alto during the Middle Formative and clearly does not have a similar degree of settlement complexity. In the Valdivia valley (Fig. 15), with the drastic decline in the size of the Loma Alta settlement, only Valdivia at the mouth of the valley remains as a village-sized site. What has survived of the site does not display any intrasite structure, nor does it measure more than two or three hectares.

At this same time, small settlements were established along the linear course of the valley bottom, as documented in both the Chanduy drainage and the

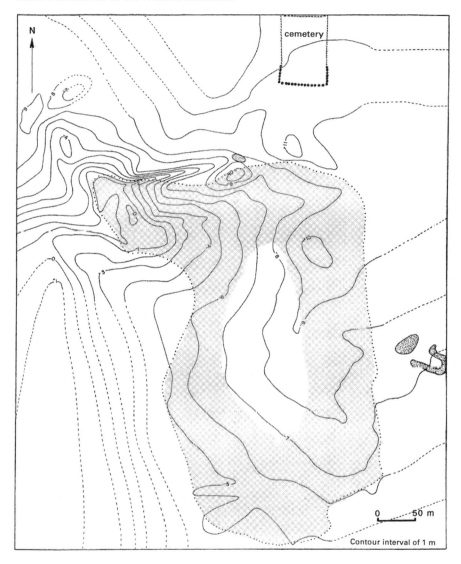

Fig. 14   San Pablo: Shaded area shows estimated distribution of midden.

Valdivia valley (Damp 1984; Raymond 1999; Schwarz and Raymond 1996; Zeidler 1986). The pattern, then, which needs to be more fully documented in other valleys, is one in which a string of relatively small settlements is punctuated with a larger settlement near the valley mouth. The unique size and complexity of Real Alto suggests that it may have served as a ceremonial center for a commu-

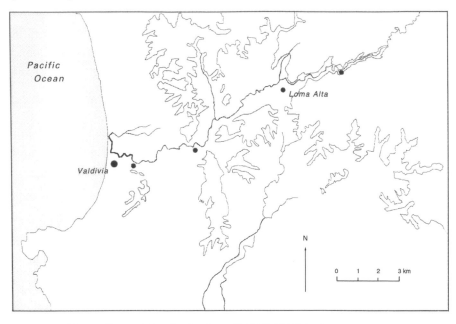

Fig. 15   Valdivia valley and the distribution of Middle Valdivia sites.

nity that extended beyond the bounds of the settlement. Small sites also now began to occur in the interfluvial areas to the west of Real Alto (Kreid n.d.), suggesting that its influence may not have been limited to a single valley system.

The pattern of dispersed small settlements is more marked in Late Valdivia. In the Valdivia valley (Fig. 16), the population was evenly distributed in a series of small settlements that follow the course of the river. The population as a whole had better access to valley bottomland than at any other time in the Formative (Schwarz and Raymond 1996). At this time there were only small hamlets in the valley, although the overall population appears to have been as large as or larger than earlier. A slightly different pattern evolved in the Chanduy valley (Fig. 17). Small hamlets were strung out along the course of the river; however, in the lower valley several satellite settlements were established in the vicinity of Real Alto, associated with local patches of alluvium. There was also an explosion in the number of hamlets or camps in the interfluvial region to the west (Kreid n.d.). At the same time Real Alto lost most of its residents but continued to function as a ceremonial center or "big house" for a regionally dispersed community.

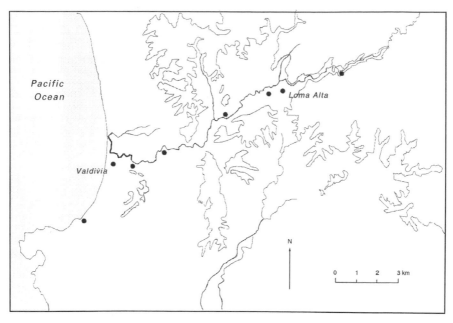

Fig. 16   Valdivia valley and the distribution of Late Valdivia sites.

Terminal Valdivia to Machalilla

During Terminal Valdivia the window on the Formative widened to include other parts of the western lowlands (Fig 18). In northern Manabí, recent surveys in the Jama valley led to the discovery of 28 Terminal Valdivia sites, known locally as the Piquigua phase. In less than 130 years, the alluvial bottomlands of the Jama valley were colonized, establishing a site hierarchy that ranged from a large civic–ceremonial center to small isolated homesteads (Zeidler 1994a,b; Zeidler and Pearsall 1994). South in El Oro province, Late to Terminal Valdivia sites, belonging to the Jelí phase, have been discovered within the Buenavista and Arenillas drainages (Staller n.d.a,b, personal communication, October 1995). Two sites larger than 10 hectares, La Emerenciana and Jumón, are separated by about 5 km and associated with the respective drainages.

Frustratingly, settlement in the Guayas basin is still attested mainly by redeposited ceramics (Raymond et al. 1980). The discovery of Late Valdivia materials in possible association with raised fields at Peñon del Río in the lower basin points to an intensification of agricultural production. But without sites to investigate or data from which to infer settlement patterns, we must leave the socioeconomic formations to our imagination (Marcos 1981).

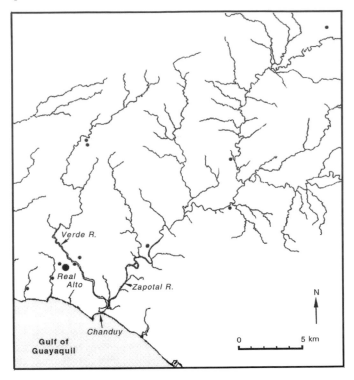

Fig. 17   Chanduy valley and the distribution of Late Valdivia sites.

In both Manabí and El Oro, the large centers are associated with ceremonial mounds; at all three sites—San Isidro, La Emerenciana and Jumón—the mounds are paired, continuing the pattern of mound building at Real Alto (Staller n.d.a,b; Zeidler and Pearsall 1994). The probable site hierarchies in both areas and the association of civic–ceremonial features with the large centers suggests that the pattern of social ranking, first evident at Real Alto, continued to develop in these two provinces. The existence of a unique large center at San Isidro in the Jama valley suggests that it served a valleywide community. Similarly, in El Oro, the positioning of La Emerenciana in the lower segment of the Buenavista drainage and Jumón in the lower Arenillas may be indicative of socioceremonial spheres defined by the drainage systems, with the large centers situated at the lower community boundaries. The site of Laguna de Caña, situated about 5 km upstream from Jumón, has a Terminal Formative/Middle Formative occupation, associated with a possible ceremonial mound, but the ceramics recovered from the site indicate that it postdates the ceremonial constructions at La

Fig. 18   Western Ecuador and the locations of Terminal Valdivia ceremeonial centers

Emerenciana and Jumón (John Staller, personal communication, October 1995).

Meanwhile in the Santa Elena peninsula, the pattern of population dispersion reached an extreme. Real Alto was abandoned completely, and the Chanduy valley system was populated by small hamlets (Zeidler 1986). Settlement in interfluvial areas boomed. In the Valdivia valley, the Valdivia type-site dwindled to a small hamlet, and with the exception of one cliff-top site south of the valley mouth, the population was evenly distributed along the course of the river. The most distinctive site in the region is that of San Lorenzo del Mate, which is not in the peninsular region per se, but on the boundary between the peninsula and the Guayas basin. Preliminary investigations at San Lorenzo indicated that it was a contemporary of La Emerenciana in El Oro and San Isidro in Manabí and had a similar scale and complexity, including ceremonial mounds (Marcos 1989).

The dispersed pattern of settlement on the peninsula has led some to propose that populations moved out of the region (Zeidler 1986, n.d.a) and that the locus of sociopolitical development shifted to areas that had formerly been frontiers (Staller n.d.a). These proposals are difficult to evaluate; however, settlement data from the Valdivia valley do not indicate a decline in the *population* during Late or Terminal Valdivia, only a decline in *average site size* (Schwarz and Raymond 1996). Deterioration in the environment, either through changes in climatic patterns and/or human degradation, may partly explain the dispersion of the population, particularly into the interfluvial areas, but without better paleoenvironmental data we are unable to confirm this. In any case, it does not provide an adequate explanation for settlement in the Valdivia valley, where the population had better access to alluvial bottomland than at any other time before or after.

Considering the expansion of settlement in the peninsular region over the full span of the Early Formative, the Late/Terminal Valdivia pattern may be predictable in terms of a process of social and economic change that began in Middle Valdivia. At that time there seems to have been a significant decrease in the mobility of the population. This is attested by a marked increase in the size and permanence of dwellings and a dispersion of small permanent settlements in the optimal resource areas (i.e., coastal estuaries and alluvial bottomland). I do not mean to suggest that there was economic specialization at this time but rather that settlements were focused on nearby resources. This seems especially apparent for the shell-midden sites in the Guayas estuary. At the same time, certain settlements grew while others dwindled. This can be seen in the growth of San Pablo and Real Alto and the decline of Loma Alta, La Lora, and La Centinela. If we discount the Valdivia type-site, which has no evidence of ceremonial construction, there was no ceremonial or community center in the Valdivia valley from the Middle Valdivia onward, nor is there any evidence of site hierarchy. The Chanduy pattern stands in marked contrast, with the large, complex center at Real Alto, a small settlement on the coast, and small settlements in the interior drainage. Does this mean that small, socially and politically independent households occupied the Valdivia valley at this time? Possibly so, but it is more likely that they were part of a larger community, tied together through common ritual at a center outside the Valdivia valley. There are several as yet uninvestigated possible centers in the Javita valley immediately south of Valdivia.

If this scenario is correct, it raises further questions about the settlement at Real Alto. Was it nucleated with a permanent population during Middle Valdivia, or was it a ceremonial center with a resident population that fluctuated in rhythm with the ritual calendar? Given the strong indications of a permanent population, I doubt that it was merely a ceremonial center; however, it seems possible that a significant portion of the population was present only on certain ritual occasions. Again, this suggests Gê-Bororo settlements were residential groups that belong to the community are structurally represented in the domestic circle, even though they may not be physically present all of the time (Lea 1995). During Late Valdivia, with Real Alto losing most of its residential population, it may have become one of several secondary regional ceremonial centers in the peninsular region that came under the shadow of more prestigious centers such as San Lorenzo del Mate.

CONCLUSIONS

The beginning of the Formative period in western Ecuador was marked by a significant transformation of local societies. The most evident changes were the aggregation of population into nucleated settlements, the establishment of settlements within the valleys, and the spatial structuring of these settlements. The earliest settlements seem to have been economically and politically separate but probably socially interdependent communities, set apart physically and conceptually from each other. A preference for placing settlements atop small hillocks may have served to emphasize the separateness and solidarity of each community, while similar distinctive settlement plans and a shared distinctive ceramic style speak of a common cultural heritage and a high degree of sociocultural integration among settlements. As noted above, though seafood was clearly not a dietary staple for the inland settlements, the presence of small quantities of seashells and fish bones at inland sites indicates that nonlocal foods were consumed occasionally. Though this may simply reflect a desire for some dietary variability, it seems just as likely—perhaps more likely—that this represents a ritual exchange of food among communities, a symbolic act that may have reinforced social ties. Such exchanges are common among lowland groups in South America. Hugh-Jones, for example, describes the following for a Tukanoan group of Northwest Amazonia.

> Visiting men give their affines large amounts of smoked meat or fish and then dance in their hosts' maloca. In return, they are supplied with vast amounts of manioc beer which they must consume before leaving, even vomiting it out to make room for more. At the end of the dancing the hosts may provide a smaller, reciprocal gift of some complementary food—fish for meat, meat for fish—a foretaste of the gift they will give when they, in turn, go to dance in the house of their erstwhile guests. (1995: 232)

The central spaces in Valdivia settlements appear to have been public spaces, enclosed and separated from the outside world by a periphery of huts and houses. They were kept clean of domestic refuse. Such spaces, or plazas, are associated with indigenous settlements and ceremonial constructions in both lowland and highland South America. Plazas are places of social encounter that may be sacred or mundane. As Moore (1996) argued, they shape and are shaped by social interactions, and their size, shape, and location are indicative of the scale and nature of the interactions. Ritual encounters, such as that described above by Hugh-Jones, may have occurred repeatedly on fixed or random occasions in the plazas of the Valdivia settlements. Participants may have glutted themselves on beer served in decorated red-polished bowls and danced until they dropped. The central space of Loma Alta, about 150 x 50 m, could have accommodated a fair-sized group of visitors as well as local participants. By Middle Valdivia, as noted above, two mounds, opposing each other from the east and west and projecting into the central space, divided the plaza at Real Alto. Atop the mounds were structures that would have provided ritual space for a small group hidden from the view of most of the populace. The ritual interactions and communications occurring in the central space at Real Alto at this time, then, seem to have been more exclusive than at earlier times, perhaps privileging some individuals above others.

The houses surrounding the domestic space may also have had an important social–symbolic role, providing a physical plan of the social world within a community. The variability in house size and the probable clustering of houses during the Middle Valdivia occupation at Real Alto are suggestive of residential groupings within the settlement. Neither the evidence from the Early Valdivia settlements at Real Alto nor from Loma Alta allows an assessment of relative house size or the discernment of clustering. Therefore, researchers cannot conclude whether such residential patterning was evident earlier. The practice of burial beneath house floors, however, as noted above, extends back to Vegas times and is suggestive of a symbolic association between ancestors and dwellings. The evidence is scant—some may say nonexistent—but I find it stimulating to speculate that in Valdivia society from the outset, houses (or house clusters) were not merely residential units but also repositories of the symbols of social identity (see Lea 1995 for an analysis of such a social pattern among the Kayapó). The high frequency of small stone figurines in the domestic refuse is more than suggestive that houses may have owned ritual objects. Additionally, such symbols may have been made of perishable material (e.g., woodcarvings, wall paintings, painted cloth).

If residents of Valdivia settlements saw themselves as members of a larger community, in which several settlements were linked through kinship relations and a shared cultural heritage, symbolic associations with houses may have defined kin relationships and connubial rules among the different settlements. The settlements were communities of people involved in everyday lives of sharing labor, food, and living space. At the same time, they represented a ritual construct related to ancestors and perpetuated through names and heirlooms. The domestic or secular world was temporary, just as settlements are ephemeral. Ritual, however, probably mediated through shamans, connected the community with the continuity of an invisible world, which was conceptually permanent.

Over time, the populations of most Valdivia settlements were dispersed into small villages or hamlets. Some settlements tripled and quadrupled in size. Settlement boundaries were less evident at this point; however, it seems probable that the populations in the dispersed settlements were associated through kinship with larger settlements. Generalizing from Real Alto, the large sites were complex settlements with formal, central civic–ceremonial arenas and residentially divided populations. Social and political ranking undoubtedly accompanied the increased complexity in settlement. By the end of the Early Formative, large centers with monumental ceremonial mounds were apparently specialized civic–ceremonial centers and the majority of the population resided in rural settlements ranging in size from single homesteads to large villages.

There is insufficient data to conclude how these patterns of social and political organization were transformed in the Middle and Late Formative, and I have chosen not to speculate. In the Valdivia valley, however, it is clear that there was a significant increase in population density in the Middle Formative, and there may have been some economic specialization among settlements (Raymond 1999; Schwarz and Raymond 1996). We now need extensive excavations at specific sites to understand how these demographic and economic changes were reflected in the social and political world.

Acknowledgments I am grateful to Elizabeth Hill Boone for inviting Richard Burger and me to organize a symposium on the Ecuadorian Formative, hence giving me the opportunity to write this essay. I am also grateful to Richard for his collaboration, initiative, and enthusiasm, and to Jeff Quilter, without whose support, encouragement, and hard work this volume may not have been published. I also thank those who have supported and contributed to my research on Ecuador over the years. It was Donald Lathrap who first stimulated my interest in the topic. Without the support and collaboration of Jorge Marcos and Presley Norton, my field research would not have been possible, and without the collaboration of Jonathan Damp I would not have dared begin excavations at Loma Alta. Peter Stahl's quick wit and inspiring ideas made the stressful conditions of the Loma Alta project more enjoyable and at times stimulating. Karen Stothert's presence in nearby Cautivo provided logistic and moral support. Among the others deserving acknowledgment are Persis Clarkson, Claire Allum, Nicholas David, Judy Sterner, Brian Kooyman, Marianne Tisdale, Juan Oralla, Lisa Valkenier, Coreen Chiswell, Diane Lyons, John Hoopes, and Eric Poplin.

BIBLIOGRAPHY

Bischof, Henning, and Julio Viteri Gamboa
　1972　Pre-Valdivia Occupations on the Southwest Coast of Ecuador. *American Antiquity* 37: 548–551.

Carsten, Janet, and Stephen Hugh-Jones
　1995　Introduction. In *About the House: Lévi-Strauss and Beyond* (Janet Carsten and Stephen Hugh-Jones, eds.): 1–46. Cambridge University Press, Cambridge.

Chernela, Janet
　1993　*The Wanano Indians of the Brazilian Amazon: A Sense of Space*. University of Texas Press, Austin.

Damp, Jonathan E.
　1982　Ceramic Art and Symbolism in the Early Valdivia Community. *Journal of Latin American Lore* 8: 155–178.
　1984　Architecture of the Early Valdivia Village. *American Antiquity* 49: 573–585.
　n.d.　Better Homes and Gardens: The Life and Death of the Early Valdivia Community. Ph.D. dissertation, University of Calgary, Alberta, 1979.

DeBoer, Warren
　1996　*Traces behind the Esmeraldas Shore: Prehistory of the Santiago–Cayapas Region, Ecuador*. University of Alabama Press, Tuscaloosa.
　1997　Ceremonial Centres from the Cayapas (Esmeraldas, Ecuador) to Chillicothe (Ohio, USA) [with comments and reply]. *Cambridge Archaeological Journal* 7(2): 225–253.

Di Capua, Costanza
　1994　Valdivia Figurines and Puberty Rituals: An Hypothesis. *Andean Past* 4: 229–279.

Estrada, Emilio
　1956　*Valdivia. Un Sitio arqueológico en la costa de la provincia del Guayas, Ecuador*. Museo Víctor Emilio Estrada Publicación 1, Guayaquil.

Estrada, Emilio, Clifford Evans, and Betty J. Meggers
　1959　*Cultura Valdivia*. Museo Víctor Emilio Estrada Publicación 6, Guayaquil.

Ford, James A.
　1969　*A Comparison of Formative Cultures in the Americas*. Smithsonian Contributions to Anthropology 11. Smithsonian Institution. U.S. Government Printing Office, Washington, D.C.

Hill, Betsy D.
　1975　A New Chronology for the Valdivia Ceramic Complex from Guayas Province, Ecuador. *Ñawpa Pacha* 10/12: 1–32.

Hugh-Jones, Stephen
　1995　Inside-Out and Back-to-Front: The Androgynous House in Northwest Amazonia. In *About the House: Leví-Strauss and Beyond* (J. Carsten and S. Hugh-Jones, eds.): 226–252. Cambridge University Press, Cambridge.

KREID, JUDITH A.

n.d.　Informe de La I Etapa (1982) del Proyecto de Rescate Arqueológico en la Peninsula de Santa Elena, Convenio CEPE/ESPOL. Manuscript on file at Escuela Superior Politécnica del Litoral, Guayaquil, 1982.

LANNING, EDWARD P.

1967　*Peru before the Incas.* Prentice Hall, Englewood Cliffs, N. J.

n.d.　Archaeological Investigation on the Santa Elena Peninsula. Report to the National Science Foundation on Research Carried Out under Grant GS-402, 1964–1965. National Science Foundation, Washington D.C., 1967.

LATHRAP, DONALD W.

1967　Review of B. J. Meggers, C. Evans and E. Estrada, Early Formative Period of Coastal Ecuador: The Valdivia and Machalilla Phases. *American Anthropologist* 69: 96–98.

1970　*The Upper Amazon.* Thames and Hudson, London.

1973a　Review of G. R. Willey, *An Introduction to American Archaeology*, vol. 2: *South America. American Anthropologist* 75(6): 175–176.

1973b　The Antiquity and Importance of Long-Distance Trade Relationships in the Moist Tropics of Pre-Columbian South America. *World Archaeology* 5(2): 171–186.

LATHRAP, DONALD W., DONALD COLLIER, AND HELEN CHANDRA

1975　*Ancient Ecuador: Culture, Clay and Creativity, 3000–300 B.C.* Field Museum of Natural History, Chicago.

LEA, VANESSA

1995　The Houses of the Mêbengokre (Kayapó) of Central Brazil—A New Door to Their Social Organization. In *About the House: Levi-Straus and Beyond* (J. Carsten and S. Hugh-Jones, eds.): 206–225. Cambridge University Press, Cambridge.

LUNDBERG, EMILY

n.d.　Reappraisal of Valdivia Figurines based on Controlled Feature Contexts: A Preliminary Report. Paper presented at the 42nd Annual Meeting of the Society for American Archaeology, New Orleans, 1977.

MARCOS, JORGE G.

1988　*Real Alto: La Historia de un centro ceremonial Valdivia* (primera y segunda partes). Corporación Editora Nacional, Quito.

1989　Informe arqueológico. In *Proyecto San Lorenzo del Mate* (J. G. Marcos, ed.): 1–19. Fundación Pedro Vicente Maldonado, Guayaquil.

n.d.　The Ceremonial Precinct at Real Alto: Organization of Time and Space in Valdivia Society. Ph.D. dissertation, University of Illinois at Urbana–Champaign.

MARCOS, JORGE G. (ED.)

1981　*Proyecto arqueológico y etnobotánico "Peñon del Río" Informe preliminar y planteamiento de continuación.* Escuela Superior Politécnica del Litoral, Guayaquil.

MARCOS, JORGE G., DONALD W. LATHRAP, AND JAMES A. ZEIDLER

1976　Ancient Ecuador Revisited. *Field Museum of Natural History Bulletin* 47(6): 3–8.

MEEHAN, BETTY
  1982   *Shell Bed to Shell Midden.* Australian Institute of Aboriginal Studies, Canberra.
MEGGERS, BETTY J.
  1966   *Ecuador.* Praeger, New York.
MEGGERS, BETTY J., CLIFFORD EVANS, AND EMILIO ESTRADA
  1965   *Early Formative Period of Coastal Ecuador: The Valdivia and Machalilla Phases.*
          Smithsonian Contributions to Anthropology 1, Smithsonian Institution. U.S.
          Government Printing Office, Washington, D.C.

MOORE, JERRY D.
  1996   The Archaeology of Plazas and the Proxemics of Ritual. *American Anthropologist*
          98(4): 789–802.

MORRIS, CRAIG, AND DONALD THOMPSON
  1985   Huanuco Pampa: An Inca City and Its Hinterland. Thames and Hudson,
          London.

NETHERLY, PATRICIA
  n.d.   Informe sobre trabajos arqueológicos efectuados durante la primera temporada
          de campo de noviembre 1978 (Valle de Arenillas, provincia de El Oro).
          Manuscript on file, Museo Antropológico, Banco Céntral del Ecuador,
          Guayaquil, 1980.

NORTON, PRESLEY
  1982   Preliminary Observations on Loma Alta, an Early Valdivia Midden in Guayas
          Province, Ecuador. In *Primer Simposio de Correlaciones Antropológicas Andino–
          Mesoamericano* (J. G. Marcos and P. Norton, eds.): 101–119. Escuela Superior
          Politécnica del Litoral, Guayaquil.

PEARSALL, DEBORAH M.
  1988   An Overview of Formative Period Subsistence in Ecuador:
          Paleoethnobotanical Data and Perspectives. In *Diet and Subsistence: Current
          Archaeological Perspectives* (B. V. Kennedy and G. M. LeMoine, eds.): 149 158.
          Archaeological Association of the University of Calgary, Calgary, Alberta.
  1999   Agricultural Evolution and the Emergence of Formative Societies in Ecuador.
          In *Pacific Latin America in Prehistory: The Evolution of Archaic and Formative
          Cultures* (Michael Blake, ed.): 161–170. Washington State University Press,
          Pullman.

PEARSALL, DEBORAH M., AND DOLORES R. PIPERNO
  1990   Antiquity of Maize Cultivation in Ecuador: Summary and Reevaluation of
          the Evidence. *American Antiquity* 55 (2): 324–337.

PIPERNO, DOLORES R.
  1988   Primer informe sobre los fitolitos de las plantas del OGSE-80 y la evidencia
          del cultivo de maíz en el Ecuador. In *La prehistoria temprana de la península de
          Santa Elena, Ecuador: Cultura Las Vegas* (K. E. Stothert, ed.): 203–214. Serie
          Monográfica 10, Miscelánea Antropológica Ecuatoriana. Museos del Banco
          Central del Ecuador, Guayaquil.

RAYMOND, J. SCOTT
  1993   Ceremonialism in the Early Formative of Ecuador. In *El mundo ceremonial
          andino* (Luis Millones and Yoshio Onuki, eds.): 25–43. Senri Ethnological

Studies 37. National Museum of Ethnology, Osaka.

1999   Early Formative Societies in the Tropical Lowlands of Western Ecuador, a View from the Valdivia Valley. In *Pacific Latin America in Prehistory: The Evolution of Archaic and Formative Cultures* (Michael Blake, ed.): 149–159. Washington State University Press, Pullman.

RAYMOND, J. SCOTT, JORGE G. MARCOS, AND DONALD. W. LATHRAP

1980   Evidence of Early Formative Settlement in the Guayas Basin, Ecuador. *Current Anthropology* 21(5): 700–701.

ROTH, WALTER. E.

1924   *An Introductory Study of the Arts, Crafts, and Customs of the Guiana Indians.* Bureau of American Ethnology 38th Annual Report, Washington, D.C.

SCHWARZ, FREDERICK A., AND J. SCOTT RAYMOND

1996   Formative Settlement Patterns in the Valdivia Valley, Southwest Coastal Ecuador. *Journal of Field Archaeology* 23(2): 205–224.

SPATH, CARL D.

n.d.   The El Encanto Focus: A Post-Pleistocene Maritime Adaptation to Expanding Littoral Resources. Ph.D. dissertation, University of Illinois at Urbana–Champaign, 1980.

STAHL, PETER W.

1985   The Hallucinogenic Basis of Early Valdivia Phase Ceramic Bowl Iconography. *Journal of Psychoactive Drugs* 17 (2): 105–123.

1986   Hallucinatory Imagery and the Origin of Early South American Figurine Art. *World Archaeology* 18(1): 134–150.

n.d.a   The Archaeofauna of Loma Alta. Department of Archaeology, University of Calgary, Calgary, Alberta, 1985.

n.d.b   Tropical Forest Cosmology: The Cultural Context of the Early Valdivia Occupations at Loma Alta. Ph.D. dissertation, University of Illinois at Urbana–Champaign, 1984.

STALLER, JOHN EDWARD

n.d.a   The Jelí Phase at La Emerenciana, a Late Valdivia Site in Southern El Oro Province, Ecuador. Paper presented at the 23rd Annual Midwest Conference on Andean and Amazonian Archaeology and Ethnohistory, Chicago, 1995.

n.d.b   Late Valdivia Occupations in Southern Coastal El Oro Province, Ecuador: Excavations at the Early Formative Period (3500–1500 B.C.), Site of La Emerenciana. Ph.D. dissertation, Southern Methodist University, Dallas, 1994.

STOTHERT, KAREN E.

1985   The Preceramic Las Vegas Culture of Coastal Ecuador. *American Antiquity* 50: 613–637.

1988   *La prehistoria temprana de la península de Santa Elena: Cultura Las Vegas.* Miscelánea Antropológica Ecuatoriana 10, Museos del Banco Central del Ecuador, Guayaquil.

SWANTON, JOHN R.

1931   *Source Material for the Social and Ceremonial Life of the Choctaw Indians.* Bulletin 103, Bureau of American Ethnology, Smithsonian Institution, Washington, D.C.

van der Merwe, Nikolaas, Julia Lee-Thorp, and J. Scott Raymond
  1993   Light Stable Isotopes and the Subsistence Base of Formative Cultures at
          Valdivia, Ecuador. In *Prehistoric Human Bone: Archaeology at the Molecular Level*
          (J. B. Lambert and G. Grupe, eds.): 63–97. Springer-Verlag, Berlin.

Zeidler, James A.
  1986   La evolución local de asentamientos formativos en el Litoral ecuatoriano: El
          caso de Real Alto. In *Arqueología de la costa ecuatoriana: Nuevos enfoques* (J. G.
          Marcos, ed.): 85–127, Corporación Editora Nacional, Quito.

  1988   Feline Imagery, Stone Mortars, and Formative Period Interaction Spheres in
          the Northern Andean Area. *Journal of Latin American Lore* 14: 243–283.

  1994a   Archaeological Testing in the Lower Jama Valley. In *Regional Archaeology in
          Northern Ecuador,* vol. 1: *Environment, Cultural Chronology, and Prehistoric
          Subsistence in the Jama River Valley* (James A. Zeidler and Deborah M. Pearsall,
          eds.): 99–110. Memoirs in Latin American Archaeology 8. University of
          Pittsburgh, Pittsburgh, Pa.

  1994b   Archaeological Testing in the Middle Jama Valley. In *Regional Archaeology in
          Northern Ecuador,* vol. 1: *Environment, Cultural Chronology, and Prehistoric
          Subsistence in the Jama River Valley* (James A. Zeidler and Deborah M. Pearsall,
          eds.): 71–98. Memoirs in Latin American Archaeology 8, University of
          Pittsburgh, Pittsburgh, Pa.

  n.d.a   The Piquigua Phase: A Terminal Valdivia Occupation in Northern Manabí
          (Ecuador). Paper presented at the 57th Annual Meeting of the Society for
          American Archaeology, Pittsburgh, Pa., 1992.

  n.d.b   Social Space in Valdivia Society: Community Patterning and Domestic
          Structure at Real Alto, 3000–2000 B.C. Ph.D. dissertation, University of Illinois
          at Urbana-Champaign, 1984.

Zeidler, James A., and Deborah M. Pearsall, (eds.)
  1994   *Regional Archaeology in Northern Ecuador,* vol. 1: *Environment, Cultural Chronology,
          and Prehistoric Subsistence in the Jama River Valley.* Memoirs in Latin American
          Archaeology 8. University of Pittsburgh, Pittsburgh, Pa.

Zevallos Menéndez, Carlos, and Olaf Holm
  1960a   Excavaciones arqueológicas en San Pablo. *Ciencia y Naturaleza* 3(2/3): 62–95.

  1960b   *Excavaciones arqueológicas en San Pablo: Informe preliminar.* Editorial Casa de la
          Cultura Ecuatoriana, Nucleo del Guayas, Guayaquil.

Settlement Process and Historical Contingency in the Western Ecuadorian Formative

JAMES A. ZEIDLER
COLORADO STATE UNIVERSITY

JOHN S. ISAACSON
LOS ALAMOS NATIONAL LABORATORY

Ultimately, the question of questions boils down to the placement of the boundary between predictability under invariant law and the multifarious possibilities of historical contingency.
—Stephen J. Gould (1989: 290)

INTRODUCTION

In spite of the 40 or more years that have transpired since the three Formative period cultures of western Ecuador were defined, surprisingly little is known about their regional settlement dynamics, site densities, and intersite relationships. Much of the archaeological attention given to the Valdivia, Machalilla, and Chorrera cultures over the years has been site-specific and geographically restricted to a narrow band along the Pacific littoral or to a handful of sites at inland locations in the Guayas basin. Few survey projects have consciously aimed at providing representative regional coverage, although some at least provide survey data from specific river valleys. Even these, however, are few and far between, leaving much of the western Ecuadorian lowlands a terra incognita as far as Formative period settlement pattern studies are concerned.

In this essay, we examine settlement data for the Formative period cultural sequences of several coastal river valleys from Esmeraldas to El Oro for purposes of (a) comparing valleywide settlement processes and (b) highlighting fundamental differences in their developmental trajectories. For comparative purposes, we also reference several inland sites where Formative period occupations have been documented. Rather than viewing all of these archaeological sequences as uniform trajectories of increasing social complexity along a continuous and gradual evolutionary path, we argue that certain Formative period settlement processes documented in less studied areas, were truncated, or at least interrupted because of the variable short-term and long-term effects of volcanic eruptions that blanketed extensive portions of the western Ecuadorian lowlands and *montaña* during the Formative period. In these areas, then, punctuated cultural sequences characterized by periodic valley abandonment and resettlement, as well as interregional migration, seem to have been the norm. These patterns can be profitably viewed as examples of historical contingency operating on long-term trajectories of cultural development.

By *historical contingency*, we mean the interaction between evolving social formations and the unpredictable historical realities played out in a specific environmental setting. In this case, unpredictability derives from the extreme environmental instability of the volcanic zone of northern Ecuador. Historical contingency represents the net effect of the stochastic nature of "history" occurring in a number of contexts, both physical and social. The interplay of these contingencies with ongoing social processes and evolutionary transformations introduces an unpredictable quality that is particularly elusive archaeologically. Historical process, then, is comprised of (a) the causal relations acted out in the course of evolving social processes and (b) the contingent relations of unpredictable events that impact the evolving social processes, sometimes altering them dramatically (Bate 1978; Sayer 1992). McGuire has described this in the following terms:

> Historical process is both contingent and unpredictable. The prior conditions of a historical sequence, material relations, social structures, culture, and ideology define a range of possible actions that people can both conceive of and perform. Which of this possible range of actions people will undertake, however, is not determined but contingent. The conditions that structure human action leave broad channels and lots of room for actions and consequences that cannot be known in advance. Small changes in events or circumstances, actions taken or not taken, can, over time, have dramatic and unforeseeable consequences for the course of history (1992: 251).

In the emerging picture of the history of northwestern Ecuador, we argue that both social contingency (e.g., Formative period population expansion from southern to northern coastal river valleys) and environmental contingency (e.g., the volcanic–tectonic instability of northwestern Ecuador) had a significant impact on the evolution of western Formative cultures.[1]

From recent compositional analyses of tephras derived from stratigraphic contexts at numerous archaeological sites throughout the western Ecuadorian lowlands, we suggest that vast areas of the central lowlands were subjected to extensive volcanic airfalls from at least three different eruptions originating in the northern highlands, which affected to varying degrees the peoples occupying their path. More specifically, we argue that the entire area indicated by rules in Figure 1 was blanketed by one or more of these volcanic ashfalls in prehistory. Two of these volcanic events affected the Formative period and are discussed in greater detail here. While the primary negative effects of these eruptions would have followed a clinal gradient with increasing distance from the source eruption (from east to west), there is also a north–south gradient along which these tephras have been documented. Both of these gradients are crucial for understanding the variable nature of Formative period settlement processes. The area above our proposed volcanic impact zone is limited to Esmeraldas province, while to the south it comprises southern Guayas, southern Los Ríos, and El Oro provinces. The affected zone comprises northern, central, and part of southern Manabí province, the *montaña* zone of western Pichincha province, and the northern portions of Guayas and Los Ríos provinces. Although our evidence is somewhat limited in spatial extent, we argue that Formative period occupations within this impact zone were significantly affected by these episodes but to varying degrees, depending on their location with respect to the source eruption. Furthermore, watersheds lying above and below the impact zone may have been indirectly affected as potential refuge areas for migrations emanating out of the impact zone immediately following these catastrophic events. We hold that these considerations may help elucidate the uneven nature of cultural development in western Ecuador as well as provide plausible reasons for substantial hiatus periods in the cultural sequences of certain areas.

---

[1] For a detailed discussion of causality and contingency in historical materialist thought, see Bate (1978) and Sayer (1992). For discussion and debate on the concepts of historical process and contingency in southwestern U.S. archaeology, see McGuire (1994), Haas et al. (1994), and the counterpoint provided by Cordell (1994) and others in Gumerman and Gell-Mann (1994).

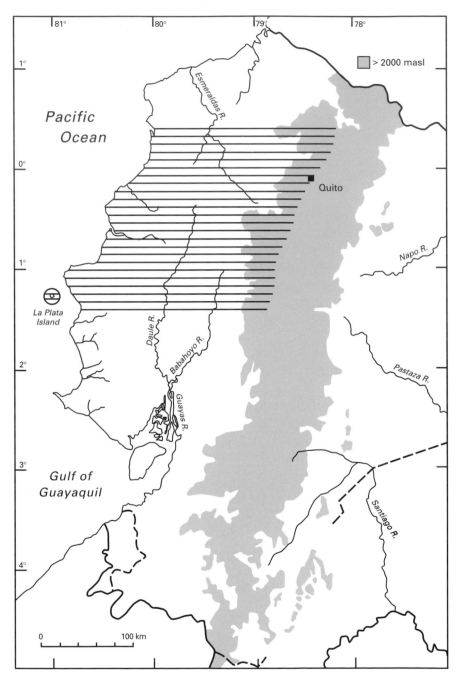

Fig. 1   Probable extent, indicated by horizontal rules, of the volcanic impact zone in the western *montaña* and lowlands of Ecuador. This area (0° 30' N, 1° 30' S) extends from the Cordillera Occidental in the east to the Pacific Ocean in the west.

VOLCANIC ZONATION IN THE NORTHERN HIGHLANDS

Background

Before our discussion of Formative period settlement dynamics and developmental trajectories, it may be useful to review briefly the geological context of Ecuadorian volcanism. The Andean range is characterized by three zones of volcanic activity: southern Colombia/northern Ecuador, southern Peru, and southern Chile, which result from segments of the Nazca Plate being subducted at angles greater than 25°. In northern Ecuador, volcanic activity is amplified by the Carnegie Ridge, a 3-km high, 300-km wide sea floor ridge formed by the passage of the Nazca Plate over the Galapagos Hot Spot (Barberi et al. 1988; Hall and Beate 1991; Hall and Wood 1985; Isaacson 1990, 1994; Sillitoe 1974; Zeil 1979). The subduction of this topographic feature is responsible for the increased uplift of the northern Ecuadorian Andes and the widespread and chemically diverse multiple rows of volcanoes.

The northern Andean volcanoes form an extensive arc of active and dormant stratovolcanoes and rhyolitic ash sheets stretching from 5°N to 3°30'S. The Colombian volcanoes are compositionally similar (Hall and Wood 1985; Herd n.d.). However, from the Ecuadorian border south, volcanism becomes more abundant and compositionally variable with the volcanoes of the Cordillera Occidental forming a continuous front some 270 km long (Fig. 2). Since the late Pleistocene, 20 or more of the northern Ecuadorian volcanoes have had major eruptions (Hall and Wood). For the last 3,000 years, radiocarbon dating has confirmed eruptions of these volcanoes: Cerro Negro, Cuicocha, Guagua Pinchincha, Ninahuilca, Pululahua, Quilotoa, and possibly Rasuyacu (Hall and Beate 1991; see also Hall and Mothes 1994).

The silicic stratovolcanoes of the Cordillera Occidental produce explosive plinian eruptions with eruption columns extending tens of kilometers high. This airborne pyroclastic material, or *tephra*, is distributed by the prevailing upper atmospheric easterlies forming fan-shaped deposits west of the volcanic vents (Eaton 1964; Johnson 1969; Sadler 1975; Schwerdtfeger 1976). The inter-Andean basins have also been mantled by these eruptions, resulting in massive ecosystem disruptions oriented on an east–west axis through northern Ecuador (Isaacson 1990, 1994, n.d.; Lathrap, Isaacson, and McEwan 1984). As noted below, samples of these tephra deposits have been recovered from a number of archaeological deposits throughout the northern highlands, western *montaña*, and coastal lowlands, permitting chemical characterization of at least three different volcanic eruptions and their tephrochronological correlations over extensive areas of the western Ecuadorian landscape. One of these eruptive events,

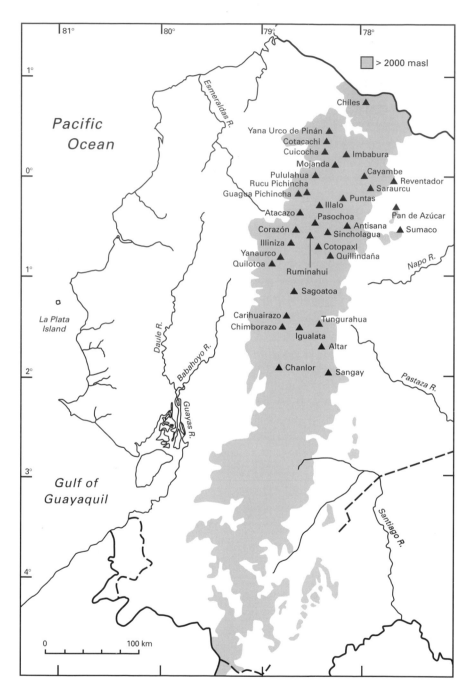

Fig. 2   Map of the northern Ecuadorian highlands, with triangles showing the location of the principal volcanoes.

the massive Pululahua eruption at the end of the Formative period, is high-lighted in this essay, as it is the *one* event for which a source volcano has been conclusively identified (Geotermica Italiana and Instituto Ecuatoriano de Mineria 1989; Hall and Mothes 1994; Papale and Rosi 1993).

Dating the Pululahua Eruption

Hall (1977) obtained a radiocarbon assay of 2305 ± 65 RYBP (SI-2128) from carbonized wood in the base surge deposits corresponding to the Pululahua eruption. Since then, a second date has been obtained for this eruption by a team of Italian and Ecuadorian volcanologists (Geotermica Italiana and the Instituto Ecuatoriano de Mineria 1989). Their sample (GP88-135) was derived from a peat deposit immediately underlying a layer of plinian airfall. The resulting assay of 2650 ± 150 RYBP is somewhat earlier than that of Hall. They have suggested an "averaged" estimate of 2450 RYBP for the Pululahua eruption, which they uncritically converted to calendar years as 500 B.C. (see also Papale and Rosi 1993). However, to correctly assess the timing of this event in calendar years for purposes of archaeological analysis, it is essential to examine the contexts of these radiocarbon specimens, as well as calculate calibrated calendrical dates from the raw radiocarbon assays.

In the first place, we question the utility of averaging or combining the two radiocarbon assays, since they are essentially dating different phenomena. The earlier assay, GP88-135, is directly dating the cumulative formation process of a peat deposit,[2] which demonstrably predates the Pululahua eruption. It should thus be considered a *terminus post quem* rather than part of the eruption. Averaging is misleading. The later assay, SI-2128, on the other hand, was made on carbonized wood extracted directly from the base surge deposits on the east flank of the volcanic cone and thus constitutes a more appropriate estimate of the eruption itself.

Secondly, the derivation of a true calendar age for a radiocarbon assay cannot be accurately carried out by simply subtracting 1,950 years from the raw radio-carbon determination. This practice does not take into account the widely accepted dendrochronological calibration curve (Stuiver, Long, and Kra 1993) and the non-Gaussian nature of radiocarbon ages when projected on that curve (Bowman 1990; see also Buck, Cavanaugh, and Litton 1996: 201–252). Calibration is thus a necessary step in the transformation of radiocarbon results into calendar years. For this purpose we have utilized the probabilistic calibration

---

[2] See Christen, Clymor, and Litton (1995) for discussion of the special problems involved in the interpretation of calibrated radiocarbon dates from peat deposits.

method of OxCal software, version 2.01 (Ramsey 1995).[3] Applying this method, then, SI-2128 gives a time range spanning from 752 to 182 cal B.C. (midpoint = 467 cal B.C.), from the three probability intervals of the 95.4 percent confidence level (Fig. 3). The sample GP88-135 gives a range of 1160 to 396 cal B.C. (midpoint = 778 cal B.C.), from the two probability intervals of the 95.4 percent confidence level (Fig. 4), and probably predates the eruption by several hundred years. Using only the SI-2128 assay, then, we argue that 752 to 182 cal B.C. represents the best approximation of the true calendar age of the Pululahua eruption. While this 570-year range is not especially helpful for precise calendrical timing, it is the best approximation available in the absence of additional radiocarbon determinations that directly date primary pyroclastic deposition.

FORMATIVE PERIOD SETTLEMENT DYNAMICS IN THE WESTERN LOWLANDS

Our limited scope does not allow detailed assessment of Formative period settlement dynamics for the entire western lowlands, nor of the political and economic contexts within which these settlement systems evolved. Here we wish to compare only the broad patterns of Formative period settlement continuity and population dynamics as a means of illustrating two very different scenarios for cultural development. Our thinking on this matter has stemmed

---

[3] The OxCal software program, version 2.01, developed by C. Bronk Ramsey at Oxford University, is available on the World Wide Web at http://www.rlaha.ox.ac.uk/orau.html. This method provides multiple probability intervals or bands for the 68.2%, 95.4%, and 99.7% confidence levels and thus allows for objective assessment of the spread and modality of a given radiocarbon assay when projected on the dendrochronological calibration curve of Stuiver, Long, and Kra. (1993). The multimodal nature and wide variability of the calibration curve for the general time range under consideration (ca. 800–400 B.C.) are well-known phenomena (Bowman 1990), and it is important to emphasize the special nature of radiocarbon results pertaining to this general time range. For the sake of simplicity, we have used the combined probability intervals of the 95.4% confidence level (±2σ error) to derive the appropriate time range in calendar years B.C. (Bowman 1990). As Bowman (1990: 49) observed, "There is nearly a one in three chance of the true result lying outside the 68.3% time range(s), and it makes much more sense to cut the chance to 1 in 20 by using the 95.4% range(s)." In Bayesian statistics this range is termed the *highest posterior density* (HPD) region (Buck, Cavanagh, and Litton 1996: 153), and it is the most appropriate way to interpret or represent calibrated radiocarbon results. For convenience, we have also provided the mathematical midpoint or median value of that range. We urge caution in the use of these midpoint values, however, as they are not intended as precise estimates of the true calendar age of these radiocarbon assays. Such measures of central tendency are somewhat spurious or, at best, incomplete summaries because of the multimodal nature of the calibrated probability distribution (Buck, Cavanagh, and Litton 1996). Figures 3, 4, 6, 8, 9, and 18 provide the computer-generated plots for these calibrations resulting from the OxCal program and illustrates the different probability intervals for all three confidence levels.

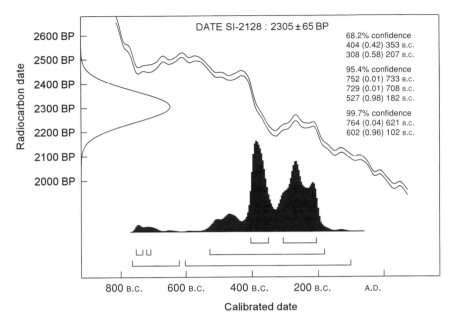

Fig. 3 OxCal computer plot of calibration results for SI-2128, carbonized wood extracted from base surge deposits on the east flank of the Pululahua *caldera* (Hall 1977).

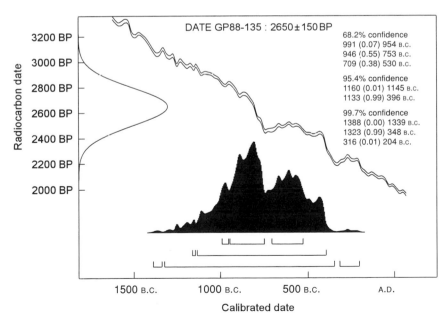

Fig. 4 OxCal computer plot of calibration results for GP88-135, peat deposits underlying pyroclastic materials on the Pululahua *caldera* (Geotermica Italiana and Instituto Ecuatoriano de Minería 1989).

from intensive field research in two areas of western Ecuador which have traditionally received less archaeological attention: the western *montaña* of Pichincha province (e.g., the Tulipe valley) and the coastal valleys of northern Manabí province (e.g., the Jama valley). In both of these localities of the central western lowlands, the Formative period cultural sequences were interrupted by major volcanic eruptions resulting in significant stratigraphic breaks or hiatuses between major cultural occupations during which the resident populations were forced to abandon their territory and migrate elsewhere. The same is true for the Formative period occupation of Cotocollao in the Quito basin (see Bruhns, this volume), which lies at approximately the same latitude. In contrast, in the lowland areas to the north and south of our proposed volcanic impact zone, where most archaeological research has traditionally been concentrated, the cultural sequences can be generally characterized as *continuous* trajectories in which gradual stylistic changes in pottery and other material items mark the transitions between major cultural occupations and no significant hiatus periods have been identified, although the Santa Elena peninsula may be an exception in this regard because of the periodic effects of drought throughout the prehistoric sequence (Paulsen 1976).

Continuous Trajectories and Cultural Transitions

To the far north of our proposed volcanic impact zone, archaeological research in northern Esmeraldas at the coastal La Tolita site (Valdez 1986, 1987) and at inland locations along the Santiago and Cayapas rivers (DeBoer 1995, 1996; Tolstoy and DeBoer 1989) has demonstrated a basal Late Formative occupation, but with a beginning date (ca. 500 B.C.) that coincides, more or less, with the ending date for Late Formative occupations farther south along the coast of Ecuador. From that point on, a continuous trajectory of six cultural occupations is documented for the Santiago–Cayapas area up to the present. These include the Mafa, Selva Alegre, Guadual, Las Cruces/Herradura, Tumbaviro, and modern Chachi phases, as defined by DeBoer (1995, 1996). At the La Tolita site, a continuous development also characterizes the Early La Tolita, Classic La Tolita, and Late La Tolita phases during the Regional Developmental period. The earliest occupation at the island, termed Early La Tolita by Valdez (1986, 1987) and pre-Tolita by Bouchard (1996), is dated to about 500 to 600 B.C. At about A.D. 350, however, the site was abandoned for unknown reasons and never reoccupied. In southern Esmeraldas, archaeological work by a team of Spanish archaeologists in the vicinity of Esmeraldas and Atacames has also produced a similar picture. A basal cultural occupation of Late Formative Chorrera culture, termed the Tachina phase, has been established (López y Sebastián 1986; López y Sebastián and Caillavet 1979; Stirling 1963), and, although it lacks radiometric dating, it has been chonologically placed at 400 to 50 B.C. (Bouchard 1996; Guinea 1986; Rivera et al. 1984). A continuous cultural trajectory is documented thereafter, which includes the Tiaone culture (Regional Developmental period), the Balao culture (Integration period) and the Nigua culture (Historic period) (Alcina Franch 1979, 1985).

The degree to which volcanic airfalls may have affected, if at all, the prehistory of Esmeraldas is yet to be determined. Although a single tephra layer has been observed and sampled along a river cut near Maldonado in the lower Santiago basin of northern Esmeraldas (Judith Kreid, personal communication, 12 April 1995), its precise stratigraphic position with regard to the pre-Hispanic cultural sequence has not been determined. To the best of our knowledge, tephras have never been identified in controlled archaeological contexts in Esmeraldas province. For the present, then, we assume that Esmeraldas lies outside of our zone of direct impact.

Just beyond the southern limit of our proposed volcanic impact zone in southern Manabí province, intensive long-term excavations at the coastal site of Salango (Norton 1992; Norton, Lunnis, and Nayling 1983) have yielded evidence of a long continuous trajectory of human occupation as early as 3500 B.C. and continuing into the Historic period. For the Formative period, the entire sequence appears to be present, including the entire eight-phase Valdivia sequence, the entire Machalilla sequence, a Chorrera and Bahia I (Engoroy) component, as well as transitional phases between these major occupations (Norton 1992). As in Esmeraldas, no evidence of volcanic ash deposits has been found in archaeological contexts from this area. For inland localities, little is known about the Late Formative period. Although two archaeological surveys have been carried out in the nearby Río Blanco and Río Ayampe valleys (Damp 1984; Smith n.d.), they have focused exclusively on Valdivia settlement patterns but at least they confirm the presence of all eight ceramic phases and offer no evidence for volcanic ash deposits in these contexts.

Farther south along the Guayas coast, the same pattern is repeated although in some areas a short hiatus existed where Valdivia 8 occupations or a Valdivia–Machalilla transitional phase have not been found in an otherwise continuous Formative sequence. In general terms, this pattern holds for the Valdivia valley (Lippi n.d.; Raymond n.d; Schwarz and Raymond 1996); the Santa Elena peninsula (Paulsen and McDougle n.d.), and the Chanduy valley (Damp 1984; Zeidler 1986, n.d.a,b). In these areas, the Terminal Valdivia phase is generally represented by a widely dispersed settlement pattern of small isolated homesteads with no evidence for local ceremonial centers. This pattern continues during the subsequent Machalilla occupation of the area. At inland sites in the Guayas basin, such as San Lorenzo del Mate (Marcos 1989), and in the Arenillas valley in El Oro province (Staller n.d.), cultural continuity is even more pronounced in that a clear Valdivia–Machalilla transition is observable in the ceramic sequences. At other inland Guayas sites along the lower Daule River (Raymond, Marcos, and Lathrap 1980; Stemper 1993), much of the Formative sequence has been documented in deeply buried alluvial contexts, but additional work is required for conclusively determining the continuous nature of the sequence from Early to Late Formative. However, Stemper (1993: 113–115) has presented limited but convincing evidence for the derivation of his early Regional Development Silencio 1 phase directly out of a Chorrera or Chorrera-like occupation at the Yumes locality.

Volcanism, Discontinuous Trajectories, and Regional Abandonment

Our narrative of discontinuous cultural trajectories and volcanic impacts in the Formative period begins in the highlands in an archaeological context from the Quito basin, at the proximal end of the eruptive events. From there, we treat three archaeological contexts in western Ecuador that lie at progressively greater distances from the source eruptions so as to highlight the attenuating effects of distance on the relative ecosystemic devastation caused by pyroclastic airfalls.

Highland Pichincha: Quito Valley (Cotocollao). The information about the excavations and the material collected at the site of Cotocollao comes from Porras (1982), who first discovered the site and performed test excavations there, and reports from the extensive excavations conducted by the Museo Arqueológico del Banco Central under the direction of Emil Peterson and later by Marcelo Villalba (Peterson n.d.; Villalba 1988).

The Cotocollao basin, which runs northwest of Quito, was once marshland surrounding a number of shallow lakes. The Cotocollao site is strategically located at the foot of a low pass or *boca de montaña* (Acosta Solís 1968) that connects the Quito basin with the subtropical and tropical forests of the western Andean foothills. The Cotocollao site has a Middle-to-Late Formative occupation dating from approximately 2000 to 500 B.C., as determined by radiocarbon assay (Villalba 1988). This component was mantled by the Pululahua eruption, which forced the site's abandonment (Geotermica Italiana and Instituto Ecuatoriano de Mineria 1989; Papale and Rosi 1993; Villalba 1988). The physical stratigraphy of the site is complex (Fig. 5), reflecting its long occupation. Three major divisions can be defined in the stratigraphic sequence. The uppermost strata are comprised of a normal bedded sequence of volcanic ash, *lapilli*, and bombs that cover the artifact-bearing paleosol. These strata represent the remnant tephra deposits from the Pululahua eruption ca. 467 B.C. The upper-most soils and later cultural materials were removed by grading prior to the discovery of the site. Below the pyroclastic debris is a thick paleosol that con-tains the Formative period component. This is a complex series of superim-posed house floors, pit features, burials, and midden, which continues from the volcanic strata for 70 cm. The upper portions of this paleosol underlying the pyroclastic deposits from the Pululahua eruption yielded a radiocarbon assay of 2410 ± 140 RYBP (GX-4764). Calibration of this value yields an age range of 819 to 168 cal B.C. (midpoint = 494 cal B.C.), based on the single probability interval of the 95.4 percent confidence level (Fig. 6). Below this cultural stra-

Cotocollao Site, Quito Basin
Profile section, 1976 excavations

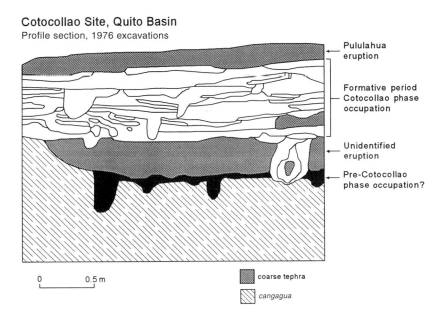

Pululahua eruption

Formative period Cotocollao phase occupation

Unidentified eruption

Pre-Cotocollao phase occupation?

0   0.5 m

coarse tephra

cangagua

Fig. 5   Physical stratigraphy at the Cotocollao site, Quito basin. This represents a 2.8-m section extracted from a longer 12-m profile drawing pertaining to the late Emil Peterson's 1976 excavations at Cotocollao (Peterson n.d.) under the auspices of the Museo Arqueológico del Banco Central del Ecuador (Quito). The drawing by Lynnette Norr is derived from unpublished field data and manuscripts of Peterson's on file in the library at the University of Illinois at Urbana–Champaign. Unfortunately, the precise location of this cut within the site is not documented, but it pertains to cut 1 of the preliminary stratigraphic trenches ("street profiles") resulting from road-cutting activity related to an urbanization project (see Villalba 1988: figs. 10–13).

tum is a 35-cm thick layer of light gray-to-white, culturally sterile tephra. It is discontinuous across the site but where it is preserved, it covers a 5-cm thick paleosol that contains archaeological features. This paleosol, which clearly predates the Cotocollao phase and may date to the Early Formative period, is at the base of the occupation and rests on the culturally sterile Cangahua Formation of Pleistocene age. Unfortunately, no pyroclastic material was collected from this pre-Cotocollao occupation, and little information exists about it. However, a tephra mantle of comparable age in the Jama valley is discussed below.

Western Pichincha: Tulipe valley (Nueva Era) and Mindo valley (Nambillo). The Nueva Era site is 35 km W by NW of Quito above the modern town of Tulipe. Tulipe is located 0°5'15" N, 78°40'57" W, at an elevation of 1,500 m. This area lies at the lower margins of the subtropical cloud forests that run along the western slopes of the Cordillera Occidental. The Nueva Era site was excavated to 3.4 m below the surface. Two prehistoric occupations were identified: the Integration Period Tulipe phase (stratum C) and the deeply buried Middle-to-Late Formative Nueva Era phase (stratum B$_1$), which is contemporaneous with

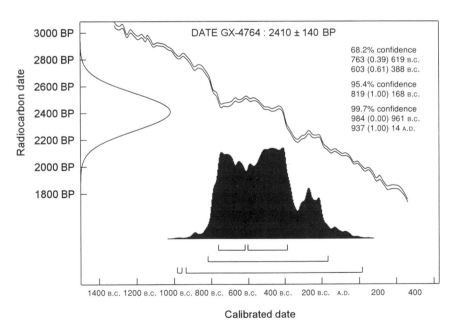

Fig. 6   OxCal computer plot of calibration results for radiocarbon assay GX-4764, Quito basin, Cotocollao site (Peterson n.d.; Porras 1982).

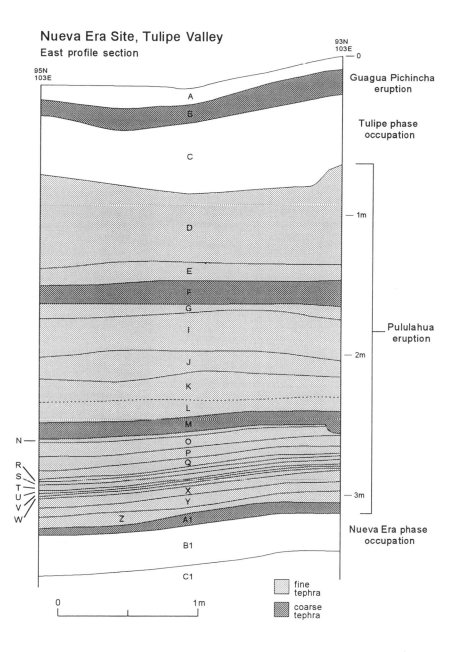

Fig. 7   Physical stratigraphy of the east profile at the Nueva Era site, Tulipe valley.

Cotocollao (Fig. 7). Overlying the Tulipe phase occupation is a 13-cm thick airfall deposit of the eruption of Guagua Pichincha in A.D. 1660 (Isaacson 1990, n.d.). Between the two occupations lie thick volcanic deposits (strata D–A_1) representing three episodes of intense volcanic activity that occurred within a relatively short period. The uppermost eruptive episode is represented by strata D, E, and F. Together they are 91 cm thick and are normally bedded from fine ash to coarse lapilli, some of which are 6 cm in diameter. These strata are interpreted as a single explosive eruption of considerable magnitude.

Below this deposit is an 86-cm thick series of tephras represented by strata G, I, J, K, L, and M. These strata represent another eruption that exhibits characteristics of a primary airfall deposit. Stratum M is comprised of 13 cm of coarse lapilli, which represent the initial deposits of this blast. Below this pyroclastic unit is evidence for a short period of quiescence, as illustrated by deep channels eroded into the underlying deposits when they were exposed at the surface. These channels are filled with the coarse lapilli from stratum M above. This bottommost series of pyroclastic deposits is made up of a 53-cm thick ash sequence (strata N–A_1) which indicates several closely spaced volcanic blasts or pulses. No evidence of erosion exists within this sequence. The three pyroclastic units can be interpreted as three stages of a single volcanic eruption cycle. Below A_1 is a 24-cm dark brown paleosol that contains the Middle-to-Late Formative materials and structure floors representing the Nueva Era phase occupation. Below this paleosol are a series of culturally sterile silts and clays that continue to bedrock.

The Nueva Era phase ceramics and the radiocarbon dates place the occupation between ca. 1500 and 400 B.C. A radiocarbon assay from a hearth context in the Nueva Era phase component yielded a value of 2620 ± 70 RYBP (ISGS-1175). The calibrated age range for this value is 915 to 520 cal B.C. (midpoint = 718 cal B.C.), on the basis of the single probability interval of the 95.4 percent confidence level (Fig. 8). This paleosol layer sets a maximum age for the erupted material above it in the stratigraphic column and supports the correlation of this material with the eruption of Pululahua at 2305 ± 65 RYBP. Thereafter, the valley was abandoned for over 1,000 years until its reoccupation by the Late Integration period Tulipe phase. With a mantle of tephra and other pyroclastic material more than 2.3 m thick, ecosystemic damage in this airfall zone was extensive and probably forced any survivors of the eruption to migrate north or south, away from the east–west axis of airfall deposition.

This eruptive sequence is also represented at the archaeological site of Nambillo, located approximately 18.5 km to the south of Tulipe, but with an interesting variation. Here Lippi (1988: table 1) documented a deep stratigraphic sequence with three distinct layers of pyroclastic deposits. His Paleosol 3 (buried anthropic epipedon) is partially contemporaneous with the Nueva Era phase of Tulipe and the Cotocollao phase of the Quito basin. Five radiocarbon assays from this context range from 2315 ± 260 to 5325 ± 110 RYBP. The youngest of these values (GX-12472: 2315 ± 260 RYBP) yields a calibrated range of 992 cal B.C. to 242 cal A.D. (midpoint = 375 cal B.C.), on the basis of the two probability intervals of the 95.4 percent confidence level (Fig. 9). Note that this estimated time range extends over four centuries later than our estimated date for the Pululahua eruption, but this is most likely because of the high sigma value assigned to this radiocarbon determination, which makes its calibrated age range even more variable. Paleosol 3 is capped by a ca. 70-cm thick series of pyroclastic deposits identified by Italian volcanologists as the Pululahua eruption (Geotermica Italiana and Instituto Ecuatoriano de Minería 1989: fig. 10.1). Following this volcanic event, another paleosol horizon (Paleosol 2) appears with ceramics similar to late Cotocollao material. A suite of four radiocarbon assays from this context ranges from 1665 ± 200 to 2515 ± 85 RYBP. This paleosol is capped by a ca. 20-cm thick layer of pyroclastic material tentatively identified as the eruption of the volcano Guagua Pichincha in A.D. 550. Note that this second volcanic event and its underlying cultural occupations are *not* represented in the Tulipe sequence a short distance to the north. A third paleosol

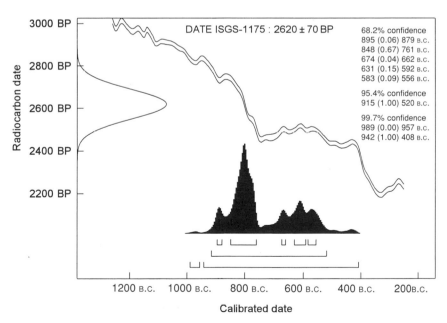

Fig. 8   OxCal computer plot of calibration results for radiocarbon assay ISGS-1175, Tulipe valley, Nueva Era site, Nueva Era phase hearth context (Isaacson n.d.).

(Paleosol 1) overlies these deposits and pertains to a late prehistoric/early colonial occupation of the area, contemporaneous with the Tulipe phase in the Tulipe valley. A suite of six radiocarbon determinations ranges from 820 ± 75 to 1665 ± 75 RYBP. This paleosol is capped by a third layer of pyroclastic material correctly identified by Lippi (1988) as the eruption of Guagua Pichincha in A.D. 1660. The final stratigraphic deposit is a humus layer representing modern occupation.

Northern Manabí: Jama valley (San Isidro and related sites). The Jama River valley is a 1,612 km² drainage located in northern Manabí province. It is a coastal valley flowing westward into the Pacific Ocean from headwaters originating in a series of low hills some 75 km inland. Three volcanic ash layers have been identified and sampled throughout the valley in archaeological contexts representing a long cultural sequence spanning more than 3,500 years (Zeidler 1994a,b; Zeidler and Sutliff 1994; Zeidler, Buck, and Litton 1998). They were first encountered in deep stratigraphic excavations in Sector XII/Area C at the archaeological site of San Isidro (Fig. 10), located at 0°22'30"S, 8°10'00" W. This site is centrally located within the drainage in a large tract of alluvial bottomland and served as a primary regional civic–ceremonial center throughout the

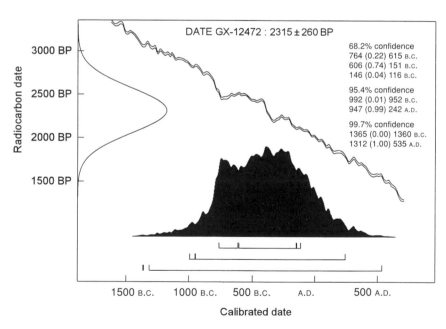

Fig. 9   OxCal computer plot of calibration results for radiocarbon assay GX-12472, Mindo valley, Nambillo site, upper portion of Paleosol 3 (Lippi 1988).

cultural sequence. Ceremonial mound building began in the Early Formative period and continued well into the Integration period. Tephra I (Fig. 11) occurs at the end of the Terminal Valdivia (Early Formative period) occupation approximately 5 m below surface and is comprised of deposits 31–33, the lower of which is a primary deposit of airfall, while the latter two are reworked tephra. Tephra II caps the Chorrera component (Late Formative period) at about 2.3 m below the surface and is represented by a single layer (deposit 21) of reworked tephra. Tephra III caps the Jama–Coaque I component of the valley and comprises two deposits of reworked tephra (deposits 5, 5c) at about 1 to 1.3 m below the surface. It provides a clear stratigraphic break between two phases of the long Jama–Coaque ceramic tradition, which is the hallmark culture of northern Manabí during the Regional Developmental and Integration periods.

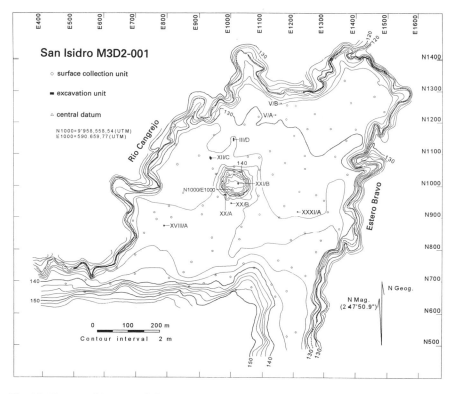

Fig. 10 Topographic map of the San Isidro site, Jama valley, showing location of various archaeological sampling units (reproduced from Zeidler [1994b: fig. 5.1] with permission of the University of Pittsburgh Memoirs in Latin American Archaeology series).

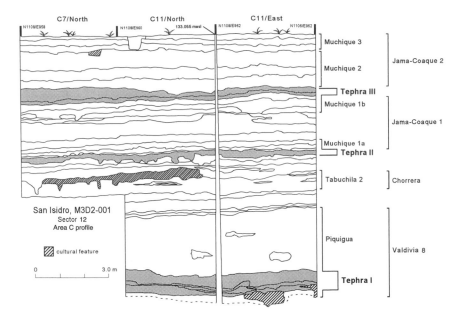

Fig. 11 Physical stratigraphy of Area XII/Unit C at the San Isidro site, Jama valley.

Since the initial test excavations at San Isidro, a systematic regional archaeo-logical survey of the Jama valley has yielded the discovery of some 239 ar-chaeological sites (Zeidler 1995, n.d.c), and additional site testing has yielded new information on the chronostratigraphy of these three tephra mantles across the valley landscape and their probable correlation within the valley and with tephras from other regions of Ecuador. Here we consider only the two erup-tions that impacted the Formative period occupations. Chronological place-ment of these tephra units is based on the bracketing of radiocarbon assays and ceramic cross-dating from archaeological sites with clearly defined stratigraphic deposition and well-seriated ceramic sequences. Tephra I is dated at 3603 ± 40 RYBP at San Isidro[4] and its source eruption is unknown at present. It may correlate with the basal tephra documented at Cotocollao (see Fig. 5 Isaacson n.d.; Villalba 1988: fig. 5). Villalba (1988) suggests an age range between 3,450 and 4,950 BP for this basal tephra, although the source of these temporal esti-

---

[4] This determination is based on the averaged value of three radiocarbon assays associ-ated with the Tephra I airfall deposits in Unit XII/C11 at San Isidro (Zeidler 1994b). These assays are as follows: 3630 ± 70 RYBP (ISGS-1221); 3560 ± 70 RYBP (ISGS-1223); and 3620 ± 70 RYBP (ISGS-1222). The calibrated age range for these combined assays is 2115–1782 cal B.C. (midpoint = 1949 cal B.C.), from four probability intervals of the 95.4% confidence level.

mates is not discussed. It is interesting, however, that these dates are consistent with the Early Formative dates from the Jama valley. Tephra I seems to have blanketed the valley toward the end of the short-lived Valdivia 8 (Piquigua phase) occupation when population densities were relatively low. However, archaeological evidence seems to indicate that the Valdivians survived the detrimental effects of the volcanic ashfall, at least for a short time. At least two occupation surfaces uncovered at San Isidro clearly postdate the tephra deposit, so no general abandonment seems to have occurred as an *immediate* result of the eruption. However shortly thereafter (perhaps in a matter of months), the region was abandoned and was not repopulated for some 475 to 560 years when the Chorrera peoples (Tabuchila phase) appeared in the valley. No evidence has been found for a Machalilla occupation of the Jama valley either in our regional survey or in our controlled excavations.

As to the post-Chorrera ash deposit (Tephra II), an approximate date of 2300 RYBP has been assumed given the high probability of correlation with the Pululahua eruption (Hall 1977) dated at 2305 ± 65 RYBP (SI-2128) and calibrated to an age range between 752 and 182 cal B.C. (midpoint = 467 cal B.C.). This age range is considerably later than that proposed for the Chorrera occupation of the Jama valley. Bayesian statistical analysis of the available calibrated radiocarbon assays for this component suggests an occupation ranging from 1300 to 750 B.C. (Table 1; see also Buck, Cavanagh, and Litton 1996; Zeidler, Buck, and Litton 1998). Three additional radiocarbon determinations from Chorrera deposits at the Dos Caminos site near San Isidro tend to confirm this early placement (Evan Engwall, personal communication, 30 September 1996).

However, there is a preponderance of stratigraphic and ceramic evidence indicating a late Chorrera component (Tabuchila 2) in the valley as well (Zeidler 1994a,b; Zeidler and Sutliff 1994). A terminal Chorrera radiocarbon determination of 2500 ± 160 RYBP (ISGS-2377) was excavated by Engwall at the Mocoral site in the lower Jama valley, where it was extracted from reworked volcanic ash deposits (Tephra II) admixed with and overlying Chorrera deposits. Calibration of this value gives a range of 979 to 196 B.C. (midpoint = 588 cal B.C.), from the two probability intervals of the 95.4 percent confidence level (Fig. 12). Late Chorrera materials (Tabuchila 2) were also found immediately underlying the Tephra II unit in several test units at the San Isidro site (Zeidler 1994b). This stratigraphic contiguity between terminal Chorrera deposits and Tephra II is especially evident in Sector V/Unit B1 (Donahue and Harbert 1994: fig. 3.4; Zeidler 1994b: fig. 5.16) and Sector XXXI/Unit A1 (Zeidler 1994b: fig. 5.19). In both cases Chorrera paleosols immediately underlie tephra deposits pertaining to the Pululahua eruption. In other cases, where

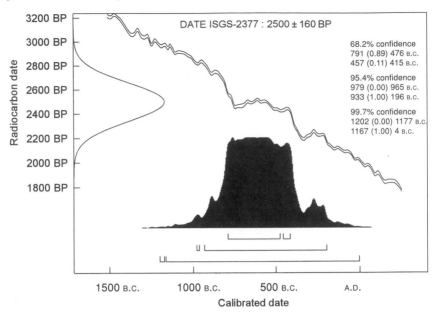

Fig. 12 OxCal computer plot of calibration results for radiocarbon assay ISGS-2377, Jama Valley, Mocoral site, Test Unit 2 Deposits 10/11 (Engwall, personal communication, 1995).

sterile deposits immediately underlie the Tephra II ashfall at San Isidro (Units XVIII/A1, XII/C11, and V/A1), they are interpreted as fluvial deposits directly related to increased rainfall and flooding slightly preceding the volcanic airfall (Donahue and Harbert 1994: 57, fig. 3.8). Unfortunately, no suitable radiocarbon samples have been encountered in these late Chorrera (Tabuchila 2) paleosol deposits. From stratigraphic evidence alone, however, it is clear that the Chorrera occupation extended later than 750 B.C., which was suggested by Bayesian statistical analysis and available radiocarbon evidence. Additional radiocarbon determinations from these later Chorrera deposits are needed to confirm this supposition. In any case, there is reasonable agreement between the calibrated age ranges for the Pululahua eruption (SI-2128: 752–182 cal B.C.) and the Tephra II deposits from the Mocoral site in the Jama valley (ISGS-2377: 979–196 cal B.C.), given the vagaries of the radiocarbon method and the slightly higher sigma on the Mocoral determination (compare Figs. 3 and 12).[5]

[5] In spite of the general agreement between these two calibrated age ranges, it would be inappropriate to average the original radiocarbon results in an attempt to improve the calibrated range for the Pululahua eruption because the charcoal sample from the upland Mocoral site was extracted from a reworked tephra layer that was probably redeposited from other slopes in its immediate vicinity. Thus the charcoal sample may actually be dating slightly earlier Chorrera deposits and not the volcanic event per se. As such, it should be considered a *terminus post quem* for the Pululahua eruption.

As at Cotocollao and Nueva Era, the Late Formative Chorrera occupation in the Jama valley was apparently devastated by the Pululahua eruption, although probably not as severely because of its much greater distance (ca. 200 km) from the source eruption. A definite stratigraphic break exists in the archaeological record, which corresponds precisely with a demonstrable break in ceramic style and technology. On the basis of calibrated radiocarbon dates bracketing the Tephra II airfall, the subsequent hiatus lasted about 250 years, at which point early Jama–Coaque peoples settled in the valley and began a long and fairly stable tradition of complex chiefdoms. Bayesian statistical analysis has

Table 1

Cultural Occupations in the Jama Valley

Cultural component	Ceramic phase	95% probability region and modal values cal B.C./A.D.		
Campace?	Muchique 5	1540	(1640)	1910 cal
		1360	(1430)	1620 cal
Spanish Conquest (1532)				
Jama–Coaque II	Muchique 4	1360	(1430)	1620 cal
		950	(1290)	1400 cal
Jama–Coaque II	Muchique 3	1180	(1260)	1430 cal
		640	(880)	970 cal
Jama–Coaque II	Muchique 2	700	(790)	990 cal
		230	(420)	550 cal
Tephra III (hiatus)				
Jama–Coaque I	Muchique 1	50 cal B.C.	(90)	350 cal A.D.
		620	(240)	100 cal B.C.
Tephra II (hiatus)				
Chorrera	Tabuchila	1050	(750)	290 cal B.C.
		1730	(1300)	1020 cal B.C.
hiatus				
Valdivia	Piquigua (late)			
	Tephra I	2000	(1880)	1540 cal B.C.
	Piquigua (early)	2320	(2030)	1880 cal B.C.

Note: Data based on Bayesian statistical analysis of available radiocarbon evidence.

placed this reoccupation of the valley at about 240 B.C. (Table 1; Zeidler, Buck, and Litton 1998).

Both the Piquigua and Tabuchila occupations of the Jama valley can be considered ranked or stratified societies having simple settlement hierarchies focused on a large ceremonial center with monumental construction, variable site sizes, and locational preference for alluvial bottomland settings. The Piquigua phase lasted about 150 years, and the Tabuchila occupation was considerably longer. Bayesian statistical analysis of available radiocarbon dates suggests a 550-year Chorrera occupation (Zeidler, Buck, and Litton 1998), while stratigraphic and ceramic evidence point to a longer Chorrera presence lasting some 800 years. The principal difference between these two Formative period cultures lies in the greater social complexity and population density exhibited by the Chorrera peoples and a trend toward upland settlement during this phase.

Figure 13 illustrates the spatial distribution of Terminal Valdivia (Piquigua phase) sites in the Jama valley. The ceramics of this phase have been described by Jadán (n.d.) and Zeidler and Sutliff (1994). Some 30 sites have been located, all of which occur on alluvial floodplain deposits along the main river channel or on the extensive tributary alluvium of the Cangrejo River where San Isidro is located. These floodplain areas were the focus of our survey effort and thus received 100 percent coverage by surface inspection and occasional shovel probing. Random quadrat sampling in the uplands failed to locate any Piquigua phase sites. Only one Piquigua site was found in the lower valley where it was eroding out of an older alluvial terrace away from the modern river channel. This suggests that more Piquigua sites probably exist in the lower valley than were located by our survey, but they are deeply buried and not discoverable without deep subsurface testing. In spite of the relatively short duration of this phase (ca. 150 years), the Piquigua peoples apparently colonized the valley bringing with them a stratified social organization, elaborate ceremonial complex, a well-developed ceramic assemblage, and a broad agricultural subsistence base (Jadán n.d.; Pearsall 1996 and this volume; Pearsall and Zeidler 1994; Zeidler 1988, n.d.b; Zeidler and Pearsall 1994). San Isidro was immediately established as the ceremonial center for the Piquigua settlement hierarchy and was characterized by dual opposed mounds oriented along a northeast-to-southwest axis (Zeidler n.d.b), following the earlier pattern of ceremonial mound building documented at Real Alto (Lathrap, Marcos, and Zeidler 1977; Marcos 1988; Zeidler n.d.d; see also Raymond 1993).

Figure 14 illustrates the spatial distribution of Chorrera (Tabuchila phase) sites in the Jama valley. The ceramics for this phase have been described by Engwall (n.d.a,b) and Zeidler and Sutliff (1994). Some 33 Tabuchila phase sites have been identified, 25 in the principal alluvial areas of the valley, and 8 in upland zones or along higher elevation tributary alluvium. While these numbers seem low when compared with the preceding Piquigua phase, it must be remembered that the 8 upland sites were discovered through random quadrat sampling (i.e., a total of 130 one-hectare quadrats over the 785 km^2 study area). Thus if the figures for the upland or nonalluvial sample are projected over the entire landscape, it becomes clear that floodplain settlement probably remained comparable to that of Terminal Valdivia times, but that an appreciable number of smaller isolated sites were scattered throughout the upland zone. As before, San Isidro remained the central ceremonial center in this more complex settlement hierarchy and the single platform mound at the center of the site was enlarged by new mound construction.

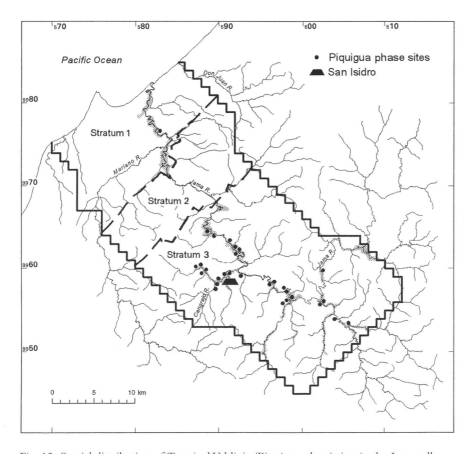

Fig. 13 Spatial distribution of Terminal Valdivia (Piquigua phase) sites in the Jama valley.

Southern Manabí province: Buena Vista valley (Agua Blanca). Archaeological research by McEwan (1992, n.d.) in the Buena Vista valley has primarily focused on a synchronic study of Manteño settlement and political organization; hence, little information exists on the archaeological contexts of the sampled tephras. Detailed descriptions, though not presented here, exist for the physical stratigraphy in the Buena Vista valley (Mosquera n.d.; see also McEwan n.d.). The Buena Vista valley represents the southern boundary of the tephra fallout zone. Here Isaacson and McEwan sampled five tephras exposed in a quebrada formed after the El Niño of 1982 and 1983 (McEwan n.d.: fig. 3.7). The lowest of these tephras (Tephra I) mantles a Chorrera paleosol and marks the end of the Chorrera presence in the valley. The remaining four tephras represent as–yet–unidentified eruptions that extend well into the Integration period. The volume of tephra

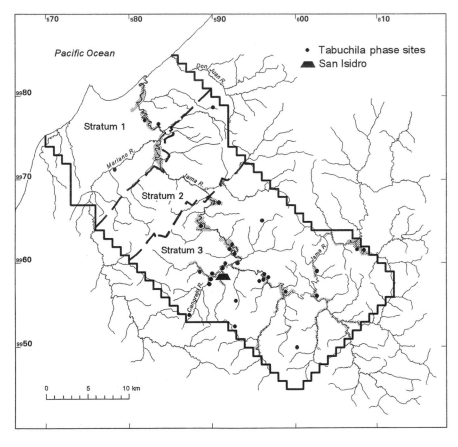

Fig. 14 Spatial distribution of Chorrera (Tabuchila phase) sites in the Jama valley.

deposited in this part of the fallout zone is less than that found farther north and east, and we can infer from this that the impacts were less severe.

COMPOSITIONAL ANALYSIS OF ARCHAEOLOGICAL TEPHRAS

Tephra Samples

A chemical characterization and correlation of tephras from archaeological contexts throughout the northern Andean volcanic zone has the potential to produce powerful chronological tools in the form of time-stratigraphic horizons. Archaeological components above and below provide independent evidence for correlation of these discontinuous ash mantles. Taken together, they also define the relative intensity and extent of natural disasters. The impacts of these events can be independently confirmed by discontinuities in ceramic styles, as well as hiatuses defined by radiometric assays. In this sense, the archaeological record plays a key role for deciphering the history of Late Holocene volcanism.

Through a cooperative effort among archaeologists working in various regions of Ecuador, we have assembled a large collection of archaeological tephras, 38 of which have been chemically analyzed by energy dispersive X-ray spectroscopy (EDS) microprobe (Fig. 15). Four source volcanoes were sampled: Cuicocha, Guagua Pichincha, Pululahua, and Quilotoa. Thirty-four samples come from archaeological contexts. These include 3 from the northern highlands (Cotocollao, La Chimba, Lake San Pablo), 4 from the western *montaña* (Nueva Era), and 27 from the coastal lowlands. The latter include 19 samples from the Jama valley, 5 from Agua Blanca, and 1 each from Colimes, Coaque, and La Plata Island. The 19 Jama valley tephra samples represent a total of 11 different archaeological sites in the lower, middle, and upper valley (Fig. 16).

EDS Microprobe Analysis

The compositional analysis of the glass fraction of archaeological tephras from coastal and highland Ecuador was carried out through EDS microprobe analysis in the scanning electron microscopy (SEM) laboratory of the Illinois State Geological Survey (ISGS) in Champaign (see Appendix on p. 119). The elemental characterization of tephras for purposes of tephrostratigraphic correlation has been achieved most successfully with neutron activation analysis (NAA), where detection is focused on trace element concentrations of glass separates. However, the purification process of archaeological tephra samples from western Ecuador did not produce pure glass separates suitable for NAA. This was due to the high clay/silt content of many of the tephra samples which, in archaeological context, are commonly found in a reworked state and

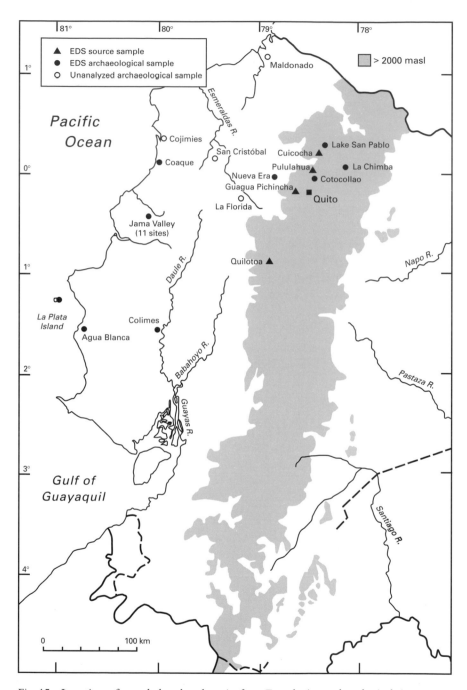

Fig. 15 Location of sampled tephra deposits from Ecuadorian archaeological sites.

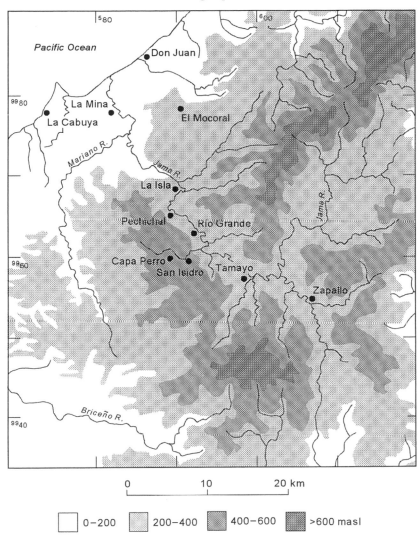

Fig. 16   Location of sampled tephra deposits from archaeological sites in the Jama valley.

intermixed with alluvial deposits. This impediment necessitated a different analytical approach to chemical characterization, namely EDS microprobe analysis. Since this technique allows visual identification and instantaneous analysis of individual glass shards with the SEM, the tedious and often fruitless purification process through heavy liquid separation becomes unnecessary, but characterization must rely on detection of major and minor elements.

While not as precise as NAA, EDS microprobe analysis of pyroclastic materials has proven successful in a number of geological and archaeological studies (e.g., see Desborough, Pitman, and Donnell 1973; Fisher and Schmincke 1984; Larsen 1981; Sheets 1983; Smith and Westgate 1969; Westgate and Gorton 1981). It provides semiquantitative data on the weight percentage of major and minor elements of the volcanic glass in each sample and permits their correlation or segregation through subsequent graphic display and multivariate statistical analysis (Westgate and Gorton 1981). Because of the semiquantitative nature of this method, 10 replicates of each sample were analyzed to control for minor fluctuations in microprobe beam intensity and intrasample variation. The Appendix provides detailed methodological information regarding sample preparation, SEM–EDS equipment and instrument parameters, and operating conditions.

Results

We screened each elemental analysis for internal variability with the standard deviation and the coefficient of variation. The oxides of aluminum (Al), silica (Si), calcium (Ca), potassium (K), and sodium (Na) exhibited the lowest levels of variability and were used for the provenance study. The 10 replicate runs were averaged to produce a characteristic value for each element in a sample. Then we graphically displayed these values and subjected them to multivariate statistical analysis. Only the 18 samples pertaining to the Formative period, Tephras I and II as determined by ceramic association, are discussed here: 13 samples were thought to correspond to the Late Formative Tephra II, while 5, all from the Jama valley, were thought to correspond to the Early Formative Tephra I. The 4 source samples are also included in these analyses.

Figure 17 is a bivariate ratio scattergram of Al_2O_3/SiO_2 versus K_2O/CaO for samples from Tephras I and II and the four source volcanoes (Wilkenson, Hill, Miceli et al. 1992). The corresponding 50 percent confidence ellipses are also plotted. We used bivariate ratios here as a means of minimizing instrument error while maintaining the relationship between elemental concentrations. Figure 17 clearly shows a tight cluster of samples from the post-Chorrera tephra and its separation from the cluster of samples from the post-Valdivia tephra. Within the post-Chorrera tephra cluster are the two source volcanoes: Pululahua and Cuicocha. The tight correlation of the Pululahua eruption with the post-Formative tephra at Cotocollao (Geotermica Italiana and Instituto Ecuatoriano de Minería 1989; Hall and Mothes 1994; Papale and Rosi 1993) identifies Pululahua as the source volcano for this eruption. The other two source samples, Guagua Pichincha and Quilotoa, both fall within the broad cluster of Tephra I samples.

Figure 18 is a ternary diagram showing the relationship between K_2O, CaO,

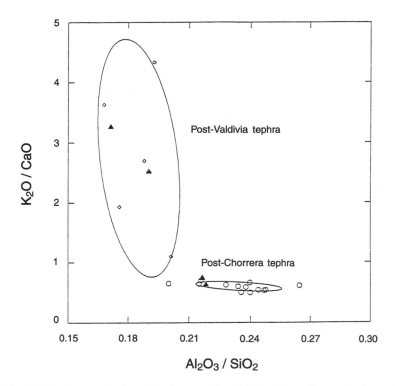

Fig. 17 Bivariate ratio plot of Tephras I and II (Al_2O_3/SiO and K_2O/SiO). Circles = Tephra II samples; diamonds = Tephra I samples; triangles = source samples.

and NaO_2 for the four source volcanoes and Tephras I and II (Wilkenson, Hill, Micelli et al. 1992). Again, the post-Chorrera tephra samples produce a tight grouping that is clearly separated from the more variable Tephra I samples, and the four source samples segregate in the same pattern as before.

Finally, we conducted a cluster analysis (Fig. 19) on four elements (the bivariate ratios Al_2O_3/SiO_2 and K_2O/CaO) with the hierarchical agglomerative method, Euclidean distance measure, and a single linkage clustering algorithm (Wilkenson, Hill, Welna, and Birkenbeuel et al. 1992; see also Aldenderfer and Blashfield 1984; Baxter 1994). The results again display a tight clustering of samples from the post-Chorrera tephra, while the post-Valdivia tephra samples are distinct yet internally more variable. We conducted a second cluster analysis (Fig. 20) on only three elements (K_2O, CaO, and NaO_2), confirming the earlier clustering while using a slightly different dataset.

From these three analytical techniques, a consistent pattern emerges. Pululahua

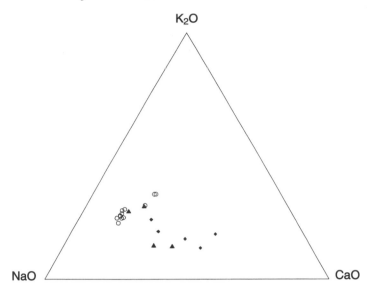

Fig. 18 Ternary diagram of Tephras I and II (K_2O, CaO, and NaO). Circles = Tephra II samples; diamonds = Tephra I samples; triangles = source samples.

volcano is correlated with the post-Formative tephra samples from the seven archaeological sites of Agua Blanca, Capaperro, Cotocollao, Mocoral, Nueva Era, San Isidro, and Tamayo (Fig. 21). These interregional correlations are consistent with independent archaeological and radiometric evidence at these sites, thus establishing the Pululahua airfall as a time-stratigraphic horizon. The results are also consistent with the stratigraphic placement of unanalyzed tephra samples from the Hacienda San Cristóbal area and the Hacienda La Florida area in western Pichincha province (Fig. 15). At Hacienda San Cristóbal, a large Jama–Coaque mound complex, and several associated sites have been reported with underlying Chorrera occupations (Tobar 1997). The Pululahua tephra is consistently found overlying the Chorrera deposits throughout the locality (Tobar 1997: gráficos 1, 2), providing a tentative northern limit for the reconstructed footprint of the eruption (Fig. 21). At the Hacienda La Florida locality northwest of Santo Domingo de Los Colorados, test excavations at two mound complexes yielded evidence of volcanic ash deposits (Lubensky 1979, n.d.; see also Isaacson n.d.:137–139), one of which overlies cultural material of Chorrera affiliation.

For the post-Valdivia tephra samples, the Jama valley sites of San Isidro and Capaperro correlate, and there is promising evidence that these coastal valley

Tree diagram

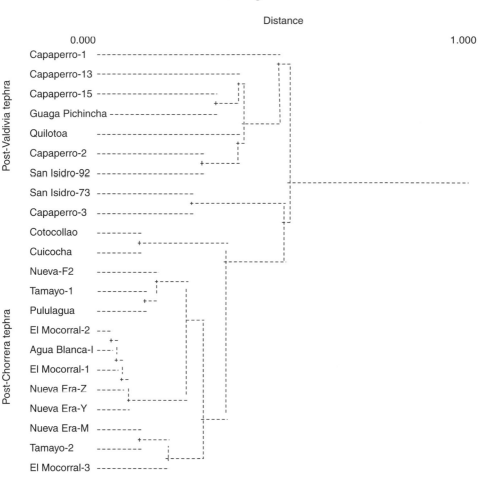

Fig. 19 Cluster analysis of Tephras I and II (Al_2O_3/SiO and K_2O/SiO).

deposits will correlate with the basal tephra at Cotocollao in the Quito basin. If that is the case, then Guagua Pichincha may prove to be the likelier source volcano because of its close proximity to Cotocollao. Establishment of this eruption as a pan-regional, time-stratigraphic horizon awaits further study, however, since our comparative collection of tephras from potential source volcanoes is still rather limited.

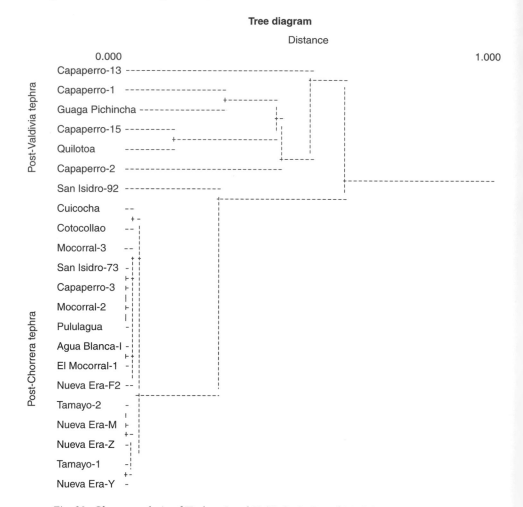

Fig. 20 Cluster analysis of Tephras I and II (K_2O, CaO, and NaO_2).

MAGNITUDE OF THE PULULAHUA ERUPTION

Defining the magnitude of volcanic eruptions is based on the total volume of tephra deposited and estimates of the height of the eruption column. Volume estimates require accurate measurements of the thickness of the distal end of tephra deposits, a difficult measurement to acquire when dealing with partially eroded deposits. Column height is estimated on the basis of wind velocity and grain size distributions. In lieu of accurate measurements, mathematical models can calculate the total volume of tephra produced by an eruption from the shape of tephra blankets.

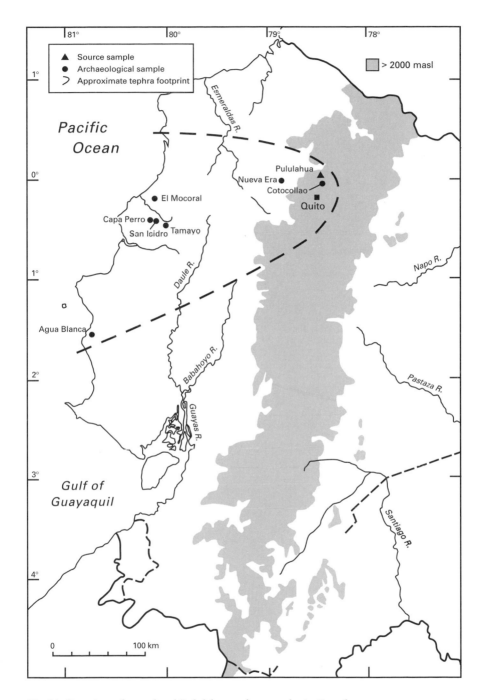

Fig. 21 Location of correlated Pululahua tephra samples in Ecuador.

Fig. 22 Present-day *caldera* of Pululahua volcano from the southeast. Note human settlement at bottom of *caldera*. Photo by Marie J. Zeidler

Papale and Rosi (1993) gave estimates on the magnitude of the Pululahua eruption with a number of these models but warned that the measurement of the distal end of the deposit "is reconstructed mainly by analogy with the general trend, and it is possible that its real pattern would indicate a greater dispersal" (1993:528).

Given this qualification, the volume of the eruption is estimated at 5 to 6 km³ with an estimated column height of between 28 km and 33 km. These estimates place the magnitude of the Pululahua eruption in the 99th percentile of the 4,815 eruptions listed in the register of volcanic events over the past 10,000 years (Simkin et al. 1981). The magnitude of the Pululahua eruption can also be gauged visually by the immensity of the modern caldera that is its legacy (Fig. 22). The expansive bottomland inside the crater measures some 3 km in diameter opening toward the west, and it is now inhabited by a large hacienda. For a modern comparison, the devastating 1991 plinian eruption of Pinatubo Volcano in the Philippines produced a tephra deposit of 5 or more cm, which covered an area of about 4,000 km². This eruption produced 2 to 4 km³ of tephra (Pinatubo Volcano 1994), or about *one half* the volume estimated for the Pululahua eruption. Now let us consider its impact on pre-Hispanic societies.

Given the respective distances of these correlated sites from the source eruptions, it is instructive to consider the probable nature of the impacts from accounts of contemporary volcanic events. Comparisons of the erosional patterns of tephra following the 1943 eruption of Paricutin volcano (Rees 1979) and the suggested impacts of the eruption at the Vidor site in Costa Rica indicate that low-lying areas suffer most from tephra fallout (Eggler 1949: 415–36, 1963: 38–68; Kerbis 1980: 125–40; Segerstrom 1950: 965A). Erosion from slopes, with gradients greater than 15°, continually blanket floodplains and level ground with fresh tephra. Ash-laden runoff smothers young crops and destroys irrigation canals. At Paricutin, erosion stabilized after 19 years so that low-lying areas stopped aggrading. By 1965, agriculture had not reached pre-eruption levels in most areas (Segerstrom 1966). The areas that seemed to experience the best recovery either trapped mixed sediments of ash and mature soil, or were cut by rill or channel erosion to expose the old soil surface. These conditions occurred in streams dammed by lava dikes and on slopes where exposed mature soils could be exploited.

This has interesting implications for Formative period agricultural practices in coastal valleys where there is a dependence on floodplain farming (Lathrap 1974, 1977; Lathrap, Collier, and Chandra 1975; Pearsall 1992, 1996, this volume; Pearsall and Zeidler 1994; Zeidler and Pearsall 1994). These may be characterized as immature systems, in that they have not reached the full range of environmental diversity that characterize agricultural systems of the Regional Developmental and Integration periods when more extensive swiddening in upland localities would have occurred. As Knapp (n.d.) demonstrated for the Ecuadorian highlands, agriculture of the late Integration period had expanded to fill both the slopes and the valley bottoms of the highland basins. This observation seems to be supported by agricultural practices in most regions of western Ecuador and is certainly the case in the Jama valley.

In the Jama valley archaeological sequence, it is interesting to note that the first two ashfalls mark major cultural breaks in the sequence (Zeidler 1994a, 1994b; Zeidler, Buck, and Litton 1998). The third ashfall occurs in the middle of the long Jama–Coaque sequence and exhibits no cultural discontinuity characteristic of the earlier two eruptions. If we compare thicknesses of ash deposits between the three strata, the Jama–Coaque tephra appears to be the thickest. It should have caused the most damage to the inhabitants if we assume a one-to-one correspondence between thickness of tephra and impact. However, the nature of the agricultural production system must be considered. At distal ends of tephra fallout zones, agricultural systems that have a significant slope exploitation may be able to weather the impacts of tephra airfalls better than systems that rely, solely or mainly, on floodplain exploitation. A second consideration is degree of political organization. Complex chiefdoms having valleywide or multivalley territorial control such as those characteristic of Jama–Coaque (Zeidler n.d.c) are inherently better organized logistically than their Formative period counterparts. This greater logistical capability was probably a distinct advantage in dealing with natural disasters such as volcanic airfalls. That may be why there was no complete cultural break and long hiatus in the Jama–Coaque sequence after Tephra III, only a ceramic phase break (Zeidler and Sutliff 1994).

These observations make a significant contribution to our understanding of the effects of volcanic eruptions and their magnitude at the distal ends of the fallout zone. It is clear that the airfall deposits in the Jama valley eroded rapidly off the slopes and uplands. Soils in these contexts were buried by tephra for only a short time, permitting resumption of upland and slope farming soon after the eruption. However, the floodplain areas of the valley were devastated. Riverbank deposits of tephra—2 m thick in some locations—indicate that the floodplain areas were buried under tremendous loads of ash. These deposits contain very little eroded soil. Thus it appears that valley bottomlands were taken out of agricultural production for a considerable time. A population movement out of the valley bottoms and onto the slopes and uplands after an eruption is a plausible reconstruction of the cultural response to these events. However, during the Formative period, when floodplain agriculture was the dominant form, tephra fallouts that quickly eroded onto the valley bottoms would have been particularly devastating for the resident population (Figs. 13, 14). Although it is during the Late Formative Chorrera occupation when upland settlement first occurs, it is limited in scope when compared to later Jama–Coaque settlement patterns and site sizes are generally smaller. In later periods when population densities were much higher, agricultural systems more diversified, and political organization more complex, reliance on slope and upland agriculture could have produced sufficient food to permit a continued Jama–Coaque presence in the valley.

The effects of the eruption on populations living closer to the vent are considerably different than those at the distal end. Nearer the volcanic source, the tephra mantle thickens considerably, is internally more variable, and behaves quite differently. Interestingly, a tephra mantle in the foothills is almost impervious to erosion. In the Tulipe valley, the landscape is blanketed with ash, both on the slopes and the uplands, as if it were cemented onto the underlying topography. Others have also observed this; Williams described a similar case with the Mazama ash in Oregon:

> *So faithfully does the pumice sheet reflect the underlying surface that test pits excavated at the tops and bottoms of large hills show thicknesses to vary only within a few inches over areas of several square miles. It is as if the ejecta had been "ducoed" onto the pre-existing slopes. Where the thickness of the mantle exceeds 2 feet, hardly a single exposure of "bedrock" may be seen for miles* (Williams 1942: 69; emphasis in the original).

The resistance to erosion of the tephra deposits in the foothill regions such as the Tulipe valley make the nature of the volcanic impacts quite different from that experienced in the coastal valleys farther west. Whereas the coastal valleys were occupied primarily by floodplain agriculturalists exploiting the expansive tropical floodplains of the coastal rivers, the foothill farmers were swiddening the slopes and ridge tops. The Pululahua eruption blanketed the whole landscape with thick deposits of ash and pumice that did not erode. In the Tulipe valley, the Late Formative period communities disappeared and, with them, the social and economic links between the western lowlands and the Quito basin. It was not until a new soil had formed in the thick ash mantle and, presumably, the landscape recovered that there was new colonization in the valley. Tulipe was not recolonized for 1,000 years. This reflects a very long period of both ecological and social recovery that together form the impetus for colonization. Once a community establishes itself in a new area, new social and economic relationships develop that make recolonization to former homelands a complex decision.

One aspect of these economic links is the obsidian trade (Burger et al. 1994). In Formative times, obsidian was traded from the Quito basin, where the obsidian sources are found, through the *boca de montaña* at Cotocollao into the western foothills and, presumably, onto the coast. Obsidian is the most common lithic material in both the Cotocollao site and the Nueva Era site during the late Formative period (Isaacson n.d.; Villalba 1988). When the Tulipe valley is recolonized long after the Pululahua eruption, obsidian is almost nonexistent in the archaeological assemblage. It appears that the obsidian trade routes out of the Quito basin had changed significantly by that time. In the later occupation, the Tulipe phase communities are on the margins of the obsidian trade instead of at its center. Obviously, as people go, so trade goes. In the Jama valley, by contrast, limited obsidian characterization analysis (Zeidler, Giauque, Asaro, and Stross 1994) suggests continued trade contacts with the Quito basin through-out the cultural sequence, although the specific routes by which the obsidian reached northern Manabí may have changed over time and were no doubt influenced by volcanic events in the western foothill region.

The negative effects of volcanic eruptions on human settlement are well documented both in prehistoric and historic periods (Sheets and Grayson 1979), yet no a priori conclusions should be drawn once a volcanic ash layer has been identified archaeologically. Rather, the effects of a tephra fallout on a given prehistoric population, as well as their response to it, should become specific research questions in and of themselves. The western Ecuadorian data suggest that cultural responses to tephra fallouts vary in relation to the intensity and timing of the event, as well as the complexity of sociopolitical organization and subsistence practices. The answers do not lend themselves to the develop-ment of universal cultural "laws," but rather highlight the importance of his-torical contingency in shaping the archaeological record of prehistoric settlement process, as well as the complex interaction between cultural systems and their environment. As Gould persuasively argues:

> A historical explanation does not rest on direct deductions from laws of nature, but on an unpredictable sequence of antecedent states, where any major change in any step of the sequence would have altered the final result. This final result is therefore dependent, or contingent, upon everything that came before—the unerasable and determining signa-ture of history. (1989: 283)

The archaeological evidence for simultaneous regional abandonments docu-mented at the Formative sites of Cotocollao, Nueva Era, San Isidro, and Agua Blanca indicates that volcanism had a major impact on the cultural trajectories of all four. In turn, the cultural response in these four areas no doubt had repercussions in the refuge zones on their peripheries. A thorough study of these processes of abandonment, migration, and recolonization is essential for an accurate analysis of settlement dynamics and culture–historical sequences in western Ecuador. Brief consideration of these processes during the terminal Formative period in northern Manabí and southern Esmeraldas provides a use-ful example.

We note that the chronological placement of the Tachina phase (Chorrera) of southern Esmeraldas immediately postdates the Tabuchila phase (Chorrera) presence in the Jama valley. Several archaeologists have commented on the relatively late appearance of Chorrera culture in this northerly region and its possible derivation from Chorrera manifestations in Manabí province. No absolute dates are available for this Late Formative manifestation, but temporal estimates range from 800 to 1 B.C. (Alcina Franch 1979: 111), 500 to 200 B.C. (Rivera et al. 1984: 16), and 400 to 50 B.C. (Bouchard 1996; Guinea Bueno 1986: 44). The latter of these estimates is generally considered to be the most likely and reasonable (Bouchard 1996). A review of the stratigraphic sections from published archaeological reports reveals no evidence of pyroclastic deposits, and an overview of the cultural chronology for Esmeraldas province (Bouchard 1996) makes no mention of tephra-related hiatuses. If we consider that the Jama valley is located at the center of the Tephra II ash sheet (Fig. 21), populations moving out of the valley toward the south would have encountered other well-established Chorrera populations in the more arid regions of southern Manabí and coastal Guayas provinces, as well as in the humid inland waterways of the Daule/Babahoyo drainages. However, populations migrating into the ash-free zones to the north would have encountered *uninhabited*, or at best *sparsely populated*, humid environments similar to those of northern Manabí. We propose as a probable explanation for this temporal lag or "Doppler effect" (Davis 1983; Deetz and Dethlefsen 1965) that southern Esmeraldas received Chorrera refugees migrating out of northern Manabí after the Pululahua eruption around 500 B.C. (752–182 cal B.C.). This is not meant to imply that no Chorrera peoples were occupying southern Esmeraldas prior to 500 B.C. Current evidence, however, suggests a sparse occupation at best, and we suggest that much of the Tachina phase occupation could have resulted from population displacements from northern Manabí after the Pululahua eruption.

CONCLUSIONS

The foregoing examination of Formative period volcanism has implications both for methodological aspects of cultural chronology building and for substantive interpretations of prehistoric settlement dynamics in western Ecuador. In the former case, the stratigraphic importance of volcanic ash layers as time-horizon markers cannot be overstated. Where stratigraphic and/or geochemical correlations can be made on these airfall deposits across a regional landscape, they provide the archaeologist with a powerful tool for constructing regional cultural chronologies and for making macroregional comparisons. Given the chronometric uncertainties of the radiocarbon dating method and the variability inherent in probabilistic calibration, the presence of event-specific ash layers in a stratigraphic column is not trivial. These sediments represent an almost instantaneous depositional event when viewed on an archaeological time scale, and in that sense are much more precise than radiocarbon dating as a means of punctuating a cultural sequence and making broad interregional correlations between multiple sequences.

The potential role of volcanism in substantive interpretations of western Ecuadorian prehistory also has far reaching implications and highlights the interplay of social process and historical contingency. It is interesting to contrast the impacts of the Pululahua eruption across the western foothills and lowlands in terms of clinal gradients (see introduction). In the Jama valley, floodplain agriculture was particularly vulnerable to the erosion of tephra off the slopes and uplands. The fine powdery tephra, almost entirely made up of glass shards, quickly made its way to the floodplain terraces and caused social and economic collapse. We suggest that it was only after considerable hill-slope swiddening developed that Jama-Coaque communities could survive these events. In the foothills of the Tulipe valley, however, swiddening was the predominant agricultural practice, but it did not afford any protection against the effects of the eruption because of its close proximity to the event itself. Since the tephra in this region was so thick and resistant to erosion, *all* farmable soils were permanently buried. Therefore, in each area along the clinal gradient of the tephra blanket, different contingencies and social processes prevailed, and it is this aspect of these catastrophic events that is so informative. What was adaptive in one area under one set of conditions failed in another. Only through the detailed regional study of these events can such a history of human settlement be reconstructed.

Two observations can be made regarding the continuous sequences in the south and the discontinuous sequences in northern Manabí. First, the Tabuchila phase of northern Manabí is arguably the most complex regional manifestation of Chorrera culture thus far investigated in Ecuador (Cummins 1992; see also Engwall n.d.a,b). Evidence of this complexity includes ceremonial mound construction, complex settlement hierarchies, maize-dependent agriculture involving both intensive floodplain farming and some upland swiddening, elaborate ceramic production (including mold made figurines), and high-status burial, all of which point to the early emergence of a localized stratified chiefdom centered around the San Isidro ceremonial center. In the one southern valley where systematic survey data permit comparisons, the Valdivia valley, the Late Formative period does not exhibit the same constellation of traits (Schwarz and Raymond 1996). One of the consequences of the Pululahua eruption appears to have been the termination of a Late Formative cultural florescence in northern Manabí. Thus, it is ironic that this northward colonization and cultural florescence in the more desirable, arable regions of northern Manabí brought these Late Formative peoples into a zone of extreme environmental instability and natural hazards that ultimately led to their demise.

Secondly, it is not surprising that the emergence of Manteño culture as a multi regional Integration period polity first appeared in the south where cultural sequences developed without interruption. If the long-term stability of centralized polity formation is essential for the development and expansion of complex political organization and multiregional interaction, then that stability would have been periodically truncated in northern and central Manabí, as well as the inland coastal plain, by massive volcanic disasters that did not permit rapid recovery.

These volcanic events and the variable cultural responses to them, as played out over large areas of western Ecuador, have dramatic implications for interaction between the highlands and lowlands, population movement north and south, long-distance trade, political organization, and alliance formation. Until the spatial distribution and correlation of these events are better defined, an accurate synthesis of Formative period settlement dynamics and social evolution will remain elusive.

Acknowledgments The tephrostratigraphic analysis and correlation study presented in this essay were supported by supplemental funding from the National Science Foundation for Grant BNS-9108548 (Jama Valley Prehistory Project) awarded jointly to us. We gratefully acknowledge the collaboration of various colleagues who graciously provided us with the tephra samples necessary to make this a macroregional analysis: J. Stephen Athens, Minard Hall, Judith Kreid, Earl Lubensky, Colin McEwan, Andrew Mudd, J. Scott Raymond, and Oswaldo Tobar. We also thank Donald Lowry of the Illinois State Geological Survey for his advice and continued collaboration in the SEM–EDS microprobe analysis of Ecuadorian tephras. We owe a special debt of gratitude to Marie J. Zeidler for her diligence in preparing Figures 1, 2, 5, 7, 10, 11, 13,14, 15, 16, 21, and 22, and to Jeanne Drennan of the University of Pittsburgh for permission to reproduce Fig. 10 from the Memoirs in Latin American Archaeology series. Finally, we thank J. Scott Raymond and Richard Burger for inviting us to participate in this Dumbarton Oaks symposium and Jeffrey Quilter for hosting it. We alone remain responsible for any errors of fact or interpretation contained herein.

APPENDIX
SEM–EDS METHODOLOGY

DONALD J. LOWRY
ILLINOIS STATE GEOLOGICAL SURVEY

A total of 44 samples of volcanic ash from Ecuador were processed in the Scanning Electron Microscopy (SEM) facility of the Illinois State Geological Survey, Champaign, for purposes of chemical composition analysis. Detection was focused on these eight major elements as follows: aluminum (Al), silica (Si), iron (Fe), calcium (Ca), potassium (K), magnesium (Mg), sodium (Na), and titanium (Ti).

Sample Preparation

A small split of each sample of volcanic ash was placed into an 8-ml glass vial containing 99 percent ethyl alcohol. The samples were dispersed within the vials with an ultrasonic and then pipetted onto an aluminum SEM stub previously coated with colloidal graphite. Each SEM stub was then coated with Au/Pd with a sputter coater. The SEM stubs were loaded into the SEM in groups of four with a specially made stub holder that included an integral Faraday-cup.

Operating Conditions

The SEM-EDS equipment and operating parameters employed in this analysis are provided in Tables A1 and A2. The SEM-EDS was turned on and allowed to stabilize for two hours prior to all analyses. When stabilized, an incident beam current reading from the integral Faraday-cup was recorded from the picoammeter. Then, 10 particles of volcanic glass (sample replicates) were analyzed with the spot mode of the SEM. After the 10 points were analyzed, another incident beam current reading was recorded. A difference of less than 2 percent between the initial picoammeter reading and the reading after the 10 data points were acquired was considered acceptable. The 10 data points were sent to a file for further analysis via Q-file software. This program lists each analysis point and the values for each of the 8 oxides. (The table also lists Au and Pd, but these points were removed from the calculations.) At the bottom of the table are values showing the average of the 10 points and the standard deviation of the analysis.

Table A1
SEM-EDS Equipment

Type	Brand
SEM	Amray 1839
EDS	Noran 5500
detector	Noran with Z-MAX window
filament	Denka LaB6
picoammeter	Keithley 480
film	Polaroid Type 55 positive/negative 4x5 sheet film

Table A2
SEM–EDS Parameters

Parameter	Description
kV	15
condenser lens	4.0
tilt	0°
working distance	20 mm
dead time	22 to 25%
counts	~2,300
analysis	standardless semiquantification program
beam current	see Operating Conditions (pp. 112)
counting time	30 s
emission	60
magnification	1000x
raster	spot mode, which allows the oxide data to be acquired on an area of the sample that is the diameter of the electron beam (~75 Å)

James A. Zeidler and John S. Isaacson

BIBLIOGRAPHY

ACOSTA SOLÍS, MISAEL
  1968   *Divisiones fitogeográficas y formaciones geobotánicas del Ecuador.* Casa de la Cultura
          Ecuatoriana, Quito.

ALCINA FRANCH, JOSÉ
  1979   *La arqueología de Esmeraldas (Ecuador): Introducción general.* Memorias de la Misión
          Arqueológica Española en el Ecuador 1. Ministerio de Asuntos Exteriores,
          Dirección General de Relaciones Culturales, Madrid.
  1985   La arqueología de Esmeraldas (Ecuador): Estado de la cuestión y perspectivas.
          Revista Andina 3(1): 213–258.

ALDENDERFER, MARK S., AND R. K. BLASHFIELD
  1984   *Cluster Analysis.* Sage, Beverly Hills, Calif.

BARBERI, F., M. COLTELLI, G. FERRARA, F. INOCENTI, J. M. NAVARRO, AND R. SANTACROCE
  1988   Plio-Quaternary Volcanism in Ecuador. *Geological Magazine* 125(1): 1–14.

BATE, LUIS F.
  1978   *Sociedad, formación económico social y cultura.* Ediciones de Cultura Popular,
          México. D.F.

BAXTER, M. J.
  1994   *Exploratory Multivariate Analysis in Archaeology.* Edinburgh University Press,
          Edinburgh.

BOUCHARD, JEAN-FRANÇOIS
  1996   Los datos de cronología cultural para el litoral del Pacífico nor-ecuatorial:
          Período Formativo Tardío y período de Desarrollo Regional—Sur de
          Colombia—Norte del Ecuador. In *Andes: Boletín de la Misión Arqueológica
          Andina* 1: 137–152. Warsaw University, Warsaw.

BOWMAN, SHERIDAN
  1990   *Radiocarbon Dating.* University of California Press, Berkeley.

BUCK, CAITLIN E., WILLIAM G. CAVANAGH, AND CLIFFORD D. LITTON
  1996   *Bayesian Approach to Interpreting Archaeological Data.* Wiley, Chicester, UK.

BURGER, RICHARD L., FRANK ASARO, HELEN V. MICHEL, FRED H. STROSS, AND ERNESTO SALAZAR
  1994   An Initial Consideration of Obsidian Procurement and Exchange in Pre-
          Hispanic Ecuador. *Latin American Antiquity* 5(3): 228–255.

CHRISTEN, J. A., R. S. CLYMO, AND C. D. LITTON
  1995   A Bayesian Approach to the Use of ^{14}C Dates in the Estimation of the Age
          of Peat. *Radiocarbon* 37(2): 431–442.

CORDELL, LINDA
  1994   The Nature of Explanation in Archaeology: A Position Statement. In
          Understanding Complexity in the Prehistoric Southwest (G. J. Gumerman and M.
          Gell-Mann, eds.): 149–162. Addison-Wesley, Reading, Mass.

CUMMINS, TOM
  1992   Tradition in Ecuadorian Pre-Hispanic Art: The Ceramics of Chorrera and

Jama–Coaque. In *Amerindian Signs: 5,000 Years of Precolumbian Art in Ecuador* (F. Valdez and D. Veintimilla, eds.): 63–81. Dinediciones, Quito.

DAMP, JONATHAN E.

1984   Environmental Variation, Agriculture, and Settlement Processes in Coastal Ecuador (3300–1500 B.C.). *Current Anthropology* 25(1): 106–111.

DAVIS, DAVID V.

1983   Investigating the Diffusion of Stylistic Innovations. In *Advances in Archaeological Method and Theory* (M. B. Schiffer, ed.) vol. 6: 53–89. Academic Press, New York.

DEBOER, WARREN R.

1995   Una sequencia cultural en la Cuenca Santiago–Cayapas, Ecuador: Implicaciones para periodización e interacción regional. In *Perspectivas regionales en la arqueología del suroccidente de Colombia y norte del Ecuador* (C. Gnecco, ed.): 111–129. Editorial Universidad del Cauca, Popayán.

1996   *Traces behind the Esmeraldas Shore: Prehistory of the Santiago–Cayapas Region, Ecuador.* University of Alabama Press, Tuscaloosa.

DEETZ, JAMES A., AND EDWARD DETHLEFSEN

1965   The Doppler Effect and Archaeology: A Consideration of the Spatial Effects of Seriation. *Southwestern Journal of Anthropology* 21: 196–206.

DESBOROUGH, G. A., J. K. PITMAN, AND J. R. DONNELL

1973   Microprobe Analysis of Biotites: A Method of Correlating Tuff Beds in the Green River Formation, Colorado and Utah. *Journal of Research, U.S. Geological Survey* 1 (1): 39–44.

DONAHUE, JACK, AND WILLIAM HARBERT

1994   Fluvial History of the Jama River Drainage. In *Regional Archaeology in Northern Manabí, Ecuador,* vol. 1: *Environment, Cultural Chronology, and Prehistoric Subsistence in the Jama River Valley* (J. A. Zeidler and D. M. Pearsall, eds.): 43–57. Memoirs in Latin American Archaeology 8. University of Pittsburgh, Pittsburgh, Pa.

EATON, G. P.

1964   Windbourne Volcanic Ash: A Possible Index to Polar Wandering. *Journal of Geology* 72(1): 1–35.

EGGLER, W. A.

1949   Plant Communities in Vicinity of the Volcano Paricutin, Mexico, after $2^1/_2$ Years of Eruption. *Ecology* 29(4): 415–436.

1963   Plant Life of Paricutin Volcano, Mexico, Eight Years after Activity Ceased. *American Midland Naturalist* 69(1): 38–68.

ENGWALL, EVAN

n.d.a   Archaeological Investigations of Chorrera Culture: Tabuchila Phase Ceramics from Northern Manabí, Ecuador. Paper Presented at the 57th Annual Meeting of the Society for American Archaeology, Pittsburgh, Pa., 1992.

n.d.b   The Tabuchila Phase: Late Formative Chorrera Culture in the Jama River Region, Manabí, Ecuador. Paper presented at the 60th Annual Meeting of the Society for American Archaeology, Minneapolis, 1995.

FISHER, R. V., AND H.-U. SCHMINCKE

1984   *Pyroclastic Rocks.* Springer-Verlag, Berlin.

GEOTERMICA ITALIANA AND THE INSTITUTO ECUATORIANO DE MINERIA (INEMIN)
>   1989   *Mitigación del riesgo volcánico en el area metropolitana de Quito: Informe final.* Geotermica Italiana 97. Pisa and Quito.

GOULD, STEPHEN J.
>   1989   *Wonderful Life: The Burgess Shale and the Nature of History.* Norton, New York.

GUINEA BUENO, MERCEDES
>   1986   El Formativo de la región sur de Esmeraldas (Ecuador): Visto desde el yacimiento del Chévele. In *Arqueología y etnohistoria del sur de Colombia y norte del Ecuador* (J. Alcina Franch and S. E. Moreno Yánez, eds.): 19–46. *Miscelánea Antropológica Ecuatoriana: Boletín de los Museos del Banco Central del Ecuador* 6.

GUMERMAN, GEORGE J., AND MURRAY GELL-MANN, ED.
>   1994   *Understanding Complexity in the Prehistoric Southwest.* Addison-Wesley, Reading, Mass.

HAAS, JONATHAN, E. J. LADD, JANET E. LEVY, RANDALL H. McGUIRE, AND NORMAN YOFFEE
>   1994   Historical Processes in the Prehistoric Southwest. In *Understanding Complexity in the Prehistoric Southwest* (G. J. Gumerman and M. Gell-Mann, eds.): 203–232. Addison-Wesley, Reading, Mass.

HALL, MINARD L.
>   1977   *El volcanismo en el Ecuador.* Instituto Panamericano de Geografía e Historia, Quito.

HALL, MINARD L., AND BERNARDO BEATE
>   1991   El volcanismo plio-cuaternario en los Andes del Ecuador. In *El paisaje volcánico de la sierra ecuatoriana: Geomorfología, fenómenos volcánicos y recursos asociados* (P. Mothes, ed.): 5–17. Corporación Editora Nacional, Quito.

HALL, MINARD, AND PATRICIA MOTHES
>   1994   Tefroestratigrafía holocénica de los volcanes principales del valle interandino, Ecuador. In *Estudios de geografía*, vol. 6 (R. Morocco, ed.): 47–67. Colegio de Geógrafos del Ecuador, Quito.

HALL, MINARD L., AND C. A. WOOD
>   1985   Volcano-Tectonic Segmentation of the Northern Andes. *Geology* 13: 203–207.

HERD, D. G.
>   n.d.   Glacial and Volcanic Geology of the Ruiz–Tolima Volcanic Complex, Cordillera Central, Colombia. Ph.D. dissertation, Department of Geology, University of Washington, Seattle, 1974.

ISAACSON, JOHN S.
>   1990   Stratigraphy. In *Yearbook of Science and Technology*: 314–315. McGraw-Hill, New York.
>   1994   Volcanic Sediments in Archaeological Contexts from Western Ecuador. In *Regional Archaeology in Northern Manabí, Ecuador*, vol. 1: *Environment, Cultural Chronology, and the Prehistoric Subsistence in the Jama River Valley* (J. A. Zeidler and D. M. Pearsall, eds.): 131–140. Memoirs in Latin American Archaeology 8. University of Pittsburgh, Pittsburgh, Pa.
>   n.d.   Volcanic Activity and Human Occupation of the Northern Andes: The Application of Tephrostratigraphic Techniques to the Problem of Human

Settlement in the Western Montaña during the Ecuadorian Formative. Ph.D. dissertation, Department of Anthropology, University of Illinois at Urbana–Champaign, 1987.

JADÁN, MARY

n.d. La cerámica del Complejo Piquigua (Fase VIII) de la cultura Valdivia en San Isidro, norte de Manabí: Un análisis modal. Tésis de Licenciatura, Centro de Estudios Arqueológicos y Antropológicos, Escuela Superior Politécnica del Litoral, Guayaquil, 1986.

JOHNSON, A. M.

1969 The Climate of Peru, Bolivia, and Ecuador. In *Climates of Central and South America* (Werner Schwerdtfeger, ed.), World Survey of Climatology, vol. 12: 147–218.

KERBIS, J.

1980 The Analysis of Faunal Remains from the Vidor Site. *Vínculos* 6(1/2): 125–140.

KNAPP, GREGORY

n.d. Soil, Slope, and Water in the Equatorial Andes: A Study of Prehistoric Agricultural Adaptation. Ph.D. dissertation, Department of Geography, University of Wisconsin–Madison, 1984.

LARSEN, G.

1981 Tephrochronology by Microprobe Glass Analysis. In *Tephra Studies* (S. Self and R.S.J. Sparks, eds.): 95–102. Reidel, Dordrecht.

LATHRAP, DONALD W.

1974 The Moist Tropics, the Arid Lands, and the Appearance of Great Art Styles in the New World. In *Art and Environment in Native North America* (M. E. King and I. Traylor Jr., eds.): 115–158. Museum of Texas Tech University Special Publications 7. Texas Tech University Press, Lubbock.

1977 Our Father the Cayman, Our Mother the Gourd: Spinden Revisited or a Unitary Model for the Emergence of Agriculture in the New World. In *Origins of Agriculture* (C. A. Reed, ed.): 713–751. Mouton, The Hague.

LATHRAP, DONALD W., DONALD COLLIER, AND HELEN CHANDRA

1975 *Ancient Ecuador: Culture, Clay, and Creativity 3000–300 B.C.* Field Museum of Natural History, Chicago.

LATHRAP, DONALD W., JOHN S. ISAACSON, AND COLIN MCEWAN

1984 On the Trail of the Finest Metallurgy of the Ancient New World: How Old Is the Classic Quimbaya Style? *Field Museum of Natural History Bulletin* (November): 10-19.

LATHRAP, DONALD W., JORGE G. MARCOS, AND JAMES A. ZEIDLER

1977 Real Alto: An Ancient Ceremonial Center. *Archaeology* 30(1): 3–13.

LIPPI, RONALD D.

n.d. *La Ponga and the Machalilla Phase of Coastal Ecuador.* Ph.D. dissertation, Department of Anthropology, University of Wisconsin–Madison, 1983.

1988 Paleotopography and Phosphate Analysis of a Buried Jungle Site in Ecuador. *Journal of Field Archaeology* 15: 85–97.

James A. Zeidler and John S. Isaacson

LÓPEZ Y SEBASTIÁN, LORENZO E.

1986   Contribución al estudio de las culturas formativas en la costa norte del Ecuador: El Sitio E-26 "La Cantera." In *Arqueología y etnohistoria del sur de Colombia y norte del Ecuador* (J. Alcina Franch and S. E. Moreno Yánez, eds.): 47–60. *Miscelánea Antropológica Ecuatoriana: Boletín de los Museos del Banco Central del Ecuador 6.*

LÓPEZ Y SEBASTIÁN, LORENZO E., AND CHANTAL CAILLAVET

1979   La Fase Tachina en el contexto cultural del Horizonte Chorrera. *Actes de 42 Congrès International des Américanistes* (1976), vol. 9A: 199–215. Société des Américanistes, Paris.

LUBENSKY, EARL H.

1979   Excavación arqueológica en la Hacienda La Florida, enero 1979: Informe preliminar. Instituto Nacional del Patrimonio Cultural, Quito.

n.d.   Unpublished field notes in possession of the senior author.

MARCOS, JORGE G.

1988   *Real Alto: La historia de un centro ceremonial Valdivia.* Biblioteca Ecuatoriana de Arqueología, vols. 4 and 5. Corporación Editora Nacional, Quito.

1989   Informe Arqueológico. In *Proyecto San Lorenzo del Mate* (J. G. Marcos, ed.): 1-19. Fundación Pedro Vicente Maldonado, Guayaquil.

McEWAN, COLIN

1992   Sillas de poder: Evolución sociocultural en Manabí, costa del Ecuador. In *5000 Años de ocupación: Parque nacional Machalilla* (P. Norton, ed.): 53–70. Centro Cultural Artes and Ediciones Abya-Yala, Quito.

n.d.   And the Sun Sits in His Seat: Creating Social Order in Andean Culture. Ph.D. dissertation, Department of Anthropology, University of Illinois at Urbana–Champaign, 1998.

McGUIRE, RANDALL

1992   *A Marxist Archaeology.* Academic Press, San Diego.

1994   Historical Process and Southwestern Prehistory. In *Understanding Complexity in the Prehistoric Southwest* (G. J. Gumerman and M. Gell-Mann, eds.): 193–201. Addison-Wesley, Reading, Mass.

MOSQUERA, I. M.

n.d.   Geología arqueológica de la zona de Agua Blanca, Puerto Lopez, provincia de Manabí. Tésis de grado, Departamento de Geología, Escuela Politécnica Nacional, Quito, 1989.

NORTON, PRESLEY

1992   Las culturas cerámicas prehispánicas del sur de Manabí. In *5000 Años de ocupación: Parque Nacional Machalilla* (P. Norton, ed.): 9-40. Centro Cultural Artes and Ediciones Abya-Yala, Quito.

NORTON, PRESLEY, RICHARD LUNNIS, AND NIGEL NAYLING

1983   Excavaciones en Salango, provincia de Manabí, Ecuador. *Miscelánea Antropológica Ecuatoriana: Boletín de los Museos del Banco Central del Ecuador* 3: 9–72.

PAPALE, P., AND M. ROSI

1993   A Case of No-Wind Plinian Fallout at Pululahua Caldera (Ecuador): Implications for Models of Clast Dispersal. *Bulletin of Volcanology* 55: 523–535.

PAULSEN, ALLISON
    1976   Environment and Empire: Climatic Factors in Prehistoric Andean Culture Change. *World Archaeology* 8(2): 121–132.

PAULSEN, ALLISON, AND EUGENE MCDOUGLE
    n.d.   A Chronology of Machalilla and Engoroy Ceramics of the South Coast of Ecuador. Paper presented at the 9th Annual Midwest Conference on Andean and Amazonian Archaeology and Ethnohistory, Columbia, Mo., 1981.

PEARSALL, DEBORAH M.
    1992   Prehistoric Subsistence and Agricultural Evolution in the Jama River Valley, Manabí Province, Ecuador. In *Gifts to the Cayman: Essays in Honor of Donald W. Lathrap* (E. C. Engwall, M. van de Guchte, and A. Zigelboim, eds.):181–207. *Journal of the Steward Anthropological Society* 20(1/2).
    1996   Reconstructing Subsistence in the Lowland Tropics: A Case Study from the Jama Valley, Manabí, Ecuador. In *Case Studies in Environmental Archaeology* (E.J. Reitz, L. A. Newsom, and S. J. Scudder, eds.): 233–254. Plenum, New York.

PEARSALL, DEBORAH M., AND JAMES A. ZEIDLER
    1994   Regional Environment, Cultural Chronology, and Prehistoric Subsistence in Northern Manabí. *In Regional Archaeology in Northern Manabí, Ecuador,* vol. 1: *Environment, Cultural Chronology, and Prehistoric Subsistence in the Jama River Valley* (J. A. Zeidler and D. M. Pearsall, eds.): 201–216. Memoirs in Latin American Archaeology 8. University of Pittsburgh and Ediciones Libri Mundi, Pittsburgh and Quito.

PETERSON, EMIL
    n.d.   Cotocollao: A Formative Period Village in the Northern Highlands of Ecuador. Paper presented at the 42nd Annual Meeting of the Society for American Archaeology, New Orleans, 1977.

PINATUBO VOLCANO
    1994   *Bulletin of Volcanic Eruptions 31* (1991): 56–58.

PORRAS, PEDRO I.
    1982   *Arqueología de Quito 1: Fase Cotocollao.* Centro de Investigaciones Arqueológicas, Pontífica Universidad Católica del Ecuador, Quito.

RAMSEY, C. BRONK
    1995   Radiocarbon Calibration and Analysis of Stratigraphy: The OxCal Program. *Radiocarbon* 37(2): 425–430.

RAYMOND, J. SCOTT
    1993   Ceremonialism in the Early Formative of Ecuador. In *El mundo ceremonial andino* (L. Millones and Y. Onuki, eds.): 25–43. Senri Ethnological Studies 37. National Museum of Ethnology, Osaka.
    n.d.   Early Formative Societies in the Tropical Lowlands of Western Ecuador: A View from the Valdivia Valley. Paper presented at the Circum-Pacific Prehistory Conference, Seattle, 1989.

RAYMOND, J. SCOTT, JORGE G. MARCOS, AND DONALD W. LATHRAP
    1980   Evidence of Early Formative Settlement in the Guayas Basin, Ecuador. *Current Anthropology* 21(5): 700–701.

James A. Zeidler and John S. Isaacson

REES, J. D.
1979   Effects of the Eruption of Paricutin Volcano on Landforms, Vegetation, and
        Human Occupancy. In *Volcanic Activity and Human Ecology* (P. D. Sheets and
        D.K. Grayson, eds.): 249–292. Academic Press, New York.

RIVERA, MIGUEL, EMMA SÁNCHEZ, A. CIUDAD, A. RODRÍGUEZ, AND A. COLÓN
1984   *La Cultura Tiaone.* Memorias de la Misión Arqueológica Española en el Ecuador
        4. Ministerio de Asuntos Exteriores, Dirección General de Relaciones
        Culturales, Madrid.

SADLER, J. C.
1975   *The Upper Tropospheric Circulation over the Global Tropics.* University of Hawaii
        Press, Honolulu.

SAYER, ANDREW
1992   *Method in Social Science: A Realist Approach.* Routledge, London.

SCHWARZ, FREDERICK A., AND J. SCOTT RAYMOND
1996   Formative Settlement Patterns in the Valdivia Valley, Southwest Coastal
        Ecuador. *Journal of Field Archaeology* 23(2): 205–224.

SCHWERDTFEGER, W., (ED.)
1976   *Climates of Central and South America.* World Survey of Climatology 12. Elsevier,
        Amsterdam.

SEGERSTROM, K.
1950   Erosion Studies of Paricutin Volcano. *U.S. Geological Survey Bulletin* 965A.
        Government Printing Office, Washington, D.C.
1966   Paricutin 1965—Aftermath of Eruption. U.S. Geological Survey, Professional
        Paper 550C. Government Printing Office, Washington, D.C.

SHEETS, PAYSON, ED.
1983   *Archaeology and Volcanism in Central America: The Zapotitán Valley of El Salvador.*
        University of Texas Press, Austin.

SHEETS, PAYSON D., AND DONALD K. GRAYSON, EDS.
1979   *Volcanic Activity and Human Ecology.* Academic Press, New York.

SILLITOE, R. H.
1974   Tectonic Segmentation of the Andes: Implications for Magmatism and
        Metallogeny. *Nature* 250: 542–545

SIMKIN, T., L. SIEBERT, L. MCCLELLAND, D. BRIDGE, C. NEWHALL, AND J. H. LATTER
1981   *Volcanoes of the World.* Hutchinson Ross, Stroudsberg, Pa.

SMITH, D. G. W., AND J. A. WESTGATE
1969   Electron Probe Techniques for Characterizing Pyroclastic Deposits. *Earth and
        Planetary Science Letters* 5: 313–319.

SMITH, R. KIMBALL
n.d.   Early Formative Occupation in Southern Manabí, Ecuador: A Reevaluation
        of Valdivia Settlement Patterns in the Puerto Lopez–Ayampe Region. Paper
        presented at the 45th International Congress of Americanists, Bogotá, 1985.

STALLER, JOHN
n.d.   Late Valdivia Occupation in Southern Coastal El Oro Province, Ecuador:
        Excavations at the Early Formative Period (3500-1500 B.C.): Site of La

Emerenciana. Ph.D. dissertation, Department of Anthropology, Southern Methodist University, Dallas, 1994.

STEMPER, DAVID M.
1993   *The Persistence of Pre-Hispanic Chiefdoms on the Río Daule, Coastal Ecuador.* Memoirs in Latin American Archaeology 7. University of Pittsburgh and Ediciones Libri Mundi, Pittsburgh and Quito.

STIRLING, MATTHEW W.
1963   A New Culture in Ecuador. *Archaeology* 16(3): 170–175.

STUIVER, MINZE, AUSTIN LONG, AND RENEE KRA, EDS.
1993   Calibration Issue. *Radiocarbon* 35(1).

TOBAR, OSWALDO
1997   Prospección controlada y excavación de cateos de prueba en la Hacienda San Cristóbal, provincia de Pichincha. Fundación ECOBARI, Informe final WW97012T15A, Quito.

TOLSTOY, PAUL, AND WARREN R. DeBOER
1989   An Archaeological Sequence for the Santiago–Cayapas River Basin, Esmeraldas, Ecuador. *Journal of Field Archaeology* 16: 295–308.

VALDEZ, FRANCISCO
1986   *Investigaciones Arqueológicas en La Tolita (Esmeraldas, Ecuador). In Arqueología y Etnohistoria del Sur de Colombia y Norte del Ecuador,* (J. Alcina Franch and S. E. Moreno Yánez, eds.): 81–107. *Miscelánea Antropológica Ecuatoriana: Boletín de los Museos del Banco Central del Ecuado*r 6.
1987   *Proyecto Arqueológico La Tolita (1983–1986).* Museo Arqueológico del Banco Central del Ecuador, Quito.

VILLALBA, MARCELO
1988   *Cotocollao: Una aldea Formativo del valle de Quito.* Miscelánea Antropológica Ecuatoriana, Serie Monográfica 2. Museos del Banco Central del Ecuador, Quito.

WESTGATE, J. A., AND M. P. GORTON
1981   Correlation Techniques in Tephra Studies. In *Tephra Studies* (S. Self and R.S.J. Sparks, eds.): 73–94. Reidel, Dordrecht.

WILKENSON, L., M. HILL, S. MICELI, G. BIRKENBEUEL, AND E. VANG
1992   *SYSTAT for Windows: Graphics, Version 5.* SYSTAT Inc., Evanston, Ill.

WILKENSON, L., M. HILL, J. P. WELNA, AND G. K. BIRKENBEUEL
1992   *SYSTAT for Windows: Statistics, Version 5.* SYSTAT Inc., Evanston, Ill.

WILLIAMS, H.
1942   *The Geology of Crater Lake National Park, Oregon.* Publication 50. Carnegie Institution of Washington D.C.

ZEIDLER, JAMES A.
1986   La evolución local de asentamientos Formativos en el litoral ecuatoriano: El caso de Real Alto (OGSECh-012). In *La arqueología de la costa ecuatoriana: Nuevos enfoques* (J. G. Marcos, ed.): 86–127. Corporación Editora Nacional, Quito.

James A. Zeidler and John S. Isaacson

1988 Feline Imagery, Stone Mortars, and Formative Period Interaction Spheres in the Northern Andean Area. *Journal of Latin American Lore* 14(2): 243–283.

1994a Archaeological Testing in the Lower Jama Valley. In *Regional Archaeology in Northern Manabí, Ecuador,* vol. 1: *Environment, Cultural Chronology, and Prehistoric Subsistence in the Jama River Valley* (J. A. Zeidler and D. M. Pearsall, eds.): 99–109. Memoirs in Latin American Archaeology 8. University of Pittsburgh and Ediciones Libri Mundi, Pittsburgh and Quito.

1994b Archaeological Testing in the Middle Jama Valley. In *Regional Archaeology in Northern Manabí, Ecuador,* vol. 1: *Environment, Cultural Chronology, and Prehistoric Subsistence in the Jama River Valley* (J. A. Zeidler and D. M. Pearsall, eds.): 71–98. Memoirs in Latin American Archaeology 8. University of Pittsburgh and Ediciones Libri Mundi, Pittsburgh and Quito.

1995 Archaeological Survey and Site Discovery in the Forested Neotropics. In *Archaeology in the Lowland American Tropics: Current Analytical Methods and Recent Applications* (P. W. Stahl, ed.): 7–41. Cambridge University Press, Cambridge.

n.d.a Early Formative Settlement in the Chanduy Valley, Southwest Ecuador. Paper presented at the 42nd Annual Meeting of the Society for American Archaeology, New Orleans, 1977.

n.d.b The Piquigua Phase: A Terminal Valdivia Occupation in Northern Manabí (Ecuador). Paper presented at the 57th Annual Meeting of the Society for American Archaeology, Pittsburgh, 1992.

n.d.c Settlement Dynamics and Political Centralization in Jama–Coaque Chiefdoms: The View from Ancient Muchique. Paper presented at the 61st Annual Meeting of the Society for American Archaeology, New Orleans, 1996.

n.d.d Social Space in Valdivia Society: Community Patterning and Domestic Structure at Real Alto, 3000–2000 B.C. Ph.D. dissertation, Department of Anthropology, University of Illinois at Urbana–Champaign, 1984.

ZEIDLER, JAMES A., CAITLIN E. BUCK, AND CLIFFORD D. LITTON

1998 The Integration of Archaeological Phase Information and Radiocarbon Results from the Jama River Valley, Ecuador: A Bayesian Approach. *Latin American Antiquity* 9(2): 160–179.

ZEIDLER, JAMES A., R. L. GIAUQUE, FRANK ASARO, AND FRED H. STROSS

1994 Trace-Element Analysis of Obsidian Artifacts from the San Isidro Site. In *Regional Archaeology in Northern Manabí, Ecuador,* vol. 1: *Environment, Cultural Chronology, and Prehistoric Subsistence in the Jama River Valley* (J. A. Zeidler and D. M. Pearsall, eds.): 141–144. Memoirs in Latin American Archaeology 8. University of Pittsburgh and Ediciones Libri Mundi, Pittsburgh and Quito.

ZEIDLER, JAMES A., AND DEBORAH M. PEARSALL

1994 The Jama Valley Archaeological/Paleoethnobotanical Project: An Introduction. In *Regional Archaeology in Northern Manabí, Ecuador,* vol. 1: *Environment, Cultural Chronology, and Prehistoric Subsistence in the Jama River Valley* (J. A. Zeidler and D. M. Pearsall, (eds.): 1–12. Memoirs in Latin American Archaeology 8. University of Pittsburgh and Ediciones Libri Mundi, Pittsburgh and Quito.

ZEIDLER, JAMES A., AND MARIE J. SUTLIFF

1994 Definition of Ceramic Complexes and Cultural Occupation in the Jama Valley. In *Regional Archaeology in Northern Manabí, Ecuador,* vol. 1: *Environment,*

Cultural Chronology, and Prehistoric Subsistence in the Jama River Valley (J. A. Zeidler and D. M. Pearsall, eds.): 111–130. Memoirs in Latin American Archaeology 8. University of Pittsburgh and Ediciones Libri Mundi, Pittsburgh, Pa., and Quito.

ZEIL, WILLIAM
1979   The Andes: A Geological Review. Beitrage zur Regionalem Geologie de Erde, Band 13, Gebruder Brontegaeger, Berlin.

Social and Cultural Development in the Ecuadorian Highlands and Eastern Lowlands during the Formative

KAREN OLSEN BRUHNS

SAN FRANCISCO STATE UNIVERSITY

INTRODUCTION

Archaeological investigations in the highlands and eastern lowlands of Ecuador have lagged far behind those on the coast. With the exception of a few areas that can be easily reached from either Quito or Otavalo, these two major regions have been traditionally seen as hard to work in because transportation is poor and the climate is considered unfavorable (too cold, hot, or damp). Hence they have been largely ignored.

Ironically, archaeological investigation began in the highlands long before coastal studies. From the sixteenth to the mid-twentieth centuries such figures as Pedro de Cieza de León, Bartolomé de las Casas, Charles-Marie de la Condamine, Francisco González Suárez, Jacinto Jijón y Caamaño, Max Uhle, Donald Collier, John Murra, and Wendell Bennett, among others, visited, mapped, and studied first the Inka remains of the southern highlands and then earlier sites in Cañar and Azuay (Barnes and Fleming 1989; Idrovo Urigüen 1990). Following these luminaries, the indefatigable Padre Porras visited, sometimes excavated, and always wrote about sites up and down the highlands and into the eastern lowlands (Porras 1987b). Although there are reasonable and deserved criticisms of Porras's excavations and interpretations, he was working in a wilderness of interpretation that was based almost entirely upon an overdependence upon scanty colonial period documents, looted materials, and the occasional excavation.

The existence of the Ecuadorian Highlands Formative was first firmly established by Max Uhle in the 1920s and further elucidated by Collier, Murra, and Bennett in the early 1940s (Bennett 1946; Collier and Murra 1943; Uhle 1922). Thirty years later investigation recommenced, first in the north—where a rapidly urbanizing Quito and adjacent valleys uncovered sites such as Cotocollao—and in the south, with an exploratory project headed by Elizabeth Carmichael of the British Museum followed by a project in the Río Jubones valley under the general directorship of Warwick Bray of the University of London (Carmichael, Bray, and Ericson 1979).[1]

In 1984 I began archaeological investigations in the Paute River valley of Azuay province. My focus was on the Formative as a regional manifestation tied closely to developments in the rest of Ecuador and northern Peru (Bruhns 1989, 1988/9, 1991, 1994, 1995; Bruhns, Burton, and Miller 1990). It rapidly became evident from excavations in Pirincay, a site at the east end of the agricultural zone of the Paute valley, that the undisturbed stratigraphy, abundant evidence of exchange with adjacent and faraway areas, and the possibility of recovering samples for radiocarbon assay in good cultural contexts, would be a key to chronological and other problems raised by former interpretations the Formative—interpretations on the basis of little to no archaeological evidence (Fig. 1).

CHRONOLOGICAL PROBLEMS OF THE HIGHLAND FORMATIVE

As someone accustomed to coastal prehistory, I found the highlands most unusual: Virtually all Formative remains known to date are Late Formative, and it appears that there was a prolonged aceramic Archaic/early farming stage. Since ceramics appear early on the coast, most have expected an equally early appearance of this technology in the highlands. On the other hand, ceramics were likewise late in Peru. The spread of technology is tied to a number of factors, including a perceived need by the receptors of the technology. It may well be that a seminomadic, incipiently agricultural people felt no need for ceramics because gourds, baskets, and wooden or leather containers were sufficient for many of their needs.

There is good evidence of Paleoindian occupations in the highlands, which are best documented for the north, where Robert Bell and, especially, Ernesto Salazar, have shown a widespread Paleoindian and Archaic adaptation (Bell 1965; Salazar 1980, 1984, 1985). In the central highlands around Riobamba, human remains have been found in association with extinct megafauna (Reinoso Hermida 1973). In the south, a sole late Paleoindian site, Chobshi cave (unfortunately badly disturbed by *guaqueros* and tourists), shows that the highlands were completely populated early on (Lynch 1989; Lynch and Pollack 1981).

---

[1] Athens (1995) postulated some very early dates for La Chimba. These dates are not really comparable to the many other ^{14}C dates for the sierra Formative, and it is probably best to wait for further excavation and dating of that site before accepting them.

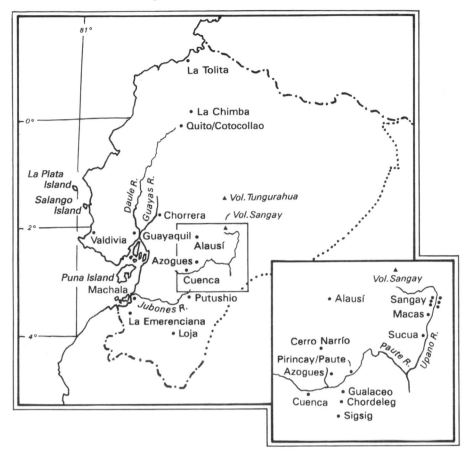

Fig. 1   Major Formative sites of Ecuador. Drawing by Tom Weller.

However, between these Paleoindian occupations and the establishment of permanent settlements, there is no archaeological evidence concerning the local cultures. It appears that foraging, trapping, hunting deer and other small-to-medium-size animals, and perhaps ruminating about the possibilities of setting up a farmstead were common. No sites pertaining to this long time span have been located, and the nature of this extended Archaic adaptation is totally unknown. There exists the remote possibility that earlier sites have not yet been found, but although a great many more Formative sites are known to exist than have been formally investigated, nothing earlier than the known ceramic traditions has yet appeared.

It could conceivably be, at least in the south, that there was an Early Formative stage characterized by small aceramic sites upon the floodplains of the larger rivers, such as the Tomebamba and Paute. These rivers flood often enough that such sites would be deeply buried. Chaullabamba, for example, is under roughly a meter of sediment and was found because the river has cut through part of the site (Fig. 2). Virtually nothing was on the surface. The spring of 1993 provided a lesson in why these sites, had they existed, might no longer be findable: after some 11 hours of torrential downpour, one of the barren hills— its loose, redeposited volcanic deposits even less stable after this drenching— slid. The landslide completely wiped out a small hamlet and its occupants; it also cut off the Paute entirely, causing the formation of a huge lake running up the Tomebamba and Azogues valleys, inundating farms, vacation homes, and archaeological sites. Eventually the natural dam broke, and the waters hurled themselves down the Paute, washing much of the floodplain down to the eastern lowlands (Fig. 3). Such cataclysms doubtless happened in the past and might partly explain the lack of Early Formative remains (López Monsalve 1993).

Because some of the earliest Late Formative sites have been found on floodplains, perhaps this indicates that floodplain sites were an older pattern of settle-

Fig. 2   Archaeological technicians from the Museo del Banco Central, Cuenca, examine the archaeological stratum of Chaullabamba, approximately 1 m below the modern ground surface, where it was exposed as the site was cut through by the Tomebamba River, July 1988.

ment. However, one of the general characteristics of highland Formative sites is that most known sites are on spurs or low ridges, which offer access to a number of ecosystems and protection from yearly floods. The two known flood-plain sites, Chaullabamba and Monjashuaycu, are single period of occupation sites and may be comparable to the evanescent villages built along the flood plain of the Río Upano today. The Upano is extremely active within its deeply cut, wide canyon, but, as the river has not changed its course for about a decade, people are moving onto the floodplain. They know that they will have to leave, probably in a hurry, but the advantages of the well-watered, rich alluvium are such that it is worth building a village that may have only a few years' lifespan (Ernesto Salazar, personal communication, October 1995).

Some archaeologists have claimed that Cerro Narrío has an Early Formative component, because of Robert Braun's seriation of the some of the collections from there (Braun 1982). This seriation, though actually first presented in 1971, circulated in unillustrated manuscript form for nearly a decade, which may explain why nonspecialists in Ecuadorian archaeology, especially, believe it. Braun drew parallels between Narrío ceramics and those of Early Formative Valdivia in Ecuador and the Initial period Paita complex of northern Peru. These arguments are unconvincing, mainly because a survey of museum and private col-

Fig. 3   Paute valley at Bullcay, across from Monjashuaycu, after the spring 1993 flood.

lections throughout Ecuador—including that of a man who has systematically looted Narrío for many decades—indicates that there is nothing earlier there than Late Formative. Most Cerro Narrío ceramics are identical or closely related to those of Pirincay (Bruhns 1989). At Pirincay the archaeological deposits are undisturbed, and a long series of radiocarbon dates firmly places these vessels in the Late Formative (the earliest are ca. 1400 B.C.), as does the existence of fairly abundant Chorreroid trade vessels from the coast in the early levels of the site (Bruhns 1989). No vessels related to either the Valdivia or the Machalilla traditions have been found at Pirincay or any other highland Formative site to date. The radiocarbon dates from Cerro Narrío are from surface contexts and lack good archaeological context. They are, respectively, 904 ± 59 BP (BM-909 associated with "coarse ceramics") and 3928 ± 60 BP (BM-896 associated with "red ceramics"); both are uncalibrated (Burleigh, Hewson, and Meeks 1972). It is the latter that is commonly quoted, although the former must be considered at least as good insofar as neither date has any firm associations with diagnostic artifacts. Coarse wares and red ceramics are found throughout the Formative and into succeeding epochs in the southern highlands. Moreover, Cerro Narrío has been so thoroughly looted and disturbed—looting began in 1912 and has continued until the present—that it would be difficult to get any kind of artifact or radiocarbon sequence (Fig. 4) (Uhle 1921). Donald Collier and John Murra described the site upon their arrival:

> The hill showed the signs of these efforts (referring to looting). A heavy, crunching carpet of Red-on-Buff sherds covered its lower reaches and upper platform. Large holes and yawning caves, only half filled by wind and rain, were everywhere, and in places the contour of the hill had been considerably altered. (Collier and Murra 1943: 36)

It is to their great credit that they were able to separate out the early and late components so well as to put together a general sequence of ceramic types that has stood the tests of time and further investigation in highland Formative sites.

Verification of Collier and Murra's artifactual sequence has now come from Pirincay, a Late Formative site located at the eastern edge of the highlands on a small spur above the valley floor. Pirincay commands two major trade routes: one to the tropical lowlands and one via the Río Guayán across the mountains to the Cañar valley (see Fig. 1). That this was an important location is demonstrated by the existence of a settlement in the same area (within less than five km away) from the Late Formative to the present. The exact locations of these sites vary through time in response apparently to changing political conditions. In the early centuries A.D. the Pirincaes moved their settlement to a higher

Fig. 4   The surface of Cerro Narrío with looters' pits and grazing sheep.

location just above Old Pirincay, one that was defensible and with a much better view of traffic along the Río Guayán. There is a later settlement (Tacalshalpa, Regional Developmental and Integration periods) on the ridge just above colonial and modern Paute; the Cañari and Inka also had a hilltop fortress across the valley from Pirincay/Paute (known today as Maras).

Pirincay was selected for excavation because of evidence of early (eggshell) ceramics and exotic materials (shell and crystal) on the surface. Most of the site was undisturbed, and the deep unmixed strata have provided a complete artifactual record further tied to some 37 radiocarbon dates. Thus Pirincay enables us to sort out the problematic chronology of Cerro Narrío and align the other known Formative sites of the southern highlands into a relatively complete chronology. Congruencies between the artifact assemblages and the radiocarbon dates of Loma Pucara, Cotocollao, and La Chimba as well as the Sucua and Río Upano sites of Harner and Porras (Harner 1972; Porras 1987a) further enable a construction of a summary chronology for the entire highlands and part of the adjacent eastern lowlands.

Throughout the highlands it appears that the Archaic aceramic foraging and incipient agricultural cultures began to have increasing contact with the more highly developed coastal cultures. By the Late Formative (ca. 1400 to 1200 B.C., calibrated ^{14}C dates), this influence resulted in the establishment of permanent villages and the appearance of ceramics. Agriculture became an important factor in the economy, as did local and interregional exchange. In the southern highlands where archaeologists have investigated a number of Late Formative sites, there was a sudden cultural florescence. The first occupations of Cerro Narrío, Chaullabamba, and Monjashuaycu are roughly coeval and should date to approximately 1400 B.C. or, just maybe, slightly earlier (Bennett 1946; Gomis S. 1989b; Greider n.d.; Uhle 1922). Pirincay was founded shortly thereafter (the earliest dates are in the 1500 to 1400 B.C. range), as were a lot of other sites that are known only through surface pickup or looting, such as Bullcay (next to Gualaceo), Cerro Llaver (Chordeleg), El Carmen Bajo and El Carmen Alto (upper Paute valley), and Villa Jubones/Santa Isabel. Chaullabamba and Monjashuaycu were definitely abandoned sometime before 400 B.C. as no evidence of the major change in ceramics that occurred at Pirincay and Cerro Narrío at this time is found at those sites. Possibly the inhabitants of one or both of those sites moved to sites along the higher terraces of the river valley on the Hacienda Huancarcuchu. Here Bennett (1946: 20–40; fig. 8) recovered ceramics like those of the later component of Pirincay and Cerro Narrío.

At approximately 400 to 300 B.C. (on the basis of ^{14}C dates from Pirincay), both Cerro Narrío and Pirincay show major changes in ceramics (see below); Pirincay also evidences major changes in economy, religion, and external contacts (Bruhns 1988/89, 1995; Bruhns, Burton, and Rostoker 1994). Similar changes are visible at Alausí, in the Valle de Las Cebadas, in the Jubones valley, and to the south in Loja (Arellano 1994, Guffroy 1987, Porras 1977). Pirincay was abandoned in the first century A.D. when its inhabitants moved up the ridge to a series of sites where they could continue to oversee the highlands–lowlands route as well as whoever was coming over the hill from Cañar. At approximately the same time at Cerro Narrío, the focus of occupation seems to have moved to the top of the hill; shortly thereafter the site was abandoned, although it was used as a cemetery in later prehistory and again in the modern era.

Not all southern sites were abandoned. Putushío had an uninterrupted occupation as did Loma Pucara, which continued to be occupied until an eruption of Sangay forced its abandonment late in the first millennium A.D. (Arellano 1994; Rehren and Temme 1994).

In the north there are fewer data. Some of Myers' survey near Laguna San Pablo in Imbabura suggests that site areas were occupied for a long time, although the degree of disturbance is such that little concerning them at any time period is known (Athens 1978, Myers 1976, 1978).[2] Cotocollao was aban-

---

[2] As above, note 1.

doned ca. 500 B.C., shortly before changes appeared in the south. There are few data from the Pichincha sites and La Nueva Era that bear on the issue of chronology. However, it seems that volcanic eruptions in the north had something to do with site histories, much as they did in the Valle de Las Cebadas (Arellano 1994, Isaacson 1987).

THE NATURE OF THE HIGHLAND FORMATIVE

Enough archaeological investigation has been done in the Ecuadorian highlands to delineate two major cultural spheres in the Formative: one that encompasses the southern highlands from Loja to the Riobamba region and another other to the north, extending into southern Colombia.[3] There may be a third sphere, in the central highlands, but there are not enough data as yet to support this possibility. These are not totally separate traditions. Exchange between the north and the south resulted in stylistic and other diffusion, and both seem to have shared a common background, evidenced in strong continuities in such artifacts as lithics, sherd tools, and bone tools. However, the ceramic traditions are sufficiently different to postulate a different source for each. Moreover the differing contacts of the north and south resulted in cultures that are qualitatively different in important ways.

The North

The northern sphere is best characterized by Cotocollao in the Quito valley (Porras 1980; Villalba 1988). Cotocollao is a small village. The earliest occupation of the site was somewhat scattered small groups of closely spaced rectangular houses made of wattle and daub. Marcelo Villalba (1988: 71) has suggested that the groups of houses pertain to coresident members of a kin group. The later occupation was a more concentrated group of oval houses. Remains of ceramics making, cooking, weaving, stonework and other activities were associated with the houses.

Cotocollao ceramics are the best described and most completely published of the northern traditions. Aside from a plethora of simple *ollas* and jars of various sizes (domestic wares used for cooking and storage), Cotocollao ceramics are best typified by a large variety of open bowls, many of them decorated. Vessels are relatively thick, and red slip is common. Most other decoration is plastic and consists of notched carinations on the bowls, notched fillets, incision, punctation, and some deeper incision/excision, all in simple geometric

---

[3] The cold highlands of southern Colombia (department of Nariño) and northern Ecuador (province of Carchi) were culturally a single unit in later times. There has been no investigation, to date, of Formative period sites in either area, although it seems likely that the cultural continuities observed later on had deep roots.

designs. Aside from the, bowls there are also relatively rare bottles, both single spout and stirrup spout (Fig. 5).

The lithic assemblage of Cotocollao is distinctive. Perhaps the most outstanding component is the presence of stone bowls. These are both rectangular and round, with the round ones being similar to the ceramic bowls. One of these bowls was found with a "trophy" head impaled on the wall (Villalba 1988: 79-81 and fig. 47). Other ground stone forms are common and include mortars, pestles, *manos, metates,* T-shaped axes, and ornaments such as ear flares, labrets, and various beads and pendants. Flaked tools are numerous and, as might be expected in a site so close to the major flows, a large percentage are obsidian. There was also a well-developed bone tool industry.

The well-analyzed floral and faunal remains indicate that Cotocollao was fully agricultural with the entire battery of Andean cultigens including potatoes (*Solanum tuberosum*), *achira* (*Canna edulis*), *oca* (*Oxalis tuberosa*), *chochos* (*Lupinus* spp. and *tarwi*), beans, (*Phaseolus* spp.), *quinoa* (*Chenopodium quinoa*), and maize (*Zea mays*). Hunting focused on deer and rabbit (*Odocoilus virginianus* and *Sylvilagus brasilienus andinus,* respectively), the two major prey of all Formative highland dwellers. Llamas (*Lama glama*) were present in the latest phase of occupation (Villalba 1988: 348).

Other northern highlands Formative sites have neither been so thoroughly investigated nor published. Ronald Lippi's work in western Pichincha province above 1,500 m in elevation centered on a number of sites with Cotocollao-related ceramics. What is interesting is that the range of pottery wares and forms recovered from these sites represents only a small part of the Cotocollao complex. As no petrographic work has been done to date, it is not known whether these few sherds represent traded-in pieces or were made locally in imitation of Cotocollao models. In general, however, a series of local Late Formative traditions with some ties with the Quito region exist. Lippi also reported that at elevations lower than 1,000 m he located sites containing small quantities of Chorrera and Machalilla or Pisagua pottery (Lippi 1986: 189–207; 1998b: 316–317 and fig. 8.6; 1998a: 120–124). Tamara Bray (personal communication, 21 Nov. 1995) reported that in her survey of the Guallabamba valley she had identified some eight sites as Formative on the basis of comparison with material from Cotocollao. J. Stephen Athens uncovered work in the north, near Otavalo, a Formative site, La Chimba, at an altitude of some 3,100 m in Imbabura province. This is close to the modern limits of agriculture. Nonetheless, the La Chimba cultural was fully agricultural with much the same variety of crops seen at Cotocollao: maize, *oca*, potatoes, beans, and *quinoa*. La Chimba's deep, stratified deposits show that it had permanent residents. The ceramics of

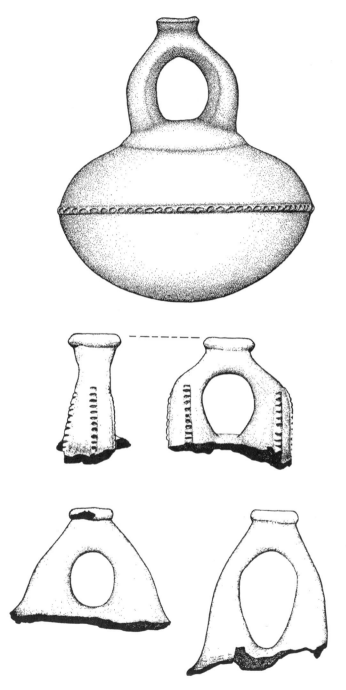

Fig. 5   Bottles from Cotocallao (after Villalba 1988, figs. 110–111).

La Chimba are simple, with some similarities in decoration to Cotocollao. These similarities include an emphasis upon open carinated bowls with simple plastic decoration (incision, punctation, notched fillet, red-on-buff slip paint), many of which are identical to examples from Cotocollao (Fig. 6). The simple *ollas* and jars are also similar (Fig. 7).

La Chimba indicates that trade with the coast and with other highland areas was well developed, as marine shell and obsidian are fairly common. Imported ceramics of Chorrera type occur in small quantities. What is perhaps more interesting is the evidence—in the form of a figurine with a quid in its cheek—of coca use at La Chimba. Whether this indicates ties with the eastern lowlands, as Athens suggested, or simply shows that coca growing was already established in nearby Ibarra is not known. Athens also suggested eastern ties on the basis of Cosanga phase-related ceramics in the site. All of these ties seem to have intensified through time, and evidences of foreign contact are strongest in the latest Formative periods. However, if the lowland pottery found at La Chimba really was Cosanga related, either the dating of Cosanga as Regional Developmental is in error or Athens's rather early dates for La Chimba are erroneous (Athens 1995a,b).

Fig. 6 Carinated bowl and plain jar neck sherds from La Chimba. Incision, notching, and painting are visible on the various pieces and a single solid leg from a tripod bowl is center, lower row. Photo courtesy of J. S. Athens.

The Formative in the Central and Southern Highlands

Little work has been done in the central highland valleys of Ecuador, and virtually all of this work has been concerned with the Inka or colonial periods because these valleys have been repeatedly buried under volcanic ash; consequently, early deposits must await the coincidence of erosion or earth-moving equipment to be uncovered. The only Formative site known to date is Loma Pucara in the Valle de Las Cebadas to the southeast of Riobamba (Arellano 1994; see also Fig. 1). Loma Pucara and related, although undescribed, sites show a sedentary hunting and foraging population making the transition toward supplementing these activities with agriculture. The role of agriculture increased through time, and at the later levels stone hoes and mortars and pestles became commonplace. White-tailed, brocket, and *pudu* deer (*Pudu mephistophiles*) were hunted, as were the rabbit and possibly the mountain dog (*Speothos venaticus*). Domestic guinea pigs (*Cavea porcellus*) were present from the earliest levels onward. The ceramics at this site show clear association with the southern ceramic sphere. Eggshell wares dominate the early levels, and later jars and *ollas* with

Fig. 7   *Olla* from La Chimba. The rounded form, punctations and, above all, the streaking burnishing (often in wide bands) is typical of many sierra Formative ceramic assemblages. Photo courtesy of J. S. Athens.

vertical red stripes on their shoulders, identical to materials from Cañar and Azuay, occur with some frequency. Eggshell wares here, as elsewhere, are associated with thicker plain wares used for cooking and storage and portage (Fig. 8). There are a few vessels that show affiliations with Cotocollao and even La Chimba ceramics in their decorated rims, applied clay disks, and ticked carinations. Rarer finds include some Chorrera-related ceramics (fine black ware) and yellowish white, thick-walled ceramics—which seem to have affiliation with the eastern slopes—and T-shaped stone axes, which the excavator would also like to see as evidence of trade with the Upano region (Fig. 9). Bone and antler tools are common as are spindle whorls, sherd tools used in the manufacture of ceramics, and a considerable quantity of obsidian chips. The obsidian has been sourced to Mullamica, north of Quito (Arellano 1994).

It is not known how typical Loma Pucara is of the central highlands Formative, and—owing to the existence of only a summary report—it is not possible to say much more about the site and its external ties, other than to note their similarity to Pirincay and, perhaps, Cerro Narrío.

More work has been done on sites in the southern highlands than in the north and central highlands. Formative period sites known to date include several localities within modern Alausí and its environs, Cerro Narrío in the Cañar valley, Pirincay and associated sites in the Paute valley, Chaullabamba in the Tomebamba valley, Villa Jubones in the Jubones valley, Putushío in southern

Fig. 8   Rims from Loma Pucara. These simple striped everted rims can be matched in virtually all southern Formative ceramics assemblages. Photo courtesy of A. Jorge Arellano.

Azuay, and a number of sites near Catamayo in Loja (Bennett 1946; Bruhns, Burton, and Miller 1990; Carmichael, Bray and Ericson 1979; Collier and Murra 1943; Gomis 1989a,b; Guffroy 1987; Idrovo 1989; Excavations at Cañar 1922; Porras 1977; Rehren and Temme 1994; Uhle 1921, 1922).

All of these sites are clearly part of a single cultural sphere of ceramics, economy, and, as best we can tell, settlement pattern. The most detailed information is on the ceramics. In 1922, Max Uhle noted a continuous distribution of a highly distinctive ware from the Nudo del Azuay to the valley of Loja. This is the ceramic he and everyone thereafter calls *eggshell*: vessels that have a thin, hard, gray paste. This paste was commonly formed into small-to-medium *ollas*, semiclosed bowls, or tiny *tecomates* (perhaps *poporos*, although none seems to have remains of lime within it). Eggshell ceramics usually have highly polished slipped rims, painted red on white in concentric stripes or simple geometric designs. In the years since Uhle's original observation, it has become possible to extend this distribution a bit to the north and a little to the east and west, but eggshell ceramics are definitely the hallmark of the earliest known pottery-making cultures of the southern highlands.

Eggshell ceramics are generally cooking wares, despite their thinness. Collier and Murra (1943: 51) reported having seen one of the few surviving unbroken pieces shivering in a light breeze as it blew down a corridor. I have also seen the same piece do exactly the same thing. Eggshell ceramics are incredibly thin and

Fig. 9   Loma Pucara: Sherds showing stylistic ties with the eastern side of the Andes and the Amazon lowlands. Both these sherds and those of Fig. 8 are from Sitio 4, Levels 40-60. Photo courtesy of A. Jorge Arellano.

Fig. 10   Pirincay: Offerings from Burial 1. The two relatively thick plates are painted red on white, whereas the eggshell *olla*, with its thick deposits of carbon on the exterior, has a highly polished rim with red-and-white geometric designs. The function of the cork-shaped rock crystal object (*center*) found near the mandible is not known.

lightweight. They are fragile and any site where they were used will have quantities of tiny, plain, gray, thin sherds throughout the deposits (along with bits of slipped rim). The majority of known eggshell ceramics are formed into *ollas* with globular or oblate globular bodies. The rims, which are generally everted or erect and fairly narrow (with a wide horizontal variant, however), are commonly either plain polished red or slipped white and painted with simple designs in red of multiple stripes or, in the earliest phases, with step frets, curlicues, or half circles. The rims are highly polished, the bodies simply wiped.

Associated with eggshell ceramics are heavier plates and bowls of various forms: flat plates, several varieties of carinated plates/bowls, flaring bowls, and hemispherical bowls, often with a deep groove around the outside rim. Bowls are painted red or white or red and white, usually with simple, crude designs (Fig. 10). The exceptions are hemispherical bowls, which are always plain red and well polished, and flaring bowls, whose interiors are slipped red or white on the bottom and have highly polished red on the interior side walls. There is a great variety of bowls and plates. There are also some plain domestic wares: small-to-medium size jars predominate.

Ceramics in the southern highlands are made from white-to-buff clays with high organic content. They were reduced fired, having been removed from the firing situation—"firing situation" because as yet no ceramics workshops date to the Formative—and exposed to the air, so that they oxidized superficially and the slip turned red. Most vessels retain a reduced core and many are superficially oxidized. The appearance of the vessels is similar to vessels manufactured in the modern village of Jatunpamba, on the ridge above the juncture of the Tomebamba and Azogues rivers. Jatunpamba potters have preserved ancient technologies, including hand building with coil, paddle and anvil, and slab construction. Firing is in the open, and vessels are stacked on their sides with their openings toward the center of the circle of pots, large *ollas* and jars on the lower level, small *ollas* and casseroles above, with layers of branches and grass separating them. Sometimes a "wall" of large broken sherds is placed around or on one side of the vessels to protect them from the flames. Firing is done without preheating the vessels; the wood is allowed to flame up into the wind to produce a high heat. Vessels are fired for about three hours by using light branches and wood at first and then heavy logs toward the end. Thereupon, the fire is pulled away from the vessels, which are allowed to cool. This kind of firing produces a paste that in its exterior and interior appearance is similar to the ancient ones, although the modern vessels are much thicker and less decorated (Sjöman 1989).

Minor constituents of the entire southern highlands ceramics group are reduced black ware bowls with line luster decoration, open bowls with pink-and-gray iridescent painting on the interior (simple stripes and dots predominate), glossy plain and incised wares in red, black, and gray. The plain and incised wares are named from the site where they were first described: for example, Narrío Glossy, Narrío Glossy Incised, and Cañar Polished. Narrío Glossy tends to be limited in forms to piriform and cylindrical vases, while the characteristic form of Cañar Polished is a basal flanged bowl (Fig. 11). There are also vessels, usually globular *ollas*, with strange-looking hollow zoomorphic(?) *adornos* on them. These little figures are another absolute hallmark of the southern highlands Formative (Fig. 12). Some bottles are also present, but it is hard to determine whether these are a minor part of local production or are imports. They are not common and at Pirincay, at least, all were imports, not local wares.

There are also a series of highly characteristic ceramic artifacts: cylinder "seals" with deeply excised patterns, flat stamps, sherd tools used for ceramics manufacture (for finishing the rim), and sherd disks and whorls (Fig. 13). The latter can be shown to be for different purposes: the disks and whorls occur in a bimodal pattern of size and weight distributions. It is evident that the unperforated disks were not blanks for whorls, but their function is unknown (Bruhns 1988/89). Sherd disks, whorls, and tools are also characteristic of the northern Formative ceramic complexes.

Associated with the southern ceramics group are a fair number of bone tools (many for weaving and basketry), white argillite pendants, and marine

141

Fig. 11 Cañar polished basal flange bowl. The scratchy incision over the highly polished red slip is characteristic of this ware. Private collection, Quito.

Fig. 12 Hollow *adornos* from Pirincay and Loma Pucara. Photo of object on left courtesy of A. Jorge Arellano.

Fig. 13 Pirincay: A handheld sherd tool held against the underside of an egg-shell rim shows its exact fit.

shells, both unmodified and made into masks, dishes, tinklers, and pendants. The most common shells in use were spondylus, strombus, mother of pearl (*Pinctada* spp.), and a number of different species of *Conus*. The characteristic decorative form is the *ucuyaya*, a little anthropomorphic or zoomorphic pendant, often ending in a sort of tusk shape (Fig. 14); however, various beads, including zoomorphic ones, tinklers, and similar simple ornaments were also made.

Stone tools in the southern sierra sites are relatively simple, mainly scrapers, drills, utilized flakes, and hammerstones of locally available stones. At Pirincay most tools were made of stones from around the site, either from the ridge or the riverbed (Jean DeMouthe, personal communication, September 1998). The rock crystal bead industry was accompanied by quartz tools–hammerstones of various sizes and drills (Bruhns 1991). Pirincay has yielded little obsidian, mainly small flake tools. Several pieces were sourced to the Quito area, although one was evidently from an obsidian pebble from much earlier volcanic activity. These pebbles, commonly called *Apache tears*, are quite common in the geological formations of the Paute, and some have been found in the cultural layers of the site, apparently collected and hoarded for use. Ground stone tools consisted of

143

Fig. 14 *Ucuyayas* of white shell (strombus?), spondylus, and bone. Collection of Colegio Benigno Malo, Cuenca; photograph by Norman Hammond and Karen Olsen Bruhns.

numerous grinding stones (both *manos* and *metates* and rocker mills, *bataanes* and *chunga*s) and rare T-shaped stone axes (all surface finds), as well as some small tools of slate and pink shale of unknown use.

Comparable material was found at Chaullabamba but nothing on it has yet been published (Dominique Gomis S., personal communication, June 1989). Wendell Bennett did not report any stone tools from the sites he investigated in 1943, although Collier and Murra (1943:67–68) briefly mentioned a few stemless points, some stone beads, two small limestone figurines, a celt and a fragmentary ax (from the upper levels). To the north, Jorge Arellano (1994: 119–129) reported that Loma Pucara yielded numerous obsidian chips, which were shown to have come from the Mullamica source.

Clearly, study of the lithic assemblages of sites has lagged far behind that of the ceramic components. Only from Cotocollao do we have anything like a complete stone tool kit analyzed and related to specific economic activities.

In those sites with continuous occupation throughout the Late Formative and earlier Regional Developmental periods, there was a major change in this ceramics assemblage about 300 to 400 B.C. (on the basis of calibrated ^{14}C dates from Pirincay). Eggshell wares and most associated bowls and plates disappeared

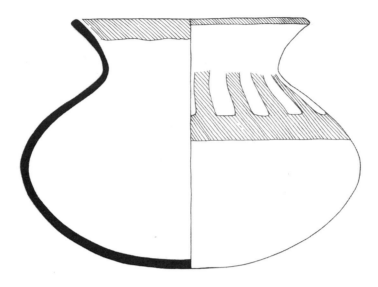

Fig. 15 Small red-on-buff jar with decorations typical
of the later Formative. Drawing by Paul Stempen.

and were replaced by a whole series of much larger, thicker vessels. These were
made from the same clays with the same construction and exhibit the same
firing techniques as the earlier components. All the simplest decoration remained: plain red rims and upper vessel exteriors, red stripes on the neck or
shoulder of jars and *ollas*, and red patches on the shoulder, etc. (Fig. 15). Plain
red hemispherical bowls, often with a channel groove around the exterior rim,
continued in popularity, although they became larger. New domestic vessel
forms include large undecorated *ollas* and medium-to-large jars with various
neck shapes. There also appeared a series of new decorated shapes: *compoteras*
(the local term for a plate or bowl on a high annular base) identical to those
Collier and Murra identified at Cerro Narrío (pl. 27; figs. 4, 5), annular base
bowls painted in red on cream or yellow (some with applied fillet and incised
decoration and with an incised and appliqué face on one side), large piriform
cups with red-on-white or yellow decoration, and ceramic stools (Fig. 16).
Minor constituents of this group include vessels with punctate and incised
decoration and a little relief modeling, vessels decorated with faded negative
painting, the peculiar quartz studded ware—these are not grater bowls, since
the quartz pebbles are generally applied to the exterior—and Red Banded

Fig. 16 Red-on-buff ceramic stool, provenance unknown. Collection of the Museo del Banco Central, Cuenca.

Incised pottery (Figs. 17, 18). These unusual and probably nonlocal wares do not form any cohesive group, despite Collier and Murra's hypothesis of a Group X coming from somewhere in the Nudo del Azuay (1943: 48–62), but are found throughout the southern (and perhaps central) highlands in small quantities. Red Banded Incised, in particular, is ubiquitous in southern highland assemblages and can be shown to have originated along the southeastern flanks of Sangay volcano (Bruhns, Burton, and Rostoker 1994).

This group of ceramics and associated artifacts are found throughout the southern highlands. This is not to say that every site has exactly the same ceramic assemblage; rather there are local preferences for specific shapes, for neck and rim forms and decorations, and quantities and types of exotica are different. This is doubtless a reflection of local site histories and contacts. For example, Pirincay has a great deal more Red Banded Incised than Cerro Narrío. Chaullabamba has more polished fine black ware and a red-on-cream ware with painted plant motifs not seen elsewhere. The Catamayo sites have more jars and *ollas* and a preference for incision as neck decoration. However, from just southeast of Riobamba to Catamayo in central Loja and west into the upper Jubones valley ceramic technology, basic forms and decorations, and a great many of the same forms and sizes are held in common. This is especially

Fig. 17 Pirincay: Red banded incised sherds from late levels.

Fig. 18 Pirincay: Quartz studded ware.

true for the earlier component (eggshell and associated wares) and is also true for those sites with a later occupation as well.

FORMATIVE SETTLEMENT PATTERNS, ARCHITECTURE, AND CRAFTS SPECIALIZATION

Settlement patterns as well as ceramics show considerable similarities in the southern highlands. Sites are small. Cerro Narrío is quite large, but the Formative settlement area seems to have been quite limited. The extent of the early settlement is blurred by the extensive looting, most of it aimed at the late prehistoric burials, which sometimes contain metal and cover the hill. Pirincay is small, about a hectare, as are a number of unexcavated sites in the immediate vicinity such as Pirincay Alto and the Chicte and Bullcay sites. Chaullabamba's absolute extent is difficult to ascertain; the exposure on the riverbank does not continue for more than about 50 m. As in the Paute and Cañar valleys, the later occupation of the area is up on the ridge above Chaullabamba on the Hacienda Huancarcuchu (Bennett 1946: 15–16). Bennett neither mapped his sites nor gave sufficient data for others to locate them again; so it is a bit difficult to gauge their size from his few illustrations. El Carmen Bajo and El Carmen Alto, which have been located, are small. Arellano's Loma Pucara and related sites in the Valle de Las Cebadas are likewise tiny hamlets, as are Guffroy's Catamayo sites in Loja (Arellano 1994; Guffroy 1987). Temme's Late Formative Putushío site is also apparently small, although the size of the earlier occupation is obscured by later use of the site, which was occupied without break until the Inka invasions (Rehren and Temme 1994). This small site size is interesting considering what is currently known of the history of the Formative period on the coast with its steady growth in size and early development of special purpose architecture (Echeverría Almeida 1983; Lippi 1996: 41-57). In the highlands there are apparently no large sites or readily identifiable special purpose architecture. The historic situation of a population scattered in farmsteads or hamlets without urban centers and no architecturally differentiated ceremonial centers appears to have had a considerable time depth in the southern highlands.

Sites in the northern highlands may be larger. Athens (1995b) has estimated about 12 hectares for La Chimba, although testing there has not been extensive. Cotocollao (Villalba 1988) covered an equivalent space. No other sites have been investigated to absolute size. Architecture, insofar as we have information, is quite variable. The houses Guffroy (1987) excavated at the La Vega site in Loja are semicircular and about 8 m x 4 m in size. They were built of wood and thatch above stone and clay lower walls (Fig. 19). Guffroy identifies Structure 1 as a familial dwelling, but speculates that Structure 2 may have had "un usage plus colectif."

Cerro Narrío, like Pirincay, revealed post holes corresponding to rectangular or apsidal structures in levels Collier and Murra (1943) identified as belonging to their later phase (figs. 4, 6, 7, 8). These structures were approximately 4 to 6 m in length and 2 to 2.5 m in width (Fig. 20).

Pirincay has evidence of changing architecture through the Formative, a record so far not uncovered elsewhere (except perhaps at Cotocollao). The earliest structure at Pirincay is a low (ca. 15 cm) platform of rock and clay with a packed clay floor atop bedrock. Only a small part of this structure could be uncovered, but it is evidently rectangular. Radiocarbon assays from this level are about 1200 B.C. (calibrated). Ceramics associated include heavy, gray, carinated bowls with notches on the carination, eggshell sherds from *ollas*, and other ceramics characteristic of the earliest Formative occupations of the southern highlands. Somewhat later, as the midden surrounding the platform rose, the area was leveled and a building with a packed cobblestone and clay floor—this time not raised on a definite platform—was constructed. The artifacts associated were identical to those associated with the first building; apparently not much time had elapsed. Following this construction, there were repeated epi-

Fig. 19 Reconstruction drawing of Structure 1, La Vega, Catamayo valley, Loja. Courtesy of Jean Guffroy.

sodes of filling and leveling. Bits of burned wattle and daub and one large lens of ash, apparently from a thatched roof, indicate that the structure or structures here were not different from precement block modern ones in construction. Then a major episode of fill followed. Loose rock from the side of the site was hauled up and on top of this a yellow clay floor was constructed. At least two more major leveling episodes followed with several individual construction phases between them (Fig. 21). Apparently the site was consolidated in the center of the hilltop, as later material is found only in the leveled and paved site center.

The area around Pirincay contains abundant lenses of a nearly pure calcium carbonate. This may have been an item of exchange, since coca chewing had been present in Ecuador from the Early Formative (Lathrap, Collier, and Chandra 1975: 48). We have no evidence of the use of coca at Pirincay itself, although, as mentioned above, a figurine depicting a figure with a quid in its cheek from La Chimba in northern Ecuador is an indication that coca use was not restricted to the coast during the Formative (Athens 1995b). At Pirincay the soft and granular calcium carbonate was used as flooring and paving. From the late centuries B.C. onward, Pirincay showed signs of being a special purpose site. Perhaps the first paving of the center was for a plaza, since it has a stone drain-

Fig. 20 Pirincay: White calcium carbonate floor with post holes. Photo by Norman Hammond and Karen Olsen Bruhns.

age system under the floor. Debris later covered this plaza and into it were dug "party pits," each containing the remains of a ritual or ceremony involving sacrificing of llamas, eating, and drinking (Fig. 22). The nearly identical contents of these pits indicates that they were made within a relatively close time span.

Later construction was not as ambitious, although there was another partial pavement and a number of individual structures with wooden frames and wattle-and-daub walls constructed at site center. Those final buildings with post holes visible in the topmost calcium carbonate floors and dating to the beginning of the CE, are definitely domestic. There was also a small circular storage structure, ca. 50 cm in diameter, constructed on the abandoned floor of a house and dating to the time of the site's abandonment. Garbage, including a trophy head, had been dumped into it, as was, and is, common with abandoned structures. At this point warfare seems to have become a problem, and Pirincay was abandoned, with the inhabitants moving up the ridge above the original site.

Fig. 21 Pirincay: Excavations M, G, F, and L showing the series of leveling episodes and floors.

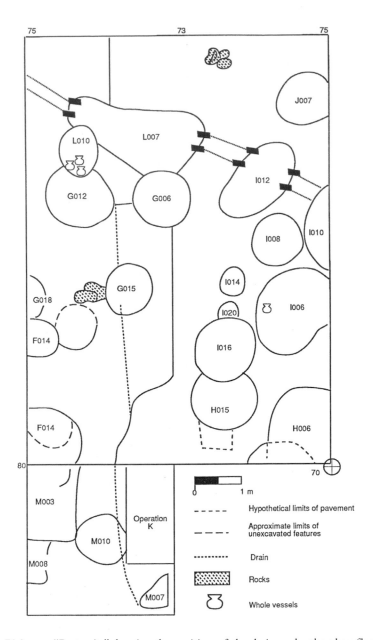

Fig. 22 Pirincay: "Party pits" showing the position of the drain under the plaza floor. At L010 is the burned llama sacrifice. The heavily charred bones of this young llama, under one year old, were tightly packed in the hole. Even the smallest bones were present save for the cranium and the two scapulae. Three domestic *ollas* accompanied the sacrifice. Drawing by Jean Sandifer.

Social and Cultural Development

Architecture such as Pirincay's is reported for a number of other sites in the region. Uhle reported what he calls *altars*, which are similar hard-packed white floors with pits full of debris in or under them, in Loja and at Chaullabamba (1922: 4–5). These altars are large enough also to have been open paved patios or plazas. Dominique Gomis S. (1989b) found lines of stones in her excavations at Chaullabamba, indicating elliptical or rectangular structures with clay floors, somewhat similar to the house Guffroy (1987) excavated at La Vega in Loja.

The apparent paucity of specialized architecture in the south does not mean a lack of specialization. Pirincay was established as a rock crystal bead manufacturing site, and workshop debris is a significant component of the midden from the first midden levels. The source of rock crystal is the Río Collay, some 15 km southeast of Pirincay (Burton n.d.). The distance from Pirincay indicates that other sites were likely involved in rock crystal bead manufacture, either as workshops or feeder sites for Pirincay. With the introduction of llamas in the late centuries B.C. textile manufacture seems to have been added to the list of specialist manufactures (Bruhns 1988/89). The party pits suggest that the site may have served as a center for rituals. Putushío has evidence of smelting on its lowest floors, and it continued as a smelter site until late in prehistory (Rehren and Temme 1994). The specialty at Cerro Narrío, if indeed it had any, is unknown. Although it has been rumored that there was spondylus working on the site, there is little evidence of shell working at the site. There is a fair amount of spondylus, all worked, but no debris at all. There should also be sites where the characteristic white argyllite pendants were worked, but these have not yet been located. Of course, many items, such as baskets, mats, and processed foodstuffs, leave no archaeological traces of their production.

Burial Patterns

Burials associated with Formative sites in the highlands are generally flexed or seated and have a few ceramic offerings. Three burials have been excavated at Pirincay. The first was the burial of a neonate, who was flexed (wrapped?) and placed in one of the party pits. This may have been fortuitous; perhaps a stillbirth occurred during one of these ceremonials, and the baby was included in the ritual disposal of the ceremonial rubbish. The neonate dates to the last centuries B.C. and is associated with the larger, coarser ceramics of the age and llama bones. Other finds in the same pit included a carved pickup stick for weaving and a gilded copper nose ornament. These artifacts may not have been deliberately included as the pits were often "topped off" with a bit of contemporary, ordinary garbage, and small artifacts such as these become lost easily.

The second and third burials, which date to the initial occupation, were placed in shallow circular pits cut in a natural lens of calcium carbonate. In one, the body had been mutilated before interment. The articulated arms and hands and legs and feet were placed in the bottom of the pit with a mandible placed on top of them. The rest of the bones were missing. The offerings consisted of a crystal cork-shaped object placed in or just above the mandible and two plates and an eggshell *olla* placed to the northeast of the body (see Fig. 10). The third burial was located just to the side of the second in a pit of much the same size and depth. This burial contained only some fragmentary teeth and an "offering" of two Narrío-style hollow *adornos* placed on the floor of the grave. Both graves were marked by large unworked rocks on the surface.

Two contemporary burials at Chaullabamba are different (Gomis S. 1989b). The bodies were loosely flexed with the heads to the north within a single circular pit. Burial 1 had a whole strombus shell, two pieces of a bone tool, and a square stone bead or spangle as offerings. Burial 2 had been laid on some sort of a mat and was accompanied by two stone beads, a ceramic disk, and a pair of white argyllite ornaments (for the ears?) in the form of stylized double birds. Burial in Pirincay and Chaullabamba seems to have been within or just to one side of the current occupation of each site.

At Cerro Narrío Collier and Murra (1943: 72–73) excavated nine burials from the late period. These were flexed in a sitting position and placed into pits about 1.5 m deep and 60 to 80 cm wide. The graves were then covered with rocks. No offerings except a few snail shells were noted.

No burials are reported for Catamayo, Putushío, or Loma Pucara. Only at Cotocollao is there abundant evidence for the disposal of the dead (Villalba 1988: 75–110). Two concentrations of burials were excavated, one dating to the later occupation and one to the earlier. These cemeteries seem to have been at the side of the occupied living space. The later cemetery shows evidence of having been used over a long period of time, as later burials disturb and cut through earlier ones.

In the earlier cemetery, which is contemporary with the Pirincay and Chaullabamba burials, were found four adults, two male and two female. The graves were cut into the soft volcanic tuff and were circular to oval, 1 to 1.5 m in diameter and shallow (20 to 30 cm), comparable in size and shape to the graves at Pirincay and Chaullabamba. In the graves a single tightly flexed body was carefully placed in the center and large rocks were placed around the body or at the feet. There may have been a preference for placing the body on its left side and the face was oriented toward the bottom of the pit. Two of the tombs may have been for secondary burials, and in the first the bones of an infant were found under some of the rocks around the body.

The later cemetery contained nearly 200 bodies in both primary and secondary burials in simple graves cut into the site soil. The bodies had the same predominantly northeastern orientation of the earlier burials and simple offerings of ceramics, stone artifacts, and personal ornaments. Not all burials had offerings.

It is evident that there are some similarities in burial customs between north and south, although the limited sample makes it difficult to elaborate. Primary and secondary burials, usually flexed, were placed in simple graves cut either into the soft bedrock or into the soil of the site. Burial was at or close to the side of the habitation area. There may be simple offerings of ceramic or other containers and, perhaps, personal adornments.

As for the populations involved, detailed data exist only for Cotocollao, where Ubelaker (1988) noted that (a) only 5 of the 27 skulls in good enough condition to study showed cranial modification, (b) the males averaged about 159 cm in height, and (c) the females were, on the average, nearly 10 cm shorter. In the early component the two men were between 30 and 40 years of age, whereas the two women were in their early-to-mid-20s. The later component contained 199 bodies in 137 burials. Of these, 42 were male and 40 female; the rest could not be sexed. The burials showed an essentially equal average age at death for women and men (34 years). There were also 17 teenagers, 7 children between ages 5 and 9, 19 toddlers (ages 2–4), and 1 infant. The lack of infants is attributable to either cultural or preservation factors, according to Ubelaker (1988: 568). However, the data correspond well with information from other early American populations, with deaths concentrated at weaning, a time when children are exposed to malnutrition and the full complement of disease vectors in the community, with resultant diarrhea, anemia, and increased mortality. The other peaks in mortality are from childbearing, dangerous work, and accidents in young adulthood.

The Cotocollao population was quite healthy. No pathologies were noted in the early cemetery; the later one had few (five bodies showed signs of infections; four showed signs of trauma). One male had a depressed fracture of the frontal bone, probably from a blow to the head. There was a low incidence of dental caries—two percent—among the later population; none was noted in the individuals of the early cemetery (Ubelaker 1988: 565–571).

Forensic study of the Pirincay burials showed that the neonate was full term, although if it had been born alive, it did not survive for more than a day or two. There was no evidence of the cause of death. The baby was somewhat shorter than standard tables for neonates indicate but more robust. None of the burials could be sexed. The fragmentary teeth were apparently milk teeth. In the other burial, those bones that would have indicated sex were missing. The person's age at death age was over 60, to judge by the entirely toothless mandible with considerable bone resorption. The height of the person, as judged by the long bones, falls into the height range of the Cotocollao burials; although the fragmentary state of this burial makes it impossible to do much more than a rough estimate (Charles Cecil, personal communication, September 1988). The Pirincay (trophy?) head was of a robust male in his thirties as was the Cotocollao one.

FORMATIVE SUBSISTENCE IN THE HIGHLANDS

Cotocollao was a fully sedentary farming village with a large number of Andean domesticates, both plant and animal. Guinea pigs and camelids were present, as well as *quinoa, oca*, beans, maize (*Zea mays*), perhaps potatoes, and a series of other cultivated and gathered crops (Villalba 1988: 334–348). La Chimba had most of the same cultigens and domesticated and hunted animals as Cotocollao, indicating that this subsistence orientation was found fairly widely in the northern highlands (Athens n.d., 1995a). Paleobotanical information is much sketchier for the southern highlands, although bone preservation is generally adequate. At Pirincay animal bone shows no real change from non-specialized, opportunistic hunting until about 300 to 400 B.C. when llamas appeared and began to dominate the faunal record (Miller and Gill 1990). Along with llamas there may have been guinea pigs. Phytolith evidence notes maize and beans as well as carbonized maize kernels (Middleton n.d.). Llamas (and alpacas) have been found in contemporary levels at Putushío. Other faunal remains indicate a broad spectrum hunting/trapping adaptation. Faunal remains from Chaullabamba are similar and include white-tailed and brocket (*Mazama* spp.) deer, agouti (*guatusa, Dasiprocta* sp.), rabbit, skunk (*Conepatus* sp.), and a local type of freshwater crab not further identified (Peña 1989). Llamas were not present at Cerro Narrío (Donald Collier, personal communication, November 1987). Collier remembered that most bone at Cerro Narrío was cervid, mainly white-tailed and brocket deer. Arellano reported much the same for Loma Pucara, with the addition of *Pudu* and *Speothos*, although guinea pigs were prominent in the bone assemblage and may have formed the commonest protein source at this site (Arellano 1994). The same is true for the Catamayo tradition of Loja (Guffroy 1987: 109–110). Faunal remains and the small amount of paleobotanical evidence then suggest a farming people, perhaps without maize (at least in the south) until quite late. They hunted a broad range of local animals, especially deer, and had the domestic guinea pig. In the later components of some sites, the domestic camelids were added to this assemblage, providing meat, wool, and a draft animal. Llamas were certainly eaten, but their preponderance at Pirincay is probably due to most of the faunal remains of the later period coming from the party pits. The llama bone in these pits were found in concentrations indicating that large chunks of the llama had been deposited. The other contents of the pits (large jars, *ollas* and fancy painted cups, all in large fragments) identify them as the scene of the careful disposal of debris from a single event, doubtless a ritual. The party pits and the find of a burned llama sacrifice in the same contexts indicate that the types of rituals still found in the central Andes had come to Ecuador.

The Eastern Lowland Formative

Not much can be said about the Formative on the eastern sides of the Andes and into the Amazon basin, largely because so little work has been done in this area. Moreover, tremendous problems have arisen in trying to synthesize the few studies that have come to the point of publication, owing to the nature of the ceramics of this region and the tendency to publish them in line drawing. There is a certain stylistic homogeneity in ceramic assemblages from the eastern slopes of the Andes and the Amazon proper (DeBoer, this volume). This includes a propensity to decorate domestic wares with corrugation and for other decoration, on both plain and elaborate pieces, to be done in simple plastic techniques such as combing, incision, circular and triangular punctation, and rocker stamping. The individual motifs are combined into geometric patterns that share many features throughout the entire eastern side of the Andes, down into the Amazon basin proper. Many vessels were slip painted as well, but surface preservation is often poor. There also appear to be numbers of shared forms whose localized nuances may not be visible on small sherds and the drawings and photographs of these. It is easy to identify a eastern lowlands sherd, but impossible to tell where it came from without both excavation data and paste analysis. Some of this information is available from the Macas region (Bruhns, Burton, and Rostoker 1994; Rostoker 1988, 1998). Unfortunately the material that has been analyzed, while Late Formative (it occurs in clearly datable contexts at Pirincay), is not in primary context in either the Sitio Sangay (Huapula) or the more southerly sites Michael Harner tested in the 1950s (Harner 1973; Rostain 1998; Salazar 1998, 1999). These sites consist of complexes of *tolas* (earthen platforms), terraces, sunken plazas and patios, drains, and causeways (Ochoa, Rostain, and Salazar 1997). The sherds are found in the fill of these structures and hence must be earlier (Porras 1987a). Also, it is quite evident from studies throughout Ecuador that the idea of building earthen platforms upon which to locate houses and other architectural units only became widespread in later periods (Salazar 1998a, b).

The Cueva de Los Tayos, on the northern slopes of the Cordillera del Condor and investigated by Padre Porras (1978), is equally enigmatic. Remains of ceramics of many types, of stone and marine shell (*Spondylus, Conus* and *Pinctada* spp.), were found within the *"sala ceremonial."* Porras reported nothing concerning the context of the material he recovered, but guano mining in the cave almost certainly mixed the archaeological deposits. It seems likely that the materials found in the cave represent offerings rather than ordinary living debris. Porras saw ties with virtually all Formative Ecuadorian and Early Horizon Peruvian cultures in the ceramics and he might well have been right. However, the material appears to have been deposited over considerable time. The Cueva de Los Tayos indicates that caves were utilized for ritual and offerings from the Formative onwards but reveals nothing concerning early cultures in the region.

The Pastaza phase is defined on the basis of Porras's excavations in a midden on the right bank of the Río Huasaga, a tributary of the Río Pastaza close to the border between Ecuador and Peru (Porras 1975). Located approximately 15 m above the current river level, the site is described as being some 300 x 50 m in size. The ceramics from this site consist of various rounded bowls with concave, rounded, or annular bases, various sizes of conical and flaring bowls, and two jar forms. Plain brown or tan wares are the commonest; about 30 percent of the sherds were decorated. Incision and punctation in simple geometric designs and simple corrugated wares predominate, although there is some red-and-white ware with incised geometric designs, which are somewhat similar to those of Red-Banded Incised. The dating of the Pastaza phase is based mainly upon similarities to other supposed Formative complexes and then by a series of ^{14}C dates, which Porras interprets as placing this culture between 2200 and 1000 B.C. Unfortunately, the samples appear to have been taken from excavations into the berm cast up when an airstrip was cut through the site. The other excavations were in areas planted to plantain and an abandoned Shuar house, so both locales had been disturbed. Thus it is not possible to conclue what, if anything, this series of dates refers to. Pastaza phase pottery is similar to materials dated anywhere between 500 B.C. and A.D. 1500. Thus the status of the "Fase Pastaza" as an exemplar of the eastern lowlands Formative is in some doubt.

In the northern Amazon of Ecuador, Evans and Meggers collected material they considered Late Formative from two sites: Puerto Miranda Hill (N-P-10) and Puerto Miranda Bank (N-P-11), close together on the right bank of the Río Napo some three km below the mouth of the Río Tiputini (Evans and Meggers 1968: 7–18). The dating is based on a single uncorrected ^{14}C assay of 2000 ± 90 BP. No archaeological context is given for the sample. The ceramics consist of a variety of decorated and undecorated bowls. Shallow and deep hemispherical bowls with round or annular bases, carinated bowls, and some rarer deep bowls with flaring upper halves and jars also occur. Most vessels are open forms. Decorative techniques consist of incision, often combined with punctation in simple geometric designs, fingernail impressions, nicked applied fillets, and red slip. One stone ax and some possible hammerstones complete the small assemblage. No evidence concerning subsistence or settlement pattern was found. The Yasuní phase seems ancestral to the later cultures of the Napo region, but the data are too scanty to support further interpretation.

Not much more can be said concerning the Formative on the eastern slopes of the Andes and the Ecuadorian Amazon. The dating of all of these Formative complexes is poor, based as it is upon seriated surface collections or collections from excavations, often in fill or disturbed earth, in arbitrary levels. Despite Porras's rather enthusiastic reconstructions (1987a,b), settlement and economic data are lacking. No evidence of religious practices—other than making offerings in a cave—has come to the fore. Ceramics show stylistic evidence, as best as can be told, of relationships with later ceramic complexes in the Amazon and, occasionally, with nearby highlands sites. The finding of sherds that stylistically appear to be eastern lowlands in nature in highlands sites and the occurrence of marine shell in eastern lowlands sites indicates that trade linked these two regions in the past just as today.

Perhaps the most that can be said with any confidence is that there probably was a first millennium B.C. occupation or perhaps even an earlier one in the eastern portion of Ecuador. Pollen and phytolith data from Lake Ayauchi in the far southeast indicates the presence of maize, not an indigenous plant, at ca. 4000 B.C. (Pearsall this volume; Piperno 1990). However, there are no cultural associations for this material, and all of the known archaeological sites are some millennia later.

Who Said What and to Whom?

One of the most interesting aspects of Formative sites in the highlands and the eastern lowlands is the mounting evidence that these peoples were avid participants in chains of short and long-distance exchange. Formative sites throughout the highlands clearly evidence regular exchange of some sort between the highlands communities, both those contiguous to one another and those at considerable distances; moreover, there was also exchange with the coast, the eastern lowlands, and, in some cases, with the central Andes—that is, Peru.

It seems quite evident that the developed Formative cultures of the southern highlands are due, at least in part, to the burgeoning Chorrera phenomenon of the Ecuadorian coast. Unfortunately, not much is known about Chorrera in any of its aspects. There are few data concerning its development, and when or how the desire for spondylus shell was implanted in those people, who could not gather the thorny oyster for themselves is a mystery. spondylus is the one exotic material that appears in all of the highlands sites and, increasingly through time, in sites in Peru, both highland and lowland. In an early Peruvian stone relief, the Smiling God of Chavín holds spondylus (and strombus) in his hands; spondylus is found in elaborate burials, such as those of Kuntur Wasi, as well as in more general midden and architectural offering contexts.[4] The appearance of spondylus in Peru may well have something to do with the emerging Chorrera elite's desires for exotica themselves, but this is little more than speculation. It is evident that, at least in the southern highlands, when coastal materials appear, the local peoples were engaged in making goods for exchange. Many sites are also neatly perched to control traffic. Pirincay, located at the point where the river turns right and begins its precipitous descent to the lowlands, is virtually on top of a rare transmontane route into the valley of Cañar. It is also above the only large piece of valley floor that can be irrigated. Perhaps significantly, this is also one of the two places in the southern highland valleys where cotton can grow. The Bullcay site controls the meeting of the Gualaceo–Santa Barbara (a major source of gold in the past) with the Paute, as does Monjashuaycu across the valley. These two sites flank the other warm cotton-growing area. Warm valleys like the Paute are also important because they do not frost. These lands can be counted on to produce *something*, even in years of cold, snow, and hail in the higher elevations. This was certainly important in local exchange networks.

Cerro Narrío controls access to the Cañar valley and a major route to the coast. The Villa Jubones and Las Juntas sites in the Jubones, another major coastal route leading to the far south coast and to northern Peru, control movement up and down that valley as well as access to the Río Rircay. Putushío, which seems to have been a metallurgical production site from the beginning, is accessible via this route as well. Loma Pucara is on a trade route to the eastern

---

[4] The distribution of shells in the Kuntur Wasi tombs is interesting. The three tombs containing remains of elderly men had rich offerings of ceramics, jewelry of gold and exotic stones and, in one case, strombus trumpets and ornaments. Tomb 4, of an elderly woman, had among its many rich offerings 849 spondylus beads of various sizes and shapes and 3,653 tiny pieces of spondylus, originally part of breastplates and necklaces. In weight the spondylus was almost 2.5 kg (Kato 1993: 216–224). Of equal interest in considering the Ecuadorian connections of Early Horizon Peruvian cultures is the use of cinnabar to pack the heads of all the principle burials. Although conventional wisdom has it that all Andean cinnabar comes from Huancavilca in Peru, there are, in fact, important cinnabar sources in the southern highlands of Ecuador (Truhan, Burton, and Bruhns n.d.).

side of the Andes. Cotocollao is near the head of the important Quito valley. The distribution of these known Formative sites indicates that a fair number of them were in strategic areas for moving goods.

Highland Exchange Systems

If we deem development of a Formative in the highlands as being tied into expansionist exchange from the coast, we need to consider what that involved. There was spondylus, of course, as it has been found in virtually all known highland sites. The amount of spondylus varies considerably. At Pirincay there is little and most of it is in the form of tiny beads, although a spondylus-and-turquoise necklace was found where it had been dropped (Fig. 23). Quantities of other marine shell have been discovered at this tiny site: *Strombus*, *Conus* of various species, *Anadara* (mangrove oyster), *Tyropecten* (scallop), and *Pinctada* (mother of pearl) have all been specialist-identified from the archaeological deposits. An interesting aspect to Pirincay and, indeed, to other Formative sites

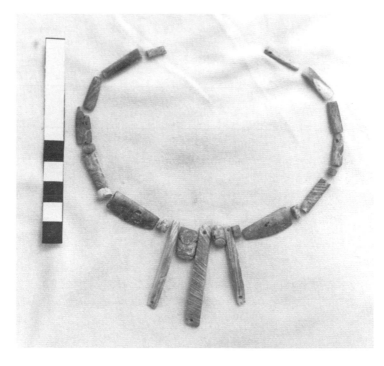

Fig. 23 Pirincay: Spondylus-and-turquoise necklace dating from the earliest occupation levels (A089). One turquoise bead is in the form of a human figure; another is a mollusk; the rest are simple pierced disks. The holes in the spondylus beads indicate that they were sewn onto a backing that probably contained perishable elements.

where the nonworked shell has been collected, is that so much of the shell is in the form of whole (though small) unmodified shells. Are these souvenirs of a highlander's first walk on the beach? This is possible, if only because so much of the unworked shell is not of types that coast dwellers would put into their packs and carry uphill.

Perhaps significant is that evidence of shell working is not common in the highlands. The types of shell found in different sites also varies somewhat. There is no evidence of shell working at Pirincay. Chaullabamba and Monjashuaycu have yielded a fair amount of shell, although only worked shell was collected at Monjashuaycu. Chaullabamba has much more mother of pearl than Pirincay. Cerro Narrío has more spondylus, to judge from collections looted from the site. Spondylus offerings have been found to the south at Putushío and in the Catamayo Formative sites. No shell has been reported from Loma Pucara, but as yet only a summary report exists for this site.

To the north are quantities of marine shell, both worked and whole, at Cotocollao and La Chimba. In all cases, however, coastal shell is not abundant, and the farther a site is from the coast, the scarcer shell is. Apparently, conditions changed through time. Spondylus, at least, seems to be limited to the early levels at Pirincay and a similar situation may exist at some of the other southern Formative sites. This may reflect changes in trade routes or even to the increase in spondylus being moved southward to Peru instead of uphill. There is no way of knowing at present, although the immense increase in spondylus in northern Peruvian sites was still quite a few centuries into the future.

Ceramics form another valuable means of analyzing what highlands sites were receiving. The art of pottery making itself apparently came from the coast in Middle-to-Late Formative times, as the southern ceramics complex, at least, features thin-walled vessels, a technology that first appeared in Chorrera. The northern highland ceramics may have a different origin. The emphasis upon open bowl forms in the north as well as the thickness of the vessels suggests a more northerly and, perhaps, a slightly earlier origin.

Paste analysis in the southern highlands shows that local settlements were exchanging pottery, or perhaps better put, something that was moved in pottery. Paste groups have now been isolated for Pirincay, Chaullabamba, and Cerro Narrío. There is some Cerro Narrío and Chaullabamba pottery at Pirincay. This discovery was fortuitous and was due in large part to analyzing a great many sherds because the traded-in vessels are the same shapes and designs as local vessels; that is to say, plain gray eggshell *ollas*, Narrío Glossy red cups, numerous types of plates and simple bowls. Narrío Engraved, which has been found in many Formative sites in the highlands, may actually come from Narrío or close by (James Burton, personal communication, September 1995). What paste analysis clearly shows in this instance is that people were going from one site to another and bringing a pot to break far from home. Home was not necessarily that far away. Chaullabamba is only some twenty km from Pirincay; Cerro Narrío is a long way by the present highway, but not nearly so far via the eastern route along the Río Guayán right by Pirincay. Many traces of ancient roads and tracks throughout the highlands remain to be studied and dated. Other source areas are more distant, but good evidence, from both style and paste analyses, exists for close contact between the sites of Azuay, Cañar, and even Chimborazo provinces. The nature of the exchange is not known. The quantities of nonlocal vessels at Pirincay, at least, are not large and may well relate to ongoing exchanges of spouses, mutual participation in each other's rituals, and similar activities between neighboring groups.

The exchange of ceramics has not really been studied in other areas. Athens (1995b) and Myers (1976) both reported some evidences of Cotocollao "influence" on their Imbabura ceramics. This, however, is probably simply due to these sites belonging to the same general tradition. Arellano, in the Valle de Las Cebadas (1994), noted evidences of both Cotocollao and southern stylistic types, perhaps because of the intermediate position of this site between the Quito/Imbabura region and Cañar/Azuay. He also notes sherds that could be from eastern lowlands vessels. Until paste analyses are done for these various sites (and the clay sources are located), we cannot know if some of the more Cotocollao "looking" vessels at Loma Pucara are actually from Cotocollao or if indeed Loma Pucara or Riobamba region vessels are at Cotocollao.

Athens and Lippi both refer to occasional Chorrera-like sherds in their various sites, although Lippi noted that these are mainly confined to sites in western Pichincha province (1998a,b: 316–317). At both Pirincay and Chaullabamba, and to a lesser extent Cerro Narrío, coastal ceramics have also been identified. These are mainly small fancy vessels: modeled, painted, or incised bottles of good Chorrera style and the unmistakable satin-like Chorrera slip have been found at Pirincay and Chaullabamba. An extremely fine black ware is probably also imported. This is quite common at Chaullabamba, where it occurs mainly in the form of double spout bottles (one spout is closed, so they are not strictly double spouted). This extremely fine, glossy black ware is in paste, thickness, and shape totally different from the black vertical-sided bowls with exterior line luster designs that form an important part of the southern ceramic complex. Rather they seem to be of nonlocal pastes and probably are from some Chorrera-related sites. At Pirincay, a single sherd of incised red and yellow on black, from a small bottle, seems to have stylistic similarities, in its design of recurved rays, with both northern "Chavín" styles such as have been found at Morropón in Piura and with Chorrerra vessels in general (Fig. 24). No other sites to date have yielded similar sherds, but most early levels at southern sites—such as Villa Jubones, Pirincay, Putushío, and even Loma Pucara—have some of the fine black ware.

Pirincay and other sites have also yielded small quantities of painted (mainly red-on-buff) modeled vessels, all fragmentary. These are of nonlocal pastes as well. Most of the infrequently occurring bottles (stirrup and single or double spout) bottles in highlands sites would seem to be imports from the coast. At Pirincay the six spouts found are all of different pastes, surface finishes, and shapes, which again suggest that they were brought into the site.

Iridescent painted pottery is quite common throughout the southern highlands ca. 1200 to 500 B.C. It has not been reported from the north, but it is quite easy to miss if excavators do not see their sherds when wet. Iridescent painted vessels occur mainly in one shape: a carinated bowl with a low ring base. The stripes or stripes and dots are on the interior, but a rare flaring bowl form also is represented. Iridescent painted vessels have been found at Pirincay, where both the gray and the pink iridescent form are present on the surface at Bullcay and Chaullabamba and with some frequency at Cerro Narrío.[5] Figurines (rare), deeply carved cylinder "seals," and ceramic stamps may either come from the coast or copy coastal forms.

Obsidian is probably the most reliable indicator to date of long-distance exchange in the highlands. The major obsidian sources in Ecuador are in the vicinity of Quito (Burger et al. 1994). All obsidian analyzed to date from highland Formative sites comes from these flows. There is considerable fall-off: northern sites are full of obsidian tools, where as southern ones have little of this desired material. It is, however, evident that there were functioning routes, perhaps down-the-line exchange, perhaps something more elaborate, which brought small quantities of obsidian to peoples up and down the *cordilleras*.

In the case of Pirincay, there is another item of northern origin: maize. The maize that appears in later period deposits is the small pointed kernel kind, which is found at Cotocollao, not a large coastal-type kernel. Unfortunately, most maize in Formative sites has been identified through pollen or phytolith methods. Thus its presence and absence is known, but not its race.

---

[5] According to Karen Stothert (personal communication, July 1991), the gray iridescent pottery is typical of Chorrera of the basin of Guayaquil and the pink of the Engoroy of the Santa Elena peninsula. Both types are present at Pirincay in approximately equal quantities. The types of iridescent painted pottery at Cerro Narrío are unknown to me. Collier and Murra did not recognize this peculiar decorative technique and so lumped the iridescent sherds with other types. When I visited the Field Museum of Natural History in 1987 to look at the Narrío collections and discuss them with Donald Collier, all the iridescent sherds had been removed for analysis by John Isaacson, who as of this writing has not made his results known. Wendell Bennett (1946, fig. 5a–e) illustrated what appears to be iridescent painted pottery sherds but classified them among his red wares. This might suggest that they are Engoroy in origin.

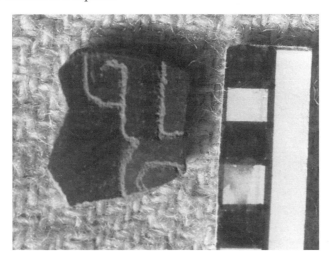

Fig. 24 Sherd with incised design of recurved rays on highly polished red-and-black slip. Of Chorrera derivation (thin, extremely smooth slip), the sherd's coloration and incised design are similar to those found on vessels from the site of Morropón in the Piura valley of far northern Peru.

The Coastal Connection

It is clear that the Formative cultures of the southern highlands, in particular, were in contact with the coast. Specialist manufacture has been most thoroughly investigated at Pirincay, which, from its founding, seems to have been a manufacturing center for rock crystal beads. The remains of over fifty workshops have now been found there, mainly debitage, quartz hammers and drills, and the remains of beads broken during their manufacture (Bruhns 1991). Later on textile manufacture seems to have been added to the specialist manufacture (Bruhns 1988/89). Putushío, which is contemporary with the latest occupations at Pirincay and Cerro Narrío, originated as a smelting settlement. This kind of information is lacking from other sites in the highlands, but because coastal goods are found in all and are especially frequent in the southern highlands, steady contact was likely maintained with coastal settlements (Bruhns 1989). The northern highland sites seem to have fewer external ties, although marine shell and coastal ceramics do appear. However, in all cases materials were preserved in nonoptimum conditions—basically ceramics, shell, and stone.

Archaeologically, salt, dried fish, textiles, songs, dances, rituals, and other items important in nonmodern exchange networks are missing. The exchange was not large scale as it is seen archaeologically. One might postulate emissary trade with a small number of highland people going down to the coast and vice versa. Yet it was important to the cultural development of both areas.

Terminal Formative Changes

Major changes in directions of trade, either augmenting existing highland–highland and highland–coast routes or, perhaps, even abandonment of some exchange systems appears in the last three or four centuries B.C.E. This is seen most clearly at Pirincay, but more diffuse data from other sites suggest that this was a widespread phenomenon. The most archaeologically visible sign of these changes is a major change in ceramics. As mentioned above, eggshell wares disappeared, as did the multiple forms of plates, bowls, and even the ubiquitous reduced black line luster bowls. The paste, construction, and firing methods did not change, and a fair number of decorative patterns, especially those on utilitarian vessels, remained the same, but new shapes were introduced and all vessels became markedly larger. Large (15- to 20-liter) jars appeared, as did large and small *ollas* of varying shapes. These became the major constituent of the ceramics complex, replacing the small open vessels that had predominated at the earlier levels. Decorated ceramics became radically different, with annular base bowls, *compoteras*, deep piriform and cylindrical cups painted red on white, or red on pale orange, and at Pirincay the *nose cup* (an annular base bowl with an appliqué human face on one side) appears. Ceramic stools are also a notable addition to the upper levels at Pirincay and are found at a great many other sites. Organic resist painting replaced iridescent painting. Moreover, no vessels of evident coastal origin appear at Pirincay or Cerro Narrío in this time frame. Chaullabamba and Monjashuaycu were abandoned, as were El Carmen Bajo and Bullcay. Surface finds indicate that the change to large cooking and storage vessels and much larger serving vessels was general and the move off of the floodplain to the spurs on the edges of the valleys which had begun with the establishment of sites such as Cerro Narrío and Pirincay, was amplified.

Along with changes in vessels, consumption of foods and evidently in the sociology of eating that this change indicates, there is evidence of an expansion of ties to the south and the east. Metallurgy appeared in the highlands. This has been investigated most thoroughly by Matilde Temme and her colleagues (Rehren and Temme 1994) at Putushío in northern Loja. This site was built on a hilltop in a valley that opens to the Pacific Ocean and has easy access to the gold-bearing tributaries of the Amazon basin, as well as smaller secondary deposits in the Río León. The first gold smelters at this site are late Formative. At Pirincay a small ingot of smelted silver-rich gold, a copper bar, and a gilded nose ornament all date from this time. There was probably Late Formative metal at Cerro Narrío, but none has been recovered by archaeologists. No one has really looked for evidences of metallurgy elsewhere, although metal began to appear on the coast in the late Chorrera or earliest Bahía phases. Metalworking is much earlier in coastal Peru, and undoubtedly this art was introduced from the south, especially since this was also the time in which llamas were introduced to highland sites. A llama sacrifice of the southern type has been found at Pirincay and the party pits with their evidences of camelid and beer(?) consumption also date to the late centuries B.C.

People were also turning to the eastern lowlands, setting a pattern that continues to the present. At Pirincay, Cerro Narrío, Alausí, Loma Pucara, Villa Jubones, and down into Loja, Red Banded Incised pottery appears. Everywhere it has been tested it is the same: It has to be, geologically speaking, from the southeastern slope region of Sangay volcano. Ceramics from the fill of *tolas* as well as from other contexts in this region have the same peculiar paste (Bruhns, Burton, and Rostoker 1995). Other eastern lowland wares have been found in the highlands. Arellano has noted ceramics that he maintains are related to the Upano ones at Loma Pucara. Pirincay has also yielded some unusual yellow and red on black sherds with fine incision in simple geometric patterns, which may have some stylistic affinity to the Bagua ceramics of the Marañon (Shady Solís 1987; Shady and Rosas LaNoire 1979).

However, pottery is only the remaining part of the picture. The important question is what came in those pots. It is, of course, possible that the pots themselves were trade items. They are certainly exotic, and we have every indication that the highlands Formative peoples liked exotic ceramics. In the highlands most seemed to favor either a wide mouthed, shoulderless jar, a variant of a form extremely common in eastern lowland assemblages, or bowls. Could the eastern lowland people be coming up for a beer party and bringing the dishes too? Although the Pirincay Red Banded Incised ware is in much better condition than the pottery Harner or Porras excavated, it is still somewhat eroded and lacks visible residues. That salt, drugs, feathers, skins, pets, and similar perishable items were brought up from the east to sell to the highlanders is in the historical record.

It is possible that this change in direction of exchange was related to population growth and the establishment of new, large sites on the eastern slopes of the Andes (Ochoa et al 1997; Rostain 1998; Salazar 1998a,b, 1999). This new interest in the east was seen elsewhere, although it has been best documented from a later time period in the north, where the Panzaleo ceramic style was a eastern lowland import (Bray 1995). Possibly the east was not an new entrant into long-distance exchange systems but only became visible when ceramics entered the equation. However, from the terminal Formative onward, current knowledge points toward increasing evidence of close ties with both the eastern lowlands and Peru (Bruhns 1989, 1995; Burger 1984). Despite the archaeological focus on the spondylus trade and how it was supposedly carried out, the clearest evidence of exchange between Ecuadorian cultures and those of Peru is in the southern provinces of Azuay and Cañar, where historic ties with the peoples of the adjacent *montaña* were crucial to local economies and politics. Ongoing research is pointing to some interesting problems in cultural development and the reciprocating role of exchange in this development. Perhaps new research will define more closely the details of this northern Andean reciprocity.

Two-Thirds of Ecuador in the Formative

The highlands and eastern tropics of Ecuador clearly comprised an essential element in the development of northern Andean cultures. It is also evident that the historic trajectory of these areas was far different from that of the coast. It is entirely possible that the precocious development of coastal cultures spurred the end of the extended Archaic adaptation of the highlands. However, the highland and eastern lowland cultures are distinct from those of the coast in virtually all aspects. Moreover, they have remained distinctive throughout centuries of contact with their western neighbors. Highland archaeological investigation has, in its turn, had a slow gestation, as have the tropical lowlands. I hope that in the near future new projects will provide a more detailed look at the origins and evolution of these societies.

Acknowledgments I would like to thank the following people, all of whom assisted greatly in the formulation of this essay: the late Cornelio Ventimilla and his family, especially Berta Ventimilla de Ordoñez, Costanza di Capua, the late Presley Norton and Olaf Holm, Hernán Crespo Toral, Karen E. Stothert, Ernesto Salazar, Myriam Ochoa, Stephén Rostain, J. S. Athens, A. Jorge Arellano, the late Donald Collier, James H. Burton, Warwick Bray and Elizabeth Carmichael, and my many friends and colleagues in Cuenca and Quito.

BIBLIOGRAPHY

ARELLANO, A. JORGE
  1994   Loma Pucara, a Formative Site in the Cebadas Valley, Ecuador. *National
          Geographic Research and Exploration* 10(1): 118–120.

ATHENS, J. STEPHEN
  1978   Formative Period Occupations in the Northern Highlands of Ecuador: A
          Comment on Myers. *American Antiquity* 43(3): 493–496.
  1995a   Cultural Chronology and Agriculture: Archaeological Investigations in the
          Northern Highlands of Ecuador, 1989 and 1994. Paper presented at the
          Symposio Internacional de Investigaciones Arqueológicas del Area
          Septentrional de América del Sur, 21–23 September 1995, Ibarra, Ecuador.
  1995b   Relaciones interregionales prehistóricas en el norte de los Andes: Evidencia
          del Sitio La Chimba en el Ecuador Septentrional. In *Perspectivas regionales en
          la arqueología del suroccidente de Colombia y norte del Ecuador* (Cristóbal Gnecco,
          ed.): 3–29. Editorial Universidad del Cauca, Popayán, Colombia.
  n.d.   Early Maize Agriculture in Northern Highland Ecuador. Unpublished
          manuscript in the possession of the author, 1994.

BARNES, MONICA, AND DAVID FLEMING
  1989   Charles-Marie de la Condamine's Report on Ingapirca and the Development
          of Scientific Field Work in the Andes, 1735–1744. *Andean Past* 2: 175–236.

BELL, ROBERT E.
  1965   *Investigaciones arqueológicas en el sitio de El Inga, Ecuador.* Casa de la Cultura
          Ecuatoriana, Quito.

BENNETT, WENDELL C.
  1946   *Excavations in the Cuenca Region, Ecuador.* Yale University Publications in
          Anthropology 35. New Haven, Conn.

BRAUN, ROBERT
  1982   The Formative as Seen from the Southern Ecuadorian Highlands. In *Primer
          Simposio de Correlaciones Antropológicas Andino-Mesoamericano* (Jorge G. Marcos
          and Presley Norton, ed.): 41–100. Escuela Superior Politécnica del Litoral,
          Guayaquil.

BRAY, TAMARA
  1995   The Panzaleo Puzzle: Non-Local Pottery in Northern Highland Ecuador.
          Journal of Field Archaeology 22(2): 137–156.

BRUHNS, KAREN OLSEN
  1988/89 Early Prehispanic Spinning and Weaving Equipment from Ecuador. *Textile
          Museum Journal* 27/28: 70–77.
  1989   Intercambio entre la sierra y la costa en el Formativo Tardío, nuevas evidencias
          del Azuay. In *Relaciones Interculturales en el Area Ecuatorial del Pácifico Durante la
          Epoca Precolombina* (J. F. Bouchard and M. Guinea, editors): 57–74. BAR
          International Series 503. British Archaeological Reports, Oxford.
  1991   Los tallares de cristal de roca en Pirincay, provincia del Azuay. *Miscelanea
          Antropológica Ecuatoriana* 7: 91–100.

Karen Olsen Bruhns

1994   *Ancient South America.* Cambridge University Press, Cambridge.

1995   Las culturas peruanas y el desarrollo cultural en los Andes septentrionales. *Memoria* 4: 251–267.

BRUHNS, KAREN OLSEN, JAMES H. BURTON, AND GEORGE R. MILLER

1990   Archaeological Investigations at Pirincay in Southern Ecuador. *Antiquity* 64(243): 221–233.

BRUHNS, KAREN OLSEN, JAMES H. BURTON, AND ARTHUR ROSTOKER

1994   La Cerámica Incisa en Franjas Rojas: Evidencia de intercambio entre la sierra y el oriente en el Formativo Tardío del Ecuador. In *Tecnología y Organización de la Producción de Cerámica Prehispánica en los Andes* (Izumi Shimada, ed.): 53–66. Pontificia Universidad Católica del Perú, Fondo Editorial, Lima.

BURGER, RICHARD L.

1984   Archaeological Areas and Prehistoric Frontiers: The Case of Formative Peru and Ecuador. In *Social and Economic Organization in the Prehispanic Andes* (David L. Browman, Richard L. Burger, and Mario A. Rivera, eds.): 33–64. BAR International Series 194. British Archaeological Reports, Oxford.

BURGER, RICHARD L., FRANK ASARO, ERNESTO SALAZAR, HELEN V. MICHEL, AND FRED H. STROSS

1994   Ecuadorian Obsidian Sources Used for Artifact Production and Methods for Provenience Assignment. *Latin American Antiquity* 5(3): 257–277.

BURLEIGH, R., A. HEWSON, AND N. MEEKS

1977   British Museum Natural Radiocarbon Measurements IX. *Radiocarbon* 19: 143–160.

BURTON, JAMES H.

n.d.   Pirincay postdata. *Miscelanea Antropológica Ecuatoriana.* In press.

CARMICHAEL, ELIZABETH, WARWICK BRAY, AND JOHN ERICKSON

1979   Informe preliminar de las investigaciones arqueológicas en el area de Minas, Río Jubones, Ecuador. *Revista de Antropología* 6: 130–153. Sección de Antropología y Arqueología del Núcleo del Azuay de la Casa de la Cultura Ecuatoriana, Cuenca.

COLLIER, DONALD, AND JOHN V. MURRA

1943   *Survey and Excavations in Southern Ecuador.* Anthropological Series 35, Field Museum of Natural History, Chicago.

ECHEVERRÍA ALMEIDA, JOSÉ

1983   Los primeros poblados. In *Nueva historia del Ecuador,* vol. 1 (Enrique Ayala Mora, ed.): 181–222. Corporación Editora Nacional, Quito.

EVANS, CLIFFORD AND BETTY JANE MEGGERS

1968   *Archaeological Investigations on the Río Napo, Eastern Ecuador.* Smithsonian Contributions to Anthropology 6. Smithsonian Institution. U.S. Government Printing Office, Washington, D.C.

THE EXCAVATIONS AT CAÑAR

1922   *Pan American Magazine* 34(4): 24–26.

GOMIS S., DOMINIQUE

1989a   La alfarería de Chaullabamba. *Catedral Salvaje* (Cuenca) 24: 4–5.

1989b   El hombre andino visto desde Chaullabamba. *Catedral Salvaje* (Cuenca) 24: 7.

GREIDER, TERENCE
    n.d.   Informe sobre estudios arqueológicos en Chaullabamba, 1995. Unpublished report submitted to the Instituto Nacional del Patrimonio Cultural del Ecuador, Subdirección del Austro, Cuenca, 1995.

GUFFROY, JEAN, (ED.)
    1987   *Loja préhispanique. Recherches archéologiques dans les Andes méridionales de l'equateur.* Editions Recherches sur les Civilizations, Synthese 27. Paris.

HARNER, MICHAEL J.
    1972   *Jibaro: People of the Sacred Waterfall.* Natural History Press, New York.

IDROVO URIGUÉN, JAIME
    1989   Chaullabamba: Una ventana hacia nuestro pasado. *Catedral Salvaje* (Cuenca) 24: 1.
    1990   *Panorama histórico de la arqueología ecuatoriana.*

ISAACSON, JOHN
    1987   *Volcanic Activity and Human Occupation of the Northern Andes: The Application of Tephrastratigraphic Techniques to the Problem of Human Settlement in the Western Montaña during the Ecuadorian Formative.* Ph.D. dissertation, University of Illinois at Urbana–Champaign, University Microfilms, Ann Arbor, Mich.

KATO, YASUTAKI
    1993   Resultados de las excavaciones en Kuntur Wasi. In *El mundo ceremonial andino.* (Luis Millones and Yoshio Onuki, eds.) Senri Ethnological Studies 37: 203–228. Osaka.

LATHRAP, DONALD W., DONALD COLLIER, AND HELEN CHANDRA
    1975   *Ancient Ecuador: Culture, Clay and Creativity.* Field Museum of Natural History, Chicago.

LIPPI, RONALD D.
    1986   Arqueología de los Yumbos. In *Arqueología y etnohistoria del sur de Colombia y norte del Ecuador* (José Alcina Franch and Segundo E. Moreno Yáñez, eds.): 189–207. Miscelanea Antropológica Ecuatoriana, Serie Monográfica 6, Museo del Banco Central del Ecuador and Ediciones Abya-Yala, Quito.
    1996   *La primera revolución ecuatoriana: El desarrollo de la vida agrícola en el antiguo Ecuador.* MARKA, Instituto de Historia y Antropología Andina, Quito.
    1998b   *Una exploración arqueológica del Pichincha occidental, Ecuador.* Museo Jacinto Jijón y Caamaño de la Pontificia Universidad Católica del Ecuador, Consejo Provincial de Pichincha, and Banco Interamericana de Desarrollo, Quito.
    1998a   Encuentros precolombinos entre serranos y costeños en el país Yumbo (Pichincha occidental, Ecuador). In *Intercambio y comercio entre costa, Andes y selva: Arqueología y etnohistoria de Suramérica* (Felipe Cardenas-Arroyo and Tamara Bray, eds.): 115–134. Department of Anthropology, University of the Andes, Bogotá.

LYNCH, THOMAS F.
    1989   Chobshi Cave in Retrospect. *Andean Past* 2: 1–32.

LYNCH, THOMAS F., AND SUSAN POLLACK
    1981   La arqueología de la Cueva Negra de Chobshi. *Miscelanea Antropológica Ecuatoriana* 1: 92–119.

López Monsalve, Rodrigo, ed.

1993   *La tragedia del austro*. Ediciones La Golondrina, Cuenca.

Middleton, William D.

n.d.   Reconstruction of Pre-Hispanic Ecuadorian Livestock Management Practices through the Extraction of Opal Phytoliths from Prehistoric and Contemporary Camelid Dental Calculus. Master's thesis, San Francisco State University, San Francisco.

Miller, George F., and Ann Gill

1990   Zooarchaeology at Pirincay, a Formative Period Site in Highland Ecuador. *Journal of Field Archaeology* 17(1): 49–68.

Myers, Thomas P.

1976   Formative Period Occupations in the Highlands of Northern Ecuador. *American Antiquity* 41(3): 353–360.

1978   Formative Period Occupations in the Highlands of Northern Ecuador: Rejoinder to Athens. *American Antiquity* 43(3): 497.

Ochoa, Myriam, Stephen Rostain, and Ernesto Salazar

1997   Montículos precolombinos en el Alto Upano. *Cultura segunda epoca* 2: 54–62.

Peña, Agustín

1989   Los restos y la subsistancia. *Catedral Salvaje* (Cuenca) 24: 6.

Piperno, Dolores R.

1990   Aboriginal Agriculture and Land Usage in the Amazon Basin, Ecuador. *Journal of Archaeological Sciences* 17: 665–677.

Porras, Pedro Ignacio

1975   El Formativo en el valle Amazónico del Ecuador: Fase Pastaza. *Revista de la Universidad Católica* (Quito) 3(10): 74–134.

1977   Fase Alausí. *Estudios arqueológicos: Antillas y tierras bajas de Sudamerica y Ecuador*. 89–160. Ediciones de la Universidad Católica, Quito.

1978   *Arqueología de la cueva de Los Tayos*. Ediciones de la Universidad Católica, Quito.

1980   *Arqueología de Quito, Fase Cotocollao*. Artes Gráficas Señal, Quito.

1987a   *Investigaciones arqueológicas a las faldas del Sangay, provincia Morona-Santiago. Tradición Upano*. Centro de investigaciones arqueológicas, Pontificia Universidad Católica del Ecuador, Quito.

1987b   *Nuestro ayer. Manual de la arqueología ecuatoriana*. Centro de Investigaciones Arqueológicas, Pontificia Universidad Católica del Ecuador, Quito.

Rehren, Thilo, and Matilde Temme

1994   Pre-Columbian Gold Processing at Putushio, South Ecuador: The Archaeometallurgical Evidence. In *Archaeometry of Pre-Columbian Sites and Artifacts* (David A. Scott and Pieter Meyers, eds.): 267–284. Getty Conservation Institute, Malibu, Calif.

Reinoso Hermida, Gustavo

1973   Punin y Chalan. *Revista de Antropología* 4: 130–175. (Sección de Antropología del Núcleo del Azuay de la Casa de la Cultura Ecuatoriana, Cuenca.)

Rostain, Stephen

1999   Excavaciones en área en un montículo de Huapula, Amazonía ecuatoriana (Proyecto Upano). In *Memorias del primer congreso ecuatoriano de antropologia,* vol. 3 (Ernesto Salazar, ed.): 227–256. Museo Jacinto Jijón y Caamaño, Universidad Católica del Ecuador, Quito.

ROSTOKER, ARTHUR G.

1996   *An Archaeological Collection from Eastern Ecuador.* Treganza Museum Papers 18, San Francisco State University, San Francisco.

1998   Recuerdos de la montaña mágica, revisitados. In *Intercambio y comercio entre costa, Andes y selva: Arqueología y etnohistoria de Suramérica* (Felipe Cardenas-Arroyo and Tamara Bray, eds.): 155–162. Department of Anthropology, University of the Andes, Bogotá.

SALAZAR, ERNESTO

1980   *Talleres prehistóricos en los altos Andes del Ecuador.* Department of Cultural Diffusion, University of Cuenca, Cuenca.

1984   *Cazadores recolectores del antiguo Ecuador.* Banco Central del Ecuador, Serie Nuestro Pasado 1, Quito.

1985   Investigaciones arqueológicas en Mullamica (provincia de Pichincha). *Miscelánea Antropológica Ecuatoriana* 5: 129–160.

1998a   De vuelta al Sangay: Investigaciones arqueológicas en el Alto Upano, Amazonia Ecuatoriana. *Bulletin de l'Institut d'Etudes Andines* 27(2): 213–240.

1998b   Naturaleza y distribución de los montículos precolombinos de la cuenca del Alto Upano, Ecuador. In *Intercambio y comercio entre costa, Andes y selva: Arqueología y etnohistoria de Suramérica* (Felipe Cardenas-Arroyo and Tamara Bray, eds.): 185–212. Department of Anthropology, University of the Andes, Bogotá.

1999   De vuelta al Sangay: Investigaciones arqueológicas en el Alto Upano. In *Memorias del Primer Congreso Ecuatoriano de Antropología* 3 (Ernesto Salazar, ed.): 183–226. Museo Jacinto Jijón y Caamaño, Universidad Católica del Ecuador, Quito.

SHADY SOLÍS, RUTH

1987   Tradición y cambio en las sociedades Formativas de Bagua, Amazona, Perú. *Revista Andina* 5(2): 457–487. Cusco.

SHADY SOLÍS, RUTH, AND HERMILIO ROSAS LANOIRE

1979   El Complejo Bagua y el sistema de establecimiento durante el Formativo en la sierra norte del Perú. *Ñawpa Pacha* 17: 109–142.

SJÖMAN, LENA

1989   *Jatunpamba, tierra de alfareras.* Cuadernos de Cultura Popular 14, Centro Interamericano de Artesanias y Artes Populares (CIDAP), Cuenca.

TRUHAN, DEBORAH L., JAMES H. BURTON, AND KAREN OLSEN BRUHNS

n.d.   El cinabrio en el mundo andino. Manuscript in possession of the author.

UBELAKER, DOUGLAS H.

1988   Restos humanos prehistoricos del sitio Cotocollao, Provincia de Pichincha, Ecuador. In *Cotocollao: Una aldea formativa del valle de Quito.* Appendix 2 (Marcelo Villalba): 557–571. Miscelanea Antropológica Ecuatoriana, Serie Monográfica 2. Museo del Banco Central del Ecuador, Quito.

UHLE, MAX

1921   Les Huacas de Cañar. *Journal de la Société des Américanistes de Paris* 13: 242-244. Paris.

Karen Olsen Bruhns

1922   *Influencias mayas en el Alto Ecuador.* Tipografía y Encuadernación Salesianas, Quito.

VILLALBA, MARCELO
1988   *Cotocollao: Una Aldea Formativa del Valle de Quito.* Museo del Banco Central del Ecuador, Quito.

The Zooarchaeological Record from Formative Ecuador

PETER W. STAHL

BINGHAMTON UNIVERSITY

T he systematic recovery and analysis of animal remains from archaeological sites in Ecuador is a recent development of the past few decades. Although we might cite Jacinto Jijón y Caamaño's pioneering work at Quinche (1912) and Cerrito de Macají (1927) as early exceptions, the potential importance of zooarchaeological data was not actually realized until the late 1950s with the work of Meggers, Evans, and Estrada (1965) at the Formative site of Valdivia. Not only did they list the frequencies and proportions of identified taxa by excavation unit but they also integrated these data into their interpretation of the site's early occupation. With the explosion of interest in Formative archaeology during the late 1960s and early 1970s, the recovery, analysis, and interpretation of archaeofaunal specimens became somewhat standard, as zooarchaeological data assumed increasing importance for archaeological inference.

Throughout the relatively brief history of Formative archaeology in Ecuador, archaeologists have used zooarchaeological data to support inferences about prehistoric subsistence and ecology. Like most forms of archaeological evidence, faunal remains were pliably manipulated to support different and often conflicting interpretations of regional prehistory. Inferential statements generally complied with the specific research biases and competing theoretical or methodological interests held by different archaeologists. Coastal sites with abundant marine and limited or no terrestrial fauna were regarded by some researchers as examples of a primary or exclusive marine subsistence orientation. These sites stood in contrast to coastal middens with lower-than-expected amounts of marine and no recovered terrestrial resources, which were believed to implicate agricultural subsistence. High proportions of juvenile human bones, recovered with nonlocal marine resources at inland sites, suggested the need to establish coastal trade connections to overcome dietary protein deficiency. Some archaeologists analogically associated identified faunal taxa with the natural histories of their contemporary counterparts to argue the primacy of both riverine alluvial foci and horticultural pursuits at inland sites. Others used diachronic fluctuations in the relative abundance of identified faunal taxa within excavated assemblages as inferential support for prehistoric environmental oscillations that underlay presumed periods of abandonment and repopulation.

Regardless of the interpretive scenario offered and the dominant research paradigm guiding it, supporting inferences from faunal data have usually been based on the manipulation of taxonomic lists and/or respective abundances. That is, archaeologists were interested in what species were present, and sometimes absent, in specific archaeological provenances. To increase the interpretive power of their zooarchaeological data, researchers occasionally analyzed changes in relative abundances of different taxa between separate archaeological contexts. These methods are not without drawbacks, which can become insurmountable, especially when specimen abundances are uncritically used as variables in ratio scale measurement.

This essay introduces the zooarchaeological record from Formative contexts throughout the western lowlands and highlands of Ecuador. I begin by presenting the geographical and temporal distribution of the database followed by a brief discussion of limitations that the record holds for subsistence and paleoecologic interpretation. Here, I focus specifically on how taxonomic lists and corresponding abundances from excavated contexts can be qualitatively and quantitatively influenced throughout assemblage formation history. This brief review of the processes, which can potentially operate on assemblages predating their original accumulation to their eventual excavation and analysis by archaeologists, serves as a guide to what we should *not* say, at the risk of being wrong. Next, I return to the database and discuss a number of inferences about ancient Formative subsistence and environment in a way that minimizes the risk of incorrect interpretation, or at least increases our chances of being right. A brief conclusion follows.

FORMATIVE ARCHAEOFAUNA

The record consists of a comprehensive faunal database compiled from 27 archaeological sites throughout highland and western lowland areas of Ecuador (Fig. 1). For purposes of comparison, the highland assemblages are chronologically keyed to the sequence established for the adjacent western lowland area. The designations Early, Middle, and Late (see Fig. 1) conform to the Valdivia, Machalilla, and Chorrera phase cultures, respectively. As some sites are multi-component occupations, the total number of chronologically discrete assemblages examined in this essay is 32.

The zooarchaeological database is presented in three tables. Table 1 lists the invertebrate and principally molluscan fauna recovered from Formative contexts mainly in the coastal lowlands. Table 2 lists all of the identified cartilaginous and bony fishes from Formative archaeological contexts. Table 3 compiles similar data for amphibian, reptile, bird, and mammal remains recovered in Formative contexts. For ease of presentation, the majority of uncertain identifications are considered in the next higher taxonomic category (e.g., cf. Rodentia is considered Rodentia). Where contemporary genera are represented by only one specific form, that species name is used.

INTERPRETIVE LIMITATIONS OF THE RECORD

To varying degrees, all archaeological samples are temporally and spatially distanced from their parent population. Many processes can subtract from, add to, and/or spatially rearrange an assemblage after it has departed a living context, is deposited, buried, and eventually excavated, and analyzed. Therefore, for purposes of subsistence or paleoecological reconstruction, it is usually difficult to refer the exact structure of an excavated sample back to its parent population, our target of interest. Here, I briefly focus on some of the more important processes that can confound this relationship, emphasizing how they can potentially affect the qualitative and quantitative structure of an excavated sample. Some points are obvious, but those that are not are very often subtly pernicious.

Animals differ in both the number and distribution of durable body parts, and these intrinsic factors alone can strongly influence the presence or absence and abundance data during each stage of assemblage formation. Certain taxa have more durable parts that are often identifiable to differing levels of accuracy when found in isolation. For example, a gastropod has one shell that can be reliably identified when complete; a fish has hundreds of bony elements, many of which are difficult to identify when separated from the rest of the skeleton. Moreover, these parts are usually recovered as fragments. Skeletal portions of diverse taxa—or even different portions of the same skeleton—often exhibit differential durability. For example, the preservation potential of a discarded marine oyster shell is unlike that of a digested microvertebrate skeleton, as is the survivorship of a durable tooth isolated from the highly fragmented skull of a small animal. These variables strongly influence the data presented

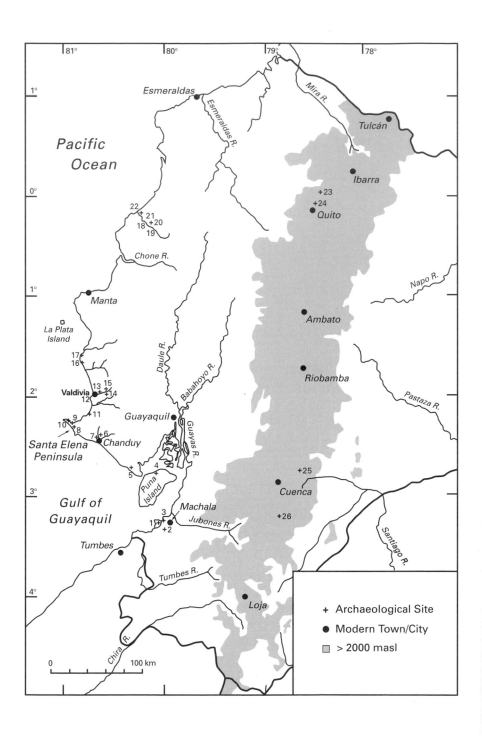

81°   80°   79°   78°

1°

Esmeraldas

Pacific
Ocean

Mira R.

Tulcán

Esmeraldas R.

0°

Ibarra

+23
+24
Quito

22
18 21
   +20
19

Chone R.

Napo R.

1°

Manta

La Plata
Island

Ambato

Daule R.

Babahoyo R.

17
16

Riobamba

Pastaza R.

2°

13 15
+14
Valdivia 12

9
+11
10 8

Guayaquil

Guayas R.

7 +6
Chanduy

Santa Elena
Peninsula

4
5

Puna
Island

+25

Cuenca

3°

Gulf of
Guayaquil

Machala

Jubones R.

+26

Santiago R.

Tumbes

1 3
  +2

Tumbes R.

4°

Loja

+ Archaeological Site

● Modern Town/City

▨ > 2000 masl

0   100 km

Chira R.

here, certainly in terms of what survives to be identified, at what level of accuracy, and in what quantity.

Obviously, for human subsistence interpretation, it is crucial to identify which portion of the zooarchaeological record was culturally accumulated and deposited as a byproduct of intentional acquisition, preparation, and consumption. Generally, the simple assumption that an archaeological bone sample was necessarily accumulated, modified, and deposited by humans is not straightforward. Any portion of the assemblage may have been introduced through noncultural mechanisms, either during or after cultural deposition. For example, small pests may be attracted to and eventually die in refuse pits. After abandonment, human habitation sites may become favored locales for roosting owls, denning carnivores, or burrowing animals, all of which could contribute faunal remains not directly associated with human involvement. These portions of the assemblage cannot provide human subsistence information but can be useful for paleoecological inference, especially if the agent of accumulation or deposition can be recognized.

If we are relatively certain that the excavated remains are those of human food resources, then inferences about prehistoric subsistence are usually based upon the kinds of animals selected and their relative importance. Archaeologists understand that taxonomic representation in cultural deposits differs notably from the original parent population. Humans, like any other predator, select their prey; therefore, any paleoecological inference must be treated accordingly. The relative cultural importance of food taxa is often evaluated with a number

---

Fig. 1 (*opposite*) Formative zooarchaeological assemblages in Ecuador. (1) Punta Brava, Late (Currie n.d.). (2) La Emerenciana, Early (Staller n.d.). (3) Guarnal, Late (Currie n.d.). (4) El Encanto, Early (Porras 1973). (5) Hormiga Shelter, Early (Spath n.d.). (6) OGCH-20, Early/Middle (Byrd n.d.: 128–129). (7) Real Alto, Early (Byrd n.d.: 113–122; Marcos 1988; Stahl and Zeidler 1988: 279, 1990: 158; unpublished). (8) OGSE-62, Early (Byrd n.d.: 104–106). (9) OGSE-46, Middle/Late (n.d. 1976: 124–126). (10) OGSE-42, Early (Byrd n.d.: 103). (11) San Pablo, Early (Zevallos and Holm 1969) (12) Valdivia, Early (Byrd n.d.: 108; Meggers et al. 1965: fig. 9), and La Cabuya, Middle (Meggers et al. 1965: 110). (13) Buena Vista, Early (Byrd n.d.: 107). (14) Loma Alta, Early/Late (Byrd n.d.: 110–112; Stahl n.d.e: 232–233, n.d.a: tables 1, 2, 1991). (15) La Ponga, Middle (Lippi n.d.: table 3). (16) Río Chico, Early (Sánchez Mosquera n.d.: 103). (17) Salango, Middle/Late (Cooke 1992; Sánchez Mosquera n.d.: 81, 103; app. 1; Stahl n.d.c). (18) Capaperro, Early (unpublished). (19) Dos Caminos, Late (unpublished). (20) San Isidro, Early/Late (Stahl n.d.d: 187; unpublished). (21) Finca Cueva, Late (unpublished). (22) El Mocorral, Late (unpublished). (23) La Chimba, Late (Athens 1990; Wing n.d.). (24) Cotocollao, Middle, and Late (Villalba 1988: 347). (25) Pirincay, Late (Miller and Gill 1990: 52). (26) Putushío, Late (Freire, personal communication, 1993; Sánchez Mosquera 1997: 87).

Peter W. Stahl

of derived measures. However, these numbers are usually confounded by the many factors associated with assemblage formation history. They often become unreliable proxy measures, either for estimating the original amount of edible dietary tissue or for understanding the quantitative structure of the original accumulation. We must critically ask how and in what proportion each food taxon was culturally accumulated and deposited (e.g., Stahl 1995). Were any durable portions lost through the differential transport of body parts? For example, were only portions of large animals, or whole bodies of small animals, introduced into the area of eventual deposition? Was there further reduction during processing and consumption? For example, were larger body parts processed into smaller portions and smaller parts left more or less intact? Finally, does the *recovered* assemblage accurately reflect the *deposited* assemblage, or was it affected by a host of postdepositional processes? Cultural assemblages can be modified by biological or physical means during and after their deposition and prior to burial.

Archaeologists have long been aware that burial environments in the neotropical lowlands are usually hostile to all but the most durable remains. High humidity and temperature, acidic soil, and significant biological activity can have profound effects on the survivorship of bone remains, especially when they enter the burial environment in fragmented condition. Furthermore, as all archaeologists who have excavated Formative middens know, stratigraphic and temporal resolution are difficult, often necessitating the need for arbitrary excavation levels. We must critically evaluate exactly what is compressed into these relatively homogenous burial contexts, for time averaging of assemblages often leaves us uncertain as to how many separate depositional events are compacted into the excavated substrates. The resultant palimpsest assemblages can mask both temporal and spatial heterogeneity (e.g., Stahl 1991). This has further importance for grouping data during counting, for regardless of which statistics we use, the arbitrary way in which data are aggregated will have an important effect on the conclusions.

Of course, *where* we choose to dig and *why* are obvious and crucial considerations. The strong coastal bias in Formative archaeology is quickly demonstrated by looking at any map of excavated sites (see Fig. 1). This bias is further compounded by the preferential excavation of the earliest assemblages. Site location was undoubtedly a prominent consideration for the Formative inhabitants of Ecuador and has important effects on *what* and *how much* is recovered. Often, where and how we excavate and what remains for us to recover are dictated by factors outside of our control like *huaquerismo,* or looting, construction, or the recent explosion of *camaroneros* (commercial shrimp farms). How we retrieve samples from any excavated site has an enormous influence both on the kinds of taxa present and their relative quantities (e.g., Stahl 1992). Some excavated collections contain no zooarchaeological data. Some were only casually recorded or partially analyzed. Some were lost, and more recently some reflect the heavy use of intensive recovery techniques. Depending upon the specific circumstances of recovery, analysis, and curation, assemblages vary in their representation of taxa, thus compromising intersite comparability.

The well-explored relationship between sample size and assemblage diversity must also be taken into consideration. As a function of increased sample size, the number of different categories (*richness*) in any sample rapidly increases to a point where fewer new categories are added at a much slower rate. This tight correlation between richness and sample size can be demonstrated for Ecuadorian faunal assemblages from the western lowlands, as can the related statistic measuring the distribution or spread of abundances across recovered categories (*evenness*). In those few cases where sample size does not correlate with assemblage diversity, separate measures of richness and evenness are controlled by either excavation sampling and/or site assemblage formation (Stahl 1992; n.d.d).

In short, the interpretation of presence or absence and relative abundance data is usually not straightforward. Years ago, Grayson (1981; see also 1979: 227–229; 1983: 100; 1984) detailed most of these problems and cogently argued that the use of relative abundance—in the form of frequencies or ratios—can be fraught with difficulty, as it makes too many assumptions about the structural relationship between the excavated sample and its parent population. Unless we can control for all the effects of assemblage formation history, and we normally cannot, then we should treat inferences from ratio scale data with healthy skepticism. Fortunately, nominal scale data, whereby taxa are parsimoniously treated as variables that can be either present or absent, make far fewer assumptions. Of course, reliable inferences asymmetrically emphasize presence over absence, as the presence of a taxonomic category in a collection is verifiable, whereas its absence is not. Along with archaeological context and analogical reasoning, we can use these qualitative data to build inferences about prehistoric subsistence and ecology. The reliability of these inferences can be corroborated through the repeated excavation of similar associations in contemporaneous archaeological deposits throughout a particular region. Their validity can be corroborated through association with other fauna that demonstrate similar evidence for diet or shared ecology and then independently checked with separate lines of botanical and contextual evidence.

SUBSISTENCE AND ENVIRONMENT

An initial impression of the Formative zooarchaeological database is one of striking richness. No less than 55 orders, 134 families, 175 genera, and 193 species belonging to nine zoological classes are represented in Tables 1, 2, and 3. The distribution of zoological categories is certainly biased by many of the previously outlined factors, particularly site location and the many variables affecting differential identifiability. Also, the majority of these data are derived from the earliest portion of the Formative continuum. Much less is known about later, especially middle, temporal sequences. However, I stress that the nature of the zooarchaeological record is no less representative or impressive than any other artifact category known thus far from Formative Ecuador. It supplies us with an impression, albeit a biased one, of the many taxa that accumulated at various times in coastal, inland, and highland archaeological settings over the years spanning Formative occupation in Ecuador.

Contemporary Ecuador is characterized by a complex and richly heterogenous environmental mosaic. The western lowlands in particular are well known for a high rate of endemism, which contributes to an overall biodiversity described as astonishing (Southgate and Whitaker 1992: 795). For example, despite occupying an insignificant land mass (< 1/28 the size of Brazil), Ecuador nevertheless possesses roughly over 83 percent as many known vertebrate species (Southgate and Whitaker 1992: 795; Stahl n.d.b). An extremely broad sampling of numerous ecological habitats are represented in the zooarchaeological record. Despite the presence of a few taxa that can inhabit offshore, moderately deep, and pelagic habitats, the majority of invertebrate fauna in the sample are representative of shallow, nearshore conditions, including intertidal and mangrove habitats. The spondylid oysters and tun shells are examples of mollusks intentionally harvested from moderately deep waters since the earliest Valdivia occupations. The well-studied fish fauna from a number of coastal sites fill out the range of represented marine habitats, with taxa typically occupying waters ranging from brackish, estuarine conditions to offshore, pelagic, and deep water. Like their marine counterparts, the vertebrate fauna from inland and highland sites reflect a variety of settings. These range from dry, semiarid habitats to semiaquatic, riverine, and humid forested environments, grasslands, high-altitude *páramo*, and uniquely anthropogenic conditions.

Although future research will undoubtedly fill in many of the zoological, ecological, temporal, and spatial lacunae that presently exist within the known archaeofaunal record, a number of taxa already emerge as consistently present throughout the entire Formative sequence. These include conch, requiem shark, sea catfish, snook, sea bass, tilefish, jack and pompano, snapper, grunt, porgy, drum, mullet, barracuda, mackerel and tuna, triggerfish and filefish, sea turtle, duck, pigeon and dove, opossum, fox, deer, squirrel, cotton rat, agouti, and rabbit. Virtually all of these taxa have also been identified in earlier Vegas contexts from the Santa Elena peninsula (Stothert 1988: 188). Without question some of these were important food sources, notably fish and the universal Native American mammalian protein source par excellence, the white-tailed deer. The remains of many taxa undoubtedly were introduced into archaeological contexts for use as tools, adornments, ritual adjuncts, or through noncultural mechanisms.

Molluscan fauna have been identified and described, mainly from a number of Early Formative contexts along the southern coast. Of course this does not imply the absence of shellfish exploitation in other areas or at later times; rather, it indicates that much archaeological work still needs to be done. The record includes marine mollusks principally from intertidal, shallow water, and mangrove habitats, at least since the first appearance of Valdivia occupations and much earlier (Stothert 1988: 191–192). This would represent a broad-based collection that certainly did not necessitate sophisticated technology. Where available, mangroves were heavily exploited. Ferdon (1981) has eloquently demonstrated how coastal uplift and sediment deposition created favorable conditions for mangrove formation along the southwestern coast. Continuation of the same processes could also have lead to the eventual disappearance of estuarine and mangrove habitats; however, nothing is comparable to the startling rate at which they are disappearing today in the wake of contemporary *camaroneros* (Southgate and Whitaker 1992).

All of these marine habitats were exploited for invertebrate fauna. In particular, arks, oysters, clams, and horn shells were consumed as food or used in food preparation. Others became tools, adornments, and ritual commodities. For example, pearl oyster (*Pinctada mazatlanica*) fishhook lures and blanks are a hallmark of early Valdivia phase assemblages, as are the frequently encountered stone reamers used in their manufacture. Pearl oysters, along with various forms of clams, scallops, and marine gastropods, were used at various sites throughout the Early Formative to produce beads, pendants, ceramic decorators, bowls or cups, hoes, and picks. It has long been suspected that concentrations of the mangrove-dwelling horn shell, or *concha prieta* (*Cerithidea* spp.), suggest a lime source used in the processing of maize or consumption of coca (e.g., Zevallos M. et al. 1977:388). Marine shells like *Pinctada mazatlanica* and *Ostrea columbiensis* were also included in earliest Formative phase burial contexts as fill or were strategically placed over anatomical articulations and crania (e.g., Norton, Lunnis, and Nayling 1984: 47; Stahl n.d.e: 229; Staller n.d.: 304–313). The shallow marine-dwelling conch (*Strombus* spp.) was fashioned into utilitarian objects like hoes and picks. It is also implicated along with its more famous partner, the spondylid oyster, as an important ritual adjunct, widely distributed from earliest times and eventually reaching far-flung points in the prehistoric Andean world (Marcos and Norton 1984; Norton et al. 1984: 42; Paulsen 1974).

Two important molluscan taxa from the Formative zooarchaeological record inhabit moderately deep waters. It is likely that they were intentionally harvested in their natural habitats. Ample evidence for early seafaring certainly corroborates this possibility. Middle Valdivia phase settlement of La Puná Island (Porras 1973), contemporaneous artifacts unearthed some 23 km from the coast on La Plata Island (Marcos and Norton 1981), and unmistakably realistic depictions of canoes and fiber boats resembling the Peruvian *caballito del mar* from Valdivia and Chorrera contexts (Lathrap, Collier, and Chandra 1975: 23–25), respectively, attest to the seafaring capacity of prehistoric inhabitants in Formative Ecuador. The sturdy tun shell (*Malea ringens*), one of the largest Panamic shells averaging up to 240 mm in height and 100 mm in diameter (Keen 1971: 499), inhabits moderately deep waters and was fashioned into spoons or shell scoops in Valdivia contexts. Lathrap has suggested that heavily worn examples may have been used in the manufacture of dugout canoes or in the decortification of tuberous crops (Lathrap et al. 1975: 23). Alternatively, these and similar instruments fashioned from a variety of shallow marine gastropods (*Ficus*, *Fasciolaria*, and *Conus*) could also have been used as shell diggers.

Tun shells could conceivably have been stranded on shore and subsequently collected; however, their deeper water counterpart, the thorny oyster (spondylus spp.), likely was not. These large tropical bivalves attach themselves to local substrates and can be harvested only by divers at depths of 15 to 50 m—their native habitat—off the tropical Ecuadorian coast (Marcos and Norton 1984: 14). Of course, much has been written about the ceremonial and economic importance of spondylus in the prehistoric Andean world, where *mullu* was especially revered as an essential offering to the gods (Murra 1975). Archaeologists have successfully traced the evolution of a vibrant trade in spondylus, often coupled with the strombus conch, beginning at least in the Early Formative. Shell products like beads, necklaces, pendants, and figurines appear later in highland contexts (e.g., Athens 1990: 72; Bruhns 1989: 63; Collier and Murra 1943: 69) and eventually expand into areas throughout the Andean world. The importance of the trade is evinced by its continued persistence, even after the cataclysmic arrival of Europeans (e.g., see Estrada 1990; Paulsen 1974; Zeidler 1991).

Identified fish bones from a number of coastal sites fill out the range of marine habitats represented in the zooarchaeological record. Certainly many of the represented taxa are denizens of easily accessible habitats, ranging from brackish and estuarine conditions, extending seaward to neighboring inshore and nearshore areas. Although certain fish, like bonefishes (*Albula vulpes*), may be beached by wave action or opportunistically scavenged along shorelines, it is reasonable to suppose that the majority identified in archaeological contexts were actively pursued, caught, processed, and consumed by prehistoric peoples. It is perhaps no coincidence that most of the represented taxa are carnivores that readily take to hook and line. As noted above, shell hook lures are common in coastal Valdivia assemblages; however, this certainly does not preclude the use of perishable materials for fishing equipment as cactus spines or plant thorns. Zevallos and Holm (1960: 7) also suggested the possibility that cotton lines were utilized; however, the use of wild fibers cannot be ruled out. In either case, many nearshore carnivores, especially the commonly encountered snooks, sea basses, jacks and pompanos, snappers, grunts, porgies, drums, barracudas and wrasses could have been captured through relatively solitary shoreline hook-and-line fishing. This method could have been supported by trapping or spearing taxa like eels, cat-fish, grunts, and drums in shallow and estuarine waters. Still other nearshore schooling fishes like herrings, croakers, pigfish, and mullets—and surface schoolers like needlefish—could have been readily procured through communal haul sein-ing. This is a common sight today along the Ecuadorian coast. These fishermen hold one end of a long net on the beach while its other end is drawn by boat around a school of fish, which is eventually hauled ashore.

Access to deeper marine environments was undeniably within the grasp of the earliest Formative inhabitants. Deepwater shell diving could easily have been supplemented by spearing of reef fishes like cornet and parrotfishes or inshore toadfishes. Spearing or hook-and-line and net fishing could also have been undertaken in deeper conditions from water craft. Coastal Valdivia assem-blages include stone netweights in their inventories. A number of taxa that frequent offshore, pelagic, and deepwater environments are included in the recovered zooarchaeological assemblages. Two notable carnivores in this group, swordfishes and tunas, take bait; however, their large size and immense power necessitate an extremely heavy line. Alternatively, their beached carcasses may also have been occasionally and opportunistically scavenged along the shore, but the quantity and ubiquity of scombrid deposits in archaeological contexts argue against this. Interestingly, these taxa have been for the most part uncov-ered in Middle Formative deposits from which bone barbs for composite har-poon heads have been illustrated (Lathrap et al. 1975: 23, 86); thus harpooning from boats remains a possibility. Similar observations apply for the remains of sea turtles found in coastal contexts.

Certain fishes may not have been eaten (e.g., certain tetraodontiforms can be poisonous) and may have been collected as they washed up on the shore. Some fish bones were worked into awls and adornments, and stingray spines, possibly having been traded from the coast (e.g., Collier and Murra 1943: 68), have been found as far as the southern highlands. On a local scale, an organized trade in marine products between coastal and inland groups has been suggested on the basis of early excavations at Loma Alta (e.g., Byrd n.d.: 67; Lathrap et al. 1975: 22–23; Norton 1982). This idea is supported by: (a) a presumed inland protein scarcity; (b) varied and abundant marine faunal assemblage lacking indication of fishing tool kits; (c) ceramic evidence suggesting the existence of coastal ethnic enclaves; and (d) a slightly exaggerated distance from the coast. However, in light of excavated evidence for preserved fishing equipment at Loma Alta (Stahl n.d.e; see also Lathrap et al. 1975: 81), the well-stocked larder of the site's inhabitants could have been supplemented through the regular exploitation of marine resources easily accessed via a moderate walk or simple dugout ride to the nearby coast (Stahl n.d.a: 15–16; 1991: 349).

Until recently, much less has been known of interior coastal and highland sites; however, the limited but expanding information available from these areas details a zooarchaeological record no less striking in richness than their coastal counterparts. A wide range of habitats is represented in the list of recovered nonmarine vertebrate fauna. These range from semiaquatic and riverine areas through forested, grassland, dry, semiarid, and anthropogenic settings. Weapons and tools used in the acquisition and processing of animals from these habitats are generally lacking. Durable antler, bone, and shell points, and hooks for use in spears and other projectiles, have been described from coastal lowland and highland contexts (e.g., Athens 1990: 72; Lathrap et al. 1975: 81, 105; Porras 1973: 64). However, weapons used in the hunt most certainly could have been fashioned from perishable materials as well (Lathrap et al. 1975: 23; Stahl n.d.e: 241).

Many of the terrestrial vertebrates identified in Formative contexts could easily have been pursued with the most rudimentary technology. Various amphibians, reptiles, and mammals could have been caught by hand or through the use of expedient projectiles. It is likely, however, that many smaller terrestrial and scansorial forest taxa were pursued by the many ingenious traps, snares, and deadfalls that are still commonly used to catch important food items like paca, agouti, spiny rats, and rabbits. Bird remains tend to be far less common in archaeological sites, perhaps because of their greater overall fragility. However, their identification in certain contexts suggest that early Formative hunters were also adept at birding the grebes, ibises, ducks, and coots that regularly frequent wet habitats like mangroves, estuaries, lagoons, and swamps. Conceivably, they used nets or some form of projectile. Similarly, forest forms, including tinamous, currasows, and a variety of small, brilliantly plumed birds could have been stalked in canopied forests, where a host of terrestrial, scansorial, and arboreal mammals could also have been hunted. It is interesting to speculate on the way in which certain arboreal taxa were obtained, especially those sloths and primates who spend much of their lives in high canopy. This could implicate projectile weapons like bows and arrows, spear throwers (e.g., Lathrap et al. 1975: 105), or even blowguns. Recent Tsátchela of the western lowlands included blowguns with clay pellets in their arsenal (Métraux 1963: 251). The Chachi of Esmeraldas province are known to have employed the poisonous darts essential for relaxing the death grip of certain arboreal game (Murra 1963: 280).

Significantly, different kinds of open habitats are represented in the list of Formative archaeofauna. Access to semiarid landscapes may be suggested by the commonly encountered remains of *Dusicyon sechurae*, which is found in the desertic, yet highly labile environment of the southwestern coast. Forested habitats of the *páramo* are suggested by the remains of the mountain tapir, as are highland grassland habitats by the late appearance of domesticated camelids. Much has been made of the feeding preferences of the white-tailed deer. These browsers tend to thrive in edge environments, and, as most suburban gardeners can attest, flourish in and around areas cleared for crops. Nevertheless, the white-tailed deer and its close allies tend to dominate the profiles of prehistoric food fauna in practically every archaeological context that does not include domesticated animals. Indeed, many of the taxa in Table 3 can be described as ecological generalists, especially opossum, armadillo, various raccoons, peccary, certain rodents, and rabbits. Usually, when flotation recovery of lowland archaeological deposits is employed, remains of the rice rat tend to be common to ubiquitous. Hershkovitz (1960: 527–528) has noted that species of *Oryzomys* can become markedly commensal with humans through residence in roof thatch. Certain pastoral rodents like grass mouse and cotton rat include croplands in their range of exploited habitats, as do doves, parrots, and toucans.

Anthropogenic manipulation of animal populations is evident in the recovery of domesticated taxa. Domesticated dogs have been identified from early Formative contexts in the coastal lowlands. The notorious difficulty in using incomplete skeletal remains for discriminating amongst the various canids is mitigated through the infrequent recovery of intentional dog burials. The interment of domesticated dogs might explain why so few canine remains are found in Early Formative midden contexts. Dogs may certainly have possessed a variety of cultural roles as hunters, protectors, and sustenance. Some time ago,

Lathrap et al. (1975: 23–25) identified a breed of dog depicted in a Chorrera vessel as the Mexican hairless, a point recently rediscovered by Cordy-Collins (1994). Bred as a food source, Lathrap et al. claimed it was eventually introduced to the prehistoric cultures of western Mexico.

The mechanism for introduction was likely the same means by which prized marine shells were transported away from their Ecuadorian habitats. In this sense, any number of smaller animals may have been introduced to far-flung areas. It is interesting to note the distribution of the domesticated guinea pig, or *cuy*, in Ecuador. Villalba (1988) claims its early appearance at Cotocalloa between 1500 and 1100 B.C.; however, it must be cautioned that the published photographs of *cuy* remains (Villalba 1988: lámina 59h,i) include those of rabbits. A sizeable sample of caviid remains were unearthed from a Late Formative context at the southern site of Putushío; otherwise, much of the evidence thus far unearthed for prehistoric *cuys* comes from the western lowlands. Lippi (n.d.: 186) has identified *Cavia* remains in his excavated materials from La Ponga; however, their archaeological context at that site unfortunately contains a mixture of Guangala and Machalilla ceramics. Nevertheless, *cuy* remains have been identified in a variety of post-Formative contexts throughout the coastal lowlands, extending from the large sites of Peñón del Río and Jerusalén near Guayaquil (unpublished data), to the cemetery at Ayalán on the southern coast (Hesse 1981) and various sites along the Santa Elena peninsula (Fuentes González, Freires Paredes, and Valero Merino n.d.; Sánchez Mosquera n.d.), north through La Ponga and Salango (Stahl and Norton 1987), to a variety of sites in the Jama valley of northern Manabí province (unpublished data). In particular, the ancient role of Salango in coastal trade and the highly portable size of domesticated cavies could implicate purposive human introduction into areas far outside the range of either wild or early domesticated varieties (Stahl and Norton 1987).

Domesticated camelids appear to have been introduced into northern and southern highland contexts by the end of the Formative. Shortly thereafter, around A.D. 100, they dominated the faunal profile at Pirincay (Miller and Gill 1990) and eventually materialized in highland sites throughout Ecuador (Stahl 1988). Because of the notorious problem of osteologically discriminating between camelid taxa, especially the domesticated llama and alpaca, it is difficult to determine which form was introduced. Llamas have been identified at Cotocollao, and both domesticated forms have been tentatively identified at Putushío. Miller and Gill (1990: 64) suggested the early presence of a previously undocumented undersized llama, whose dimensions are transitional between either domesticated variety. At present, the nature of camelid utilization by Formative populations remains speculative; however, they appeared later on the coast in burial contexts at Ayalán (Hesse 1981) and El Azúcar (Reitz n.d.). Their possible role in long-distance trade at Peñón del Río has been discussed (Stahl 1988).

Limited evidence, particularly from highland sites, suggests the use of mammal bone in the manufacture of needles, awls, spatulas, scoops, and ladles, as well as musical instruments and ornamentation. In particular, carnivore tooth pendants are found in Formative assemblages. In Vegas context, Wing (1988) noted the relationship of *Dusicyon* teeth, particularly in larger communal grave contexts, which she considered to be offerings. She further suggested that wild fox populations may have been minimally controlled, and possibly even domesticated prior to the Formative (Wing 1988: 185). Certainly, we have seen the ritual disposal of other Ecuadorian domesticates in Formative dog burials, as well as post-Formative *cuy* and camelid grave associations in the southwestern lowlands.

Clear evidence for the ritual use of animals during the Formative comes from the Jama valley of northern Manabí province. Zeidler (1988) has discussed the archaeological and religious context of feline effigy mortars uncovered in Terminal Valdivia context at the large ceremonial mound at San Isidro. Both feline and reptilian imagery have long been postulated to be included within the range of early decorative motifs found in the Northern Andean area (Damp 1982: 171; Stahl n.d.e: 168, 1985; Zeidler 1988: 250). Not surprisingly, nearby deposits also yielded burned fragments of the large tropical lowland jaguar (Stahl 1994: 189; Zeidler 1988: 264). Feline faunal remains, including those of the ocelot and puma, are found in different contexts throughout lowland and highland areas during the entire temporal span of Formative occupation. Perhaps the most dramatic example of ritual comes from recent excavations at the site of Capaperro, where one Terminal Valdivia burial yielded convincing evidence for shamanistic ritual. This feature included the close association of a miniature ceramic *coquero*; a polished green stone pendant; remains of a large fruit-eating bat (*Artibeus* sp.); and a ceramic figurine nestled within the mouth of an ocelot (*Felis pardalis*), whose snout rested on the midsection of a young woman (Zeidler et al. 1998).

CONCLUSIONS

The word *precocious* has crept into the literature on Formative Ecuador, and it is commonly used to underscore its early achievements. It is certainly my favorite descriptive term for the Ecuadorian Formative, as it richly conveys different meanings. It suggests to me the delight, astonishment, and mildly condescending amusement we experience when confronted with the gifted exploits of a beloved inferior who has obviously been underestimated. At the same time, it reveals our own prejudices and naïveté in assuming that prehistoric maturity or complexity should somehow have been achieved at some later time or in some other place. With great fondness, I remember my visits to the magnificent exhibit of the famed Norton/Pérez collection housed in the Museo Arqueológico del Banco del Pacífico in Guayaquil. Liberated from the dry pages of archaeological reports and assembled into one magnificent visual presentation, this corpus of Formative artifacts can instill an overwhelming feeling of precocious achievement even in the most hardened skeptic. It is in this spirit, albeit in a less spectacular format, that I present the archaeofaunal record from Formative Ecuador.

Only a relatively recent development in the history of Ecuadorian archaeology, zooarchaeological research has nonetheless contributed archaeofaunal data from at least 32 chronologically discrete assemblages at 27 Formative sites. Because of the many factors that can influence the life history of any faunal assemblage, it is usually difficult to refer the exact structural relationship of our samples back to their parent populations. Parsimoniously treating these data as variables that can be either present or absent makes fewer assumptions about this relationship. Asymmetrically emphasizing presence over absence also overcomes the presumption that our "telephone booth" excavations and coarse screens are capable of capturing an intact past, somehow preserved in its entirety. Through this conservative approach, which minimizes our chances of being woefully wrong, the record remains as astonishing as any other catalog of Formative remains.

The Formative zooarchaeological record is strikingly rich in represented taxa. Some may have entered archaeological contexts surreptitiously, whereas others were intentionally exploited as food, used in the manufacture of tools and adornments, or performed some capacity in the realm of ritual and ceremony. Numerous habitats, characteristic of the richly heterogenous environments of contemporary Ecuador, are represented. If we picture a transect through the country, we can plot along its Formative course the diverse habitats found within: deep, offshore pelagic waters; moderately deep and shallow nearshore conditions; shallow inshore, estuarine, and brackish zones; intertidal flats; mangroves and coastlines; riverine areas; dry, semiarid scrublands; forests; secondary growth; croplands; grasslands; and high *páramo*. The necessary exploitative technology is no less diverse, as it ranges from simple collection or opportunistic scavenging, through sophisticated weaponry and significant ocean-going skill, employing either solitary or communal effort. We also see what are normally considered as hallmarks of human achievement, including the manipulation of domesticates and the organization of long-distance trade. In special circumstances, the record also enables us to contemplate concepts of Formative afterlife. In any case, the nature of the surviving archaeofaunal record is no less representative or impressive than any other artifact category thus far described from the precocious Formative of Ecuador.

Acknowledgments I thank Dumbarton Oaks and the symposium organizers for inviting me to contribute to the conference proceedings. I acknowledge a continuing debt to Steve Athens, Evan Engwall, Judy Kreid, Jorge Marcos, Mike Muse, Debby Pearsall, Scott Raymond, Jim Zeidler, and the late Presley Norton for generously including me in various projects throughout Ecuador over the past years.

In this regard, I thank various staff members at the Museum of Vertebrate Zoology in Berkeley, Calif., especially Jim Patton, the British Museum (Natural History) in London, and the American Museum of Natural History, New York, as well as the Social Sciences and Humanities Research Council of Canada and the National Science Foundation, Washington, D.C., for facilitating my research.

Friends and colleagues, particularly Steve Athens, Richard Cooke, Evan Engwall, Ana Maritza Freire, Franklin Fuentes, the late Olaf Holm, Ron Lippi, Mike Muse, Alan Osborn, Elizabeth Reitz, Amelia Sánchez, Marie Sutliff, Elizabeth Wing, Jim Zeidler, and an anonymous reviewer provided me with advice and data for this essay. However, I alone remain responsible for any act of omission or commission.

Table 1

Invertebrate Fauna Identified in Formative Archaeological Provenances from Ecuador

Fauna, taxon, and common name		Site	Habitat	Formative context
Mollusca Bivalvia (bivalves)				
Mytiloida				
Mytilidae (mussels)				
Mytella strigata	strigata mussel	Hormiga Shelter	intertidal mud	Early
Mytilus edulis	bay mussel	La Emerenciana	shallow rocks	Early
Arcoida				
Arcidae				
Anadara emarginata	emarginate ark	La Emerenciana	shallow	Early
Anadara esmerarce	ark shell	La Emerenciana	shallow	Early
Anadara grandis	ark shell	La Emerenciana, Real Alto	intertidal sand	Early
Anadara labiosa	ark shell	La Emerenciana	shallow	Early
Anadara multicostata	ark shell	Valdivia	mod. shallow	Early
Anadara obesa	ark shell	La Emerenciana	shallow mud	Early
Anadara similis	ark shell	La Emerenciana	shallow	Early
Anadara tuberculosa	ark shell	La Emerenciana, Guarmal, El Encanto, Hormiga Shelter, Real Alto, Valdivia, Loma Alta	mangrove	Early/Late
Arca pacifica	ark shell	Valdivia	intertidal rocks	Early
Glycymeridae				
Glycymeris inaequalis	bittersweet shell	Valdivia	shallow mud	Early
Ostreoida				
Pectinidae (scallops)				
Aequipecten circularis	scallop	Valdivia	shallow	Early
Argopecten circularis	scallop	Hormiga Shelter	intertidal	Early
Nodipecten subnodosus	scallop	Valdivia	mod. deep	Early
Spondylidae (thorny oysters)				
Spondylus	thorny oyster	Real Alto, Valdivia, La Cabuya, Salango, Loma Alta, San Isidro, La Chimba, Pirincay	mod. deep	Early/Middle/Late
Spondylus princeps	thorny oyster	La Emerenciana, Valdivia	mod. deep	Early
Ostreidae (oysters)		Real Alto, Valdivia	shallow	Early/Late
Crassostrea	oyster	Guanal	intertidal mud	Late
Ostrea columbiensis	mangrove oyster	Punta Brava, La Emerenciana, Guanal, Hormiga Shelter	mangrove	Early/Late
Ostrea corteziensis	mangrove oyster	Hormiga Shelter	mangrove	Early
Ostrea fischeri	mangrove oyster	Hormiga Shelter, Valdivia	mangrove	Early
Ostrea iridescens	oyster	Valdivia	intertidal rocks	Early
Pinctada	oyster	Loma Alta	shallow	Early
Pinctada mazatlanica	pearl oyster	Valdivia, La Cabuya, Salango	mod. shallow	Early/Middle
Veneroida				
Chamidae				
Chama echinata	jewel box	Valdivia	mod. shallow rocks	Early
Carditidae				
Cardita megastropha	cardita	La Emerenciana	mod. shallow	Early
Cardiidae (cockles)		Pirincay	mod. shallow	Late
Trachycardium	cockle	Loma Alta	mod. shallow	Early
Trachycardium senticosum	cockle	Valdivia	mod. shallow	Early

Fauna, taxon, and common name		Site	Habitat	Formative context
Mollusca Bivalvia (bivalves) *(cont.)*				
Mactridae				
Mactra augusta	mactra clam	La Emerenciana	mod. shallow	Early
Mactra velata	surf clam	Valdivia	mod. shallow	Early
Tellinidae				
Tellina ecuatoriana	tellin	La Emerenciana	shallow	Early
Sanguinolariidae				
Tagelus	jackknife clam	La Emerenciana, Valdivia	intratidal shallow mud	Early
Tagelus irregularis	jackknife clam	La Emerenciana, Hormiga Shelter	intratidal shallow mud	Early
Semelidae				
Semele tortuosa	semeles	Hormiga Shelter	shallow mud	Early
Corbiculidae				
Polymesoda inflata	marsh clam	La Emerenciana	shallow mud	Early
Veneridae				
Anomalocardia subimbricata	Venus clam	Valdivia	mod. shallow	Early
Anomalocardia subrugosa	Venus clam	El Encanto, Valdivia, La Cabuya	mod. shallow	Early/Middle
Chione	Venus shell	Loma Alta	intertidal	Early
Chione subimbricata	Venus shell	Hormiga Shelter	intertidal	Early
Chione subrugosa	pointed venus	Punta Brava, La Emerenciana	intertidal	Early/Late
Dosinia dunkeri	disk dosinia	La Emerenciana	shallow mud	Early
Pitar concinnus	Venus clam	Valdivia	shallow	Early
Protothaca ecuatoriana	protothaca	Punta Brava, La Emerenciana, Guanal	intratidal mud	Early/Late
Protothaca grata	Venus clam	Valdivia	intertidal mud offshore	Early
Corbulidae				
Panamicorbula inflata	basket clam	Valdivia	shallow rocks	Early

		Gastropoda (univalves)		
Archaeogastropoda				
Fissurellidae				
Fissurella airescens	limpet	Valdivia	shallow rocks	Early
Trochidae				
Tegula reticulata	reticulate top	Valdivia	shallow rocks	Early
Turbinidae				
Astraea buschi	busch's turban	Valdivia	shallow rocks	Early
Turbo squamiger	turban	Valdivia	shallow	Early
Neritidae				
Neritina latissima	virgin nerite	La Emerenciana	shallow	Early
Mesogastropoda				
Turritellidae				
Turritella radula	turret shell	El Encanto	mangrove	Early
Littorinidae				
Littorina	periwinkle	Valdivia	intertidal	Early

(cont.)

193

Table 1 (*cont.*)

Invertebrate Fauna Identified in Formative Archaeological Provenances from Ecuador

Fauna, taxon, and common name		Site	Habitat	Formative context
Gastropoda (univalves) (*cont.*)				
Potamididae				
Cerithidea	horn shell	Loma Alta	intertidal mud	Early
Cerithidea pulchra	*concha prieta*	Hormiga Shelter	intertidal mud	Early
Cerithidea valida	horn shell	Punta Brava, La Emerenciana, Guarmal, Hormiga Shelter, Valdivia, Real Alto	intertidal mud	Early/Late
Cerithiidae				
Cerithium	horn shell	La Emerenciana	shallow	Early
Cerithium adustum	horn shell	La Emerenciana, Valdivia	shallow	Early
Cerithium stercusmuscarum	horn shell	El Encanto	shallow	Early
Strombidae (conchs)		Valdivia, La Cabuya, La Chimba, Salango	mod. shallow	Early/Middle/Late
Strombus galeatus	winged conch	La Emerenciana, Valdivia	mod. shallow	Early
Strombus granulatus	conch	Valdivia	shallow	Early
Calyptraeidae				
Crepidula marginalis	slipper shell	La Emerenciana	shallow	Early
Triviidae				
Trivia radians	sea button	Valdivia	intertidal	Early
Cypraeidae (cowries)				
Cypraea arabicula	little Arabian cowry	Valdivia	shallow	Early
Cypraea robertsi	cowry	Valdivia	shallow	Early
Atlantidae (Atlantas)		Loma Alta	pelagic	Early
Naticidae				
Natica	moon shell	Loma Alta	shallow	Early
Natica chemnitzi	moon shell	El Encanto, Valdivia	shallow sand	Early
Polinices	moon shell	La Emerenciana	shallow	Early
Ficidae				
Ficus	fig shell	San Pablo	mod. shallow	Early
Tonnidae				
Malea ringens	tun shell	El Encanto, Real Alto, San Pablo	mod. deep	Early
Neogastropoda				
Muricidae				
Phyllonotus regius	rock shell	Valdivia	shallow	Early
Thaididae				
Thais crassa	dye shell	Valdivia	shallow	Early
Columbellidae				
Columbella major	dove shell	Valdivia	shallow	Early
Buccinidae				
Triumphis distorta	whelk	El Encanto, Valdivia	intertidal mud	Early
Nassariidae				
Nassarius	dog whelk	La Emerenciana	variable	Early

Fauna, taxon, and common name		Site	Habitat	Formative context
Gastropoda (univalves) *(cont.)*				
Fasciolariidae				
Fasciolaria	tulip shell	San Pablo	intertidal mud	Early
Opeatostoma pseudodon	tulip shell	Hormiga Shelter	intertidal rocks	Early
Olividae				
Oliva	olive shell	Loma Alta	intertidal	Early
Oliva callosa	Pacific white Venus	La Emerenciana	intertidal	Early
Oliva peruviana	olive shell	Valdivia	intertidal	Early
Olivella	olive shell	La Emerenciana, Loma Alta	shallow	Early
Vassidae				
Vasum muricatum	vase shell	Valdivia	intertidal	Early
Conidae (cone shells)		La Chimba	shallow	Late
Conus	cone shell	San Pablo	shallow	Early
Conus purpurascens	purple cone	Valdivia	mod. shallow	Early
Cephalaspidea				
Bullidae				
Bulla aspera	true bubble shell	Valdivia	intertidal mud	Early
Stylommatophora				
Strophocheilidae				
Strophocheilus	land snail	La Emerenciana, Loma Alta	terrestrial	Early
Naesiotus quitensis	land snail	La Chimba	terrestrial	Late
Crustacea				
Decapoda (crabs)	crab	Hormiga Shelter, Loma Alta, San Isidro		Early/Late
Calappidae	box crab	Loma Alta	intertidal mud	Early
Majidae	spider crab	Loma Alta	intertidal mud	Early/Late
Xanthidae	mud crab	Loma Alta	intertidal mud	Early

Notes: taxon = a listing by zoological category and common name. Nomenclature and habitat conform to a number of authoritative reference sources (Keen 1971; Morris 1966; Olsson 1961; Turgeon et al. 1988).

Table 2

Fish Fauna Identified in Formative Archaeological Provenances from Ecuador

Fauna, taxon, and common name		Site	Habitat	Formative conte:
Chondrichthyes (cartilaginous fishes)				
Lamniformes				
Orectolobidae (carpet sharks)		Real Alto	shallow	Early
Carcharhinidae (requiem sharks)		OGCH-20, Real Alto, Valdivia, Loma Alta, La Ponga, Salango	variable	Early/Middle/Late
Sphyrnidae				
Sphyrna	hammerhead shark	Loma Alta	inshore, offshore	Early
Rajiformes				Early
Dasyatidae (stingrays)		Real Alto, Loma Alta	variable	Early
Myliobatidae				
Aetobatus narinari	spotted eagle ray	Salango	inshore, offshore	Middle
Osteichthyes (bony fishes)				
Elopiformes				
Albulidae				
Albula vulpes	bonefish	OGSE-62	brackish, inshore	Early
Anguilliformes				
Anguillidae (eels)		Salango	variable	Middle/Late
Clupeiformes				
Clupeidae (herrings)		Salango	shallow schools	Middle/Late
Siluriformes				
Ariidae (sea catfishes)		OGCH-20, Real Alto, OGSE-62, OGSE-46, OGSE-42, Valdivia, Loma Alta, La Ponga, Río Chico, Salango	estuarine	Early/Middle/Late
Arius	sea catfish	OGCH-20, Real Alto, OGSE-62, OGSE-46, Valdivia, Buena Vista, La Ponga	estuarine	Early/Middle
Arius seemani	sea catfish	Río Chico	estuarine	Early
Bagre	chihuil	OGSE-62, Valdivia, Buena Vista, La Ponga, Río Chico	estuarine	Early/Middle
Bagre panamensis	chihuil	OGCH-20, Real Alto, OGSE-62, OGSE-46, Buena Vista, Valdivia, Loma Alta, Río Chico, Salango	estuarine	Early/Middle
Ophidiiformes				
Ophidiidae (cusk-eels/brotulas)		Salango	variable	Middle
Brotula	brotula	Salango	variable	Middle
Brotula clarkae	brotula	Salango	variable	Middle

196

Fauna, taxon, and common name		Site	Habitat	Formative context
Osteichthyes (bony fishes) *(cont.)*				
Batrachoidiformes				
Batrachoididae (toadfishes)		OGCH-20, Real Alto, OSGE-46, Loma Alta	inshore	Early/Middle
Batrachoides pacificum	toadfish	Salango	inshore	Middle
Daector	toadfish	Salango	inshore	Middle
Daector reticulata	toadfish	Salango	inshore	Middle
Atheriniformes				
Exocoetidae (flyingfishes/ halfbeaks)		Salango	surface, offshore, schools	Middle
Belonidae (needlefishes)		Salango	surface, nearshore, schools	Middle/Late
Strongylura	needlefish	Salango	surface, nearshore, schools	Late
Strongylura exilis	California needlefish	Salango	surface, nearshore, schools	Middle
Strongylura stolzmanni	needlefish	Loma Alta	surface, nearshore, schools	Early
Tylosurus	needlefish	Salango	surface, nearshore, schools	Middle
Tylosurus fodiator	needlefish	Salango	surface, nearshore, schools	Middle
Gasterosteiformes				
Fistulariidae (cornetfishes)		Salango	concealed reefs	Late
Fistularia	cornetfish	Salango	concealed reefs	Middle/Late
Fistularia corneta	cornetfish	Salango	concealed reefs	Middle
Scorpaeniformes				
Scorpaenidae (scorpionfishes)		Río Chico, Salango	shallow rocks	Early/Middle
Scorpaena	scorpionfish	Río Chico, Salango	shallow rocks	Early/Middle
Perciformes				
Centropomidae				
Centropomus	snook	OGCH-20, Real Alto, OGSE-62, OGSE-46, OGSE-42, Valdivia, Buena Vista, Salango	brackish, inshore	Early/Middle/Late
Centropomus armatus	snook	Río Chico	brackish, inshore	Early
Centropomus nigrescens	snook	Salango	brackish, inshore	Middle
Centropomus pectinatus	tarpon snook	Río Chico	brackish, inshore	Early
Serranidae (sea basses)		OGCH-20, Real Alto, OGSE-62, OGSE-46, Valdivia, La Ponga, Salango	inshore	Early/Middle/Late
Epinephelus	grouper	Salango	inshore	Middle/Late
Epinephelus acantaistius	grouper	Salango	inshore	Middle
Epinephelus analogus	spotted cabrilla	Salango	inshore	Middle
Epinephelus multiguttatus	grouper	Río Chico, Salango	inshore	Early/Middle
Hemilutjanus	grouper	Río Chico	inshore	Early
Mycteroperca	grouper	Real Alto, OGSE-62, Valdivia, Salango	inshore	Early/Middle/Late
Mycteroperca xenarcha	broomtail grouper	OGSE-62, Río Chico, Salango	inshore	Early/Middle
Paralabrax	sea bass	Salango	inshore	Middle/Late
Paralabrax callaensis	sea bass	Salango	inshore	Middle/Late
Malacanthidae (tilefishes)		Río Chico	shallow, offshore	Early
Caulolatilus affinis	tilefish	Río Chico, Salango	shallow, offshore	Early/Middle/Late
Caulolatilus princeps	ocean whitefish	Salango	shallow, offshore	Middle

(cont.)

Table 2 (*cont.*)

Fish Fauna Identified in Formative Archaeological Provenances from Ecuador

Fauna, taxon, and common name		Site	Habitat	Formative conte:
Osteichthyes (bony fishes) (*cont.*)				
Nematistidae (roosterfish)		Río Chico	shallow sand, inshore	Early
Nematistius pectoralis	roosterfish	Río Chico, Salango	shallow sand, inshore	Early/Middle
Coryphaenidae (dolphins)		Salango	surface, inshore and pelagic	Late
Coryphaena hippurus	dolphin	Salango	surface, inshore and pelagic	Middle/Late
Carangidae (jacks and pompanos)		OGCH-20, Real Alto, OGSE-62, OGSE-46, Valdivia, Buena Vista, Loma Alta, La Ponga, Salango, San Isidro, Río Chico	shallow, nearshore	Early/Middle/Late
Alectis ciliaris	pompano	Salango	shallow, nearshore	Late
Caranx	jack	Valdivia, Loma Alta, Río Chico, Salango	shallow, nearshore	Early/Middle
Caranx caballus	green jack	Río Chico, Salango	inshore and pelagic, schools	Early/Middle
Caranx caninus	jack	Río Chico, Salango	brackish and inshore, schools	Early/Middle/Late
Caranx hippos	crevalle jack	Real Alto, OGSE-62	shallow, nearshore	Early
Caranx otrynter	jack	Río Chico, Salango	shallow, nearshore	Early/Middle
Caranx speciosus	jack	Salango	shallow, nearshore	Middle
Caranx vinctus	jack	Salango	shallow, nearshore	Middle
Hemicaranx	bluntnose jack	Loma Alta	shallow, nearshore	Early
Oligoplites	leatherjacket	Salango	shallow, nearshore	Middle
Oligoplites altus	leatherjacket	Salango	shallow, nearshore	Middle
Selar crumenophthalmus	bigeye scad	Salango	shallow, nearshore	Middle
Selene	lookdown	Real Alto, Río Chico, Salango	shallow, nearshore	Early/Middle/Late
Selene brevoorti	lookdown	Río Chico, Salango	shallow, nearshore	Early/Middle
Selene peruviana	lookdown	Salango	inshore schools	Middle
Seriola	amberjack	Río Chico	shallow, nearshore	Early
Seriola lalandi	jack	Salango	inshore schools	Middle
Seriola rivoliana	almaco jack	Salango	brackish inshore, pelagic	Middle
Trachinotus kennedyi	pompano	Salango	shallow, nearshore	Middle
Trachinotus paitensis	paloma pompano	Salango	inshore sand	Middle
Trachinotus rhodopus	gafftopsail pompano	Salango	inshore sand	Middle
Vomer	moonfish	OGSE-62, Loma Alta	shallow, nearshore	Early
Vomer declivifrons	Pacific moonfish	OGSE-62	shallow, nearshore	Early
Lutjanidae (snappers)		Río Chico, Salango	shallow inshore reefs	Early/Middle/Late
Lutjanus	snapper	OGCH-20, Real Alto, OGSE-62, OGSE-46, Valdivia, Loma Alta, Río Chico	shallow inshore reefs	Early/Middle/Late
Lutjanus apatus	snapper	Salango	shallow inshore reefs	Middle
Lutjanus argentiventris	snapper	Salango	shallow inshore reefs	Middle
Lutjanus colorado	snapper	Río Chico, Salango	shallow inshore reefs	Early/Middle
Lutjanus guttatus	snapper	Río Chico, Salango	shallow inshore reefs	Early/Middle
Lutjanus inermis	snapper	Salango	shallow inshore reefs	Middle
Lutjanus novemfasciatus	snapper	Salango	shallow inshore reefs	Middle
Lutjanus peru	snapper	Salango	shallow inshore reefs	Middle
Lobotidae				
Lobotes pacificus	tripletail	Salango	brackish	Middle
Gerreidae				
Eugerres brevimanus	mojarra	Salango	shallow brackish inshore, sand, mud	Middle
Pomadasyidae (grunts)		OGCH-20, Real Alto, OGSE-62, OGSE-46, Valdivia, Buena Vista, La Ponga, Salango	shallow schools	Early/Middle/Late
Anisotremus	grunt	OGSE-62, La Ponga, Río Chico	shallow schools	Early/Middle
Anisotremus dovii	grunt	Salango	shallow schools	Middle
Anisotremus pacifici	grunt	Salango	shallow schools	Middle
Haemulon	grunt	OGSE-62, OGSE-46	shallow schools	Early/Middle/Late
Haemulon scudderi	grunt	Río Chico, Salango	shallow schools	Early/Middle

Fauna, taxon, and common name		Site	Habitat	Formative context
		Osteichthyes (bony fishes) (*cont.*)		
Pomadasyidae				
Haemulon steindachneri	grunt	Río Chico, Salango	shallow schools	Early/Middle
Orthopristis	pigfish	Real Alto, OGSE-62, Río Chico, Salango	shallow schools	Early/Middle
Orthopristis chalceus	pigfish	Río Chico, Salango	shallow schools	Early/Middle
Pomadasys	grunt	Río Chico, Salango	shallow schools	Early/Middle
Pomadasys bayanus	grunt	Salango	shallow schools	Middle
Pomadasys branicki	grunt	Río Chico	shallow schools	Early
Pomadasys leuciscus	grunt	Salango	shallow schools	Middle
Pomadasys macracanthus	grunt	Salango	shallow schools	Middle
Pomadasys nitidus	grunt	Salango	shallow schools	Middle
Pomadasys panamensis	grunt	Salango	shallow schools	Middle
Sparidae (porgies)		Río Chico, Salango	nearshore, sand, bottom	Early/Late
Calamus	porgy	OGCH-20, OGSE-46, La Ponga	nearshore, sand, bottom	Early/Middle/Late
Calamus brachysomus	Pacific porgy	OGSE-62, OGSE-46, Valdivia, Río Chico, Salango	nearshore, sand, bottom	Early/Middle/Late
Sciaenidae (drums)		OGCH-20, Real Alto, OGSE-42, Loma Alta, La Ponga, Río Chico Salango	estuarine, shallow, brackish, inshore, bottom	Early/Middle/Late
Bairdiella	bairdiella	Real Alto	estuarine, shallow, brackish, inshore, bottom	Early
Bairdiella ensifera	bairdiella	Salango	estuarine, shallow, brackish, inshore, bottom	Middle
Cynoscion	sea trout	OGCH-20, OGSE-62, OGSE-42, OGSE-46, Loma Alta, La Ponga	estuarine, shallow, brackish, inshore, bottom	Early/Middle/Late
Cynoscion albus	sea trout	Río Chico	estuarine, shallow, brackish, inshore, bottom	Early
Cynoscion phoxocephalus	sea trout	Salango	estuarine, shallow, brackish, inshore, bottom	Middle
Cynoscion stolzmanni	sea trout	Salango	estuarine, shallow, brackish, inshore, bottom	Middle
Larimus	drum	OGCH-20, Real Alto, Loma Alta, Río Chico	estuarine, shallow, brackish, inshore, bottom	Early/Middle
Larimus golosus	drum	Salango	estuarine, shallow, brackish, inshore, bottom	Middle
Menticirrhus	kingfish	Salango	estuarine, shallow, brackish, inshore, bottom	Middle
Menticirrhus elongatus	kingfish	Salango	estuarine, shallow, brackish, inshore, bottom	Middle
Menticirrhus nasus	kingfish	Salango	estuarine, shallow, brackish, inshore, bottom	Middle
Menticirrhus panamensis	kingfish	Salango	estuarine, shallow, brackish, inshore, bottom	Early/Middle
Micropogon	croaker	OGCH-20, Real Alto, Loma Alta, La Ponga	estuarine, shallow, brackish, inshore, bottom	Early/Middle
Micropogon fusiari	croaker	La Ponga	estuarine, shallow, brackish, inshore, bottom	Middle
Micropogonias	drum	Salango	estuarine, shallow, brackish, inshore, bottom	Middle
Micropogonias altipinnis	drum	Salango	estuarine, shallow, brackish, inshore, bottom	Middle/Late
Paralonchurus	drum	Real Alto, La Ponga	estuarine, shallow, brackish, inshore, bottom	Early/Middle
Paralonchurus dumerilii	drum	Salango	estuarine, shallow, brackish, inshore, bottom	Middle
Paralonchurus goodei	drum	Salango	estuarine, shallow, brackish, inshore, bottom	Middle

(*cont.*)

Table 2 (*cont.*)

Fish Fauna Identified in Formative Archaeological Provenances from Ecuador

Fauna, taxon, and common name		Site	Habitat	Formative contex
Osteichthyes (bony fishes) (*cont.*)				
Umbrina	croaker	Río Chico, Salango	estuarine, shallow, brackish, inshore, bottom	Early/Middle/Late
Umbrina roncador	yellowfin croaker	Salango	estuarine, shallow, brackish, inshore, bottom	Middle
Umbrina xanti	croaker	Río Chico, Salango	estuarine, shallow, brackish, inshore, bottom	Early/Middle
Kyphosidae (sea chubs)		Real Alto	inshore reefs, schools, rocks	Early
Kyphosus elegans	sea chub	Salango	inshore reefs, schools, rocks	Middle
Sector ocyurus	sea chub	Salango	inshore reefs, schools, rocks	Middle
Ephippidae				
Chaetodipterus	spadefish	La Ponga	inshore reefs, schools, rocks	Middle
Chaetodipterus zonatus	Pacific spadefish	Salango	inshore reefs, schools, rocks	Middle
Cirrhitidae (hawkfishes)		OGSE-46	reefs, rocks	Late
Cirrhites	hawkfish	Loma Alta	reefs, rocks	Early
Mugilidae (mullets)		OGCH-20, Río Chico, Salango	brackish, estuarine, inshore, schools	Early/Middle/Late
Mugil	mullet	Real Alto, OGSE-62, Loma Alta, Salango	brackish, estuarine, inshore, schools	Early/Middle/Late
Mugil carema	mullet	Río Chico	brackish, estuarine, inshore, schools	Early
Mugil cephalus	striped mullet	OGSE-62	brackish, estuarine, inshore, schools	Early
Sphyraenidae (barracudas)		Río Chico, Salango	nearshore, surface, schools	Early/Late
Sphyraena	barracuda	Salango	nearshore, surface, schools	Middle
Sphyraena barracuda	great barracuda	Loma Alta, Salango	nearshore, surface, schools	Early/Middle
Sphyraena ensis	barracuda	Río Chico, Salango	nearshore, surface, schools	Early/Middle/Late
Polynemidae (threadfins)		Salango	inshore, mud	Middle
Polydactylus	threadfin	Salango	inshore, mud	Middle
Polydactylus approximans	blue bobo	Salango	inshore, mud	Middle
Polydactylus opercularis	yellow bobo	Salango	inshore, mud	Middle
Labridae (wrasses)		OGCH-20, Real Alto, OGSE-46, Valdivia, Río Chico, Salango	shallow sand	Early/Middle
Bodianus	hogfish	Salango	shallow sand	Middle
Bodianus diplotaenia	hogfish	Salango	shallow sand	Middle
Scaridae (parrotfishes)		Salango	reefs, schools	Middle/Late
Scarus perico	parrotfish	Salango	reefs, schools	Middle
Acanthuridae (surgeonfishes)		Río Chico, Salango	variable	Early/Middle
Prionurus	surgeonfish	Salango	variable	Middle
Scombridae (mackerels and tunas)		OGCH-20, OGSE-62, OGSE-46, Valdivia, Loma Alta, La Ponga, Salango	inshore, offshore, epipelagic, schools	Early/Middle/Late
Acanthocybium solanderi	wahoo	La Ponga, Salango	inshore, offshore, epipelagic, schools	Middle/Late
Auxis	mackerel	Loma Alta, Salango	inshore, offshore, epipelagic, schools	Early/Middle
Auxis thazard	frigate mackerel	Salango	inshore, offshore, epipelagic, schools	Middle
Euthynnus	skipjack tuna	La Ponga, Salango	inshore, offshore, epipelagic, schools	Middle/Late

Fauna, taxon, and common name	Site	Habitat	Formative context
Osteichthyes (bony fishes) (*cont.*)			
Euthynnus lineatus black skipjack	Salango	inshore, offshore, epipelagic, schools	Middle/Late
Euthynnus pelamis skipjack tuna	Salango	inshore, offshore, epipelagic, schools	Middle/Late
Sarda bonito	Salango	inshore, offshore, epipelagic, schools	Middle
Scomber mackerel	Salango	inshore, offshore, epipelagic, schools	Middle
Scomber japonicus mackerel	Salango	inshore, offshore, epipelagic, schools	Middle/Late
Scomberomorus sierra sierra	Salango	inshore, offshore, epipelagic, schools	Middle
Thunnus tuna	Salango	inshore, offshore, epipelagic, schools	Middle/Late
Thunnus albacares yellowfin tuna	Salango	inshore, offshore, epipelagic, schools	Middle/Late
Eleotriidae (sleepers)	Real Alto	brackish, inshore, mud	Early
Xiphidae (swordfishes)	Salango	shallow, offshore, deepwater	Middle
Tetraodontiformes			
Balistidae (triggerfishes/filefishes)	OGCH-20, OGSE-46, Río Chico, Salango	nearshore and pelagic	Early/Middle/Late
Sufflamen verres triggerfish	Salango	nearshore and pelagic	Middle
Diodontidae			
Diodon hystrix porcupinefish	Salango	inshore, bottom and shallow, bottom	Middle
Tetraodontidae (puffers)	OGCH-20, Loma Alta	nearshore	Early/Middle
Sphoeroides puffer	Salango	nearshore	Middle
Sphoeroides annulatus bullseye puffer	Salango	nearshore	Middle
Sphoeroides lobatus puffer	Salango	nearshore	Middle

Notes: taxon = a listing by zoological category and common name. Nomenclature and habitat conform to a number of authoritative reference sources (Eschmeyer et al. 1983; Jordan 1963; Nelson 1994; Robins et al. 1980).

Table 3

Non-fish Vertebrate Fauna Identified in Formative Archaeological Provenances from Ecuador

Fauna, taxon, and common name		Site	Habitat	Formative context
Amphibia				
Caudata (salamanders)		Dos Caminos	terrestrial, semiaquatic	Late
Anura (frogs/toads)		Hormiga Shelter, Loma Alta, Capaperro, Dos Caminos, San Isidro, El Mocorral	terrestrial, semiaquatic	Early/Late
Bufonidae (toads)		Loma Alta, El Mocorral	terrestrial, semiaquatic	Early/Late
Ranidae (frogs)		Loma Alta	terrestrial, semiaquatic	Early/Late
Reptilia				
Chelonia				
Kinosternidae				
Kinosternon	mud turtle	Loma Alta, La Ponga	terrestrial, semiaquatic	Early/Middle
Emydidae	emydid turtles	Valdivia, La Cabuya, Loma Alta, La Ponga	terrestrial, semiaquatic	Early/Middle
Rhinoclemmys	brown land terrapin	Loma Alta, San Isidro	terrestrial, forest	Early
Cheloniidae (sea turtles)		OGCH-20, Real Alto, OGSE-46, OGSE-48, OGSE-42, Valdivia, Buena Vista	marine, aquatic	Early/Middle/Late
Lepidochelys	sea turtle	OGSE-46	marine, aquatic	Middle/Late
Sauria (lizards)		Hormiga Shelter, Dos Caminos, Cotocollao	variable	Early/Late
Iguanidae	iguanid lizards	Dos Caminos	variable	Late
Serpentes				
Boidae				
Boa constrictor	boa constrictor	Loma Alta	terrestrial, forest, variable, riverine	Early
Viperidae				
Bothrops	fer-de-lance	Loma Alta	terrestrial, variable	Early
Crotalus	rattlesnake	La Ponga	terrestrial, variable, dry, semiarid	Middle
Aves				
Tinamiformes				
Tinamidae (tinamous)		Loma Alta	terrestrial, forest, secondary growth	Early
Tinamou	tinamou	La Chimba	terrestrial, forest, secondary growth	Late
Podicepediformes				
Podicepedidae	grebes	La Ponga	semiaquatic, riverine	Middle
Procellariiformes				
Diomedeidae				
Diomedea irrorata	Galapagos albatross	Salango	marine aquatic, volant	Middle

Fauna, taxon, and common name		Site	Habitat	Formative context
		Aves *(cont.)*		
Pelecaniformes				
Pelecanidae				
Pelecanus occidentalis	brown pelican	OGSE-46	marine aquatic	Late
Ciconiformes				
Threskiornithidae (ibises)		Loma Alta	semiaquatic, riverine	Early
Anseriformes				
Anatidae (ducks)		Real Alto, Loma Alta, La Ponga, San Isidro	semiaquatic, riverine	Early/Middle/Late
Falconiformes				
Accipitridae (hawks)		Loma Alta	variable	Early
Buteo	hawk	Loma Alta	variable	Early
Falconidae (falcons)		Loma Alta	variable	Late
Falco peregrinus	peregrine falcon	Loma Alta	variable	Early
Galliformes				
Cracidae (currasows)		Loma Alta	arboreal, forest, secondary growth	Early
Penelope	guan	Loma Alta	arboreal, forest, secondary growth	Early/Late
Grulliformes				
Rallidae (coots)		Loma Alta	semiaquatic, riverine	Early
Charadriiformes				
Laridae (gulls)		Loma Alta, Salango	marine aquatic, variable	Early/Middle
Larus	gull	Salango	marine aquatic, variable	Early?
Sterna	tern	Salango	marine aquatic, variable	Late
Columbiformes				
Columbidae (pigeons/doves)		Hormiga Shelter, Loma Alta, La Ponga, Dos Caminos	variable	Early/Middle/Late
Columba	pigeon	La Chimba	variable	Late
Zenaida	dove	Loma Alta, Cotocollao	variable, open areas, croplands	Late
Columbina	ground dove	Loma Alta	variable, open areas	Late
Claravis	dove	Loma Alta	variable, open areas	Late
Psittaciformes				
Psittacidae (macaws/parrots)		Loma Alta	variable	Early/Late
Amazona	parrot	Cotocollao	variable	Late
Strigiformes				
Strigidae (owls)		La Ponga	arboreal	Middle

(cont.)

Table 3 (*cont.*)

Non-fish Vertebrate Fauna Identified in Formative Archaeological Provenances from Ecuador

Fauna, taxon, and common name		Site	Habitat	Formative context
		Aves (*cont.*)		
Piciformes				
Capitonidae (barbets)		Loma Alta	arboreal, forest	Early
Picidae (woodpeckers)		Loma Alta	arboreal, forest	Early
Ramphastidae (toucans)		Loma Alta	arboreal, forest, secondary growth	Early/Late
Passeriformes (passerine birds)		Hormiga Shelter, Loma Alta	variable	Early
		Mammalia		
Marsupialia				
Didelphidae (opossums)		Loma Alta, La Ponga, Cotocollao	arboreal, scansorial, terrestrial, variable	Early/Middle/Late
Chironectes	water opossum	La Chimba	semiaquatic, riverine	Late
Didelphis marsupialis	common opossum	Loma Alta, La Chimba	arborial, scansorial, terrestrial, variable	Late
Marmosa	mouse opossum	Hormiga Shelter, Loma Alta, Capaperro, El Mocorral	arborial, terrestrial, forest, secondary growth	Early/Late
Xenarthra				
Bradypodidae (sloths)		San Isidro	arboreal, forest	Early
Dasypodidae				
Dasypus novemcinctus	nine-banded armadillo	Loma Alta, Capaperro, Dos Caminos, San Isidro, Finca Cueva, El Mocorral	terrestrial, fossorial, semifossorial, forest, open areas	Early/Late
Chiroptera				
Phyllostomidae				
Artibeus	fruit-eating bat	Capaperro	volant, arboreal, forest	Early
Primates				
Cebidae (monkeys)		Loma Alta	arboreal, forest	Early
Cebus albifrons	capuchin monkey	Salango	arboreal, forest	Late
Saimiri	squirrel monkey	La Chimba	arboreal, variable	Late
Carnivora				
Canidae (dogs)		Hormiga Shelter, Loma Alta, Capaperro, La Chimba	terrestrial, variable	Early/Late
Canis	dog	OGSE-46, Loma Alta, Pirincay	terrestrial, variable	Early/Late
Canis familiaris	domestic dog	Real Alto, OGSE-46, Loma Alta	domesticated	Early/Late
Dusicyon	fox	Hormiga Shelter, OGCH-20, Loma Alta, La Ponga, Pirincay	terrestrial, variable	Early/Middle/Late
Dusicyon sechurae	fox	OGSE-46, Loma Alta	terrestrial, variable, dry, semiarid	Early/Late
Speothos	bush dog	Loma Alta	terrestrial, variable, forest	Early
Ursidae				
Tremarctos ornatus	spectacled bear	La Chimba, Pirincay	scansorial, terrestrial, forest, croplands	Late
Procyonidae (raccoons)		La Chimba	arboreal, terrestrial, forest, croplands	Late
Nasua	coati	La Chimba	arboreal, terrestrial, forest, croplands	Late
Potus flavus	kinkajou	La Chimba	arborial, forest	Late

Fauna, taxon, and common name		Site	Habitat	Formative context
Mammalia *(cont.)*				
Mustelidae (weasels)				
Mustela	weasel	La Chimba	terrestrial, forest	Late
Mustela frenata	long-tailed weasel	Cotocollao	terrestrial, forest	Middle
Felidae (cats)				
Felis pardalis	ocelot	Capaperro	arboreal, terrestrial, variable	Early
Felis concolor	puma	Loma Alta, La Chimba, Cotocollao, Pirincay	terrestrial, variable	Late
Panthera onca	jaguar	Real Alto, San Isidro	terrestrial, scansorial, variable, dry, semiarid, forest	Early
Perissodactyla				
Tapiridae (tapirs)				
Tapirus bairdii	baird's tapir	Loma Alta, San Isidro	terrestrial, variable, forest	Early
Tapirus pinchaque	mountain tapir	La Chimba, Pirincay	terrestrial, *páramo*	Late
Artiodactyla				
Tayassuidae				
Tayassu	peccary	Valdivia, Loma Alta, Dos Caminos, San Isidro	terrestrial, variable, forest, croplands	Early/Late
Camelidae				
Lama glama	llama	Cotocollao, Putushío	domesticated	Late
Lama pacos	alpaca	Putushío	domesticated	Late
Cervidae (deer)		OGCH-20, Real Alto, OGSE-42, OGSE-46, Valdivia, Buena Vista, La Chimba, Loma Alta, La Ponga, San Isidro, El Mocorral, Pirincay, La Chimba	terrestrial, variable	Early/Middle/Late
Odocoileus virginianus	white-tailed deer	Real Alto, OGSE-42, Valdivia, La Cabuya, Buena Vista, Loma Alta, La Ponga, Salango, Capaperro, Dos Caminos, San Isidro, Cotocollao, La Chimba, Pirincay, Putushío	terrestrial, variable	Early/Middle/Late
Mazama	brocket deer	Real Alto, OGSE-42, Valdivia, Loma Alta, El Mocorral, La Chimba, Pirincay	terrestrial, forest, open areas	Early/Late
Pudu mephistophiles	northern pudu	La Chimba, Pirincay	terrestrial, forest	Late
Rodentia (rodents)		Hormiga Shelter, Loma Alta, La Ponga, Capaperro, San Isidro, Finca Cueva, El Mocorral, La Chimba, Cotocollao, Pirincay	variable	Early/Middle/Late
Sciuridae (squirrels)				
Sciurus	squirrel	Loma Alta	arboreal, scansorial, forest	Early
Muridae (mice)		La Ponga	variable	Middle
Oryzomys	rice rat	Loma Alta, Capaperro, Dos Caminos, San Isidro, Finca Cueva, El Mocorral	arboreal, scansorial, terrestrial, commensal	Early/Late
Phyllotis	leaf-eared mouse	Cotocollao	scansorial, variable	Late
Akodon	grass mouse	Dos Caminos, San Isidro	terrestrial, variable, open areas, grasslands	Late
Sigmodon	cotton rat	Hormiga Shelter, Loma Alta, La Ponga, Capaperro, Dos Caminos, San Isidro, Finca Cueva	terrestrial, open areas, grasslands, croplands, commensal	Early/Middle/Late

(cont.)

Table 3 *(cont.)*

Non-fish Vertebrate Fauna Identified in Formative Archaeological Provenances from Ecuador

Fauna, taxon, and common name		Site	Habitat	Formative context
		Mammalia *(cont.)*		
Caviidae				
Cavia porcellus	*cuy*	La Ponga, Cotocollao, Putushío	domesticated	Middle?/Late
Agoutidae				
Agouti paca	paca	Loma Alta, San Isidro	terrestrial, forest, croplands	Early/Late
Agouti taczanowskii	mountain paca	La Chimba, Cotocollao, Pirincay, Putushío	terrestrial, forest	Late
Dasyproctidae				
Dasyprocta	agouti	OGSE-46, Loma Alta, San Isidro	terrestrial, forest, dry deciduous forest	Early/Middle/Late
Dasyprocta punctata	agouti	Loma Alta	terrestrial, forest, dry deciduous forest	Early
Echimyidae				
Proechimys	spiny rat	Loma Alta, Salango, Dos Caminos	terrestrial, forest	Early/Late
Lagomorpha				
Leporidae (rabbits/hares)		La Ponga	terrestrial, variable	Middle
Sylvilagus	rabbit	Hormiga Shelter, Loma Alta, Pirincay	terrestrial, variable	Early/Late
Sylvilagus brasiliensis	rabbit	Hormiga Shelter, Loma Alta, Salango, Dos Caminos, San Isidro, La Chimba, Cotocollao, Pirincay, Putushío	terrestrial, variable	Early/Middle/Late

Notes: taxon = a listing by zoological category and common name. Nomenclature and habitat conform to a number of authoritative reference sources (Albuja 1991; Eisenberg 1989; Emmons and Feer 1990; Freiberg 1981, 1982; Hilty and Brown 1986).

BIBLIOGRAPHY

ALBUJA, LUIS
  1991 Mamíferos. *Politécnica* (Revista de Información Técnico-Cientifica, Quito) 16(3): 163–203.

ATHENS, J. STEPHEN
  1990 *Prehistoric Agricultural Expansion and Population Growth in Northern Highland Ecuador: Interim Report for 1989 Fieldwork.* International Archaeological Research Institute, Honolulu.

BRUHNS, KAREN O.
  1989 Intercambio entre la costa y la sierra en el Formativo Tardío: Nuevas evidencias del Azuay. In *Relaciones interculturales en el area ecuatorial del Pácfico durante la época precolombina* (J. F. Bouchard and M. Guinea, eds.): 57–74. BAR International Series 503. British Archaeological Reports, Oxford.

BYRD, KATHLEEN M.
  n.d. Changing Animal Utilization Patterns and Their Implications: Southwest Ecuador (6500 B.C.–A.D. 1400). Ph.D. dissertation, University of Florida, Gainesville, 1976.

COLLIER, DONALD, AND JOHN V. MURRA
  1943 *Survey and Excavations in Southern Ecuador.* Anthropological Series 35. Field Museum of Natural History, Chicago.

COOKE, RICHARD
  1992 Prehistoric Nearshore and Littoral Fishing in the Eastern Tropical Pacific: An Ichthyological Evaluation. *Journal of World Prehistory* 6: 1–49.

CORDY-COLLINS, ALANA
  1994 An Unshaggy Dog Story. *Natural History* 2/94: 34–41.

CURRIE, ELIZABETH J.
  n.d. New Evidence on the Late Formative Period in El Oro Province, Southwestern Ecuador. Manuscript in possession of the author, 1992.

DAMP, JONATHAN E.
  1982 Ceramic Art and Symbolism in the Early Valdivia Community. *Journal of Latin American Lore* 8: 155–178.

EISENBERG, JOHN F.
  1989 *Mammals of the Neotropics,* vol. 1: *The Northern Neotropics.* University of Chicago Press, Chicago.

EMMONS, LOUISE H., AND FRANÇOISE FEER
  1990 *Neotropical Rainforest Mammals: A Field Guide.* University of Chicago Press, Chicago.

ESCHMEYER, WILLIAM N., EARL S. HERALD, AND HOWARD HAMMAN
  1983 *A Field Guide to Pacific Coast Fishes of North America from the Gulf of Alaska to Baja California.* Houghton Mifflin, Boston.

ESTRADA, JENNY
  1990 *La Balsa en la historia de la navegación ecuatoriana.* Instituto de Historia Maritima Armada del Ecuador, Guayaquil.

FERDON, EDWIN N. JR.
1981   Holocene Mangrove Formations on the Santa Elena Peninsula, Ecuador: Pluvial Indicators or Ecological Response to Physiographic Changes. *American Antiquity* 46: 619–626.

FREIBERG, MARCOS
1981   *Turtles of South America.* TFH Publications, Neptune, N.J.
1982   *Snakes of South America.* TFH Publications, Neptune, N.J.

FUENTES GONZÁLEZ, FRANKLIN, MARITZA FREIRES PAREDES, AND PEDRO VALERO MERINO
n.d.   Arqueología de rescate en el malecón de Salinas: Sitio La Fiorella. Paper presented at the Primer Congreso Ecuatoriano de Antropología, Quito, 1996.

GRAYSON, DONALD K.
1979   On the Quantification of Vertebrate Archaeofauna. In *Advances in Archaeological Method and Theory,* vol. 2 (M. B. Schiffer, ed.): 199–237. Academic Press, New York.
1981   A Critical View of the Use of Archaeological Vertebrates in Paleoenvironmental Reconstruction. *Journal of Ethnobiology* 1: 28–38.
1983   The Paleontology of Gatecliff Rockshelter: Small Mammals. In *The Archaeology of Monitor Valley,* vol. 2: *Gatecliff Shelter* (D. H. Thomas, ed.): 99–126. Anthropological Papers 59. American Museum of Natural History, New York.
1984   *Quantitative Zooarchaeology.* Academic Press, Orlando, Fla.

HERSHKOVITZ, PHILIP
1960   Mammals of Northern Colombia, Preliminary Report 8: Arboreal Rice Rats, a Systematic Revision of the Subgenus *Oecomys,* Genus *Oryzomys. Proceedings of the United States National Museum* 110: 513–568.

HESSE, BRIAN
1981   The Association of Animal Bones with Burial Features. In *The Ayalán Cemetery: A Late Integration Period Burial Site on the South Coast of Ecuador* (D. H. Ubelaker, ed.): 134–138. Smithsonian Contributions to Anthropology 29. Smithsonian Institution Press, Washington, D.C.

HILTY, STEVEN L., AND WILLIAM L. BROWN
1986   *A Guide to the Birds of Colombia.* Princeton University Press, Princeton, N.J.

JIJÓN Y CAAMAÑO, JACINTO
1912   *Contribución al concimiento de los aborígenes de la provincia de Imbabura en la república del Ecuador.* Estudios de Prehistoria Americana 2. Blass y Cía., Madrid.
1927   Puruhá. Contribución al conocimiento de las aborígenes de la provincia del Chimborazo de la república del Ecuador. *Boletín de la Academia Nacional de Historia*: 6, 12, 14.

JORDAN, DAVID STARR
1963   *The Genera of Fishes and a Classification of Fishes.* Stanford University Press, Stanford, Calif.

KEEN, A. MYRA
1971   *Sea Shells of Tropical West America.* Stanford University Press, Stanford, Calif.

LATHRAP, DONALD W., DONALD COLLIER, AND HELEN CHANDRA
1975   *Ancient Ecuador: Culture, Clay and Creativity, 3000–300 B.C.* Field Museum of Natural History, Chicago.

LIPPI, RONALD D.
  n.d.   La Ponga and the Machalilla Phase of Coastal Ecuador. Ph.D. dissertation, University of Wisconsin–Madison, 1983.

MARCOS, JORGE G.
  1988   *Real Alto: La historia de un centro ceremonial Valdivia (primera parte).* Corporación Editora Nacional, Quito.

MARCOS, JORGE G., AND PRESLEY NORTON
  1981   Interpretación sobre la arqueología de la Isla de La Plata. *Miscelánea Antropológica Ecuatoriana* 1: 136–154.

  1984   From the Yungas of Chinchay Suyo to Cuzco: The Role of La Plata Island in *Spondylus* Trade. In *Social and Economic Organization in the Prehispanic Andes* (David L. Browman, Richard L. Burger, and Mario A. Rivera, eds.): 7–20. BAR International Series 194. British Archaeological Reports, Oxford.

MEGGERS, BETTY J., CLIFFORD EVANS, AND EMILIO ESTRADA
  1965   *Early Formative Period of Coastal Ecuador: The Valdivia and Machalilla Phases.* Smithsonian Contributions to Anthropology 1. Smithsonian Institution. U.S. Government Printing Office, Washington D.C.

MÉTRAUX, ALFRED
  1963   Weapons. In *Handbook of South American Indians,* vol. 5: *The Comparative Ethnology of South American Indians* (J.H. Steward, ed.): 229–263. Cooper Square, New York.

MILLER, GEORGE R., AND ANNE L. GILL
  1990   Zooarchaeology at Pirincay, a Formative Period Site in Highland Ecuador. *Journal of Field Archaeology* 17: 49–68.

MORRIS, PERCY A.
  1966   *A Field Guide to Pacific Coast Shells* (2d ed.). Houghton Mifflin, Boston.

MURRA, JOHN V.
  1963   The Cayapa and Colorado. In *Handbook of South American Indians,* vol. 4: *The Circum-Caribbean Tribes* (J. H. Steward, ed.): 277–291. Cooper Square, New York.

  1975   *Formaciones económicas y políticas del mundo andino.* Instituto de Estudios Peruanos, Lima.

NELSON, JOSEPH S.
  1994   *Fishes of the World* (3rd ed.). Wiley, New York.

NORTON, PRESLEY
  1982   Preliminary Observations on Loma Alta, an Early Valdivia Midden in Guayas Province, Ecuador. In *Primer Simposio de Correlaciones Antropológicas Andino-Mesoamericano* (Jorge G. Marcos and Presley Norton, eds.): 101–119. Escuela Superior Politécnica del Litoral, Guayaquil.

NORTON, PRESLEY, RICHARD LUNNIS, AND NIGEL NAYLING
  1984   Excavaciones en Salango, provincia de Manabí, Ecuador. *Miscelánea Antropológica Ecuatoriana* 3: 1–80.

OLSSON, AXEL A.
  1961   *Mollusks of the Tropical Eastern Pacific.* Paleontological Research Institution, Ithaca, N.Y.

PAULSEN, ALLISON C.
1974   The Thorny Oyster and the Voice of God: *Spondylus* and *Strombus* in Andean Prehistory. *American Antiquity* 39: 597–607.

PORRAS, PEDRO
1973   *El Encanto—La Puná: Un sitio insular de la Fase Valdivia asociado a un conchero anular.* Quito.

REITZ, ELIZABETH J.
n.d.   Vertebrate Fauna from El Azúcar, Ecuador. Manuscript on file with the Museum of Natural History, University of Georgia, Athens, 1990.

ROBINS, C. RICHARD, REEVE M. BAILEY, CARL E. BOND, JAMES R. BROOKER, ERNEST A. LACHNER, ROBERT N. LEA, AND W. B. SCOTT
1980   *A List of Common and Scientific Names of Fishes from the United States and Canada* (4th ed.). Special Publication 12. American Fisheries Society. Bethesda, Md.

SÁNCHEZ MOSQUERA, AMELIA M.
n.d.   Patrones de pesca precolombinos de la costa central ecuatoriana. Tésis de grado, Centro de Estudios Arqueológicos y Antropológicos. Escuela Politécnica del Litoral, Guayaquil, 1992.
1996   Fauna vertebrada del sitio La Balsa, provincia del Guayas, Ecuador. *Boletín Arqueológico* 5: 72–92.
1997   *Ecuador aborigen.* Arqueólogos Asociados and Vicerrectorado de Asuntos Estudiantiles y Bienestar. Escuela Politécnica del Litoral, Guayaquil.

SOUTHGATE, DOUGLAS, AND MORRIS WHITAKER
1992   Promoting Resource Degradation in Latin America: Tropical Deforestation, Soil Erosion, and Coastal Ecosystem Disturbance in Ecuador. *Economic Development and Cultural Change* 40: 787–807.

SPATH, CARL DAVID
n.d.   The El Encanto Focus: A Post-Pleistocene Maritime Adaptation to Expanding Littoral Resources. Ph.D. dissertation, University of Illinois at Urbana–Champaign, 1980.

STAHL, PETER W.
1985   The Hallucinogenic Basis of Early Valdivia Phase Ceramic Bowl Iconography. *Journal of Psychoactive Drugs* 17: 105–123.
1988   Prehistoric Camelids in the Lowlands of Western Ecuador. *Journal of Archaeological Science* 15: 355–365.
1991   Arid Landscapes and Environmental Transformations in Ancient Southwestern Ecuador. *World Archaeology* 22: 346–359.
1992   Diversity, Body Size, and the Archaeological Recovery of Mammalian Fauna in the Neotropical Forests. *Journal of the Steward Anthropological Society* 20: 209–233.
1994   Qualitative Assessment of Archaeofaunal Taxa from the Jama Valley. In *Regional Archaeology in Northern Manabí, Ecuador,* vol. 1: *Environment, Cultural Chronology, and Prehistoric Subsistence in the Jama River Valley* (J. A. Zeidler and D. M. Pearsall, eds.): 185–199. Memoirs in Latin American Archaeology 8. University of Pittsburgh, Pittsburgh, Pa.
1995   Differential Preservation Histories Affecting the Mammalian Zooarchaeological Record from the Forested Neotropical Lowlands. In

Archaeology in the Lowland American Tropics: Current Analytical Methods and Recent Applications (Peter W. Stahl, ed.): 154–180. Cambridge University Press, Cambridge.

n.d.a   The Archaeofauna of Loma Alta, Ecuador. Manuscript on file with the Instituto Nacional de Patrimonio Cultural, Quito, 1985.

n.d.b   Encountering Paradise Lost: The Archaeological Recovery of Ancient Biodiversity in the Lowlands of Western Ecuador. Paper presented at the 91st Annual Meeting of the American Anthropological Association, San Francisco, December 1992.

n.d.c   La fauna no marina del sitio Salango, Manabí, Ecuador: Informe preliminar. Manuscript on file with the Instituto Nacional de Patrimonio Cultural, Quito, 1985.

n.d.d   Interpreting Ancient Mammalian Diversity from the Archaeofaunal Record in the Forested Lowlands of Western Ecuador. 13th Annual Northeast Conference on Andean Archaeology and Ethnohistory, Ithaca, N.Y., 1994.

n.d.e   Tropical Forest Cosmology: The Cultural Context of the Early Valdivia Occupations at Loma Alta. Ph.D. dissertation, University of Illinois at Urbana–Champaign, 1984.

STAHL, PETER W., AND PRESLEY NORTON

1987   Precolumbian Animal Domesticates from Salango, Ecuador. *American Antiquity* 52: 382–391.

STAHL, PETER W., AND J. A. ZEIDLER

1988   The Spatial Correspondence of Selected Bone Properties and Inferred Activity Areas in an Early Formative Dwelling Structure (S20) at Real Alto, Ecuador. In *Recent Studies in Pre-Columbian Archaeology* (N. J. Saunders and O. de Montmollin, eds.): 275–298. BAR International Series 421. British Archaeological Reports, Oxford.

1990   Differential Bone Refuse Accumulation in Food Preparation and Traffic Areas on an Early Ecuadorian House Floor. *Latin American Antiquity* 1: 150–169.

STALLER, JOHN E.

n.d.   Late Valdivia Occupation in Southern Coastal El Oro Province, Ecuador: Excavations at the Early Formative Period (3500–1500 B.C.), Site of La Emerenciana. Ph.D. dissertation, Southern Methodist University, Dallas, 1994.

STOTHERT, KAREN E.

1988   *La Prehistoria temprana de la peninsula de Santa Elena, Ecuador: Cultura Las Vegas.* Serie Monográfica 10, Miscelánea Antropológica Ecuatoriana, Guayaquil.

TURGEON, DONNA D., ARTHUR E. BOGAN, EUGENE V. COAN, WILLIAM K. EMERSON, WILLIAM G. LYONS, WILLIAM L. PRATT, CLYDE F. E. ROPER, AMELIE SCHELTEMA, FRED G. THOMPSON, AND JAMES D. WILLIAMS

1988   *Common and Scientific Names of Aquatic Invertebrates from the United States and Canada: Mollusks.* Special Publication 16. American Fisheries Society, Bethesda, Md.

VILLALBA, MARCELO

1988   *Cotocollao: Una aldea formativa del valle de Quito.* Serie Monográfica 2. Museos del Banco Central del Ecuador, Quito.

WING, ELIZABETH S.

1988   Dusicyon Sechurae, en contextos arqueológicos tempranos. In *La Prehistoria temprana de la peninsula de Santa Elena, Ecuador: Cultura Las Vegas* (Karen E. Stothert, ed.): 179–185. Serie Monográfica 10. Miscelánea Antropológica Ecuatoriana, Guayaquil.

n.d.   Prehistoric Subsistence Patterns of the Central Andes and Adjacent Coast and Spread in the Use of Domestic Animals. Manuscript submitted to the National Science Foundation, Washington, D.C., 1977.

ZEIDLER, JAMES A.

1988   Feline Imagery, Stone Mortars, and Formative Period Interaction Spheres in the Northern Andean Area. *Journal of Latin American Lore* 14: 243-283.

1991   Maritime Exchange in the Early Formative Period of Coastal Ecuador: Geopolitical Origins of Uneven Development. *Research in Economic Anthropology* 13: 247-268.

ZEIDLER, JAMES A., PETER STAHL, AND M. J. SUTLIFF

1998   Shamanistic Elements in a Terminal Valdivia Burial, Northern Manabí, Ecuador: Implications for Mortuary Symbolism and Social Ranking. In *Recent Advances in the Archaeology of the Northern Andes: In Memory of Gerardo Reichel-Dolmatoff* (Augusto Oyuela-Caycedo and J. Scott Raymond, eds.): 109–120. Institute of Archaeology, University of California, Los Angeles.

ZEVALLOS M., CARLOS, WALTON C. GALINAT, DONALD W. LATHRAP, EARL R. LENG, JORGE G. MARCOS, AND KATHLEEN M. KLUMPP

1977   The San Pablo Corn Kernel and Its Friends. *Science* 196: 385–389.

ZEVALLOS M., CARLOS, AND OLAF HOLM

1960   *Excavaciones aqueológicas en San Pablo. Informe preliminar.* Casa de la Cultura, Guayaquil.

Plant Food Resources of the Ecuadorian Formative: An Overview and Comparison to the Central Andes

DEBORAH M. PEARSALL

UNIVERSITY OF MISSOURI

ISSUES IN FORMATIVE PERIOD SUBSISTENCE

In my 1988 overview of subsistence in the Ecuadorian Formative, I concluded:

> The few data available to date suggest that the Formative of Ecuador was characterized by diversity in subsistence strategies, with maize playing a role even before the appearance of ceramics. (Pearsall 1988: 156)

Perhaps the best way to begin this effort at the same task is to ask what we have learned since then. The short answer is that I believe this conclusion still holds; maize *did* play a role in Formative period subsistence. Documenting the trajectory of subsistence change during the Formative still eludes us, however. While the database has grown steadily, it is still difficult to answer this question: Is Formative subsistence agriculturally based, and if so, on *what* crops? It also continues to be difficult to look beyond subsistence, to issues such as use of plants in ritual and medicine, the relationship of patterns of food production to gender and social status, or the roles played by plant commodities in trade.

Part of the difficulty is a simple lack of archaeological botanical data. For example, there is still only one set of data from the florescence of Valdivia (Real Alto Valdivia 3) and two limited datasets from Machalilla (La Ponga and Río Perdido). The greatest growth is in information on Chorrera; from the Jama River valley, Manabí province, come four new datasets on Tabuchila phase subsistence. New data from the La Chimba site in the northern Andes greatly enhance the understanding of subsistence during the Middle Formative. But limited data from Esmeraldas only hint at subsistence during the Formative in this important region.

Another difficulty for understanding the nature of Formative period subsistence is more fundamental and has to do with the nature of the paleoethnobotanical record. I have written elsewhere on the problems of "doing" paleoethnobotany in the lowland tropics (Pearsall 1995a) and hence do not discuss methodology in depth here. There are two methodological issues that must be considered, however. First, botanical remains that are charred and become part of the archaeological record can be lost from that record over time. Fig. 1, from the Finca Cueva site (M3D2-009), for example, shows a fairly typical curve for wood recovery per flotation sample from sites in the Jama valley. The graph represents some 3,000 years of occupation at this village site, from Terminal Valdivia (Piquigua) through Muchique 3 (Evan Engwall, personal communication, 1996). Artifact densities indicate that the site was intensely occupied during Muchique 2 and 3 (surface through 120 cm in this test pit), with a much lighter occupation for Muchique 1, Tabuchila, and Piquigua (120–240 cm). Although artifact densities are high through 120 cm below the surface, there is a decline in wood charcoal density beginning at 40 cm below surface. This drop-off in charred material in a part of the sequence with dense occupational debris suggests that charred plant remains have been subject to postdepositional destruction. Since quantitative comparisons of macroremain assemblages require equal conditions of preservation and recovery (Pearsall 2000), such patterned loss of data means that assemblages should not be compared quantitatively. Measures such as percentage presence or ratios may give false indications of subsistence change if substantial material has been lost from the older datasets. Stahl (1995; this volume) illustrates these points convincingly for the Formative faunal assemblage. The second point is that phytolith preservation is not subject to the same patterned loss. There are abundant, well-preserved phytoliths throughout the Finca Cueva sequence. This example is typical of the Jama project phytolith database.

It is important to assess the robustness of the botanical database before drawing comparisons among sites or site components. For example, I argue that demonstrating similar preservation conditions is essential before applying quantitative measures, such as ubiquity of plants by site or richness of cultivated taxa (numbers of crops present), to charred macroremain data from Formative sites. I have examined some of the Jama data in this light (see Fig. 1 for Finca Cueva), and hold that quantitative comparisons are only possible within the post-Formative Muchique phases (Pearsall 1996). The quantities of charred materials preserved in Terminal Valdivia (Piquigua) and Chorrera (Tabuchila) phase samples

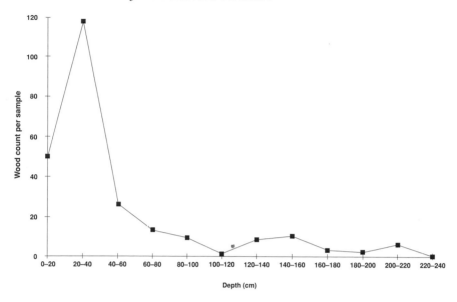

Fig. 1 Decline of charred wood with depth, Finca Cueva site (M3D2-009), Jama valley.

in the Jama valley indicate that most are not directly comparable to the Muchique dataset. While I have not examined the Real Alto and Loma Alta data from this perspective, the overall low quantities of charred materials recovered from these early Formative village sites suggest that these charred data cannot be compared quantitatively in any meaningful way with later samples.

For "economic" plants that produce diagnostic phytoliths (e.g., maize, bean, palm, sedge, arrowroot, *achira*, squash, and gourd), phytoliths often provide a more reliable indicator of the presence of a plant in the record than do charred macroremains. (Table 1 contains a list of the common and scientific names of plants discussed in text.) This is certainly the case if preservation of charred materials is poor, or if older flotation technology was used. I rely on the phytolith record to fill these gaps whenever possible. Not all sites have been sampled for phytoliths, however, and phytolith studies from the 1970s through the early 1980s should be revisited to search for new diagnostics (i.e., squash/gourd, bean, arrowroot, *llerén*). I have done this for only a small number of samples from Loma Alta and Real Alto.

I list plant resources used by Formative peoples in Table 2, which presents macroremain and phytolith data by site. The antiquity of the appearance of various resources can be assessed cautiously from this table. For macroremain datasets for which preservation and recovery is especially good, for example at the La Chimba site, percentage presence (ubiquity) of various foods provides some indication of the relative importance of different resources.

The data presented below illustrate that a rich array of wild, tended, and domesticated plant food resources was used by Formative peoples on the coast

Table 1
Glossary of Plants Referred to in Text

Name		
Common	Scientific	Botanical family
achira	*Canna edulis*	Cannaceae
amaranth	*Amaranthus* spp.	Amaranthaceae
arrowroot	*Maranta* spp.	Marantaceae
avocado	*Persea americana*	Lauraceae
bean, common bean	*Phaseolus vulgaris*	Fabaceae
bedstraw	*Galium* spp.	Rubiaceae
begonia	*Begonia geraniifolia*	Begoniaceae
bottle gourd	*Lagenaria siceraria*	Cucurbitaceae
chenopod	*Chenopodium* spp.	Chenopodiaceae
chili, *aji*	*Capsicum* spp.	Solanaceae
ciruela de fraile	*Bunchosia armeniaca*	Malpighiaceae
cotton	*Gossypium barbadense*	Malvaceae
grass (wild)		Poaceae
guava	*Psidium guajava*	Myrtaceae
hackberry	*Celtis* spp.	Ulmaceae
jack bean	*Canavalia* spp.	Fabaceae
jicama	*Pachyrrhizus* spp.	Fabaceae
llerén	*Calathea* spp.	Marantaceae
lima bean	*Phaseolus lunatus*	Fabaceae
lucuma	*Pouteria lucuma*	Sapotaceae
lupine	*Lupinus* spp.	Fabaceae
maize, corn	*Zea mays*	Poaceae
manioc, *yuca*	*Manihot esculenta*	Euphorbiaceae
oca	*Oxalis tuberosa*	Oxalidaceae
pacae	*Inga feuillei*	Fabaceae
palm		Arecaceae
peanut, *maní*	*Arachis hypogaea*	Fabaceae
potato	*Solanum tuberosum*	Solanaceae
quinoa	*Chenopodium quinoa*	Chenopodiaceae
sedge	*Cyperus* or *Scirpus*	Cyperaceae
soursop, *cherimoya, guanábana*	*Annona* spp.	Annonaceae
squash	*Cucurbita* spp.	Cucurbitaceae
squash/gourd		Cucurbitaceae
sweet potato	*Ipomoea batatas*	Convolvulaceae
tree legume	*Acacia, Prosopis,* or similar	Fabaceae
ullucu	*Ullucus tuberosus*	Basellaceae

and in the sierra of Ecuador. The Ecuadorian Amazon remains the least known region. Annual seed crops like maize, jack bean, common bean, and lupine were used in combination with wild or tended tree fruits such as palm, soursop, hackberry, and legume and Sapotaceae trees, among others. Use of root and tuber resources, including sedge, *achira, arrowroot,* potato, and *oca,* is documented. Cotton and gourd or squash were used. The introduced Mesoamerican grain—maize—was integrated into coastal and Andean subsistence systems that each included local domesticates (cotton, jack bean, squash, arrowroot, and *achira* on the coast; common bean, potato, *oca,* and lupine in the sierra). The record is silent on several important crops, including manioc. Many fragmented charred remains can be identified only as root/tuber or as fragments of the cotyledons or endosperm tissue of seeds.

Comparing Ecuadorian Formative plant remains to those from coastal Peru, where excellent preservation of dried macroremains has resulted in an especially rich database for examining the timing of plant cultivation and agriculture, suggests that agriculturally based societies emerged earlier in coastal Ecuador than in Peru and that maize was introduced earlier and became important earlier in Ecuador. As I illustrate below, however, there were many similarities in plant use during the Ecuadorian Valdivia period (early Formative, 3500–1500 B.C.)[1] and the Peruvian Cotton Preceramic (2600/2200–1800/1500 B.C.; these dates vary by region; see Table 3). Both were periods when a variety of domesticated and wild plants were used and no single domesticate dominated. In coastal Ecuador, site location, among other factors, suggests that a shift to agriculturally based economies was underway at this time, while to the south in Peru, settlements were oriented to maximize access to maritime resources. In Peru, the types of plants used stayed much the same through the Initial period (2000/1500–1100/800 B.C.), but a shift in site locations to riverine settings signaled the increasing importance of agriculture. In Ecuador during this time period (Machalilla and Chorrera on the coast, Middle Formative in the sierra), there are clear indications that subsistence *was* agriculturally based.

ECUADORIAN FORMATIVE BOTANICAL DATABASE

Table 2 presents the tally of remains at 27 sites or site components and two lake core records chronologically, and by region (Guayas and Manabí coasts, Esmeraldas, the Andes, and the Amazon) (Fig. 2).

---

[1] All radiocarbon dates are uncorrected unless otherwise indicated.

Table 2

Botanical Database for the Ecuadorian Formative

Site	Culture/phase	Sample (yr/type)	N	Dense	Porous	Rind
		Coast				
Loma Alta	Valdivia 1, 2	1980/CS	20			
		1982/CS	27			
		1982/Fl	172			
Real Alto	Valdivia 1, 2	1974–75/Fl	14	❖	❖	❖
		1984/CS	35			
		1986/CS	80		❖	
		1974–75/Ph	4			
	Valdivia 3	1974–75/Fl	24	❖	❖	❖
		1974–75/Ph	71			
	Valdivia 4, 5, 6, 7	1974–75/Fl	13	❖	❖	❖
		1974–75/Ph	13			
Río Perdido	Machalilla	1974–75/Fl	3	❖	❖	❖
		1974–75/Ph	7			
La Ponga	Machalilla	Fl	15			
Anllulla	Valdivia D	CS				
San Isidro	Valdivia/Piquigua	1988/Ph	6			
		1988/Fl				
	Chorrera/Tabuchila	1988–89/Ph	21			
		1988–89/Fl	21			
Capaperro	Valdivia/Piquigua	1989–90/Fl	10			
Dos Caminos	Chorrera/Tabuchila	1994/Fl	22			
Finca Cueva	Chorrera/Tabuchila	1991/Fl	3			
		1991/Ph	2			
El Mocorral	Chorrera/Tabuchila	1991/Fl	9			
		1991/Ph	9			
Perdomo	Selva Alegre	Ph	1			
	Guadual	Ph	7			
Herradura	Herradura	Ph	4			
Selve Alegre	Selva Alegre	Ph	1			
	Guadual	Ph	5			
R30	Selva Alegre	Ph	1			
	Las Cruces	Ph	3			
C69	Mafa	Ph	1			
	Guadual	Ph	1			
		Andes				
Cotocollao	Formative	CS	22			
		Ph	35			
Nueva Era	Formative	1980, 82–83 CS	26	❖	❖	
		1980, 82–83 Fl	90			
La Chimba	Formative/Early	1989 Fl	13			❖
	Formative/Middle	1989 Fl	21			❖
	Formative/Late	1989 Fl	4			❖

218

	Arboreal							Root/tuber	
Tree fruit rind, pit fragment	Tree legume	Palm	cf. Sapotaceae	Annona	cf. Celtis	Dense cotyledon		Sedge	Canna
				Coast					
❖		❖	❖	❖		❖			
❖					❖	❖		❖	
❖						❖			
❖									
❖								❖	
❖						❖			
❖									❖
❖	❖								❖
									❖
❖									
		❖						❖	❖
		❖						❖	❖
❖						❖			
❖						❖			
❖									
		❖						❖	❖
❖		❖						❖	❖
		❖						❖	❖
		❖						❖	
		❖							
		❖							❖
		❖						❖	❖
		❖						❖	
		❖						❖	❖
		❖							
		❖						❖	
				Andes					
❖						❖			
❖						❖		❖	
❖									

(cont.)

Table 2 (*cont.*)
Botanical Database for the Ecuadorian Formative

Site	Culture/phase	Sample (yr/type)	N	Root/tuber (cont.)			
				Arrowroot	Potato	Oca	Root/tuber
		Coast					
Loma Alta	Valdivia 1, 2	1980/CS	20				❖
		1982/CS	27				
		1982/Fl	172				❖
Real Alto	Valdivia 1, 2	1974–75/Fl	14				
		1984/CS	35				
		1986/CS	80				❖
		1974–75/Ph	4				
	Valdivia 3	1974–75/Fl	24				
		1974–75/Ph	71				
	Valdivia 4, 5, 6, 7	1974–75/Fl	13				
		1974–75/Ph	13				
Río Perdido	Machalilla	1974–75/Fl	3				
		1974–75/Ph	7				
La Ponga	Machalilla	Fl	15				
Anllulla	Valdivia D	CS					❖
San Isidro	Valdivia/Piquigua	1988/Ph	6	❖			
		1988/Fl					
	Chorrera/Tabuchila	1988–89/Ph	21	❖			
		1988–89/Fl	21				
Capaperro	Valdivia/Piquigua	1989–90/Fl	10				
Dos Caminos	Chorrera/Tabuchila	1994/Fl	22				
Finca Cueva	Chorrera/Tabuchila	1991/Fl	3				
		1991/Ph	2	❖			
El Mocorral	Chorrera/Tabuchila	1991/Fl	9				
		1991/Ph	9	❖			
Perdomo	Selva Alegre	Ph	1	❖			
	Guadual	Ph	7	❖			
Herradura	Herradura	Ph	4				
Selve Alegre	Selva Alegre	Ph	1				
	Guadual	Ph	5	❖			
R30	Selva Alegre	Ph	1				
	Las Cruces	Ph	3				
C69	Mafa	Ph	1				
	Guadual	Ph	1				
		Andes					
Cotocollao	Formative	CS	22				
		Ph	35				
Nueva Era	Formative	1980, 82–83 CS	26				❖
		1980, 82–83 Fl	90				❖
La Chimba	Formative/Early	1989 Fl	13		❖		❖
	Formative/Middle	1989 Fl	21		❖	❖	❖
	Formative/Late	1989 Fl	4		❖		❖

Notes: CS = carbon sample (collected in situ or in excavation screen); Fl = flotation sample; Ph = phytolith sample; N = number of samples analyzed, except for Real Alto 1974-1975: these are numbers of provenances analyzed; ❖ = present.

Root/tuber		Nonarboreal							
Dicot	Monocot	Maize	Jack bean	Common bean	Lupine	Squash/Gourd	Gourd	Cotton	Porous endosperm
					Coast				
	❖	❖	❖						
			❖						
	❖	❖	❖						❖
			❖						
			❖						
			❖					❖	
		❖							
			❖						
		❖	❖						
		❖							
		❖							
		❖							
		❖				❖			
							❖		
		❖				❖			
		❖							
		❖		❖					❖
									❖
		❖							❖
		❖							
		❖							
		❖							
		❖							
		❖							
		❖							
		❖							
					Andes				
❖	❖	❖			❖				
		❖							
❖		❖							
		❖						❖	
		❖						❖	
		❖						❖	

221

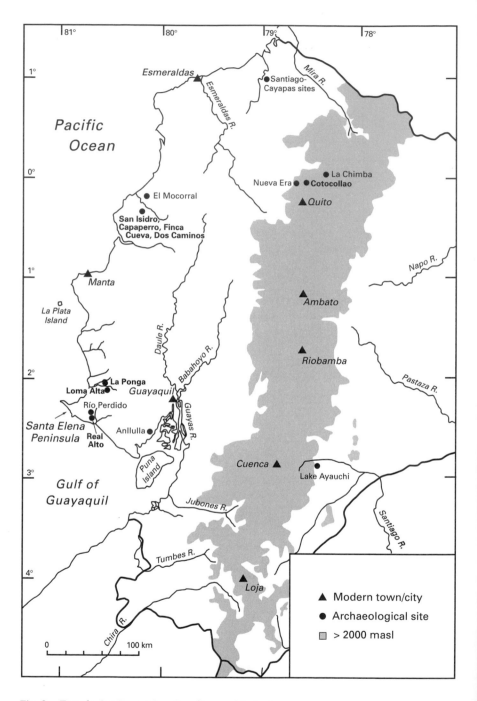

Fig. 2   Ecuadorian Formative sites discussed in text.

Coast: Valdivia 1 and 2

Loma Alta. Raymond and colleagues excavated Valdivia 1 and 2 deposits at the Loma Alta site in 1980 and 1982 as part of a survey and site-testing program in the Valdivia River valley, southern Manabí province. Loma Alta is located on a relict Pleistocene river terrace 12 km from the coast. Occupied beginning at 5000 BP, it is the largest of the Valdivia 1 and 2 sites in the valley (Raymond 1988). In situ material (carbon samples) from the 1980 excavation and both in situ and flotation-recovered materials from the 1982 excavation form the database discussed here. Raymond et al. processed and sorted 172 flotation samples. All charred remains submitted to me for identification were from the Valdivia sector of the site. In addition to analyzing these materials, I tested eight phytolith samples. The final report on the botanical materials is in preparation; I reexamined all remains for this essay.

Overall, few food remains were present in flotation samples. For example, fewer than 20 percent of the samples contained sturdy cotyledon fragments, the most durable type of food remain recovered. Many samples contained nothing but a few pieces of wood. The poor recovery is likely the result of the age of the site, the flotation technology employed (a manual flotation device constructed with window screen), and the small volume of soil processed per sample (Pearsall 1995a). Flotation did enhance recovery of some interesting materials, however, such as very "glossy" monocot root material, which was much more common in flotation than carbon samples. Other root material was also better represented in the flotation samples, and most maize kernels were recovered by flotation. Overall, in spite of the poor preservation, flotation did enhance the recovery of food remains.

Identifiable fragments of fruits from the Sapotaceae and palm families were recovered in situ at the site. This suggests that these families were among those contributing the fragmentary tree fruit and dense cotyledon remains observed in flotation samples. One almost entire sedge root was also recovered from the carbon samples. The glossy monocot root does not appear to be sedge; perhaps it is a more sugary root.

Maize kernel fragments were recovered from six different contexts at the site.[2] Jack bean is somewhat more abundant than maize. Not all the robust cotyledon fragments in the Loma Alta samples are jack bean, however. Kaplan examined some of these fragments following his study of Real Alto jack beans (Damp, Pearsall, and Kaplan 1981) and determined that their cell structure differed from that of jack bean (Lawrence Kaplan, personal communication,

---

[2]   Accelerator mass spectrometry (AMS) dates on the Loma Alta maize kernels do not support an early Formative date for the charred maize remains.

1986). Lacking attachment areas, these fragments remain difficult to identify; they are tallied as dense cotyledon in Table 2. Size suggests they may be fragments of tree fruits.

I extracted phytoliths from eight Loma Alta samples both to evaluate the presence of maize and to determine what other plants were utilized at the site. Maize phytoliths occurred in two samples. Palm, arrowroot, *achira*, and squash or gourd phytoliths were also present. Because of high soil pH, phytoliths were not well preserved, however.

Real Alto. Lathrap and associates excavated at Real Alto on the Río Verde in the Chanduy region of southwestern Guayas province between 1974 and 1975 (Lathrap, Marcos, and Zeidler 1977). Chronologically the first site in Ecuador on which systematic botanical recovery techniques were employed, these Real Alto excavations yielded more than 900 flotation samples spanning Valdivia 1 through 7. Phytolith samples were also systematically collected. During early Valdivia times, Real Alto was a small village (ca. 1 hectare in Valdivia 1; 2.25 hectares in Valdivia 2), located in the northwestern sector of the larger Valdivia 3 village. The beginning of the ceremonial precinct dates to Valdivia 2 (Zeidler 1991). Following Zeidler (1991), the Valdivia sequence is dated as follows: Valdivia 1 and 2 (early), 4500 to 2900 B.C.; Valdivia 3, 2900 to 2600 B.C.; Valdivia 4 through 7 (my grouping), 2600 to 2100 B.C.; Valdivia 8, 2100 to 2000 B.C., with all dates calibrated.

I analyzed a sample of the Lathrap et al. flotation and phytolith samples from contexts that could be assigned to a phase on the basis of associated ceramics. The flotation method I used—a manual system with window screen bucket, small (7-liter) samples—did not result in good recovery. Charred remains from 14 provenances (provenance, rather than sample, is the unit of analysis) dating to Valdivia 1 and 2 are in Table 2; phytolith data are from four samples. For a more detailed presentation of these results, see Pearsall (1979) and Pearsall and Piperno (1990).

Excavations conducted by Damp in the early Valdivia village at Real Alto in 1977, 1984, and 1986 resulted in recovery of additional food remains. Specifically, botanical materials were excavated in situ in 1984 from 35 contexts and recovered by fine sieving in 1986 from 80 contexts. Damp and Pearsall (1994) discuss cotton remains recovered from these excavations. Damp (1984, 1988) dates the excavated contexts at 3500 to 3000 B.C. by association.

I could not separate the charred botanical remains in the 1974 through 1975 flotation samples precisely by plant part or type. The "dense" class includes both fragments of tree fruit rinds and meats and small fragments of jack beans.

The "porous" class is a mixture of seed endosperm fragments and root/tuber fragments. Rind includes both fragments of woody tree fruits and robust seed coats (Pearsall 1979). While not directly comparable to materials analyzed later, these remains indicate that a variety of foods in addition to jack bean were used at the site during the early Valdivia period. The 1984 and 1986 materials flesh out the picture, adding sedge and cotton to the assemblage, and indicating that tree fruits were fairly common.

There is a striking difference in recovery of cotton between the 1984 and 1986 samples (see Table 2). There is no cotton in the 1984 samples and cotton in half the 1986 samples. This is a good illustration of recovery bias and why it is impossible to discuss the Formative database quantitatively. Cotton seeds are so small as to be difficult to spot during excavation but were recovered in the fine sieves used in 1986 by Damp. No recognizable cotton seeds came out of the 1974 and 1975 flotation samples because the fragile seeds were probably broken during flotation. Damp (personal communication, 1987) experimented with recovery techniques during the later excavations and observed this phenomenon. This led to his decision to employ fine sieving rather than flotation. Lee Newsom (personal communication, 1995) has also suggested that if charred remains are dry most of the time, as in the more arid areas of the Caribbean where she has worked, wetting during flotation may lead to increased breakage. Cotton was a commonly used plant at the early Valdivia village at Real Alto; whether it was domesticated or wild cannot be determined from the remains.

Large cross-shaped phytoliths were recovered from three of four samples I analyzed from early Valdivia contexts; these were identified on the basis of size as likely to have come from maize (Pearsall 1979). No *achira* phytoliths were observed. Reanalysis of these four samples by using size and cross variant to identify maize and a discriminant function to separate maize and wild grasses confirmed that maize was present in one Valdivia 2 sample and was likely in one Valdivia 1 sample. Crosses from the other two samples were reclassified as wild grass (Pearsall and Piperno 1990). Rescanning also led to the identification of *achira* in both Valdivia 1 and 2 samples, Cucurbitaceae in a Valdivia 1 sample, and arrowroot in a Valdivia 2 sample. While recovery technique is the primary factor contributing to the lack of charred maize remains in Real Alto flotation samples, it is also likely that maize was uncommon in early Valdivia times and that several types of tree fruits, root/tuber foods, wild and cultivated legumes, and wild/weedy annuals contributed substantially to the plant portion of diet (Pearsall 1979).

Coast: Valdivia 3

Real Alto. I analyzed flotation samples from 24 Valdivia 3 provenances excavated in 1974 through 1975 (incorporating numerous individual samples). The recovery and identification biases discussed above apply to this dataset as well. I also processed and scanned 71 Valdivia 3 phytolith samples during my dissertation research. Recently I reanalyzed 14 of these samples from six different Valdivia 3 house floors by using an improved processing procedure (Zhao and Pearsall 1998), and by applying a new discriminant function for separating maize and wild grasses (Pearsall, Piperno, and Benfer n.d.). The Valdivia 3 village at Real Alto was a large (12.4 hectares), elliptical settlement with a central ceremonial precinct. This is the period of maximum village size and residential population (Marcos n.d.; Zeidler 1991).

Botanical data recovered from Valdivia 3 contexts were similar in many ways to those from the early Valdivia village. The mixed categories of charred remains described above were present in many flotation samples, suggesting that a mixed subsistence strategy continued. Maize, *achira*, and Cucurbitaceae phytoliths were identified. Charred jack beans were recovered. Since no follow-up data are available in Valdivia 3 areas of the site, presence of cotton or specific tree fruits cannot be confirmed.

To evaluate how common maize was at the Valdivia 3 village, I reanalyzed 14 phytolith samples from six different house floors. If maize was commonly used at the site, I reasoned that evidence for it should appear routinely in the compacted refuse that made up house floors. In other words, percentage presence (ubiquity) should be high. The details of this study are presented in Pearsall (2000); to summarize, I identified maize in 79 percent of the individual samples with the multiple indicator method described in Pearsall (2000), and in 86 percent of samples by using the discriminant function (Pearsall et al. n.d.). Maize was present in all the houses.

Coast: Valdivia 4 through 7

Real Alto. Flotation samples from 13 Valdivia 4 through 7 provenances excavated in 1974 through 1975 have been studied. The recovery and identification biases discussed above apply to this dataset. I also analyzed 13 Valdivia 4 through 7 phytolith samples. Real Alto population and site size declined during this period (late Middle and Late Valdivia), with the population moving to satellite settlements. The site remained a ceremonial center, however. I consider Phases 4 through 7 together because there are relatively few samples from the post-Valdivia 3 occupations at the site. Real Alto was abandoned after Valdivia 7.

Maize phytoliths occur in many contexts, *achira* in a few. All categories of charred food remains are well represented, including jack bean. Overall, preservation of charred materials appears better in the Valdivia 4 through 7 samples, perhaps because strata are younger and less deeply buried.

Coast: Terminal Valdivia

San Isidro. Zeidler and Pearsall and colleagues have worked at the San Isidro site (M3D2-001) in the middle Jama River valley, northern Manabí province since 1982. From 1988 through 1991, we carried out a valleywide survey and site testing program; results of the early stages of this research are published in Zeidler and Pearsall (1994). Final analyses by Zeidler of survey and excavation data are nearing completion (Pearsall n.d.c). San Isidro is a regional ceremonial center some 25 km inland on a major left bank tributary of the Jama. The site, which lies beneath the modern town of San Isidro, is 40 hectares, with stratified archaeological and natural deposits ranging between 3 and 6 m deep. Occupation at the site began during Valdivia 8 (Piquigua phase, 2030–1880 B.C.) and continued through the Chorrera (Tabuchila phase, 1300–750 B.C.) and Jama–Coaque I and II (Muchique phases 1–5) periods. In broad terms, the modal calibrated date ranges given above, which are from Zeidler, Buck, and Litton (1998), may be applied to all Formative sites or site components from the Jama valley (i.e., San Isidro, Capaperro, Finca Cueva, Dos Caminos, and El Mocorral).

Because Piquigua deposits were deeply buried, and areas available for excavation restricted, Zeidler and colleagues were able to expose relatively few contexts dating to this period during test excavations at San Isidro. Those that were available were at the bottom of deep test pits; little horizontal exposure was possible in the Piquigua or Tabuchila occupations of San Isidro. Flotation was carried out with an Illinois Department of Transportation-style device, made with 0.5-mm wire cloth (Pearsall 2000). We increased soil volumes from 10 to 30 or more liters during the course of the project in an attempt to improve poor recovery. Phytolith samples were taken from all contexts. Few charred materials are present in Formative samples, probably because of the depth of the deposits, the claylike nature of the soil, and choice of flotation system. For additional information on subsistence results to date, see Pearsall (1994b,c, 1996) and Pearsall and Stahl (n.d.).

The full array of food plants identified in sites in the Jama valley were present beginning with the Piquigua occupation of San Isidro. Maize, arrowroot, *achira*, squash or gourd, palm, and sedge are identified in the phytolith samples (maize in four of six samples tested); charred gourd rind was also recovered. No charred maize remains have been recovered to date in Terminal Valdivia contexts at San Isidro.

Capaperro. The Capaperro site (M3D2-065) is adjacent to San Isidro and was excavated in 1989 and 1990 as part of the Jama Valley Project. Flotation samples come from 10 Piquigua contexts. Few charred materials were present, and recovery of food remains was poor, being limited to tree fruit and dense cotyledon fragments and small pieces of porous endosperm tissue. Analysis of phytolith samples is in progress.[3]

Anllulla. The Anllulla shell mound, located on a small *estero* leading into the Estero Salado south of Guayaquil, was tested by Lubensky in 1973. This multiple component site has a thick Valdivia occupation (from 140 to 280 cm in the test pit) that was characterized throughout by Valdivia D or Terminal Valdivia ceramics (Earl Lubensky, personal communication, 1995). A ^{14}C date of 3560 BP, uncorrected, at 180 cm below surface is consistent with the dating on the basis of associated ceramics. Lubensky collected charred material during excavation; analysis is in progress. I have identified maize kernels at a depth of 210 and 220 cm below surface. Root/tuber material occurred at 220 cm and below; tree fruit fragments occurred at 320 cm.

Coast: Machalilla

Río Perdido. Lippi carried out test excavations at Río Perdido (OGCh-20) in 1975 in conjunction with the Real Alto project (Lippi n.d.). This small site, located less than 1 km east and north of the ceremonial precinct of Real Alto, provides a limited Machalilla sample for the Chanduy region. The site is not dated but can be placed by association in the 1200 to 800 b.c. time range proposed by Lippi (n.d.; Lippi, Bird, and Stemper 1984) for Machalilla. It is one of some 26 Machalilla hamlets (average size 0.46 hectare) recorded by Zeidler (1986) during a pedestrian survey in the valley.

Given the small number of provenances analyzed (three for charred materials and seven for phytoliths), it is difficult to conclude anything except that maize continued to be used, as was *achira*, and dense, porous, and rind materials occurred. I identified no jack bean remains.

La Ponga. La Ponga is 15 km from the coast in the Valdivia River valley in southern Manabí province. Lippi excavated in the Machalilla areas of the site in

---

[3] Analyses of all botanical datasets from the Jama project have been completed. Post-Formative materials will be published in Pearsall (n.d.c). Formative materials are in lab report form. Results from research completed in 2000 and 2001 could not be added to this essay.

1978. The site is dated by association to 1200 through 800 B.C. (Lippi n.d.; Lippi et al. 1984). Only the analysis of maize remains has been reported (Lippi et al. 1984; Stemper n.d.). Maize was recovered in all flotation samples, including those associated with the earliest Machalilla strata at the site. Two varieties of small-kerneled maize may have been present.

Coast: Chorrera

San Isidro. The Chorrera (Tabuchila phase) occupation at San Isidro in the Jama River valley, northern Manabí province, follows a hiatus in occupation after Piquigua (for details on the sequence, see Zeidler and Sutliff [1994] and Zeidler et al. [1998]). Tabuchila is capped by the Tephra II volcanic ashfall event (see Zeidler and Isaacson, this volume). To date we have analyzed 21 phytolith samples from two long profiles pertaining to the Tabuchila occupation of the site. Maize phytoliths were present in 15 of the samples tested. Charred maize kernels were recovered from three of the same contexts, including one feature with a ^{14}C date of 2845 BP (Pearsall 1994b). Phytoliths from *achira*, arrowroot, squash or gourd, palm, and sedge have also been identified (Pearsall 1994c).

Finca Cueva. Finca Cueva (M3D2-009) is a multi-component site located adjacent to San Isidro. Engwall tested the site in 1991 as part of the Jama Valley Project, and conducted further excavations there in 1994. I discuss only the 1991 data here, since analysis of the 1994 samples is in progress. Tabuchila phase deposits occur from 180 to 240 cm in the test excavation (Evan Engwall, personal communication, 1995). Two phytolith samples have been analyzed; the same two contexts, plus one additional sample, were floated. Maize, *achira*, arrowroot, palm, and sedge phytoliths were recovered from the samples. Recovery of charred materials was poor; only tree fruit rind and porous endosperm fragments were present.

Dos Caminos. Dos Caminos (M3D2-008) is a large, multi-component site located on the Río Congrejo alluvium 500 m from San Isidro. Engwall tested the site in 1994. I have analyzed 22 Tabuchila phase flotation samples from the site (one or two samples from Tabuchila strata in 11 test pits). Soil volume averaged 30 liters per sample. Phytolith analysis is in progress.

This is perhaps the best macroremain sample to date for Chorrera. With flotation of large quantities of soil, more material was recovered than at other sites of this age, but still much less than 1 g per sample. Charred maize remains occurred in 18 samples. Tree fruits of various kinds and common bean were also present. No charred root/tuber remains were recovered, however.

El Mocorral. El Mocorral (M3B4-031) is a multi-component site located during the Jama Valley Project survey in the Narrows, a stretch of the river with rugged topography and no active alluvium. El Mocorral is the only nonalluvial site excavated during the project. It was tested by Engwall in 1991. Nine Tabuchila phase contexts were sampled for flotation and phytolith analysis. Maize occurred in both phytolith and flotation samples, but charred materials were not abundant. I also identified arrowroot, *achira*, palm, and sedge phytoliths in samples.

Coastal Esmeraldas

Archaeological survey and excavation in the Cayapas and Santiago river drainages of Esmeraldas province by DeBoer, Tolstoy, and colleagues have resulted in identification of numerous sites and the establishment of a regional chronology of some 2,500 to 3,000 years (DeBoer 1996; Tolstoy n.d.; Tolstoy and DeBoer 1989). The results of phytolith analysis from five sites are available in Pearsall (1993) and Pearsall and DeBoer (1996).

All sites show the background phytolith assemblages typical of moist, lowland, tropical forest vegetation. Maize phytoliths occurred at all sites, but not always at the earliest levels. At the post-Formative Selva Alegre site, for example, maize occurred in three of four Guadual phase strata dated to ca. A.D. 250, but not in the single older Selva Alegre phase sample. A Selva Alegre phase sample from site R30 documented maize, however. Maize occurred in a single sample of the Mafa phase, dated at ca. 1000 to 500 B.C., at site C69. Evidence for presence of *achira*, arrowroot, palm, and sedge is good at most of the sites.

Sierra

La Chimba. As part of ongoing research into the prehistory of northern highland Ecuador between the Guayllabamba and Chota river valleys (northern half of Pichincha and all of Imbabura province in the highlands), in 1989 Athens excavated at La Chimba (Pi-1), a multi-component site located at 3,180 m. The site was continuously occupied from 2640 BP to 1700 BP. Three periods are represented at the site, Middle Formative (2640–2390 BP), Late Formative (2390–1910 BP), and post-Formative (1910–1700 BP) (Athens 1990; personal communication, 1995).[4]

In situ charred botanical materials (carbon samples) and flotation-recovered remains are available for each period from undisturbed deposits. Preservation

---

[4] Athens refers to these ceramic periods as Early Ceramic (2640–3390 BP), Middle Ceramic (2390–1910 BP), and Late Ceramic (1910–1700 BP).

was excellent—the best of any Formative site I have analyzed. Large pieces of charred tubers and maize cob fragments were common in samples. Both maize and potato were ubiquitous in strata dating to the Middle Formative. Maize and potato both occurred down to the lowest level of the site (Level 28), which dates to 2640 BP. Cotton was somewhat less common but occurred down to Level 23, which dates to 2565 BP. Root/tuber fragments (probably more potato, with perhaps some other Andean tubers) were nearly ubiquitous at the site. The pattern of food remains was similar in Late Formative strata, in which an identifiable *oca* tuber also occurred, and in post-Formative deposits.

A variety of small seeds from wild/weedy annuals, including wild legume, sedge, bedstraw, lupine, Malvaceae, chenopod, amaranth, and several grasses occurred throughout the La Chimba sequence. Carbon samples contained many of the same plant taxa as the flotation samples, with the addition of common bean in a Late Formative period sample. Small seed and carbon sample data are not presented in detail here since analysis is ongoing.

The La Chimba botanical data suggest that subsistence was quite stable over the 1,000 years of site occupation and that root crop and maize agriculture was supplemented by use of wild, gathered resources. The antiquity of this subsistence system is likely to be considerably earlier than the 2640 BP date for the beginning of occupation at La Chimba. Coring in Lake San Pablo has revealed maize pollen and charcoal particles from maize at the base of a short core dated to 4000 BP (Athens 1990).

Nueva Era. The Nueva Era site is at 1,500 m in the *montaña* region of the western slopes of the western *cordillera* in Pichincha province in the northern Ecuadorian Andes. Isaacson excavated at the site during 1980 and between 1982 and 1983. Nueva Era is a stratified site with an upper Late Prehistoric–Protohistoric occupation and a lower Middle to Late Formative occupation. The latter dates from 1100 B.C. to 500 B.C. (Isaacson 1987). Formative levels were capped by over 2 m of sterile volcanic ash, representing a series of violent eruptions (see Zeidler and Isaacson this volume). I examined 26 samples of in situ charred remains and 90 flotation samples from the Formative occupation at the site. The Formative deposits were excavated in five levels. Details on the botanical analysis are in Pearsall (n.d.a).

Root/tuber remains were relatively common at the site, with large seeds (tree fruits and other robust taxa) and maize also present. Carbon samples documented that at least two types of root/tubers were present, an unidentified dicot tap root and sedge roots. Maize kernels were small, identical in size range to smaller examples of kernels from the coastal La Ponga site (Lippi et al. 1984;

Stemper n.d.), and virtually identical to maize from Formative deposits at Cotocollao in the Quito basin. Cupules were relatively deep and triangular. These kernel and cupule characteristics are consistent with a primitive popcorn race. Maize cupules, kernels, and a cob fragment were recovered from a hearth (Hearth 1, Level 3) dated by ^{14}C to 670 B.C. (Isaacson 1987). A second hearth, dated to 760 B.C., also contained kernel and cupule remains. While most of the maize recovered from carbon samples was contemporaneous with these finds, I also identified charred maize in one carbon sample from the lowest level (Level 5) of the site, although not in direct association with the earliest date (1120 B.C.).

Cotocollao. Cotocollao is in the Quito basin of the Ecuadorian Andes. It has been excavated several times; the botanical data discussed here come from excavations by Peterson and Villalba. The earliest date for the site is 1545 B.C.; the Formative occupation ended around 500 B.C. with the destruction of the village by volcanic eruption (Peterson and Rodriguez n.d.). The site is at 2,810 m on a volcanic fan on the northeast slope of Pichincha volcano. I have examined 22 carbon samples and 35 phytolith samples from the site (Pearsall n.d.b).

Maize was present in both phytolith and carbon samples. Carbon samples also contained tree fruit fragments, two types of root/tubers, and lupine. One phytolith and one carbon sample with maize come from the earliest level at the site, Capa D. Robert Bird examined the charred maize and reported to me that it was similar to one type from La Ponga and to Swasey Types 1 and 2 from the Cuello site, Belize. The Cotocollao maize is virtually identical to that recovered from the Formative occupation at Nueva Era. The dicot and monocot root material recovered from these two sites is also similar. Presence of lupine seeds adds another potential cultigen to the assemblage.

It is noteworthy that macroremain evidence for maize is roughly contemporaneous at La Chimba (where maize occurs in all strata dating to the Middle Formative) and Nueva Era and that a few charred remains occur in older levels at Nueva Era and Cotocollao. The 2000 B.C. date for maize remains in the San Pablo lake core indicate that we should be looking for maize in Preceramic and Early Ceramic sites in the sierra, however.

Ecuadorian Amazon

Lake Ayauchi Core. Lake Ayauchi in the Ecuadorian Amazon was cored to recover a Holocene record of landscape modification in the eastern Andean foothills (Bush, Piperno, and Colinvaux 1989; Piperno 1990). Pollen, phytolith, and charcoal records revealed that from 5100 to 3300 B.C. mature forest indicators dominated, with slight occurrence of disturbance taxa. Maize occurred at 3300 B.C. in association with increased disturbance indicators and abundant carbon particles, indicating that swiddening was ongoing in the lake watershed at this time. By 500 B.C., maize was increasingly abundant, and vegetation indicators indicated that agriculture had intensified. While of limited utility in characterizing the overall nature of subsistence in the region, this core provides the first evidence of the introduction of maize into the eastern foothills and documents the timing and nature of landscape modifications associated with agriculture.

DISCUSSION

Subsistence in the Ecuadorian Formative

Were societies agricultural during the Ecuadorian Formative, and, specifically, was subsistence based on maize agriculture? Without going into a detailed discussion of domestication and agriculture (see Pearsall 1995b), I look for the following characteristics in a society with an agricultural base: presence of domesticated plants, including productive carbohydrate sources; reduced reliance on wild plant resources; evidence that domesticates were important in diet and economy (ubiquitous occurrence, supporting isotope and health data in the case of maize, and presence of storage facilities and caches); and orientation of sites to agricultural lands.

Available data support an agricultural basis for Formative period societies in Ecuador. The case is stronger for the later part of the sequence than for the earlier, however. Preservation of charred remains is poor overall; few of the databases can be examined quantitatively in any meaningful way. Thus while the presence of cultivated plants is easily established, it is impossible in most cases to evaluate how common crops were in relation to wild plant resources. The situation on the coast is further complicated because manioc remains largely undocumented in the botanical record. This makes it difficult to assess the full extent to which root crops were used with the tree fruits, jack beans, maize, and *achira* and arrowroot remains that do occur in the record. If all the charred bits of root/tuber tissue in coastal sites were from cultivated taxa, a tighter case for early Formative agriculture could be made. The development of methods to identify such remains (Hather 1993; Hather and Hammond 1994) may permit clarification of this issue in the future. Starch grain analysis may also prove helpful in identifying manioc (e.g., Piperno and Holst 1998). Among the most persuasive data are site locations: Formative sites typically allow easy access to alluvial and other good agricultural lands and, in the case of Real Alto, provide access to coastal as well as riverine resources. This pattern begins in southwest coastal Ecuador with the Preceramic Vegas tradition (Stothert 1985, 1988).

The La Chimba site in the northern Andes is the exception to the pattern of poor preservation. Here there are abundant remains of cultivated plants. Both maize and potato are present in all strata; bean, cotton, and *oca* also occur. Co-occurrence by maize and potato dates from the Middle Formative (beginning 2640 BP). While the remains of wild seeds are also common, the suite of cultivated plants present, which includes three carbohydrate sources (maize, potato, and *oca*), makes La Chimba look agricultural. The less well-preserved databases from Cotocollao and Nueva Era also document maize, root/tubers, and beans from this period and earlier (ca. 1100 B.C., Nueva Era, and ca. 1500 B.C., Cotocollao). Further, the presence of maize pollen and charred maize tissue at the 2000 B.C. level and after in the San Pablo Lake core is suggestive: Did agriculturally based societies exist in the northern Andes beginning in the late Preceramic or in an earlier ceramic phase? More than a single core is needed to answer this—a program of lake coring and deep site-testing seems called for.

Chorrera sites in the Jama valley and Machalilla sites in coastal Manabí and southwest Guayas provide glimpses at coastal subsistence that overlap with the developments summarized above for the sierra. While the macroremain database is much weaker on the coast than at La Chimba, maize is nearly ubiquitous at Dos Caminos, the best Chorrera dataset available, and is ubiquitous at the Machalilla La Ponga site. Phytolith analysis reveals the presence of arrowroot, *achira*, sedge, and palm; there is some evidence for other tree fruits and common bean. The relative importance of these resources and maize cannot be assessed quantitatively. However, since data from the subsequent Muchique phases in the Jama valley indicate that tree fruits, tubers, and maize were all important (Pearsall 1996), proposing a late Formative agricultural base of maize and tubers, with gathering (or tending?) of tree fruits, seems a reasonable hypothesis for further testing.

Isotope data from Chorrera period skeletons at the Loma Alta and Salango sites in southern Manabí province (van der Merwe, Lee-Thorp, and Raymond 1993) provide the only direct evidence to date for clarifying the importance of maize in the late Formative period on the coast. The mean $\Delta^{13}C$ collagen value of the Loma Alta samples ($N = 13$) is -10.1‰, just below the range for populations dependent on C_4 terrestrial resources (i.e., a diet high in maize and/or animals feeding in maize fields; see Norr 1995). This indicates that C_3 plants foods (e.g., tree fruits and tubers) and some marine foods (indicated by slightly elevated $\Delta^{15}N$ levels) were also present in the diet. Intrasite variability is high (collagen $\Delta^{13}C$ values range from -14.1 to -8.4‰), indicating considerable individual variation in the mixture of foods consumed. Isotope data from 7

Chorrera period skeletons at the Salango site indicate somewhat less maize use among that population (average $\Delta^{13}C$ value: -12.5‰; range: -14.0 to -10.3‰). Interestingly, data from 10 Machalilla skeletons from Salango have virtually the same average carbon isotope value, but a broader range, as the later population (average $\Delta^{13}C$ collagen value: -12.3‰; range: -14.6 to -8.41‰). ^{15}N values suggest higher use of marine resources by both Salango populations (van der Merwe et al. 1993). The available isotope data thus lend support to a late Formative coastal diet that included considerable (but variable) consumption of maize, within the context of a broadly diverse diet, and a Machalilla diet that, at the coastal Salango site at least, included marine foods and possibly some maize.

This takes us back to Valdivia and the case for an agricultural base for this early Formative culture. With the exception of common bean, all the crops and utilized resources documented later on the coast appear by the early Formative. In the Jama case, for example, phytolith assemblages for Terminal Valdivia (Piquigua) contexts are virtually identical to those for Chorrera (Tabuchila). Many Valdivia sites, including Real Alto, Loma Alta, and the sites in the Jama valley, are located on or near river alluvium. By Valdivia 3, Real Alto is a large village with a ceremonial precinct and two earthen mounds. The presence of burials within one mound suggests the emergence of an elite. Bell-shaped pits indicate the capacity for storage of food surpluses. These features of the Valdivia 3 village at Real Alto are all consistent with an agriculturally based economy. As Ubelaker (this volume) discusses, occurrence of dental caries at Real Alto (8.5%) is in the range usually associated with agricultural populations. Additionally, I have proposed elsewhere (Pearsall 1999) that the movement of peoples into new territories, such as that associated with Terminal Valdivia, was a response to the increased instability of early agricultural systems. Unfortunately, the available botanical data are simply not strong enough to test the relative importance of crops versus gathered plant and animal foods. If early Formative villages were agriculturally based, as suggested by site location, the suite of crops—including carbohydrate sources—present, and evidence for storage, I would expect a narrowing of the subsistence base over the course of Valdivia as a core group of crops assumed primary importance. Future research should allow testing of this prediction.

Isotope data are available for nine individuals from early-to-middle Valdivia contexts (eight from Loma Alta Valdivia 1–2 strata; one from Real Alto Valdivia 3 contexts) (van der Merwe et al. 1993). This population has a unique isotopic signature: depleted $\Delta^{13}C$ (in the range of populations consuming C_3 vegetation and/or terrestrial animals), with slightly enriched $\Delta^{15}N$ (too high for a strictly terrestrial diet). Van der Merwe et al. tested four taxa from riverine/

estuarine habitats; these gave depleted $\Delta^{13}C$ and enriched $\Delta^{15}N$ values, suggesting that consumption of fish and invertebrates from such habitats contributed to diet at these sites. The mean $\Delta^{13}C$ collagen value from Loma Alta Valdivia skeletons, -19.0‰, indicates that maize was not the basis of subsistence at that site, nor at Real Alto; in the latter case, only a single datum point is available.

On the basis of available site data, botanical remains, and skeletal indicators, then, it seems reasonable to propose that early Formative coastal subsistence depended on root crops (*achira*, and arrowroot, and perhaps manioc, and sweet potato), tree fruits, jack bean, squash, and local wild foods, including both estuarine and terrestrial animals, with some input of maize, and that this constituted agriculture. There was no single dominant carbohydrate source; rather Valdivia agriculture fits the tropical forest pattern (Lathrap 1970), with a broad base of root crops, tree crops, and seed crops and continued use of a wide diversity of wild, tended, and weedy plants and animals. Whether a shift to increased maize use on the coast occurred in terminal Valdivia, in association with the movement of populations into new territories referred to above or is a characteristic of Chorrera period subsistence, is as yet unknown. It seems reasonable to propose, however, that a shift to increased reliance on cultivated plants occurred prior to the emergence of maize as a dominant dietary component. In other words, agriculture *preceded* maize agriculture on the coast, and in the sierra maize and other indicators of agriculture *appeared simultaneously* in the record.

Archaeobotanical Record of the Peruvian Coast

Now I turn to the occurrence of cultivated plants at 20 sites on the arid coast of Peru, spanning from 6200 B.C. to 400 B.C., or slightly later (Middle Preceramic through Early Horizon). My objectives are to compare the Ecuadorian data with contemporary data from this adjoining region, to look at the antiquity of agriculture in each, and to assess, to the extent possible, whether the Ecuadorian Formative was "precocious" in its shift to agriculture. I selected sites for this review with two criteria: subsistence reconstruction was a focus of the research design, and systematic botanical recovery procedures employed, minimally, use of quarter-inch excavation screens; better, fine sieving, flotation, coprolite analysis; and phytolith or pollen analysis. Included are Quebrada de Las Pircas sites (Dillehay, Netherly, and Rossen 1989; Rossen n.d.; Rossen, Dillehay, and Ugent 1996); Paloma (Benfer 1982, 1984, 1990; Dering and Weir n.d.a,b; Weir and Dering 1986); Chilca 1 (Jones n.d.); Los Gavilanes (Bonavia 1982; Popper 1982); La Galgada (Grieder et al. 1988; Smith 1988), two components, a western midelevation site; Huaca Prieta (Bird, Hyslop, and Skinner 1985); Huaynuná, Las Haldas (three components), Pampa de Las Llamas–Moxeke,

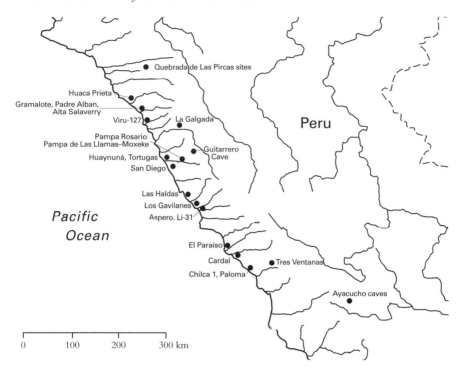

Fig. 3   Coastal Peruvian sites discussed in the text.

Tortugas, San Diego, Pampa Rosario (S. Pozorski and T. Pozorski 1987), Padre Alban, Alto Salaverry, Gramalote (Pozorski 1983), El Paraíso (Quilter et al. 1991; Pearsall unpublished lab data), Cardal (Burger 1987; Burger and Salazar-Burger 1991; Umlauf n.d.); Aspero, Li-31 (Feldman n.d.); and site Viru-127 from the Viru valley (Ericson et al. 1989) (Fig. 3).

Table 3 summarizes the occurrence of cultivated plants at the Peruvian sites discussed. Abundance estimates were available for some. Given that different recovery techniques were used at the sites and that even in a desert, preservation is not perfect (foods leaving inedible residues are overrepresented, for example), these should be used with caution. Detailed information on occurrence of wild plants was available from only a few sites; therefore I do not discuss these data. Fig. 4 represents the numbers of cultivated plant taxa present (richness) at the sites versus time.

Middle Preceramic.   The three earliest sites/site groups, the Quebrada de Las Pircas sites (6200–5500 B.C.), Paloma (5700–3000 B.C.), and Chilca 1 (3700–

237

Table 3
Botanical Database for Coastal Peruvian Sites

Plant	Middle Preceramic				Cotton Preceramic							
	Quebrada de Las Pircas[a] 6200–5500 B.C.	Paloma[b] 5700–3000 B.C.	Chilca 1[c] 3700–2400 B.C.	Los Gavilanes[d] 2700–2200 B.C.	La Galgada[e] 2662–2000 B.C.	Aspero[f] 2410–2200 B.C.	Huaca Prieta[g] 2400–1200 B.C.	Huaynuná[h] 2250–1775 B.C.	Las Haldas[i] 2010–1795 B.C.	Padre Alban[j] 1980–1729 B.C.	Alto Salaverry[k]	El Paraíso[l] 1800–1500 B.C.
cotton				P	P	P	P	A	A	P	P	A
gourd		P	P	P	P	P	P	A	A	P	P	R
squash	P	P	P	P	P	P	P	MA			P	MA
chili, *ají*		P	P	P	P	P	P	R		P	P	R
quinoa	P											
potato								R				
sweet potato				P				R				
achira			P	P	P	P	P	R				R
manioc, *yuca*	P			P								
jícama			P	P								
lucuma				P	P		P	MA			P	MA
guava		P		P	P	P	P		VR		P	A
avocado				P	P	P			VR		P	A
pacae				P	P	P					P	MA
ciruela de fraile	P				P	P						
soursop				P			P				P	
common bean				P	P		P		VR		P	R
lima bean		P	P	P	P	P	P				P	R
Phaseolus spp.			P	P		P						
peanut	P						P	R				
jack bean			P		P		P					
maize, corn												

TABLE 8 (cont.)

	Initial Period						Early Horizon				
Plant	La Galgada[m] 2085–1395 B.C.	Pampa de Las Llamas-Moxeke[n] 1785–1120 B.C.	Las Haldas[o] 1645–1190 B.C.	Gramalote[p] 1650–1100 B.C.	Cardal[q] 1100–850 B.C.	Tortugas[r]	Las Haldas[s] 1040–895 B.C.	San Diego[t] 810–450 B.C.	Pampa Rosario[u] 550–295 B.C.	Li-31[v]	Viru-127[w]
cotton	P	VA	A	A	P	VA	MA	A	A	P	
gourd	P	A	A	A	P	A	MA	A	A	P	
squash	P	A	R	A	P	MA	R	R	R	P	
chili, *ají*	P	A		P	P	MA	R	MA	MA	P	P
quinoa						R					
potato			R			R	R		R		
sweet potato		MA to A						MA			
achira		MA to A						MA	R	P	
manioc, *yuca*		MA to A				R	R				
jícama						R	R				
lucuma	P	A	A	P	P	A		R	VR	P	
guava		MA			P	VR	R	R	MA	P	
avocado	P	A		P	P	VR	R	R	MA	P	P
pacae	P	R	R				R	R	VR	P	
ciruela de fraile	P	R	R		P	P		R	A		
soursop											
common bean		R to MA	MA	P		VR	R	A	A		
lima bean		R to MA	R			MA		A	A		
Phaseolus spp.				P	P					P	
peanut	P	VA	MA	A	P	A	MA	A	A	P	P
jack bean		R		P			R	R	R	P	P
maize, corn	P		MA		P	P	MA	A	A	P	P

Notes: A = abundant; MA = moderately abundant; P = present; R = rare; VA = very abundant; VR = very rare. [a] No. of domesticates = 5; preservation good; Rossen 1991, Rossen et al. 1996. [b] No. of domesticates = 6; preservation good; Benfer 1982, 1984; 1990; Dering and Weir n.d.a, n.d.b; Weir and Dering 1986. [c] No. of domesticates = 6; preservation good; Jones n.d. [d] No. of domesticates = 15; preservation good; Bonavia 1982, Popper 1982. [e] No. of domesticates = 13; Grieder, Mendoza, Smith, and Malina, 1988, Smith 1988. [f] No. of domesticates = 8; Feldman n.d. [g] No. of domesticates = 11; Bird, Hyslop, and Skinner 1985. [h] No. of domesticates = 9; preservation good; Pozorski and Posorski 1987. [i] No. of domesticates = 5; preservation poor; Pozorski and Posorski 1987. [j] No. of domesticates = 3; preservation poor; Pozorski 1983. [k] No. of domesticates = 11; preservation moderate; Pozorski 1983. [l] No. of domesticates = 11; preservation good; Quilter et al. 1991, Pearsall unpublished lab data. [m] No. of domesticates = 10; Grieder et al. 1988, Smith 1988. [n] No. of domesticates = 17; preservation good; Pozorski and Posorski 1987. [o] No. of domesticates = 10; preservation good; Pozorski and Posorski 1987. [p] No. of domesticates = 10; preservation good; Pozorski 1983. [q] No. of domesticates = 10; preservation good; Pozorski and Posorski 1987. [r] No. of domesticates = 14; preservation good; Bird et al. 1985. [s] No. of domesticates = 12; preservation moderate; Pozorski and Posorski 1987. [t] No. of domesticates = 16; preservation very good; Pozorski and Posorski 1987. [u] No. of domesticates = 16; preservation very good; Pozorski and Posorski 1987. [v] No. of domesticates = 14; Feldman n.d. [w] No. of domesticates = 4; preservation poor; Ericson, West, Sullivan, and Krueger 1989.

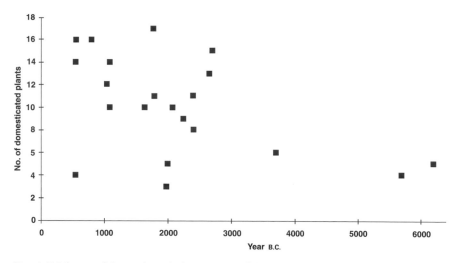

Fig. 4 Richness of domesticated plants at coastal Peruvian sites.

2000 B.C.), were occupied before the Late or Cotton Preceramic, a convenient horizon marked by the appearance of abundant cotton remains in coastal sites. Paloma and Chilca 1 on the central coast (Fig. 3) have excellent botanical preservation and good recovery techniques, including fine sieving and analysis of coprolites (see Benfer 1982, 1984, 1990; Dering and Weir n.d.a,b; Weir and Dering 1986). The low richness of cultivated plants (four and six taxa, respectively) at these sites thus reflects the minor role cultivated taxa played in subsistence, rather than preservation or recovery biases. At both sites a wide variety of wild plant resources were present, as were remains of marine shellfish, fish, and mammals. Marine resources were undoubtedly a dietary staple. A local tuber, *Begonia geraniifolia*, may also have been cultivated. The Quebrada de Las Pircas botanical materials are not as abundant; relatively few remains were recovered from these north coastal sites. Five cultivated plants were present; that is, richness is consistent with the pattern at the later Paloma and Chilca 1 sites.

The earliest cultivated plants to appear on the coast, at the Quebrada de Las Pircas sites, were peanut, manioc, *quinoa*, squash, and *ciruela de fraile*.[5] While the *ciruela de fraile* and squash were likely local domesticates or semidomesticates (*Cucurbita ecuadorensis* occurs just over the border in coastal Ecuador), peanut

[5] As discussed in detail in Rossen et al. (1996), direct accelerator mass spectrometry (AMS) dates on desiccated squash, peanut, and charred quinoa returned modern dates, while dates on charred wood in direct association with the food remains and ancient living surfaces returned Middle Preceramic dates. Rossen et al. (1996) argue that the AMS dates

and manioc were likely domesticated east of the Andes, and *quinoa* is considered an Andean crop (Pearsall 1992). The Quebrada de Las Pircas assemblage thus provides early evidence for plant introductions.[6] The Paloma site added gourd, some type of *Phaseolus* bean, and guava to the cultivated plant list, as well as squash. None of the plants recovered from Paloma were dietary staples; none showed morphological change; all but gourd probably occurred naturally in the *lomas* near Paloma or in the Chilca River valley. I consider these four taxa cultivated plants for the purposes of this discussion because they underwent morphological change or occurred in abundance later.

Three new cultivated taxa were present at the Chilca 1 site, the tubers *achira* and *jicama* and jack bean, yielding a total of 11 cultivated taxa for the Middle Preceramic. The three tubers (*achira, jicama*, and manioc) are not native to the coast; nor are *quinoa* or peanut. Traded or brought in by populations moving seasonally among altitudinal zones, these plants were likely maintained under cultivation. The proposed cultivated taxa occurred at the sites with a variety of wild plant foods.

Cotton Preceramic. Richness of cultivated plants by site was noticeably higher during the next period, the Cotton Preceramic (2600/2200–1800/1500 B.C., depending on the region), in comparison to the sites discussed above. At most sites 9 to 15 cultivated plant taxa were represented in the record, with two exceptions that represent poorer than usual preservation.

A total of 18 cultivated plants have been documented at Cotton Preceramic sites, including seven new taxa: cotton, chili peppers, four tree fruits (*lucuma*, avocado, *pacae*, and soursop), and one tuber (sweet potato).[7] In addition, remains of common bean and lima bean show morphological changes from wild species. Jack bean, gourd, squash, *achira, jicama*, manioc, peanut, and guava oc-

---

should be rejected, since, among other things, the morphologies of the *quinoa*, peanut, and squash are not modern. I find the multiple lines of evidence convincing and include these data; omitting them would not change my conclusions, however.

[6] It is beyond the scope of this essay to review the debate concerning climate and vegetation on the north Peruvian coast in the early to mid-Holocene. There is some evidence for well-watered conditions in the late Pleistocene/Early Holocene in some valleys in north and north central Peru. Whether this is due to increased run-off from the sierra onto the desert coast or an extension southward of the seasonal rains that characterize coastal Ecuador depends on how one interprets the same few datasets. Peanut and manioc do not grow wild in coastal Ecuador, however, so an extension of forest from the north would not explain their occurrence in the Zaña valley.

[7] As discussed in Pearsall (1992), evidence for late Preceramic maize on the Peruvian coast is clouded by problems in establishing clear Preceramic context of remains in some cases, and contradictions in dating in others.

curred at Cotton Preceramic sites, while *quinoa* dropped out of the record. While the tree fruits and cotton are probably local, all the other new taxa are likely introductions from the sierra or eastern lowlands (Pearsall 1992). This jump in the number of introduced, planted species and local taxa clearly maintained under cultivation later in time indicates increased reliance on plants in general and on cultivated plants in particular. As abundance estimates in Table 3 suggest, no single plant food dominated; cotton, however, was widespread and abundant, with a mixture of seed crops, root crops, and perennials.

Initial period. The next two cultural periods, Initial (marked by appearance of ceramics, 2000/1500–1100/800 B.C.) and Early Horizon (defined by the appearance in some areas of Chavín-style pottery, 800–400 B.C.), were quite similar in richness of cultivated taxa present at sites. All sites with the greatest richness (14 to 17 cultivated taxa) date to one of these periods. Some sites with good preservation fall in the same richness range as Cotton Preceramic sites, however. As noted by Moseley (1975), Initial period centers are located inland relative to Late Preceramic centers.

During the Initial period, the rate of introduction of new cultivated plant taxa slowed. Maize was present in reliable contexts for the first time, potato appeared, and soursop dropped out of the record. This brings to 19 the number of cultivated plant taxa present. Maize and manioc occurred at only two sites; peanut was widespread. Tree crops continued in use, with avocado and *ciruela de fraile* becoming more common in comparison to low Cotton Preceramic occurrences. Occurrence of root crops was erratic, partially because of preservation problems. It appears that the Cotton Preceramic pattern of use of a wide variety of food resources continued during the Initial period and that the crop base was not narrowing. There is no evidence that either maize or a single root crop like manioc or *achira* assumed primary dietary importance during the Initial period.

Early Horizon. Three root crops present earlier in the record, potato, sweet potato, and *jicama*, did not occur at sites I reviewed for this period, leaving a total of 16 cultivated plant taxa for the Early Horizon. This is a slight net drop in richness and an apparent narrowing of the root crop component of subsistence—only *achira* and manioc were present. At sites where abundance estimates were provided, tree fruits were rarer than at earlier sites. Maize was widespread, occurring at all five sites I reviewed. These data may mark the beginning of a narrowing of the subsistence base with use of some crops in decline and others becoming more widespread.

Plant Food Resources of the Eduadorian Formative

A study of stable carbon and nitrogen isotopes of skeletons from the Viru valley, which included Early Horizon populations (Ericson et al. 1989), showed consistent and abundant use of marine resources at coastal sites, with 10 to 20 percent of energy input coming from maize compared with 40 to 60 percent later in time. Burger and van der Merwe (1990) found similar levels of maize use in a small contemporary sample from the sierra. These studies suggest that while maize increased in the Early Horizon, it was not a mainstay of diet.

Emergence of Agriculture on the Coast of Peru

To draw some conclusions concerning when agriculture developed in coastal Peru, it is useful to consider the archaeobotanical record in its archaeological context. We are fortunate to have several sequences with systematically recovered floral and faunal data within the context of valleywide settlement studies, as well as a number of single-site studies, which provide the detail needed for examining subsistence change in the broader contexts of cultural change and continuity.

The Casma valley sequence (S. Pozorski and T. Pozorski 1987) is fairly representative, in my view. Both late Preceramic sites investigated, Huaynuná and Las Haldas, were oriented toward good areas for fishing and shellfish collection. Neither is located in the river valley: Las Haldas is at the edge of the *lomas*, some 20 km south of the river. As expected from site locations, all faunal materials from Huaynuná were marine, mostly shellfish from rocky substrates, while materials from the levels at Las Haldas combined abundant shellfish with use of land snails from the *lomas*. As Table 3 shows, cultivated plants were present at both sites; S. Pozorski and T. Pozorski (1987) have emphasized the abundance of "utility" plants like cotton and gourd, both useful for marine exploitation. All other plant taxa are very rare, rare, or moderate in occurrence. But note that three tubers are present at Huaynuná. The Casma valley sites, then, document an orientation toward marine resources. Other late Preceramic sites that illustrate a pattern of marine settlement orientation and faunal exploitation combined with plant cultivation include Aspero adjacent to a coastal marsh in the broad lower part of the Supe valley (Feldman n.d.); Padre Alban and Alto Salaverry in the Moche valley (Pozorski 1983); and Huaca Prieta in the Chicama area (Bird et al. 1985).

Where were crops grown? Undoubtedly in fields in the valleys; there is no rainfall cultivation on the coast of Peru. Coastal rivers run mainly between January and May, with cultivation beginning with the onset of water flow. Simple water control features to distribute water and use of areas with high water tables were likely mechanisms for cultivation in the lower reaches of the valley. There is no evidence for permanent canal structures at this period. In the Casma case, survey revealed no late Preceramic sites in the valley itself (Malpass 1983); perhaps there were (seasonal?) settlements near fields that have been lost over the centuries of intensive use of the lower valley.

While most Central and North coast valleys show the pattern I have outlined above for the Casma—late Preceramic sites, often substantial, oriented to take advantage of marine resources—major sites were also established in valley settings. El Paraíso is an impressive example (Quilter et al. 1991). This late Cotton Preceramic site, which occupies 50 hectares and includes eight or nine stone buildings, is near the mouth of the Chillón valley, adjacent to the river. As summarized in Table 3, 11 crops were present, and cotton and tree fruits were abundant. Fish and molluscs were also common, but land mammals (deer, fox, and rodents) and birds were relatively rare. These patterns led Quilter et al. to propose that fish were the major animal food at the site and that subsistence was relatively broad, incorporating a variety of cultivated and wild plant foods. Site location adjacent to agricultural land perhaps signaled the importance of controlling production of cotton for textile manufacture. Note that two root crops were among the foods crop present, however.

This settlement shift—to locations adjacent to productive lands in the lower and middle valleys—occurred throughout the central and north coast during the subsequent Initial period. This is not to say the shore was abandoned; on the contrary, sites like Tortugas in the Casma valley and Gramalote in the Moche valley were established in productive shellfish and fishing areas along the arid shore. However, such sites appear to have been involved in exchange of marine foods for agricultural products with inland valley sites (Pozorski 1983; S. Pozorski and T. Pozorski 1987). The real growth of major sites with ceremonial architecture was in the river valleys, including locations where canal irrigation could be practiced. At major inland sites, like Pampa de Las Llamas–Moxeke in the Casma valley and Caballo Muerto in the Moche valley, while marine resources dominated the animal component of diet, there was also evidence of increased use of terrestrial animals. At the Cardal site, one of four late Initial period ceremonial centers in the Lurín valley, 15 km from the coast, there was ready access to both agricultural land and *lomas* vegetation (Burger 1987; Burger and Salazar-Burger 1991). Most animal protein was maritime in origin; however, *lomas* land snails and some small game also occurred.

In a study of skeletal remains from Cardal, Vradenburg (n.d.) demonstrated that general community health was poor at this late Initial period site. Infectious disease, identified by Vradenburg as chronic endemic (nonvenereal) syphilis, was prevalent and contributed to enhanced childhood morbidity and mortality and to adult morbidity. Caries data indicated a rate of infection characteristic of a mixed horticultural subsistence base; there were some indications that elite individuals consumed more cariogenic foods. Vradenburg (n.d.) suggested that poor health, with possible reduced fecundity, may have contributed to the ultimate abandonment of the site, rather than warfare or conquest from the outside, as suggested for the abandonment of Initial period sites in the Casma region (S. Pozorski and T. Pozorski 1987).

The trends of growing numbers of sites in the valleys and orientation of sites to productive land continued into the subsequent Early Horizon period, when there was also evidence for irrigation. In the Casma valley, for example, animal foods continued to be dominated by marine taxa. This was more prevalent at sites close to the coast and less so at sites further inland (S. Pozorski and T. Pozorski 1987). Virtually all fauna was marine at the San Diego site (5.5 km inland), for example, while both marine and terrestrial animals, including camelids, fox/dog, guinea pigs, and land snails, occurred at the Pampa Rosario site (16 km inland). At site Viru-127 in the lower Viru valley, faunal remains were dominated by marine taxa (Ericson et al. 1989). In the Supe valley, the Early Horizon Li-31 site located near Aspero combined a wealth of plant remains (some five times the abundance as at the late Preceramic site) with marine fauna use, including shellfish, fish, and sea lion (Feldman n.d.).

To summarize, then, the Cotton Preceramic (beginning 2600 B.C. to 2200 B.C., depending on the region) saw the first appearance of monumental architecture on the Peruvian coast. In association with this development, richness of cultivated plants jumped; 18 different crops were present at sites. Site location, with notable exceptions such as El Paraíso, was to take advantage of rich shellfish and fishing areas; sites were typically not oriented toward productive agricultural lands, although such lands were undoubtedly used. Thus while the abundance of cultivated plant taxa present suggests an increase in reliance on plants in general and on domesticated plants in particular, during the late Preceramic, site location argues for a primary maritime focus of subsistence. In a number of cases, utility plants like gourd and cotton were the most abundant crop remains. People did not live by either molluscs or tubers alone, but, unfortunately, detailed dietary and health data are largely lacking for this period. This complicates evaluating how much agricultural resources supported these early ceremonial centers. The plant subsistence base of Initial periods sites was similar to that of the late Preceramic, although increased abundances of plant remains characterized a number of sites. New sites were largely located in areas adjacent to agricultural lands, including locations suitable for short irrigation works. These trends in site orientation and subsistence base also characterized a number of Early Horizon centers. Vradenburg's findings (n.d.) concerning the health of the late Initial period Cardal population suggest that new or intensified stressors were affecting coastal populations by this time.

What are the implications of the settlement and subsistence shifts outlined above for the emergence of agriculture on the Peruvian coast? The available botanical and faunal data from late Preceramic coastal sites are not robust enough to reconstruct caloric input of the various plant and animal foods, but I agree with Raymond (1981) that the input of roots crops such as *achira* in the late Preceramic period diet has been underestimated. Furthermore, the correlation of large Preceramic sites with the narrowest coastal plain is illuminating: it is along this stretch of coast that the best fishing was closest to land that could be cropped without irrigation, that is, in valley mouth areas. Likewise, Feldman (n.d.) notes that the location of the Aspero site at the edge of a marsh near the shore maximized access to fishing, gathering of shellfish and wild plants, and hunting, and provided easy access to agricultural lands in the lower Supe valley. Such positioning characterized many large Preceramic sites with access to *lomas* being another consideration. As Sandweiss (1996) notes, a rising sea level at 5000 to 6000 BP (the beginning of the late Preceramic) brought fishermen and farmers into close proximity in the central coast, the area in which early monumental architecture is concentrated. Thus the human settlement pattern appears to coevolve with changes in physical landscape (width of coastal plain, estuary development, and changes in lower reaches of rivers) (Wells and Noller 1999).

I also think it significant that the subsistence bases of both the late Preceramic and Initial periods broaden and resemble one another when recovery techniques designed to recover the full size range of botanical and faunal materials were employed or when coprolites were studied (Jones n.d.; Quilter et al. 1991). This occurred at the late Preceramic El Paraíso site (Quilter et al. 1991) and Initial period Cardal (Burger and Salazar-Burger 1991; Umlauf 1988). More wild plant foods join the diet; fish and birds are more common; marine, estuarine, marsh, *lomas*, and river valley resources occur together.

The adaptation of late Preceramic coastal populations on the Peruvian coast seems best characterized as one based primarily on the rich resources of the maritime province, which in fact included a number of important resources besides fish and shellfish. Terrestrial faunal played an insignificant role as a protein source, but plant foods, including seaweed, were key sources of carbohydrates, vitamins, and minerals. The widespread change of settlement pattern in the Initial period signaled a shift in resource emphasis, to an increasingly important role for cultivated plants and provides evidence for the emergence of agriculturally based subsistence at this time.

Comparing the Ecuadorian and Peruvian Sequences

First, it is important to realize that the coastal Peruvian data discussed here are not without interpretive problems. Preservation on the dry coast, though vastly superior to coastal and Andean Ecuador, is not uniformly excellent. Some changes in abundance or occurrence of crops are undoubtedly from preservation or recovery biases. Still, it appears that maize arrived later on the Peruvian coast than in coastal Ecuador. There were otherwise many similarities in plant use during the early Ecuadorian Formative (Valdivia, 3500–1500 B.C.) and the Peruvian Cotton Preceramic (2600/2200–1800/1500 B.C.). Richness of plants used was high in both areas and no single domesticate dominated assemblages. A mixture of tubers, tree fruits, and annual seed crops were used, as were a variety of wild plant and animal resources, both terrestrial and maritime. Crops were a mixture of local domesticates and plants introduced from the eastern lowlands and sierra. I characterize this adaptation as coastal tropical forest agriculture. Antecedents to this tradition can be seen in the Preceramic Vegas culture of southwest Ecuador, for which there is evidence of a subsistence system based on horticulture (maize, squash, gourd, and the root crop *llerén*), hunting, gathering, and fishing in Late Las Vegas times (6000–4000 B.C.) (Byrd 1996; Piperno 1988a,b; Piperno and Pearsall 1998; Stothert 1985, 1988), and in the Quebrada de Las Pircas sites of the Zaña valley of northern Peru (6200–5500 B.C.) (Dillehay et al. 1989; Rossen n.d.; Rossen et al. 1996).

The better preserved Peruvian data document an explosion of cultivated plants in the late Preceramic, with new local taxa and introduced plants appearing in the record to increase the number of taxa present by more than 50 percent over the Middle Preceramic period. Site locations suggest that maritime resources played a larger role in subsistence in the Peruvian case than the Ecuadorian, likely the result of the greater maritime and lesser terrestrial productivity (in the absence of irrigation technology) of the former region. The Ecuadorian macroremain database is much weaker, but phytolith data show a parallel trend of richness in numbers of utilized plants.

A broad-based subsistence strategy continued to characterize the coastal Peruvian sequence through the Initial period (2000/1500–1100/800 B.C.), while in Ecuador during this period (Machalilla and Chorrera on the coast; Middle Formative in the sierra), there are indications of the emergence of agriculturally based societies with somewhat narrower bases. Maize appeared to have been important in both the Ecuadorian coast and sierra; parallel with its introduction, maize assumed greater dietary importance earlier in Ecuador than in Peru.

Deborah M. Pearsall

CONCLUSIONS

It is still difficult to answer the question, "Is Ecuadorian Formative subsistence agriculturally based—and if so, on what crops?" It also continues to be difficult to look beyond subsistence, for example, to the use of plants in ritual and medicine or the role of plant commodities in exchange. As this overview of the available data has shown, part of the difficulty is a simple lack of archaeobotanical data. More fieldwork incorporating modern data recovery techniques is needed. The best way to address issues of diet and subsistence, however, is to focus on multiple lines of evidence: charred macroremains, phytoliths, pollen, and faunal data from sites, settlement pattern data, landscape studies, and chemical and physical analyses of human bone.

As the Ecuadorian Formative botanical database has grown, it has come to resemble contemporary patterns of plant use in coastal Peru. The differences, especially the early acceptance and earlier importance of maize in Ecuador, may have their roots in ecological differences between the regions (Pearsall 1994a). The dry tropical forests, estuaries, and river floodplains of the lowlands of coastal Ecuador provided congenial habitats for the introduced grain, as well as for locally domesticated plants and crops introduced from the sierra and east of the Andes. The rich resources of the cold waters off the coast of Peru and more restricted terrestrial plant and animal resources tipped the balance toward a maritime subsistence focus in that region.

In Ecuador, the western lowlands appear to take priority over the adjoining sierra in initial crop domestication and in the appearance of agriculturally based societies during the Early Formative (i.e., by late Valdivia). However, the lack of evidence for early domestication in the sierra may be a function of the difficulties of discovering and excavating sites deeply buried by volcanic ash. A program of lake coring focused on determining human and landscape interrelationships would provide a means of documenting the antiquity of cultivation practices in the Andean region. From evidence at Chorrera sites in the Jama valley and northern Andean sites like La Chimba, Middle Formative cultures of both the coast and sierra appear to have been agriculturally based.

In Peru several datasets from the Andes suggest that the appearance and development of agriculture was as early in the sierra as on the coast. I have reviewed the record for La Galgada; this highland site is similar to contemporary coastal sites in showing an association of cultivated plants and ceremonialism during the late Preceramic and Initial periods. While stable carbohydrate sources were few in the La Galgada record (i.e., *achira* is present but not common), the site is adjacent to land that could be cropped under irrigation. The earliest evidence for domesticated plants in the Andes comes from Guitarrero cave (common bean, lima bean, *oca*, chili peppers, *lucuma*; 8000–7500 B.C.; Kaplan 1980; Lynch 1980; Lynch et al. 1985; Smith 1980), caves in the Ayacucho region (gourd, *quinoa*, squash; 5800–4400 B.C.; MacNeish, Nelken-Terner, and Vierra 1980), and Tres Ventanas in the upper Chilca valley (*jicama*, potato, *ullucu*, manioc, sweet potato; 8000–6000 B.C.; Engel 1973). As I have reviewed elsewhere (Pearsall 1992), data from these dry cave sites are difficult to interpret because of the potential of redeposition of food remains by burrowing animals or late prehistoric use of caves for burials. For example, accelerator mass spectrometry (AMS) dating of a common bean seed from Guitarrero cave yielded a date of 2430 BP, while dates on two lima beans yielded ages of 3495 BP and 3325 BP (Kaplan 1994), many millennia younger than dates on associated charcoal (Lynch et al. 1985), and also younger than many *Phaseolus* finds on the coast (see Table 3). Given that most of the crops documented in the archaeological record of coastal Peru were not native there, one would expect earlier evidence of their use to the east in the low- and mid-elevation Andes and the dry tropical forest. Redating alone will not resolve this issue; further research in the areas of origin of the crops is needed.

As a result of writing and revising this overview, I find myself fascinated again by Valdivia 3, the phase in which the Real Alto site reached its peak. From the limited data available, subsistence during this period was a mixture of cultivated and wild plant use, with maize widely available but apparently of little dietary importance. Abundant caries (Ubelaker this volume) suggest that sticky carbohydrates were eaten—the botanical data suggest several carbohydrate sources besides maize, including *achira*, jack bean, and tree legume seeds; perhaps the "invisible" manioc was also contributing. Did the expanding ceremonial function of the site require a shift in food production? What happened to cotton? Did cloth become an item of exchange, a social marker? Maize phytoliths occurred in many samples. Was this the beginning of a shift to a more easily stored carbohydrate source? More research on this important period of the Ecuadorian Formative is needed.

Acknowledgments I thank all the archaeologists who have entrusted their botanical materials to me over the years. The Jama research was supported by grants from the National Science Foundation to James A. Zeidler and me. This essay was revised for content in 1996.

Deborah M. Pearsall

BIBLIOGRAPHY

ATHENS, J. STEPHEN
  1990   Prehistoric Agricultural Expansion and Population Growth in Northern Highland Ecuador: Interim Report for 1989 Fieldwork. International Archaeological Research Institute, Honolulu.

BENFER, ROBERT A., JR.
  1982   Proyecto Paloma de la Universidad de Missouri y el Centro de Investigaciones de Zonas Aridas. *Zonas Aridas* 2: 34–73.
  1984   The Challenges and Rewards of Sedentism: The Preceramic Village of Paloma, Peru. In *Paleopathology at the Origins of Agriculture* (Mark N. Cohen and George J. Armelagos, eds.): 531–558. Academic Press, New York.
  1990   The Preceramic Period Site of Paloma, Peru: Bioindications of Improving Adaptation to Sedentism. *Latin American Antiquity* 1(4): 284–318.

BIRD, JULIUS B., JOHN HYSLOP, AND MILICA D. SKINNER
  1985   The Preceramic Excavations at the Huaca Prieta, Chicama Valley, Peru. Anthropological Papers 62, pt. 1. American Museum of Natural History, New York.

BONAVIA, DUCCIO (ED.)
  1982   *Precerámico peruano. Los gavilanes. Mar, desierto, y oasis en la historia del hombre.* Corporacíon Financiera de Desarrollo (COFIDE). Oficina de Asuntos Culturales, Instituto Arqueológico Alemán, Comisión de Arqueología General y Comparada. Editorial Ausonia-Talleres Gráficos, Lima.

BURGER, RICHARD L.
  1987   The U-shaped Pyramid Complex, Cardal, Peru. *National Geographic Research* 3(3): 363–375.

BURGER, RICHARD L., AND LUCY SALAZAR-BURGER
  1991   The Second Season of Investigations at the Initial Period Center of Cardal, Peru. *Journal of Field Archaeology* 18: 275–296.

BURGER, RICHARD L., AND NIKOLAAS J. VAN DER MERWE
  1990   Maize and the Origin of Highland Chavín Civilization: An Isotopic Perspective. *American Anthropologist* 92: 85–95.

BUSH, MARK B., DOLORES R. PIPERNO, AND PAUL A. COLINVAUX
  1989   A 6,000-Year History of Amazonian Maize Cultivation. *Nature* 340: 303–305.

BYRD, KATHLEEN M.
  1996   Subsistence Strategies in Coastal Ecuador. In *Case Studies in Environmental Archaeology* (Elizabeth J. Reitz, Lee A. Newsom, and Silvia J. Scudder, eds.): 305–316. Plenum, New York.

DAMP, JONATHAN
  1984   Architecture of the Early Valdivia Village. *American Antiquity* 49: 573–595.
  1988   La primera ocupación Valdivia de Real Alto. Patrones económicos,

arquitectónicos, e ideológicos. Biblioteca Ecuatoriana de Arqueología 3. Escuela Politécnica del Litoral, Centro de Estudio Arqueológicos y Antropológicos, Guayaquil.

DAMP, JONATHAN, AND DEBORAH M. PEARSALL
1994   Early Cotton from Coastal Ecuador. *Economic Botany* 48: 163–165.

DAMP, JONATHAN, DEBORAH M. PEARSALL, AND LAWRENCE KAPLAN
1981   Beans for Valdivia. *Science* 212: 811–812.

DEBOER, WARREN R.
1996   *Traces behind the Esmeraldas Shore. Prehistory of the Santiago–Cayapas Region, Ecuador.* University of Alabama Press, Tuscaloosa.

DERING, PHILLIP, AND GLENDON H. WEIR
n.d.a   Analysis of Plant Remains from the Preceramic Site of Paloma, Chilca Valley, Peru. Manuscript on file, University of Missouri, Columbia, 1979.
n.d.b   Preliminary Plant Macrofossil Analysis of La Paloma Deposits. Manuscript on file, University of Missouri, Columbia, 1981.

DILLEHAY, TOM D., PATRICIA J. NETHERLY, AND JACK ROSSEN
1989   Middle Preceramic Public and Residential Sites on the Forested Slope of the Western Andes, Northern Peru. *American Antiquity* 54: 733–759.

ENGEL, FREDERIC A.
1973   New Facts about Pre-Columbian Life in the Andean Lomas. *Current Anthropology* 14: 271–280.

ERICSON, JONATHAN E., MICHAEL WEST, CHARLES H. SULLIVAN, AND HAROLD W. KRUEGER
1989   The Development of Maize Agriculture in the Viru Valley, Peru. In *The Chemistry of Prehistoric Human Bone* (T. Douglas Price, ed.): 68-104. Cambridge University Press, Cambridge.

FELDMAN, ROBERT A.
n.d.   Aspero, Peru: Architecture, Subsistence Economy, and Other Artifacts of a Preceramic Chiefdom. Ph. D. dissertation, Harvard University, Cambridge, Mass., 1980.

GRIEDER, TERENCE, ALBERTO B. MENDOZA, C. EARLE SMITH JR., AND ROBERT M. MALINA
1988   *La Galgada, Peru. A Preceramic Culture in Transition.* University of Texas Press, Austin.

HATHER, JON G.
1993   *An Archaeobotanical Guide to Root and Tuber Identification*, vol. 1: *Europe and South West Asia.* Oxbow Monograph 28, Oxbow Books, Oxford.

HATHER, JON G., AND NORMAND HAMMOND
1994   Ancient Maya Subsistence Diversity: Root and Tuber Remains from Cuello, Belize. *Antiquity* 68: 330–335.

ISAACSON, JOHN S.
1987   *Volcanic Activity and Human Occupation of the Northern Andes: The Application of Tephrostratigraphic Techniques to the Problem of Human Settlement of the Western Montaña during the Ecuadorian Formative.* Ph.D. dissertation, University of Illinois, University Microfilms, Ann Arbor, Mich.

JONES, JOHN G.
  n.d.   Middle to Late Preceramic (6000–3000 BP) Subsistence Patterns on the Central Coast of Peru: The Coprolite Evidence. Master's thesis, Department of Anthropology, Texas A&M University, College Station, 1988.

KAPLAN, LAWRENCE
  1980   Variation in the Cultivated Beans. In *Guitarrero Cave. Early Man in the Andes* (Thomas F. Lynch, ed.): 145–148. Academic Press, New York.
  1994   Accelerator Mass Spectrometry Dates and the Antiquity of *Phaseolus* Cultivation. Annual Report of the Bean Improvement Cooperative 37: 131–132.

LATHRAP, DONALD W.
  1970   *The Upper Amazon.* Praeger, New York.

LATHRAP, DONALD W., JORGE G. MARCOS, AND JAMES A. ZEIDLER
  1977   Real Alto: An Ancient Ceremonial Center. *Archaeology* 30: 2–13.

LIPPI, RONALD D.
  n.d.   La Ponga and the Machalilla Phase of Coastal Ecuador. Ph. D. dissertation, Department of Anthropology, University of Wisconsin–Madison, 1983.

LIPPI, RONALD D., ROBERT McK. BIRD, AND DAVID M. STEMPER
  1984   Maize Recovered at La Ponga, an Early Ecuadorian Site. *American Antiquity* 49: 118–124.

LYNCH, THOMAS F. (ED.)
  1980   *Guitarrero Cave: Early Man in the Andes.* Academic Press, New York.

LYNCH, THOMAS F., R. GILLESPIE, JOHN A. J. GOWLETT, AND R.E.M. HEDGES
  1985   Chronology of Guitarrero Cave, Peru. *Science* 229: 864–867.

MACNEISH, RICHARD S., ANTOINETTE NELKEN-TERNER, AND ROBERT K. VIERRA
  1980   Introduction. In *Prehistory of the Ayacucho Basin, Peru,* vol. 3: *Nonceramic Artifacts* (Richard S. MacNeish, Robert K. Vierra, Antoinette Nelken-Terner, and C. J. Phagen): 1–34. University of Michigan Press, Ann Arbor.

MALPASS, MICHAEL A.
  1983   The Preceramic Occupations of the Casma Valley, Peru. In *Investigations of the Andean Past. Papers from the First Annual Northeast Conference on Andean Archaeology and Ethnohistory* (Daniel H. Sandweiss, ed.): 1–20. Latin American Studies Program, Cornell University, Ithaca, N.Y.

MARCOS, JORGE G.
  n.d.   The Ceremonial Precinct at Real Alto: Organization of Time and Space in Valdivia Society. Ph.D. dissertation, Department of Anthropology, University of Illinois at Urbana–Champaign, 1978.

MOSELEY, MICHAEL E.
  1975   *The Maritime Foundations of Andean Civilization.* Cummings, Menlo Park, Calif.

NORR, LYNETTE
  1995   Interpreting Dietary Maize from Bone Stable Isotopes in the American Tropics: The State of the Art. In *Archaeology in the Lowland American Tropics. Current Analytical Methods and Recent Applications* (Peter W. Stahl, ed.): 198–223. Cambridge University Press, Cambridge.

PEARSALL, DEBORAH M.

1979   *The Application of Ethnobotanical Techniques to the Problem of Subsistence in the Ecuadorian Formative.* Ph.D. dissertation, Department of Anthropology, University of Illinois. University Microfilms, Ann Arbor Mich.

1988   An Overview of Formative Period Subsistence in Ecuador: Palaeoethnobotanical Data and Perspectives. In *Diet and Subsistence: Current Archaeological Perspectives. Proceedings of the Nineteenth Annual Chacmool Conference* (Brenda V. Kennedy and Genevieve M. LeMoine, eds.): 149–164. Archaeological Association of the University of Calgary, Calgary, Alberta.

1992   The Origins of Plant Cultivation in South America. In *Origins of Agriculture: An International Perspective* (C. Wesley Cowan and Patty Jo Watson, eds.): 173–205. Smithsonian Institution Press, Washington, D.C.

1993   Contributions of Phytolith Analysis for Reconstructing Subsistence: Examples from Research in Ecuador. In *Current Research in Phytolith Analysis: Applications in Archaeology and Paleoecology* (Deborah M. Pearsall and Dolores R. Piperno, eds.): 109–122. MASCA Research Papers in Science and Archaeology, vol. 10. MASCA, University Museum of Archaeology and Anthropology, University of Pennsylvania, Philadelphia.

1994a   Issues in the Analysis and Interpretation of Archaeological Maize in South America. In *Corn and Culture in the Prehistoric New World* (Sissel Johannessen and Christine A. Hastorf, eds.): 245–272. Westview Press, Boulder, Colo.

1994b   Macrobotanical Analysis. In *Regional Archaeology in Northern Manabí, Ecuador,* vol. 1: *Environment, Cultural Chronology, and Prehistoric Subsistence in the Jama River Valley* (James A. Zeidler and Deborah M. Pearsall, eds.): 149–159. Memoirs in Latin American Archaeology 8. University of Pittsburgh, Pittsburgh, Pa.

1994c   Phytolith Analysis. In *Regional Archaeology in Northern Manabí, Ecuador,* vol. 1: *Environment, Cultural Chronology, and Prehistoric Subsistence in the Jama River Valley* (James A. Zeidler and Deborah M. Pearsall, eds.): 161–174. Memoirs in Latin American Archaeology 8. University of Pittsburgh, Pittsburgh, Pa.

1995a   "Doing" Paleoethnobotany in the Tropical Lowlands: Adaptation and Innovation in Methodology. In *Archaeology in the Lowland American Tropics. Current Analytical Methods and Recent Applications* (Peter W. Stahl, ed.): 113–129. Cambridge University Press, Cambridge.

1995b   Domestication and Agriculture in the New World Tropics. In *Last Hunters– First Farmers: New Perspectives on the Prehistoric Transition to Agriculture* (T. Douglas Price and Anne B. Gebauer, eds.): 157–192. School of American Research, Santa Fe, N.M.

1996   Reconstructing Subsistence in the Lowland Tropics: A Case Study from the Jama River Valley, Manabí, Ecuador. In *Case Studies in Environmental Archaeology* (Elizabeth Reitz, Lee Newsom, and Silvia Scudder, eds.): 233–254. Plenum, New York.

1999   Agricultural Evolution and the Emergence of Formative Societies in Ecuador. In *Pacific Latin America in Prehistory: The Evolution of Archaic and Formative Cultures* (Michael Blake, ed.): 161–170. Washington State University Press, Pullman.

Deborah M. Pearsall

2000   *Paleoethnobotany: A Handbook of Procedures* (2d ed.) Academic Press, San Diego.

n.d.a   Final Report on Analysis of Plant Macroremains and Phytoliths from the Nueva Era Site, Pichincha Province, Ecuador. Report on file at the American Archaeology Division, University of Missouri, Columbia, 1986.

n.d.b   Informe del análisis de fitolitos y semillas carbonizadas del Sitio Cotocollao, provincia de Quito, Ecuador. Report on file at the American Archaeology Division, University of Missouri, Columbia, 1984.

n.d.c   *Plants and People in Ancient Ecuador: The Ethnobotany of the Jama River Region.* Wadsworth, Belmont, Calif. in press.

PEARSALL, DEBORAH M., AND WARREN R. DEBOER

1996   Phytoliths. In *Traces behind the Esmeraldas Shore. Prehistory of the Santiago–Cayapas Region, Ecuador* (Warren R. DeBoer): 216–220. University of Alabama Press, Tuscaloosa.

PEARSALL, DEBORAH M., AND DOLORES R. PIPERNO

1990   Antiquity of Maize Cultivation in Ecuador: Summary and Reevaluation of the Evidence. *American Antiquity* 55: 324–337.

PEARSALL, DEBORAH M., DOLORES R. PIPERNO, AND ROBERT A. BENFER JR.

n.d.   Identifying Crops through Phytolith Analysis. Paper presented at the 59th Annual Meeting of the Society for American Archaeology, Anaheim, Calif., 1994.

PEARSALL, DEBORAH M., AND PETER W. STAHL

n.d.   Multidisciplinary Perspectives on Environmental and Subsistence Change in the Jama River Valley, Manabí, Ecuador. Paper presented at the 61st Annual Meeting of the Society for American Archaeology, New Orleans, 1996.

PETERSON, EMIL, AND EUGENIA RODRIGUEZ

n.d.   Cotocollao. A Formative Period Village in the Northern Highlands of Ecuador. Paper presented at the 42nd Annual Meeting of the Society for American Archaeology, New Orleans, 1977.

PIPERNO, DOLORES R.

1988a   *Phytolith Analysis: An Archaeological and Geological Perspective.* Academic Press, San Diego.

1988b   Primer informe sobre los fitolitos de las plantas del OGSE-80 y la evidencia del cultivo de maíz en el Ecuador. In *Prehistoria temprana de la península de Santa Elena, Ecuador: Cultura Las Vegas* (Karen E. Stothert): 203–214. Serie Monografica 10. Museos del Banco Central del Ecuador, Guayaquil.

1990   Aboriginal Agriculture and Land Usage in the Amazon Basin, Ecuador. *Journal of Archaeological Science* 17: 665–677.

PIPERNO, DOLORES R., AND IRENE HOLST

1998   The Presence of Starch Grains on Prehistoric Stone Tools from the Humid Tropics: Indications of Early Tuber Use and Agriculture in Panama. *Journal of Archaeological Science* 25: 765–776.

PIPERNO, DOLORES R., AND DEBORAH M. PEARSALL

1998   *Origins of Agriculture in the Lowland Neotropics.* Academic Press, San Diego.

POPPER, VIRGINIA

1982   Análisis general de las muestras. In *Precerámico peruano. Los gavilanes. Mar, desierto, y oasis en la historia del hombre* (Duccio Bonavia, ed.): 148–156. Corporación

Financiera de Desarrollo (COFIDE), Oficina de Asuntos Culturales, Instituto Arqueológico Alemán, Comisión de Arqueólogia General y Comparada. Editorial Ausonia–Talleres Gráficos, Lima.

POZORSKI, SHELIA G.
    1983   Changing Subsistence Priorities and Early Settlement Patterns on the North Coast of Peru. *Journal of Ethnobiology* 3: 15–38.

POZORSKI, SHELIA G., AND THOMAS POZORSKI
    1987   *Early Settlement and Subsistence in the Casma Valley, Peru*. University of Iowa Press, Iowa City.

QUILTER, JEFFREY, BERNARDINO OJEDA E., DEBORAH M. PEARSALL, DANIEL H. SANDWEISS, JOHN G. JONES, AND ELIZABETH S. WING
    1991   Subsistence Economy of El Paraíso, an Early Peruvian Site. *Science* 251: 277–283.

RAYMOND, J. SCOTT
    1981   The Maritime Foundations of Andean Civilization: A Reconsideration of the Evidence. *American Antiquity* 46: 806–821.
    1988   Subsistence Patterns during the Early Formative in the Valdivia Valley, Ecuador. In *Diet and Subsistence: Current Archaeological Perspectives. Proceedings of the Nineteenth Annual Chacmool Conference* (Brenda V. Kennedy and Genevieve M. LeMoine, eds.): 159–163. Archaeological Association of the University of Calgary, Calgary, Alberta.

ROSSEN, JACK
    n.d.   Ecotones and Low-Risk Intensification: The Middle Preceramic Occupation of Nonchoc, Northern Peru. Ph.D. dissertation, Department of Anthropology, University of Kentucky, Lexington, 1991.

ROSSEN, JACK, TOM D. DILLEHAY, AND DONALD UGENT
    1996   Ancient Cultigens or Modern Intrusions? Evaluating Plant Remains in an Andean Case Study. *Journal of Archaeological Science* 23: 391–407.

SANDWEISS, DANIEL H.
    1996   The Development of Fishing Specialization on the Central Andean Coast. In *Prehistoric Hunter-Gatherer Fishing Strategies* (Mark G. Plew, ed.): 41–63. Department of Anthropology, Boise State University, Boise, Idaho.

SMITH, C. EARLE JR.
    1980   Plant Remains from Guitarrero Cave. In *Guitarrero Cave: Early Man in the Andes* (Thomas F. Lynch, ed.): 87–119. Academic Press, New York.
    1988   Floral Remains. In *La Galgada. Peru. A Preceramic Culture in Transition* (Terence Grieder, Alberto B. Mendoza, C. Earle Smith Jr., and Robert M. Malina): 125–151. University of Texas Press, Austin.

STAHL, PETER W.
    1995   Differential Preservation Histories Affecting the Mammalian Zooarchaeological Record from the Forested Neotropical Lowlands. In *Archaeology in the Lowland American Tropics. Current Analytical Methods and Recent Applications* (Peter W. Stahl, ed.): 154–180. Cambridge University Press, Cambridge.

STEMPER, DAVID
    n.d.   Paleoethnobotanical Studies at La Ponga (OGSE-186). Report on file at the American Archaeology Division, University of Missouri, Columbia, 1980.

STOTHERT, KAREN E.
    1985   The Preceramic Las Vegas Culture of Coastal Ecuador. *American Antiquity* 50: 613–637.
    1988   Prehistoria temprana de la península de Santa Elena, Ecuador: Cultura Las Vegas. Serie Monográfica 10. Museos del Banco Central del Ecuador, Guayaquil.

TOLSTOY, PAUL
    n.d.   An Archaeological Sequence for the Santiago–Cayapas River Basin, Esmeraldas, Ecuador. Paper presented at the 52nd Annual Meeting of the Society for American Archaeology, Toronto, 1987.

TOLSTOY, PAUL, AND WARREN R. DEBOER
    1989   An Archaeological Sequence for the Santiago–Cayapas River Basin, Esmeraldas, Ecuador. *Journal of Field Archaeology* 16: 259–308.

UMLAUF, MARCELLE
    n.d.   Paleoethnobotanical Investigations at the Initial Period Site of Cardal, Peru. Master's thesis, Department of Anthropology, University of Missouri, Columbia, 1988.

VAN DER MERWE, NIKOLAAS J., JULIA A. LEE-THORP, AND J. SCOTT RAYMOND
    1993   Light, Stable Isotopes and the Subsistence Base of Formative Cultures at Valdivia, Ecuador. In *Prehistoric Human Bone: Archaeology at the Molecular Level* (Joseph B. Lambert and Gisela Grupe, eds.): 63–97. Springer-Verlag, Berlin.

VRADENBURG, JOSEPH A.
    n.d.   Analysis of the Human Skeletal Remains from the Late (1150–800 B.C.) Initial Period Site of Cardal, Lurin Valley, Peru. Master's thesis, Department of Anthropology, University of Missouri, Columbia, 1992.

WEIR, GLENDON, AND PHILLIP DERING
    1986   The Lomas of Paloma: Human–Environmental Relationships in a Central Peruvian Fog Oasis—Archaeobotany and Palynology. In *Andean Archaeology* (Ramiro M. Matos, Solveig A. Turpin, and J. Herbert H. Eling Jr., eds.): 18–44. Monographs of the Institute of Archaeology. Institute of Archaeology, Los Angeles.

WELLS, LISA ESQUIVEL, AND JAY STRATTON NOLLER
    1999   Holocene Coevolution of the Physical Landscape and Human Settlement in Northern Coastal Peru. *Geoarchaeology* 14: 755–789.

ZEIDLER, JAMES A.
    1986   La Evolución local de asentamientos formativos en el litoral ecuatoriano: El Caso de Real Alto. In *Arqueológia de la costa ecuatoriana: Nuevos enfoques*: 85–127. Corporación Editora Nacional, Quito.
    1991   Maritime Exchange in the Early Formative Period of Coastal Ecuador: Geopolitical Origins of Uneven Development. In *Research in Economic Anthropology*, vol. 13: 247–268. JAI Press, Greenwich, Conn.

ZEIDLER, JAMES A., CAITLIN E. BUCK, AND CLIFFORD D. LITTON
   1998   The Integration of Archaeological Phase Information and Radiocarbon
           Results from the Jama River Valley, Ecuador: A Bayesian Approach. *Latin
           American Antiquity*: 160–179.

ZEIDLER, JAMES A., AND DEBORAH M. PEARSALL (EDS.)
   1994   *Regional Archaeology in Northern Manabí, Ecuador,* vol. 1: *Environment, Cultural
           Chronology, and Prehistoric Subsistence in the Jama River Valley.* Memoirs in Latin
           American Archaeology 8. University of Pittsburgh, Pittsburgh, Pa.

ZEIDLER, JAMES A., AND MARY JO SUTLIFF
   1994   Definition of Ceramic Complexes and Cultural Occupation in the Jama
           Valley. In *Regional Archaeology in Northern Manabí, Ecuador,* vol. 1: *Environment,
           Cultural Chronology, and Prehistoric Subsistence in the Jama River Valley* (James A.
           Zeidler and Deborah M. Pearsall, eds.): 111–130. Memoirs in Latin American
           Archaeology 8. University of Pittsburgh, Pittsburgh, Pa.

Health Issues in the Early Formative of Ecuador: Skeletal Biology of Real Alto

DOUGLAS H. UBELAKER
NATIONAL MUSEUM OF NATURAL HISTORY, SMITHSONIAN INSTITUTION

INTRODUCTION

The Early Formative of Ecuador is generally recognized as a period of transition (Meggers 1966). Presumably, prior populations of Ecuador were relatively small, more nomadic, and lived in more dispersed settlements. During the Early Formative, populations began to shift their subsistence base in favor of agriculture and animal domestication (Lathrap 1975), although overall subsistence likely remained mixed (Zeidler and Pearsall 1994). This not only involved a likely change in subsistence but also in settlement patterns. Agriculture and other forms of food production involved a lifestyle transition toward more sedentism, larger population size and density, and increased social stratification and complexity.

Although much of the shift described above is cultural, it includes a substantial biological component. Subsistence and settlement pattern are two important variables in the multifactorial evolution of disease systems. Diet affects nutrition, which in turn affects skeletal growth and maintenance. Population sedentism and density are important factors contributing to the spread of infectious disease. Thus, careful study of well-documented samples of human skeletal remains offers a unique opportunity to examine aspects of community health and understand the dynamic interplay between biology and culture.

Since 1973, I have collaborated with many archaeologists working in Ecuador to assemble and carefully study well-documented samples of human remains from archeological contexts (Ubelaker 1988f). Through this work, I have published analyses of about 1,637 skeletons from 23 distinct samples (Table 1) ranging in antiquity from 192 Preceramic Vegas Complex skeletons (6300–4650 B.C.

Table 1

Chronological Sequence of Skeletal Samples by Culture and Period

Site and no. of samples	Date	Location	Culture
	Preceramic		
Santa Elena complex 192	8250–6600 BP	Guayas	Vegas complex
	Early Formative		
Real Alto 100	3400–1500 B.C.	Guayas	Valdivia
	Intermediate Precontact		
Cotocollao 199	1000–500 B.C.	Pichincha	Cotocollao
La Libertad (OGSE-46) 24	900–200 B.C.	Guayas	Engoroy
Early La Tolita 7	600–200 B.C.	Esmeraldas	Early Tolita
Cumbayá 20	400 B.C.–A.D. 100	Pichincha	Cumbayá
OGSE-MA-172 30	100 B.C.	Guayas	Guangala
Classic La Tolita 20	200 B.C.–A.D. 90	Esmeraldas	Classic Tolita
Late La Tolita 54	90–400	Esmeraldas	Late Tolita
	Late Precontact		
Ayalán (non-urn) 51	500 B.C.–A.D. 1155	Guayas	Milagro
La Florida 76	340	Pichincha	Chaupicruz
Agua Blanca 7	800–1500	Manabí	Manteño
Ayalán (urn) 384	730–1730	Guayas	Milagro
	Early Historic		
Convento de San Francisco			
hallway 30	1500–1570	Pichincha	Historic
Santo Domingo 46	1500–1650	Pichincha	Historic
Convento de San Francisco			
strata cut, upper level 74	1540–1650	Pichincha	Historic
strata cut, lower level 46	1580–1700	Pichincha	Historic
atrium 19	1600–1725	Pichincha	Historic
	Late Historic		
Convento de San Francisco			
church 119	1535–1858	Pichincha	Historic
superficial collection, lower level 52	1670–1709	Pichincha	Historic
main cloister 33	1730–1858	Pichincha	Historic
superficial collection, upper level 21	1770–1890	Pichincha	Historic
boxes 33	1850–1940	Pichincha	Historic

uncorrected radiocarbon years) from the Santa Elena peninsula (Ubelaker 1980a, 1988d) to 33 skeletons from a component of Convento de San Francisco in Quito, dating from the late 19th and early 20th centuries (Ripley and Ubelaker 1992; Teran de Rodriguez 1988; Ubelaker 1994).

Although the skeletal samples referred to above form a column of time representing much of Ecuador's human past, relatively few remains are available from the Early Formative. This essay focuses on the analysis of 100 human skeletons from the Early Formative recovered during excavations at the coastal Ecuador site of Real Alto, OGCH-12 (Fig. 1) initiated in 1974 by Jorge G. Marcos and the late Donald W. Lathrap of the University of Illinois. The site is located near the coastal town of Chanduy and was occupied for a long period during the Early Formative (Damp 1988; Lathrap, Marcos, and Zeidler 1977; Marcos 1988; Marcos, Lathrap, and Zeidler 1976). The recovered human remains date from Valdivia 1 through Valdivia 7. The archaeologists reported evidence of a ceremonial center and considerable social specialization. Some have also argued that diet at Real Alto and related early Formative Ecuadorian sites included maize, perhaps even involving intensive maize agriculture (Zevallos et al. 1977).

At the invitation of Ecuadorian officials, I studied most of the remains from the Real Alto excavations in 1981 in a makeshift laboratory outside of Quito in the Ecuadorian highlands. Since the materials had not been cleaned, I first washed them with water. After they were dry, I conducted a skeletal inventory and collected data that had proven to be of interest in previous studies of Ecuadorian samples (e.g., Ubelaker 1980a,b, 1981). Estimations of age and sex were based on standard techniques (Bass 1987; Ubelaker 1989).

A relatively small portion of the Real Alto cemetery sample had been sent to the University of Illinois at Urbana–Champaign (UIUC). Rather than publish information gleaned from the partial sample studied in Ecuador, I chose to wait until the entire sample had been examined. This opportunity materialized in March 1995 when research assistant Erica Jones and I traveled to Urbana at the invitation of Linda Klepinger of the UIUC Department of Anthropology. We first washed most of this sample and then studied it in the same manner as with the previous material in Ecuador. Some additional data were collected at this time, reflecting expanded protocols developed in recent years (Buikstra and Ubelaker 1994).

DEMOGRAPHY

The entire sample of 100 individuals originates from a variety of time periods within the Early Formative. Linda Klepinger provided a chronological clas-

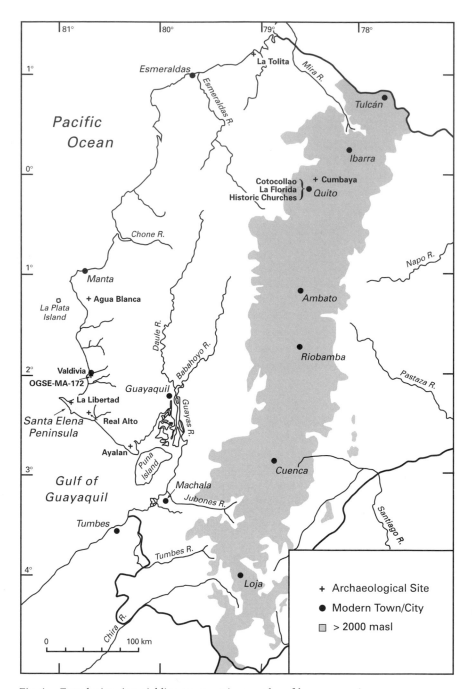

Fig. 1   Ecuadorian sites yielding comparative samples of human remains.

sification of the burial features that had been assembled and given to her by the archaeologists in charge of the Real Alto excavations. Additional information on the chronological affiliation of burials is available in Marcos (1988: 161–173). According to our study of the number of individuals within each feature and this chronological classification, the 100 individuals were assigned to the following periods: 1 from Valdivia 1, 5 from Valdivia 2, 64 from Valdivia 3, 1 from Valdivia 2 through 3, 1 from 3 through 4, 4 from Valdivia 4, 1 from Valdivia 4 through 5, 1 from Valdivia 5, 3 from Valdivia 5 through 6, 14 from Valdivia 6, 1 from Valdivia 1 through 7, and 4 of unknown phase but presumably from sometime within the Early Formative occupations represented by the site. The question marks and multiple designations reflect uncertainty on the part of the archaeologists involved regarding the classification of those particular features. Since the individuals had been assigned to so many closely affiliated cultural levels, for purposes of this essay, they were grouped into one sample of 100 individuals representing the Early Formative. Any attempt to separate out subsamples beyond the large number from Valdivia 3 would produce individual samples too small to be useful in statistical comparisons.

The entire sample of 100 contained individuals of all ages and of both sexes, thus presenting no evidence for cultural exclusion of any particular sex or age group. Of all individuals in the sample, 8 percent were below the age of 1 year and about 21 percent were less than age 5. The ratio of the number of individuals less than age 15 (37) to the number 15 years or greater (63) was 0.59. The mean age at death for males was 38.7 years compared with 33.9 years for females. Summary data on each of the burial features are presented in Table 2. Inventory columns explain the relative completeness of the skeleton. Some remains were not available for analysis, some could be identified as being present but were in some way incomplete, and other materials were relatively complete and present.

Table 3 presents a life table reconstructed from the entire Real Alto sample. The life table suggests that 8 percent of the sample died prior to age 1. An additional 13 percent died during the following five years. Life expectancy at birth was about 24 years with a first-year mortality of 8 percent. Mortality during the first five years was about 21 percent. Life expectancy at age 15 was about 20 years. Thus, a 15-year-old could expect to live until about age 35.

Comparative data on the demographic variables as well as others are available from additional samples from Ecuador. Klepinger's (1979) previous demographic study of the Real Alto remains focused exclusively on those she attributed to the Valdivia 3 phase. Her published life table suggests 22 percent died before the age of 5, a life expectancy at birth of 20.7 years, life expectancy at age 5 of

Table 2
Individual Burial Data from Real Alto

Burial no.	Individual	Sex	Age (yr)	Stature	Cranial deformation	Bone Condition				Valdivia (V) period
						Cranium	Mandible	Long bones	Other	
4	A	M?	40–45		no	I	I	I	I	V 3
4	B	F	30–60			I	I	A	A	V 3
5		F	ca. 20	(145.6)		I	I	I	I	V 3
6		M?	40–45		no	I	I	I	I	V 3 or 2
7		F	30–35	(141.7)		I	C	I	I	V 6
8		M	30–35	(143.7)	no	I	C	C	I	V 3
9		F	35–40		no	I	I	I	I	V 6
10		?	18–45			I	A	A	I	V 6–7
12		?	4–5			I	A	I	I	V 3
13		M	32–40	(155.0)	no	C	C	I	A	V 5–6
14		?	9–11			A	C	C	I	V 5–6
15	A	M	25–30	162.4		I	I	C	I	V 3
15	B	M	30–35		maybe?	I	I	A	A	V 3
15	C	?	ca. 15			I	A	A	A	V 3
15	D	?	2–3			I	A	A	A	V 3
15	E	?	8–10			I	A	A	A	V 3
15	F	M?	20–30			I	A	A	A	V 3
15	G	?	3–4			I	A	A	A	V 3
15	H	?	5–6			I	A	A	A	V 3
16		?	ca. 9			A	A	I	I	V 6
17		M	33–40	160.4	no	C	C	C	I	V 3
18		M	35–40	(156.8)	no	I	I	C	I	V 3
19		?	10–11			C	C	C	C	V 3
20	A	?	ca. 2			I	I	I	I	V 3

No.	Grp	Sex	Age	Ht								V
20	B	?	ca. 2			A	I	A	I	A	A	V 3
21		?	40–50		no	I	C	I	C	I	I	V 3
22		F	35–40	(139.9)		I	I	C	I	C	I	V 3
23	A	F?	15–16		no	I	I	I	I	I	I	V 3
23	B	F?	32–35	157.2	no	I	I	C	I	C	I	V 3
24		M?	40–45		no	I	I	I	I	I	I	V 3
25		M	30–37	(156.8)	no	C	C	C	C	C	C	V 5
26	A	M	35–42			I	I	I	C	I	I	V 6
26	B	F	28–35			A	A	A	I	I	I	V 6
27		F	17–20			I	I	C	C	C	I	V 6
28		?	40–50			I	A	I	I	I	I	V 3
29		F?	30–40			A	A	I	I	I	I	V 3
30		?	ca. 4			I	A	I	A	A	A	V 3
32	A	M	35–45	165.4	no	C	C	C	I	C	I	V 4
32	B	M	Adult			I	A	A	A	A	A	V 4
32	C	F	20–35			I	A	A	A	A	A	V 4
32	D	?	7–9			A	A	I	I	I	I	V 4
33		F	40–45		no	I	I	I	I	I	I	V 5–6
34		?	ca. 0.5			I	I	I	A	A	A	V 4 or 5
36		M	40–50		no	C	C	C	C	I	I	V 3
37		?	15–16			I	C	C	C	I	I	V 3
38		?	0.5–0.75			I	C	I	I	I	I	V 2
39		?	2–2.5			I	C	I	I	I	I	V 3
40	A	?	3–4.5			I	I	I	I	I	I	V 6
40	B	?	10–12			I	I	I	I	I	I	V 6
41		F	40–45	(143.0)	no	I	I	C	I	I	I	V 3
42		F	35–40			A	A	I	I	A	I	V 3
43	A	?	18–20			A	A	I	I	A	I	V 3
43	B	?	15–18			A	A	A	A	A	A	V 3
44		M	40–45	(159.0)	no	I	I	I	I	A	I	V 3

(cont.)

Table 2 (*cont.*)
Information on Individual Burials from Real Alto

Burial no.	Individual	Sex	Age (yr)	Stature	Cranial deformation	Bone Condition				Valdivia (V) period
						Cranium	Mandible	Long bones	Other	
45		F	34–38	145.1	no	I	I	C	I	V 3
46		F?	40–45		no	I	C	I	I	V 3
47		F	20–35	(143.0)		A	A	I	I	V 3
48		?	ca. 5			A	A	I	I	V 3
49		M	50–60		no	C	I	I	I	?
50		?	5–6			I	C	I	I	V 3
51		?	0–.25			I	I	A	I	V 3
52	A	M?	40–50	150.0		I	I	C	I	V 3
52	B	?	10–12			A	C	A	A	V 3
53		M	50–55	164.9	no	C	C	I	I	V 3
55		?	2–3			I	C	I	I	V 3
56	A	F	50–60		no	I	I	I	I	V 2
56	B	?	5–7			I	A	A	A	V 2
57	A	M	adult			A	C	C	I	V 6
57	B	?	2–4			I	C	A	A	V 6
58	A	F	adult		no	I	A	I	A	V 3
58	B	?	5–6			I	C	I	I	V 3
59		?	10–11			C	C	C	I	V 3
63		?	NB			A	I	I	A	V 3?
67		M	adult			I	A	A	A	V 3
68		M?	35–40			I	I	I	I	?
70	A	?	NB			I	I	I	I	V 3
70	B	?	NB			I	A	I	I	V 3
71	A	M	35–40	167.2		C	C	I	A	V 2

71	B	?	5–6	I	I	C	I	C	I	V 3
72		?	0–0.25	I	I	I	I	I	I	V 3
73		?	15–18	C	C	I	C	I	I	V 3
74	A	M	40–60	I	A	A	A	A	A	V 6
74	B	?	10–12	I	I	A	A	A	A	V 6
75	A	F	20–25	I	I	C	I	C	I	V 3
75	B	M	23–28	I	I	I	I	I	I	V 3
75	C	M	35–40	I	I	I	C	I	I	V 3
75	D	?	0.25	A	A	A	I	A	A	V 3
75	E	?	4–5	A	A	A	I	I	I	V 3
75	F	?	6–7	I	I	I	I	A	A	V 3
75	G	?	ca. 15	I	A	A	A	A	A	V 3
76		M	35–40	I	I	I	I	I	I	V 3
81		?	2.5–3	I	C	C	I	C	I	V 3
83		F	22–26	I	I	I	C	C	A	V 6
84		M	40–45	I	C	C	I	I	I	?
87		M	40–45	A	I	C	C	C	A	V 3
92		M	30–35	A	A	A	C	A	A	?
93		?	ca. 15	I	I	A	I	A	I	V 6
118		?	35–50	I	I	I	I	A	A	V 1
A15–9		?	4–5	I	I	A	A	A	A	V 3
S–20f–a–1		M	30–35	no	I	I	I	I	I	V 3 or 4

Notes: A = absent; C = complete; F = female; I = incomplete; M = male.

Table 3

Life Table Reconstructed from the Real Alto Sample

	Dx	dx	lx	qx	Lx	Tx	e°x (life expectancy in years)
0-.9	8.00	8.00	100.00	.0800	96.000	2413.300	24.13
1-4.9	13.00	13.00	92.00	.1413	342.000	2317.300	25.19
5-9.9	10.00	10.00	79.00	.1266	370.000	1975.300	25.00
10-14.9	6.00	6.00	69.00	.0870	330.000	1605.300	23.27
15-19.9	9.00	9.00	63.00	.1429	292.500	1275.300	20.24
20-24.9	3.24	3.24	54.00	.0600	261.900	982.800	18.20
25-29.9	5.40	5.40	50.76	.1064	240.300	720.900	14.20
30-34.9	9.72	9.72	45.36	.2143	202.500	480.600	10.60
35-39.9	14.04	14.04	35.64	.3939	143.100	278.100	7.80
40-44.9	11.88	11.88	21.60	.5500	78.300	135.000	6.25
45-49.9	5.40	5.40	9.72	.5556	35.100	56.700	5.83
50-54.9	2.16	2.16	4.32	.5000	16.200	21.600	5.00
55-59.9	2.16	2.16	2.16	1.0000	5.400	5.400	2.50
60-64.9	0.00	0.00	0.00	0.0000	0.000	0.000	0.00

Notes: Dx = number who died before reaching the next age group; dx = percentage of the Dx data; lx = percentage of survivors who reached the next age group. See Ubelaker (1989) for further discussion of life tables.

20.9 years, and at age 15 of 17.8 years. She suggested that relatively few individuals lived beyond age 50. Comparison with my Table 3 suggests relatively lower life expectancy values for all younger ages in the Klepinger reconstruction, but greater adult longevity. These differences may suggest that the later time periods exhibited increased life expectancy values. They also could reflect, at least partially, differences in methods utilized to estimate age at death and the fact that Klepinger's estimates were generated from field observations on the remains prior to cleaning.

Comparative data from other archaeologically recovered Ecuadorian samples are available from the numerous published studies summarized in Table 1. For broad comparative purposes, these samples have been grouped into six general successive temporal periods. The earliest comprises solely the 192 individuals from the Preceramic Vegas Complex sample from Santa Elena, dating about 8250 to 6600 BP. Greater detail and more rigorous statistical presentation of these data are available in the individual publications of these samples listed in the literature cited. As noted, the Early Formative sample consists entirely of the 100 Real Alto skeletons discussed in detail in this essay.

The Intermediate Precontact period includes skeletons from the sites of Cotocollao (Ubelaker 1980b; 1988e), La Libertad (Ubelaker 1988a), La Tolita (Ubelaker 1988b), Cumbayá (Buys and Dominguez 1988a,b; Ubelaker 1990), and OGSE-MA-172 (Ubelaker 1983, 1993). Dates from these sites range from 1000 B.C. to A.D. 400.

The Late Precontact period includes both components of the Ayalán site (Ubelaker 1981), as well as Agua Blanca (Ubelaker 1988c) and the highland site of La Florida (Doyon 1988; Ubelaker, Katzenberg, and Doyon 1995). Dates from these samples range from 500 B.C. to A.D. 1730.

The Historic remains originate from two Quito churches and have been divided into early and late groupings. Dates of the five early samples range from 1500 to 1725, while those of the later group range from 1535 to as late as 1940 (Ubelaker 1994).

Although these six temporal groupings generally represent a temporal sequence, they do not correspond exactly with traditional archeological or Historic classifications. The dates of individual component samples of these groupings overlap somewhat as well. For example, the latest date for the Late Precontact sample is 1730 for the Ayalán urn component, while the earliest date for the succeeding Early Historic period is 1500 and the latest date is only 1725. In spite of the overlap, the sequence makes sense because evidence suggests all Late Precontact samples, including Ayalán urn, predominantly represent Indian groups prior to Spanish contact. The Early Historic samples all present evidence that they date from the period of European contact. It also is important to note that many, if not most of the Historic samples likely originate from relatively high-status individuals of European ancestry. In contrast, the samples from the four earlier periods all represent Indians in nonurban settings.

As shown in Figure 2, the life expectancy at birth value of 24 for the Early Formative is slightly less than the Preceramic period and the following Intermediate Precontact, but higher than in the more recent periods. Life expectancy at birth represents the number of years a newborn can expect to survive, and thus reflects the influence of the infant mortality rate as well as adult longevity. Collectively, these data suggest overall mortality did not increase significantly until the Late Precontact and accelerated during the Historic periods.

Figure 3 presents comparative values for life expectancy at age 5. It reveals similar trends but excludes the important infant mortality and considers adult longevity. The Early Formative value drops from the Preceramic levels, gradually increases in successive Precontact periods, and then declines in the Historic periods.

Life expectancy at age 15 was only 20 years during the Early Formative, the lowest value for any period considered here (Fig. 4). This suggests that more adults died as young adults than in any other period of Ecuadorian history. Adult maximum longevity was 55 years, among the lowest values reported.

LIVING STATURE

Estimates of living stature were calculated from long bone measurements by using published regression equations (Ubelaker 1989). Stature values for males from Real Alto ranged from 150 to 167 cm with a mean of 162 cm. This value is similar to mean values from other periods (Fig. 5) suggesting little change in stature among males throughout time. As expected, mean female stature (151 cm) from the Real Alto sample is substantially less than that of males, but within the range of mean values from the other periods. As with males, female stature shows little variation throughout time. These values are Preceramic, 149 cm; Intermediate Precontact, 152 cm; Late Precontact, 151 cm; Early Historic, 151 cm; and Late Historic, 154 cm. The slightly higher value in the Late Historic sample probably reflects European rather than the exclusively Indian constituency of the earlier periods.

TRAUMA

Twelve bones from 10 individuals, all adult, showed evidence of trauma in the Real Alto sample. These individuals consisted of seven likely males and

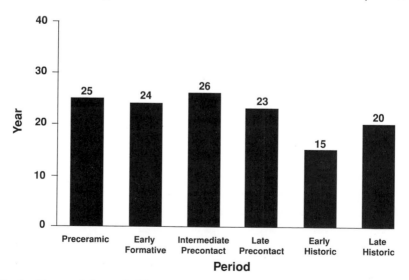

Fig. 2   Temporal change in life expectancy at birth.

three females, mostly from the older age categories. All of these fractures showed evidence of healing; thus they were not directly related to the deaths of the individuals. Various parts of the skeleton were involved, including the cranium, ribs, ulna, femur, fibula, and foot bones (Table 4). Four of these examples represented depressed fractures of the cranium, likely produced by interpersonal

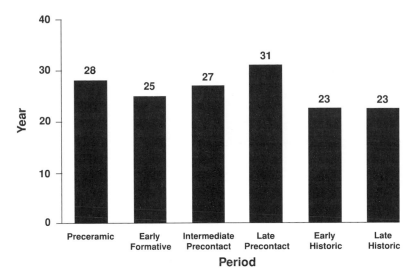

Fig. 3   Temporal change in life expectancy at age 5.

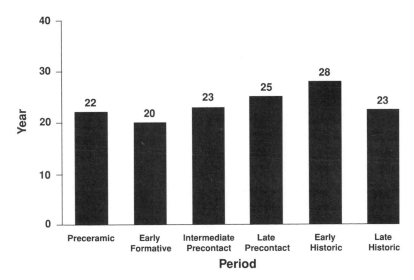

Fig. 4   Temporal change in life expectancy at age 15.

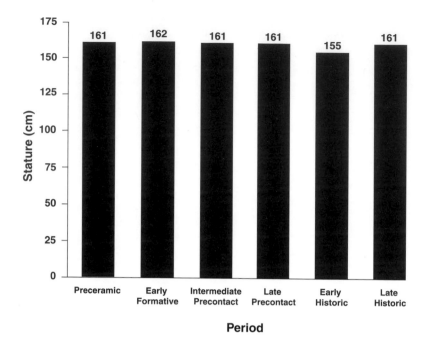

Fig. 5   Temporal change in male stature.

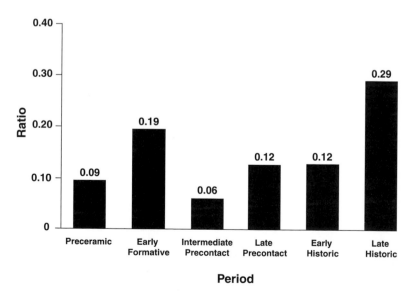

Fig. 6   Temporal change in the ratio of bones with trauma to the number of adults.

272

Table 4
Evidence for Trauma in the Real Alto Sample

Burial no.	Sex	Age (yr)	Fracture site	Description
8	M	30–35	left frontal	depressed 33 mm above left orbit
9	F	35–40	rib	healed near vertebral end
15B	M	30–35	right parietal	healed depressed
23B	F?	32–35	left ulna	healed midshaft; bone shortened 5 mm; radius not affected
24	M?	40–45	right frontal	depressed 25 mm above right orbit
33	F	40–45	right frontal rib	depressed 35 mm above right orbit fracture
49	M	50–60	right femur left 4th metatarsal	large callus involved remodeling at proximal end
71A	M	35–40	right 4th metatarsal	healed at distal end
84	M	40–45	fibula	healed complete
87	M	40–45	proximal foot phalanx	healed

Note: F = female; M = male.

violence. Three of these individuals date to Phase 3 and one from Phases 5 through 6.

The ratio of the number of bones with evidence of trauma compared with the number of adults in the sample was 0.19 for Real Alto. As shown in Figure 6, this value was higher than for all periods but the Late Historic.

PERIOSTEAL LESIONS

Periosteal lesions represent abnormal bone formation on the outer periosteal bone surface. Although a variety of conditions can stimulate such alterations, they are usually interpreted as indicators of infection. If soft tissue infection is sufficiently severe, the periosteum can be stimulated to produce bone deposits on the preexisting cortical bone surface. Although such bone deposits cannot always be linked to infection, they provide strong evidence of morbidity within the individual. The ratio of bones with periosteal lesions to adults in the Real Alto sample is 0.14. As shown in Figure 7, this value is intermediate between the low Preceramic value and the higher Intermediate Precontact value and substantially lower than the Historic values. In context, the value suggests gradually increasing frequencies of infection, likely correlated with increasing population

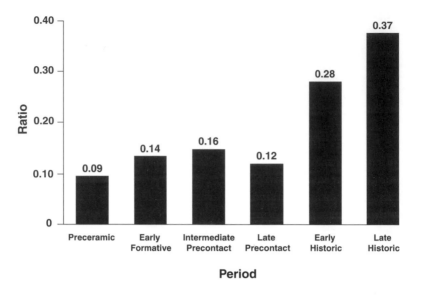

Fig. 7   Temporal change in the ratio of bones with periosteal lesions to the number of adults.

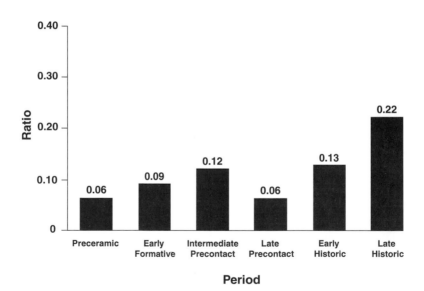

Fig. 8   Temporal change in the ratio of bones with periosteal lesions to the number of individuals.

density. A similar trend is seen when the ratio of bones with periosteal lesions to total number of individuals (of all ages) is plotted through time (Fig. 8). The comparatively high values from the Historic samples likely reflect the obviously elevated levels of infectious disease that contemporary sources documented for that time. The lower value for the Late Precontact is more difficult to explain, since presumably it represents the Precontact period with greatest population density and thus the greatest opportunity for the spread of infectious disease.

DENTAL HYPOPLASIA

Dental hypoplasia represents a structural defect in the tooth produced when tooth formation is temporarily disrupted (Goodman, Martin, Armelagos, and Clark 1984; Goodman, Thomas, Swedlund, and Armelagos 1988; Ubelaker 1992a). Although many factors can influence the formation of dental hypoplasia, the alterations are significantly correlated with morbidity and malnutrition. Although they cannot be linked directly to a specific disease condition or dietary deficiency, they seem to suggest general health problems at the time of their formation.

Ten hypoplastic teeth were found in the Real Alto sample, seven in maxillary teeth but only three in mandibular teeth. Of the maxillary teeth, three were from incisors, three were from canines, and one was from a premolar. Of the mandibular teeth, one was a canine and two were molars. Three teeth were from males, one from a female, and the remaining six from individuals of undetermined sex. Frequencies of affected teeth were 1.2 percent of male teeth and only 0.5 percent of female teeth. The overall frequency of affected teeth was 1.7 percent.

Figure 9 plots the frequency of permanent teeth with hypoplastic defects in the chronological periods. The Real Alto figure is higher than the Preceramic figure, equal to the Intermediate Precontact period and considerably lower than the Late Precontact and Early Historic periods. In fact, the Precontact values show a general temporal trend of increasing hypoplasia frequency with time. The reduction in the Historic values is perplexing, but two explanations are plausible. The hypoplastic defects may represent sites on the tooth especially conducive to caries formation. Thus, the elevated caries frequency, apparent especially in Late Historic times, combined with increased longevity, may have created especially high frequencies of tooth loss for the hypoplastic teeth, thus eliminating them from the sample prior to the death of these individuals.

The other possible explanation may be that the Historic samples represent a different population, both genetically and socially, than the earlier samples. The individuals of predominantly European ancestry and higher social class may have enjoyed better childhood nutrition than the earlier populations.

DENTAL CARIES

Dental caries represents a disease of the teeth. Generally, it is believed that certain foods, especially refined sugar, adhere to the tooth surface, providing an ideal environment for bacteria to multiply and colonize (Larsen, Shavit, and Griffin 1991). Left uninterrupted, these bacterial colonies can produce substances that break down the tooth surface, leading to tissue collapse and formation of a cavity. In the absence of adequate dental hygiene and dentistry, the process continues until much of the tooth surface is destroyed. Eventually, such destruction may produce exposure of the pulp cavity of the tooth, allowing bacteria to enter and infect the inner-tooth structure. The result of such bacterial encroachment is likely an apical abscess and eventual loss of the tooth (Ubelaker 1992b).

Dental caries has attracted considerable attention in anthropological analysis because it continues to be a universal health problem and archaeologically recovered samples reveal a dietary component in its development. The consumption of certain foods promotes the formation of dental caries.

The caries data are especially relevant in studies of Early Formative samples from Ecuador because (a) the literature contains considerable debate regarding

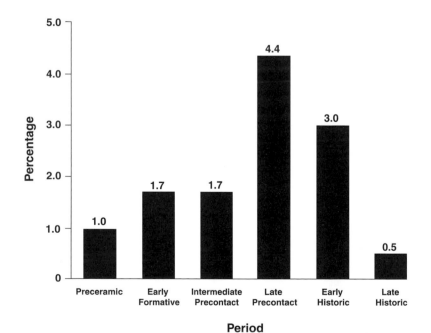

Fig. 9   Temporal change in the frequency of dental hypoplasia.

subsistence (Pearsall 1988; Zevallos et al. 1977) and (b) some data have been published from the Early Formative in Ecuador citing low-caries frequencies and interpreting them as evidence for the lack of consumption of carbohydrates, and thus the lack of the practice of intensive maize agriculture (Turner 1978).

In the Real Alto sample, 8.5 percent of all teeth displayed at least one carious lesion. In this study, a carious lesion was defined as a defect in the tooth at least 1 mm in diameter displaying clear evidence of tissue collapse resulting from caries. Of 209 teeth from males, 29 (13.9%) were carious. Of 183 teeth from adult females, 14 (7.6%) were carious. Three of 149 teeth of unknown sex were carious (2.0%). Of the 21 maxillary teeth with caries, 2 were incisors, 2 were canines, 3 were premolars, and 14 were molars. Of 25 mandibular teeth, not one was from incisors, 3 were from canines, 5 from premolars, and 17 from molars.

The carious teeth in the Real Alto sample originated from 22 individuals, 12 probable males, seven probable females, and three individuals of undetermined sex. As shown in Table 5, one of these individuals was from Valdivia 2, 15 from Valdivia 3, one from Valdivia 5, one from Valdivia 5 through 6, one from Valdivia 6, and 3 of unknown cultural affiliation.

Of the 52 individuals in the sample with at least one tooth sufficiently well preserved to allow observations for carious lesions, 22, or 42.3 percent, had at least one carious lesion. Frequencies for percentage of individuals affected for each phase within the sample were 100 percent (1 of 1) for Phase 2; 44.1 percent (15 of 34) for Phase 3; 0 percent (0 of 1) for Phase 4; 100 percent (1 of 1) for Phase 5; 12.5 percent (1 of 8) for Phase 6; 50 percent (1 of 2) for Phase 5 through 6; 0 percent (0 of 1) for Phase 3 through 4; and 75 percent (3 of 4) for those of unknown phase.

Figure 10 provides temporal perspective for the Real Alto caries data. The Real Alto figure of 8.5 percent of teeth is sharply higher than the previous Preceramic value of 3.0 percent and also markedly higher than the later Intermediate Precontact value of 2.3 percent, and even slightly higher than the Early Historic figure of 5.6 percent.

Turner (1978) summarized much of the relevant literature on caries frequency. He noted that elevated occurrence of caries is frequently associated with intensive maize agriculture, since many of the products, especially maize, involved in such practice are thought to be cariogenic. Of 76 teeth from six individuals of the Early Formative Valdivia sample from the Buena Vista site and 14 teeth from one individual from a nearby Machalilla phase site (La Cabuya), Turner found absence of caries in the Valdivia teeth and two possibly carious teeth from the later Machalilla phase individual. This suggested an overall frequency of 2.2 percent for the entire sample. He suggested that the low fre-

Table 5

Individuals with Dental Carious Lesions by Period

Period	Burial no.	Sex	No. of lesions
Valdivia 2	71A	Male	1
Valdivia 3	5	Female	1
	8	Male	1
	18	Male	2
	21	?	1
	22	Female	3
	24	Male?	5
	28	?	1
	41	Female	3
	43A	?	1
	44	Male	6
	45	Female	3
	46	Female?	2
	53	Male	2
	58A	Female	2
	76	Male	3
Valdivia 5	25	Male	1
Valdivia 5–6	13	Male	2
Valdivia 6	7	Female	1
?	49	Male	1
	68	Male?	2
	92	Male	3

quency offered "no physical anthropological support for the idea of early intensive agriculture in Ecuador" (Turner 1978: 696).

The data presented here suggest that in the Ecuadorian samples, a simple relationship between caries frequency and subsistence remains elusive. In contrast to the data Turner gleaned from his small Early Formative sample, the Real Alto data suggest relatively high caries frequency (8.5%) for the Early Formative and much lower frequencies for the later Intermediate Precontact samples.

Note that the 8.5 percent figure applies, like all other data discussed herein, to the *entire* Real Alto sample, even though a considerable time range is involved. As noted above, the 22 individuals with carious lesions originated from several different cultural phases within the Early Formative. The data show that 68.2 percent of the carious individuals in the sample were from the Valdivia 3 phase and 76.1 percent of carious teeth originated from Valdivia 3. Only 4.5

percent of individuals with caries were from Valdivia 2, and only 2.2 percent of teeth with lesions were from Valdivia 2.

Turner (1978) notes that crown caries and root caries may represent different phenomena. He indicates that the two carious lesions found in his Machalilla sample were located at the crown–root junction and did not involve enamel destruction. He suggests that crown caries are more significantly correlated with intensive agriculture than root caries. He further suggests that root lesions could result from "(a) actual caries, (b) incipient caries, (c) root caries (a wasting process associated with old age), or (d) a form of preservation damage" (Turner 1978: 696).

The Real Alto lesions located in cementum were not judged to result from postmortem factors. Rather, they were scored as present if they appeared to show evidence of structural damage from disease. Of the 46 teeth with lesions, 7 displayed lesions of the cementum that did not involve the crown. The remaining 39 teeth with enamel involvement suggest a crown caries frequency of 7.2 percent. This figure is still high in relationship to the other comparative data from Ecuador. The root carious lesions were found within the dentitions of predominantly young adults suggesting they were not caused by factors relating to old age. It is also worth noting that all comparative data from Ecuador reported here are for total caries frequency, grouping teeth with both crown and cementum lesions.

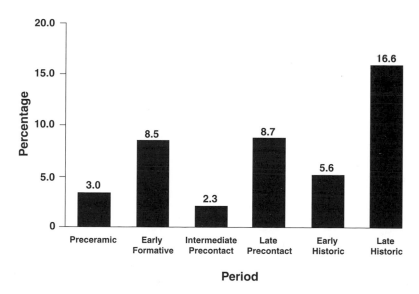

Fig. 10 Temporal change in the frequency of dental caries.

Obviously, extensive maize consumption during Early Formative times would explain the comparatively high frequency of dental caries in the Real Alto sample. Although if maize relating to intensive maize agriculture is the primary explanation, then why are the caries frequencies during the Intermediate Precontact period so low? The answers likely relate to both the dynamics of caries formation, as well as the complexity of food production and preparation. There may be other foods in addition to maize that were consumed during the Early Formative that were cariogenic. The population at Real Alto may have been exploiting a local food source not available to their earlier Preceramic neighbors. They may have favored a method of food preparation that rendered their food especially prone toward caries formation. All of these factors also may have been operating on the later Intermediate Precontact group to limit their caries involvement.

ALVEOLAR ABSCESSES

When the destruction of the tooth surface by caries, attrition, or trauma is such that the pulp cavity is exposed, bacteria can penetrate to the tip of the root and form an abscess in the surrounding bone. Such an alveolar abscess frequently leads to tooth loss, after which the involved area of the bone gradually remodels, destroying the evidence for the abscess as well as the perforations in the bone for the roots.

In the Real Alto sample, alveolar abscesses were found in 8.9 percent of observations for the trait. The frequencies were 11.3 percent in males and 9.7 percent in females. As shown in Figure 11, the overall 8.9 percent value is highest of any of the groupings depicted. It displays a remarkable increase over the low Preceramic value. The high value likely represents a combination of dental problems because of considerable attrition of the occlusal surfaces, combined with a relatively high caries rate. The young mean age of death of the adults in the Real Alto sample also is a contributing factor, since in older individuals many previously abscessed teeth would have been lost, with the alveolus remodeled to the point that a previously existing abscess would not have been detected.

ANTEMORTEM TOOTH LOSS

The final outcome of dental disease is tooth loss. Loss of teeth in these samples usually results from caries or occlusal attrition leading to pulp exposure and apical abscesses. The associated bone loss allows the tooth to be easily extracted. Severe and prolonged periodontal disease also can create bone remodeling and reduction that can lead to tooth loss.

In the Real Alto sample, 10.1 percent of all permanent teeth had been lost antemortem. The values were 10.9 percent for males and 15.6 percent for females. Figure 12 compares the percentage of permanent tooth loss antemortem from the Real Alto sample with the other six temporal samples from Ecuador. The data demonstrate a regular increase in antemortem tooth loss with time. This seems to reflect the general temporal increase in both dental disease and adult longevity.

OTHER PATHOLOGY

In addition to the dental disease discussed above, two examples of interproximal grooves were found. One was found on the mesial surface of the left mandibular first premolar from a male, age 40 to 45, of Feature 84 (Fig. 13). This male also displayed extensive dental attrition, arthritic changes on the glenoid cavity of the scapulae and the left temporomandibular joint, and a well-remodeled fracture of a fibula. Microscopic examination revealed fine parallel striations extending along the long axis of the alteration.

A second interproximal groove was found on the buccal aspect of a large

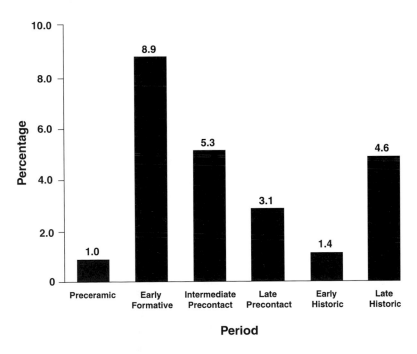

Fig. 11 Temporal change in the frequency of alveolar abscesses.

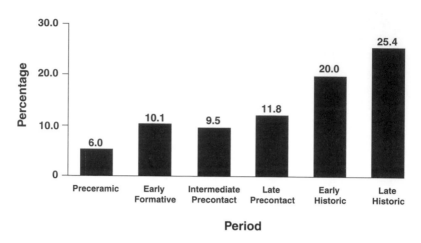

Fig. 12 Temporal change in the frequency of antemortem tooth loss.

carious lesion located in the distal cervical area of a maxillary right second molar of a likely male, age 35 to 40, of Feature 68. The groove extends into the carious lesion.

Both of these lesions appear to represent the use of toothpick-like instruments. Apparently, the instrument was inserted between the teeth with sufficient frequency that grooves were eventually worn. The association of the groove with the carious lesion in Feature 68 likely suggests the instrument was inserted in response to discomfort associated with the carious lesion. Similar type grooves have been reported from numerous other archeological samples throughout the world (Ubelaker, Phenice, and Bass 1969). The fine, parallel striations likely were produced by many individual insertions of the instrument.

Additional pathology, not included in the categories discussed above, includes various examples of congenital disorders. These consist of fused foot phalanges from a likely male, age 40 to 45, of Burial 4; fusion of the second and third cervical vertebrae in a child, age 10 to 11, of Feature 19; fused cervical vertebrae from a female, age 34 to 38, from Feature 45; and an apparent cervical rib from a female, age 22 to 26, from Feature 83.

Only one possible nondefinitive example of cranial deformation was noted in this sample, the Phase 3 male, age 30 to 35, of Burial 15B. In other early samples from Ecuador, cranial deformation was not found at the Vegas Complex site OGSE-80 (Munizaga 1976; Ubelaker 1980a). Cranial deformation

Fig. 13 Interproximal groove on premolar from Feature 84.

has been suggested for Valdivia remains from San Pablo and Engomala (Munizaga 1976) as well as Machalilla (La Cabuya) and various coastal Chorrera samples (Munizaga 1976) and the highland site of Cotocollao (Ubelaker 1988d). Munizaga suggests aspects of this custom began in Ecuador about 2000 B.C.

CONCLUSIONS

The Real Alto data provide much of the missing link in the previously published information on health trends within Ecuador. As expected, the data suggest that tooth loss, most demographic variables, living stature, dental hypoplasia, and skeletal evidence of infection were transitional between the Preceramic and later samples. These data suggest that evidence of infectious disease, growth disruption, and levels of infection were increasing during the Early Formative but had not yet achieved the higher values of later periods. Porotic hyperostosis had not yet appeared, suggesting that subsistence and population density had not yet created conditions conducive to severe anemia in the populations. Such evidence appears to be confined to the coast beginning during Guangala times (what has been called the Intermediate Precontact period) and may represent anemia brought on by severe hookworm infection (Ubelaker 1992b,c).

Douglas H. Ubelaker

Unusual features of the Real Alto data consist of the elevated frequencies of trauma, dental caries, and dental abscesses. Although conclusions must be tempered by the small sample sizes involved, the data suggest that during the Early Formative in Ecuador, trauma, including interpersonal violence, may have been on the increase. This may suggest intergroup conflict, competition over territory or resources, or domestic violence. The high levels of dental caries seem to be subsistence related and lend some credence to the archaeological evidence for extensive maize consumption at this time. Other interpretations, relating to subsistence and food preparation cannot be ruled out, however, especially since lower levels of dental caries are found in the later Intermediate period samples. Clearly, simplistic explanations relating dental disease to single foods are not tenable. The interrelationship between biology and culture is both dynamic and complex and a complete explanation likely must await additional research on other well-documented samples.

Acknowledgments   Access to the Real Alto samples was graciously provided by Jorge Marcos and Olaf Holm. Access to the portion of the sample at the University of Illinois was graciously provided by Linda Klepinger. Helpful assistance at the Smithsonian Institution was provided by M. Bakry in the preparation of the map and Erica Jones in data collection at the University of Illinois and general manuscript preparation.

BIBLIOGRAPHY

Bass, William M.
1987   *Human Osteology* (3d ed.). Missouri Archaeological Society, Columbia.

Buikstra, Jane E., and Douglas H. Ubelaker (eds.)
1994   Standards for Data Collection from Human Skeletal Remains. *Proceedings of a Seminar at the Field Museum of Natural History.* Arkansas Archeological Survey Research Series 44. Arkansas Archeological Survey, Fayetteville.

Buys, Jozef, and Victoria Dominguez
1988a   Un cementerio de hace 2000 años: Jardín del este. *Quito antes de Benalcazar* (I. C. Cevallos, ed.): 31–50. Centro Cultural Artes, Quito.
1988b   *Hace dos mil años en Cumbayá.* Instituto Nacional de Patrimonio Cultural, Quito.

Damp, Jonathan
1988   *La primera ocupación Valdivia de Real Alto: Patrones económicos, arquitectónicos, e ideológicos.* Escuela Politécnica del Litoral, Guayaquil.

Doyon, Leon G.
1988   Tumbas de la nobleza en La Florida. In *Quito antes de Benalcazar* (I. C. Cevallos, ed.): 51–66. Centro Cultural Artes, Quito.

Goodman, Alan H., Debra L. Martin, George J. Armelagos, and George Clark
1984   Indications of Stress from Bone and Teeth. *Paleopathology at the Origins of Agriculture* (M. N. Cohen and G. J. Armelagos, eds.): 13–49. Academic Press, New York.

Goodman, Alan H., R. Brooke Thomas, Alan C. Swedlund, and George J. Armelagos
1988   Biocultural Perspectives on Stress in Prehistoric, Historical, and Contemporary Population Research. *Yearbook of Physical Anthropology* 31: 169-202.

Hill, Betsy
1975   A New Chronology of the Valdivia Ceramic Complex from the Coastal Zone of Guayas Province, Ecuador. *Ñawpa Pacha* 10-12: 1-39.

Klepinger, Linda L.
1979   Paleodemography of the Valdivia III Phase at Real Alto, Ecuador. *American Antiquity* 44: 305-309.

Larsen, Clark Spencer, Rebecca Shavit, and Mark C. Griffin
1991   Dental Caries Evidence for Dietary Change: An Archaeological Context. *Advances in Dental Anthropology* (Marc A. Kelley and Clark Spencer Larsen, eds.): 179–202. Wiley-Liss, New York.

Lathrap, Donald W.
1975   *Ancient Ecuador: Culture, Clay and Creativity 3000–300* b.c. Field Museum of Natural History, Chicago.

Lathrap, Donald W., Jorge G. Marcos, and James A. Zeidler
1977   Real Alto: An Ancient Ceremonial Center. *Archaeology* 30: 2–13.

Douglas H. Ubelaker

MARCOS, JORGE G.
1988   Real Alto: La historia de un centro ceremonial Valdivia. Escuela Politécnica del Litoral, Guayaquil.

MARCOS, JORGE G., DONALD W. LATHRAP, AND JAMES A. ZEIDLER
1976   Ancient Ecuador Revisited. Field Museum of Natural History Bulletin 47: 3–8.

MEGGERS, BETTY J.
1966   Ecuador. Praeger, New York.

MUNIZAGA, JUAN R.
1976   Intentional Cranial Deformation in the Pre-Columbian Populations of Ecuador. American Journal of Physical Anthropology 45: 687–694.

PEARSALL, DEBORAH M.
1988   La producción de alimentos en Real Alto: La aplicación de las técnicas etnobotánicas al problema de la subsistencia en el período formativo ecuatoriano. Escuela Politécnica del Litoral, Guayaquil.

RIPLEY, CATHERINE, AND DOUGLAS H. UBELAKER
1992   The Ossuary of San Francisco Church, Quito, Ecuador (abstract). American Journal of Physical Anthropology Suppl. 14: 139.

TERAN DE RODRIGUEZ, PAULINA
1988   Estudio de investigación arquelógica, Convento de San Francisco de Quito, Sitio: OPQSF-2. Informe al Instituto de Cooperación Ibero Americana de España, Quito.

TURNER, CRISTY G. II
1978   Dental Caries and Early Ecuadorian Agriculture. American Antiquity 43: 694–697.

UBELAKER, DOUGLAS H.
1980a   Human Skeletal Remains from Site OGSE-80, a Pre-ceramic Site on the Sta. Elena Peninsula, Coastal Ecuador. Journal of the Washington Academy of Sciences 70: 3–24.

1980b   Prehistoric Human Remains from the Cotocollao Site, Pichincha Province, Ecuador. Journal of the Washington Academy of Sciences 70: 59–74.

1981   The Ayalán Cemetery: A Late Integration Period Burial Site on the South Coast of Ecuador, vol. 29, Smithsonian Contributions to Anthropology. Smithsonian Institutión Press, Washington, D.C.

1983   Human Skeletal Remains from OGSE-MA-172, an Early Guangala Cemetery Site on the Coast of Ecuador. Journal of the Washington Academy of Sciences 73: 16–26.

1988a   Human Remains from OGSE-46, La Libertad, Guayas Province, Ecuador. Journal of the Washington Academy of Sciences 78: 3–16.

1988b   Prehistoric Human Biology at La Tolita, Ecuador, a Preliminary Report. Journal of the Washington Academy of Sciences 78: 23–37.

1988c   A Preliminary Report of Analysis of Human Remains from Agua Blanca, a Prehistoric Late Integration Site from Coastal Ecuador. Journal of the Washington Academy of Sciences 78(1): 17–22.

1988d   Restos de esqueletos humanos del sitio OGSE-80. In Prehistoria temprana de la península de Santa Elena, Ecuador: Cultura Las Vegas (K. E. Stothert, ed.): 105–132. Museos del Banco Central del Ecuador, Guayaquil.

1988e   Restos humanos prehistóricos del sitio Cotocollao, provincia del Pichincha, Ecuador. In *Cotocollao: Una Aldea Formativa del valle de Quito* (M. Villalba, ed.): 557–571. Serie Monográfica 2. Miscelania Antropológica Ecuatoriana, Museos del Banco Central del Ecuador, Quito.

1988f   Skeletal Biology of Prehistoric Ecuador: An Ongoing Research Program. *Journal of the Washington Academy of Sciences* 78: 1–2.

1989   *Human Skeletal Remains. Excavation, Analysis, Interpretation* (2d ed.). Taraxacum, Washington.

1990   Human Skeletal Remains from "Jardín del Este," Cumbayá, Pichincha, Ecuador. In *La Preservación y promoción del patrimonio cultural del Ecuador*. Cooperación Técnica Ecuatoriana–Belga 4: 22–52. Instituto Nacional de Patrimonio Cultural, Quito.

1992a   Enamel Hypoplasia in Ancient Ecuador. *Journal of Paleopathology, Monographic Publications* 2: 207–217.

1992b   Patterns of Demographic Change in the Americas. *Human Biology* 64(3): 361–379.

1992c   Porotic Hyperostosis in Prehistoric Ecuador. In *Diet, Demography, and Disease: Changing Perspectives on Anemia* (P. Stuart-Macadam and S. Kent, eds.): 201–217. Aldine de Gruyter, New York.

1992d   Temporal Trends of Dental Disease in Ancient Ecuador. *Anthropologie* 30(1): 99–102.

1993   Restos humanos esqueléticos de OGSE-MA-172, un sitio "Guangala temprano" en la costa del Ecuador. In *Un sitio de Guangala temprano en el suroeste del Ecuador*: 99–112. Banco Central del Ecuador, Guayaquil.

1994   The Biological Impact of European Contact in Ecuador. In *In the Wake of Contact: Biological Responses to Conquest* (C. S. Larsen and G. R. Milner, eds.): 147–160. Wiley-Liss, New York.

UBELAKER, DOUGLAS H., M. ANNE KATZENBERG, AND LEON G. DOYON
1995   Status and Diet in Precontact Highland Ecuador. *American Journal of Physical Anthropology* 97(4): 403–411.

UBELAKER, DOUGLAS H., TERRELL W. PHENICE, AND WILLIAM M. BASS
1969   Artificial Interproximal Grooving of the Teeth in American Indians. *American Journal of Physical Anthropology* 30(1): 145–150.

ZEIDLER, JAMES. A., AND DEBORAH M. PEARSALL
1994   El proyecto arqueológico/paleoetnobotánico del valle de Jama. In *Regional Archaeology in Northern Manabí, Ecuador*, vol. 1: *Environment, Cultural Chronology, and Prehistoric Subsistence in the Jama River Valley* (James A. Zeidler and Deborah M. Pearsall, eds.): 2–12. Memoirs in Latin American Archaeology 8. University of Pittsburgh, Pittsburgh, Pa.

ZEVALLOS M., CARLOS, WILTON C. GALINAT, DONALD W. LATHRAP, EARL R. LENG, JORGE G. MARCOS, AND KATHLEEN M. KLUMPP
1977   The San Pablo Corn Kernel and Its Friends. *Science* 196: 385–389.

Ceramic Assemblage Variability in the Formative of Ecuador and Peru

WARREN R. DeBOER

QUEENS COLLEGE

CITY UNIVERSITY OF NEW YORK

INTRODUCTION

In attempts to establish reliable chronologies for the Formative of Ecuador and Peru, much energy has been devoted to the study and comparison of ceramic remains. This effort is basic and necessary. This essay, however, approaches pottery in a different, although hardly novel manner. Emphasis is placed on the definition of ceramic assemblages, those contemporary suites of vessels used for eating, drinking, cooking, storage, transport, or sheer ostentation. The purpose is to identify what assemblages were doing rather than slot them on a space–time grid.

To attribute function to the vessel forms that comprise assemblages, the archaeologist ideally should have information on food or other residues adhering to pot surfaces, traces of use–wear (e.g., Halley 1983), performance characteristics (e.g., A. Alvarez n.d.), and the context in which pottery was used (e.g., Moore 1989). For most Formative ceramic assemblages, however, the appropriate investigations designed to obtain these kinds of information have yet to be initiated. As a recourse, I follow the conventional and risk-laden procedure of inferring function from form. To do this, I have developed a general model for relating ceramic form and function that is based upon a survey of extant or historically reported assemblages from tropical forest groups in Ecuador and Peru. This broad-based comparison indicates a significant degree of correlation between vessel form and function and also relates vessel size and decorative elaboration to varying contexts of use such as feasts, everyday domestic tasks, and travel.

Although these guidelines should not be extrapolated uncritically into deep prehistory, they nonetheless provide a framework for isolating key inclusions and omissions in Formative assemblages. That is, the ethnographically based model is a device for highlighting contrasts in the archaeological record and, thereby, for directing attention to the ways in which ceramic assemblages of the past were constructed in ways fundamentally different from those of the present. Following the well-worn principle of proceeding from the known to the unknown, I begin with "old friends"—the Shipibo of the Central Ucayali, Peru.

SHIPIBO CERAMIC ASSEMBLAGE OF PERU

The Shipibo of the Central Ucayali, Peru, are famous for their elaborate pottery. In the early 1970s, when I lived among the Shipibo, pottery continued to be made and used in a largely traditional manner, although metal and plastic containers had made inroads. Shipibo pottery is the subject of a large literature (DeBoer 1990; DeBoer and Lathrap 1979; Gebhart-Sayer 1984; Lathrap 1970, 1976, 1983, n.d.a.; Roe 1980; Vossen 1969). Here, emphasis is placed on the form and function of vessels.

An initial and basic distinction is between cooking pots, or *ollas*, and noncooking pots. The former are wide-mouthed vessels that come in three functionally distinct sizes and are decorated with fingernail impressions, punctations, incision, or other texturing techniques (Fig. 1). The large *olla*, *kenti ani*, is used for cooking the batches of manioc that are needed in producing beer for fiestas. Everyday cooking pots are of medium size, although two submodes are recognized, a larger *kenti anicha* and a smaller *kenti anitama*. The smallest *olla*, *kenti vacu*, is used to heat medicines and can also serve as a portable cook pot. *Olla*s customarily have smudged interiors.

Noncooking vessels consist of jars and bowls that, like cookware, come in three sizes (Fig. 2). Large jars, *chomo ani*, are used as beer kegs for fiesta gatherings. The everyday jar, *chomo anitama*, is the standard water- or beer-carrying and storage vessel. The small jar, *chomo vacu*, is a handy canteen carried by an individual while away from the village. Serving bowls are of two basic kinds: an incurving beer mug and an open food bowl. Beer mugs include a large form (*kenpo ani*) passed from individual to individual during fiestas; a medium-sized bowl (simply called *kenpo*), which is the everyday drinking vessel; and a small mug (*kenpo vacu*) inverted over a small jar to form a kind of lunchbox, or thermos bottle, for the traveler. Food bowls follow a similar pattern: an extra-large form for fiestas (*Pascua kencha*); a medium-sized form for daily meals (*kencha*); and a small size for children or, increasingly, for sale to tourists (*kencha vacu*).

Unlike cookware, jars and serving bowls are painted. The most common paint schemes are a resin-coated polychrome black-and-red-on-white applied

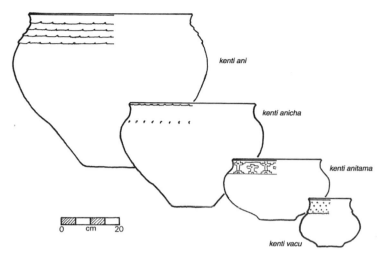

Fig. 1   Shipibo cooking pots.

to the necks of jars and to the exteriors of beer mugs, and an unresined white-on-red bichrome primarily found on the exteriors of food bowls. Food bowls are frequently smudged on their interiors, whereas beer mugs typically have their interiors resined after firing.

This sketch of the Shipibo assemblage can be summarized in terms of a 3 X 4 matrix in which each cell contains a particular vessel form (Table 1). The columns of this matrix distinguish three contexts: (a) fiestas attended by dozens or even hundreds of celebrants; (b) the quotidian or day-to day domestic sphere; and (c) transport or travel in which small, portable vessels are favored. The rows of the matrix correspond to the four major form classes of *ollas*, jars, beer mugs, and food bowls. Table 1 also gives the estimated volume of the modal vessel size on the basis of rim diameter within each form class. (Note that this measure is *not* the same as mean volume.) These volumetric estimates are of some interest when expressed as ratios, in which the volume of jars or *ollas* is divided by the volume of individual serving bowls. Thus, fiesta ratios are high, the transport ratio is low, and the quotidian values are intermediate. These findings are in general accord with Turner and Lofgren (1966), who proposed that capacities of *ollas* and jars should be related to the number of individuals being served. They also offer an intriguing parallel to Blitz's (1993) arguments for the recognition of ceramic feasting assemblages. Perhaps the one ill-fitting datum in Table 1 is the 17.1 value for the ratio of *kenti anicha* volume to *kencha* volume, a value much higher than other quotidian ratios. This discordance, however, is only seeming when it is remembered that the daily eating unit among the Shipibo may vary from the individual house (typically containing a nuclear family) to the household or residential compound of three to four houses arranged around a common plaza, presumably a vestige of the traditional *maloca*. *Kenti anitama* would apparently be the *olla* for the smaller group, *kenti anicha* for the larger.

The preceding simplified observations indicate that the Shipibo ceramic assemblage, one that Donald Lathrap called "the most complex of extant American Indian ceramic industries still made in a largely indigenous tradition" (Lathrap n.d.a.), can be understood in terms of a few functional and contextual dimensions of a general nature—cooking, storing, eating, and drinking while on the move, while at home, or during periodic fiestas.

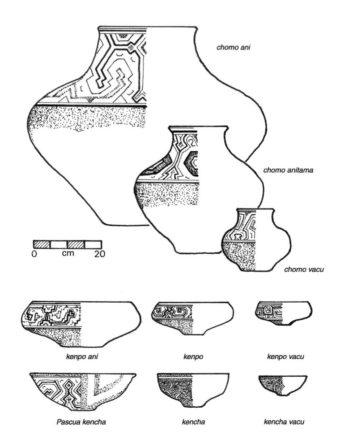

Fig. 2   Shipibo jars and serving bowls.

HISTORIC UPPER AMAZON CERAMIC INTERACTION SPHERE (HUACIS)

The Shipibo case is not unique, but only the hub of a field of ceramic interaction that extends over 1,200 km from north to south along the eastern base of the Andes. Laterally, this field envelopes the eastern foothills and reaches to the modern border with Brazil (Fig. 3). It is German scholarship that has documented the reality of this interaction sphere. Tessmann (1930) laid the groundwork in his monumental survey, weak on social organization but generally reliable on material culture; Vossen (1969) codified Tessmann's and other data on ceramic materials; and, more recently, Kästner (1992) covered much the same ground in another expansive monograph. I venture to call this vast network of interaction *HUACIS.* Although a somewhat awkward acronym, it may help to recall that the Huallaga basin occupies a central position within this network and that the overall shape of the network is cis-Andean.

Table 1
Vessel Form, Volume (in liters) of Shipibo Pottery, according to Context, Function, and Corresponding Volume Ratio

	Context		
Use	Fiesta	Quotidian	Transport
cooking 27%	*kenti ani*	*kenti anicha*	*kenti vacu*
N = 84	80.2	29.0	5.0
		kenti anitama	
		11.1	
storing liquids 31%	*chomo ani*	*chomo anitama*	*chomo vacu*
N = 94	103.3	16.5	2.4
serving liquids 10%	*kenpo ani*	*kenpo*	*kenpo vacu*
N = 31	7.5	2.8	1.2
serving foods 32%	*Pascua kencha*	*kencha*	*kencha vacu*
N = 97	3.8	1.7	0.7
	Volume ratio		
kenti ani to kencha	47.2		
kenti anicha to kencha		17.1	
kenti anitama to kencha		6.5	
chomo ani to kenpo	36.9		
chomo anitama to kenpo		5.9	
chomo vacu to kenpo vacu			2.0
N = 306	17%	67%	16%

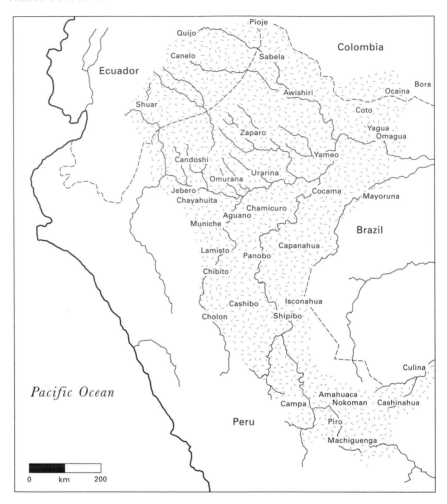

Fig. 3   Distribution of groups included in the Historic Upper Amazon Ceramic Interaction Sphere (HUACIS).

In the following, I have relied heavily on Tessmann. When possible, I have supplemented his original insights with the results of later research. It is clear from this effort that the Shipibo 12-cell matrix is a basic structure engulfing much of the Upper Amazon. Wide-mouthed *ollas*, necked jars, incurving beer mugs, and open food bowls are basic forms throughout the area. Multimodality of vessel size is common. Decorative canons also are patterned. Table 2 summarizes the results of the 44 groups sampled (missing data play a substantial role in these arrays), whereas Figure 3 plots the distribution of these groups. *Olla*s are customarily decorated by texturing techniques. The Shipibo penchant for white-on-red food bowls, frequently smudged on the interior, is widely shared. Beer mugs and jars tend toward black-and-red-on-white color schemes with resined and thereby waterproofed interiors. Although the degree of elaboration and formal properties of design styles vary widely, all of these ceramic assemblages can be viewed as differential participants in, or precipitates of, the same field of play.

One must also recall that in the Upper Amazon, we are "at play in the fields of the gourd." In the 1960s, Lathrap was famous for his classroom exhibition of how just about every ceramic form could be derived from slicing a gourd in this or that plane. Mesoamericanists have made the same argument for gourd skeuomorphy (e.g., Clark and Blake 1994; Flannery and Marcus 1994). Table 2 suggests that gourds are most likely to impinge on the category of drinking vessels. In a lesser way, gourds also way serve as food bowls or jars. They are not effective cooking vessels (but see Speck 1941).

ORIGINS OF HUACIS

Since Eric Wolf's *Europe and the People without History* (1982), history is again respectable among many anthropologists. This rapprochement, however, has taken a course that, I believe, runs contrary to Wolf's intent. In a kind of "Indian-giving," history is bestowed with one hand while taken back by the other — taken back in the sense that native history is seen as a reaction to, or forged by, the colonial and expansionary ventures of Europe and its attendant anthropologists.

I once suggested that the Shipibo design style may have been formed in a historic revitalization movement (DeBoer 1990). With even greater ahistoric hubris, Gow (1994) has argued that the whole *ayahuasca*-based shamanic complex of the Upper Amazon may be a recent concoction forged in response to European restructuring of the region. In a similar vein, Reeve (n.d.: 114) cited her own Quichua informants to suggest that fancy polychrome pottery was unknown before the coming of priests and that design styles were disseminated by merchants linking the far-flung missions of the Ecuadorian and Peruvian Amazon. In these accounts, there is no prehistory, nothing at all before ourselves. To escape such hubris, one must turn to the archaeological record.

The archaeological evidence is quite clear. Almost every aspect of the HUACIS 12-celled matrix paradigm can be derived from the Cumancaya ceramic complex of the Upper Ucayali, dated to about A.D. 900 (DeBoer 1990; Raymond, DeBoer, and Roe 1975). In terms of basic vessel shapes, size modalities, and color schemes, one could hardly imagine a more appropriate prototype than that offered by Cumancaya, a site which is recognized as an ancient ancestral settlement by both Shipibo and Conibo. Although some Cumancaya

Table 2

Characteristics of 44 Ceramic Assemblages Included in the Historic Upper Amazon Ceramic Interaction Sphere (HUACIS)

Characteristic	Food bowl	Drinking bowl	Jar	*Olla*
Groups represented (*N* = 44)	55%	70%	80%	98%
Vessel exterior				
white-on-red or red slip alone	52%	0	0	0
postfire red or black	10	11	20	0
black-and-red-on-white or red-on-white; resined	0	74	50	0
plain	29	5	17	14
textured	10	11	0	86
"painted"[a]	0	0	13	0
Vessel interior				
smudged	89%	7	0	67
plain	11	21	20	33
resin-over-plain	0	36	80	0
"painted"[a]	0	7	0	0
"painted" and resined	0	29	0	0
groups with gourd containers; groups with ceramic vessels	0.19	1.00	0.14	0.00

Notes: Tessmann (1930) remains the basic source supplemented by Vossen (1969) and Kästner (1992). See also Dole (1974) for Amahuaca; see Shell (1959); Trujillo (1960); Frank (1994) for Cashibo; see papers in Dwyer (1975) for Cashinahua; see Hanke (1954); Prost (1970) for Chacobo; see Erickson (1990) for Mayoruna; see d'Ans (1970) for Pánobo; see Tessmann (1928); DeBoer and Lathrap (1979); Roe (1982) for Shibibo-Conibo, see Farabee (1922); Baer (1969) for Machiguenga; see Matteson (1968); Gow (1988); Alvarez (n.d.) for Piro; see Adams (1976) for Culina; Girard (1958); Faust (1972) for Cocama and Omagua; Fejos (1943); Chaumeil (1994) for Yagua; see Espinosa (1955) for Yameo; see García (1993) for Chayahuita; see Bellier (1994) for Coto or Mai Huna; see Kelley and Orr (1976); Porras (1975); Whitten (1981); Whitten and Whitten (1978); Reeve (n.d.) for Canelo; see DeBoer (n.d.) for Lamisto; see Stirling (1938); Harner (1972); Bianchi (1982); Zeidler (1983) for Shuar-Achuar; see Califano (1982) for Mashco; see Nimuendajú (1952); Goulard (1994) for Ticuna; see Morales (1992) for Urarina. Other information was collected during visits to the Summer Institute of Linguistics Museum, Yarinacocha, Peru, summers 1971 and 1975.

[a] No other information available.

forms are adumbrated in the preceding Pacacocha complex (Myers n.d.), the Cumancaya design style is without local antecedents. In tracing the HUACIS lineage beyond A.D. 900, some scholars (Roe n.d.; Lathrap, Gebhart-Sayer, and Mester, 1985) have looked to the Ecuadorian Amazon.

Here I chose not to review the debate concerning the nature of this Ecuadorian connection (DeBoer and Raymond 1987; Lathrap, Gebhart-Sayer, Myers, and Mester 1987). However, similarities between Cumancaya designs and the Ecuadorian materials generally glossed as Red Banded Incised (RBI) are sufficiently specific to argue for a historical relationship between the two, and the available chronological evidence indicates a temporal priority of this design style in Ecuador. Furthermore, these similarities extend beyond designs to include some of the basic structural features of HUACIS as outlined above.

At Pirincay in the Paute valley, Red Banded Incised pottery occured as an apparent import in levels dated between 400 B.C. and A.D. 1 (Bruhns, Burton, and Miller 1990; Bruhns, Burton, and Rostoker 1994). RBI materials are dominant at the site of Sangay, north of Macas (Porras 1987). Porras proposed that the Sangay chronology spans more than three millennia. This is unlikely, however, as the chronology is based upon radiocarbon dates for samples from arbitrary levels often excavated in structural fill; given this excavation procedure, it is not surprising that few patterned changes are seen in the ceramic remains. As Athens (1986) pointed out, the majority of radiocarbon dates for Sangay cluster from 330 B.C. to A.D. 170, an age conformable with the Pirincay evidence.

The most complete description of an RBI assemblage is provided by Arthur Rostoker (n.d.), who reanalyzed a collection made by Michael Harner at the site of Yaunchu, near Macas (Harner 1972: 13–14). In his analysis, Rostoker reconstructs more than 60 vessels that divide about evenly between shallow plates, deeper bowls, and a combined class of necked jars and *ollas*. The most common treatment of plates is a red-slipped exterior combined with a smudged interior, a scheme recalling the HUACIS food bowl. Bowls have the most elaborately decorated exteriors (Red Banded Incised), although interiors tend to be plain (an organic resin, however, is unlikely to be preserved). Jar–*ollas* tend to have textured exteriors, whereas interiors may be plain or smudged. Plates and bowls come in two size modes, but three modes are indicated for jar–*ollas*. Overall, the form and decorative schemes at Yaunchu fit into HUACIS. I know of no earlier ceramic assemblage from Peru or Ecuador that could so readily serve as a HUACIS prototype.

METHOD AND CONSTRAINTS

If its trail ends two millennia ago in the forests of Ecuador, then HUACIS would hardly seem useful for shedding light on earlier Formative assemblages of Ecuador and Peru. Nonetheless, the HUACIS construct is useful in examining the form and function of these Formative assemblages. My rationale for this procedure is as follows. First, from the standpoint of culture history, *why not?* Although it would be excessive to stretch a direct historical approach several millennia into prehistory (but see Schlesier 1994), nevertheless, it is probably better to employ a geographically proximate and perhaps even phylogenetically related HUACIS than, let us say, the Polish Neolithic. Although this point may be weak and readily contested by committed functionalists, such criticism can be deflected by noting that HUACIS is not being extrapolated tentatively into deeper prehistory so much as it is being used as a foil to highlight the contrasts or differences of what came before. This use obviates the just criticism that Andeanists are often prone to a kind of "homunculus" notion in which such historically recorded Andean institutions as *ayllus, minkas, chicha (asua),* verticality, and dual organization are all there in the beginning, albeit in embryonic form, and just waiting to unfold according to some ontogenetic program. Such a notion is bad evolutionary theory (e.g., Blute 1979) and a faulty premise for sound culture history (e.g., Tschauner 1994).

On the other hand, it is possible to eschew phylogenetic constraints altogether and to argue that functionally specific pots, anywhere and at any time, are apt to share certain performance characteristics. For example, serving bowls for solid foods are likely to be open to facilitate access, whereas liquid-containing bowls are likely to be incurving to avoid spillage (Smith 1985). In this sense, phylogenetic and functional perspectives do not lead to contrary test implications. It becomes a largely empirical matter to evaluate the relative explanatory efficacy of the two approaches (e.g., Oliver 1962).

But these general concerns pale in comparison to other problems. A basic problem is the need for reliably recorded and representative ceramic samples for which vessel forms and sizes are provided. This basic criterion is often not met. Frequently site reports present ceramic data in terms of "types" that are then counted. This sherd-oriented, typological approach may be adequate for purposes of quantitative seriation, but it is clearly unsuited for understanding ceramic assemblages.

A vessel-oriented assemblage analysis needs: (a) a presentation of vessel forms based on whole or, more commonly, reconstructable pots; (b) a sufficient sample for determining size modes, usually recorded as rim diameters; and (c) some indication that ceramics residues were collected representatively, that is, that drab *olla* rims were not selectively discarded (by the archaeologist) in preference for fancy bowl rims. Even if these conditions are met, other daunting problems remain. For example, without detailed conjoinability analysis, how are rim sherd counts to be converted into whole vessels? Despite the amount of attention that archaeologists have given this issue (e.g., Orton and Tyers 1992), Lynda Carroll and I (DeBoer and Carroll 1992) have argued that simple rim counts are neither better nor worse, but are certainly easier to calculate than various other rim-to-vessel conversions offered by archaeologists. Another problem is that of context. Although it is a basic archaeological tenet that provenience and association determine the interpretive value of an artifact, this fundamental canon must often be compromised when dealing with the literature. Thus, it is often necessary to assume that potsherds from middens, or even from fill, are sampling activities carried out in general proximity to the site of deposition. These are imperfect accommodations, but until more rigorous recording and reporting techniques and methods become standardized, the option is paralysis.

Finally, when appropriate shape and size data are present, it is possible to estimate vessel volume. With the help of Rostoker, this task initially was carried out with the stacked cylinder method described by Nelson (1985). Recently HALFPOT computer software has become available and greatly facilitates vessel capacity estimation from scaled profile drawings (Senior and Birnie 1995).

Below is an overview of Formative ceramics considered in terms of form, size, and function. The space–time chart of Table 3 and the map of Figure 4 plot the scope of this project.

Valdivia

Although not the earliest pottery in northwestern South America (Raymond, Oyuela-Caycedo, and Carmichael 1994), Valdivia ceramics are precocious. At present, the origins of this ceramic tradition are unknown. I am willing to regard it as a development *sui generis* on the Ecuadorian coast. Real Alto, a large site with a long and complex history, is perhaps the best known Valdivia settlement; it certainly provides the most thoroughly documented ceramic remains (Marcos 1988). The following observations are based on Marcos's reconstruction of more than 500 vessels from Real Alto and also incorporate Zeidler's (n.d.) functional categorization of Valdivia pottery.

Major Valdivia vessel forms consist of *ollas*, jars, and serving bowls. Serving bowls, in turn, can be partitioned into open or incurving variants. Table 4 gives the frequency and volumes of these forms throughout the Real Alto sequence. Phases are paired (i.e., 2–3, 4–5, and 6–7) in order to compile reasonable and comparably sized samples.

Table 3
Chronology of Ceramic Assemblages Discussed in Text

Year	Valdivia (Real Alto)	Cotocallao	Catamayo	Far north coast, Peru	Pacopampa	Huacaloma	Cerro Blanco	Huaricoto	La Pampa	Waywaka	Kotosh	Ucayali
200 B.C.												Late Shakimu
400		Late				Layzon	Sotera				Chavin	
600			D	Pechiche		EL			La Pampa			Early Shakimu
800		Middle	C			Late Huacaloma	Cerro Blanco					
1000		Early	B			Early Huacaloma	La Conga				Kotosh	Late Tutishcainyo
1200			A						Yesopampa			
1400				Early Paita	Pandanche					Muyo Moqo A	Waira-jirca	Early Tutishcainyo
1600	8							Toril				
1800	6–7											
2000	4–5											
2200												
2400	2–3											
2600												
2800	1											
3000												

Note: The scale is based on uncalibrated radiocarbon ages.

Ceramic Assemblage Variability in the Formative of Ecuador and Peru

Table 4 reveals several patterns of note. First, although the basic triad of bowl–jar–*olla* is present in all phases, *ollas* decrease over the sequence while incurving bowls increase. It is possible that this trend is a ceramic monitor of the postulated shift of Real Alto from a large, permanently occupied settlement, in which a full suite of domestic vessels would be expected, to a largely vacant ceremonial center to which congregations periodically flocked and where

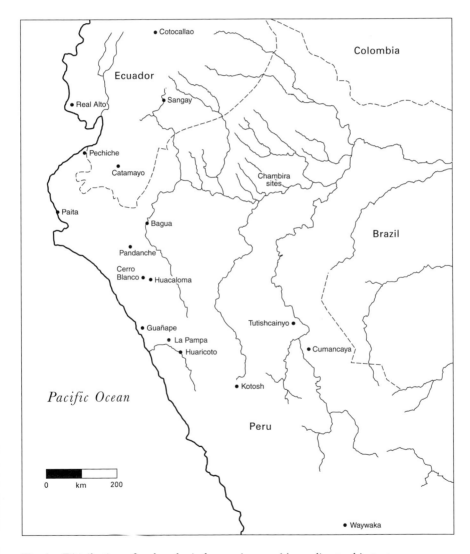

Fig. 4 Distribution of archaeological ceramic assemblages discussed in text.

Table 4

Vessel Form, Volume (in liters), and Volumetric Ratio for Pottery from the Real Alto Site

	Valdivia		
Vessel form	2–3 (*N* = 241)	4–5 (*N* = 94)	6–7 (*N* = 179)
olla	34%	22%	12%
	2.4	3.4	2.4
jar	17%	24%	25%
	5.9	4.3	3.0
incurving bowl	35%	40%	57%
	2.4	1.2	2.4
open bowl	8%	13%	7%
Mode 1	0.8	0.3	0.8
open bowl	6%		
Mode 2	3.9		
	Volume ratio		
olla to open bowl	3.0	11.3	3.0
jar to incurving bowl	2.5	3.6	1.3

serving vessels played an accordingly prominent role (Lathrap, Marcos, and Zeidler 1977). It is even possible that the small bowl sizes characterizing Valdivia 4–5 represent a version of the HUACIS transport principle, namely "bring your own bottle." These observations, however, are mere guesses without stronger evidence.

A second pattern is that Valdivia vessels are usually small. The largest size mode only approaches a modest six liters, and the volumetric ratios given in Table 4 generally suggest a small, domestically based eating and drinking unit. The one exception is the 11:3 *olla*/open bowl ratio, but this high value is determined by the peculiarly diminutive size of Valdivia 4–5 open bowls. One last observation is the general unimodality of Valdivia vessel size. The singular exception is the double mode of Valdivia 2–3 open bowls. It would be interesting to know if this bimodality in vessel capacity maps onto the bimodality in house floor areas that Zeidler (n.d.: 286) noted.

In an admirable summary, Raymond wrote of Valdivia pottery:

There is no "fine ware" which might have been reserved for special occasions, but significantly greater attention, care, and energy were put into finishing and decorating the bowls than into the jars. Furthermore, although both jars and bowls were decorated, bowl designs are more complex and intricate. . . . An obvious implication is that bowls were more than domestic serving vessels, that they at least occasionally participated in events which were more public or special than daily eating and drinking within the household. A salient possibility, which has been suggested by others as well, is ritualized drinking. (1993: 39–39)

Some evidence supports this possibility. John Staller (personal communication; see also Thompson and Staller 2001) reports that maize phytoliths have been recovered from the interior of a ceramic bottle found at the Valdivia site of La Emerenciana, El Oro province. This residue could be interpreted to indicate *chicha*, the Andean maize beer. Despite this singular piece of evidence, the vessel volume data suggest that Valdivian hosts were, at best, "pikers" by HUACIS standards. It is difficult to imagine the Valdivia vessel assemblage supporting the kind of celebration that Lathrap described for the Shipibo, the purpose of which "was to give a fiesta which lasted longer, expended more beer, and unleashed more drunken brawls than any other fiesta in memory" (Lathrap 1970: 54). Perhaps the Valdivians supplemented their half-pint draughts of beer with small but potent chugs of *ayahuasca* millennia before Gow (1994) "reinvented" this hallucinogen to counter the misery of European domination.

Cotocollao

Villalba (1988) produced a handsome site report for this Formative community in the Quito basin of Ecuador. Unfortunately, although diameter ranges are given for 34 vessel types, size modes are not. In estimating the volumes of these vessel types, I, therefore, have adopted the risky procedure of taking the midpoint of the range, unless the illustrated vessels for a particular type indicate a skewed size distribution. Even by taking such liberties, however, volumetric estimates could not be made for all vessel types. Furthermore, Villalba's 34 vessel types are much more than we need and have been collapsed accordingly into the major forms illustrated in Figure 5. Bottle forms seriate nicely across the three major chronological periods recognized by Villalba (see Fig. 5, top). Other forms are less chronologically sensitive, and I have lumped together Early and Middle Cotocollao (Fig. 5, bottom).

Table 5 gives the frequency and volume of major forms. *Ollas*, which come in a number of size modes, remain a rather constant part of the assemblage

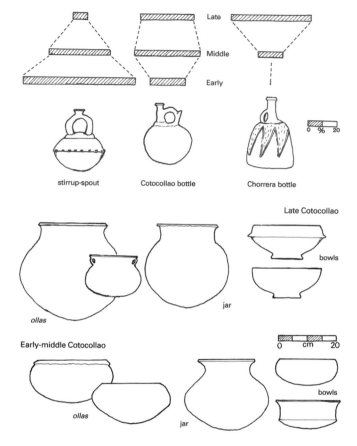

Fig. 5   Seriation of bottles and profiles of major vessel forms.

across all three periods. The large *olla* with an estimated capacity of 25 liters, however, is restricted to the Late period. Jars are rare at Cotocollao, their place presumably being taken by bottles. Taken together, jars and bottles decline from 34 percent to 23 percent, whereas their volumes tend to increase over the sequence. Never common, incurving bowls decrease over time; open bowls—the most consistently and lavishly decorated of Cotocollao vessels—increase dramatically. Types assigned to the latter category vary from 1.7 to 2.2 liters during Early and Middle periods, rising substantially to 3.4 liters in the Late.

Although vessels tend to become larger throughout the Cotocollao sequence, volumetric ratios conform to what would be expected of a domestic or quotidian context by HUACIS standards. No large-scale fiestas are in evidence.

Table 5
Vessel Form, Volume (in liters), and Volumetric Ratio for Pottery from the Cotocollao Site

Vessel form	Early (N = 524)	Middle (N = 1735)	Late (N = 1951)
olla	37%	32%	31%
	0.9		3.7
	6.0		4.7
	8.1		6.0
			25.1
jar	2%	4%	9%
	10.3	10.3	15.9
		15.9	
bottle	32%	25%	14%
	1.3	4.1	5.1
incurving bowl	13%	6%	7%
	2.2	2.2	2.8
open bowl	16%	32%	39%
	1.7	1.8	3.4
	1.8	1.9	
	1.9		
	2.2		
Volume ratio			
olla to open bowl	3.0		1.1
	4.1		1.4
			1.8
			7.4
jar to incurving bowl	4.7	4.7	7.2
		7.2	

Note: Volumes are those determined for Villalba's (1988) vessel types, which here have been reassigned to major vessel forms.

Catamayo

Although the two are contemporary and separated by only some 400 km, Cotocollao and Catamayo ceramics are worlds apart. Recovered from generally small sites in the vicinity of Loja, the Catamayo materials have been arranged into a four-phase sequence A–D (Guffroy et al. 1987). Although I have not been able to extract complete rim sherd counts from Guffroy's report, the percentages of major vessel forms are given. Modal sizes are not provided, but the few whole–vessel reconstructions are said to be typical. Major forms are illus-

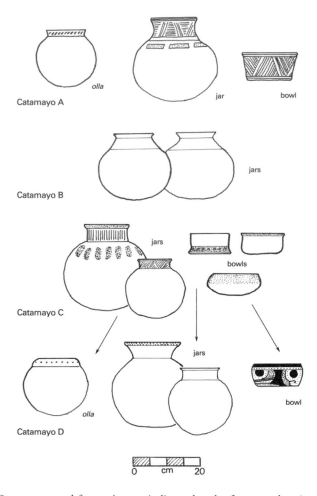

Fig. 6   Catamayo vessel forms. Arrows indicate that the form overlaps into D.

trated in Figure 6, and Table 6 provides the vessel frequencies and volume estimates.

Catamayo pottery has peculiarities. Jars are the predominant vessel form, constituting virtually the entire B and C assemblages. Simple globular *ollas* are common only in Phases A and D. Bowls are exceedingly rare throughout most of the sequence, rising to 10 percent only in the last phase. Other forms, such as bottles, are too few to figure in percentage calculations. Given the rarity of bowls, the jar-to-bowl and *olla*-to-bowl ratios shown in Table 6 are of questionable value.

Table 6
Vessel Form, Volume (in liters), and Volumetric Ratio for Catamayo Pottery

Vessel form	Catamayo			
	A	B	C	D
olla	30%	—	—	40%
	5.2			4.9
jar	70%	100%	100%	50%
	9.5	8.3	2.7	8.6
	12.2		14.2	10.6
bowl	+	—	+	10%
	2.1		0.9	0.9
			1.3	2.2
	Volume ratio			
olla to bowl	2.5	—	—	2.2
				5.4
jar to bowl	4.5	—	2.7	3.9
	5.8		14.2	4.8
				9.6
				11.8

Note: + indicates form is present but volume is indeterminate; — indicates absence of form.

The depauperate or unbalanced nature of Catamayo vessel assemblages is difficult to explain. There is no evidence to suggest that the assemblages come from specialized sites devoted to, for example, water carrying or storage. Turning to a HUACIS analogy, it is tempting to postulate a rich gourd-based inventory of containers fulfilling the functions of "missing" ceramic bowls.

In its penchant for jars, Catamayo is not unique. Jars also dominate the Paita assemblages of the Piura–Chira coast. As Lanning (1963: 153) noted, the entire Paita sequence is characterized by the "extreme rarity of bowls, bottles, and other non-jar forms." Jar-based assemblages, however, are not universal during the Formative of the far north coast. Pechiche ceramics from the Tumbes valley, coeval with Catamayo C–D, display a more balanced composition: 36 percent jars, 34 percent *ollas*, 27 percent bowls, and a few distinctive handled beakers (Izumi and Terada 1966). My reworking of the Pechiche data indicates typically quotidian jar-to-bowl (2.5) and *olla*-to-bowl (5.6) volume ratios.

The postulation of perishable gourds, unsatisfying enough, does not solve

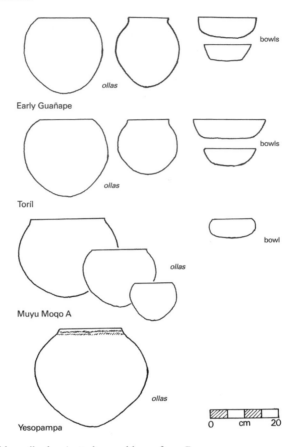

Fig. 7   Neckless *olla*-dominated assemblages from Peru.

the mystery of Catamayo cooking utensils. Where are they? Are the jars, in fact, multifunctional jar–*ollas* that subsume the tasks of cooking, storage, and transport? In the case of Catamayo and other Formative assemblages, more specific information is needed on ceramic use–wear (e.g., see Hally 1983; Skibo 1992). In addition, systematic evidence on the prevalence of fire-cracked rock, earth ovens (the Andean *pachamanka*), and other cooking features would facilitate understanding the role of pottery in culinary culture.

NECKLESS OLLA-DOMINATED ASSEMBLAGES OF PERU

James Ford (1969: 94) observed that, whereas neckless *ollas* are rare or absent in Ecuador, they are salient in the Formative of Peru. Here a brief look at four Peruvian assemblages in which the neckless *olla* predominates is in order. As

Table 7
Vessel Form, Volume (in liters), and Volumetric Estimate for Assemblages Dominated by
Neckless *Ollas*

Vessel form	Early Guañape (N = 512)	Toríl (N = 57)	Yesopampa[a] La Pampa	Muyu Moqo A Waywaka
olla	95%	82%	88%	—
	3.4	2.7	27.3	1.0
	4.8	4.9		3.6
				12.2
bowl	5%	18%	12%	—
	0.4	0.5	1.4	0.4
	0.9	1.8		
		Volume ratio		
olla to bowl	3.8	5.4	19.5	2.5
	5.3	9.8		9.0
	12.0			30.5

Note: — indicates absence of form.

[a] Yesopampa bowl volume is based on later La Pampa phase examples, as no illustrated
bowls can be associated securely with the Yesopampa component.

plotted in Figure 4, the cases are Early Guañape (Strong, Evans, and Lilien
1952), the Yesopampa component at La Pampa (Onuki and Fujii 1974, Terada
1979), the Toríl component at Huaricoto (Burger 1988; Burger and Salazar-
Burger 1985), and, as a southern outlier, the Muyu Moqo A assemblage from
Waywaka (Grossman 1983). These examples were chosen because they meet
some of the criteria for assessing the frequency and size of vessels.

Following the same format as above, vessel forms are presented in Figure 7;
frequency and volume specifications for these forms appear in Table 7. Neckless
ollas are egg-shaped vessels, usually undecorated, but occasionally bearing brushed
or other textured exteriors. These *ollas* come in size modes. Those of Muyu
Moqo show a clear trimodality; two modes seem to characterize Guañape and
Toríl; a small sample indicates a single large-sized mode for Yesopampa. In the
four considered assemblages, all dating to the early- to mid–second millennium
B.C., more than 82 percent of all rims pertain to neckless *ollas*; the remainder
come from generally small and undistinguished bowls. (Thomas Zoubek [n.d.]
reports that bowls are more common in Guañape deposits at Huaca El Gallo in
the Viru valley.) Only Toríl has a somewhat large bowl or pan, a form that may
be antecedent to a minor but consistently represented vessel found in later

Formative assemblages. Volume ratios generally fall within the HUACIS quotidian range, although the Yesopampa and highest Muyo Moqo ratios are conformable with a large-sized eating or drinking group.

I know of no comparative, functional study of neckless *ollas*, although it would be useful to have one. I sense that there is a general belief that these vessels are indeed *ollas*, that is, cooking pots. As with Catamayo, however, this functional inference could be based more on reasonable impression than on demonstrated fact. Rather drably decorated, if adorned at all, Peruvian neckless *ollas* are distinct from the comparatively showy or even show-off *tecomates,* which constitute 89 percent of the Barra assemblage from coastal Chiapas that Clark and Blake (1994: 27) have involved in competitive beer bashes among nascent and jockeying elites. Different media or processes must have been at work in Formative Peru, as perhaps seen at Kotosh.

Kotosh

It was at a Dumbarton Oaks conference on Chavín that Donald Lathrap (1971: 94) first proposed a dual tradition for Kotosh pottery, as it is found at Kotosh proper as well as numerous other Formative sites in the Upper Huallaga and neighboring regions. He noted that Kotosh neckless *ollas* relate to the coastal and highland materials considered in the preceding section, whereas an array of fancy bowls bearing carinations, flanges, and elaborate incisions impregnated with post-fired pigments ultimately point to a different source. On the basis of similarities to Tutishcainyo and later Shakimu material from the Ucayali basin, Lathrap suggested that this other source was, or at least involved, the forested lowlands of the Upper Amazon. As far as I know, research of the last quarter-century has not overturned Lathrap's diagnosis.

Of course, the dual tradition hypothesis need not imply ceramic "schizophrenia," anymore than "fine china" ever saved English food from its essential dreariness. It is to whole Kotosh assemblages that we now turn. Figure 8 presents major vessel forms (the earlier Waira-jirca and Kotosh phases are combined); Table 8 gives vessel frequencies, volume estimates, and volume ratios.

A word is needed about the Kotosh sample used to construct Table 8. In his 1971 article, Lathrap relied upon all the illustrated vessels from construction levels H–D, with G–H corresponding to the Waira-jirca occupation, F to the Kotosh phase, and D–E to Kotosh Chavín. As illustrated by Izumi and Sono (1963), however, these vessels apparently represent a selection that does not conform to the actual relative frequencies of respective forms. This is evident in the fuller data given by Izumi and Terada (1972) where the actual frequency of rim sherds is recorded. In the latter report, *ollas* were much more abundant than indicated in the 1963 volume, and jars and flamboyantly decorated or contoured bowls were accordingly fewer. Table 8 and the following comments are based on the more complete data published in 1972.

As seen in Table 8, *ollas* dominate all three phases of the Kotosh Formative. These pots primarily consist of neckless *ollas*, often decorated with incised arcades of triangles pendant from the rim exterior, but also include a wide-mouthed and low-necked form. Jars with constricted necks, and bottles as well, are rare in all phases. There is a plethora of fancy, sometimes eccentric bowl shapes: boat-shaped and triangularly sectioned bowls are common in Waira-jirca; carinated and sublabially flanged bowls are a highlight of Kotosh; shallow, flat-based incurving bowls are conspicuous in Chavín. These bowls all show a high degree of decorative investment and clearly present the ostentatious face of the Kotosh tradition.

Kotosh volumetric ratios are of interest. The small *olla*/bowl and jar/carinated bowl ratios are in the quotidian range. The large *olla*/bowl ratio, however, is large indeed, exceeding the highest ratios known from HUACIS (compare with Table 1). One is prompted to see a fiesta-based feasting pattern in full swing. Two observations, however, should condition this seduction by analogy. First, we are dealing with *ollas*, or what seem to be cooking pots. Jars, the beer kegs of a later HUACIS, were minor forms. One might even suggest that it was food, not the alcoholic libations of HUACIS, behind the large-sized Kotosh *ollas*. Secondly, the volumes for modal vessels given in Table 8 are potentially misleading because they do not convey the actual frequencies of differing size modes within the same form. Figure 9 conveys this fact with respect to *ollas*. Big *ollas* were common in Waira-jirca and Kotosh phases; they are rare in Chavín. If big pots are a signature for feasts, then feasting was a comparatively uncommon activity during the Chavín component at Kotosh; if big pots mean beer-based fiestas, then the Chavín episode at Kotosh was a relatively abstemious time.

The latter implications, however, are unlikely to be pursued to a reliable conclusion from the perspective of the Kotosh site alone. Onuki (1993: 84) has pointed out that Upper Huallaga settlement patterns underwent major disruptions with the advent of the Chavín phase; most sites—Kotosh being an exception—were abandoned, but new centers were established at Paucarbamba and possibly at Sajarapatac. Without contextualization in this shifting political and social landscape, it is difficult to interpret the ceramic evidence. Another obvious point concerns sampling: At fairly large sites that include varying degrees of monumental architecture, what are sondages sampling? La Pampa may provide a glimpse of the problems attendant to intrasite variability in ceramic remains.

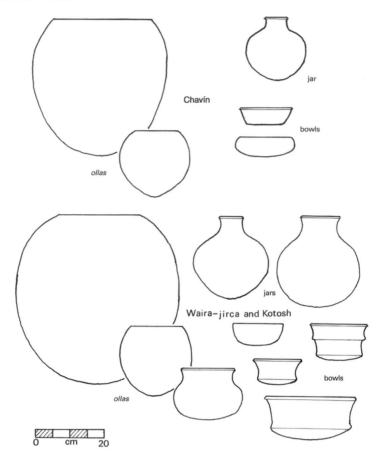

Fig. 8   Major vessel forms from the Formative of the Kotosh site.

La Pampa

Situated at 1,800 m elevation on the Manta, a tributary of the Santa, La Pampa was a major center at the beginning of the Early Horizon. Two archaeological campaigns have been carried out at La Pampa, the first concentrating on the M4 sector of the site (Onuki and Fujii 1974); the second was a more substantial excavation in the M8 sector (Terada 1979). The pottery recovered from these two probes differs significantly. Although it is not totally clear that M4 and M8 were indeed contemporary, Terada suggested:

> The Chavín-related pottery sherds are not numerous at M8, while M4, excavated in 1969, yielded a lot of sherds showing Chavín ele-

Table 8

Vessel Form, Volume (in liters), and Volumetric Ratio for Pottery from the Kotosh Site by Phase

Vessel form	Waira-jirca (N = 925)	Kotosh (N = 1,566)	Chavín (N = 1,244)
olla	71%	51%	62%
	4.1	5.0	4.7
	5.0	77.0	67.1
	77.0		
plain carinated basin	+	2%	+
		6.1	
jar	2%	1%	5%
	5.6	8.3	4.3
bottle	2%	2%	2%
incurving bowl	3%	+	25%
			1.1
open bowl	4%	9%	
	0.9	1.4	3%
flaring bowl	—	1%	3%
			0.7
flanged or carinated bowl	2%	33%	+
	0.9	1.1	1.1
boat-shaped or triangular bowl	15%	2%	+
Volume ratio			
large *olla* to bowl	85.6	55.0	61.0
			95.8
small *olla* to bowl	5.6	4.2	4.3
jar to carinated bowl	6.2	7.3	3.9

Note: + indicates form is present but volume is indeterminate: — indicates absence of form.

ments in a more sophisticated and diverse manner. We wonder if M4 was a mound where the elites and foreigners who had introduced the Chavín culture resided, while at M8 native people continued to live.

On the basis of the illustrated vessel profiles given in the two Japanese reports, Figure 10 presents modal sized pots from M4 and M8, while Table 9 gives the corresponding frequency and volume indices for major vessel forms.

M8, an alleged hoi polloi deposit, is characterized by large *ollas*, small jars, and simple bowls. It smacks of the quotidian. In contrast, M4 is characterized by

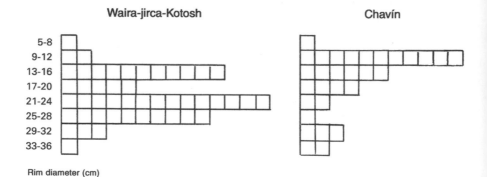

Fig. 9   *Olla* rim diameters for the combined Waira–jirca and Kotosh phases and for the Chavín phase at Kotosh. The mean rim diameters for the two groups are significantly different; $p = .0223$, t test.

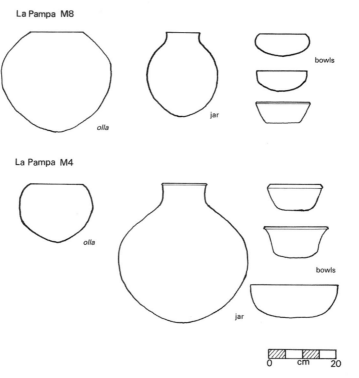

Fig. 10   Major vessel forms from the M4 and M8 sectors of the La Pampa site.

comparatively rare and small *ollas*, large jars, and a plethora of fancy serving vessels. If the M4 and M8 deposits are indeed contemporary, then we must imagine distinct food preparation and food-dispensing theaters within this complex site. This inference, however, says little about alleged intrusive Chavín "elites" or equally putative "nonelite indigenes." The lesson is that big sites are likely to be functionally differentiated into feasting and quotidian zones. Identification of such zones requires excavation programs designed specifically to document contemporary variability. The La Pampa lesson conditions all that has been said before.

Cerro Blanco and Huacaloma

Our final Andean sortie is to the Cajamarca basin, where the small center of Huacaloma is located, and to the site of Cerro Blanco nestled, just across the Continental Divide, in the upper watershed of the Jequetepeque. Again, it is the Japanese who have furnished the relevant information (Terada and Onuki 1985,

Table 9

Vessel Form, Volume (in liters), and Volumetric Ratio for Pottery from the La Pampa Site by Sector

Vessel form	La Pampa M8 ($N = 72$)	La Pampa M4 ($N = 289$)
olla	53%	23%
	15.8	1.5
	4.0	
jar	7%	15%
	5.5	27.8
bottle	10%	11%
incurving bowl	7%	1%
	1.0	
open bowl	17%	22%
	0.7	1.4
	4.3	
flaring bowl	4%	21%
	0.9	2.0
Volume ratio		
olla to open bowl	20.4	0.9
jar to open bowl	7.1	6.5
		19.4
jar to flaring bowl	5.9	14.0

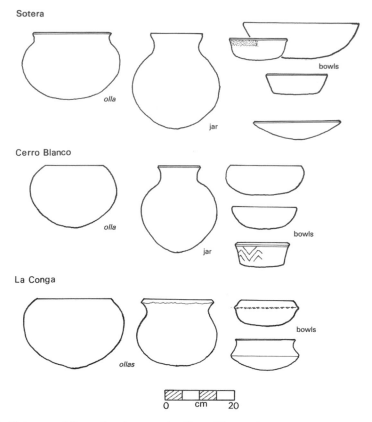

Fig. 11 Major vessel forms for phases at the Cerro Blanco site.

1988). (The Onuki [1995] study dealing with excavations at Kuntur Wasi and Cerro Blanco arrived too late to be incorporated into this analysis, but a quick scan of its contents suggests no major conflicts with the following text) Figures 11 and 12 illustrate major vessel forms from Cerro Blanco and Huacaloma; the corresponding frequency and volume data are in Tables 10 and 11.

The earliest phase at Cerro Blanco, La Conga, and the earliest phase at Huacaloma, Early Huacaloma, yield similar ceramic assemblages, and the two appear to have been contemporary (Terada and Onuki 1988: 15). *Ollas* dominate both assemblages, but incurving bowls are also common. (These vessel proportions are identical to those reported by Kaulicke [1981] for Pandanche A to the north, and I accept Terada and Onuki's [1985: 267] verdict that La Conga, Early Huacaloma, and Pandanche A should be contemporary.) In subsequent phases at both Cerro Blanco and Huacaloma, *ollas* decreased in fre-

Table 10

Vessel Form, Volume (in liters), and Volumetric Ratio for Pottery from the Cerro Blanco Site by Phase

Vessel form	La Conga (N = 138)	Cerro Blanco (N = 1,811)	Sotera (N = 211)
olla	65%	34%	8%
	4.7	6.2	9.7
	9.7		
jar	—	2%	18%
		6.2	11.6
bottle	—	6%	+
incurving bowl	26%	33%	—
	1.0	3.1	
open bowl	—	5%	61%
		1.4	1.4
			6.4
carinated bowl	9%	—	—
	1.6		
flaring bowl	—	20%	11%
		2.2	1.2
large plate	—	—	3%
			2.1
		Volume ratio	
olla to bowl	3.6	2.8	7.5
	7.5	4.4	
jar to bowl	—	2.0	8.9
		2.8	
		4.4	

Note: + indicates form is present but volume is indeterminate; — indicates absence of form.

quency and jars increased, whereas a variety of bowls, often elaborately decorated, proliferated. By the time of the Sotera phase at Cerro Blanco and the contemporary Layzón phase at Huacaloma, bowls comprised three-fourths of all vessel forms. Particularly noteworthy are the large bowls that comprise 23 percent of the Layzón assemblage. These basin-shaped vessels resemble containers that in later Moche times were used in *chicha* production (e.g., Shimada 1994: fig. 8.41). Throughout both the Huacaloma and Cerro Blanco sequences, the shift from *ollas* to jars and bowls suggests changing culinary activities, with serving activities ultimately preponderant over cooking. This attractive hypothesis, however, is not clearly matched by the volume data. As seen in Tables 10 and

Warren R. DeBoer

Layzón

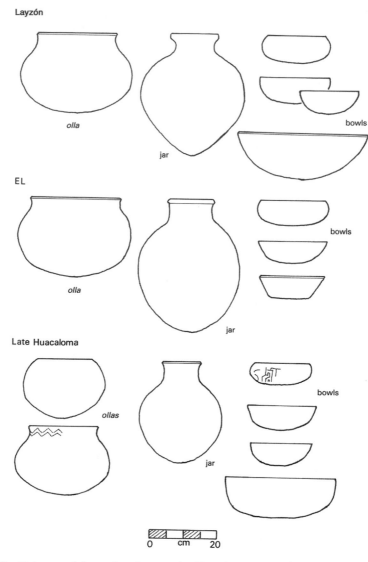

Fig. 12   Major vessel forms for phases at the Huacaloma site. Early Huacaloma phase excluded because of a dearth of specimens.

11, *olla*-to-bowl and jar-to-bowl volume ratios tended to remain low and only in the EL phase at Huacaloma did they even approach the feasting signature of HUACIS.

Table 11

Vessel Form, Volume, and Volumetric Ratio for Pottery from the Huacaloma Site

Vessel form	Early Huacaloma (N = 144)	Late Huacaloma (N = 4,026)	EL (N = 872)	Layzón (N = 269)
olla	72%	15%	8%	4%
		5.4	19.7	15.3
		7.9		
jar	2%	3%	14%	24%
		7.8	23.3	18.7
bottle	—	+	+	—
incurving bowl	21%	6%	4%	3%
		0.9	1.1	2.3
open-flaring bowl	5%	76%	71%	46%
		1.2	1.5	1.4
		1.6		2.0
large bowl	—	+	2%	23%
		8.0	8.0	10.3
		Volume ratio		
olla to open bowl	—	3.8	13.2	9.0
		5.6		
jar to incurving bowl	—	7.8	20.4	8.0
jar to open bowl	—	5.6	15.5	11.0

Notes: + indicates form is present but volume is indeterminate; — indicates absence of form. Early Huacaloma based on material from HL-MB; Late Huacaloma based on material from HL-IV (20 + 27 V-Y); EL and Layzón based on material from NS (29-30x). See Terada and Onuki (1985: 112) for definition of excavation units.

THE TYRANNY OF BILATERAL SYMMETRY

Up to this point, I have emphasized common and countable vessel forms in order to assess the role of ceramics in *la vida cotidiana,* a phrase in Spanish that seems to capture more than *quotidian*. Thus I have ignored the noteworthy but rather atypical remains that often characterize mortuary contexts such as Tumba I at Cerro Blanco (Terada and Onuki 1988). Here, however, I digress briefly in order to consider an odd assortment of vessels that had a wide distribution along the eastern base of the Andes and into the Ecuadorian sierra during Late Formative times. In this effort, I am retracing the steps of Lathrap (1971), who argued that tropical forest and highland cultures were members of the same

Formative "interaction sphere." As a specific datum, Lathrap cited the case of the double-spout-and-bridge bottle.

Although his basic argument was not chronological, Lathrap implied that the salient double-spout-and-bridge bottle probably appeared earliest in the Tutishcainyo pottery of the Central Ucayali basin. From this proximate Ucayali source, the form was transmitted to Ecuador only to become transmuted, through a merging of two spouts into one (Lathrap 1971: fig. 13). The result was the stirrup-spout bottle first evinced in Machalilla, thus initiating a form that came to play such a conspicuous role in the later ceramic prehistory of the northern Andes. Although this scenario has a certain geometric elegance, thorny empirical troubles have surfaced largely since Lathrap's seminal article. Specifically, the Cotocollao evidence indicates that the stirrup-spout form clearly preceded, at least in numerical frequency, a version of double-spout-and-bridge bottle in which one spout is peculiarly shortened to form a perforated stub, perhaps to serve as a finger hold to facilitate pouring (see Fig. 5, top). It is remarkable that Cotocallao stirrup-spouts, dating as early as 1500 B.C., should revert to the alleged, albeit mutated, ancestral form of the double-spout-and-bridge. Secondly, Staller's excavations in El Oro province demonstrate that stirrup-spout bottles were part of coastal Valdivian assemblages during the early second millennium B.C., an age that presses even the speediest of diffusions from a Tutishcainyo source (Staller n.d.: 384–387).

A third problem, however, is perhaps even more telling. I am not sure that any solid evidence for classical, symmetrical double-spout-and-bridge bottles exists anywhere before 1000 B.C. This perhaps startling charge requires further investigation.

The basis for this claim is that complete double-spout-and-bridge bottles recovered from the Formative of eastern Peru and Ecuador almost always display a decided asymmetry in which one spout is attentuated or even atrophied to a mere perforation. Alleged exceptions are always *reconstructions* based on the assumption that one spout with bridge attachment can be bilaterally reflected to generate a vessel profile at home in such familiar and later styles as Paracas or Nasca, where symmetrically spouted vessels were the rule. All of Lathrap's reconstructions (n.d.b.: figs. 35h, 49a,e,f, 71a) for Tutishcainyo and Shakimu were based on such mirror reflections, as was my own for the Shakimu component at Iparía (DeBoer 1975). The correlative Kotosh evidence is equally exiguous. Although stirrup-spout bottles are recorded for Kotosh Chavín, the only candidates for provenianced double-spout-and-bridge bottles are woefully incomplete (Izumi and Sono 1963: pl. 138: 22–23). Available evidence, therefore, indicates that the mirror can deceive.

At the risk of introducing two dubious acronyms in the same essay, let me nonetheless offer the concept of <u>A</u>symmetric <u>S</u>pouts of the <u>U</u>pper <u>A</u>mazon, or ASUA. Sites or localities yielding ASUA materials are plotted in Figure 13; these range from Cotocollao in the Ecuadorian highlands to the upper Purús on the Peru–Brazil border. An array of candidates for ASUA membership is illustrated in Figure 14; although variable, this array shares the common feature of spout asymmetry. The pervasiveness of such asymmetric and otherwise eccentric vessels may suggest a certain degree of historical and functional unity

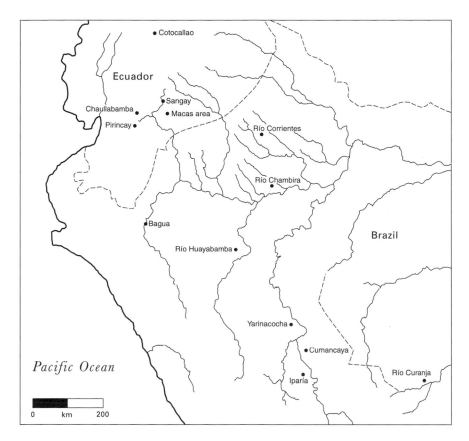

Fig. 13 Sites or localities bearing materials: Cotocollao (Villalba 1988); Sangay area (Porras 1987); Macas area (Bushnell 1946, Tellenbach, n.d.); Chaullabamba (Gomís 1989); Pirincay (Bruhns, Burton, and Miller 1990); Río Corrientes (Fung 1981; Ravines 1981); Río Chambira (Morales 1992, 1993; Bartholomew Dean, personal communication; Josea Kramer, personal communication); Bagua (Shady 1987, 1992; also see Miasta [1979]); Río Huayabamba (Ravines 1981); Yarinacocha (Lathrap n.d.b, 1970); Cumancaya (DeBoer, field notes); Iparía (DeBoer 1975); Río Curanja (Richard Montag, personal communication).

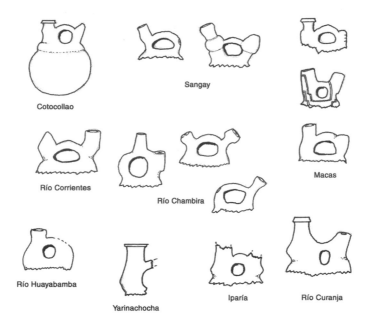

Fig. 14 Asymmetrically spouted bottles of varying scales, by location.

and might even agitate those imaginations that see social tensions embedded in ceramic form (e.g., Burger and Salazar-Burger 1993: 106).

Only scant information exists for dating ASUA. Bruhns, Burton, and Miller (1990: 228) reported that "double-spout-and-bridge bottles with one spout closed and nonfunctional" are known from Pirincay and nearby Chaullabamba in contexts dating to about 900 to 800 B.C. Porras (1987: figs. 114, 115) illustrated similar specimens from the vicinity of Sangay, but none is associated securely with excavated materials from Sangay proper; in fact, their absence from Sangay suggests that they are chronologically disjunct from the RBI style that dominates this site. The Chambira drainage of the Marañon appears to have been a hotbed of ASUA activity. Collections that Kramer noted in the 1970s and Bartolomew Dean in the 1990s are being contextualized through the work of Morales (1992, 1993). Typical ASUA vessels, as well as a distinctive assortment of figurines, now define a Chambira phase, although I think that Morales errors wildly in attributing a 3000 B.C. antiquity to this material. Farther south, radiocarbon dates for ASUA Shakimu remains indicate a mere 850 to 650 B.C. time depth (DeBoer 1975; Lathrap 1970), age estimates more or less conformable with the Pirincay evidence.

I suggest that ASUA is a flash horizon dated to about 800 B.C., perhaps a bit earlier, that spread across the same terrain of a later HUACIS and, not coincidentally, followed the same riverine routes traversed by seventeenth-century Jesuits from Quito to the Upper Ucayali, *entradas* whose historical and geopolitical significance continues to be contested by the modern nations of Peru and Ecuador. From the standpoint of archaeology, however, ASUA remains an enigmatic collection of far-flung oddities whose function, context, and meaning escape understanding. Another exciting and doable research project is lurking.

CONCLUSIONS

Millennia and thousands of kilometers have been covered and some summation is in order. One salient fact is the sheer diversity in the composition of Formative ceramic assemblages. Phylogenists who seek a singular origin for these assemblages are likely to be disappointed. The Ecuadorian assemblages of late Valdivia, Cotocollao, and Catamayo are decidedly different from each other, whereas the rather drab neckless *olla* assemblages of early second millennium B.C. Peru seem to be in a separate world. Nor do the latter appear to have much to do with the flamboyantly decorated *tecomates* of coastal Chiapas, putative Mesoamerican cognates of the South American neckless *olla*. The quest for a unitary origin for New World ceramics appears to be receding, either into deeper time or into theoretical forfeiture (Hoopes 1994). This verdict, of course, does not deny diffusion nor the still unappreciated nuances of "stimulus diffusion," but it does suggest that archaeological methods for detecting diffusion are wanting and based upon rather naïve, mechanical, and essentially "copycat" notions of emulation or, for that matter, "anticopycat" resistance.

A second point stems from our HUACIS foil. Ethnographically known ceramic assemblages, whose basic structure can be extended back 2,000 years into prehistory, typically contain a balance of *ollas* for cooking, jars for liquid transport and storage, and serving bowls. These three basic categories occur in essentially equivalent proportions among the contemporary Shipibo and many of their HUACIS compatriots. The Formative record is much more variable.

Figure 15 portrays this variability in the form of a tripolar graph. The Shipibo assemblage is situated in its center and its neighbors include all phases of the Cotocollao sequence, Pechiche, with Valdivia 2–3 and the Cerro Blanco phase as outliers. All of these cases would appear to be balanced domestically oriented assemblages. However, a grave technical problem emerges. One cannot rightfully compare the frequency of vessels *in use* (the Shipibo case) with the frequency of vessels *discarded* into archaeological middens. As I (1974) pointed out elsewhere, differing vessel categories have different lifespans that determine their

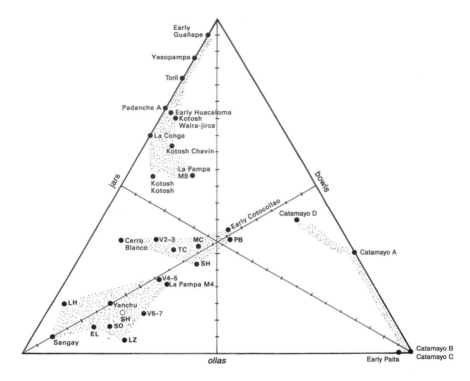

Fig. 15 Percentage frequency of *ollas*, jars, and bowls for assemblages discussed in text. V2–3 = Valdivia 2–3; V4–5 = Valdivia 4–5; V6–7 = Valivia 6–7; MC = Middle Cotocollao; TC = Late Cotocollao; PE = Pechiche; SO = Sotera phase at Cerro Blanco; LH = Late Huacaloma phase at Huacaloma; EL = EL phase at Huacaloma; LZ = Layzón phase at Huacaloma. The solid circle SH stands for the in-use Shipibo assemblage, while the open circle SH indicates the Shipibo discard assemblage.

representation in the archaeological record. Furthermore, these differing lifespans are not randomly distributed but relate directly to vessel size (DeBoer 1983), suggesting that they have more than localized relevance. Taking the differential longevity of vessels into account, the Shipibo profile is shunted well toward the bowl-dominated assemblages of Figure 15.

The center of Figure 15 shows that all phases of the Cotocollao sequence and Pechiche occupy this central position with Valdivia 2–3 and the Cerro Blanco phase as possible outliers. All of these cases would appear to be balanced domestically oriented assemblages. Other groupings differ markedly. The upper apex of the triangle includes assemblages dominated by neckless *ollas*, all three phases at the Kotosh site, as well as Pandanche A, La Conga, Early Huacaloma, and the M8 deposit at La Pampa. With the exception of M8, all members of

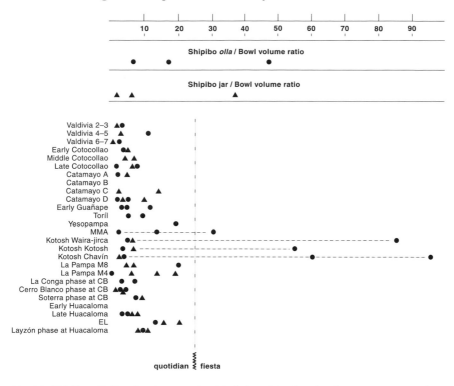

Fig. 16 Shipibo *olla*/bowl volume ratios (circles) and jar/bowl volume ratios (triangles), shown at top, contrasted with archaeological assemblages for which corresponding vessel volume data are available. CB = Cerro Blanco; MMA = Muyu Moqo A.

this group are also chronologically early in the Peruvian sequence, suggesting that temporal factors are a force in conditioning ceramic assemblage variability. A third grouping consists of all four Catamayo phases and Early Paita. In these northern assemblages, jars overwhelm and make us question, "Where is everything else?"

A fourth grouping tends toward bowls, typically decorated in an ornate manner. In this group, M4 at La Pampa and Valdivia 4–5 fall as outliers, whereas Valdivia 6–7, Late Huacaloma, EL, and Layzón phases at Huacaloma, Sotera at Cerro Blanco, and the probably post-Formative Yaunchu and Sangay assemblages, the latter two in the) Oriente, constitute its major constituency. The transformed Shipibo assemblage occupies center stage in this grouping. In contrast, Sangay is a peripheral member of this group, its elaborately decorated and shaped bowls comprising over 90 percent of the vessels Porras (1987) illustrated. Clearly the Sangay assemblage represents a special kind of ceramic deposit. It

could represent a prehistoric version of world renewal ceremonies as still practiced by the Achuar (Pita Kelekna, personal communication) and by the Quichua
speakers of Curacay (Reeve n.d.). During the course of these ceremonies, quantities of serving vessels are used and then ritually smashed (compare DeBoer and
Lathrap 1979: 135). The ceremonial nature of the Sangay site seems likely as
humdrum residential midden is scarce throughout the mound-bearing precinct
(Arthur Rostoker, personal communication; see also Kelekna 1998).

Vessel shape, however, is only half of the story. Vessel size, as measured in
terms of modal volume, presents another picture. Recall the confidence with
which Lathrap asserted:

> On surveying the average size of each of the functional classes of
> pottery used by the various surviving Tropical Forest groups, one is led
> to the conclusion that a vessel with a maximum diameter of more
> than 40 cm is very likely to be a fermentation vessel. The presence of
> such large containers in an archaeological deposit can be taken as evi-
> dence that beer was present and that the whole fiesta pattern was in
> full swing. (1970: 55)

When applied to Formative ceramic assemblages, Lathrap's criterion leaves most
"sober" rather than "swinging." Figure 16 summarizes the volumetric data
marshaled for Formative ceramic assemblages.

By HUACIS standards, almost all Formative assemblages fall within the quotidian or even transport range. With the exception of the Kotosh phases, *olla*-
to-bowl and jar-to-bowl volume ratios do not approach the Shipibo feasting
signature. Even in the case of Kotosh, the high values pertain to the *olla* to bowl
ratio, not to the ratio of jars to bowls, the forms most central to the serving of
beer. These results suggest either of two possibilities: (a) beer-based fiestas, or
the Andean institution of the *minka* in which hosts rewarded laborers with
draughts of *chicha* were not widely in place during the Formative; or (b) such
fiestas were part of Formative culinary culture, but their expression in ceramic
form was quite different from that found in later times. For example, might
four 25-liter jars be functionally equivalent to one 100-liter jar?

In late prehistoric and historic times, large *chicha* brewing and storage vessels,
the largest with capacities approaching 2,000 liters, were common in the Andean
highlands and on the coast (Marcus 1987: 50; fig. 30). In a famous passage,
Padre Bernabe Cobo commented on the focal role of *chicha* in Andean domestic economy:

> The majority of their household equipment . . . are earthen jars or
> jugs. They keep no other liquor, not even water, except their wine or

chicha, and this does not last them a long time. For this reason, they make it often ... To make this beverage, store it, and drink it, they have more instruments and containers than they have for their meals. The largest ones contain from four to six arrobas [ca. 60 to 90 liters]. (1970: 194–195)

Formative pottery intimates a different Andean world, one that was "unformed" or better formed in ways distinct from its sequel.

BIBLIOGRAPHY

ADAMS, PATSY
    1976   Cerámica culina. *Comunidades y Culturas Peruanas* 7. Summer Institute of Linguistics, Yarinacocha, Peru.

ALVAREZ, AURELIO
    n.d.   Cooking Pots, Liquid Jars and Breakable Fiesta Wares: Selecting the Right Kind of Paste at Real Alto. Paper presented at the 91st Annual Meeting of the American Anthropological Association, San Francisco, 1992.

ALVAREZ, RICARDO
    n.d.   *Hijos de dioses.* Santiago Valverde, Lima.

ATHENS, J. STEPHEN
    1986   The Site of Pumpuentsa and the Pastaza Phase in Southeastern Lowland Ecuador. *Ñawpa Pacha* 24: 111–124.

BAER, GERHARD
    1969   Reise und Forschung in Ost–Peru. *Verhandlungen der Naturforschenden Gesellschaft in Basel*, Band 80/2.

BELLIER, IRENE
    1994   Los Mai Huna Tucano occidentales. In *Guía etnográfica de la Alta Amazonía* (F. Santos and F. Barclay, eds.), 1: 1–180. FLACSO–SEDE, Quito.

BIANCHI, CÉSAR
    1982   *Artesanías y técnicas Shuar.* Mundo Shuar, Morona–Santiago, Ecuador.

BLITZ, JOHN H.
    1993   Big Pots for Big Shots: Feasting and Storage in a Mississippian Community. *American Antiquity* 58(1): 80–95.

BLUTE, MARION
    1979   Sociocultural Evolutionism: An Untried Theory. *Behavioral Science* 24: 46–59.

BRUHNS, KAREN O., JAMES H. BURTON, AND GEORGE R. MILLER
    1990   Excavations at Pirincay in the Paute Valley of Southern Ecuador, 1985–1988. *Antiquity* 64: 221–233.

BRUHNS, KAREN O., JAMES H. BURTON, AND ARTHUR ROSTOKER
    1994   La cerámica incisión en fajas rojas: Evidencia de intercambio entre la sierra y el oriente durante el Formativo Tardío de Ecuador. In *Tecnología y organización de la producción de cerámica prehispánica en los Andes* (Izumi Shimada, ed.): 53–66. Pontificia Universidad Católica del Perú, Fondo Editorial, Lima.

BURGER, RICHARD
    1988   The Beginning of Ceramic Use in Peru as Viewed from Huaricoto. *Paleoetnología* 5: 259–266.

BURGER, RICHARD, AND LUCY SALAZAR–BURGER
    1985   The Early Ceremonial Center of Huaricoto. In *Early Ceremonial Architecture in the Andes* (C. B. Donnan, ed.): 111–138. Dumbarton Oaks, Washington, D.C.

1993 The Place of Dual Organization in Early Andean Ceremonialism: A Comparative Review. In *El mundo ceremonial andino* (L. Millones and Y. Onuki, eds.): 97–116, Senri Ethnological Studies 37. National Museum of Ethnology, Osaka.

CALIFANO, MARIO
1982 *Etnografía de los Mashco de la Amazonía sud occidental del Perú.* Fundación para la Educación, la Ciéncia y la Cultura, Buenos Aires.

CHAUMEIL, JEAN–PIERRE
1994 Los Yagua. In *Guía etnográfica de la Alta Amazonía* (F. Santos and F. Barclay, eds.), 1: 181–309. FLACSO–SEDE, Quito.

CLARK, JOHN E., AND MICHAEL BLAKE
1994 The Power of Prestige: Competitive Generosity and the Emergence of Rank Societies in Lowland Mesoamerica. In *Factional Competition and Political Development in the New World* (M. Brumfiel and J. W. Fox, eds.): 17–30. Cambridge University Press, Cambridge.

COBO, BERNABE
1970 *Inca Religion and Customs.* University of Texas Press, Austin.

D'ANS, ANDRÉ–MARCEL
1970 *Materiales para el estudio del grupo lingüistico Pano.* Universidad Nacional Mayor de San Marcos, Lima.

DeBOER, WARREN R.
1974 Ceramic Longevity and Archaeological Interpretation: An Example from the Upper Ucayali, Eastern Peru. *American Antiquity* 39(2): 419–433.
1975 Bino Style Ceramics from Iparía. *Ñawpa Pacha* 10–12: 91–107.
1983 The Archaeological Record as Preserved Death Assemblage. In *Archaeological Hammers and Theories* (J. Moore and A. Keene, eds.): 19–36. Academic Press, New York.
1990 Interaction, Imitation, and Communication as Expressed in Style: The Ucayali Experience. In *The Uses of Style in Archaeology* (M. Conkey and C. Hastorf, eds.): 82–104. Cambridge University Press, Cambridge.
n.d. Archaeological Reconnaissance in the Central Huallaga, Northeastern Peru. Unpublished manuscript in the possession of the author, 1984.

DeBOER, WARREN R., AND LYNDA CARROLL
1992 Full Circle on the Rim Sherd. *Journal of the Steward Anthropological Society* 20(1/2): 265–281.

DeBOER, WARREN R., AND DONALD W. LATHRAP
1979 The Making and Breaking of Shipibo Conibo Ceramics. In *Ethnoarchaeology: Implications of Ethnography for Archaeology* (C. Kramer, ed.): 102–138. Columbia University Press, New York.

DeBOER, WARREN R., AND J. SCOTT RAYMOND
1987 Roots Revisited: The Origins of the Shipibo Art Style. *Journal of Latin American Lore* 13(1): 115–132.

DOLE, GERTRUDE
1974 Types of Amahuaca Pottery and Techniques of Its Construction. *Ethnologische Zeitschrift* 1: 145–157.

329

Warren R. DeBoer

DWYER, JANE P. (ED.)
1975   *The Cashinahua of Eastern Peru*. Studies in Anthropology and Material Culture 1. Haffenreffer Museum of Anthropology, Brown University, Providence, R.I.

ERICKSON, PHILIPPE
1990   How Crude Is Mayoruna Pottery? *Journal of Latin American Lore* 16(1): 47–68.

ESPINOSA, LUCAS
1955   *Contribuciones lingüísticas y etnográficas sobre algunos pueblos indígenas del Amazonas peruano, Tomo I.* Consejo Superior de Investigaciones Científicas, Instituto Bernardino Sahagún, Madrid.

FARABEE, WILLIAM C.
1922   *Indian Tribes of Eastern Peru*. Papers of the Peabody Museum of American Archaeology and Ethnology 10. Cambridge, Mass.

FAUST, NORMA
1972   *Gramática Cocama: Lecciones para el aprendizaje del idioma Cocama.* Instituto Lingüístico de Verano. Serie Lingüística Peruana 6. Yarinacocha, Peru.

FEJOS, PAUL
1943   *Ethnography of the Yagua.* Viking Fund Publications in Anthropology 1.

FLANNERY, KENT V., AND JOYCE MARCUS
1994   *Early Formative Pottery of the Valley of Oaxaca, Mexico.* Memoirs of the Museum of Anthropology 27. University of Michigan, Ann Arbor.

FORD, JAMES A.
1969   *A Comparison of Formative Cultures in the Americas.* Smithsonian Institution Press, Washington, D.C.

Frank, Erwin H.
1994   Los Uni. In *Guía etnográfica de la Alta Amazonía* (F. Santos and F. Barclay, eds.) 2: 131–237. FLACSO–SEDE, Quito.

FUNG, ROSA
1981   Notas y comentarios sobre el sitio Valencia en el Río Corrientes. *Amazonia Peruana* 4(7): 99–137.

GARCÍA, MARÍA
1993   *Buscando nuestras raices: Historia y cultura Chayahuita.* Centro Amazónico de Antropología y Alicación Practica, Lima.

GEBHART–SAYER, ANGELIKA
1984   *The Cosmos Encoiled: Indian Art of the Peruvian Amazon.* Center for Inter–American Relations, New York.

GIRARD, RAFAEL
1958   *Indios selváticos de la Amazonía peruana.* Libro Mex, México, D.F.

GOMÍS, DOMINIQUE
1989   La Alfarería de Chaullabamba. *Catedral Salvaje* 24: 4–5. Cuenca, Ecuador.

GOULARD, JEAN–PIERRE
1994   Los Ticuna. In *Guía etnográfica de la Alta Amazonía* (F. Santos and F. Barclay, eds.) 1: 311–442. FLACSO–SEDE, Quito.

GOW, PETER
    1988   Visual Compulsion: Design and Image in Western Amazonian Cultures. *Revindi* 2: 19–32.
    1994   River People: Shamanism and History in Western Amazonia. In *Shamanism, History, and the State* (N. Thomas and C. Humphrey, eds.): 90–113. University of Michigan Press, Ann Arbor.

GROSSMAN, JOEL W.
    1983   Demographic Change and Economic Transformation in the South Central Highlands of pre–Huari Peru. *Ñawpa Pacha* 21: 45–126.

GUFFROY, JEAN, N. ALMEIDA, P. LECOQ, C. CAILLAVET, F. DUVERNEUIL, L. EMPERAIRE, AND B. ARNAUD
    1987   *Loja prehispanique. Recherches archeologiques dans les Andes meridionales de l'equateur.* Synthèse 27. Institut Français d'Etudes Andines, Paris.

HALLEY, DAVID J.
    1983   Use Alteration of Pottery Vessel Surfaces: An Important Source of Evidence for the Identification of Vessel Function. *North American Archaeologist* 4: 3–26.

HANKE, WANDA
    1954   The Chacobo in Bolivia. *Ethnos* 23 (2–4): 100–126.

HARNER, MICHAEL J.
    1972   *The Jivaro: People of the Sacred Waterfalls.* Doubleday/Natural History Press, Garden City, N.Y.

HOOPES, JOHN
    1994   Ford Revisited: A Critical Review of the Chronology and Relationships of the Earliest Ceramic Complexes in the New World, 6000–1500 B.C. *Journal of World Prehistory* 8(1): 1–50.

IZUMI, SEIICHI, AND TOSHIHIKO SONO
    1963   *Andes 2—Excavations at Kotosh, Peru, 1960.* Kadokawa, Tokyo.

IZUMI, SEIICHI, AND KAZUO TERADA
    1966   *Andes 3—Excavations at Pechiche and Garbanzal, Tumbes Valley, Peru.* Kadokawa, Tokyo.
    1972   *Andes 4—Excavations at Kotosh, Peru, 1963 and 1966.* University of Tokyo Press, Tokyo.

KÄSTNER, KLAUS–PETER
    1992   *Historisch–Ethnographische Klassifikation der Stämme des Ucayali–Beckens (Ost– Peru).* Band 46, Monographien 8. Abhandlungen und Berichte des Staatlichen Museums für Völkerkunde.

KAULICKE, PETER
    1981   Keramik der Frühen Initialperiode aus Pandanche, Cajamarca, Peru. *Beitrage zur Allgemeinen und Vergleichenden Archäologie* 3: 363–389.

KELEKNA, PITA
    1998   War and Theocracy. In *Chiefdoms and Chietaincy in the Americas* (Elsa Redmon, ed.): 164–168. University Press of Florida, Gainesville.

KELLEY, PATRICIA, AND CAROLYN ORR
    1976   *Sarayacu Quichua Pottery.* Summer Institute of Linguistics 1, Dallas.

LANNING, EDWARD P.
1963   *A Ceramic Sequence for the Piura and Chira Coast*. Publications in American Archaeology and Ethnology 46(2), University of California.

LATHRAP, DONALD W.
1970   *The Upper Amazon*. Thames and Hudson, London.
1971   The Tropical Forest and the Cultural Context of Chavín. In *Dumbarton Oaks Conference on Chavín* (E. Benson, ed.): 73–100. Dumbarton Oaks, Washington, D.C.
1976   Shipibo Tourist Art. In *Ethnic and Tourist Arts: Cultural Expressions from the Fourth World* (N. Graburn, ed.): 197–207. University of California Press, Berkeley.
1983   Recent Shipibo–Conibo Ceramics and Their Implications for Archaeological Interpretation. In *Structure and Communication in Art* (D. Washburn, ed.): 25–39. Cambridge University Press, Cambridge.
n.d.a.   Shipibo–Conibo Ceramic Form Categories and Comparative Material from the Isconahua. Paper distributed at the Annual Meeting of the Society for American Archaeology, México, D.F., 1970.
n.d.b.   *Yarinacocha: Stratigraphic Excavations in the Peruvian Montaña*. Ph.D. dissertation, Harvard University, 1962.

LATHRAP, DONALD W., ANGELIKA GEBHART–SAYER, AND ANN MESTER
1985   The Roots of the Shipibo Art Style: Three Waves on Imiriacocha or There Were "Incas" before the Incas. *Journal of Latin American Lore* 11: 31–119.

LATHRAP, DONALD W., ANGELIKA GEBHART–SAYER, THOMAS P. MYERS, AND ANN MESTER
1987   Further Discussion of the Roots of the Shipibo Art Style: A Rejoinder to DeBoer and Raymond. *Journal of Latin American Lore* 13: 225–271.

LATHRAP, DONALD W., JORGE G. MARCOS, AND JAMES ZEIDLER
1977   Real Alto: An Ancient Ceremonial Center. *Archaeology* 30(1): 2–13.

MARCOS, JORGE
1988   *Real Alto: La historia de un centro ceremonial Valdivia*, 2 vols. Biblioteca Ecuatoriana de Arqueología 4/5. Corporación Editora Nacional, Quito.

MARCUS, JOYCE
1987   *Late Intermediate Occupation at Cerro Azul, Perú*. Museum of Anthropology Technical Report 20. University of Michigan, Ann Arbor.

MATTESON, ESTHER
1965   *The Piro (Arawakan) Language*. Publications in Linguistics 42, University of California.

MIASTA, JAIME
1979   *El alto Amazonas: Arqueología de Jaen y San Ignacio, Perú*. Seminario de Historia Rural Andino, Universidad Nacional Mayor de San Marcos, Lima.

MOORE, JERRY D.
1989   Pre–Hispanic Beer in Coastal Peru: Technology and Social Context of Prehistoric Production. *American Anthropologist* 91(3): 682–695.

MORALES, DANIEL
1992   Chambira: Alfareros tempranos de la Amazonía peruana. In *Estudios de arqueología peruana* (D. Bonavia, ed.): 149–177. FOMCIENCIAS, Lima.

1993   *Compendio histórico del Perú. Historia arqueológica. Tomo 1.* Editorial Milla Batres, Lima.

MYERS, THOMAS P.
n.d.   The Late Prehistoric Period at Yarinacocha, Peru. Ph.D. dissertation, University of Illinois at Urbana–Champaign, 1970.

NELSON, BEN
1985   Reconstructing Ceramic Vessels and Their Systemic Contexts. In *Decoding Prehistoric Ceramics* (B. Nelson, ed.): 310–329. Southern Illinois University Press, Carbondale.

NIMUENDAJÚ, CURT
1952   *The Tukuna.* Publications in American Archaeology and Ethnology 45, University of California.

OLIVER, SYMMES C.
1962   *Ecology and Cultural Continuity as Contributing Factors in the Social Organization of the Plains Indian.* University of California Publications in American Archaeology and Ethnology 48.

ONUKI, YOSHIO
1993   Las actividades ceremoniales tempranas en la Cuenca del Alto Huallaga y algunos problemas generales. In *El mundo ceremonial andino* (L. Millones and Y. Onuki, eds.): 69–96. Senri Ethnological Studies 37. National Museum of Ethnology, Osaka.

ONUKI, YOSHIO (ED.)
1995   *Kuntur Wasi y Cerro Blanco: Dos sitios del Formativo en el norte del Perú.* Hokusen-sha, Japan.

ONUKI, YOSHIO, AND TATSUHIKO FUJII
1974   Excavations at La Pampa, Peru. *Proceedings of the Department of Humanities, College of General Education, University of Tokyo* 59: 45–109.

ORTON, CLIVE, AND P. TYERS
1992   Counting Broken Objects: The Statistics of Ceramic Assemblages. *Proceedings of the British Academy* 77: 163–184.

PORRAS, PEDRO
1975   *Supervivencia de tradición cerámica común a las culturas del Alto Amazonas y de manera especial a las de la Zona Oriental del Ecuador en Sudamérica.* Imprenta Universitaria, Panamá.
1987   *Investigaciones arqueológicas a las faldas del Sangay.* Artes Gráficas Señal, Quito.

PROST, MARIAN D.
1970   *Costumbres, habilidades y cuadro de la vida humana entre los Chacobos.* Instituto Lingüístico de Verano. Riberalta, Bolivia.

RAVINES, ROGGER
1981   Yacimientos arqueológicos de la región nororiental del Perú. *Amazonia Peruana* 4(7): 139–175.

RAYMOND, J. SCOTT
1993   Ceremonialism in the Early Formative of Ecuador. In *El mundo ceremonial andino* (L. Millones and Y. Onuki, eds.): 25–44. Senri Ethnological Studies 37. National Museum of Ethnology, Osaka.

RAYMOND, J. SCOTT, WARREN R. DeBOER, AND PETER G. ROE
 1975   *Cumancaya: A Peruvian Ceramic Tradition.* Occasional Papers 2, Department of Archaeology. University of Calgary, Alberta.

RAYMOND, J. SCOTT, AUGUSTO OYUELA–CAYCEDO, AND PATRICK CARMICHAEL
 1994   Una comparación de los tecnologías de la cerámica temprana en Ecuador y Colombia. In *Tecnología y organización de la producción cerámica prehispanica en los Andes* (I. Shimada, ed.): 33–52. Pontificia Universidad Católica, Lima.

REEVE, MARY–ELIZABETH
 n.d.   Identity as Process: The Meaning of Runapura for Quichua Speakers of the Curaray River, Eastern Ecuador. Ph.D. dissertation, University of Illinois at Urbana–Champaign, 1985.

ROE, PETER G.
 1980   Art and Residence among the Shipibo Indians of Peru: A Study in Microacculturation. *American Anthropologist* 82: 42–71.
 1982   *The Cosmic Zygote: Cosmology in the Amazon Basin.* Rutgers University Press, New Brunswick, N.J.
 n.d.   Cumanacaya: Archaeological Excavations and Ethnographic Analogy in the Peruvian Montaña. Ph.D. dissertation, University of Illinois at Urbana–Champaign, 1973.

ROSTOKER, ARTHUR
 n.d.   *An Archaeological Collection from Eastern Ecuador.* Master's thesis, San Francisco State University, 1985.

SCHLESIER, KARL, ED.
 1994   *Plains Indians A.D. 500–1500: The Archaeological Past of Historic Groups.* University of Oklahoma Press, Norman.

SENIOR, LOUISE, AND DUNBAR BIRNIE III
 1995   Accurately Estimating Vessel Volume from Profile Illustrations. *American Antiquity* 60(2): 319–334.

SHADY, RUTH
 1987   Tradición y cambio en las sociedades formativas de Bagua, Amazonas, Perú. *Revista Andina* 5(2): 457–487.
 1992   Sociedades formativas del nororiente peruano. In *Prehistoria Sudamerica: Nuevas perspectivas* (B. Meggers, ed.): 343–357. Taraxacum, Washington, D.C.

SHELL, OLIVE
 1959   *Vocabulario Cashibo–Castellano.* Instituto Lingüistico de Verano, Yarinacocha, Peru.

SHIMADA, IZUMI
 1994   *Pampa Grande and the Mochica Culture.* University of Texas Press, Austin.

SKIBO, JAMES
 1992   *Pottery Function: A Use–Alteration Perspective.* Plenum, New York.

SMITH JR., MARION
 1985   Toward an Economic Interpretation of Ceramics: Relating Vessel Size and Shape to Use. In *Decoding Prehistoric Ceramics* (B. Nelson, ed.): 254–309. Southern Illinois University Press, Carbondale.

SPECK, FRANK
    1941   *Gourds of the Southeastern Indians.* New England Gourd Society, Boston.

STALLER, JOHN
    n.d.   Late Valdivia Occupation in El Oro Province Ecuador: Excavations at the
            Early Formative Period (3500–1500 B.C.), Site of La Emerenciana. Ph.D.
            dissertation, Southern Methodist University, Dallas, 1994.

STIRLING, MATHEW
    1938   *Historical and Ethnographical Material on the Jivaro Indians.* Bureau of American
            Ethnology Bulletin 117, Washington, D.C.

STRONG, WILLIAM D., CLIFFORD EVANS JR., AND ROSE LILIEN
    1952   Appendix 1: Description of Pottery Types. In *Cultural Stratigraphy in the Viru
            Valley, Northern Peru,* by W. D. Strong and C. Evans Jr., Columbia University
            Press, New York.

TERADA, KAZUO
    1979   *Excavations at La Pampa in the North Highlands of Peru, 1975.* Report 1 Japanese
            Scientific Expedition to Nuclear America. University of Tokyo Press, Tokyo.

TERADA, KAZUO, AND YOSHIO ONUKI
    1985   *The Formative Period in the Cajamarca Basin, Peru: Excavations at Huacaloma and
            Layzon, 1982.* Report 3, Japanese Scientific Expedition to Nuclear America.
            University of Tokyo Press, Tokyo.

    1988   *Las excavaciones en Cerro Blanco y Huacaloma, Cajamarca, Perú, 1985.* University
            of Tokyo Press, Tokyo.

TESSMANN, GÜNTER
    1928   *Menschen ohne Gott.* Strecker und Schröder, Stuttgart.

    1930   *Die Indianer Nordost–Perus.* Friederichsen, De Gruyter, Hamburg.

THOMPSON, ROBERT, AND JOHN STALLER
    2001   An Analysis of Opal Phytoliths from Food Residues of Selected Sherds and
            Dental Calculus from Excavations at the Site of La Emerenciana, El Oro
            Province, Ecuador. *Phytolitharien Bulletin of the Society for Phytolith Research* 13
            (2/3): 8–16.

TRUJILLO, ALONSO
    1960   Análisis del comportamiento económico de los Kashibo frente a los efectos
            aculturativos. *Revista do Museu Paulista* (Nova Serie) 12: 199–309. Sao Paulo.

TSCHAUNER, HARTMUT
    1994   Archaeological Systematics and Cultural Evolution: Retrieving the Honour
            of Culture History. *Man* 29: 95–115.

TURNER, CHRISTY, AND LAUREL LOFGREN
    1966   Household Size of Prehistoric Western Pueblo Indians. *Southwestern Journal
            of Anthropology* 22: 117–132.

VILLALBA, MARCELO
    1988   *Cotocollao: Una aldea formativa del valle de Quito.* Serie Monográfica 2. Miscelanea
            Antropológica Ecuatoriana.

VOSSEN, RUDIGER
  1969   *Archäologische Interpretation und Ethnographischer Befund: Eine Analyse
          Anhandrezenter Keramik des Westlichen Amazonasbeckens,* 2 vols. Verlag Klaus
          Renner, Munich.

WHITTEN, DOROTHY
  1981   Ancient Tradition in a Contemporary Context: Canelos Quichua Ceramics
          and Symbolism. In *Cultural Transformations and Ethnicity in Modern Ecuador* (N.
          Whitten, ed.): 749–775. University of Illinois Press, Urbana.

WHITTEN, DOROTHY, AND NORMAN WHITTEN JR.
  1978   Ceramics of the Canelos Quichua. *Natural History* 87(8): 90–99.

WOLF, ERIC R.
  1982   *Europe and the People without History.* University of California Press, Berkeley.

ZEIDLER, JAMES
  1983   La etnoarqueología de una vivienda Achuar y sus implicaciones arqueológicas.
          Miscelanea Antropológica Ecuatoriana 3: 155–193.
  n.d.   Social Space in Valdivia Society: Community Patterning and Domestic
          Structure at Real Alto, 3000–2000 B.C. Ph.D. dissertation, University of Illinois
          at Urbana–Champaign, 1984.

ZOUBEK, THOMAS
  n.d.   Guañape Period Ceremonialism at Huaca El Gallo, Viru Valley, Peru. Paper
          presented at the 14th Annual Northeast Conference on Andean Archaeology
          and Ethnohistory, Providence, R.I., 1995.

Expression of Ideology
in the Formative Period of Ecuador

KAREN E. STOTHERT

CENTER FOR ARCHAEOLOGICAL RESEARCH,
UNIVERSITY OF TEXAS AT SAN ANTONIO,
AND MUSEO ANTROPÓLOGICO, BANCO CENTRAL DEL ECUADOR

INTRODUCTION

In this study an understanding of ideology in the long Formative period was developed upon the basis of archaeological evidence from sites in Ecuador. The essay draws upon interpretations generated by many scholars who have employed analogical arguments from ethnographic information on South America. The discussion illustrates the value and limitations of ethnographic analogies for making interpretations of ancient thought.

Ideology is a term that refers to the thought habits of the ancient people, especially the ideas that governed their activities and that were expressed in material remains. These thought habits included beliefs about (a) the place of people, animals, and things in the cosmos; (b) the nature of life and the values generated by those beliefs; (c) the nonordinary realms of the spirits, supernaturals, and dead ancestors (cosmology and religious ideology); and (d) human society (political and economic ideology), including the nature of women, men, and their interrelationships (gender ideologies).[1] Ancient ideologies were expressed in rituals whose remains are found in the archaeological record and in expression in symbols encoded in ancient material remains.

Many scholars recognize that each religious symbol system plays a key role in the maintenance of all other aspects of cultural life (Coe 1981; Demarest

---

[1] In reconstructing gender ideologies, archaeologists hope to grasp how ancient people understood "the meaning of male, female, masculine, feminine, sex, and reproduction in any given culture" (Spector and Whelan 1989: 69). This aspect of belief, encompassing prescriptions and sanctions for appropriate male and female behavior or cultural rationalizations and explanations for social and political relationships between males and females" (Spector and Whelan 1989: 69–70), is closely linked to cosmology and social and religious philosophy.

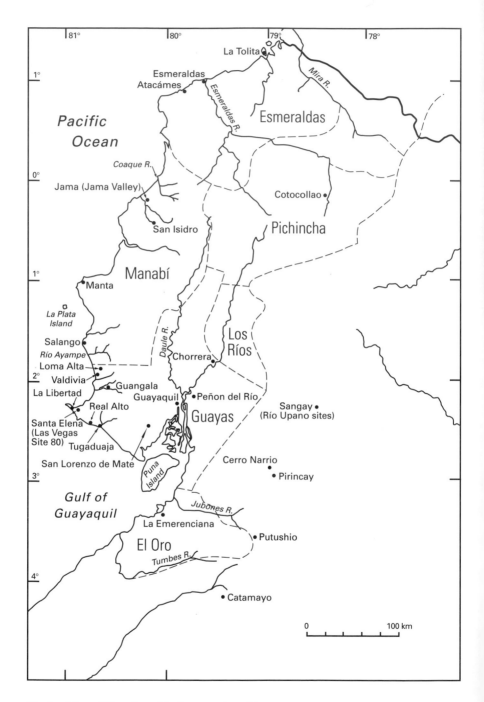

Fig. 1   Map of Ecuador with sites mentioned in text.

and Conrad 1992; Keatinge 1981). Reichel-Dolmatoff expresses this in the following way:

> [a]boriginal cosmologies and myth structure . . . represent . . . a set of
> ecological principles . . . [which] formulate a system of social and
> economic rules that have a highly adaptive value in the continuous
> endeavor to maintain a viable equilibrium between the resources of
> the environment and the demands of society. (1976: 308)

The challenge facing archaeologists is how to infer ancient ideology and behavior from material remains and how to decode the meaning of ancient symbols and their social functions. One approach involves employing the living traditions of native peoples of South America as interpretive tools for suggesting the possible meanings of ancient material remains.

Interpretation, however, is complicated by human creativity. In Ecuador, one of the salient features of the Formative archaeological record is its variability. In the ancient communities, local and regional expressions of South American religious ideas were creatively innovated. Goldman's (1972: 192) observation about variation in the ethnographic present is applicable to the Formative: "One of the striking characteristics of the [cultures of the] entire Amazon drainage is the ready way in which form and content separate and recombine in new ways."

For example, today on the Santa Elena peninsula in Ecuador (Fig. 1), the rural inhabitants speak Spanish and wear European-style clothing but express some ideas that are unique within Ecuador. Furthermore, villages a few kilometers apart that share the same ideology express it in distinct ways. Figures 2 and 3 show specialists who make *cordones*, or belts, for the dead. Believers maintain that the dead use the *cordón* as defense against the Evil Spirit (*El Maligno*) on the after-death journey. The belts are made in a variety of local styles (Stothert and Freire 1997). Residents of Tugaduaja want one kind of belt, even though residents of Guangala laugh at Tugaduaja belts, and declare them to be inadequate for giving really good whip lashes to *El Maligno*.

The diverse expressions of ideology apparent in the archaeological record of the Formative period probably involved both simple variations in style and more fundamental differences in thought and practice. The ability of archaeologists to interpret patterns of similarity and difference will be enhanced by improved descriptions of local archaeological phases such as Piquigua and Jelí (Late Valdivia phases), Machalilla, Early Cotocollao, Cerro Narrío, Pirincay, and the distinct Chorreroid phases of the coast, including Engoroy, Bellavista, Guayaquil, Tabuchila, Tachina, and Chorrera (which refers to both ceramics

Fig. 2 (*above*) Moisés Suárez Villón makes a *cordón*, or mortuary belt, in the plaited style of Tugaduaja on the Santa Elena peninsula. (*below*) Two plaited-style belts from Tugaduaja and La Puná Island. Photos by Neil Maurer.

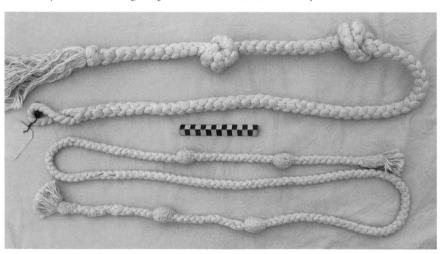

Fig. 3   Nicolás Humberto Pilay Limón completes a mortuary belt in the twisted style preferred in Manantial de Colonche. Photo by Neil Maurer.

from scientifically excavated middens and looted mortuary vessels without archaeological contexts).

While recognizing great variability among the Formative communities, most archaeologists believe that the Formative evidence reveals a philosophical tradition shared by both past and present native peoples all over America. The Native American traditions that exist today in the tropical forest regions of South America are believed to be derived with modification from ancient traditions. In her durable synthesis of Ecuadorian archaeology, Meggers (1966: 41) inferred Valdivia curers and made modest use of analogies from the tropical forest cultures. Many scholars have found that the cosmologies of the peoples of the lowland tropical forest regions of South America can be employed fruitfully to visualize Formative period ceremonialism and ideology (Damp n.d.a,b; DeBoer 1996; Lathrap, Collier, and Chandra 1975; Lathrap, Marcos, and Zeidler 1977; Marcos 1978, 1988; Raymond 1993; Stahl 1984, 1986; Stothert 1985, 1988; Zeidler 1984, 1988; Zeidler, Stahl, and Sutliff 1998).

The approach taken in this essay is to identify the practice of shamanism from evidence in the archaeological record and emphasize the central role of shaman–leaders in ancient societies.[2] The non-American term *shamanism* refers to a complex of pan-American behaviors involving a belief system,[3] social institutions, focal practitioners (intermediaries), and a set of rituals (expressing the aforementioned ideology) involving trances, drug use, curing, divination, the pursuit of power, and expressions of power in art, such as ceramic sculpture, poetry, chanting, music, costume, and dance. Recent studies of shamanism in various culture areas of North and South America demonstrate the "similarity of worldview and logic of beliefs found in all":

---

[2] The term and concept of shamanism are probably misapplied in America (see Kehoe 2000); however for many scholars the shaman is a religious leader, male or female, who (a) acts as an intermediary between the living and the realm of the spirits, (b) is a repository of esoteric knowledge, and (c) may function as a healer, diviner, adjudicator, agent of social control, or political leader. Ethnography shows many kinds of shamans, with variable functions (Langdon 1992: 14–15). Many acquire and control power by mastering ecstatic experiences and acquiring spirit helpers and songs. The practice of shamanism principally involves activities designed to communicate with and control spirits and, ultimately, to amass power. Rather than the general term *shaman*, one could use other terms for American practitioners: *priest*, *doctor*, *healer*, or in Spanish *brujo*, *curandero*, *doctor*, *sabio* (*sabia*), and *hechicero*; or in Native American languages a large number of terms including *paje* or *payé* (in the Colombian Amazon, see Reichel-Dolmatoff 1971: 125 ff., 135 ff.), or *pone* (in Tsafiqui, the language of the Tsachila, or Colorado Indians, in Ecuador).

[3] This core of common beliefs and practices includes both "the belief in souls of inanimate objects, animate beasts, and humans" (Langdon 1992: 7) and a wide range of human activities designed to communicate with spirits in other realms and manipulate supernatural forces.

They share the idea of a multi-layered cosmos, as well as a vision of two different realities composed of the extrahuman and the human. However, these two realities are linked through a general principle of energy to form an undivided universe in which all is related to the cycles of production and reproduction, life and death, growth and decay. The extrahuman domain exerts its energies and forces on the human. Through the shaman, the human, in turn, exercises forces on the extrahuman. Shamanism is a religious institution representing the culture's preoccupation with the flow of these energies as they affect human well-being. It attempts to make sense out of events and to possibly influence them. In its broadest sense, shamanism is preoccupied with the well-being of society and its individuals, with social harmony, and with growth and reproduction of the entire universe. It encompasses the supernatural, as well as the social and ecological. Thus shamanism is a central cultural institution, which, through ritual, ties together the mythic past and worldview, and projects them into daily life and activities. (Langdon 1992: 13)

Ethnologists believe that the ideology of those who practice shamanism affects nearly all other aspects of cultural behavior, including ecological regulation, community social reproduction, the creation and exercise of leadership, and the cultural expression of gender. The idea that shamans are "central" to many societies today and to "the expression of the cultural system" (Langdon 1992: 20) gives archaeologists confidence that they can model many aspects of ancient sociocultural systems by analogy. In this essay, the inference of shamanistic practice helps to account for many aspects of the Formative archaeological record.

The inference of tropical forest-style shamanism works best if an hypothesis of cultural continuity between the Formative peoples and the ethnographically known peoples of tropical America is accepted. Many archaeologists believe there to be sufficient evidence for shared features of organization, economy, and ideology among the ancient and modern cultures in question: in other words, a continuous tradition. This method has stimulated productive research and is the basis for plausible interpretations of the Ecuadorian past; nevertheless, specific historical continuities between the Formative and the ethnographic present have not been demonstrated. The concept of Tropical Forest Culture, which assumes continuity in adaptation across time and space, has helped scholars to visualize the ancient culture as complex and fascinating, thus carrying archaeologists beyond trait lists toward more interesting interpretations.

The idea of Tropical Forest Culture and the inference of ancient shamanism should be employed cautiously because the modern tropical forest peoples are in no way fossilized representatives of any ancient group. No feature of any recent culture should be projected back onto the deep past without supporting evidence from the archaeological record. Similarly, while there is good evidence of some shamanistic practices in the distant past, this should not lead to the conclusion that specific ideas present today also were present in antiquity because material remains can express a variety of ideas that may not cooccur predictably. There was surely greater variability in the past than we observe today.

RITUAL AND THE ARCHAEOLOGICAL RECORD

Ceremonial Centers

Village plans for the Preceramic and Early Formative periods support the idea that ancient Americans created villages as expressions of ideology. Late Las Vegas Preceramic people of Site 80 lived and buried their dead on a low natural hill between 8000 and 6500 BP. Although 25 Las Vegas sites were studied, burials were recovered only at Site 80. Because of its extraordinary size and depth, Site 80 has been interpreted as a community center with the cemetery as its ceremonial focus. The evidence of protracted funerary activity at this central place is indicative of an ideology that served the social and spiritual needs of Late Las Vegas people.

The early Formative Valdivia settlements that followed Las Vegas on the coast had circular village plans with open, central areas and small ceremonial platforms (Fig. 4), but only limited evidence of central burial features (Raymond 1993). In the highland Ceramic site of Cotocollao, household clusters were focused on a cemetery. The contrast might have to do with the degree of settlement permanence. The focal burial grounds at Site 80 and Cotocollao may be characteristic of seasonally sedentary people, and they have different ideological underpinnings than those characteristic of more permanent Valdivia communities.

The circular and oval-shaped plans of the Early Formative villages of the coast have been interpreted as constructed sacred landscapes and cosmic metaphors (Damp n.d.b: 2; Lathrap et al. 1977; Raymond 1993). Because Native American village layouts commonly have both cosmic and social significance (Nabokov and Easton 1989), this interpretation seems acceptable. Valdivia houses themselves may map ideological structures such as those inferred for ethnographic peoples: that is, the house is a cosmic model (Damp n.d.b: 22–24;

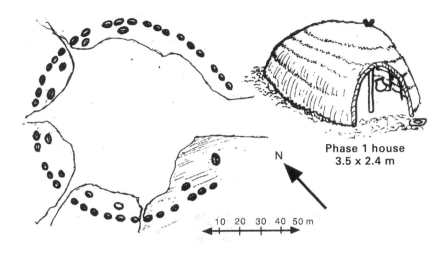

Fig. 4   An imaginative reconstruction of an Early Valdivia house (*right*) and a speculative plan of the early phase village of Real Alto (*left*). At the southern extreme is the large structure beneath the later Charnel House platform. Redrawn from Marcos (1990: 179, fig. 4).

Raymond 1993: 36; Zeidler 1984: 597–598).[4] Because of the orientation of structures at Real Alto, Zeidler (1984: 598) concluded that the Valdivia people had the same "system of ethnoastronomy and cosmology shared throughout much of tropical South America." On the basis of the well-studied settlement of Real Alto, several scholars have inferred an organization analogous to the structure of Gê-Bororo villages (Damp 1984a; Lathrap et al. 1977; Marcos 1978; Zeidler 1984: 588–599): the center (male) is associated with the ceremonial, spiritual, and ideological and the periphery (female) with the quotidian and domestic life (Damp 1984a: 582; Zeidler 1984). Of course, had these scholars chosen other analogs, they might have associated the village with the feminine and the domesticated and the hinterland with the wild, the untamed, and the masculine (Pollock 1992).

An important feature of early Formative ceremonialism is the appearance

---

[4] The shamanic *axis mundi* is, in many ethnographic cases, associated with house posts or the orientation axes of houses or villages. No good examples of ceremonial poles, central posts, ancestor poles, or vertically oriented stone monuments are known from Formative sites in Ecuador, although archaeological examples from later periods exist. Some iconography of incised Chorrera vessels suggest the four-part universe and *axis mundi* and the use of shaman's sticks or clubs (*Arte precolombino del Ecuador* 1977: 93; Cummins this volume, figs. 30, 32, 35a,b,c; Lathrap et al. [1975: figs. 39 and item 404: 98]).

of nondomestic precincts in the plaza of Real Alto (Fig. 4). As early as Phase 2b, Marcos (1988: 176, 185) believes that ceremonial activities took place in a pair of structures facing each other across the plaza. In Valdivia Phase 3, as the settlement became more rectangular (Fig. 5), these precincts were rebuilt successively, becoming platforms (mounds) topped by "public structures." The building to the west, the Charnel House, contained the remains of 20 individuals dated as Valdivia Phase 3 (Marcos 1988: 65–73), and the eastern building, the Fiesta House, showed evidence of communal feasting (Marcos 1988: 46–64, 163).

Marcos and others have described an ideological transformation: at Real Alto the egalitarian, kin-based society characterized by small houses and dual organization was transformed into a "hierarchical" social group, with new relations of production and larger, extended family houses, in which the two segments of the community had their own small meeting houses, in addition to the principal public structures with focal, high-status burials (Marcos 1988: 187; Marcos and García 1988; Zeidler 1984: 631–641). While I doubt the degree of hierarchy in these small independent communities, evidence of community ceremonies has been found not only at Real Alto but also at many

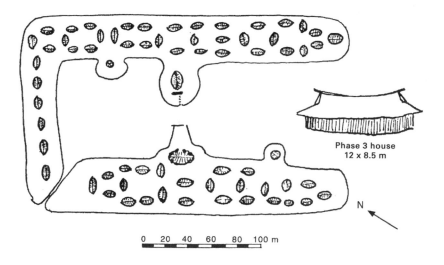

Phase 3 house
12 x 8.5 m

0 20 40 60 80 100 m

N

Fig. 5 A reconstruction of a Valdivia Phase 3 house (*right*) and a plan of the expanded village at Real Alto (*left*). The Charnel House and platform, which protrudes into the plaza from the southwest, face the Fiesta House across the central plaza. Two small meeting houses are associated with the northern and southern halves of the settlement. Redrawn from Marcos (1990: 179–180, fig. 5).

Valdivia sites identified in the Río Ayampe region, where some had "large ceremonial mounds (up to four meters high)" (Damp n.d.a: 53; 1984b). Raymond (1993: 36, note 4) has identified an analogous early Valdivia community structure at Loma Alta.

In summary, the idea of a community focused around a sacred center has various expressions in ancient Ecuador. In the Preceramic, a natural hill with elaborate burial features was at the center of the Las Vegas community. The Valdivia sites of Real Alto and Loma Alta featured one or two plazas. A burial area located in the plaza at Real Alto has been mentioned but not described. Nevertheless, the center of that site featured two large and elevated structures with evidence of ceremonial activity and a few extraordinary burials. By the end of the Valdivia period, many settlements had central platforms, some with focal burials.

Later in the Formative period, ceremonial centers continued to be the foci of integrative activities for prehistoric societies in Ecuador (Raymond 1993: 28).[5] These centers represented the elaboration of an old idea of group action, shamanic ritual, and ancestor worship, but Late Formative communities were capable of mobilizing more impressive human and material resources than was feasible in earlier times.

Formative houses and settlement layouts were regionally diverse, suggesting both variation in ideology and alternative expressions of common ideologies. During the Late Formative at Cotocollao in the Quito valley, domestic structures were rectangular rather than oval, as they were on the coast, and the settlement consisted of household clusters. These clusters were focused on an intensively utilized, central cemetery that Villalba (1988: 108–109) associates with the rituals of a kin group who stressed its corporate continuity and territorial rights for some 700 years, with evidence of escalating rank and privilege.

In the southern highlands during the late Formative period, a variety of stone-faced terraces were located at Cerro Narrío, Chaullabamba, Chinguilanchi, Putushío (Temme n.d.: 9–11), and in the upper Catamayo valley (Guffroy et al. 1987). These terraces may have supported public or ceremonial buildings, but

---

[5] Several Machalilla nondomestic platforms are also known from Salango, San Lorenzo de Mate, and the Jama valley, but none is reported in detail. Although the building of platforms has been poorly documented for the Late Formative period, the hierarchy of settlements in the Jama valley includes apparently two centers with stupendous "mounds" that may be the result of platform construction in several periods, including in Tabuchila (Late Formative) times (Zeidler 1994: 71–97, esp. 81; Zeidler and Sutliff 1994: 115). In Esmeraldas, several Tachina phase *tolas,* or *montículos,* have been identified near the mouth of the Río Esmeraldas (Alcina Franch 1979: 111).

their functions have not been documented. East of the Ecuadorian Andes, earthen platforms along the upper Upano River (sites collectively known as *Sangay*) have been described as superordinant centers, but their dating and function are still under study (Ochoa, Rostain, and Salazar 1997). Even if these platforms are dated to the Late Formative, they still cannot be taken as evidence of a stratified society or centralized polities because they also support the hypothesis that ancient people lived in dispersed hamlets and were integrated by a religious ideology that brought them occasionally to their empty ceremonial centers in the manner of the modern Chachi (DeBoer 1996) or Kogi (Zuidema 1992).

Worshipping the Dead

The manipulation of the remains of the dead is an ubiquitous feature of the behavior and ideology of Formative people in Ecuador. At the Las Vegas ceremonial site, a long series of funerary rituals was indicated by primary inhumations, secondary burial bundles, cremated remains, ceremonial pits containing selected human bones, and ossuaries containing from 25 to 40 disarticulated bodies of all ages, plus offerings (Fig. 6). The complex manipulation of human remains seen in the Las Vegas cemetery suggests an ancestor cult involving the ritual use of the bones of deceased relatives, with a shamanic goal of communicating with the dead and asking for their intercession on behalf of the living. The living may have asserted rights to their territory in this way (see Raymond this volume). In a later period, the people of Real Alto manipulated the remains of the dead in various ways, and charred human bone was identified in pits in the Charnel House mound (Marcos 1988: 70, 161–173). The manipulation of the bones of ancestors is a familiar Andean practice also found among peoples of tropical South America.

Crania were objects of special manipulation at Las Vegas, as they were at the Valdivia site of Real Alto where an adult skull was found in a child's burial (Marcos 1988) and an adult skull was interred in a ceramic bowl in an Engoroy cemetery (Zevallos 1995: 144, fig. 39). At the communal cemetery of Cotocollao, there were both secondary burials and other evidence of the manipulation of all body parts. The later burial assemblage from Cotocollao presented a differential treatment of skulls, called *cabezas ceremoniales*, which Villalba (1988: 89) identified with an ancestor cult. To contact and acquire the help of dead ancestors, the powerful head was used. According to Villalba, the rituals involving heads contributed to community cohesion and to the continuation of the social group. In his opinion this manipulation of heads was independent of trophy head taking, for which there is later evidence only.

While the manipulation of human remains is a persistent behavior indica-

Fig. 6 (*above*) A partially excavated preceramic ossuary (Feature 25b) in Las Vegas site OGSE-80 and (*below*) the polished stones (Feature 53) interred in the grave.

tive of certain beliefs about the dead, scholars are cautious when inferring human sacrifice and endocannibalism. Nevertheless, certain evidence, including partially dismembered bodies and human bones in apparent "special" contexts and midden in both Early and Late Formative sites (Estrada 1958: 78), suggests the sacramental consumption of human bodies. The sacrifices might include the bones of ancestors or the bodies of enemies or other members of the community represented as the bound captives in Late Chorrera ceramic sculpture (Cummins this volume, fig. 17).

That the Formative people were concerned with their deceased relatives is consistent with shamanic ideology, according to which both funerary activities and rituals of communication with ancestors are important to community well-being. In many cases the grave became a shrine and focus of communication with the spirit world.

Many peoples of lowland tropical America propitiate and celebrate ancestors through music (singing, chanting, playing instruments) and rhetorical speech. The Cubeo invoke their ancestors during the celebration of rites of passage and their ancestors are symbolized by musical instruments (Goldman 1972: 190–210). The Cubeo also re-create the origin of the world in rituals with "senior elders seated on ritual stools at the center of the communal longhouse" (Goldman 1993: 142). At ritual events involving intoxication, people share in world re-creation and use ritual gifts that encourage contact with ancestors, animals, and spirits. These shamanic gifts include songs, instrumental music, dances, body paints and ornaments, and hallucinogens, which transport participants "back into the ancestral era" (Goldman 1993: 145).

Today in Santa Elena, traditional families feed their beloved dead each year with the best food (Fig. 7), and at the end of the Day of the Dead the living people feast, drink, and dance to say goodbye to their dead for another year. The details of this non-Catholic celebration vary from community to community, but there is an ideology about the continuing relationship between the dead and the living community that contemporary people share with other Native American societies.

In the Preceramic, some burials appeared to be communal, but others involved single individuals who received special treatment. In the Valdivia tradition, most burials were made under the floors of houses (Damp 1984a: 580), indicating that the family was the important social unit, but some ossuaries and burials in nondomestic structures have been recovered. In both periods several extraordinary burials suggest that family or lineage ancestors were being honored by special burial locations and that some important lineage figures were female (see also Zeidler 1984). At Las Vegas Site 80, a woman (older than 45

Fig. 7 Ulberta Filomena Soriano Láinez views the table set with handwoven textiles and food offered to her deceased relatives during the Day of the Dead celebration in Santa Elena. Photo by Neil Maurer.

years) was buried beneath the doorway of a northeast-facing circular structure (Stothert 1988: 134). Similarly, a "high-ranking" woman (Fig. 8), about 35 years old at death, was recovered from a pit lined with grinding stones at the entrance of the northeast-facing Valdivia Charnel House at Real Alto (Marcos 1988: 164–167). She was associated with a large ceramic sherd bearing an excised face (Phase 3 style), not unlike the Huaca Prieta gourds that also were found in a mature woman's grave.

Changing Burial Patterns and Mortuary Offerings

Change and variation in grave goods, burial postures, head deformation, and other features are indicative of shifts in ideology and shamanic practice in the Formative. However, because burial patterns have not been well described for the entire Formative, trends are difficult to assess.

There are similarities between the reconstructed burial customs of the Late Las Vegas period and Phase 3 of Valdivia at Real Alto. In addition to the special burials in the Charnel House, burials in domestic contexts at Real Alto were common (Zeidler et al. 1998: 110–112). Domestic units, perhaps extended families, may have carried out prolonged burial programs to deal with the spirits of the deceased and reinforce their corporate identities, as Las Vegas people had done earlier.

Few durable burial offerings accompanied Las Vegas and Valdivia dead. Apparently in the Preceramic and Early Formative periods, it was not the custom to express social differentiation or gender with durable burial goods; however, since some individuals were interred in more central locations at Real Alto and La Emerenciana, a few Valdivia individuals were likely of unusual social status or memorialized as powerful ancestors. The presence of burials in both the Charnel House and in domestic contexts at Real Alto has been taken to indicate the existence of ranked lineages in Middle Valdivia times (Marcos 1978, 1988; Zeidler 1984). At La Emerenciana a few Jelí phase burials were recovered in the special central platform, but the entire burial pattern is not known. The Jelí phase burials (Late Valdivia phase) were interred in seated or "upright" postures (Staller 1994).

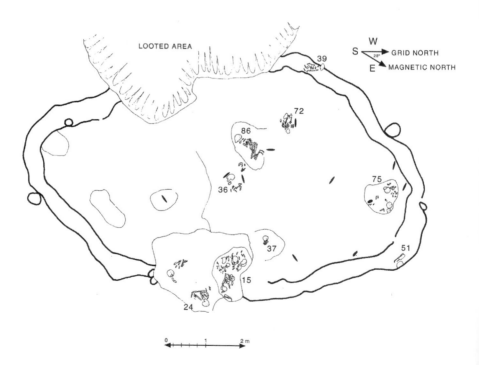

Fig. 8   Floorplan of the Charnel House (OGSECh-12, Structure E-7) at Real Alto. Note the distribution of human burials from Phase 3 including the stone-lined grave of a woman buried beneath the threshold in Burial 24, and some of the anthropomorphic figurines (black ovals). Redrawn from Marcos (1988: *mapa* 16e).

The seated position of the flexed burials of La Emerenciana is distinctive, since both Las Vegas, most Valdivia skeletons, and the early burials at Cotocollao were flexed and resting on their right or left sides. The seated burial posture was characteristic of some Machalilla and only a few Cotocollao burials, but it became more common in the Late Formative period. The choice of the seated burial posture for some individuals but not others might be indicative of social ranking. At Cotocollao the variability in burial posture, combined with the use of individual graves for some people rather than communal burial, are the basis for Villalba's hypothesis that there was social differentiation among the lineages at that site (Villalba 1988: 94–108) and that rank was inherited and derived from degree of relationship to certain ancestors. From the burials at Cotocollao, Villalba suggested that the ancient ideology included a belief in continuity between the living and the dead and that the dead were the focal points of community organization and access to land. Despite the opinions of the excavators of Real Alto and Villalba, the apparent differentiation among the dead should not be translated hastily into political hierarchy, since alternative explanations for extraordinary burials exist.

On the coast, the basic Las Vegas and Valdivia burial pattern continued into the next period at the site of Salango, from which only 28 Machalilla graves have been described briefly (Norton, Lunniss, and Nailing 1983). Only one burial had a preserved offering: Norton suggested that the flexed body was that of a shaman who had been covered with a ceramic vessel in the form of a turtle shell. Head deformation, observed frequently in Machalilla burials, may have been ideologically significant and indicative of new ways of achieving aesthetic, social, and spiritual goals. According to Villalba (1988: 104), at Cotocollao the optional cranial modification, different from that practiced on the coast, may be evidence of social differentiation. At La Emerenciana, no cranial modification was observed among the Late Valdivia skeletons, but a young woman with a modified skull was recovered from the Engoroy cemetery at Los Cerritos (Zevallos 1995: 156). Among the four adult crania recovered from Engoroy graves in La Libertad on the Santa Elena peninsula, three males and one female showed occipital flattening (Ubelaker 1988: 14). It has not been demonstrated that cranial modification in the Formative was associated with high rank.

Only a few Late Formative burials have been reported, but it is clear from a comparison with earlier Valdivia patterns that burial modes, and particularly ideas about what should be furnished to the dead, had evolved. The evidence for escalating social differentiation is equivocal.

The Engoroy cemetery excavated in La Libertad, contained numerous secondary burials of fragmentary skeletons, including a bundle of bones recovered resting on a bed of shells; other bodies had been seated and apparently wrapped in textiles (Fig. 9), with offerings, including a fine pedestal bowl (Fig. 10), which were enclosed inside the shroud with the human remains (Bushnell 1951: 85–94; Stothert n.d.). Several had green stone beads or fragments of green stone material in association (Fig. 11). Identical green stone (serpentine) ornaments were recovered at Cerro Narrío in the highlands of Ecuador and in Catamayo sites (Guffroy et al. 1987). Zevallos's excavations at Los Cerritos showed both secondary interments and seated burials associated with fancy Engoroy bottles, ordinary ceramic vessels, green stone ornaments, and one small sheet of copper in a burial dated around 800 B.C. (Zevallos 1965/66: 69; 1995: 181).

The Guayaquil phase burials excavated near the city of the same name, which might be considered Terminal Formative, were flexed and reclining in the Vegas–Valdivia pattern, although they reclined on pavements of potsherds or shell (R. Parducci Z. and I. Parducci 1975). The graves were equipped with "special offerings," such as discoidal, serpentine (green stone) charms interred between the bed of sherds and the cadaver. Other offerings included ceramic vessels, spondylus beads, *metate* and *mano* fragments, clay flutes and ocarinas, and obsidian, although some skeletons had no offerings at all.

These Engoroy and Guayaquil phase cemeteries are variable: in one, for instance, many musical instruments were recovered, and the seated position of the dead, which was common, is evidence of some popular ideology. This variability in the Late Formative has not been adequately described or accounted for,[6] but the observed proliferation of burial types and durable offerings in the Late Formative probably corresponds to an intensification of ritual activity and may be evidence of political development.

Only limited evidence from graves supports an hypothesis of hierarchy (see Zeidler and Isaacson this volume, for a contrasting interpretation). Late Formative tombs from Manabí, some with spectacular ceramic offerings (see Cummins this volume), and others constructed with stone slabs might constitute evidence of social differentiation, but they have not been described in print. The ubiquity of green stone offerings argues against their interpretation as elite markers. The growing ability of communities to acquire green stone and other raw materials may signal economic well-being, as well as the existence of questing shamans, economic or political elites, or other individuals who concerned them-

[6] Burial assemblages from the Guayas basin have not been described in detail, but at the site called Peñon del Río, Chorrera phase graves contained domestic pottery (Zedeño n.d.: 143).

Fig. 9   Two Engoroy burials from Site 46, La Libertad. Grave 19 (*left*) contained the skeleton of a male, about 35 years old at death, whose body was seated upon a layer of marine
shells and was associated with a green stone bead and a ceramic vessel pressed against its
right side. Grave 4 (*right*) held a secondary burial. Grave 3 (H.3, or Hallazgo 3) lies to the
lower left, mostly outside of the photographic frame.

selves with the distribution of symbolically charged raw materials. The location of the cemeteries in the Late Formative of Ecuador hints at new ideology.
Although no Late Formative settlement has been mapped, it seems that cemeteries with large numbers of burials may have developed adjacent to villages.
This is true for Engoroy cemeteries at Los Cerritos and La Libertad and for
Chorreroid cemeteries in Manabí province (Norton 1992: 28). While funerary
ceremonialism may have continued as a focus of community life, the dead no
longer were interred under houses or in the village center. The exterior location may indicate that individual households no longer were responsible for

Fig. 10 (*above*) Exterior of a red pedestal bowl with negative decoration associated with an Engoroy phase skeleton, Burial 19, Site 46, La Libertad, and (*below*) its interior; 13 cm high and 19.5 cm in diameter.

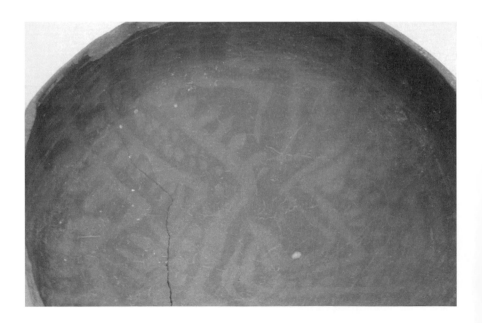

Fig. 11 Green stone ornaments usually identified as serpentine or jadeite: (*above*) beads and cut material from Engoroy burials in Site 46, La Libertad, and (*below*) a perforated nose ornament, probably from a Late Formative Chorreroid context, San Isidro, Manabí province; 3.5 cm x 2.5 cm, Cruz-De Perón Collection.

burial activities; rather it seems that each lineage in the nucleated settlement may have laid its members to rest in its own cemetery outside the village.

The Late Formative witnessed an expanded emphasis upon feeding the dead and propitiating them with certain gifts. The belief that the dead require offerings of food and drink may reflect a developing social ideology: social relations, including asymmetrical ones between hosts and guests, can be expressed and reinforced by feasting and drinking. This ideology seems to have been reflected in the elaboration of ceramic bottles and fancy serving bowls. Also, the widespread use of both green stone artifacts, or pieces of green raw material, and musical instruments as grave offerings in this period suggests a cognitive link between death and fertility. These offerings may be conceived as pump primers: because the dead were the ultimate source of life, sacrificing to them was an investment that would yield future benefits. In any case, the escalation of durable funerary offerings in the Late Formative is indicative of innovative social practices and ideology.

Similar arguments may be made for gold, another ideologically significant raw material employed in the confection of burial offerings (Helms 1981; Hosler 1994; Reichel-Dolmatoff 1988). Gold and gold alloy art objects, widely used in later prehistory in rituals, expressed religious concepts, accompanied the dead, and also adorned and protected the living on ritual and political occasions. Worked gold began to appear in Ecuadorian sites dated to the Late Formative, such as Salango (Bruhns 1994a: 143; Rehren and Temme 1992: 268), and a drop of molten gold was recovered at Pirincay (Bruhns, Burton, and Miller 1990). At the highland site of Putushío, Temme (Rehren and Temme 1992) excavated a workshop where evidence of gold working was associated with domestic refuse dated to the Late Formative, indicating a lower level of specialization than was characteristic of the greatly expanded workshops in the same site in the subsequent Regional Development period. No Late Formative gold objects with iconography are known from Ecuador, but similar technology was employed for the manufacture of personal ornaments in the Calima region of Colombia (Cardale de Schrimpff 1992: 50–57) and ornaments from Peru made at this time expressed religious ideologies.

Many aspects of the philosophy and ritual practices of ancient Ecuadorians were similar to those of other Native Americans, and the dynamic evolution in Formative mortuary practices occurred in tandem with similar changes elsewhere in America. The dramatic growth in the popularity of green stones in mortuary contexts occurred at about the same time in Mesoamerica. Grove and Gillespie (1992: 29–30) identified an ideological transformation around 500 B.C. when important symbols were transferred from the ceramic medium, which was available to everyone, to the medium of precious green stone, which was "available to only a few."

Creative social processes involve both the development of appropriate ideologies and change on the material level. It is of great interest that green stones (serpentine, sodalite, jadeite, and turquoise) became widespread in domestic and mortuary contexts in the Late Formative on the coast and in the highlands.[7] The belief in the power of green stone and its escalating use as a mortuary offering in the Late Formative no doubt corresponds to several processes in ancient social life. Scholars have concluded that the desire for green stone was fomented by individuals who were active in designing new ideologies to enhance their positions by creating new social roles for both themselves and the dead. The desire for raw materials and manufactured items apparently motivated local economic activities and stimulated the exchange of exotic goods over long distances. String-cutting technology, formerly used for the manufacture of shell artifacts, was adapted for use with exotic green stones (Holm 1969). Ideological demands also stimulated gold working and rock crystal bead manufacture, known from the Late Formative site of Pirincay (Bruhns 1987, this volume).

An interpretation of the development of various technologies and the increase in the number of burial offerings in the Late Formative can be derived from Helms's understanding that the offerings functioned as markers of the potency of leaders: Helms (1993: 142–145) wrote, "[The] quantity of burial goods . . . testifies to the deceased person's qualifications to become a beneficent ancestor [and the goods themselves] create a functioning ancestor." The burial of goods meant that they were returned to the cosmos. This was like pump priming or "refresh[ing] the ancestral stock itself," with the expectation that the precious offerings are to be redistributed to the living. The growing emphasis in the Late Formative on burying crafted items and cosmically endowed materials (like green stone and gold) in graves suggests that some individuals were committed to the ideology of acquiring goods that allowed them

---

[7] These green stones are exotic in most areas and would have been sought in exchange over long distance (like spondylus). There are likely sources in the southern highlands of Ecuador. At a Catamayo site near Loja (Guffroy et al. 1987: 192–3) excavators found a votive offering consisting of a whole spondylus shell containing two jadeite artifacts dated between 1000 and 1300 B.C. Rock crystal also was invested with meaning and widely traded. There is evidence of a rock crystal bead workshop at the site of Pirincay, which can then be understood as one of the points of origin of material that circulated in the exchange system. Formative sites at Salango and on La Plata Island were other nodes in the exchange of ideologically charged goods.

to be prestigious leaders in life and/or helped the community to create effective ancestors as they buried their dead.

In summary, the evidence shows that burial ceremonialism changed in the Formative. The locus of burial was altered, communal graves lost popularity, burial posture changed, and novel patterns of mortuary offerings developed. Some of the observed variation can be understood as indicative of extraordinary events, like special deaths, but some of the variation seems to have been the result of regional diversity in the expression of ideology. The remarkable objects looted from graves in Manabí suggest the development of a great religious centers characterized by distinctive burial cults. Increasing social differentiation may have marked the communities at such centers.

Dramatic change in burial rituals may have taken place in Late Valdivia times and again at the end of the Formative when extended burials replaced seated ones over a wide area in southwestern Ecuador in the Regional Development period[8] (Bischof 1982: 161; Stothert 1993). In this period, elaborate tombs were constructed in a few areas and mortuary ceramics, such as those of the Jama-Coaque region, included representations of men and women showing differentiated ritualistic roles. This might be evidence of a process in which elites expressed the concept of political hierarchy, or it might be evidence of competition among charismatic shaman–leaders in relatively egalitarian contexts. The intensification of shamanic ritual practice may have constituted an effective community alternative to centralized political hierarchy.

The Shaman

Formative period evidence suggests that shamanistic practices forged contact with the spirit world and the ancestors. Some aspects of shamanic belief and practice are demonstrated by a Piquigua phase burial (Zeidler et al. 1998) from the site of Capaperro in the Middle Jama valley of Manabí province that dates to the Terminal Valdivia period. The Piquigua skeleton, the remains of a woman, 15 to 20 years of age at death, showed no identifiable pathologies. She was found in an unusual, extended burial posture accompanied by offerings with shamanic connotations. These offerings include a small ceramic lime pot, associated ethnographically with the chewing of coca leaf; a bat skeleton associated with magical flight and sometimes with bloodletting; a broken Valdivia-style figurine placed within the jaws of a feline skull (*Felis paradalis*), which

---

[8] A similar transition from flexed to extended burials took place in northern Peru, on the coast and in the highlands, at about the same time—evidence of the sharing of ideology over great distances and across the boundaries of interaction spheres.

may have been part of an ocelot pelt cape of the sort worn by shamans in order to suggest their feline alter egos; a polished green stone pendant signaling fertility and power; over 250 "unworked light green clay stone fragments"; and a milling stone (a tool with symbolic significance; see Graham 1992), which capped the burial. If not a shaman in her lifetime, this woman may have become a shamanic intermediary, especially if she had died in childbirth, which, in many cultures, changes the deceased's status and destiny.

This burial is just one eloquent example of archaeological contexts that seem to express elements of shamanic thought. In the Preceramic and Formative periods, there is clear evidence of small-scale rituals performed in domestic and communal contexts, and in the post-Formative, ceramic sculptures celebrate the ritual roles of shamans.

Archaeologists are keenly interested in identifying shamans because of the perception that they were leaders. However, great variability is expected. For example, the Formative shamans might have been either male or female, and there might have been one or a few in each community, or all adult men and women may have been involved in shamanic practice. Leadership in communities might have followed many different patterns.[9] The individuals represented by the Formative anthropomorphic figurines may have been shamans or adults involved in shamanic rituals, both of whom may have had responsibilities in maintaining harmony in all areas of community life.

Animal Symbolism

Animal spirits were mobilized by shamans in many contexts, particularly in healing rituals (Reichel-Dolmatoff 1971: 177–180). Moreover, animal myths, metaphors, and symbols are central in ancient art, and they persist in contemporary Native American thought and expression (e.g., Urton 1985).

Las Vegas people symbolically manipulated animal bodies as part of burial rituals. For example, Wing (1988) noticed the differential concentration in burial contexts of the bones and teeth of *Dusicyon* (desert fox, or *lobo del monte*). Tidy stacks of selected fox teeth were associated with human bone bundles within a Vegas ossuary. The fox, who must have been a symbol or mythic actor in Late

---

[9] Until 1930 among the Mai Huna (Bellier 1991: 151–155), there were three powerful village leaders: a *jefe civil*, responsible for social harmony; a *jefe guerrero*, presumably responsible for external conflicts, who also controlled conflicts that erupted at feasts; and the shaman (a category including curers and sorcerers) noted for wisdom, who was a specialist in communication with the spirit world and also had social functions. For a good description of shamans and leadership in modern juropolitical contexts, see Whitten 1976; 1978: 850–852.

Las Vegas's thought system, later appears, in natural or anthropomorphized form, as a participant in mythic scenes in Moche art and also is represented in the paraphernalia of modern Peruvian folk healers (Sharon and Donnan: 1974: 56, plates 2, 18–20).

Valdivia sites exhibit evidence of the use of the bodies of animals in ceremonies. Dogs were buried carefully in graves at Real Alto (Marcos 1988: 159). At many Formative sites, unusual faunal remains have been found in special contexts, often accompanied by ceramic vessels and figurine fragments. At Real Alto pits within ceremonial structures contained the remains of ritual meals or curing events and included fish, crab, razor clams, deer bone, and turtle shell not common in domestic midden.

Near Salango, in the Valdivia site of Río Chico, an articulated egret (or heron) was removed from an Engoroy context where it had been interred with care (Weintz et al. n.d.). This animal apparently was kept as a pet or "ritual companion" (n.d.: 10), since it had recovered from a leg injury. The Piquigua burial described above contained portions of a feline skull, much of a bat skeleton, and other animal parts. Pirincay exhibited evidence of a camelid sacrifice and ceremonial burial (Bruhns et al. 1990); and, as early as Machalilla times at La Ponga, ducks and guinea pigs were used in rituals. This can be understood as evidence for animal sacrifices, consumption of ritual food, and generally for the importance of animal metaphor and symbolism in ancient Ecuadorian thought habits.

Some mollusk shells carried great symbolic weight in the ancient world (Furst 1966). In Preceramic midden, a variety of molluskan shells were modified into containers, whistles (David Blower, personal communication, June 5, 2000), and shell trumpets. Their presence in Las Vegas graves indicated their importance as ritual paraphernalia and symbols. Several Las Vegas burials (Stothert 1988), and at least one Valdivia skeleton from Loma Alta, were interred with mollusk shells "placed over the shoulder articulations" (Stahl 1984: 229). The Preceramic idea of sacramental shells was emphasized and given more elaborate expression in the Formative. Remains of shell offerings were recovered at San Pablo (Zevallos and Holm 1960: láminas 5, 7), and at La Emerenciana shells marked the mouths of Late Valdivia pits in the ceremonial precinct (Staller 1994).

Later, spondylus and strombus shells became symbols that formed what Marcos (1990: 172) calls the creative core of Andean cosmovision. Perhaps the most important aspect of this ideology is that it was shared with those living beyond the natural distribution of the shellfish species. Some scholars believe that the ideology, which developed from an understanding of the biology and ecology of the living mollusk (the thorny oyster, spondylus), originated in coastal Ecuador and was exported to the Central Andes along with the shell itself (Davidson 1982; Marcos 1995; Murra 1975; Paulsen 1974).[10]

The symbolic manipulations of both female-associated spondylus shell and the male strombus shell are thematic in Central Andean religion. Although the ritual association of the duo is expressed in Chavín art, it is less obvious in ancient Ecuador. Marcos (1995: 99) has asserted that the concept of the "sacred dyad" received its earliest expression at Real Alto, but the evidence of association is equivocal.[11] In the highlands of Ecuador, Uhle briefly described his excavation of a platform or altar near Loja where, under a yellow clay floor, he recovered groups of spondylus shells containing alabaster plaques, pieces of green stone, and beads. At a distance of 7 m from the altar, Uhle found strombus shells arranged symmetrically (Jijón y Caamaño 1951:140, cited in Marcos 1988: 188; 1995: 114). The two species of mollusk appeared together in the same Late Formative context, but it is not clear if they were offered ritually as a symbolic dyad.

The meaning of spondylus shell itself is clear from various late Andean

---

[10] Alternatively, when the shell was imported into Peru as a powerful natural symbol, it may have been refitted with meaning there: perhaps it was in Peru that spondylus and strombus together came to express the Central Andean idea of "dynamic dualism" (Richard Burger, personal communication, March 1996; Burger and Salazar-Burger 1993). This concept may have been part of the creation and maintenance of larger, more complex social organizations, and it persisted as an important ideology within the Central Andean tradition (Allen 1988; Sharon 1978; J. Topic and T. Topic 1997).

A dual concept was functioning in Formative Ecuadorian mythology, ideology, aesthetics, and society. Some Valdivia figurines have two heads or faces, and the two plazas and two ceremonial structures at Real Alto may indicate dual organization. Secondly, the stirrup-spout bottle, an apparent symbol of *tincu* or dynamic dualism (Burger and Salazar-Burger 1993: 106), makes its earliest appearance in a Late Valdivia context (Staller 1994). Yet this vessel form, which later became a fixture in the Central Andean tradition, disappeared in the Northern Andes after Machalilla. Thirdly, pairs of extraordinary Chorrera vessels (Fig. 19) are recovered frequently from Late Formative funerary contexts (Iván Cruz, personal communication, August 1997; Valdez and Veintimilla 1992: fig. 17, 195).

[11] At Real Alto, a *Strombus peruvianus* shell trumpet was recovered in the apparent ramp leading to the primitive ceremonial structure identified at the bottom of the earliest mound dated to Construction Epoch 1a/Valdivia Phase 2 (Marcos 1978: 531; 1988: 72–73). Marcos also found a *Spondylus princeps* shell in the access ramp leading to the Phase 3 mortuary structure that overlay the earlier ceremonial structure described above (Marcos 1988: 188). Both shells were found in the western ceremonial mound known as the *Montículo del Osario*. Nevertheless, Marcos asserted erroneously on the same page that strombus and spondylus appear "como ejes rituales en los montículos de la Casa de Reuniones y del Osario, respectivamente" (Marcos 1988: 188–189). According to the evidence, both finds were recovered from one mound (the western one known as the *Osario*), where the two shells were removed from contexts separated from each other by a considerable length of time.

sources outside Ecuador (Davidson 1982), and excavated contexts in Ecuador also illuminate the ideology underpinning this symbol in the Formative period. One votive offering that consisted of a spondylus shell containing some pieces of jade, probably associated with fertility and rainfall, was recovered from a site near Catamayo (see note 7).

Another important context was an Engoroy earthen structure that functioned as an *albarrada* at the Achallán site (Stothert 1995). This semicircular catchment structure, with 8-m high walls designed to retain rainwater from season to season, may have been characterized by abundant vegetation, some cultivated plots, and concentrated animal resources. During a relatively short period in the Late Formative, Engoroy people moved about 24,000 m³ of artificial fill to construct the walls of the *albarrada*. The construction of the *albarrada* probably depended upon motivated communal labor but required little leadership (Stothert 1995: 148).

In my view, the Engoroy people intentionally constructed this artificial mountain as a water shrine. The refuse in the catchment structure contained both broken water jars and complete ceramic drinking and serving bowls decorated with iridescent paint, which becomes luminescent when wet, suggesting that ceremonial activities at the *albarrada* might have included drinking and other rituals designed to contact and propitiate the spirits who controlled rainfall. One episode of coordinated effort at the *albarrada* involved the entombment of an earlier earthen bank beneath a cap of yellow soil and the burial of an offering consisting of three large valves of spondylus (Fig. 12). Ethnohistoric and ethnographic sources in the Andes agree that sacrifices of spondylus shell can influence weather and fertility. Male deities receive burnt offerings, and female deities receive buried ones, or those sacrificed in "water sources" (Davidson 1982: 334). The Achallán offering testifies to an early community ritual of propitiation. This ceremonial context demonstrates the association of water catchment, rainfall, and spondylus shell with the ancient belief that the successful functioning of the *albarrada* could be magically ensured.

The use of shell in expressive contexts is one of many cases of important animal metaphors and symbols. The most famous involve jaguars, snakes, birds, and bats, animals still associated with shamans and shamanic journeying. In Valdivia times the manipulation of the animals themselves, as seen in the Piquigua burial, was joined by artificial representations of animals. Staller (1994: 390–391) reports several fragments of figurines in Late Valdivia contexts, including a human arm wrapped with a snake, another modeled snake, and a caiman head. The motifs on Valdivia drinking bowls are suggestive of serpents and felines (Figs. 13, 14), represented by repetitive, geometric motifs thought to be related

Fig. 12 (*above*) A trench excavated through the highest bank of the Albarrada de Achallán reveals the stratification of this water catchment structure. (*below, detail*) Three spondylus shells were ritually entombed in a sloping layer of yellow fill in the Engoroy period.

Karen E. Stothert

to patterns perceived by drug users in excited states (Damp 1982: 163 and fig. 4e). Similar designs persisted in Machalilla ceramics (Lathrap et al. 1975: 32, fig. 27). It is believed that the drinking bowls are evidence of ceremonial drinks, including both fermented beverages and hallucinogenic brews (Damp 1982; Stahl 1984, 1985a, 1986).

Feline and bird-morph mortars, presumably used for preparation of psycho-active drugs, were manufactured by both Terminal Valdivia and later Formative artisans (Fig. 15). These artifacts are indicative of the importance of power animals so closely associated with shamans in later art and in ethnographic descriptions (Di Capua 1986; Zeidler 1988). Several categories of material culture, including miniature zoomorphic stools for figurines made by Valdivia people (Fig. 16), indicate the use of hallucinogenic substances and the transfor-mation of shamans into their animal alter egos.

The association between the shaman and the jaguar is well known (Di Capua 1986; Reichel-Dolmatoff 1971, 1988), but feline imagery was a minor theme in Valdivia art (Figs. 16, 17). Although this imagery persisted in later styles (Fig. 18), it is curious that evidence of human-into-feline transformation is weak in the Formative period in Ecuador. Furthermore, while the feline became most prominent in Peru in the later Initial and Early Horizon periods, it was not prominent in Ecuador, where other animal symbols appeared more frequently in Chorrera art. Zeidler (1988: 245) points out that the jaguar, frequently an-thropomorphized in ancient Peruvian art, was not so treated in the Ecuadorian Formative.

The Late Formative ceramic evidence shows the intensification of some shamanic practices but little fundamental change in ideology. If elaborate ce-ramic vessels, especially bottles, were manufactured for sacrifice, then they can be interpreted as an elaboration upon the theme of the sacrifice of plants and animals known from earlier periods. Such sacrifices are well documented in later prehistory. The elaborate material culture of the Late Formative is indica-tive of a novel expression of traditional ideology. Whereas a small community might perform a shamanic ritual by using shells or real animals, in more com-plex settings, a larger group might perform the same ritual in an embellished form with additional accoutrements. A group seeking to differentiate itself from other households or from less well-to-do lineages might perform the traditional sacrifices with extraordinary props to create greater visual impres-sions and more emotional responses. Producing better theater may have begun in Valdivia times.

In Manabí province and around the regional center of San Isidro, zoomor-phic mortars (Zeidler 1988) and later spectacular mortuary ceramics also de-

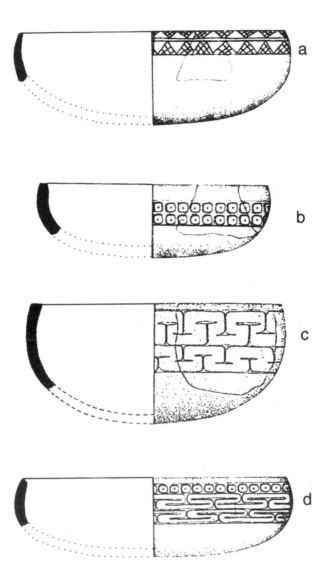

Fig. 13 Valdivia Phase 1 through 2 ceramic vessels from Real Alto reconstructed from sherds and interpreted by Damp (1982, n.d.a): (a) hatched triangles, which may refer to snake markings, (b) circle and dot designs related to jaguar pelage, (c) the *T*-shaped motif, interpreted as a stylized feline face, and (d) a combination of the two feline motifs. Redrawn from Damp (1982: 166, figs. 4e,s,t; n.d.a: fig. 51).

Fig. 14 A Valdivia Phase 1 through 2 bowl showing the *T*-shaped motif interpreted as a stylized version of a feline face; 13 cm high and 26.8 cm in diameter (Damp 1979, 1982b). Museo Antropológico del Banco Central del Ecuador, Guayaquil (GA-16-915-78).

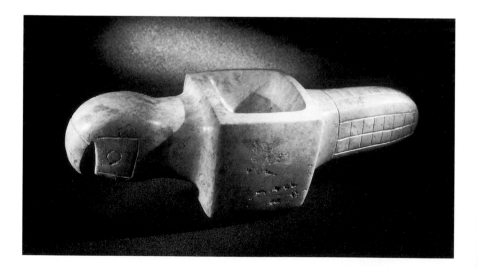

Fig. 15 A parrot effigy mortar of greenish stone in the Chorrera style, probably used for ritual grinding of sacrificial substances or hallucinogens; 22.5 x 6.5 x 7 cm. Private Collection, Ecuador.

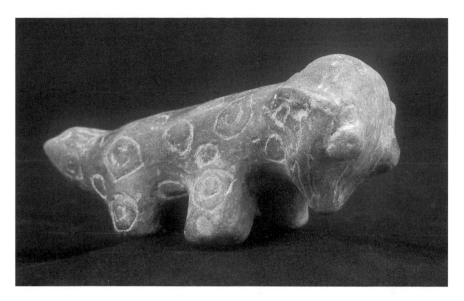

Fig. 16 A miniature ceramic stool in the form of a spotted feline, possibly designed as a tablet for snuff or seating Valdivia figurines; 12.8 x 5.5 x 5.4 cm. Museo Antropológico del Banco Central del Ecuador, Guayaquil (GA-32-1248-79).

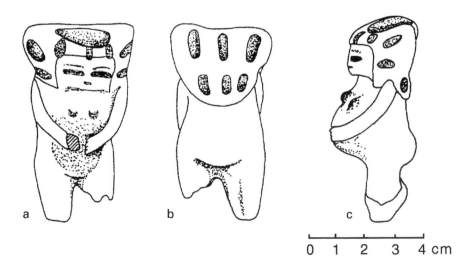

Fig. 17 A Valdivia style ceramic figurine representing a pregnant woman wearing a head-dress with markings suggestive of feline pelage. Anhalzer Collection. Redrawn from Di Capua (1994: fig. 44).

Fig. 18   A Late Chorrera whistle/figurine with a headdress fashioned from an animal pelt; 16 x 12 x 5 cm. The animal's paws appear on the headdress and its tail hangs down. Cruz–De Perón Collection.

picted naturalistic plants, animals, and humans (Figs. 19, 20; see also Lathrap et al. 1975: 92–97; Cummins this volume). Whereas real animals and fruits had long been sacrificed to the ancestors and other spirits, in Manabí the artistic images of animals and plants became meaningful and imbued with power. Scholars strive to describe the social context of the production of these artistically crafted objects that manifested religious ideology. The idea proposed by Helms (1993)—that finely crafted items are expressions of the concept of divinity and that those who make or control such objects can effectively communicate their power and authority through them—helps explain the production of extraordinary material culture in the Late Formative.

Psychoactive Substances

Another vital feature of Native American ideology and cosmology is the belief that communicating with nonordinary realms is beneficial. One mechanism of communication is the use of psychoactive plants. In the ethnographic literature the use of tobacco and mind-altering substances to achieve nonordinary states may be experienced either by an adult population at large or restricted to the shaman in the community. In the latter case, the knowledge and use of sacred plants is part of the shaman's role as intermediary with the spirit world

Fig. 19 A pair of whistling Chorrera-style snake effigy vessels with geometric motifs on the animal heads; approx. 27 cm long. Private Collection, Ecuador.

Fig. 20   A Chorrera bottle in the form of a recumbent woman; 19.5 x 26 x 17 cm. Private Collection, Ecuador.

and seeker of esoteric knowledge useful in exorcism and other forms of personal healing or divination. Drug iconography has been identified widely in South America and in the Formative of Ecuador (Lathrap et al. 1975: 48, fig. 66; Stahl 1985a, 1986; Staller 1994: 426–439; Wilbert 1987; Zeidler 1988).

   A pair of probable lime containers found in a Las Vegas burial is evidence that the ingestion of snuff or coca leaves may have been part of Preceramic spirituality and shamanic mediation (Fig. 21).[12] Drug paraphernalia has been identified in sites inhabited by Valdivia people (Fig. 22), who apparently prepared psychotropic drinks, chewed coca, and also used snuff, as do modern peoples in South America (Stahl 1984: 98–101 and 1986; Lathrap et al. 1975: 79, items 122–130, and figs. 64 and 66). At Loma Alta the only Valdivia burial

[12] The interpretation of these modified shells is difficult because of their large perforations, which expose the interior *columella* (possibly evocative of the World Tree) and make them useful as whistles or containers.

Fig. 21   Perforated, immature *Malea ringens* shells from a Las Vegas burial (Ossuary 34); 4 to 5 cm in diameter. They may have been whistles or receptacles for ritual snuff or for the lime powder employed in the mastication of coca leaves. Museo Antropológico del Banco Central del Ecuador.

with grave goods contained a Phase 1 or 2 skeleton interred with a probable lime pot that had been placed in the left hand of the deceased (Raymond 1993: 36, note 4; Stahl 1984: 226–229). This paraphernalia proliferated in Terminal Valdivia times, and later material culture (in the Chorrera style) includes anthropomorphic and zoomorphic lime pots (Fig. 23), shell receptacles, ceramic inhalers, snuffing tablets, and ritual grinding equipment (Lathrap et al. 1975: figs. 62, 65; Cummins this volume).

The evolution of paraphernalia, as evidence of social and ideological change, might correspond to the institutionalization of the shamanic specialty in the Late Formative period, this likely driven by competition among shamans. The potential for ideological change would have been great, as novel forms of organization, such as cults directed by charismatic leaders, were being generated or specialists labored to create a Great Tradition. In this scenario people worked to innovate social practices and modify the existing ideology to generate myths and images supportive of new roles and relations.

Sacred Stones

Stones are evidence of magico-religious thought habits that we associate

Fig. 22   A Valdivia lime pot (ceramic) with incised decoration;
2.5 cm high. Cruz-De Perón Collection.

with shamanism. At Preceramic Site 80, groups of selected stones were discovered in graves and interred in the midden among the burials, indicating symbolic or magical acts. Twenty-five extraordinary stones were deposited in one of the ossuaries dominating the center of the preserved Las Vegas site (Fig. 6b). They may represent the number of adults in the ossuary. The stones may have served as votive offerings or perhaps as shamanic aids buried after manipulation in curing rituals. Among the modern Canelos Quichua, polished pebbles are manipulated as receptacles for the souls of shamans and powerful ancestors (Whitten 1985: 109, 110, 120, 150; 1987: 177). The gathering and depositing of selected small stones might have been part of a domestic ritual, as among the late prehistoric Tairona and the modern Kogi. In this case the shaman collects stones (to be interred under house floors) and other items that symbolize members of the household who are magically protected. The objects function both as offerings to spirit masters and food for the dead (Reichel-Dolmatoff 1953: 41).

On La Plata Island, 147 small stones (Figs. 24, 25) were found beneath the floor of a Valdivia structure (Damp and Norton 1987). On the Fiesta House

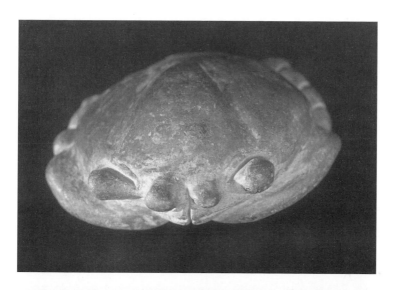

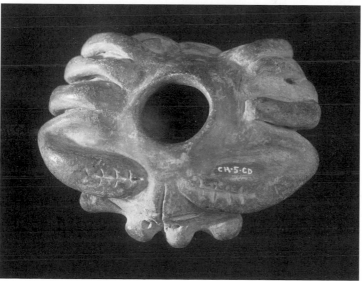

Fig. 23   A Chorrera lime pot (ceramic) in the form of a crab, seen from both sides; 5.5 x 5 x 3 cm. Cruz–De Perón Collection.

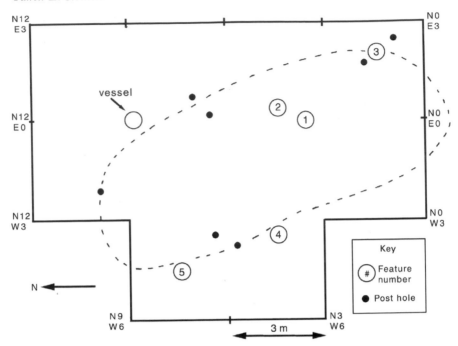

Fig. 24   Floor plan of a Valdivia Phase 6 structure on La Plata Island (Site OMPLIL-083). Feature 3, a cluster of stones, is shown in Fig. 25. Redrawn from Damp and Norton (1987: 112).

Mound at Real Alto, in a clay-lined pit, 136 pebbles, from 5 to 6 cm in diameter, were buried as an offering along with some *mano* and *metate* fragments and three large sherds (Marcos 1988: 64). Magico-religious use is inferred for small, spherical stones found at Cotocollao (Villalba 1988: 306–307).

Stones have various meanings in burial contexts. At Site 80, the large stones recovered from the top of an infant burial and the grave of the Lovers of Sumpa (Fig. 26) indicate a magico-religious gesture meant either to shield the dead from evil spirits or protect the living from the dead. Tiny polished red stones (like those in and near Las Vegas graves) were found also at Real Alto as markers for various points of the focal skeleton in the Charnel House. Their pattern is reminiscent of the placement of stones on the grave of the Lovers of Sumpa (Marcos 1988: 164–165; Stothert 1988: 137, 142). In both cases the stone were placed over the major anatomical joints, considered by some Native Americans to be the bodily source of vitality.

The mortuary use of stones is recognized in the Piquigua burial, described above, which was capped by a fragment of ground stone, and at Salango, Machalilla

Fig. 25 Feature 23, partially excavated and consisting of 147 pebbles found in the wall trench of the Valdivia structure depicted in Fig. 24. Photo courtesy of Jonathan Damp.

period burial pits were topped by stones. In the highland site of Cotocollao, a layer of cobbles covered the entire cemetery and large stones were found next to flexed skeletons (Fig. 27) in the earlier graves (Villalba 1988).[13]

Magical stones have been employed in various contexts by shamans and others all over the New World. Stones were venerated by late Andean peoples throughout prehistory (Eliade 1964; Meggers 1966: 83; Metraux 1963; Sharon 1978), and contemporary Chachi (Cayapa) shamans employ sets of three black pebbles in healing (Mitlewski 1989).

It is important that in the Las Vegas ceremonial center naturally aesthetic stones were selected for ritual use, whereas in the Formative period more labor was invested in producing a progressively wider variety of paraphernalia that

[13] The recurrence of three large stones in several of the early Cotocollao graves dated around 1000 B.C. (Villalba 1988: 94–99 and fig. 68–73) is suggestive of a belief also expressed in an early Guangala cemetery used some 800 years later. The cemetery's excavator found in several graves groups of three beads, shark teeth, or pebbles (Stothert 1993: figs. 17, 19). The symbolism of three stones in Maya cosmology merits mention: the three-stone hearth is where creation is symbolically reenacted each day as the fire is lit, and the Maya farmer sets up three stones in his newly prepared field to repeat "the acts of Creation first enacted by First Father when he set up the three stones of Creation to establish the cosmic center" (Freidel, Schele, and Parker 1993: 130, 178).

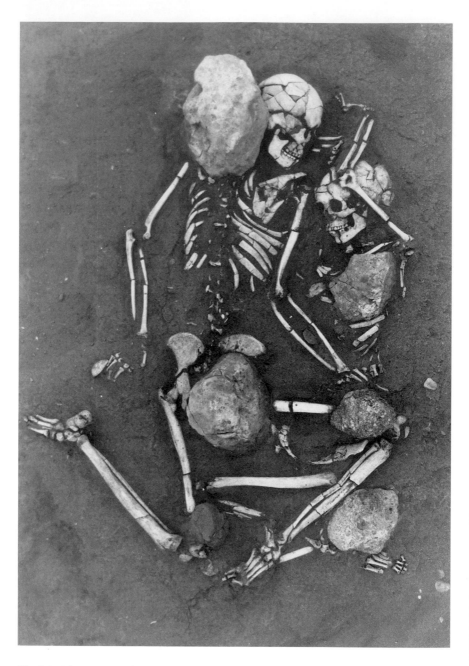

Fig. 26 The Lovers of Sumpa (*Los Amantes de Sumpa*). These entwined skeletons of a woman and a man (*left*) were buried together 7,000 years ago in Las Vegas Site 80. The arrangement of six large stones over their bodies may have been a gesture of magical protection. Photo by Neil Maurer.

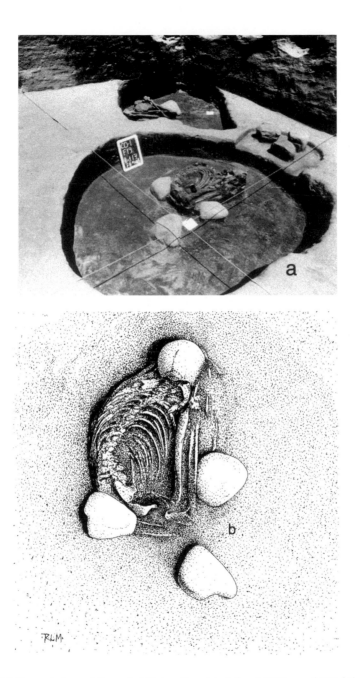

Fig. 27 (a) General view of Grave 1 at Cotocollao, dated about 1100 B.C. (b) Tightly flexed remains of the adult male in Grave 1 who, in typical style, was buried facedown with three large stones nearby. Photo courtesy of Marcelo Villalba. Drawing by Richard McReynolds following Villalba (1988: 97, fig. 70).

functioned as shamanic aids: artifacts such as *manos* and *metates*, polished stone axes, anthropomorphic figurines,[14] ornaments of exotic material such as rock crystal, serpentine, and obsidian. The more elaborate expression of ideology reflects the growing power and complexity of societies, the shift of the locus of rituals from domestic to more public contexts, and growing competition among shamans.

Color Symbolism

Color symbolism is a prominent feature of Native American thought (Stahl 1984: 96–98), and the recovery of colored pigments in archaeological contexts likely means that ancient people also used paint to transform themselves and their possessions, protect and purify, confer or concentrate power, and symbolize powerful concepts like life, health, luck, or affiliation with some creator spirit (e.g., Baer 1992: 84–85; Reichel-Dolmatoff 1961: 231). Modern peoples, like the Tsachila of coastal Ecuador, understand that body painting and ornamentation are part of the necessary personal and spiritual preparation for participation in ritual activities, including dancing.

In early archaeological sites, only mineral colors have been recovered. However, traditional people in Ecuador today prefer vegetal colors for body painting: red from *Bixa orellana*, or *achiote*, and black from *Genipa americana*, or *huito*. Among the modern Chocó, red and black are the appropriate colors for painted representations of spirit helpers and power animals (Reichel-Dolmatoff 1961: 231).

Evidence of color expression is found in the presence of red, black, yellow, and white pigments in Las Vegas graves. Las Vegas people ground the pigment, leaving some of the grinding equipment in burial contexts, and they also painted human bones and deposited shell receptacles containing red pigment in graves. These colors were associated with the cardinal directions in later American thought systems. In the Early Formative, Valdivia figurines and drinking bowls were slipped red and in the middle Valdivia period vessels were decorated in both black and red, thanks to innovative firing technology. The zoomorphic mortars carved from semiprecious stone in the Chorrera period frequently show vestiges of an applied red pigment, probably cinnabar. Blue-green pigments were often used in Chorrera ceramics to express the nonordinary status of humans and animals (Fig. 28; Cummins this volume, fig. 35c; Valdez and

---

[14] The earliest anthropomorphic figurines of the Valdivia style were made of stone, and these were gradually replaced by ceramic images (Meggers, Evans, and Estrada 1965: 95–109). Interestingly, evidence of the development of the use of stones in the period between Las Vegas and Valdivia is available from the north coast of Peru, where Sandweiss (1996) reported the presence of neatly incised pebbles from the Preceramic Ostra Base Camp site occupied from 6250 to 5500 BP.

Veintimilla 1992: 60, fig. 44). Body and face paint are represented in the anthropomorphic figurines of both the Machalilla and Chorrera styles, reflecting the ancient belief that color and the act of painting magically ensured the well-being of individuals. Ceramic pintaderas, called stamps or roller seals for duplicating designs with paint, appear in Machalilla and Chorrera sites and proliferate later in history (Cummins, Burgos Cabrera, and Mora Hoyos 1996: 20).

Ideas and Interaction

In Formative Ecuador exchange was driven by religious and ideological concerns. This is evident because the items traded in that period were related to shamanic thought and practice. Shamanism has a built-in mechanism for promoting the exchange of ideas, songs, dances, costumes, styles, technology, magical plants, and exotic materials and artifacts among the far-flung peoples of ancient America.

Helms (1979, 1992, 1993) accounts for these patterns in her model of questing shamans who created and managed the ceremonial centers described by early Europeans. To attract clients, shamans sought knowledge and acquired goods that became their sacred symbols and paraphernalia. Helms (1993) shows how both skillfully crafted items and naturally endowed materials brought from

Fig. 28 Late Chorrera vessel with a modeled owl head emerging from a plaque like a portal. Its blue color suggests otherworldliness. Private Collection, Ecuador; 18 x 19 x 18 cm.

a distance are associated with divinity, signifying the power and virtue of the acquirer and actually generating power for that person.

In discussing chiefly authority, Helms suggested that the success of a leader depended less upon managerial (political and economic) ability within the social unit and much more upon the ability to link geographically remote people with their ancestors and the spirits. She promotes the idea that in the world view of ancient Americans the contact between the shaman/chief and geographically distant people is the equivalent of contact with supernaturals, like ancestors, culture heroes, and deities (Helms 1992: 191–192). This conflation of political and religious ideology, a feature of some modern tribal groups, may have been characteristic of ancient systems as well.

Both archaeological settlement pattern data and trade goods support Helms's descriptive model. In early Formative times, most communities were economically and socially self-sufficient and had nucleated settlements, with focal ceremonial structures. These sites can be interpreted as versions of Helms's (1993) acquisitional centers, from which shamanic practitioners quested horizontally across space and brought back "political–ideological regalia." By the Middle Formative as a result of competition among centers, there emerged several "superordinant" ceremonial centers that emphasized the direct, vertical connection to the divine and produced ideology and paraphernalia. It is lamentable that we know so little about San Isidro or Sangay in this time period, but somewhat later on these sites and others like La Tolita became extraordinary pilgrimage centers and nodes of interaction.

By the Late Formative, people increasingly sought exotic products from different geographical zones. Many durable magico–ritual items, including rock crystal beads, obsidian,[15] semiprecious green stones, spondylus and strombus shells, ritual ceramic bottles, and figurines are evidence for religion-driven traffic in the Formative. At the end of the Formative, the coast of Ecuador shared a variety of traits with archaeological cultures of Peru, Central America (Coe 1960; Paulsen 1977), and Mesoamerica (Evans and Meggers 1966), evidence of the exchange of ideologically charged regalia or cosmically endowed goods. For this reason it seems likely that long-distance interaction was in the hands of elite specialists who were ideologically and politically motivated and that exchange was not a commercial endeavor in the modern sense.

---

[15] Anthropologists have not given adequate emphasis to the magico-religious significance of obsidian, a cosmically endowed (luminescent) raw material used for ritual paraphernalia in many places in ancient America. The production and consumption of bladelets in coastal Ecuador do not indicate solely "utilitarian" functions. These tools were probably preferred for rituals of sacrifice and surely were sought by shamans as darts just as modern shamans seek *chonta* slivers and razor blades (Whitten 1976: 175).

According to Helms's model, the ability to acquire exotic knowledge and materials was the basis for chiefly and shamanic authority. In fact, individuals depicted in later figurines are adorned with sumptuous items and associated with badges of shamanic office, such as coca ritual paraphernalia, pairs of roller stamps (worn by women), and stools, understood as seats of power. If one accepts the relationship between shamanic practice and authority, a plausible cause for the growing vitality of the exchange network in the Formative period is identifiable.

The system responsible for the long-distance diffusion of ideas and practices in the Formative must have included many interconnected spheres of local interaction and exchange. Perishable trade items that moved in these spheres might have included both ideological and utilitarian commodities: coca and other psychotropic drugs, feathers, pigments and domesticated plants, as well as food, salt, and dogs. Adopting Helms's model, which helps clarify the interaction among ideology, economy, and politics in prehistoric systems, we can view each Formative village as an economically self-sufficient center integrated by an actively expressed cosmology interpreted by part-time or full-time shaman–leaders. According to Staller (1994: 440–441), the late Valdivia shamans developed political power through participation in regional cults that depended on sacred knowledge and the control of narcotic plants and other exotic items. Surely these shamans helped their communities manage risk by predicting and controlling nature and maintaining channels of communication with other peoples, which generated multiple practical benefits.

The quest for sacred knowledge within a multilayered universe, in which moving across distance was analogous to moving vertically among the layers, may have caused ancient people to visit oracles and distant cult centers. In the late prehistoric period, according to Estete (1872: 82–83), people came with gold, silver, and cloth from Catámez (modern Atacámez, a port in northern Ecuador) to the oracle at Pachacamac every year. Were these pilgrims ambitious shamans, aspiring shamans, or traders? They were certainly motivated by religious zeal, and the ideology they shared with others in distant communities must have made travel and trade possible (Keatinge 1981: 184). This ideology not only motivated the quest to gain knowledge but also created an opportunity for interaction and exchange. These stimulated production at home and the accumulation of food and trade goods, which may have lowered risk and promoted stability in local ecosystems.

Some important cult centers began to develop in the Late Formative. While it is perilous to project late patterns into the deep past, sites like San Isidro, La Plata Island, and Sangay have been nominated as Formative centers, perhaps each with its own brand of orthodoxy. These religious centers, the homes of extraordinary shamanic practitioners, may have produced not only a doctrine but also a line of material culture, including Chorrera figurines from Manabí and Red Banded Incised pottery from Sangay (Bruhns et al. 1990: 230–231). Perhaps, then, pilgrims, including aspiring shaman–leaders, ventured to distant religious centers in the Formative, long before La Tolita, Chavín de Huántar, and Pachacamac. According to Helms's model, such visits, motivated by the needs of local shamanic cults, also promoted local production and exchange, which became increasingly robust in Late Formative Ecuador.

Nevertheless, Burger et al. (1994) found the popular model of extensive trade networks (inferred from ethnohistoric models for the late prehistoric period) inadequate for application in the Formative period. They noted a lack of evidence of highly developed exchange networks in Formative Ecuador and found evidence of neither extensive interregional distribution of obsidian,[16] nor specialized production, nor long-distance trade specialists, nor local markets. Instead they suggest that weak political organization may have impeded the procurement of large quantities of obsidian (Burger et al. 1994: 250). An alternative interpretation can be suggested.

It seems likely that in the Formative period coastal people viewed obsidian not as a utilitarian, but as an exotic and magical (cosmically endowed in Helms's sense) material suitable for shamanic performances or for rituals of animal sacrifice and personal sacrifice (bloodletting and tattooing) in religiously charged domestic and communal contexts. If obsidian were sought by local shamans and used and distributed in small quantities, this would account for the "patchy distribution pattern" observed by Burger et al. (1994: 250). Instead of "sociopolitical and economic obstacles" to the development of trade (Burger et al. 1994: 250), shaman–leaders sought to control the supply of the material and associate themselves with the precious commodity. The perceived patchiness of the distribution of trade items would have been caused by their successful control of the inflation of the value of obsidian, as well as by variations in fashion in

---

[16] Burger et al. (1994: 242–250) surveyed the distribution of obsidian in Formative sites, showing its extensive use at sites near the highland sources and its patchy distribution in time and space elsewhere in Ecuador. Several flakes were identified in Late Valdivia contexts (Santa Elena and La Emerenciana), but obsidian was abundant in Piquigua phase midden at San Isidro; it was present in Machalilla contexts at Salango; there was little in the Late Formative in Santa Elena, but it was present in Chorrera contexts at Loma Alta and abundant in the Guayas basin at this time (Peñon del Río and the Guayaquil phase site); obsidian was found in Esmeraldas from the Late Formative onward; there were a few flakes at Pirincay but none in Catamayo sites of the Late Formative. During the Regional Development period large quantities of obsidian were imported into some areas, but later on this procurement ceased.

shamanic paraphernalia, fluctuations in alliance patterns, and the presence of distinct spheres of interaction (as described by Burger et al. 1994: 249).

Local Formative communities flourished because of their religious ideology and practice, which modestly stimulated economies but also promoted stability. Las Vegas people may have adopted a shamanic notion of questing to promote exchange relations: they apparently invested labor in productive activity—enough to sustain their interaction in a wide social network. One older female was interred with a pristine, ground-stone axe of the kind manufactured at Preceramic sites near Siches, in northern Peru (Richardson 1978: 282–283; Richardson and Brown n.d.). The axe seems to be evidence of the exchange of nonutilitarian items, since the artifact was unique in Las Vegas contexts where apparently axes were neither made nor used. Later, a Valdivia-contemporary woman of Huaca Prieta in northern Peru was interred with rare pyroengraved gourds bearing Valdivia iconography.

In Ecuador trade may not have been necessary to satisfy the basic necessities, but it may have been desirable for a host of reasons. It is useful to view the societies of early Formative Ecuador as small systems in which people were motivated by a complex ideology to invest energy and talent in maintaining social relations beyond the borders of their communities. Technology diffused rapidly, so that features like bottle forms, whistling bottles, rocker stamping, negative decoration, iridescent paint, thin polished ceramics, and "napkin ring" earplugs were widely adopted by shaman–leaders, who recognized the potential of new knowledge and paraphernalia. People in these relatively open systems would have been aware of ideas that could be employed or modified to meet the changing sociocultural needs of each community.

While exchanging items such as spondylus shell, ancient Ecuadorian communities also shared ideology: for example, the meaning and symbolism of the sacred shell developed out of local magical modes for addressing the problem of environmental risk (Davidson 1982; Marcos 1995; Stothert 1995). Other exports from Ecuador might have included the ritual use of stirrup-spout bottles (Fig. 29), anthropomorphic figurines, moldmade figures, ceramic vessels representing life forms, iridescent paint, resist decoration, clay stamps, pedestal bowls, and zoomorphic mortars. It is possible that the perceived technological superiority of ancient Ecuadorians, with their effective maize agriculture and their excellent ceramic artifacts, combined with their sophisticated iconography (expressed, for example, on the Huaca Prieta gourds) made their ideological and material products desirable in the Formative period interaction sphere.

Archaeological evidence is consistent with religious and political leaders who were motivated to quest for knowledge, regalia, and paraphernalia. Sha-

Fig. 29 Stirrup-spout bottles: (*above*) Machalilla phase vessel with red painted decoration; 18.5 cm high. Collection of the Museo Antropológico del Banco Central del Ecuador (GA-1-2033-81). (*below*) Early Cotocollao phase bottle, brown polished (1500 to 1100 B.C.); 17 cm high. Photo courtesy of Marcelo Villalba.

mans must have competed for clientele, and centers surely vied to attract pilgrims. In the Formative, people likely acquired knowledge about people, places, and ideas by making pilgrimages and by receiving traveling shamans. Even today the most prestigious shamans are from exotic homelands, and magical curers frequently cross from one ecological zone to another in the coastal, highland, and Amazonian regions of western South America.[17]

Ceramics and Feasting

More than 5,000 years ago, ceramic containers became vehicles of symbolic expression in coastal Ecuador. Both Valdivia ceramics, which display sophisticated iconography, and the later Formative wares, which are some of the most intriguing and beautiful in the New World, responded well to the ideological and social needs of ancient people. Ceramic culinary and storage vessels also served their practical needs, but much of ancient pottery is "art–tool": religious and mortuary paraphernalia with a functional component (Graham 1992).

Valdivia pottery made of fired clay, one of the world's first synthetic materials, must have inspired admiration. These durable earthen vessels were hot with symbolism and featured awesome colors like red and, later on, black. Through time the people of the Valdivia, Machalilla, and Chorrera periods produced progressively more amazing and ideologically charged ritual paraphernalia from ceramic material: more polished and shiny, more colorful, lighter and thinner, iridescent later on, with designs modeled and painted to "blow your mind." Vessels had esoteric shapes and symbols as well as naturalistic representations of animals, especially snakes; others whistled like spirit voices when liquids were being poured. Imagine experiencing these artifacts when "stoned" on a psychedelic brew!

Nonordinary ceramics have long been associated with communal celebrations, which are key activities among South American peoples, including both egalitarian and hierarchically arranged groups in the tropical forest and in the high Andes. Formative ceramic assemblages have been taken as evidence that people prepared and consumed fermented and hallucinogenic brew during feasts that were social expressions of their ecstatic religion (see Damp n.d.a, 1982b; DeBoer this volume; Lathrap et al. 1977; Marcos 1988; Stahl 1984, 1985a,b, 1986; Staller 1994; Raymond 1993: 38–39; Zeidler 1984: 432). Studies of the

---

[17] *Brujos, curanderos,* and *chamanes* from Ecuador, Peru, and Bolivia, sporting exotic costumes and paraphernalia, held a fraternal ceremony on the international bridge between Ecuador and Peru. Focusing on the populist president-elect of Ecuador, whose portrait was surrounded with talismans representing power, wisdom, leadership, strength, and dignity, their ritual involved song, dance, speeches, candles, incense, tobacco, and liquor. They asked the saints and the gods of the *altiplano* for peace, happiness, and prosperity for all people (*El Universo,* 1996).

iconography on drinking vessels (Damp n.d.a: 88–109 and 1982; Stahl 1985a, 1986) have revealed symbolic serpents and felines implicated in shamanic trans-formations. Even today, drinking and trancing are part of curing ceremonies of the shamans, funerals, rituals of cosmic mediation, seasonal celebrations, and other events in the social lives of tropical forest people like the Chachis and the Canelos Quichua (DeBoer this volume; Einzmann 1985; Whitten 1976).

Ceramics are our best evidence of ancient ritual practice and symbolic ex-pression. In Valdivia sites, ceramic vessels were frequently smashed in place, left in pits or under caps of broken grinding stones, and employed to cover infant burials (Marcos 1988; Norton 1984; Staller 1994: 356). Narrow-necked bottles (Fig. 30), apparently innovated by Late Valdivia people, are well-documented from a ceremonial context at La Emerenciana (Staller 1994: 406–409) and are known from the Guayas basin (González de Merino 1984: 97). Bottles later had wide currency as preferred burial offerings and as paraphernalia associated with serving and drinking fermented beverages in sacred and elite contexts in Ecua-dor and elsewhere in the Andes (Lathrap et al. 1975; Lumbreras 1993). The degree of elaboration of fine ceramic bottles is a measure of the importance of ritual libations in many Formative cultures throughout America (Evans and Meggers 1957: 244).

This elaboration may have been motivated by both religious and political factors. In comparison with Mesoamerican and Central Andean peoples, the Formative Ecuadorians invested less energy in architecture, but evidence exists for elaborate ritual events involving food and intoxication. By analogy, these inferred ritual events are indicators of a complex ideology. In my view, the Formative people lacked a political hierarchy focused on a dominant group of elites; instead they were characterized by a complex, heterarchical organization (Ehrenreich, Crumley, and Levy 1993) in which power was multifarious: people communicated with their ancestors and other spirits, managed kin and other political and economic relationships, and achieved effective ecological regula-tion with the guidance of a variety of adult male and female leaders operating in various spheres and contexts.

The complex social systems of living people alert us to the probable com-plexity of ancient systems, even though the details of the Formative mythology and ritual practice are difficult to reconstruct. Like the modern Cubeo, the For-mative people may have shared in efforts to re-create the origin of the world in rituals and used their "ritual gifts" (including dance, body paint, and finely crafted ceramics) to make contact with ancestors, animals, and spirits (Goldman 1993: 145, quoted above). These rituals serve, at the same time, to "focus and intensify" a group's "experience of their ethnicity" (Goldman 1993: 153) and provide a

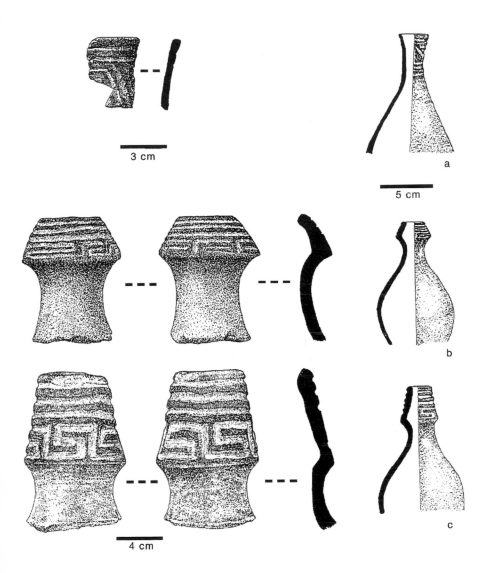

3 cm

5 cm

a

b

c

4 cm

Fig. 30   Late Valdivia (Jelí phase) bottles from La Emerenciana (Site OOSrSr-42). Rim sherds and reconstructed vessel shapes including the (a) long-neck bottle form; (b) and (c) carinated bottle forms. Redrawn from Staller (1994: figs. 45a, 47a, 48a, 49, 50).

context for making leaders and leadership and controlling their authority. Among the Cubeo, leadership might include several ritual specialists, priest–shamans who manage the collective welfare of the group, take charge of lineage concerns, and are elite representatives of the first ancestors; others "scavenge for lost souls and for fragments of soul for clients" (Goldman 1993: 155). These leaders would include the questing shaman described in Helms's model. It is these women and men who may be represented in the anthropomorphic figurines.

Helms (1993: 17–44, 75) wrote that behind the production of skillfully crafted goods like Formative ceramics is an ethnographically and historically widespread ideology of "supernatural energetics" in which skilled crafting is equated with magical transformation by morally superior individuals with access to divine and cosmic power. She suggested, "[In some societies] art is the only pursuit that provides the opportunity to manipulate, exploit and even create the images and ideas on which community well-being is believed to depend" (1993: 71). The Valdivia ceramics and the more elaborate late Formative vessels may indicate the existence of this ideology and its use by community leaders to build and exercise power.

Feasting was surely at the center of ancient socio-politico-religious activity, just as it is in some tribal contexts in the present. The feast probably involves exchanging or sharing food (symmetrically or asymmetrically), expressing gender relations, and feeding the dead and other spirits. Archaeologists interpret the food remains, recovered in graves and in refuse pits excavated in nondomestic contexts, as evidence of communal feasting. Twin pits in one of the structures on the summit of the Fiesta Mound at Real Alto contained burned material, pottery fragments, lithic items, and food remains not normally found in domestic rubbish. Some pits, like one at the Las Vegas type-site and another at Pirincay, contained both human bones and sacrificed animals. The anthropomorphic figurines found in pits may have been substitutes for human sacrifices.

In the absence of strong political stratification, these community rituals expressed the ideology of connectedness with the spirit world. These events also created the basis for both cooperation and competition, regulated relations with the environment, demonstrated the productive power of families, allowed for the accumulation of prestige, attracted affines and allies, cemented alliances, and reinforced other social relations. Any cult ideology that increased the sense of connectedness would have been attractive to local community leaders. Feasting has a great potential to manifest connectedness, and, in that context, awe-inspiring ceramics in the Formative surely heightened the symbolic impact of giving and receiving food and drink. Women and men may have reaffirmed their roles and authority in these rituals.[18] Important ideas about social and cosmic organization might also have been expressed by the manipulation of ceramics during feasts: some scholars identify expressions of duality in the Formative ceramics (see note 10), which may support the hypothesis of dual social organization in the Ecuadorian Formative.

Feasting, on the one hand, may serve to unite segments of the community and to strengthen kin group relations. Or a feast may be the venue for making alliances among factions and activities involving "prestige cycles" designed to create and maintain hierarchy (Marcos 1988: 192; Zeidler 1986: 100). The innovation of ceramics in Early Valdivia times probably accompanied a radical change in ideology and behavior. This innovation can be explained with an idea that has been expounded recently by thinkers who recognize the importance of factional competition in explaining the transition to "transegalitarian systems" in prehistory. Clark and Blake (1994: 29) have suggested that the elaborate vessels in the Barra phase of Early Guatemala may be evidence of competitive feasting and "the self-interested pursuit of prestige, or competition for followers, by using a strategy of competitive generosity" (1994: 21). Individual male[19] aggrandizers can achieve prestige (public recognition of their "status, rights, and responsibilities") and successfully create permanent social inequality through "self-promotion" (Clark and Blake 1994: 28).

Valdivia ceramics support the idea of limited competitive feasting, and the growth in household size, village size, and nucleation at Real Alto is consonant with the centripetal effect of attractive lineage and community leaders on people. Nevertheless, Valdivia settlements exhibit strong communal tendencies. The development of competing factions may explain the trajectory of growth and the elaboration of material culture and long-distance exchange in the later Formative in Ecuador. One element in the Clark and Blake model is that "[e]ffective competition within one's community requires that aggrandizers traffic outside their respective communities and establish enduring ties with individuals elsewhere (Clark and Blake 1994: 29)."

---

[18] Zeidler (1984: 482, map 64) has suggested that there is evidence of ancient gender relations in the distribution of fancy tetrapod bowl fragments in relative high numbers in the "peripheral male area" within Valdivia 3 houses. He wrote: "If our assumption is correct that these vessels served as the household 'fancy ware', then they were most likely utilized only on special occasions or exclusively for serving the adult males of the household, as in the case among many tropical forest groups" (1984: 482).

[19] Clark and Blake (1994: 30, note 1) specify that "aggrandizers" are more likely to be male because a man may have more "immediate access to the productive labor of his wife (or wives) and children, a form of familial exploitation socially justified by gender ideology." This raises questions about the flexibility of "gender ideology" and "political ideology." The ethnographic record shows that under some circumstances female leaders may control the labor and products of others.

Karen E. Stothert

If pottery was perceived as potent by ancient people, then possibly its manufacture was an ideologically charged activity. Among the Kogi and other groups of the Sierra Nevada of Colombia, shaman–priests made the ritual vessels (Reichel-Dolmatoff 1953: 40). Among many peoples craft production is itself viewed as a religious activity or personal meditation: among the Warao the skilled basketmaker becomes a powerful shamanic craftsman by virtue of his production (Wilbert 1975: 5–6; 82).

Formative ceramic production loci have not been identified in Ecuador and no studies of fingerprints have determined the identity of the potters. Although men are dominant in ritual activity in many societies (Stahl 1984), adult women may have participated in the dominant discourse of Valdivia social life. Likewise, modern Canelos Quichua women (Whitten and Whitten 1988) contribute to an intelligible material culture that makes socio-religious rituals possible and enhances the community's experience of the sacred. If it is assumed that early ceramic manufacture in Ecuador was in the hands of Valdivia women, then their participation in the thought and ritual of their society could be demonstrated, since the iconography must have been executed by ideologically skillful and knowledgeable individuals. Women in general may have gained prestige, and elderly ones social security, through ceramic production. This scenario is also compatible with self-aggrandizing shaman–leaders who promoted and underwrote the manufacture of ritual vessels for religious and political purposes.

The continuous development of decorated bowls, necked decanters, and narrow-necked bottles in the Ecuadorian Formative, culminating in the transcendental Chorreroid pottery styles, is evidence of a persistent and potent ideology expressed by the material culture of ritual drinking[20] and feasting.

Music and Dance

Music and dance are sacred activities in Native American thought (Sullivan 1988) and belong in any discussion of ideology. Cieza de León (1553 [1962]) described dancing as a principal activity in native ceremonials in coastal Ecuador in the sixteenth century (Di Capua 1986: 158). Dancers may have mimicked a particular animal as the spirit of that species was evoked, and dancing shamans may have been transformed into jaguars during curing rituals. In eth-

---

[20] While drunkenness may accompany many feasts described in the ethnographic literature, there is variation in this aspect as well. In his summary of Chocó religion, Stout (1948: 275) stated that *chicha* is stored in zoomorphic and anthropomorphic jars and that an "important episode in the ceremonies is the consecration of *chicha* by the shaman. The *chicha* drinking does not, however, have the character of a drinking bout."

nographic celebrations dancers wore feline costumes, examples of which are observed in ancient figurines (Figs. 17, 18), and they also employed drums, bells, rattles (Reichel-Dolmatoff 1961: 238), acrobatics, and mythic narrations about the ancestors (Di Capua 1986: 158). Helms includes among the potential skills of a shamanic leader who fulfills the "kingly ideal," the ability to (a) dance and craft instrumental music, (b) compose songs, poems, and oratory, and (c) manufacture marvelously transfiguring costumes and other paraphernalia. Song, music, other sonic effects, and dance are key transformative processes in curing rituals in many cultures (Hill 1992; Luna 1992; Pollock 1992; Sullivan 1988) and were important in Formative times.

Some Valdivia figurines may represent women dancing (Fig. 31). This interpretation is based on the habitual dance posture of modern Shuar women (Fig. 32). The so-called *hieratic* poses of men and women in the static figurative art of the Formative evoke the rhythmic yet trancelike dancing performed all night by modern Native American dancers.

The Formative peoples must have danced to music produced by flutes of wood and bamboo and other sound-producing instruments constructed of perishable materials including gourds and strings of seeds and shells. We have conch shell trumpets and whistles from the Preceramic, and the Valdivia people manufactured some rattling, pregnant female ceramic figures (Hickmann 1987: 28; Holm 1987), one of which also was a whistle (Idrovo 1987: 63). Bone flutes appear in Machalilla contexts (Parducci Z. and Burgos 1982: 27). Most authors, basing their interpretations upon ethnographic analogs, associate these instruments with fertility and note that they are commonly played in rituals relating to warfare—often itself an expression of human concern with fertility and regeneration (Redmond 1994).

Among Native Americans, wind instruments are associated with the spirits, the dead, rain, and sex (e.g. Whitten 1978: 848–849). Reichel-Dolmatoff (1971: 116) explains that when the Desana of Colombia dance to drumbeats, playing *maracas* and stomping the ground to make their ankle rattles sound, they perform "an act of creation in which male and female energy have united." For the Desana, playing a wind instrument symbolizes male sexuality and "is compared directly with the sex act" (Reichel-Dolmatoff 1971: 112), while the number of tubes played corresponds to the age of the player. According to Reichel-Dolmatoff, playing in the forest contributes to the fertility of game animals; playing a large flute is a cause of "hilarity" because it is associated with youthful, erotic games (1971: 112); rattling sticks, which are phallic symbols related to the cosmic axis, are manipulated by shamans as ritual objects associated with family groups (1971: 113); and drums represent the "uterus" of a

Fig. 31 Red polished Valdivia figurine (height: 3.9 cm) possibly in a stylized pose representative a dancing woman. Museo Antropológico del Banco Central del Ecuador (GA-8-471-77).

a

b

Fig. 32 Modern Shuar women in customary dance postures. Redrawn (a) from Bianchi (1993: 130) and (b) from Rovere (1977: 90).

lineage—striking it with a stick imitates cosmic regeneration (1971: 113–114).

In Native American myths, the themes of death, renewal, and fertility are intertwined (Hall 1979: 258–265). Burial ceremonialism and flute playing are probably two manifestations of the ideology that the well-being of the living community depends on its relationship with the parallel world of the dead and the spirits. Many musical instruments have been recovered in ancient graves.

An innovation of the Late Formative was the production of a variety of musical instruments in durable materials that reflected the vitality of shamanic performance that probably accompanied feast events (Idrovo 1987: 45–46).[21] In the Late Formative, bone flutes including several from Cerro Narrío (see Idrovo 1987: 85, fig. 29), whistling bottles, ceramic drums, magnificent ceramic rattles in the form of human phalluses, and ceramic whistles and ocarinas all appeared in middens and in graves (Hickmann 1986). The bat, important in tropical forest myth and frequently invoked by shamans because of its connection to blood and fertility, is represented in Chorreroid zoomorphic ocarinas (Fig. 33; Hickmann 1986: fig. 3). Many instruments are zoomorphic, but anthropomorphic whistles and ocarinas appeared in the Chorrera–Bahía transitional style, and their manufacture continued in the Regional Development period. Of the Chorrera–Bahía examples, nearly all represent women decked with necklaces and earrings: one represents a female with a panpipe (Fig. 34), an instrument played almost exclusively by male figures in later representations. Anthropomorphic instruments never occured in the highlands (Hickmann 1987: 8).

From ethnographic studies we know of the symbolic and social significance of "sacred flutes" and drums that are taboo to women in contemporary tropical forest groups; furthermore, among many Native Americans musical instruments in the hands of shamans make it possible to communicate with the spirits. The importance of musical instruments in the ideology and ritual practice of the Ecuadorian Formative is signaled by the fact that many musical instruments are held by individuals represented in anthropomorphic figures (Cummins this volume, figs. 13b, 27; Idrovo 1987: 101, fig. 51). The elaboration of ceramic and bone musical instruments began at the end of the Formative period and are most frequently recovered from later sites.[22] This evidence signifies an evolution in the nature of leadership and an intensification of ritual strategies concerned with the maintenance of fertility and abundance.

[21] Another innovation of the Late Formative in coastal Ecuador is the manufacture of ceramic *pintaderas*, often called stamps or seals, *sellos* (for example, Estrada 1958: 88, fig. 44b; Lathrap et al. 1975: 106, figs. 515–537). This technology permits the faithful repetition of designs that may have been part of ritual practice at that time. It is thought that the stamps were used to create elaborate painted designs on human bodies, an important part of dance rituals and healing rituals even today.

Fig. 33 Chorrera–Bahía style ocarina in the form of a bat, decorated with incision and post-fired paint; 15 x 11 cm. Museo Antropológico del Banco Central del Ecuador.

Fig. 34 A Chorrera–Bahía ceramic ocarina in the form of a woman playing a panpipe; 27 cm high. Museo Antropológico del Banco Central del Ecuador (GA-1-278-77).

Warfare

The ideology of tribal and chiefly warfare is complex, and the nature and objectives of warfare are variable (Redmond 1994; J. Topic and T. Topic 1997). In ancient America warfare was religious and constituted a mechanism by which communities gained access to supernatural power and leaders developed both spiritual and political power.

Las Vegas and Early Valdivia communities might have been involved in hostilities, but there is no evidence of warfare in either case.[23] The hypothesis that conflicts were more common from the Late Valdivia period on is supported by the proliferation of personal ornaments, musical instruments used in war rituals, and other sumptuous goods given as rewards by war leaders. Warfare also helps to explain the intensification of feasting, trading, initiation and burial rites, trophy heads (at Cotocollao?), and settlement nucleation in the Late Formative. It is curious that warriors are not prominent in Chorrera art, although one whistling bottle represents a bound individual (Cummins this volume, fig. 17; Lathrap et al. 1975: 60, fig. 86, no. 398). While this may be evidence that captive-taking was practiced, it might instead refer metaphorically to human sacrifice. Warfare was not expressed as frequently in the iconography of Formative Ecuador as in Initial period Peru, where ritual battle was depicted dramatically on the walls at Cerro Sechín (J. Topic and T. Topic 1997). The mostly female images in the art of Formative Ecuador may be taken as evidence of the different historical trajectories in the two neighboring regions. Later in the Regional Development period in Ecuador, ceramic sculptures show evidence of warriors, weaponry, and trophy heads; male figures are represented playing panpipes, which may have been associated with battle. This area of behavior merits further study because the kind of warfare practiced would have affected gender relations and ideology.

---

[22] Masks, frequently used by Native Americans as cult objects and as part of costumes that facilitated communication with and travel to parallel animal and spirit worlds, only rarely were manufactured of durable material in the Formative period. Ceramic figurines, which show humans with face paint, are not shown with masks. Some Valdivia spondylus shell masks are evidence that similar items made of wood, skin, or fiber were part of ritual costume in the Formative period. Like musical instruments, masks experienced a florescence in the succeeding Regional Development cultures in coastal Ecuador.

[23] While the archaeologist can expect few remains of low-tech warfare in the tropics, there is some evidence of personal violence in Valdivia burial assemblages (Ubelaker this volume). For example, one Late Formative Engoroy skull was recovered with a projectile wound (Zevallos 1995: figs. 44, 45), and prisoners are represented in Chorrera art.

Karen E. Stothert

GENDER IDEOLOGY AND ANTHROPOMORPHIC FIGURINES

A detailed analysis of Formative figurines is beyond the scope of this essay, but the ceramic images produced in coastal Ecuador frequently are interpreted as evidence of shamanic thought and practice. They also have the potential for generating insights into ancient gender ideologies (Stothert 1999: 189–208). If shamanism is seen as central and a focus of crucial ideology, then the same argument can be made about gender, which also is a key dynamic in human society regulated by custom and ideology. According to Handsman

> [G]ender . . . is actually the pivotal domain and terrain where histories of social and productive relations were made, resisted, and challenged in the past. As gender is intertwined throughout alliance, exchange, and kinship; the organization of labor and the production of surplus; the specialization of work and the ordering of space; and the social reproduction of communities—in short, throughout everyday life, its representations, and transformations—then gender is embedded within and surrounds culture, society, and politics. (1991: 338)

Because the anthropomorphic figures from Ecuador represent female bodies, they invite discussion about feminine symbols, women as actors in ancient society, and the evolution of gender ideologies. However, upon analysis the images are difficult to read. A review of ethnographic cases reveals a dazzling array of possible models for the roles, relations, and ideologies of ancient American women and men.

For instance, among the contemporary Canelos Quichua of eastern Ecuador, women celebrate their ancestral past through ceramics and paint their faces to represent cosmic union. The Canelos men enter into seance and make music to celebrate ancestors.

> [In this modern group] the apex of each segment of the social system . . . is the shaman. He achieves his position through his knowledge of and experience in traditional and contemporary worlds. Each powerful shaman has a sister and/or a wife who is a master potter, and these knowledgeable men and women together transmit the symbolism of tradition and modernity.

> [these] men and women are as familiar with their counterparts' gender role as with their own, and each may serve as an interpreter for the other. A powerful image-making woman "clarifies" a shaman's visions while he is in seance, and a shaman himself, while chanting, may bring to consciousness symbolism deeply embedded in his wife's or sister's

ceramic art. What binds these distinct yet merged male/female do-mains is an ancient, enduring cosmology. (D. Whitten and N. Whitten 1988: 15–16)

Ethnographic cases show us how the roles of men and women in life and in ritual practice are woven out of mythic materials (Bellier 1991; Karsten 1988), and the resulting social fabric is intricate and difficult to reconstruct. The variability of sociocultural patterns among modern tropical forest-dwelling ethnic groups suggests that the features of their ideologies and social organizations may not be so "ancient and enduring" as variable and changing. Although male dominance in ritual may be common today among Amazon peoples, this may not have great antiquity. Recent ethnographic research (Bellier 1991) in Mai Huna communities shows a powerful female shaman (1991: 157), a ceremony in which men render homage to a primal mother (1991: 158), a social concept that the unwed are wild and the married are cultural, and an ideology of gender complementarity reinforced by rituals involving food, its consumption, and pottery (1991: 178).

Ancient communities showed variation in gender roles and ideology across space and time, and the archaeological record of the Formative gives testimony of changing expressions of gender ideologies.

The Meaning of Valdivia Figurines

Female bodies were metaphors for powerful ideas throughout the Formative. Just as animals and plants are important natural symbols in Native American thought, so too are the human female body with its miraculous reproductive power and the male body with its marvelous capacity to inseminate. The concept of biological sex serves as a metaphor for crucial cultural and cosmic processes among many Native Americans (Bellier 1991; Kehoe 1970). For example, Reichel-Dolmatoff's (1971) description of Desana religion is full of vaginal, uterine, phallic, and seminal symbols expressing shamanic attempts to control cosmic and human fertility.

One important ceramic metaphor, invented in Valdivia times and developed by Chorrera artists, is the modeling of a container in the form of the body of a plant, an animal, or a human (Figs. 19, 20). Frequently women's bodies were modeled and equipped with spouts or whistling devices. With this imagery, the ancient artists and thinkers expressed the powerful idea and mythic theme that the female body is a metaphor for cosmic creation and regeneration.

In early and middle Valdivia phase sites, broken figurines are found on house floors and in domestic refuse, as well as in burials and more public ritual contexts. The figurines, often slipped red, portray females characterized by elaborate coiffeurs. These objects, some of which are both phallic and feminine (Marcos and García 1988), could have symbolized a variety of ideas, depending on whether they were manipulated by shamans as repositories for guardian spirits or by adults as teaching aids or as talismans for promoting fertility. Women may have performed rituals and manipulated fetishes around the hearths in domestic structures (Zeidler 1984: 435–443). The figurines might have been used for protecting the living and the dead: for instance, a figurine placed in a burial could alleviate the loneliness of the deceased who otherwise might return to take a loved one with him (Reichel-Dolmatoff 1961).

In the Río Chico site near Salango in Manabí province, Erick López excavated a small platform structure where a Valdivia phase 2 through 3 pit contained animal and fish bones, seashells, mother of pearl fishhooks, cut and perforated shells, 15 intentionally broken figurines, and five vessels (López Reyes 1996: 163). Similar pits in ceremonial precincts are widely interpreted as the results of ceremonies involving drinking and food sacrifices. López Reyes (1996) argued (see Holm 1987; Stahl 1986) that the figurines were made to be sacrificed. This ceremonial event may have been extraordinary because many of the sacrificed figurines were gigantic (Fig. 35). Greater than ordinary skill would have been required to make these showy artifacts, and their size may be taken as evidence of a public gathering involving a larger-than-usual group of people.

López Reyes understands these artifacts as representations of an ancestral creator goddess (with androgynous characteristics), who at the beginning of time participated in creating the world by being sacrificed. López Reyes (1996: 169–170, following Jensen 1966) posits that the icons were employed in ritual dramatizations of the original mythic event and that they served as a nexus for the ancestors, the events of the original time, and the living. The inferred religious ritual reenacted the goddess's sacrifice, thereby fostering an awareness among the participants of the order created by the deity when the world came into being. This is a widespread American mythic pattern expressed in rituals of intensification in Mesoamerica and other places.

One of the strengths of this interpretation is that the Valdivia figurines are seen as mythic ancestors who performed beneficial acts, not just abstract (and passive) symbols of fertility. Scholars have avoided calling the Valdivia figurines supernaturals, although female supernaturals are at least as old as Chavín art and persist into the ethnographic present (Bellier 1991; Lyon 1978; Niles 1988). Lineage goddesses, who in recent times are often involved in Native American initiation rites, marriages, and funeral ceremonies (Roosevelt 1988: 17), may have been part of Formative religious thought and practice. Figurines also may have served as shamanic aids employed during healing rituals in which spirits were contacted ecstatically and temporarily lodged in an object (Reichel–Dolmatoff 1961; Stahl 1986). It is curious that Stahl did not mention the apparent sex of the figurines. The predominance of female images suggests that the ultimate source of shamanic power was a female spirit helper and that both male and female practitioners needed access to her power. Some female figurines with animal skin headdresses (Figs. 17, 18) evoke the idea of shaman/jaguars who ethnographically function as promoters of fertility (Di Capua 1994: 239; Reichel-Dolmatoff 1971: 129). Valdivia figurines in the form of pregnant females whose heads were modeled as snuff tablets (Lathrap et al. 1975:47, fig. 64) are evidence that the female body was interpreted as a source of power in shamanistic ritual.

Some Valdivia figurines, which seem to represent several stages in the maturation of females (Figs. 31, 35a,b, 36, 37), may have been made and used by women and girls in celebrations marking life transitions. Di Capua (1994) identifies the figurines as part of household rituals that served to celebrate changing social status and magically protect those involved. The development of the rituals and other ideational, social, and material aspects of a cult of female initiation would have contributed to the integration of the extended family households that appeared during Valdivia Phase 3 (Zeidler 1984: 574–579). More effective family work units might have been achieved by the ideas expressed in the domestic rituals and dedicatory burials innovated in this period (Zeidler 1984: 581).

For purposes of discovering the ideology of the Formative, the figurines are of limited value because it is unknown what the images represented, but it seems plausible that at least sometimes women made and used these images in order to create an important social narrative favoring their interests within Valdivia society. The Valdivia figurines may themselves represent female shamans in trance or adult women performing sacred activity characteristic of shamanic traditions. The representation of women's ritual activity in highly crafted images seems to celebrate or sacralize certain women's roles and relationships. Some of the figurines show women dancing, which is one of the most sacred activities in the Native American tradition (Fig. 31). Women dance to celebrate lineage; show off status; express connectedness to supernaturals; impersonate primordial beings and their acts; enforce ecological regulations; or express solidarity with other women in the lineage or to compete with other lineages or factions.

Undoubtedly, complex mythology and cosmology undergirded the ritual activities involving figurines, and likely a great intensification of symbolic activities in the middle and late Valdivia phases ensued because of both the abun-

Fig. 35   Large Valdivia figurines with missing left legs dated to phases 2 through 3 from ceremonial context in a site near Salango in Manabí province. (*left*) Red-slipped and polished figure representing a mature woman; 31 cm high. (*right*) Unslipped figurine of a mature woman with no arms represented; 27.8 cm high. Photos courtesy of Eric Lopez.

dance of figurines and the escalating production of novel vessel forms (e.g., Fig. 38).

Hollow Figurines of the Late Formative

Subsequent to Valdivia, later Formative peoples persisted in using solid figurines in domestic rituals, but at some sites artists began to produce large, hollow figurines, less suited as shamanic aids and more appropriate as icons (Fig. 39;

Fig. 36 A Valdivia figurine possibly representative of a prepubescent girl with a partially depilated head, an unusual chest garment, and a lower abdominal protrusion; 6.5 x 2.5 x 1.0 cm. Cruz-De Perón Collection.

Fig. 37 A red-slipped Valdivia figurine/ rattle of a pregnant woman; 10 cm high. Museo Antropológico del Banco Central del Ecuador (GA-5-2356-82).

Cummins 1992, this volume). This may reflect sociopolitical change and the innovation of new ways to express traditional ideas. Whereas Valdivia communal rituals focused on domestic and lineage rites in which biological sex was an important theme, by Late Formative times some ceremonies involved more broadly constituted groups and more elaborate paraphernalia. The best ceramics made in the Chorrera style seem to indicate that ideas about gender and status had changed.

In the corpus of Chorrera art, female images are numerically predominant, but women and men seem to have had similar iconographic roles. This similarity may be a reiteration of an ideal of social equality and female–male complementarity. Some figurines lack clear evidence of biological sex, and the cultural trappings of ornament and costume are not gendered. This unisex art could have meant that female and male roles in worship, personal sacrifice, shamanic practice, or lineage ancestry were not being contested or that roles and statuses in that ancient society were not as gender marked as they became later all over America.[24] Alternatively, the apparent equality and complementarity in the figurines could mask a less balanced social reality.

Chorrera artists modeled both women and men with headdresses, tattoos, body paint, and personal ornaments, all associated ethnographically with the initiation into adulthood of both girls and boys and with adult ritual activity (Fig. 39). This group of features, however, may indicate an evolving concept of status and role. In larger, more complex social worlds, players distinguish themselves by personal markers. Personal ornamentation is evidence of a differentiation of statuses and roles (beyond male and female). Chorrera figurines, which seem to be more concerned with signaling ritual status than gender, may memorialize and propitiate the ancestors of certain lineages, thereby supporting the status and influence of certain political leaders.

A comparison of the Valdivia and Chorrera figurines draws attention to both continuity and changes in style, technology, craftsmanship, and function (Figs. 31, 39). Hollow figurines seem to have been related to the appearance of larger and more complex social groups and the development of new ritual practices at elaborate ritual centers. In the Late Formative, male images were more

---

[24] The Chorrera style lacks all the variable representations of male and female roles that make the art of the subsequent Regional Development period so brilliant. The Jama-Coaque figurines suggest that men were pioneering new roles, whereas women maintained traditional ones. In the Jama-Coaque style, only women take the posture characteristic of both men and women in Chorrera period art (Cummins 1992: 77); at the same time, Jama-Coaque figurines showed marked differences between male and female clothing and ornaments; primary and secondary sexual characteristics were ignored. It is only in the Regional Development styles that male dominance in shamanic ritual is evident.

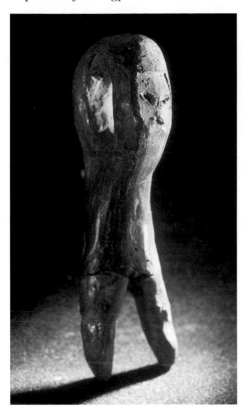

Fig. 38   A red polished Valdivia figurine that combines anthropomorphic legs with a large loop decorated with a pair of Janus-style faces; 12 x 5 x 2 cm. Cruz–De Perón Collection.

common, and male actors seem to have joined female personages in performing the same ritual roles and adopting the same hieratic postures. While the basic shamanic religious tradition persisted and both art and burials seemed to express an ideal of gender complementarity and balance, there may have been important shifts in political, religious, and gender ideology. By the end of the Formative, men had developed a stronger voice in ceramic art, the result of an ongoing negotiation at the level of symbols between women and men about their roles. Perhaps ceremonial activity was increasingly managed by male shaman–leaders, a pattern that grew clearer in the post-Formative period.

CONCLUSIONS

In this essay various kinds of evidence have been used to infer shamanic rituals and ideology in the Formative of Ecuador. It has been shown that while

Fig. 39 A pair of Chorrera figurines, front (*above*) and rear (*below*). Evidence of a continuous tradition of thought and practice initiated by Valdivia peoples, these female images exhibit extraordinary ornaments and body paint or tattooing. One has a ritual, asymmetrical haircut (*below, left*); approximately 20 x 7 x 5 cm. Private collection, Ecuador.

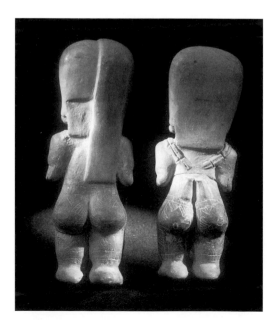

there was continuity in symbolic expression throughout the Preceramic and Formative periods, some aspects of ideology became more elaborate in the Late Formative. Shamanic ideology and ritual were used by Preceramic and Formative peoples to construct and order their social lives, but proliferation of paraphernalia in the Late Formative period at some sites may indicate special roles for members of some families or lineages. At some centers, specialized shaman–priests may have managed theatrical cult activities and attracted clients. The work of Helms (esp. 1993) has been useful for modeling Formative communities and their ideology.

I believe that the Early Formative people lived in independent villages, each with a communal, ceremonial focus and that through time there emerged a pattern of "acquisitional" communities whose elites (not to be construed as *economic* elites) developed their power base and reinforced their legitimacy as leaders by exploiting certain tenets of the shamanic cosmology. These shamanic leaders undertook beneficial rituals, sponsored feasts, and manipulated skillfully crafted items and exotic, naturally endowed materials in ways that elevated them above their ordinary comrades and associated them with the distant, the divine, and morally worthy ancestors. These shaman–leaders were the sources of knowledge of the other (spirit) world that they used for the benefit of their factions or communities. Such charismatic leaders may have had little economic power or ability to coerce, but they must have been members of productive and influential families. The idea of competition among lineages or other factions (Brumfiel and Fox 1994) helps to account for the escalation in various areas of cultural expression in the Late Formative.

This model accounts for both of the key features of Formative communities: their political autonomy and their apparent connectedness across geographical space. If members of each community were involved in questing for knowledge and acquiring skillfully crafted goods, including songs, dances, music, and theatrical techniques, as well as naturally endowed materials from great distances, then each community can be seen as a node in a system characterized by multidirectional flow of ideology and materials. Ideological motivation must have been potent to overcome transportation and communication challenges that we can hardly imagine.

Archaeologists are just beginning to map routes of exchange and describe the flow (and lack of flow) of ideas with respect to ancient frontiers (Bruhns 1994b; Burger 1984). Although there may have been significant boundaries, such as that between the Northern Andean and Chavín interaction spheres (Burger 1984), it is clear that diverse peoples were in communication across great distances throughout the Formative and even earlier. Shared ideas and style became progressively more evident in the later periods of the Formative (see Makowski et al. 1994). With better chronology, it will be possible to identify several influential Formative centers and evaluate the impact of their ideologies and material culture upon other communities.

Recognizing that religious systems play a key role in the maintenance of all aspects of culture, I have argued that shamanic ideology and practice helped Formative people to maintain flexible, heterarchical societies. In Formative Ecuador, independent and successful communities seemed to have avoided some forms of political centralization and escalating social hierarchy.

The archaeological evidence has revealed variation in the expression of ideologies across space and change through time. It also demonstrates a pattern of intensification of artistic expressive and ritual activity in Middle Valdivia Phase 3, again in the Late Valdivia period, and at the end of the Formative. Largely self-sufficient and politically autonomous communities had similar social and ecological arrangements and also shared features like ecstatic religion and ancestor worship. Many of these Formative communities may have cultivated relationships to a few superordinate centers, but, because they recognized no centralized political authority, they were free to adopt, reject, or innovate independently.

This kind of community, integrated by a strong and flexible ideology and having both autonomy and interconnectedness as central features, was established in the Formative period and maintained long-term stability in prehistoric Ecuador.[25] These communities were linked in multiple, overlapping interactive spheres. This meant that knowledge of technology, styles, modes of religious expression, and burial practices diffused widely, if not evenly, across America.

The discussion of gender ideology and anthropomorphic figurines demonstrates that female bodies were sources of symbols in the Formative. Both female figurines and several extraordinary burials of adult women suggest that among the Formative people there were female supernaturals and women had important roles in social and ritual activity. Late Formative images celebrate the roles of both men and women, suggesting that gender complementarity was a theme in social discourse. Neither the burial data nor the art of the Formative period supports an hypothesis of gender hierarchy or of societies dominated

---

[25] The evidence from the Late Formative shows a series of small, only weakly stratified sociocultural groups, bound by shamanistic religious ideology and practice, widely shared and with roots in both the earlier Formative and the Preceramic. This is analogous to Peru, where early Initial period religious expression in several valleys showed continuity with earlier Preceramic expressions in the same valley (see Burger 1992: 75–76).

by men. The theme of the aggressive, virile, inseminating male is neither ideo-logically ascendant nor iconically focal in Formative art.

All aspects of culture during the Formative period changed, but compared with the sociocultural escalation observed in neighboring Peru, the communi-ties of Ecuador may have undergone less reworking. These communities ap-parently developed ideologies that satisfied human needs, gave both women and men valuable social roles, and allowed for sociocultural growth and ritual and economic elaboration. They also helped avoid major ecological, sociocul-tural, and political disruptions in the Formative period.

Karen E. Stothert

BIBLIOGRAPHY

ALCINA FRANCH, JOSÉ
1979   *La arqueología de Esmeraldas (Ecuador): Introducción general.* Memorias de la Misión
Arqueológica Española en el Ecuador. Ministerio de Asuntos Exteriores,
Madrid.

ALLEN, CATHERINE J.
1988   *The Hold Life Has: Coca and Cultural Identity in an Andean Community.*
Smithsonian Institution Press, Washington, D.C.

ARTE PRECOLOMBINO DEL ECUADOR
1977   Salvat Editores Ecuatoriana, Quito.

BAER, GERHARD
1992   The One Intoxicated by Tobacco. In *Portals of Power: Shamanism in South
America* (E. Jean Matteson Langdon and Gerhard Baer, eds.): 79–100. University
of New Mexico Press, Albuquerque.

BELLIER, IRENE
1991   *El temblor y la luna: Ensayo sobre las relaciones entre las mujeres y los hombres Mai
Huna. Tomo I.* Colección 500 años, 44. Institut Français d'Etudes Andines and
Ediciones Abya-Yala, Quito.

BIANCHI, CÉSAR
1993   *Hombre y mujer en la sociedad Shuar.* Ediciones Abya-Yala, Quito.

BISCHOF, HENNING
1982   La Fase Engoroy: Períodos, cronología y relaciones. In *Primer Simposio de
Correlaciones Antropológicas Andino-Mesoamericano* (J. Marcos and P. Norton,
eds.): 135–176. Escuela Superior Politécnica del Litoral, Guayaquil.

BRUHNS, KAREN OLSEN
1987   Los Talleres de Cristal de Roca de Pirincay, provincia del Azuay. *Miscelanea
Antropológica Ecuatoriana* 7: 91–100.
1994a   *Ancient South America.* Cambridge University Press, Cambridge.
1994b   Las culturas peruanas y el desarrollo cultural en los Andes septentrionales.
Memoria 4: 251-268. Quito.

BRUHNS, KAREN OLSEN, JAMES BURTON, AND GEORGE MILLER
1990   Excavations at Pirincay in the Paute Valley of Southern Ecuador, 1985–1988.
Antiquity 64(243): 221–233.

BRUMFIEL, ELIZABETH M., AND JOHN W. FOX (EDS.)
1994   *Factional Competition and Political Development in the New World.* Cambridge
University Press, Cambridge.

BURGER, RICHARD
1984   Archaeological Areas and Prehistoric Frontiers: The Case of Formative Peru
and Ecuador. In *Social and Economic Organization in the Prehispanic Andes* (D. L.
Browman, R. L. Burger, and Mario A. Rivera, eds.): 33–71. BAR International
Series 194. British Archaeological Reports, Oxford.
1992   *Chavin and the Origins of Andean Civilization.* Thames and Hudson, London.

BURGER, RICHARD, AND LUCY SALAZAR-BURGER
1993   The Place of Dual Organization in Early Andean Ceremonialism: A Comparative Review. In *El mundo ceremonial andino* (Luis Millones and Yoshio Onuki, eds.): 97–116. Senri Ethnological Studies 37, National Museum of Ethnology, Osaka.

BURGER, RICHARD L., FRANK ASARO, HELEN V. MICHEL, FRED H. STROSS, AND ERNESTO SALAZAR
1994   An Initial Consideration of Obsidian Procurement and Exchange in Prehispanic Ecuador. *Latin American Antiquity* 5(3): 228–255.

BUSHNELL, G. H. S.
1951   *The Archaeology of the Santa Elena Peninsula in Southwest Ecuador.* Cambridge University Press, Cambridge.

CARDALE DE SCHRIMPFF, MARIANNE
1992   La gente del período Ilama. In *Calima: Diez mil años de historia en el suroccidente de Colombia* (Marianne Cardale de Schrimpff, Warwick Bray, Theres Gahwiler-Walder, and Leonor Herrera): 23–71. Fundación Pro Calima, Bogotá.

CIEZA DE LEÓN, PEDRO DE
1553 [1962] *La crónica del Perú.* Espasa-Calpe, Madrid.

CLARK, JOHN E., AND MICHAEL BLAKE
1994   The Power of Prestige: Competitive Generosity and the Emergence of Rank Societies in Lowland Mesoamerica. In *Factional Competition and Political Development in the New World* (Elizabeth M. Brumfiel and John W. Fox, eds.): 17–30. Cambridge University Press, Cambridge.

COE, MICHAEL D.
1960   Archeological Linkages with North and South America at La Victoria, Guatemala. *American Anthropologist* 62(3): 363–393.
1981   Religion and the Rise of Mesoamerican States. In *The Transition to Statehood in the New World* (Grant Jones and Robert Kautz, eds.): 157–171. Cambridge University Press, Cambridge.

CUMMINS, THOMAS
1992   Tradition in Ecuadorian Pre-Hispanic Art: The Ceramics of Chorrera and Jama-Coaque. In *Amerindian Signs: 5000 Years of Precolumbian Art in Ecuador* (F. Valdez and Diego Veintimilla, eds.): 63–82. Dinediciones, Quito.

CUMMINS, THOMAS, J. BURGOS CABRERA, AND C. MORA HOYOS
1996   *Arte prehispánico del Ecuador, huellas del pasado: Los sellos de Jama-Coaque.* Serie Monográfica 11. Miscelánea Antropológica Ecuatoriana, Banco Central del Ecuador, Guayaquil.

DAMP, JONATHAN E.
1982   Ceramic Art and Symbolism in the Early Valdivia Community. *Journal of Latin American Lore* 8(2): 155–178.
1984a   Architecture of the Early Valdivia Village. *American Antiquity* 49(3): 573–585.
1984b   Environmental Variation, Agriculture, and Settlement Processes in Coastal Ecuador (3300–1500 B.C.). *Current Anthropology* 25(1): 106–111.
n.d.a   Better Homes and Gardens: The Life and Death of the Early Valdivia Community. Unpublished Ph.D. dissertation, Department of Archaeology, University of Calgary, Alberta, 1979.

n.d.b   Structure as House, House as Structure: Early Valdivia Social and Economic Design. Paper presented at the 47th Annual Meeting of the Society for American Archaeology, Minneapolis, Minn., 1982.

DAMP, JONATHAN, AND PRESLEY NORTON
1987   Pretexto, contexto y falacias en la Isla de La Plata. *Miscelánea Antropológica Ecuatoriana* 7: 109–121.

DAVIDSON, JUDITH
1982   Ecology, Art, and Myth: A Natural Appraoch to Symbolism. In *Pre-Columbian Art History: Selected Readings* (A. Cordy-Collins, ed.): 331–343. Peek, Menlo Park, Calif.

DEBOER, WARREN R.
1996   *Traces behind the Esmeraldas Shore: Prehistory of the Santiago–Cayapas Region, Ecuador.* University of Alabama Press, Tuscaloosa and London.

DEMAREST, ARTHUR A., AND GEOFFREY W. CONRAD, (EDS.)
1992   *Ideology and Pre-Columbian Civilizations.* School of American Research and Advanced Seminar Series. SAR Press, Santa Fe, N.M.

DI CAPUA, COSTANZA
1986   Shamán y jaguar: Iconografía de la cerámica prehistórica de la costa ecuatoriana. In *Arqueología y etnohistoria del sur de Colombia y norte del Ecuador* (J. Alcina F. and S. Moreno, eds.): 157–169. In *Miscelánea Antropológica Ecuatoriana, Número Monográfico* 6: 157–169.
1994   Valdivia Figurines and Puberty Rituals: An Hypothesis. *Andean Past* 4: 229–279.

EHRENREICH, ROBERT, CAROL CRUMLEY, AND JANET LEVY, (EDS.)
1993   *Heterarchy and the Analysis of Complex Societies.* American Anthroplogical Association, Washington, D.C.

EINZMANN, HARALD
1985   Artesanía indígena del Ecuador: Los Chachis (Cayapas). *Revista del Centro Interamericano de Artesanías y Arte Popular (CIDAAP)* 19: 13–78.

ELIADE, MIRCEA
1964   *Shamanism: Archaic Techniques of Ecstasy.* Princeton University Press, Princeton, N.J.

ESTETE, MIGUEL
1872   Report of Miguel de Estete on the Expedition to Pachacamac. In *Reports on the Discovery of Peru* (Clements R. Markham, trans.): 74–109. Burt Franklin, New York.

ESTRADA, EMILIO
1958   *Las culturas pre-clásicas, formativas o arcaicas del Ecuador.* Publicación del Museo Víctor Emilio Estrada 5. Guayaquil.

EVANS, CLIFFORD, AND BETTY J. MEGGERS
1957   Formative Period Cultures in the Guayas Basin, Coastal Ecuador. *American Antiquity* 22(3): 235–247.
1966   Mesoamerica and Ecuador. In *Handbook of Middle American Indians,* vol. 4: *Archaeological Frontiers and External Connections* (G. F. Ekholm and G. R. Willey, eds.): 243–264. University of Texas Press, Austin.

Expression of Ideology in the Formative Period

FREIDEL, DAVID, LINDA SCHELE, AND JOY PARKER
    1993   *Maya Cosmos: Three Thousand Years on the Shaman's Path.* Morrow, New York.

FURST, PETER
    1966   *Shaft Tombs, Shell Trumpets and Shamanism: A Culture–Historical Approach to Problems in West Mexican Archaeology.* Ph.D. dissertation, University of California, Los Angeles. University Microfilms International, Ann Arbor, Mich.

GOLDMAN, IRVING
    1972   *The Cubeo: Indians of the Northwest Amazon.* University of Illinois Press, Urbana.
    1993   Hierarchy and Power in the Tropical Forest. In *Configurations of Power: Holistic Antrhpology in Theory and Practice* (John S. Henderson and Patricia J. Netherly, eds.): 137–159. Cornell University Press, Ithaca, N.Y.

GONZÁLEZ DE MERINO, JUANA
    1984   Investigación científica de arqueología en el Sitio Milagro 1. Cantón Milagro–Provincia del Guayas. University of Guayaquil, School of Philosophy, Arts and Educational Sciences, Guayaquil.

GRAHAM, MARK MILLER
    1992   Art–Tools and the Language of Power in the Early Art of the Atlantic Watershed of Costa Rica. In *Wealth and Hierarchy in the Intermediate Area* (Frederick W. Lange, ed.): 165–206. Dumbarton Oaks, Washington, D.C.

GROVE, DAVID C., AND SUSAN D. GILLESPIE
    1992   Ideology and Evolution at the Pre-State Level: Formative Period Mesoamerica. In *Ideology and Pre-Columbian Civilizations* (Arthur A. Demarest and Geoffrey W. Conrad, eds.): 15–36. School of American Research Press, Santa Fe, N.M.

GUFFROY, J., N. ALMEIDA, P. LECOQ, C. CAILLAVET, F. DUVERNEUIL, L. EMPERAIRE, AND B. ARNAUD
    1987   *Loja Prehispanique: Recherches Archéologiques dans les Andes Meridionales de l'Equateur.* Institut Français d'Etudes Andines, Editions Recherché sur les Civilisations, Syntèse 27, Paris.

HALL, ROBERT L.
    1979   In Search of the Ideology of the Adena–Hopewell Climax. In *Hopewell Archaeology: The Chillocothe Conference* (D. Brose and N. Greber, eds.): 258–265. Kent State University Press, Kent, Ohio.

HANDSMAN, RUSSELL G.
    1991   Whose Art Was Found at Lepenski Vir? Gender Relations and Power in Archaeology. In *Engendering Archaeology: Women and Prehistory* (J. Gero and M. Conkey, eds.): 329–365. Basil Blackwell, London.

HELMS, MARY W.
    1979   *Ancient Panama: Chiefs in Search of Power.* University of Texas Press, Austin.
    1981   Precious Metals and Politics: Style and Ideology in the Intermediate Area and Peru. *Journal of Latin American Lore* 7(2): 215–238.
    1992   Political Lords and Political Ideology in Southeastern Chiefdoms: Comments and Observations. In *Lords of the Southeast* (A. W. Barker and T. R. Pauketat, eds.): 191–192. Archaeological Papers of the American Anthropological Association 3. Washington, D.C.

Karen E. Stothert

1993   *Craft and the Kingly Ideal: Art, Trade, and Power.* University of Texas Press, Austin.

HICKMANN, ELLEN

1986   Instrumentos musicales del Museo Antropológico del Banco Central del Ecuador, Guayaquil. Ocarinas. *Miscelánea Antropológica Ecuatoriana* 6: 117–141.

1987   Instrumentos musicales del Museo Antropológico del Banco Central del Ecuador, Guayaquil. Parte 2. Figurines antropomorfos con significado musical. *Miscelánea Antropológica Ecuatoriana* 7: 7–30.

HILL, JONATHAN D.

1992   A Musical Aesthetic of Ritual Curing in the Northwest Amazon. In *Portals of Power: Shamanism in South America* (E. Jean Matteson Langdon and Gerhard Baer, eds.): 175–210. University of New Mexico Press, Albuquerque.

HOLM, OLAF

1969   *Cortadura a piola (una técnica prehistórica). Joa 1.* Casa de la Cultura Ecuatoriana, Núcleo del Guayas, Guayaquil.

1987   *Valdivia: Una Cultura Formativa del Ecuador.* Museo de Arte, Lima.

HOSLER, DOROTHY

1994   *The Sounds and Colors of Power: The Sacred Metallurgical Technology of Ancient West Mexico.* MIT Press, Cambridge, Mass.

IDROVO URIGUÉN, JAIME

1987   *Instrumentos musicales prehispánicos del Ecuador: Estudio de la Exposición "Música Milenaria."* Museo del Banco Central, Serie Nuestro Pasado 2, Cuenca.

JENSEN, ADOLF E.

1966   *Mito y culto entre pueblos primitivos.* Fondo de Cultura Económica, México, D.F.

JIJÓN Y CAAMAÑO, JACINTO

1951   *Antropología prehispánica del Ecuador,* La Prensa Católica, Quito. [reprint ed., 1997, Museo Jacinto Jijón y Caamaño, Quito.]

KARSTEN, RAFAEL

1988   La fiesta femenina de tabaco (*Noa Tsangu*). In *La vida y la cultura de los Shuar, Tomo I* (M. C. Montaño, Genny Iglesias, and Ing. Hector Dueñas, trans.): 215–234. Banco Central del Ecuador (Guayaquil) and Ediciones Abya-Yala, Quito. [original 1935: *The Head Hunters of Western Amazonas: The Life and Culture of the Jivaro Indians of Eastern Ecuador and Peru*].

KEATINGE, RICHARD W.

1981   The Nature and Role of Religious Diffusion in the Early Stages of State Formation: An Example from Peruvian Prehistory. In *The Transition to Statehood in the New World* (Grant Jones and Robert Kautz, eds.): 172–187. Cambridge University Press, Cambridge.

KEHOE, ALICE BECK

1970   The Function of Ceremonial Sexual Intercourse among the North Plains Indians. *Plains Anthropologist* 15: 99–103.

2000   *Shamans and Religion. An Anthropological Exploration in Critical Thinking.* Waveland Press, Prospect Heights, Ill.

414

LANGDON, E. JEAN MATTESON
    1992   Introduction, Shamanism and Anthropology. In *Portals of Power: Shamanism in South America* (E. Jean Matteson Langdon and Gerhard Baer, eds.): 1–24. University of New Mexico Press, Albuquerque.

LATHRAP, DONALD, DONALD COLLIER, AND HELEN CHANDRA
    1975   *Ancient Ecuador: Culture, Clay and Creativity, 3000–300 B.C.* Field Museum of Natural History, Chicago.

LATHRAP, DONALD, JORGE MARCOS, AND JAMES ZEIDLER
    1977   Real Alto: An Ancient Ceremonial Center. *Archaeology* 30: 2–13.

LÓPEZ REYES, ERICK
    1996   Las Venus Valdivia gigantes de Río Chico (OMJPLP-170a): Costa sur de la provincia de Manabí, Ecuador. *Boletín Arqueológico (ARAS)* 5: 157–174. Arqueólogos Asociados, Guayaquil.

LUMBRERAS, LUIS GUILLERMO
    1993   Chavín de Huántar: Excavaciones en la galería de las ofrendas. Verlag Philippe Von Zabern, Mainz am Rhein, Germany.

LUNA, LUIS EDUARDO
    1992   Icaros: Magic Melodies among the Mestizo Shamans of the Peruvian Amazon. In *Portals of Power: Shamanism in South America* (E. Jean Matteson Langdon and Gerhard Baer, eds.): 231–253. University of New Mexico Press, Albuquerque.

LYON, PATRICIA JEAN
    1978   Female Supernaturals in Ancient Peru. *Ñawpa Pacha* 16: 95–140.

MAKOWSKI, KRZYSZTOF, CHRISTOPHER B. DONNAN, IVÁN AMARO BULLÓN, AND LUIS JAIME CASTILLO
    1994   *Vicús.* Colección Arte y Tesoros del Peru, Lima.

MARCOS, JORGE
    1978   *The Ceremonial Precinct at Real Alto: Organization of Time and Space in Valdivia Society.* Ph.D. dissertation, University of Illinois at Urbana–Champaign. University Microfilms International, Ann Arbor, Mich.
    1988   *Real Alto: La historia de un centro ceremonial Valdivia. Primera parte.* Biblioteca Ecuatoriana de Arqueología 4. Corporación Editora Nacional, Quito.
    1990   Economía e ideología en andinoamérica septentrional. In *Nueva historia del Ecuador,* vol. 2: *Epoca aborigen 2* (Enrique Ayala, ed.): 167–188. Corporación Editora Nacional and Editorial Grijalbo Ecuatoriana, Quito.
    1995   El mullo y el pututo: La articulación de la ideología y el tráfico a larga distancia en la formación del estado Huancavilca. In *Primer encuentro de investigadores de la costa ecuatoriana en Europa: Arqueología–Etnohistoria, antropología sociocultural* (A. Alvarez, S. Alvarez, C. Fauria, and J. Marcos, eds.): 97–142. Ediciones Abya-Yala, Quito.

MARCOS, JORGE, AND MARIELLA GARCÍA
    1988   De la dualidad fertilidad–virilidad a lo explícitamente femenino o masculino: La relación de las figurinas con los cambios en la organización social Valdivia, Real Alto. In *Real Alto: La historia de un centro ceremonial Valdivia. Segunda parte* (Jorge Marcos, ed.): 315–332. Biblioteca Ecuatoriana de Arqueología 4.

Corporación Editora Nacional, Quito. [also in *The Role of Gender in Precolumbian Art and Archaeology* (V. Miller, ed.): 35–51. University Press of America, Lanham, Md., 1988.]

MEGGERS, BETTY J.
1966   *Ecuador.* Ancient Peoples and Places. Praeger, New York and Washington, D.C.

MEGGERS, BETTY J., CLIFFORD EVANS JR., AND EMILIO ESTRADA
1965   *Early Formative of Coastal Ecuador: The Valdivia and Machalilla Phases.* Smithsonian Contributions in Anthropology 1. Smithsonian Institution, U.S. Government Printing Office, Washington, D.C.

METRAUX, ALFRED
1963 [1949]   Religion and Shamanism. In *Handbook of South American Indians*, vol. 5: 559–599. Bureau of American Ethnology, Bulletin 143. Cooper Square, New York.

MITLEWSKI, BERND
1989   Los Chachila: "Los Mirucula ya no saben volar": Interpretación de la tradición a la luz de los nuevos valores de la "cultura nacional." *Antropología del Ecuador: Memorias del primer simposio europeo sobre antropología del Ecuador* (Segundo E. Moreno Yanez, ed.): 293–299. Ediciones Abya-Yala, Quito.

MURRA, JOHN V.
1975   El tráfico de mullu en la costa del Pacífico. In *Formaciones económicas y políticas del mundo andino.* Instituto de Estudios Peruanos, Lima.

NABOKOV, PETER, AND ROBERT EASTON
1989   *Native American Architecture.* Oxford University Press, New York and Oxford.

NILES, SUSAN
1988   Pachamama, Pachatata: Gender and Sacred Space in Amantani. In *The Role of Gender in Precolumbian Art and Architecture* (V. E. Miller, ed.): 135–151. University Press of America, Lanham, Md.

NORTON, PRESLEY
1984   La connexión Loma Alta. In *Tesoros del Ecuador antiguo*: 25–36. Instituto de Cooperación Iberoamericana y Museo Arqueológico Nacional, Madrid.
1992   Las culturas cerámicas prehispánicas del sur de Manabí. In *5000 Años de ocupación: Parque Nacional Machalilla* (P. Norton, ed.): 9–40. Centro Cultural Artes and Ediciones Abya-Yala, Quito.

NORTON, PRESLEY, RICHARD LUNNISS, AND NIGEL NAILING
1983   Excavaciones en Salango, provincia de Manabí, Ecuador. *Miscelánea Antropológica Ecuatoriana* 3: 9–72.

OCHOA, MYRIAM, STÉPHEN ROSTAIN, AND ERNESTO SALAZAR
1997   Montículos precolombinos en el Alto Upano. *Cultura: Revista del Banco Central del Ecuador* 2 (Segunda epoca): 54–61. Quito.

PARDUCCI Z., RESFA, AND JULIO BURGOS
1982   *Instrumentos musicales de viento del litoral ecuatoriano prehispánico.* Comisión Permanente para la Defensa del Patrimonio Cultural, Guayaquil.

PARDUCCI Z., RESFA, AND IBRAHIM PARDUCCI Z.
1975   Vasijas y elementos diagnósticos: Fase Guayaquil. *Cuadernos de historia y*

arqueología 42: 155–284. Publicación de la Casa de la Cultura Ecuatoriana, Núcleo del Guayas, and Museos del Banco Central del Ecuador, Guayaquil.

PAULSEN, ALLISON C.

1974   The Thorny Oyster and the Voice of God: *Spondylus* and *Strombus* in Andean Prehistory. *American Antiquity* 39(4): 597–607.

1977   Patterns of Maritime Trade between South Coastal Ecuador and Western Mesoamerica, 1500 B.C.–A.D. 600. In *The Sea in the Pre-Columbian World* (E. Benson, ed.): 141–166. Dumbarton Oaks, Washington D.C.

POLLOCK, DONALD

1992   Culina Shamanism: Gender, Power, and Knowledge. In *Portals of Power: Shamanism in South America* (E. Jean Matteson Langdon and Gerhard Baer, eds.): 25–40. University of New Mexico Press, Albuquerque.

RAYMOND, J. SCOTT

1993   Ceremonialism in the Early Formative of Ecuador. In *El mundo ceremonial andino* (L. Millones and Y. Onuki, eds.): 25–43. Senri Ethnological Studies 37. National Museum of Ethnology, Osaka.

REDMOND, ELSA M.

1994   *Tribal and Chiefly Warfare in South America*. Studies in Latin American Ethnohistory and Archaeology, vol. 5 (Joyce Marcus, gen. ed.): 28. Memoirs of the Museum of Anthropology, University of Michigan, Ann Arbor.

REHREN, THILO, AND MATHILDE TEMME

1992   Pre-Columbian Gold Processing at Putushio, South Ecuador: The Archaeometallurgical Evidence. In *Archaeometry of Pre-Columbian Sites and Artifacts. Proceedings of a Symposium, UCLA Institute of Archaeology* (David A. Scott and Pieter Meyers, eds.): 267–283. Getty Conservation Institute, Los Angeles.

REICHEL-DOLMATOFF, GERARDO

1953   Contactos y cambios culturales en la Sierra Nevada de Santa Marta. *Revista Colombiana de Antropología* 1(1): 17–122.

1961   Anthropomorphic Figurines from Colombia, Their Magic and Art. In *Essays in Pre-Columbian Art and Archaeology* (Samuel K. Lothrop et al.): 229–241. Harvard University Press, Cambridge.

1971   *Amazonian Cosmos*. University of Chicago Press, Chicago.

1976   Cosmology as Ecological Analysis: A View from the Rain Forest. *Man: Journal of the Royal Anthropological Institute* 11: 307–318.

1988   *Goldwork and Shamanism: An Iconographic Study of the Gold Museum*. Editorial Colina. Compañía Litográfica Nacional, Medellín.

RICHARDSON, JAMES B.

1978   Early Man on the Peruvian North Coast, Early Maritime Exploitation and the Pleistocene and Holocene Environment. In *Early Man in America from a Circum-Pacific Perspective* (A. L. Bryan, ed.): 274–289. Occasional Papers 1, Department of Anthropology, University of Alberta, Edmonton, Alberta.

RICHARDSON, JAMES B., AND C. BARRINGTON BROWN

n.d.   El Estero Site, *T*-Shaped Ground Stone Axes and Stone Bowls. Paper presented at the 32nd Annual Meeting of the Society for American Archaeology, Ann Arbor, Mich., 1967.

ROOSEVELT, ANNA C.
    1988   Interpreting Certain Female Images in Prehistoric Art. In *The Role of Gender in Precolumbian Art and Architecture* (V. E. Miller, ed.): 1–34. University Press of America, Lanham, Md.

ROVERE, FRANCO
    1977   El peinado y las posiciones corporales. *Mundo Shuar: Serie B, Fasciculo 12.* Centro de Documentación, Investigación y Publicaciones, Sucua (Morona Santiago), Ecuador.

SANDWEISS, DANIEL H.
    1996   Mid-Holocene Cultural Interaction between the North Coast of Peru and Ecuador. *Latin American Antiquity* 7(1): 41–50.

SHARON, DOUGLAS
    1978   *Wizard of the Four Winds: A Shaman's Story*. Free Press, New York.

SHARON, DOUGLAS, AND CHRISTOPHER B. DONNAN
    1974   Shamanism in Moche Iconography. In *Ethnoarchaeology* (C. Donnan and C. William Clewlow Jr., eds.): 51–77. Archaeological Survey, Monograph 4, Institute of Archaeology, University of California, Los Angeles.

SPECTOR, JANET, AND MARY K. WHELAN
    1989   Incorporating Gender into Archaeology Courses. In *Gender and Anthropology: Critical Reviews for Research and Teaching* (Sandra Morgen, ed.): 65–94. American Anthropological Association, Washington, D.C.

STAHL, PETER W.
    1984   *Tropical Forest Cosmology: The Cultural Context of the Early Valdivia Occupations at Loma Alta*. Ph.D. dissertation, University of Illinois at Urbana–Champaign. University Microfilms International, Ann Arbor, Mich.

    1985a   The Hallucinogenic Basis of Early Valdivia Phase Ceramic Bowl Iconography. *Journal of Psychoactive Drugs* 17(2): 105–123.

    1985b   Native American Cosmology in Archaeological Interpretation: Tropical Forest Cosmology and the Early Valdivia Phase at Loma Alta. In *Status, Structure and Stratification: Current Archaeological Reconstructions* (M. Thompson, M. T. Garcia, and F. Kense, eds.): 31–37. Archaeological Association, University of Calgary, Calgary, Alberta.

    1986   Hallucinatory Imagery and the Origin of Early South American Figurine Art. *World Archaeology* 18(1): 134–150.

STALLER, JOHN E.
    1994   *Late Valdivia Occupation in Southern Coastal El Oro Province, Ecuador: Excavations at the Early Formative Period (3500–1500 B.C.) Site of La Emerenciana*. Ph.D. dissertation, Southern Methodist University. University Microfilms International, Ann Arbor, Mich.

STOTHERT, KAREN E.
    1985   The Preceramic Las Vegas Culture of Coastal Ecuador. *American Antiquity* 50 (3): 613–637.

    1988   *La prehistoria temprana de la península de Santa Elena: Cultura Las Vegas*. Miscelánea Antropológica Ecuatoriana, Serie Monográfica 10. Museos del Banco Central del Ecuador, Guayaquil.

1993   *Un sitio de Guangala temprano en el suroeste del Ecuador.* National Museum of Natural History, Smithsonian Institution, Washington, D.C., and Museo Antropológico, Banco Central del Ecuador, Guayaquil.

1995   Las albarradas tradicionales y el manejo de aguas en la Península de Santa Elena. *Miscelánea Antropológica Ecuatoriana* 8: 131–160.

1999   Women and Religion (Figurines; Pebble Imagery of the Lower Pecos; The Transformation of Imagery in Coastal Ecuador; and New Worship and New Roles). In *Women in Ancient America* (Karen Olsen Bruhns and Karen E. Stothert): 189–204. University of Oklahoma Press, Norman.

n.d.   Informe preliminar de excavaciones en el Sitio OGSE-46B, La Libertad. Report presented to the Museo Antropológico, Banco Central del Ecuador, Guayaquil, August 1994.

STOTHERT, KAREN E., AND ANA MARITZA FREIRE
1997   *Sumpa: Historia de la Península de Santa Elena.* Banco Central del Ecuador y Plan Internacional Guayaquil, Guayaquil.

STOUT, DAVID B.
1948   The Chocó. In *Handbook of South American Indians* (J. H. Steward, ed.) 4: 269–276. Bureau of American Ethnology, Bulletin 143, Smithsonian Institution. U.S. Government Printing Office, Washington, D.C.

SULLIVAN, LAWRENCE E.
1988   *Icanchu's Drum: An Orientation to Meaning in South American Religions.* Macmillan, New York.

TEMME, MATHILDE
n.d.   El Formativo en Putushio—Sierra sur del Ecuador. Unpublished report, Museo Antropologico, Banco Central del Ecuador, Guayaquil, 1993.

TOPIC, JOHN R., AND THERESA LANGE TOPIC
1997   Hacía una comprensión conceptual de la guerra andina. In *Arqueología, antropología e historia en los Andes: Homenaje a María Rostworowski* (Rafael Varón Gabia and Javier Flores Espinoza, eds.). Instituto de Estudios Peruanos y Banco Central de Reserva del Perú, Lima.

UBELAKER, DOUGLAS H.
1988   Human Remains from OGSE-46 La Libertad, Guayas Province, Ecuador. *Journal of the Washington Academy of Sciences* 78(1): 3–16.

El Universo
1996   [Encuentro internacional de chamanes]. 5 de agosto, Primera sección, 12.

URTON, GARY
1985   *Animal Myths and Metaphors in South America.* University of Utah Press, Salt Lake City.

VALDEZ, FRANCISCO, AND DIEGO VEINTIMILLA
1992   *Amerindian Signs: 5000 Years of Precolumbian Art in Ecuador.* Dinediciones, Quito.

VILLALBA, MARCELO
1988   *Cotocollao: Una aldea formativa del valle de Quito.* Serie Monográfica 2, Miscelánea Antropológica Ecuatoriana. Museos del Banco Central del Ecuador, Quito.

Karen E. Stothert

WEINTZ, STEVEN C. F., J. WATERBERRY, ERICK LÓPEZ, AND PRESLEY NORTON
 n.d.   A Bird Burial from an Early Context in Coastal Ecuador, 1991.

WHITTEN, DOROTHEA S., AND NORMAN E. WHITTEN JR.
 1988   From Myth to Creation: Art from Amazonian Ecuador. University of Illinois Press,
         Urbana.

WHITTEN JR., NORMAN E.
 1976   Sacha Runa: Ethnicity and Adaptation of Ecuadorian Jungle Quichua. University
         of Illinois Press, Urbana.
 1978   Ecological Imagery and Cultural Adaptability: The Canelos Quichua of
         Eastern Ecuador. American Anthropologist 80: 836–859.
 1985   Sicuanga Runa: The Other Side of Development in Amazonian Ecuador. University
         of Illinois Press, Urbana.
 1987   Sacha Runa: Etnicidad y adaptación de los Quichua hablantes de la Amazonía
         ecuatoriana (Ileana Soto, Luis Uriarte, Annette de Uriarte, and Diego Quiroga,
         trans.). Ediciones Abya-Yala, Quito.

WILBERT, JOHANNES
 1975   Warao Basketry: Form and Function. Occasional Papers of the Museum of
         Cultural History 3, University of California, Los Angeles.
 1987   Tobacco and Shamanism in South America. Yale University Press, New Haven,
         Conn.

WING, ELIZABETH S.
 1988   Dusicyon Sechurae en contextos arqueológicos tempranos. In La prehistoria
         temprana de la Península de Santa Elena: Cultura Las Vegas (K. Stothert, ed.):
         179–186. Serie Monográfica 10, Miscelánea Antropológica Ecuatoriana. Banco
         Central del Ecuador, Guayaquil.

ZEDEÑO, MARÍA NIEVES
 n.d.   Análisis de cerámica Chorrera del Sitio Peñon del Río. Tésis de grado, Escuela
         Superior Politécnica del Litoral, Escuela de Arqueología, Guayaquil, 1985.

ZEIDLER, JAMES
 1984   Social Space in Valdivia Society: Community Patterning and Domestic Structure at
         Real Alto, 3000–2000 B.C. Ph.D. dissertation, University of Illinois at Urbana–
         Champaign. University Microfilms International, Ann Arbor, Mich.
 1986   La evolución local de asentamientos formativos en el litoral ecuatoriano: El
         caso de Real Alto. In Arqueología de la costa ecuatoriana: Nuevos enfoques (J. G.
         Marcos, ed.): 85–127. Corporación Editora Nacional, Quito.
 1988   Feline Imagery, Stone Mortars, aned Formative Period Interaction Spheres in
         the Northern Andean Area. Journal of Latin American Lore 14(2): 243–283.
 1994   Archaeological Testing in the Middle Jama Valley. In Regional Archaeology in
         Northern Manabi, Ecuador, vol. 1: Environment, Cultural Chronology, and Prehistoric
         Subsistence in the Jama River Valley (James A. Zeidler and Deborah M. Pearsall,
         eds.): 71–98. Memoirs in Latin American Archaeology 8. University of
         Pittsburgh, Pittsburgh, Pa.

ZEIDLER, JAMES, PETER STAHL, AND MARIE SUTLIFF
 1998   Shamanistic Elements in a Terminal Valdivia Burial, Northern Manabí, Ecuador:
         Implications for Mortuary Symbolism and Social Ranking. In Recent Advances

in the *Archeology of the Northern Andes: In Memory of Gerardo Reichel-Dolmatoff* (Augusto Oyuela-Caycedo and J. Scott Raymond, eds.): 109–120. Institute of Archaeology, University of California, Los Angeles.

ZEIDLER, JAMES, AND MARIE J. SUTLIFF

1994   Definition of Ceramic Complexes and Cultural Occupation in the Jama Valley. In *Regional Archaeology in Northern Manabi, Ecuador,* vol. 1: *Environment, Cultural Chronology, and Prehistoric Subsistence in the Jama River Valley* (James A. Zeidler and Deborah M. Pearsall, eds.): 111–130. Memoirs in Latin American Archaeology 8. University of Pittsburgh, Pittsburgh, Pa.

ZEVALLOS MENÉNDEZ, CARLOS

1965/66   Nota preliminar sobre el cementerio Chorrera, Bahía de Santa Elena, Ecuador. *Revista del Museo Nacional* (Peru) 34: 20–27.

1995   Un cementerio Chorrera. Fase Engoroy en la Bahía de Santa Elena "Los Cerritos." In *Nuestras Raices Guancavilcas* (C. Zevallos): 139–182. Casa de la Cultura Ecuatoriana "Benjamín Carrión," Núcleo del Guayas, Guayaquil.

ZEVALLOS MENÉNDEZ, CARLOS, AND OLAF HOLM

1960   *Excavaciones arqueológicas en San Pablo: Informe preliminar.* Editorial Casa de la Cultura Ecuatoriana, Núcleo del Guayas, Guayaquil.

ZUIDEMA, TOM

1992   The Tairona of Ancient Colombia. *The Ancient Americas: Art from Sacred Landscapes* (Richard Townsend, ed.): 245–257. Art Institute of Chicago, Chicago.

Nature as Culture's Representation: A Change of Focus in Late Formative Iconography

TOM CUMMINS

HARVARD UNIVERSITY

INTRODUCTION

Chorrera—as a culture, as an art style, as a concept—occupies a distinct place in the definition of Ecuador's Formative period. Whereas Valdivia has garnered for Ecuador pride of place in the New World because of its early agricultural development and ceramic production, Chorrera can be said to define Ecuador as a place with a distinct, self-contained culture and society. These are the necessary qualities that lend themselves to historical precedent and give mythic definition and boundaries to the modern nation state. Emilio Estrada (1958) was clear about this role when he defined Chorrera:

> Chorrera is the quintessential Ecuadorian culture—it was the most extensive of cultures and the initiatior of traits that later evolved into other, more recent cultures of the country. It maintained relations with Mesoamerica and Chavín, in Peru, but was sufficiently authochtonous to affirm that it is the nucleus of our national identity. Its iridescent ceramics have no equal in any other country. Technologically highly developed, it was extensive and covered a great part of the Ecuadorian coast.[1] (trans. eds.)

[1] Chorrea es la cultura netamente ecuatoriana—es la más extendida y es la iniciadora de rasgos que evolucionaron posteriormente hacia otras culturas más modernas del país. Guarda relación con Mesoamérica y con Chavín en Perú, pero es suficientemente autóctona para afirmar que es núcleo de la nacionalidad nuestra. Su cerámica iridiscente no tiene igual en ningún otro país. Altamente desarrollada tecnológicamente, fue muy extendida y cubrió gran parte del litoral de Ecuador (Estrada 1958: 12-13).

Evans and Meggers agreed with Estrada's position and restated it in 1971: "La cultura Chorrera fue descrita por Estrada como 'el verdadero fundamento de la nacionalidad propiamente ecuatoriana' por dos razones 1) es la primera tradición que se la encuentra distribuìda sobre la mayor parte del país, y 2) sirvió como base común del cual se desarrollaron y se diferenciaron los diferentes complejos del Periódo Desarrollo Regional" (Evans and Meggers 1982: 124).

423

Chorrera in the 1950s performed the same role for Estrada's Ecuador as Chavín did for Tello's Peru[2] and Olmec did for Covarrubias's Mexico.[3] Each ancient culture was attributed a generative power that extended beyond its own historical time and geographic space. For Ecuador, this attribution was particularly important for its cultural self-image in that the Formative past went from being a passive or receptive—feminine—culture[4] to an active or generative—masculine—culture that disseminated its seed to Mexico and Peru.[5]

Chorrera, however, unlike Olmec or Chavín, has not translated into sustained archaeological investigation. There is no Chavín de Huantar or La Venta for Chorrera, no defining site that, in addition to producing a cluster of attributes physically identifying the culture, spatially captures the historical imagination despite the existence of the site of Chorrera (Fig. 1). So, 13 years after Estrada linked Chorrera to an Ecuadorian national identity, his colleagues Clifford Evans and Betty Meggers (1982: 121) wrote:

[2] "Logró así adaptarse al medio geográfico asegurar su conservación y progreso y echar los fundamentos de una nacionalidad, y una civilización típica: la civilización aborigen andina." (Tello 1923: 123).

[3] "It is possible to establish a common early horizon for Middle and South America, with elaborate mother cultures—'Olmec' and Chavín—which must have been largely instrumental in the development and characterization of Middle American and Andean civilizations" (Covarrubias 1954: 79–80).

[4] Estrada participated in the formation of the theory that Valdivia ceramics were brought from Japan by Jomon fisherman (Meggers, Evans, and Estrada 1965) and is even credited with the theory (Meggers 1966: 43).

[5] Estrada's positioning of Chorrera as the generative culture of Ecuador is not held by all. Meggers, who worked with Estrada, posited a diametrically opposed view, suggesting that Chorrera, like Valdivia, originated from someplace else:

> The evidence to postulate Mesoamerican influence is much like that used to reconstruct the transpacific origin of the Valdivia Phase. The same coastal currents that brought the Jomon canoe to the coast of Ecuador brought the Mesoamericans to nearly the same place. The immigrants must have encountered both Valdivia and Machalillia Phase villagers; why they joined forces only with the latter is a puzzle that may never be solved. Whatever the reason the Valdivia Phase became extinct, and subsequent Ecuadorian cultures show no traces of its influence. (Meggers 1966: 62)

Lathrap, Collier, and Chandra (1975), on the other hand, argue the reverse:

> The early dating of the Ecuadorian examples, as well as other evidence for Ecuadorian influence on Mesoamerica discussed elsewhere in this text, leads to the conclusion that the figurine tradition of Mesoamerica was directly derived from that of the Ecuadorian (Chorrera) Formative.

Marcos, on the other hand, attributes Machalilla with being the Formative culture that put Ecuador on the New World archaeological stage: "Posiblemente Machalilla fue una de las más influyentes expresiones en la cerámica del Nuevo Mundo (Marcos 1983: 14).

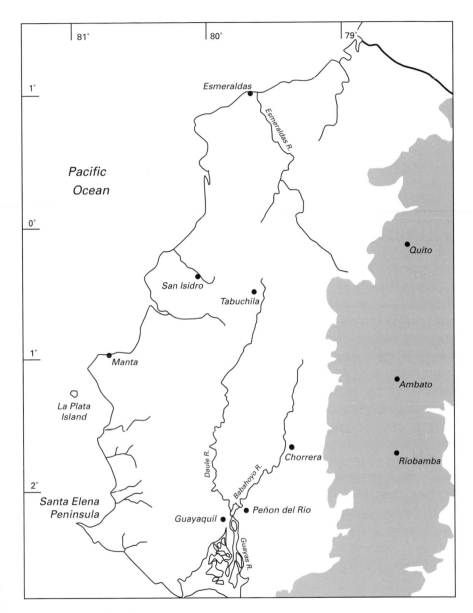

Fig. 1   Map of Ecuador.

425

conjuntamente con Tutishcainyo en el este del Perú y Barrancoide en la desbocadura del Orinoco, la Cultura Chorrera del Ecuador ha sido más frecuentemente discutida, en base de menos datos publicados que cualquier otro complejo cerámico Formativo sudamericano.[6]

Another 12 years later, the situation had improved only marginally so that Jorge Marcos (1983) could write:

en comparación con lo que sabemos sobre la cultura Valdivia, la cultura Chorrera con su magnífica cerámica se mantiene enigmática con referencia a su estructura social, tamaño de la aldea, patrón de asentamiento y vida diaria.

The same could be said for the interpretive analysis of Chorrera ceramics.[7] Even today, almost 40 years after Estrada's comments, we have advanced only slightly in our knowledge, with the published results from San Isidro in northern Manabí (Zeidler and Pearsall 1994) and the Guayas basin site of Peñon del Río (Nieves Zedeño n.d.).

Yet in the same 40 years of minimal archaeological work at Chorrera sites, excavations for certain kinds of Chorrera ceramic objects have increased almost expedientially in order to meet the market demands of private and public collections, giving a specificity and materiality to the claims made about Chorrera. These are the fine vessels and figurines that Estrada first used to categorize Chorrera as being a culture that was "altamente desarrollada tecnológicamente [highly developed technologically]" and had caught the general public's attention (Fig. 2). Donald Lathrap recognized the comparative aesthetic value of this type of Chorrera ceramics in the catalog for the 1976 Field Museum of Natural History exhibition of the Norton/Pérez collection, which now belongs to the Banco del Pacífico in Guayaquil. In regard to the human figures (Fig. 3), he wrote: "The hollow Chorrera figurines are a high point in the ceramic art of the New World" (Lathrap et al. 1975: 41). About the vessels (Fig. 4), he was equally enthusiastic: "The lively, realistic sculpture embodied in

[6] This paper was originally presented in 1971 at the Primer Simposio de Correlaciones Antropólogicas Andino–Mesoamericano in Salinas, Ecuador, but proceedings were not published until 1982; see also Bischof (1982), which attempts to differentiate areas of regional Chorrerea style.

[7] Interpretive analysis of Valdivia ceramics and ceramic designs (Damp 1982, 1984, 1988; Lathrap et al. 1975; Marcos 1973; Stahl 1985, 1986), as well as Valdivia sites (Damp 1988; Lathrap, Marcos, and Zeidler 1976), are much more developed than the far fewer studies of Chorrera ceramics (Cummins 1992, 1994; Cummins and Holm 1991; Lathrap et al. 1975) and sites (Nieves Zedeño n.d.).

Fig. 2   Chorrera vessel with spiral wall and bridge spout; 16.1 x 16.2 cm. Museo del Banco Central del Ecuador, Guayaquil (GA 3-273-77).

Fig. 3   Chorrera standing female figurine with tattoo or face painting. Hollow, partially mold-made with red slip; 27.7 x 11.8 cm. Museo del Banco Central del Ecuador, Guayaquil (GA 1-1286-79).

Fig. 4   Chorrera hollow bird vessel with whistling bridge spout handle and cream slip; 22.1 x 14.6 x 30 cm. Museo del Banco Central del Ecuador, Guayaquil (GA 1-2141-82).

427

Fig. 5   Chorrera hollow vessel in the form of a coati with a whistling bridge spout; resist painting; 18 x 15 cm. Museo del Banco Central del Ecuador, Guayaquil (GA 2-79-76).

the Chorrera whistling bottles is a summit in New World ceramic art (Lathrap et al. 1975: 59).

There are, to be sure, several reasons why these ceramic objects are aesthetically compelling. They are finely crafted, exhibiting qualities of refinement across a broad spectrum such as iridescent paint (Fig. 5), sculptural handling, expanded iconographic motifs, vessel forms, and the whistling spout. Many of these attributes have been used to indicate Chorrera's contact with both Peru and Mesoamerica, some scholars positing that these technologies were introduced from outside (Meggers 1966: 62) and others, like Estrada, suggesting (Lathrap et al. 1975: 53) that they were transferred from Ecuador to other areas. The status of their origination and diffusion is not, however, of concern for an interpretive study of the object unless an overt reference is made to that origin as part of the object's ontology. Most radically, this appears in the form of direct copying, best recognized in the intentionally archaized pieces produced in both Peru and Mexico (Burger 1976; Rowe 1971; Umberger 1987). But too little is known about pre-Columbian Ecuador to suggest that such practices occurred there as well.[8] Rather, what is important for an interpretive analysis of Chorrera

---

[8]   The continuous use of molds from Chorrera to the colonial period for figurine making permits the possibility that later cultures may have reemployed earlier molds to produce figurines that were stylistically distinct from their own. However, there is no evidence for this. We do know, however, that ancient ceramic figurines were recovered from areas washed by the sea and used by natives well into the 18th century. Fray Juan de Santa Gertrudis visited these *tolas*, or mounds, on the north coast of Ecuador in the 18th century and noted that Indians went to the mounds where they collected "por regular varias figuritas hechas de barro con mucha perfección." (cited in Barney-Cabera 1975: 224–225).

ceramics, I believe, is a description of Chorrera form and style, and the images they produce within the culture for which they were meaningful. We know, for example, that spondylus and strombus are shell goods from the coastal waters of Ecuador, but their use and meaning in Peruvian art and mythology do not make external reference to that origin (Marcos 1977/1978; Murra 1975; Paulsen 1974). The exchange network by which they were acquired surely factored into their meaning as valued sacred entities; however, that does not mean they maintained any semblance of their significance of the culture, time, or place from which they originated.[9] As Arjun Appadurai wrote:

> [There] is the constant tension between the existing frameworks (of price, bargaining, and so forth) and the tendency to breach these frameworks. This tension itself has its source in the fact that not all parties share the same 'interests' in any specific regime of value, nor are the interests of any two parties in a given exchange identical. (Appadurai 1986: 57)

Whatever contribution Chorrera iconography and style made to Peruvian or Mesoamerican artistic representation may rest on some trade network that disseminated objects well beyond the cultural orbit of their production. But Appadurai's point is that frameworks through which they were received do not ensure that their significance remains constant or stable.

TOWARD AN INTERPRETIVE FRAMEWORK OF CHORRERA FIGURAL CERAMICS

What I, as an art historian, discuss here are the Chorreran "interests" that seem to be visually exhibited in their finest ceramic pieces and what might be said about those "interests," recognizing that it is precisely these "interests" that in grand part contribute to both the scholarly and public image of Chorrera. This means recognizing that in the elaborate Chorrera ceramic pieces a refinement in style, technology, and expressive content goes beyond earlier Formative ceramic traditions. Moreover, the refinement seems directed toward a purposeful concern with the object's physical qualities: its color, shape, texture, and sound. These qualities seem to be brought into play so as to elicit an experiential relationship to the vessel by drawing different sensory attention to the

---

[9] This seems to be true for the central and southern areas of Peru, but there seems to be direct reference to the collection of these shells in Chimu art and architecture from the north coast of Peru (Cordy-Collins 1990; Marcos and Norton 1981: 148; Pillsbury 1996). In this case there is sustained, direct experience with the place of origin of these luxury goods that would enter into their meaning for the area's inhabitants.

object: visual, tactile, auricular, and perceptual. The sensual focus on the object's physical qualities is also coupled with an expansion of motifs in Chorrera ceramics that seems to emphasize a heightened sense of direct observation of selected elements of the natural environment. This is manifested not only in the iconography but also by a stylized realism that exhibits some regional variation, yet nonetheless transcends these differences. The broad use of realistic style allows for a descriptive visual analysis of a varied sample of ceramic types on the basis of this commonality and at the same time recognizing that there surely were regional differences.[10] Furthermore, there is, I believe, a conceptual coherency between the physical qualities of Chorrera ceramics and the general focus of Chorrera representation and iconography that tends toward an idealized state of the "natural" world. Chorrera "realism" in this sense is different from the "realism" of Valdivia 3 through 6 ceramics, as described by Zevallos Menéndez (1971: 22) and others (Lathrap et al. 1975).

The analytical focus of this essay, therefore, is limited to the internal consistencies of Chorrera style and iconography in relation to realism; and it does not attempt to track the antecedents in Valdivia and Machalilla in any systematic fashion. Therefore, this study does not consider Chorrera in some teleological sense, but as a corpus of cultural objects united by an expressive logic that at some level can be articulated through descriptive terms of the shared formal and iconographic features. The formal characteristics of Chorrera realism are what render these ceramics pieces aesthetically pleasing for contemporary appreciation; however, more importantly, these characteristics seem to indicate a different expression of the pre-Hispanic Ecuadorian coastal perception of cosmological experience in relation to the object itself. It is this different plastic expression of perception that continued into subsequent Ecuadorian coastal ceramic traditions allowing Estrada to claim Chorrera as "a purely Ecuadorian culture . . . and the initiator of traits that evolved toward other more modern cultures of the country." Estrada is correct in that many formal and technical innovations carried through to subsequent Ecuadorian ceramic traditions. At the same time, some fundamental differences separate Chorrera ceramic representations from those that follow. For, whereas later Ecuadorian cultures tended to emphasize cultural objects in ceramic representation, the major Chorreran expression focused primarily on "natural" things, including the human figure, making for a different expressive relationship in ceramic figurines between realism, culture, and nature than that which comes later.[11]

[10] The "sample" of Chorrera is impressionistic rather than scientific in that the ceramics I studied by and large came from already formed collections rather than archaeological excavations.
[11] As I have discussed elsewhere (Cummins 1992: 74–81), the ceramic figurines of the

All of my observations, comments, and analysis must derive from a close study of the objects themselves because, although the majority of examples either come from buried offerings or an elaborate funerary context of shaft tombs as described by the *huaqueros* who found them (James Zeidler, personal communication, 1997), few examples have been scientifically excavated. Even the recent excavations at San Isidro in Manabí, one of the areas known to be a major source of fine Chorrera ceramics, have not yielded examples of this type of Chorrera ceramics (Zeidler and Sutliff 1994: 115). Nor are there any examples recorded from the site of Peñon del Río (Nieves Zedeño n.d.: 122–123). Only Estrada, in discussing the Chorrera ceramics coming from Tabuchila (1957: 82–86; 1958: 69), which include zoomorphic whistling spout vessels with iridescent decoration, mentioned the context in which they were found: "fueron obtenidas de sepulcros hechos con lajas de piedras, los que se nos asegura hay en la zona de Manta [they were obtained from tombs made from stone slabs we were sure were found in the Manta region]" (1957: 86).[12] All my interpretive comments must perforce be phrased in the conditional. Nonetheless, the objects themselves present compelling evidence for venturing the interpretations.

I begin my descriptive analysis of Chorrera ceramic representation with the human figurine (Fig. 6). It serves as an introduction to what I mean by a more idealized state of the "natural" world because the human figurine is one of the earliest representational ceramic forms in Ecuador. In fact, small solid figurines were still produced, and they exhibit the continuation of many Valdivia characteristics (Lathrap et al. 1975: 41). However, hollow and larger figurines (up to 40 cm), which first appeared in the preceding Machalilla phase (Fig. 7), also form a part of the Chorrera corpus. Like Valdivia and Machalilla examples, the major emphasis is on an immobile female figure, although males are also represented. Most examples are depicted naked and posed standing with arms held at the side at a slight diagonal (Fig. 8). The rigid appearance of the figure comes from the bilateral symmetry organized along a central vertical axis.[13] There is,

---

Regional Development, especially Jama-Coaque, are oriented iconographically toward a display of symbolic objects, many of which are already found archaeologically in a Chorrera context but do not occur in Chorrera ceramic representation.

[12] Many of the best pieces that formed the Norton Presley collection are said to come from the Río Chico area. Until there is better archaeological evidence, it is difficult to establish the exact distribution of the more elaborate Chorrera ceramics. However, they tend to come from central and northern Manabí. This collection now forms a part of the collection of the Banco del Pacífico, Guayaquil.

[13] In many cases single piece molds were used to make the front of the figure, and the back was modeled by hand (Cummins 1994; Holm and Crespo 1980:150), a technological feature that continued until the Spanish Conquest and beyond (Estrada 1957).

Fig. 6 (*above, left*) Chorrera "standing" figurine in the form of a female. Hollow, partially mold-made with red slip and incised abstract design; 32 x 14.2 cm. Banco del Pacífico, Guayaquil.

Fig. 7 (*above, right*) Machalilla "standing" figurine in the form of a female. Ears, lips, and shoulders perforated for metal adornments, hollow, cream-colored slip with red slip paint for body decoration; 21 x 12.5 cm. Museo del Banco Central del Ecuador, Guayaquil (GA 1-222-82).

Fig. 8 (*lower, left*) Chorrera "standing" figurine in the form of a female. Hollow, red, and buff slip; 34.5 x 15 cm. Banco del Pacífico, Guayaquil.

however, greater general attention to human physiognomy than before. The facial plane is more rounded and the primary features—nose, eyes, and mouth— although generalized forms, are nonetheless raised or recessed in more or less correct proportion. The dimensions and shapes of the arms and legs are not anatomically precise; yet the much greater attention to surface detail and modulation of the surface plane suggest the structure of musculature below the surface. The anatomical articulation of sculptural volume allows the surface to become recognized independently and as a part of the body. Therefore, it can be marked and differentiated by color and/or incision into zones of unadorned skin, or areas that are tattooed, painted (Holm 1953), or clothed. These features and the negative space created by the independent arms and legs give Chorrera figurines a much greater three-dimensional appearance and less architectonic structure than their antecedents. The more corporeal appearance suggests the dynamic potential of movement. This potential is fully realized in other pieces that radically depart from the traditional standing pose in which the body is shown in a variety of poses and sometimes in contorted movement (Fig. 9).

Even in the more traditional figurines (Fig. 10), the added detail and sculptural handling imply a different cultural relationship to the figurine, perhaps

Fig. 9 Chorrera figurine/vessel in the form of a male in a contorted position. Red slip, bridge spout handle with whistle; 20.4 cm. Museo del Banco Central del Ecuador, Guayaquil (1-12-84).

Fig. 10 (*left*) Chorrera female standing figure with painted or tattooing around the eyes; hollow with brownish and cream slip; 37.7 x 13.4 cm. Museo del Banco Central del Ecuador, Guayaquil (GA 16-916-78).

Fig. 11 (*opposite, left*) Chorrera–La Tolita transitional hollow, seated female figurine holding a small human figure in her lap. Museo del Banco Central del Ecuador, Guayaquil.

Fig. 12 (*opposite, right*) Chorrera bottle-shaped vessel with monkey head and bridge spout. Excavated by Jorge Marcos and Presley Norton on La Plata Island; 13 cm. Museo del Banco Central del Ecuador, Guayaquil. Photo by Kenneth Griffiths.

beginning in the Machalilla period but more fully articulated in Chorrera ceramics. These pieces suggest both a closer visual correspondence between the image and what it represents and the demand of the viewer's recognition of that correspondence. The viewer is meant to see the burnished surface and different colors. The figurine's volume demands the recognition of independent presence. All this suggests that these figurines may have had a more autonomous or iconic function, made specially to be placed in graves, as Estrada's observation made clear, as well as forming ritual caches, or being set up in sacred precincts. None of these possibilities is mutually exclusive, and each one might have provided a spatial context in which the figurines performed as some kind of visible presence of the sacred in a locus of interaction between object and viewer.

A late transitional-style Chorrera figurine, a female seated with another smaller human figure held in her lap (Fig. 11), clearly conveys a relationship of both presence and presentation. The figurine also suggests a type of image that was interpreted at the time of contact as having an iconic status (Cummins 1992: 68). De Sámano and de Xerez (1528/1842: 200) recorded that a female figure with a child in her lap was kept in a temple on an island just off the coast,

perhaps La Plata Island, to which natives brought offerings in order to be cured of their ailments.[14] Of course, this description must be read through Christian pilgrimage practices and images of the Madonna and Child, but such a reading is understandable if the 16th-century image was anything like this Chorrera piece. Equally important, La Plata Island was not just a late Integration period pilgrimage site. It had been used as a ceremonial center even before the Chorrera time period and continued to be visited throughout the pre-Hispanic period as a place of pan-coastal religious importance. It is no accident that one of the few archaeologically excavated fine Chorrera ceramics, a whistling vessel with a monkey figure (Fig. 12), was found on the island, in a Machalilla platform

[14] De Sámano and de Xerez (1842 [1528]: 200) mention four villages on the coast under the control "de un Señor, que son Çalangone y Tusco y Seracapez y Çalango . . . Hay una isla en la [sic] mar junto a los pueblos donde tienen una casa de oración hecha a manera de tienda de campo, toldada de muy ricas mantas labradas, adonde tienen un imágen de una mujer con un niño en los brazos que tiene por nombre Mara Mesa: cuando alguno tiene alguna enfermedad en algún miembro, hácele un miembro de plata ó oro, y ofrécesela, y le sacrifican delante de la imágen ciertas ovejas (llamas) en ciertos tiempos." Çalango is Salango of today, and the island of Salango is just offshore, whereas La Plata Island is some 40 km from Salango.

mound, which had been continuously reused as a ceremonial area (Marcos and Norton 1981: 146). Bahía, La Tolita, and Jama-Coaque figurines, all deriving from Chorrera forms, were also found in a different ceremonial deposit at the same site (Marcos and Norton 1981: 147).[15]

Whether any kind of sacred Chorrera precinct was set up on La Plata Island or elsewhere, in which an image functioned as the focus of ritual practice as described by de Sámano and de Xerez, is certainly not clear. The offertory cache of figurines uncovered by Marcos and Norton is, however, suggestive. Moreover, figurines similar to the Chorrera example (Fig. 11) come from the intervening Regional Developmental period (300/200 B.C.–A.D. 700/800). The main figure, a seated female with outstretched legs, holds a smaller, rigid figure in her lap, which is unmistakably recognizable as a small male or female adult figure, representing either a human being or a figurine (Figs. 13a,b). In these pieces, there is a clear hierarchical relationship between the two figures that connotes the supernatural power of the sacred, which is to be recognized by a visual economy of scale.

The iconic concept exhibited in the Chorrera seated figure, as well as in other Chorrera human figurines, implies not only a formal difference but also a conceptual one. Here I am assuming that all highly elaborated ceramic objects operated within a religious ritual context so as to intensify experience, most probably based on a shamanic system.[16] However, shamanic practices and the way ceramic objects were understood to participate in these rituals need not have remained static throughout the Formative period. What, in fact, is significant about Chorrera figurines in an interpretive context is the fact that though few Chorrera figurines have been found in a controlled archaeological circumstance, it nonetheless may be suggested that they represent a change in function from those made and used in Valdivia rituals. This interpretation is due to their size and appearance and also by the state of their preservation. Unlike Valdivia figurines, the large hollow Chorrera ones, although often broken, have been found complete. This better state of preservation, in addition to greater

---

[15]   Stahl (1986:141–142) noted that both Dorsey (1901: 279) and Estrada (1962: 73) found numerous fragmented figurines and almost no utilitarian ceramics at La Plata, which further suggests that it may have been the ceremonial site de Sámano mentioned.

[16]   We, of course, have no real idea about the particular forms of Valdivia or Chorrera ritual practice other than the objects that by their form and decoration seem to have been used in distinctive ways. However, if ritual acts can be defined as "fundamentally a way of doing things to trigger perception that these practices are distinct (in comparison to other, usually more quotidian, practices) and the associations they engender are special" (Bell 1992: 74, 220), then ritual objects can suggest the distinctiveness of these practices and the kinds of perceptions that are to be triggered.

Fig. 13 (*left*) Bahía, seated female figurine with a small human figure playing a
flute in her lap; 26.7 cm. Museo del
Banco Central del Ecuador, Guayaquil
(GA 6–2200–80), and (*below*) detail.

formal detail, more complicated production techniques, and decorative features, implies that some figurines were not so actively used as their Valdivia counterparts. That is, whereas the vast majority of Valdivia figurines are found within a domestic context (Meggers and Evans 1958; Stahl 1986: 142; Zevallos Menéndez 1971) and seem to have been intentionally broken (Stahl 1986: 142-144), Chorrera examples are not found in this state, and they do not seem to occur significantly in domestic refuse.

It has been suggested that religious practitioners manipulated Valdivia figurines in rituals analogous to those performed in curing rites by contemporary shamans (Damp 1982; Evans and Meggers 1958; Lathrap et al. 1975: 47; Meggers 1966: 41; Stahl 1985, 1986). Sámano's and de Xerez's comments about the image on La Plata Island also suggest that cures were effected by the use of images, although his description sounds more like the Christian tradition of ex-*votos* than shamanic practice. Nonetheless, it is evident that certain Chorrera figurines were to be seen and handled differently from Valdivia examples. This is what I mean by the word *iconic*. According to the *Oxford English Dictionary*, *icon* refers to "an image, figure or representation." The Chorrera figurines manifest a greater iconic quality than their Valididvian and Machalilla predecessors in that there is greater artistic effort to make them appear more as the likeness of something else. That is, the Chorrera figurines are made to be seen as being in the likeness of something else, even though the figurines may have been understood to be what they represented. In the case of these Chorrera pieces, *extreme* likeness—as opposed to the *vague* likeness in Valdivia figurines—produces an image through which the sacred is to be accessed. Qualities of detail and surface are to be recognized, and as such the figurines are intended to be looked at independently from physical manipulation. This is evidenced in technique, curation, and appearance. This is different from Valdivia figurines whose ontology, as understood through archaeological evidence and ethnographic analogy, is as a physical object that simultaneously visualizes and manifests action and transaction. A Valdivia object is no less sacred or involved in ritual than a Chorrera one. But what they are is simply *different*.

It might be argued that the formal and iconographic differences seen in these Chorrera figurines are minor and are merely a continuation of traditions established in Valdivia and Machalilla, maintaining the same basic referential system. However, we must see the different handling of the human figure in relation to the greatly expanded representational field, focusing on plants and animals, and almost always found on whistling vessels (Fig. 14). If the human figurines and the figural whistling vessels are interpreted as relational elements in Chorrera imagery, as opposed to separate iconographic categories, then the

Fig. 14 Chorrera vessel with snail placed on a stepped platform; 14 cm. Banco del Pacífico, Guayaquil.

human figurines cannot be regarded as being simply an undifferentiated continuation of a tradition begun in Valdivia.[17]

The figural images incorporated into the corpus of the Chorrera whistling vessels are quite varied as to subject but are all handled in a similar way. The figures have a soft, swelling appearance achieved by rounded, highly burnished forms. There is clearly an idealized sense of a species type, as each figure seems to be represented at the moment of its completeness or maturity: the perfection of its being. The modern viewer recognizes this quality most clearly in the modeled representations of fruits and vegetables. Their surfaces seem to be stretched to their limits, and they contain, but just barely, the fullness within. These are the same qualities used to imbue the human figure but with a greater sense of realism. Although there seems to have been no attempt at individuation of features, many animal figures exhibit dynamic poses like the anteater

[17] The terms *Chorrera* and *Valdivia* are used here to denote temporally constituted archaeological Formative cultures defined by certain shared characteristics found over a geographical area. I cannot say whether Chorrera human figurines and Chorrera figural whistling pots were produced at the same time or even by people who had a shared cultural tradition in any meaningful sense for them. However, the ceramics were both produced within the area and time period of Chorrera, and both manifest enough similar stylistic characteristics to be seen in relation to one another as manifestations of common Chorrera ceramic concerns.

with its head tilted upward (Fig. 15) or the monkey twisting to look to its side (Fig. 16). Even the human figure, when combined with the whistling vessel, is contorted like an acrobat or bound prisoner (see Figs. 9, 17). The poses denote careful observation and lend a kinetic quality of realism to the idealized figures.

Some animal images are clearly meant to represent domesticated species such as dogs and monkeys, the only animals associated with a cultural artifact, some kind of necklace or collar (Figs. 18, 19).[18] Others, such as anteaters, owls, turtles, and pelicans might be classified as wild or at least undomesticated animals (Figs. 20, 21, 22, 23). Certain cultigens such as squash and pineapple, as well as insects and grubs, are also sculpted in the same style as the animals (Figs. 24, 25). Therefore, the relationship between the variety of species represented cannot be based upon what Lévi-Strauss called a "relationship of substance" (1966: 135), whereas this might be said of Valdivia figurines, which are overwhelmingly human and female. That is, just as the care and use of Chorrera figurines radically change, the basis of the relationship between one image and the others also seems to have changed in the late Formative period. Certainly Chorrera human figurines, many made in molds, suggest a continuation of seriality that is based upon a single type. However, this serialization is complicated because other figural images in the Chorrera corpus are radically different in their outward appearance: A squash does not appear as a human.

In whatever form of ritual context these figurines were used, their relationship as a set of images cannot be understood only within the analytical context of the ritual in the manner Damp (1982) and others have suggested for Valdivia figurines. The range of Chorrera types constitutes a selected group of images indicating that their reference reached beyond the immediacy of the ritual. Hence they were not themselves conditional objects whose physical and metaphysical state was meant to be transformed within the ritual itself, as seems to have been the case of Valdivia figurines and is the case of the eucharistic host in Roman Catholic ritual. Rather, the expanded iconography of Chorrera ceramics also seems to appeal to a "set of beliefs and practices directly or indirectly linked to classificatory schemes that allow the natural and social universe to be grasped as an organized whole" (Lévi-Strauss 1966: 135). It is a cosmology that allows the grub, turtle, bird, monkey, and human to be seen in a representational continuum (Lévi-Strauss 1966: 136). It is also probable that the

---

[18] Lathrap et al. (1975: 45) noted that many animals depicted in Chorrera ceramics may be types that were caught and raised as pets, and they specifically mentioned monkeys. Lathrap et al. also noted that many modern tropical forest communities keep such animals as pets. This does not explain, however, why they became the subject of Chorrera representation.

Fig. 15 Chorrera vessel in the form of an anteater; 21 cm. Collection of Iván Cruz, Quito.

Fig. 16 Chorrera whistling vessel with bridge spout in the form of a monkey; 45.3 x 17.2 cm. Museo del Banco Central del Ecuador, Guayaquil (GA 1-2270-82).

Fig. 17 Chorrera whistling vessel in the form of seated male with hands bound behind his back; 26.5 cm. Banco del Pacífico, Guayaquil.

Fig. 18 Chorrera whistling vessel in the shape of a dog; 27.5 cm. Banco del Pacífico, Guayaquil.

Fig. 19 Chorrera whistling vessel in the form of a howler spider monkey (*ateles paniscus*); 18.8 x 14.2 x 16 cm. Museo del Banco Central del Ecuador, Guayaquil (232-14-65).

system of classification existed in some similar manner in the myths of Valdivia and Machalilla cultures. But in this type of Chorrera ceramic production, made as permanent rather than ephemeral objects, the elements of this set of relationships are moved out of the structural order of oral myth into the physical presence of visual image. What initiated this material reification cannot be determined or even guessed, but it produced a type of visualization that was new in Formative Ecuador.

What is important about this visualization is that the system of relationship was based, in the images at least, on a classification that links all these categories through this idealized state; yet, it could maintain discrete and recognizable differences among each. Hybrid or fantastic shapes are rare; rather, one can recognize genus and species. That is, certain categories of direct observation are used to create distinctions between one form and another, and stylistic qualities are used to overrule those distinctions: A squash may appear different from a dog, but they exist equally in a perfect state.

The figuration of these elements is not part of any kind of visual narrative structure, however. Each figure appears discrete. One cannot, therefore, begin

Fig. 20 Chorrera whistling vessel in the form on an anteater; 25 cm. Banco del Pacífico, Guayaquil.

Fig. 21 Chorrera open neck vessel in the shape of an owl; 14.5 x 14.5 cm. Banco del Pacífico, Guayaquil.

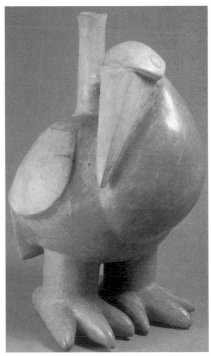

Fig. 22 Chorrera open neck vessel in the form of a turtle, one of a pair; 18 cm. Banco del Pacífico, Guayaquil.

Fig. 23 Chorrera vessel in the form of a pelican; 26.5 cm. Museo del Banco Central del Ecuador, Guayaquil.

to recover the classificatory system that underlies the appearance of the images nor the particularities of mythical discourse of which they are a part.[19] Yet at the same time, there is a rhetoric of realism employed in these images that is used not so as to create exact individual copies or duplicates from nature, but to create a cultural affinity among unlike natural entities.[20] There is a conscious choice not to distort anatomical characteristics or to metamorphose them into fantastic and imaginary qualities.

What is significant about this rhetoric is that it calls upon the sense of sight, a condition that recognizes implicitly, if not explicitly, the distinction between the viewer and the viewed, but without moving the relationship out of daily experience. The ceramic object becomes endowed with its own being because it is phenomenologically separate from the being of the viewer. This integrity seems to be marked by the careful preservation of these ceramics. More importantly, this condition of the vessel's "selfhood" is based not only upon being seen but also being touched and heard. Almost all these realistic representations of natural forms are incorporated into a vessel type whose long tubular spout is attached to one end of a looped handle (Fig. 26). A whistle was usually formed at the join of the vessel handle, and it makes a soft, almost ethereal sound when liquid in the vessel pressures air through the chamber.[21]

The sound may have been thought of as the animated presence of the sacred, but however else these sound chambers may have been interpreted, I must emphasize that they add another sensory dimension to Chorrera ceramics, which I discuss at the end of this essay. Not only is one visually and tactilely attracted to the object by color and form but one also hears it; hence the engagement with the ceramic object is multisensory. The object takes on an autonomy in the classic sense of *the other*. But unlike Sartre in a Parisian park, the exchange— between being seen and seeing, between hearing and being heard—is, in coastal Formative Ecuador, a metaphysical engagement that conducts a continuum among naturally unlike things through a relationship of shared realism in artistic form. Moreover, this engagement is conducted simultaneously through various

---

[19]   This remains a constant feature of Ecuadorian ceramic production until the arrival of the Spaniards. Thus, there seems to be good evidence for sustained contact between the northern coastal cultures of Peru and the coastal cultures of Ecuador; however, a visualized narratization is absent from Jama-Coaque ceramics unlike for the Moche.

[20]   The human figurines are differentiated by body adornment, perhaps identifying kin or other social affiliations, but they are not given any particularizing physical features.

[21]   Simply blowing into the vessel produces a sharper, less ethereal, softer whistling sound than that produced when liquid is moved inside the jar. Because the whistle chamber is purposely embedded within a vessel form, it seems more likely that the desired sound was produced by the movement of liquid rather than by direct human agency.

Fig. 24 Chorrera whistling vessel in the form of a squash; 28 x 20 x 26.5 cm. Museo del Banco Central del Ecuador, Guayaquil (GA 5-1861-81).

Fig. 25 Chorrera vessel in the form of the larva of a palm grub; 20 cm. Museo del Banco Central del Ecuador, Guayaquil (4-41-79).

senses. It is, perhaps, meaningful that many human figures on these vessels are playing musical instruments, most often the panpipe (Lathrap et al. 1975: 37). Musical performance is one of the few cultural acts depicted in Chorrera ceramics, and the sense of the vessel's whistling sound as music is perhaps reified by the image of music's production (Fig. 27). Regardless, there is a common auditory style just as there a common visual style in these objects, and it further binds them as a complex of objects, conceptually related in part through the senses.

Chorrera Visionary Worlds

I have stressed above the realism of Chorrera visual representation in terms of the imitation of natural forms and as an index of its difference from earlier ceramic traditions. It is important, however, to emphasize that in the imagining and picturing of such metaphysics realism is not a necessary or exclusive condition of representational style in the way that unity of style is a condition of Western art and an index of meaningfulness. In pre-Hispanic Ecuadorian art, as in many other artistic traditions, abstraction can coexist with realism without abstraction disassembling the illusion of mimetic reproduction or realism diminishing abstraction's capacity to produce equally meaningful signifiers. For

445

Fig. 26 (*above*) Chorrera whistling vessel in the form of a gourd and (*below*) detail. Museo del Banco Central del Ecuador, Guayaquil.

example, other Chorrera vessel types effortlessly combine two-dimensional abstract designs and three-dimensional representational motifs into a single composition. One type of vessel, a large globular storage or transport vessel,[22] is commonly decorated with a snake motif on its red slip surface. The design begins as a polychrome flat diamond band near the base. The design winds upward around the vessel and quickly becomes recognizable as the body of a snake, ending in the full three-dimensional representation of its head and eyes which are inlaid with obsidian (Figs. 28a,b).[23]

Jonathan Damp (1982: 172–173) has suggested that the markings so clearly identifying this snake as a fer-de-lance were already present in the abstract triangular designs of Valdivia 1 and 2 ceramic vessels. Damp and Stahl (1985: 114–115) also suggested that these designs and the predominate use of red slip in the Valdivia vessels are to be understood as functioning within the hallucinogenic visions of shamanic ritual. It may well be that this type of Chorrera vessel, of which I know at least four examples, was also used in the storage and/ or preparation of intoxicants.[24] But what seems critical in the Chorrera example is that the metonymic design elements that are thought to refer to the snake on the Valdivia vessels become attached to the complete image of the snake. Both Damp and Stahl have suggested that the repetitive Valdivia design units in relation to the color red refer to the visionary experience itself, helping to properly cue it.[25] The Chorrera vessel and its image seem instead to reference the sense of the visionary experience itself. That is, whatever else the fer-de-lance is meant to reference by its visual presence on both Valdivia and Chorrera vessels, one is meant to see a dynamic image on the Chorreran example as it seemingly metamorphoses from the multicolored design on the

[22] These vessels range between 26 and 35 cm high.

[23] Other examples are illustrated in Lathrap et al. (1975: figs. 74, 88) and cat. nos. 376 and 377.

[24] Certain types of vessels, such as stone mortars in the form of felines used presumably to grind hallucinogens, continued to be made throughout the Formative period and perhaps beyond. Therefore, it is possible that there is some type of relationship between this type of Chorrera vessel and the Valdivia bowls Damp and Stahl discussed. However, the morphology of the vessels is different; hence, the relationship as detected by the design elements indicates a functional connection in relation to the ritual itself.

[25] Both Damp and Stahl have based their interpretations of the Valdivia designs and colors on ethnographic analogies with shamanic visionary experience as produced in relation to the ingestion of hallucinatory drugs. Two crucial assumptions are embedded in the analogy. First, the physiology of drug does not change over 2,500 years. Second, shamanic practices and experiences are static. Although both propositions may be true, they have not been analyzed.

Fig. 27 Chorrera whistling vessel in the form of a man playing a cane flute; 22 cm. Banco del Pacífico, Guayaquil.

vessel's surface to become an independent three-dimensional form, which is realistically rendered as the head rises from the vessel's wall.

Moreover, as the image of the snake reaches the state of three-dimensionality, the idea of sight itself seems to be intensified by the use of a different material, obsidian, that is set into the clay as the snake's eyes (Fig. 28). The

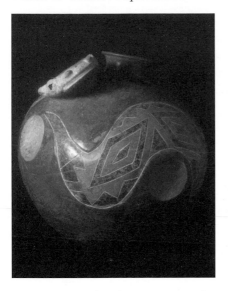 

Fig. 28 Views of a Chorrera open neck vessel with a snake painted and modeled on the exterior surface; eyes of the snake are inset with obsidian; 32 cm. Museo del Banco Central del Ecuador, Guayaquil.

qualities of obsidian make it an ideal material to stand for visionary experience.[26] An image reflected in obsidian appears to lie just slightly below the surface inhabiting the material and having a temporal condition such that it can suddenly appear clearly against the impenetrable blackness of the material; with the change of an angle the image disappears leaving only opacity. But unlike an obsidian *mirror*, which is an object through which a vision is seen, the obsidian as *eye* stands either metaphorically or metonymically for the organ of vision, not as the object through the visionary experience is achieved.[27] One might say that in this ceramic figure the hallucinatory vision returns a look through the eyes of the object of its vision.[28]

The vessels with the snake image raise further the issue of realism as a stylistic convention seemingly developed and used to form objects meant to help heighten states of experience. Clearly the image is meant to be recognized not

[26] This is the attribute the Aztecs gave to obsidian and its personification in the Aztec god Tezcatlipoca (see Carasco 1991: 42–43).

[27] Polished obsidian mirrors exist in the archaeological collections of the Banco Central in Guayaquil and Quito. Also, one Jama-Coaque ceramic piece in the Guayaquil (GA 1-100-76) appears to have been a frame for a one of these mirrors.

[28] Something of the unstable or illusory nature of vision is also manifested in the iridescent slip used to decorate some Chorrera vessels (Cummins 1992: 70–1).

only as a snake but also as a particular type of snake; yet the image also conjures up other elements of knowledge less empirically based; a snake *does not have* obsidian eyes. This knowledge, whether articulated in particular chants, myths about origins and cosmology, or curing ceremonies, is in some important way manifested in these objects; a snake in this form *does have* obsidian eyes. Moreover, a squash *does have* something fundamentally in common with a turtle. The visualization of commonality between seemingly unlike things through style, therefore, presupposes a capacity to experience that relationship as actual, a capacity often realized in some kind of ecstatic state.

The visionary world implied in the design of the snake, as well as the material of its eyes, also seems to be manifested differently but even more clearly in one substyle of Chorrera ceramic production. Here, in a series of finely crafted, thin-walled vessels, a purposeful antithesis to the smooth curvilinear forms of the natural world of appearances—be they human beings, animals, or flora—is carefully articulated. These have an abstract rectilinear form. Some, such as a pair of whistling vessels (Fig. 29), retain the general spherical shape of a gourd or some other natural form. However, the surface is divided into interlocking pentagonal shapes defined by raised borders. The repetitive abstract shapes are arranged such that they meet at the top and bottom on two parallel planes to form the sides of the vessel's flat base and top.

The geometrically modulated surface of this pair of vessels might be interpreted as a highly stylized representation of a fruit such as pineapple or a *chirimoya*;

Fig. 29 One of a pair of Chorrera polyhedral vessels; 18 x 13.2 cm. Museo del Banco Central del Ecuador, Guayaquil (GA 1-2709-84).

Fig. 30 Chorrera bowl; abstract geometric design centered on a swastika; 13.2 cm. Museo del Banco Central del Ecuador, Guayaquil.

however, other Chorrera ceramic pieces suggest a highly constructed unnatural vision of the world. They may well give the experience of an ecstatic state a concrete visual form. The image is produced both by the vessel's form and its surface design, and it is most clearly recognized among the examples that have a much more angular (Fig. 30), sometimes rectilinear form, almost like the shape of an open box (Fig. 31). These ceramic objects suggest, by their regular geometric shape and abstract linear surface design, a separate and constructed cultural space quite distinct from that of nature as expressed by curvilinear forms. The high thin walls joined at right angles imply a bounded space of order and of architectural regularity. The square or rectangular shape is not meant, however, to be a reference to an actual architectural structure in the sense of similitude on the basis of a specific building type. First of all, the vessel's four outer walls are decorated with abstract geometric curvilinear designs, usually created by incising the red slip colored surface to reveal the buff color beneath. Second, there is no reference to actual architectural elements other than the shape itself. Such references may be implied here, but more recognizable building types do occur on other Chorrera ceramic pieces (Fig. 32) in which the structural elements such as the thatched roof supported by four posts are clearly represented.[29]

[29] Until more controlled archaeological work is done at Chorrera sites, these latter representations are the best visual evidence for Chorrera architectural forms, although we do not know how closely these representations correspond to reality. Nonetheless, the two kinds of conceptualizations of ordered space do not mean that we are looking at different kinds of architecture, one sacred and one profane. Rather, the two forms may very well represent the same kind of structure, one representing its outward appearance and the other representing the essential qualities of a sacred structure.

Fig. 31 Chorrera rectangular vessel in two tiers. The bottom tier is reddened by slip and the upper tier is darkened by smudging. The surface of both tiers is incised and filled with white pigment to reveal an abstract design; 14.5 x 15.9 cm. Museo del Banco Central del Ecuador, Guayaquil (GA 539-200-76).

The four-sided angular shape of the vessel (Fig. 31) nonetheless implies an ordered structure. I suggest that at one level it may be a visual expression of a quadripartite universe, a cosmological structure so often imagined in Native American religions. Such a cosmological scheme may be referenced in the swastika design incised on Chorrera vessels (Fig. 30). In this sense, these vessel forms may refer at once to both the cosmological structure of the universe and the temporal architectural structures that mark the *axis mundi*. The actual temples may have been simple buildings, as the more realistic models imply (Fig. 32), built on raised earthen mounds.[30] But what these temple structures were imagined to have been in Chorrera cosmology may possibly be seen in these more imaginative vessel types.[31] This interpretation may also explain the relatively unusual shape and color of the vessel in Figure 31. The vessel is square, but the walls are stepped all around, forming two tiers. The movement between the two tiers is further emphasized by color differentiation. The first or bottom tier is finished with the usual brick red color, and the surface of the second tier was blackened by smudging. The form and color differential seem to imply a base supporting a superstructure. Later Jama-Coaque ceramic examples (500 B.C.–

[30] Clearly, the large central mound at San Isidro served this purpose such that it was reused and enlarged over a long period of time. It is possible that it had some kind of structure at the summit.

[31] The representation of an actual sacred structure as an imagined performative space of spiritual interaction rarely attends to the visual appearance of the structure itself. One need only think of Charlemagne's chapel at Aachen and how it is rendered in the first two pages of the *Gospel Book of St. Emmeram of Regensburg*.

Fig. 32 Chorrera whistling vessel with bridge spout in the form of a house or temple; 31 x 16.5 cm. Museo del Banco Central del Ecuador, Guayaquil (GA 1-895-78).

A.D. 500) clearly show a stepped structure of several tiers at the top of which is a seated figure either in the open or under a pitched roof (Figs. 33, 34). These fanciful Jama-Coaque examples are often decorated with a tendril-like vegetal form that flowers and may represent *ayahuasca*, or another hallucinogenic plant.

The suggestion that the rectilinear form of the Chorrera vessels may reference a building structure is perhaps substantiated by a different Chorrera–Bahía transitional vessel (Fig. 35a,b). Three of the four red walls rise vertically, and all four walls are incised with the tightly controlled curvilinear abstract forms. A clear directional orientation is created by the form of the fourth wall. Here a platform projects from the wall and in the center stands a modeled human figure (Fig. 35c). The area of the wall behind the figure is painted blue as if the figure has emerged from, or is standing before, an entrance into the vessel itself. The color seemingly marks the liminal passageway from one space to another and forms a visual transition from the flat vessel wall to the fully sculptural representation of the human figure.[32] This late Chorrera example is the clearest indication that these square ceramic forms were more than vessels with abstract

[32] While ethnographic analogy is always problematic, especially as to specific interpretation of archaeological details, I was struck by a passage in Reichel-Dolmatoff's *Amazonian Cosmos* (1971). I read it after having interpreted the blue "doorway" painted on this Chorrera piece. Describing the metaphysical world of the Tukano people of the Northwest Amazon, he wrote: "The color blue occupies a somewhat ambivalent position. Being associated with the Milky Way and the hallucinatory sphere, it is the *color of communication, of contact with the supernatural and the extraterrestrial*" [emphasis mine] (1971: 123).

Fig. 33 Jama-Coaque round architectural structure, once connected to a vessel; 24.4 x 12.5 cm. Museo del Banco Central del Ecuador, Guayaquil (GA 1-1717-80).

Fig. 34 Jama-Coaque stepped tower with a figure seated in a structure at the top; 19 cm. Museo del Banco Central del Ecuador, Guayaquil.

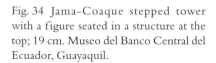

decorous surface designs. One is meant to see a human actor interacting with the shapes and designs of the vessel. The implication of a passageway through the wall certainly conveys the idea of movement through one space and another, whatever those spaces might be.

These square or rectangular vessels do not imitate natural forms like most Chorrera figurative ceramics; instead they suggest a similar sense of concreteness of the imaginary. The metaphysical world of vision is given a material form and shape that reifies the sensual experience of an hallucination, an experience already ordered by social categories, but given here an independent objective presence.[33] This is different from the Valdivia vessels that Damp and Stahl suggested made reference through their color and design to the structured images of hallucinogenic experience. These Valdivia objects were primarily shaped as functional objects, most probably for ritual consumption of food and/or liquid. Whatever the designs on the rim may signify, they are inextricably a part of the physical act of ritual, much like Valdivia figurines. It is difficult to conceive of the square and rectangular shaped Chorrera vessels in the same manner. Their shape consciously removes them from this particular functional use.[34] Ritual objects, bodies, and/or other objects may have been placed inside them, but their delicate walls suggest that they were not actively used. If these vessels were brought out in a ritual context as the containers of a sacred or venerable entity, they might have provided an appropriate locus for the aura of that entity, demarcating it, perhaps in an analogous way that a reliquary does for a Christian relic. Like the Chorrera figurines, these vessels demand to be looked

[33] The vessel's abstract designs and the figure in front of a doorlike form may appear closer to a Chorrera structure than it might first seem. Reichel-Dolmatoff described the painted longhouse, or *maloca*, of the Tukano (Taibano), which has the figure of a human painted near the door and a series of abstract symbols on either side. The figure is the Master of the Animals, a mythical figure who owns all animals and their increase. The abstract elements are based on phosphenes (i.e., fleeting perception of the human eye of specks, stars, or irregular patterns independent of an external light source and often induced by drugs). These images are coded with specific Tukano meaning (Reichel-Dolmatoff 1974: 173 and figs. 41, 42).

[34] The shape of these objects suggests a specific kind of use or function that seemingly precludes the element of liquid. If they were used as containers, it would likely have been for more solid forms. Until such objects are found in situ, one can only suggest possibilities. It may have been used for special secondary burials of particularly important ancestors. I suggest this because of a later Jama-Coaque ceramic piece of a kind of charnel house where the bones of the dead rest on the roof of a post-and-lintel structure and living figures sit below. The Museo del Banco Central del Ecuador, Guayaquil owns this piece (GA 1-2852-85), which seems to correspond with early 16th-century descriptions of such structures where the skin of dead ancestors was dried, stuffed with straw, and then hung from the roof, (Estete 1968: 360; Zeidler n.d.).

at as objects/images and separate from their physical functions. They are connected to those who may have manipulated through the abstract designs themselves. That is, the volutes and inwardly spiraling forms that appear both as positive and negative designs through raised red and recessed (incised) white areas on the walls of vessels (Fig. 31, 35a,b,c) also occur on the body and facial ornamentation of Chorrera female figurines, appearing through the same technique (Figs. 3, 6, 10). The designs also have resonance among the ceramic seals in the Chorrera corpus, proliferating in the Regional Development period (500 B.C.–A.D. 500), especially within the Jama-Coaque corpus (see Cummins et al. 1996, figs. 8b, 16a,b, 17b, 21a,b, 22b, 35b). In Jama-Coaque ceramic figurines, seals and the design of seals on the body are almost exclusively a female domain. This also may be true for Chorrera ceramics (Cummins et al. 1996 63–67). The sharing of designs between the female body, as represented by figurines, and the surface of vessels may indicate a far greater and complex set of relationships. It not only may suggest roles that are based on gender within the creative process in which domains of expression overlap and intersect, but also differing realms of Chorrera aesthetic experience intersecting through their performance.

CONCLUSIONS: SYNETHESIA/SYNAESTHETICS

In the absence of a written record and other artifacts, Chorrera ceramics, as the archaeological metonyms of an almost completely unknown culture, offer the few specifics through which something can be publicly seen and generally said about this important Formative culture. In summary, we can see today that Chorrera artisans intentionally created certain objects with a realistic appearance that—in addition to whatever magical or ritual properties they may have had—were intended to be seen as images. By calling them *images*, I refer to Socrates' definition that an "image must not by any means reproduce all the qualities of that which it imitates, if it's to be an image."[35]

In this sense, Chorrera succeed as images and are different from Valdivia figurines. Chorrera images are successful and have modern appeal because in their realism they do not attempt to duplicate nature or the cosmos. The qualities of Chorrera realism seem to evoke a broad set of relations to the world/cosmos in a most material form. Therefore, I have stressed that this style appears to be specific in this evocation, creating an interaction with the object as image,

---

[35] My use of this passage from Plato's *Cratylus* in terms of how Chorrera ceramic images might be discussed has come through Mitchell's specific discussion (1989: 92) and his broader analysis in chap. 3.

Fig. 35a   Chorrera–Bahía Transitional rectangular shaped vessel, back wall; 15.3 cm. Museo del Banco Central del Ecuador, Guayaquil.

Fig. 35b   Side wall.

Fig. 35c   Front wall with standing male figure; 14 cm.

as something that is tangible in the realm of sensual experience. It is also through the sensory aspect of Chorrera realism that these figurines and vessels might be related back to the sphere of interaction in ritual, not necessarily just as depictions or objects of ritual, although they may be that as well, but as participants in the performance of ritual.

Lawrence Sullivan (1986) described ritual performance as *synesthesia*, a term he defined as the unity of the senses such that one type of stimulation evokes the sensation of another. "Performance" he wrote, "displays the *symbolic expressions* of synesthesia as it is imagined in a culture. In doing so, it renders perceptible a symbolism of the unity of the senses. The symbolic experience of the unity of the senses enables a culture to entertain itself with the idea of the unity of meaning . . . Ritual performance [as an act of communication], repeatedly floods all the senses with redundant messages" (Sullivan 1986: 7). Sight, smell, hearing, movement, and taste are all brought together, not as separate experiences but as a totality. What Sullivan emphasized are the ephemeral aspects of ritual; these, of course, are precisely the elements of Chorrera ritual that cannot be recovered.

The unity of senses, however, does not fully encapsulate ritual as a unitary phenomenon because it focuses only on the human participant. To bring to fulfillment the unitary sense of the experience, there is the material environment in which it takes place. It is the creation of such an environment that brings objects such as the Chorrera vessels into Sullivan's understanding of the multiple sensory nature of performance. Angelika Gebhart-Sayer (1985), in analyzing the geometric designs of Shipibo–Conibo, used the term *synaesthetics* as the unitary category that brings the material and performative aspects together. It is a process through which "visual, auditory and olfactory perceptions are introduced as a connecting link and bound together" (1985: 172). Within Shipibo–Conibo ritual practices, various aesthetic codes (music, dance, visual design, fragrance, and speech) are understood to be experienced mutually. That is, "A visual experience is transformed into an audio sign" (1985: 170). This aspect of media interconnection is rather easy to comprehend within Western aesthetic/ritual criteria. It is at one level comprehensible as akin to the performance of Catholic and Anglican Christian ritual[36] and at another almost intuitively. Shipibo–Conibo abstract linear designs are understood within the community in which they are produced and experienced to be patterns that,

---

[36] Certainly, synaesthetics is not alien to Western religious performance, the integration of music, sculpture, and architectural space, as interrelated media are best exemplified at the medieval cloister of Cluny and in Bernard of Clairveux's writings (see Rudolph 1990).

by being traced as one speaks or sings, reveal a narrative or music, much in the way we process text and musical notation so that they become speech and music. The dance formations also create formations that correspond to two-dimensional patterns. The significance of synaesthtics is more difficult to appreciate in regard to how the Shipibo–Conibo understand the efficacy of such an aesthetic. For example, their healing design operates such that it may be sung onto a human body while malevolent spirits causing the disease may sing evil-smelling, antisongs (Gebhart-Sayer 1985: 171).[37] Here visual design, sound, and smell interact with the body of the participant to bring about the desired effect.

We, of course, can never recover the sounds, smells, colors, and dance of Chorrera culture. We only can presume that there were Chorrera rituals conducted by men and or woman with special knowledge, perhaps accessed or intensified by *ayahuasca* or some other hallucinogenic drug as achieved by Shipibo–Conibo practitioners. Moreover, the concepts of synesthesia and synaesthetics are extremely broad and could be used as descriptive categories for many different rituals. They most probably could be used to categorize and describe Valdivia and Machalilla rituals if we knew about them. Synesthesia and synaesthetics are nonetheless particularly useful concepts in thinking about Chorrera ceramic expression, as I have so broadly outlined it. The refined human figurines and elaborate vessels of Chorrera suggest an aesthetic that recognized heightened sensuality as something existing in nature and brought together in all its diverse forms (tactile, auditory, visual, taste, and olfactory) in ritual performance. More importantly though, the aesthetic of Chorrera ceramics seems to be directed at more than just producing a conceptual form in the manner manifested among the Shipibo–Conibo. A concreteness or materiality of the senses resides in the images themselves. The slip, sculptural handling, and the sound chamber combine with the iconography to produce an iconology of the senses. One is also tempted then to think about this reification within the increased mastery of ceramic production itself. The technical refinement that allows for plastic shapes, thin-walled vessels, evenly fired ceramics, sound chambers, iridescent slip, and obsidian eyes is on display through these objects and the images into which they are formed. There is an element of mastery and knowledge as social and perhaps political power that is ever so subtly on dis-

[37] It is tempting to read the abstract designs on Chorrera ceramics as having served in some similar way to Shipibo–Conibo designs. In fact, abstract geometric designs seem to be reserved only for elaborate vessels and headrests and human figurines. The relationship between visions produced by psychotropic drugs and dreams produced by sleep may also be the connecting element between these two disparate objects and their common design elements.

play—but without it ever becoming the overt subject of Chorrera ceramics.

By and large, the natural beings of the Chorrera environment—be they human, animal, or plant—are the subject of these images. The significance of cultural objects is not on display as image. However, these Chorrera vessels are part of a culture that placed great value on the object as a discrete presence in relation to the interrelated phenomena of the senses. Along with Chorrera technical innovations, this is the lasting ideological and artistic legacy for the ceramic traditions of coastal cultures of Ecuador. In Jama-Coaque, La Tolita, and, to a lesser degree, Bahía figurative ceramic pieces, there is a distinct reorientation away from just the natural state of being to a modification through objects and their presentation as values of social and religious power and/or status (Cummins 1992; Cummins, Burgos Cabera, and Mora Hoyos 1998). It may well be that there is increased sociopolitical stratification in Regional Developmental cultures that finds its expression in their images. But if that is true, the mode by which it is expressed in ceramics has its precedents in the realistic images of Chorrera and their relation to the senses.

Acknowledgments My research, first funded by a grant from the Getty Research Program to the Center for Materials Research in Archaeology and Ethnography at the Massachusetts Institute of Technology, is based on public and private collections in Ecuador. I am extremely grateful to Olaf Holm who not only allowed me access to the collections of Chorrera ceramics in the Museo del Banco Central del Ecuador, Guayaquil, but also shared his vast knowledge and experience of Ecuador and Ecuadorian archaeology.

BIBLIOGRAPHY

APPADURAI, ARJUN
1986   Introduction: Commodities and the Politics of Value. In *The Social Life of Things* (A. Appadurai, ed.): 3–63. Cambridge University Press, Cambridge.

BARNEY-CABERA, E.
1975   Tumaco, escultura en arcilla. *Historia del Arte Colombiano* 11/12: 213–240.

BELL, CATHERINE
1992   *Ritual Theory, Ritual Practice.* Oxford University Press, Oxford.

BISCHOF, HENNING
1982   La Fase Engoroy—Períodos, cronología, y relaciones. In *Primer Simposio de Correlaciones Antropológicas Andino–Mesoamericano* (J. Marcos and P. Norton, eds.): 135–176. Escuela Superior Politécnica del Litoral, Guayaquil.

BURGER, RICHARD
1976   The Moche Sources of Archaism in Chimu Ceramics. *Ñawpa Pacha.* 14: 95–104.

CARASCO, DAVÍD
1991   The Sacrifice of of Tezcatlipoca: To Change Place. In *To Change Place: Aztec Ceremonial Landscapes*: 58–73. University of Colorado Press, Boulder.

CORDY-COLLINS, ALANA
1990   Fonga Sigde, Shell Purveyor to the Chimu Kings. In *The Northern Dynasties: Kingship and Statecraft in Chimor* (M. Moseley and A. Cordy-Collins, eds.): 393–419. Dumbarton Oaks, Washington D.C.

COVARRUBIAS, MIGUEL
1954   *The Eagle, the Jaguar and the Serpent.* Knopf, New York.

CUMMINS, TOM
1992   Tradition in Ecuadorian Pre-Hispanic Art: The Ceramics of Chorrera and Jama-Coaque. In *Pre-Columbian Signs: 5000 Years of Art in Ecuador* (Francisco Valdez, ed.): 63–81. Imprenta Mariscal, Quito.
1994   La tradición de figurinas de la costa ecuatoriana: Estilo tecnológico y el uso de moldes. In *Tecnología y organización de la cerámica prehispanica en los Andes* (Izumi Shimada, ed.): 157–172. Pontificia Universidad Católica Fondo Editorial, Lima.

CUMMINS, TOM, AND OLAF HOLM
1991   The Pre-Hispanic Art of Ecuador. In *Ancient Art of the Ancient World* (Shozo Masuda and Izumi Shimada, eds.): 167–184. Iwanami Shoten, Tokyo. (Japanese)

CUMMINS, TOM, JULIO BURGOS CABERA, AND CARLOS MORA HOYOS
1998   *Arte prehispanico del Ecuador: Huellas del pasado, los sellos de Jama-Coaque.* Serie Monográfica 2, Miscelánea Antropológico Ecuatoriana. Banco Central del Ecuador, Guayaquil.

DAMP, JONATHAN
1982   Ceramic Art and Symbolism in the Early Valdivia Community. *Journal of Latin American Lore* 8(2): 155–178.

1984   Architecture of the Early Valdivia Village. *American Antiquity* 49(3): 573–585.

1988   *La primera ocupación Valdivia de Real Alto.* Biblioteca Ecuatoriana de Arqueología, Quito.

DORSEY, GEORGE

1901   *Archaeological Investigations on the Island of La Plata, Ecuador.* Columbian Museum Publication 56, Anthropological Series 2(5). Field Museum of Natural History, Chicago.

ESTETE, MIGUEL

1968   *Noticia del Perú.* In *Biblioteca peruana, primera serie.* (1535): 347–402. Editora Técnica Asociados, Lima.

ESTRADA, EMILIO

1957   *Prehistoria de Manabí.* Publicación del Museo del Victor Emilio Estrada 4. Guayaquil.

1958   *Las culturas pre-clásicas, formativas o arcaicas del Ecuador.* Publicación del Museo del Victor Emilio Estrada 5. Guayaquil.

1962   *Arqueología de Manabí Central.* Publicación del Museo del Victor Emilio Estrada 7. Guayaquil.

EVANS, CLIFFORD, AND BETTY J. MEGGERS

1957   Formative Period Cultures in the Guayas Basin, Coastal Ecuador. *American Antiquity* 22: 235–246.

1958   Valdivia, an Early Formative Culture of Ecuador. *Archaeology* 2(3): 175–182.

1961   Cronología relativa y absoluta en al costa del Ecuador. *Cuadernos de Historia y Arqueología,* año 11, vol. 10 (27). Guayaquil.

1982   Técnicas decorativas diagnósticas y variantes regionales Chorrera, un análisis preliminar. In *Primer Simposio de Correlaciones Antropologicas Andino–Mesoamericano* (J. Marcos and P. Norton, eds.): 121–134. Escuela Superior Politécnica del Litoral, Guayaquil.

GEBHART-SAYER, ANGELIKA

1985   The Geometric Designs of Shipibo–Conibo in Ritual Context. *Journal of Latin American Lore* 11(2): 143–175.

HOLM, OLAF

1953   El Tatuaje entre los aborígenes prepizzarinos en la costa ecuatoriana. *Cuadernos de Historia y Arqueología* 3: 7–8. Casa de Cultura Ecuatoriana, Guayaquil.

HOLM, OLAF, AND H. CRESPO

1980   Las culturas formativas. In *Historia del Ecuador,* tomo 1: 87–191. Salvat Editores, Barcelona.

LATHRAP, DONALD W., DONALD COLLIER, AND HELEN CHANDRA

1975   *Ancient Ecuador: Culture, Clay, and Creativity, 3000-300 B.C.* Field Museum of Natural History, Chicago.

LATHRAP, DONALD W., JORGE G. MARCOS, AND JAMES A. ZEIDLER

1977   Real Alto: An Ancient Ceremonial Center. *Archaeology* 30(1): 3–13.

LÉVI-STRAUSS, CLAUDE

1966   *The Savage Mind.* University of Chicago Press, Chicago.

MARCOS, JORGE
1973 Tejidos hechos en telar en un contexto Valdivia Tardío. *Cuadernos de Historia y Arqueología*. Casa de Cultura Ecuatoriana, Guayaquil.
1977/1978 Cruising to Acapulco and Back with the Thorny Oyster Set: A Model for a Lineal Exchange System. *Journal of the Steward Anthropological Society* 9(1/2): 99–132.
1983 Breve prehistoria del Ecuador. In *Tesoros del Ecuador antiguo* (9–22). Instituto de Cooperación Iberoamericano, Madrid.

MARCOS, JORGE G., AND PRESLEY NORTON
1981 Interpretación sobre la arqueolgía de la Isla de La Plata. *Miscelania Antropólogica Ecuatoriana* 1(1): 136–154.

MEGGERS, BETTY
1966 *Ecuador*. Thames and Hudson, London.

MEGGERS, BETTY, CLIFFORD EVANS, AND EMILIO ESTRADA
1965 *The Early Formative Period of Coastal Ecuador: The Valdivia and Machalilla Phases*. Smithsonian Contributions to Anthropology 1. Smithsonian Institution. U.S. Government Printing Office, Washington, D.C.

MEJIA XESSPE, TORIBIO
1965/66 Técnica negativa en la decoración de la cerámica peruana. *Revista del Museo Nacional* [Peru], 34: 28–32.

MITCHELL, W. J. T.
1989 *Iconology: Image, Text, Ideology*. University of Chicago Press, Chicago.

MURRA, JOHN V.
1975 El tráfico de mullu en la costa del Pacífico. In *Formaciones económicas y políticas del mundo andino* (275–313). Instituto de Estudios Peruanos, Lima.

NIEVES ZEDEÑO, MARIA
n.d. *Análisis de cerámica Chorrera del sitio Peñon del Río*. Centro Estudio Arqueológicos y Antropológicos. Guayaquil, 1994.

OVIEDO Y VALDES, DE GONZALO FERNÁNDEZ
1944 (1557) *Historia general y natural de las Indias* . . . (José Natalicio González, ed.), vol. 12. Editorial Guaranía, Asunción.

PAULSEN, ALLISON C.
1974 The Thorny Oyster and the Voice of God. *American Antiquity*: 597–607.

PILLSBURY, JOANNA
1996 The Thorny Oyster and Origins of Empire Implications of Recently Uncovered Spondylous Imagery from Chan Chan. *American Antiquity* 7: 313–340.

REICHEL-DOLMATOFF, GERARDO
1971 Amazonian Cosmos: *The Sexual and Religious Symbolism of the Tukano Indians*. University of Chicago Press, Chicago
1974 *The Shaman and the Jaguar*. Temple University Press, Philadelphia.

ROWE, JOHN
1971 The Influence of Chavín Art on Later Styles. *Dumbarton Oaks Conference on Chavín* (E. Benson, ed.): 101–124. Dumbarton Oaks, Washington D.C.

RUDOLPH, CONRAD
1990   The *"Things of Greater Importance": Bernard of Clairvaux's Apologia and the Medieval Attitude toward Art.* University of Pennsylvania Press, Philadelphia.

DE SÁMANO, JUAN, AND FRANCISCO DE XEREZ
1842 (1528)   Relación de los primeros descubrimientos de Francisco Pizarro y Diego de Almargo, sacada del Códice CXX de la Biblioteca Imperial de Viena." In *Colección de documentos inéditos para la historia de España* 5 (193–210). Madrid.

STAHL, PETER
1985   The Hallucinogenic Basis of Early Valdivia Phase Ceramic Bowl Iconography. *Journal of Psychoactive Drugs* 17(2): 105–123.
1986   Hallucinatory Imagery and the Origin of Early South American Figurine Art. *World Archaeology* 18(1): 134–50.

STOTHERT, KAREN, KATHLEEN EPSTEIN, THOMAS CUMMINS, AND MARITZA FREILE
1991   Reconstructing Prehistoric Textile and Ceramic Technology. In *Impressions of Cloth in Figurines from Ecuador. Proceedings of the Materials Research Society*: 767–776.

SULLIVAN, LAWRENCE
1986   Sound and Sense: Toward a Hermeneutics of Performance. *History of Religions* 26(1).

TELLO, JULIO C.
1923   Wirakocha. In *Inka* 1: 94–320.

UMBERGER, EMILY
1987   Antiques, Revivals, and Reference to the Past in Aztec Art. *Res: Anthropology and Aesthetics* 13: 62–105.

ZEIDLER, JAMES A.
1977/78   Primitive Exchange, Prehistoric Trade, and the Problems of a Mesoamerican–South American Connection. *Journal of the Steward Anthropological Society* 9 (1/2): 7–39.
1981   Pothunting and Vandalism of Archaeological Sites: An Ecuadorian Example. In *Rescue Archaeology: Papers Presented at the First New World Conference on Rescue Archaeology* (R. Wilson and G. Loyola, eds.): 49–58. Preservation Press, Washington, D.C.
1988   Feline, Stone Mortars, and Formative Period Interaction Spheres in the Northern Andean Area. *Journal of Latin American Lore* (14)2: 243–283.
n.d.   The Chronicles of Coaque and Pasao: Ethnohistorical Perspective on Jama-Coaque II Polity of Coastal Ecuador at A.D. 1531. Paper presented at the 86th Annual Meeting of the American Anthropological Association, Chicago, 1987.

ZEIDLER, JAMES A., AND MARIE J. SUTLIFF
1994   Definition of Ceramic Complexes and Cultural Occupation in the Jama Valley. In *Regional Archaeology in Northern Manabí Ecuador* (J. Zeidler and D. Pearsall, eds.): 112–130. Memoirs in Latin American Archaeology 8. University of Pittsburgh, Pittsburgh, Pa.

ZEVALLOS MENÉNDEZ, CARLOS
1971   *La agricultura en el Formativo Temprano del Ecuador: Cultura Valdivia.* Casa de Cultura Ecuatoriana, Guayaquil.

Conclusions: Cultures of the Ecuadorian Formative in Their Andean Context

RICHARD L. BURGER

YALE UNIVERSITY

In this concluding chapter, I step back from the detailed consideration of the particulars of the Ecuadorian Formative and contemplate its broad outline within a larger Andean context. Presented originally as the concluding comments of the 1996 Dumbarton Oaks conference, I have elected to retain the general character of these remarks, updating them where necessary to take into account the progress that has been made since they were presented.

SOME TERMINOLOGICAL CONCERNS

This review best begins with the framing of concept of an Ecuadorian Formative. In his contribution to this volume, Jorge Marcos looks closely at the history of the evolutionary concept of Formative as it has been applied in Ecuador. It can be added here that if one employs the well-known Willey and Phillips (1958: 144) definition of Formative as the presence of agriculture or any other subsistence economy of comparable effectiveness, and by the successful integration of such an economy into well-established sedentary village life, then the cultures of the Late Preceramic in Peru, and perhaps even some of the pre-Valdivia cultures in Ecuador would have to be considered as Formative. Nevertheless, many authors who favor evolutionary terminology have continued to refer to these cultures as Archaic. The crucial feature most investigators seem to be utilizing to determine the beginning of the Formative is the introduction of pottery, apparently on the assumption that it provides a reliable index of well-established agriculture and sedentism despite ethnographic and archaeological research that suggests that the relationship among ceramics, agriculture, and sedentism is far more complex than once thought. In reality, the Formative, as it is applied to the cultures of Ecuador and Peru, is a chronological rather than an evolutionary term.

Moreover, the concept of an Ecuadorian Formative is something of a misnomer, since Ecuador did not exist in the distant past and only became a nation in 1830. Before that time, the area was unified politically with what we now know as Colombia and Venezuela, and in the centuries preceding that the Ecuadorian area was joined administratively with portions of Peru, Chile, and Argentina as part of Tawantinsuyu. A skeptic might ask whether it is fundamentally misleading to take a set of pre-Hispanic cultures more than two millennia old and organize them within a political frame initiated only a century and a half ago. Even an archaeologist unresponsive to the critiques of post-processualists might fear that our meager authority as neutral scholars is being manipulated to legitimize the modern Ecuadorian nation state by linking to it with a putative ancient phenomenon called the *Ecuadorian Formative*.

Would it not be more appropriate to set these modern political concerns aside and refer only to an *Andean Formative*? After all, the Andes are a phenomenon several million years old and have no obvious self-interest or political agenda. As a geological formation rather than a historical invention or cultural construction, they are, in some sense, above suspicion. By speaking of an Andean Formative, the modern and somewhat arbitrary boundaries of contemporary nations could be put aside in the hope that a more scientific and meaningful picture might emerge. This is by no means a new idea, and several of the more recently initiated specialized journals, including the *Gaceta Arqueológica Andina*, *Revista Andina*, *Bulletin de l'Institut Français d'Etudes Andines*, and *Andean Past*, are devoted to Andean rather than Peruvian or Ecuadorian archaeology. Similarly, in an effort to eschew the inherent nationalist bias in treatments of Peruvian or Ecuadorian archaeology, two of my Peruvian colleagues, Luis Lumbreras (1981) and Rogger Ravines (1982), have written syntheses on Andean prehistory, and two others from the United States, Karen Bruhns (1994) and David Wilson (1999), have recently taken this trend even further by offering a continental overview. While any effort to achieve a more comprehensive vision is laudable, it is also difficult, and in these volumes and journals the Formative cultures from Ecuador and Peru often seem to be treated apart from each other—as separate as two meatballs in a plate of spaghetti.

Moreover, employing the alternative of an Andean Formative, as opposed to an Ecuadorian or Peruvian Formative, is not as neutral and unassailable as it appears. The idea that one can meaningfully group pre-Hispanic developments within an Andean frame derives from a particular view of cultural history as well as from South American geography. John Murra (1975) and others have discussed at length a common Andean culture, which has expressions from Ecuador to Chile and Peru to Colombia; discussions of "Andean" agriculture and cosmology as well have been widespread and gained considerable acceptance. However, before we accept this idea of *lo andino,* which lies at the heart of the argument in favor of reconceptualizing previous work within the framework of Andean archaeology, we should subject it to the same skeptical consideration as already applied to the paradigms of distinct Peruvian and Ecuadorian archaeologies. By joining Peru and Ecuador within a single framework, are we not merely projecting back into time a naïve ethnographically based model of undifferentiated Quechua culture? Is not the basis for many of the shared cultural traits viewed as typically Andean the result of late 15th- and early 16th-century Inka hegemony over both areas, the spread of Quechua as a lingua franca after the Inka defeat, or more recent responses to the expansion of the nation state? Moveover, if we decide to forge ahead with a unified Andean archaeology, are we not consciously or unconsciously being used to legitimize the pan-Andean agenda that has been favored by a subset of Latin American politicians since the time of Simón Bolivar?

Whatever one's perspective, it is likely that the pressures to view Peruvian and Ecuadorian prehistory within a single Andean framework will only continue to increase as a result of the 1999 peace treaty between Peru and Ecuador. Significantly, the two countries chose to mine the archaeological record in their search for a symbol of the new accord (Museo Arqueológico Rafael Larco Herrera 1999). The selection of the spondylus (i.e., the spiny oyster, *Spondylus* sp., or *mullu*) shell as this symbol of peace dramatized the long-standing links between the two countries. The models of spondylus transport as part of long-distance exchange networks during pre-Hispanic times resonated with the late 20th-century neoliberal dream of a new era of expanded trade and cooperation between Ecuador and Peru.

POLITICAL CONSIDERATIONS

Why is it so difficult to present a coherent and integrated picture of an Andean prehistory or, in this case, an Andean Formative? To some degree, it reflects the impact of contemporary politics on scholarship. The laws and bureaucracy governing archaeology in the modern nations of Peru and Ecuador are distinct and at times at odds with one another. Over the last half-century, the military tensions and, on occasion, armed conflicts between the two countries have acted to discourage investigators regardless of nationality from working in both nations. There are exceptions to this rule. Pioneers of Andean archaeology, like Max Uhle, Jacinto Jijón y Camaño, Wendell Bennett, and Edward Lanning come to mind. More recently, contemporary scholars Karen Stothert, Patricia Netherly, Terence Grieder, and Jean Guffroy have investigated sites in both Ecuador and Peru. However, those investigators who have tried to carry out research in both Peru and Ecuador are exceptional; most have chosen to specialize in either one or the other. As a result of political and academic pressures, few archaeological careers incorporate field or laboratory experience in both countries, and most scholars tend to be much more knowledgeable about one or the other.

To make matters worse, since Uhle's time, archaeologists in each country have developed their own local frameworks and terminology, making the literature resistant to the efforts of well-meaning pan-Andeanists. For example, it may come as a surprise to some that what is known as the *Late* Formative in Ecuador is roughly contemporary with what is sometimes referred to as the *Middle* Formative just a few kilometers away across the border in Peru.

In addition to the factors mentioned above, security concerns in the crucial frontier area between modern Peru and Ecuador have hampered archaeological investigation. This is not merely a problem in theory; less than a year before the Dumbarton Oaks conference that inspired this volume, the two countries were actively fighting in the Cordillera del Condor along the disputed border. More than one archaeological project has been canceled because of sudden flare-ups between the two countries, and granting agencies have traditionally been skeptical about whether such studies are feasible. Military authorities are often suspicious about whether archaeologists can be "trusted" in sensitive zones and whether their projects might be covers for intelligence operations. Justified or not, an artificial buffer zone of ignorance has separated the two nations. Fortunately, this situation has begun to improve with recent work on Formative sites near the border, including investigations by Netherly (Netherly, Holm, Marcos, and Marca n. d.) and Staller (1994) in El Oro, Guffroy (1987, 1994) in Loja and Piura, Shady (1987) and Olivera (1999) in the Utcubamba drainage, and Morales (1992) in the Río Chambira.

Archaeologists have long been aware of the obstacles to archaeological knowledge and interpretation created by modern political boundaries. At several meetings, including a 1971 meeting in Salinas (Marcos and Norton 1982), archaeologists working in Ecuador and Peru have met to share ideas on overcoming these artificial barriers. Frequently, these efforts have been supported by organizations based outside the Andes, such as the Ford Foundation, the Institut Français d'Etudes Andines, the United Nations Educational, Scientific, and Cultural Organization (UNESCO), and others (e. g., Lumbreras 1979a,b).

There are no simple solutions to the concerns touched upon here, but awareness of their existence and the way they affect archaeological research and theory in both subtle and not so subtle ways is a necessary first step in considering the heuristic devices we use to understand the Formative cultures that existed in the prehistoric Andes.

FIELDS OF INTERACTION AND THE ECUADORIAN FORMATIVE

An implicit or explicit theme in this volume is that throughout Ecuador's Early, Middle, and Late Formative, a pattern of cultural interrelatedness often has been expressed through stylistic similarity and the exchange of goods. This pattern extended over the coast, highlands, and perhaps into the poorly known eastern lowlands of Ecuador. For example, in the Late Formative, Chorrera-related cultures are found along most of the Ecuadorian coast, and the coeval highland groups at small sites like Cotocollao in the north and Pirincay in the south were linked by exchange with these coastal centers. Although politically independent and culturally distinguishable from each other, the groups appear to have been much more closely linked with each other than with the contemporary Initial Period and Early Horizon cultures found in Peru. In Warren DeBoer's words (see p. 323), "The rather drab neckless *olla* assemblages of early second millennium B.C. Peru seem to be in a separate world" from the more elaborate coeval Valdivia from Ecuador. The cultural contrast is particularly sharp between the late Chorrera manifestation and the Chavín horizon cultures to the south, but it is also true for the earlier Initial Period cultures (Burger 1984; Hocquenghem 1991). Despite the considerable amount of fieldwork and looting at Formative sites in Ecuador over the last 15 years, the conclusion that Chavín iconography does not occur in Ecuadorian sites remains valid (Burger 1984: 39–42; 1992).

Separate Peruvian and Ecuadorian spheres of interaction can be demonstrated in many ways. The pattern of obsidian distribution is a particularly unambiguous one. Obsidian from the Mullumica and Quiscatola–Yanaurco sources east of Quito were exchanged during the Formative as far south as La Emerenciana in El Oro, just north of the Peruvian frontier, but it has yet to be found at archaeological sites within the borders of modern Peru (Burger et al. 1994; Burger, Asaro, and John Staller unpublished data). Conversely, Quispisisa type obsidian whose source was recently located near Sacsamarca in the south central highlands of Peru (Burger and Glascock 2000), was widely traded within the Chavín sphere of influence and appears as far north as Pacopampa, only 150 km from Peru's frontier. It has yet to be documented within the borders of modern Ecuador. Significantly, the inhabitants of Pacopampa acquired obsidian from the Peruvian Quispisisa source despite being significantly closer to the obsidian sources in northern Ecuador (Burger 1984).

The existence of two separate spheres of interaction or cultural fields, what

Bennett called separate cotraditions, has its roots at least as far back as Ecuador's Early Formative and, as Karen Stothert suggests in this volume, probably long before the Formative. The pottery-producing agricultural societies of the Valdivia culture that figure so prominently within these pages offer a sharp contrast to the prepottery cultures of the Peruvian coast, the so-called Cotton Preceramic that were their contemporaries. In the third millennium B. C. , the late Preceramic highland cultures of central and northern Peru at sites like Galgada, Huaricoto, and Kotosh were closely linked with their coastal counterparts through exchange networks. They also shared a tradition of monumental architecture (Burger 1992), an observation that has been reinforced by the recent discovery of ceremonial hearths at Preceramic sites in Supe and Casma (S. Pozorski and T. Pozorski 1996; Shady 1998). However, these Peruvian Preceramic sites bear little relation to the cultural patterning known from the coeval Formative cultures of the Ecuadorian highlands or coast.

By recognizing the distinctive nature of the Ecuadorian Formative, I am not arguing that this phenomenon can be understood completely in isolation from the developments in Peru. On the contrary, there is ample evidence of contact between Formative Ecuadorian cultures and their contemporaries in Peru. Nor do we suggest that the nature of these contacts or even the extent of the distributions of these cultures was set in stone. In fact, existing evidence suggests the distribution and limits of cultures changed dramatically. For example, on the coast toward the end of the Early Formative, a variant of the Valdivia culture appears to extend into the northern extreme of what is now Peruvian territory. In another case, the analysis of pottery from Manachaqui Cave in the Peruvian montane forest above Gran Pajatén demonstrated that the later Initial Period pottery had strong links with the Yasuni, Upano, Chorrera, and Engoroy styles of Ecuador rather than its Peruvian counterparts. Located along an ancient road system, the Manachaqui Cave results imply interregional travel and communication in pre-Chavín times between the *ceja de selva* of what is now northern Peru and the Ecuarorian highlands and coast (Church 1996).

More commonly, as in the work of Guffroy (1994), the cultures occupying the modern border region from Piura to Tumbes do not appear to be exclusively linked to either Peruvian or Ecuadorian cultures; rather they appear to be distinctive while mutually sharing elements with both. These cultures, such as the Paita or Ñañañique, can be understood as frontier culture phenomena in which groups serve as mediators between distinctive cultural areas. The discovery by looters of a gold Chavín repoussé plaque in Upper Piura at the archaeological site Loma de Macanche, which lacks other Chavín features, serves to illustrate the mediating status of this frontier zone (Kaulicke 1998: 34).

During the Formative, land routes leading from the headwaters of the Río Catamayo (a tributary of the Río Chira) into the Río Yapatera (a tributary of the Río Piura), and then across the Río Olmos and Río Motupe into the Lambayeque drainage connected the two regions (Hocquenghem, Idrovo, Kaulicke, and Gomis 1993: fig. 5). This inland route, along which Spondylus and other goods moved, avoided the problems posed by the extensive desert of Sechura, and continued to be utilized in much later times, although the expansion of Tawantinsuyu and the integration of Ecuador into this Andean empire made it feasible to use coastal Tumbes as a port of entry for these goods (Hocquenghem et al. 1993: fig. 2).

In calling attention to distinctive cultural areas during the Formative, I am not denying the existence of the enormous variation within each area. As Zeidler and Isaacson, Raymond, and others in this volume emphasize, there was a pattern of uneven development in Formative Ecuador, and the historical trajectories of neighboring valleys were often quite different. Elsewhere I (Burger 1992) have suggested that this was equally true for the late Preceramic and Formative in Peru. Yet this observation of internal variability in no way undermines the utility differentiating between a distinctive Ecuadorian Formative from the coeval field of cultures to the south during the Formative. This latter observation leads us back to Donald Lathrap's conviction that the Ecuadorian Formative might best be understood as a variant of the Tropical Forest Culture. Since no contributors to this conference volume specifically criticize this view and Karen Stothert and Scott Raymond draw upon it for inspiration, I presume that most specialists agree with Lathrap's perspective. If we accept this contention, as several authors implicitly do, it would be worth considering the degree to which the differentiation between the Ecuadorian and Peruvian culture areas essentially conforms to cultural adaptations to two dissimilar climatic regimes— the moist tropical regime that characterized and continues to characterize much of Ecuador compared with the arid regime associated with the Humbolt Current, which characterizes much of coastal and highland Peru. It is the heavy rainfall in western Ecuador that permitted a Tropical Forest Culture pattern to flourish, and it can be argued that its absence in Peru would have made its expansion into that zone unfeasible. The "modern" climatic pattern already characterized the Ecuadorian Formative, but prior to 3000 B.C., the northern Peruvian coast as far south as Chimbote may have been wetter, warmer, and more like Ecuador than it is today (Sandweiss et al. 1996). After Valdivia 2a, the arid Humbolt-dominated climate regime extended near the current Peru–Ecuador border and thus during almost all of the Formative, the sharp environmental contrasts between the Ecuadorian and Peruvian zones resembled their current configuration.

Richard L. Burger

Let us briefly review some ramifications of Ecuador's climate because it helped shape Formative cultural features that distinguish it from the Peruvian Formative. The strong rainfall along the coast and western slopes supported large rivers throughout the year along most of the coast. This in turn permitted water transport to flourish within the valleys and linked these valley populations to the Pacific coast into a single transportation network. The rains also supported the tropical forest vegetation that included balsa wood and other trees that could be used to manufacture canoes and rafts. This early development of water transport played a role in the exploitation of deepwater fauna, as illustrated in this volume by Peter Stahl's reconstruction of harpoon-wielding fishermen bagging tuna and swordfish from their boats. Water transport also played a prominent role in promoting long-distance exchange along the Pacific coast, as Marcos (1978) has forcefully argued. While an analogous pattern of riverine trade is well-known within the eastern tropical forests of the Orinoco and Amazon drainages (Lathrap 1973), it has no parallel in coastal Peru where (a) the rivers are usually dry for part of the year and never navigable and (b) the arid climate could not support vegetation suitable for the production of wooden boats.

Reed boats, of course, were produced in antiquity along the Peruvian coast, but whether they were used for long voyages during the Formative remains unknown. Modern artesanal fishermen employ them only for short off-shore runs rather than for longer journeys because they become waterlogged. Thor Heyerdahl (1981: 15–16), on the basis of his observations in Iraq, has suggested that reeds will resist waterlogging if properly harvested, but we have no way of knowing whether they were in the Central Andes during Formative times. These challenges were eventually overcome by the importation of balsa wood for boats to the Peruvian coast and Lake Titicaca, but this occurred in the context of expansive states long after the Formative. It may be significant that the earliest evidence for off-shore voyages in ancient Ecuador coincide with the occupation of La Plata Island during the Middle Formative (i. e., Machalilla; Stothert this volume), while the earliest materials known from islands off the coast of Peru are from the Moche culture, more than 1,000 years later (Kubler 1948).

Thus, the current evidence suggests that during the Formative, the contrast between a dependence on water transport to the north and land transport to the south had important implications for understanding the distinctive character of pre-Hispanic Ecuador. Moreover, while transportation along Ecuador's rivers and oceanfront would have been straightforward and probably common according to Hocquenghem et al. (1993), roundtrip travel into the Humboldt Current would have been technically difficult, if not impossible. There is no consensus on this question, and other scholars believe that pre-Hispanic Andean watercraft could tack against the wind making southerly trips possible. Whether or not such long-distance maritime trips were undertaken between the two culture areas during the Formative, the currents would clearly have favored more frequent travel within the Ecuadorian region and, as a consequence, reinforced the integration of this zone.

Another ramification of Ecuador's relatively abundant rainfall was adequate conditions for farming without primary dependency on irrigation; this pattern, of course, is analogous to the situation in the tropical forests east of the Andes. While the aridity of the Santa Elena peninsula caused artificial holding ponds (*albarradas*) to be built during the Late Formative (Stothert 1995, this volume) and the unusually poor drainage at the mouth of the Guayas led to the construction of ridged field systems (Buys and Muse 1987), most zones in Ecuador did not require large-scale public works and their attendant maintenance. This was equally true for the Ecuadorian highlands, where small-scale irrigation seems to have been introduced only in post-Formative times as a way to promote nucleation and/or safeguard the maize crop.

Contrast this situation with that in Peru where coastal agriculture is almost impossible without irrigation and where experience with irrigation had already been developed in the third millennium B.C. at centers like Caral, El Paraíso, and La Galgada (Grieder, Bueno, Smith, and Malina 1988; Quilter et al. 1991; Shady 1998). By Initial Period times, coeval with late Valdivia and Machalilla, the population in most coastal valleys of Peru were largely dependent on irrigation agriculture, and hydraulic systems had been introduced into many highland areas as well. Thus, the agricultural system in the Peruvian area was one in which communal labor for construction and maintenance was central. Ultimately it tied families to their lands because of the enormous investment required in their infrastructure. In the Central Andes, irrigation and terracing lay at the heart of their subsistence strategy; in the Ecuadorian area, they were apparently more of an afterthought or something reserved for special cases.

It is well-known that the differences between the Humbolt and the Ecuatorial Counter Current not only impact the precipitation patterns but they also affect the yield of marine resources. The Humboldt has a far greater biomass and consequently better fishing, shellfish gathering, and hunting of sea mammals and birds. Edward Lanning, Michael Moseley, and others have argued that the unusual abundance of marine resources facilitated the success of Late Preceramic coastal cultures whose success at fishing and collecting limited their dependence on supplemental agriculture. Nevertheless, the importance of Preceramic cultivation has probably been underestimated because of a focus on shoreline sites. Indeed, the work at Caral in the mid–Supe and La Galgada in mid–Santa suggested that many of the centers were agriculturally oriented long before the introduction of pottery. Despite this, the riches of the Humbolt Current made it feasible to delay a shift to dependence on agriculture in many areas, in contrast to what had occurred to the north in the Ecuadorian area. In any case, although many of the same crops were probably being grown in both areas (Pearsall this volume), the difference between the coastal cultures of Peru and Ecuador during the third millennium B. C. was dramatic. By the time the peoples of the Peruvian coast became fully committed to agriculture as their primary subsistence strategy, the people of coastal Ecuador had already been farmers for many centuries. Clearly they were well down a different path. Similarly, the cultivation of maize as the most important food crop seems to have occurred in Ecuador many centuries before this shift took place in the Central Andes (Pearsall this volume).

In the contrasts between Tropical Forest and Andean farmers, on the basis of ethnographic data, Steward and Faron (1959) signaled substantial differences in population density. While the precision of their figures is dubious, the contrast may be germane when considering the demographic ramifications of the two agricultural systems. One of the features that I found noteworthy in the description of the Early Formative settlement systems described here for coastal Ecuador is the comparatively small size of the documented populations. While information is far from adequate even in Peru, a substantial population is implied by the numerous contemporary Initial Period centers that have been documented in almost every valley of the central and north coast; when compared with the data on Preceramic sites, this suggests a significant increase of population with the expansion of irrigation farming in the lower valleys. The existing data seem to point to much less dense populations among Formative Ecuadorian groups than those in Peru. This contrast continues and even deepens during the final millennium B.C. , during which large centers with populations numbering in the thousands are found in several locations in Peru, while the numerous coeval settlements in Ecuador apparently remained comparatively modest in size.

HIGHLANDS AND COAST IN THE ECUADORIAN FORMATIVE

In considering the chapters herein, I was struck by another major distinction between the Ecuadorian and Peruvian areas during the Formative—a difference in the relative importance of the highlands compared with the coast. In the Central Andes throughout prehistory, the economic and demographic "center of gravity" was in the highlands; in Ecuador, as was evident here in the chapters by Bruhns and Zeidler and Isaacson, the highlands appear to have been lightly occupied throughout the Formative (see also Arellcno 2000). In some areas, there is little evidence of any occupation before the Late Formative, and even the best known Late Formative sites—Cotocollao in the north and Pirincay and Cerro Narrio in the south—appear to be little more than small villages with populations numbering only from a few hundred to, in the view of some, just a few dozen. While this pattern could be a product of preservation and sampling, the amount of investigation and the quantity of destructive development in major highland valleys should have yielded much more evidence of large Formative settlements, if such settlements existed.

As indicated, this pattern from highland Ecuador is in sharp contrast to Peru. In the latter, large populations already existed in many areas by the Late Preceramic, and numerous large centers are documented for the Initial Period and Early Horizon. By the mid-first millennium B.C., highland centers like Chavín de Huántar, Kuntur Wasi, and Pacopampa had large residential populations as well as numerous surrounding village sites (Burger 1992). Indeed, the demographic "heartland" in the Peruvian area was traditionally in intermontane valleys, and this was already the case during the Formative. With ample evidence of monumental constructions at many of these highland sites, it is clear that the developments of the Peruvian Formative was the result of interconnected and parallel processes in the coast, highlands, and eastern slopes. This pattern differs sharply from the situation documented for Ecuador in which the highland population appears relatively late and sparse (Bruhns this volume), thereby suggesting a less important and more asymmetric relationship than in Peru.

Two critical environmental factors are relevant to the constrained Formative developments in the Ecuadorian highlands: (a) the prominence of volcanic activity and (b) the initial absence of wild and domesticated camelids. In this volume Zeidler and Isaacson convey the seriousness of some 20 eruptions that occurred in Ecuador since the Pleistocene and of at least 2 major eruptions in northern Ecuador during the Formative, one during late Valdivia times and the second during Late Formative (i.e., Chorrera) times. In both cases, the bottomland agriculture in the intermontane valleys was vulnerable to the resulting ashfall and other consequences of the eruptions. It appears that lengthy periods of abandonment followed each cataclysmic event in a sizable region in the north. These unpredictable catastrophes must have occasioned considerable chaos, producing disruption and in some cases massive migration. For example,

Zeidler and Isaacson argue that the flourishing of the Chorrera culture on Ecuador's north coast was linked to the migration of highland peoples departing from areas impacted by a major eruption. It seems reasonable to hypothesize that these natural events had a chilling effect on the development of autochthonous highland cultures capable of supporting dense populations, despite the wide range of cultigens like potatoes and *oca* that they had at their disposal. Unlike the famous El Niño events that are the bane of the northern Peruvian coast, the eruptions in highland Ecuador had impacts that lasted for generations, as opposed to the year or two necessary to recover from even the most severe El Niño event. This situation, of course, is not unique to Ecuador; an analog may be found in the impact of volcanic activity on highland Maya development when compared with the less vulnerable Maya lowlands (Dull, Southon, and Sheets 2001; Sheets 1983).

While the entire Andes are volcanic in origin, there are no active volcanoes in central or northern Peru, nor have there been in the relatively recent past. Consequently, the development of Peruvian cultures in most areas was not affected by the violent eruptions such as those that occurred in highland Ecuador. It is interesting, however, to consider the case of Arequipa in southern Peru where there is considerable volcanic activity. While Arequipa is one of the most productive and prosperous centers in contemporary highland Peru, its role in Peruvian prehistory remains poorly understood. Arequipa's absence from recent syntheses of Peruvian archaeology contrasts with its prominence in the socioeconomic and political world of the modern Peruvian nation. Archaeologist José Chavez (1993: 158–161) has argued that Arequipa's prehistory can only be understood within the context of the volcanic eruptions in its past. In contrast, the highlands of central and northern Peru were spared these disruptions during the Formative and in later times.

Secondly, as mentioned above, at the time of first settlement the moist *páramo* grasslands of Ecuador did not support wild camelids (i. e. , vicuñas and guanacos [e. g., Lynch 1989]). Furthermore, while domesticated llamas are able survive on these northern grasslands, they do not appear to have been introduced in significant numbers until after the Formative (Stahl this volume). If George Miller and others are correct in this assessment (Miller and Gill 1990: 49; cf., Miller and Burger 1995), the *páramo*, one of the Ecuadorian highlands largest and richest habitats, would have been underexploited by its inhabitants during most of the Formative. Furthermore, the absence of llamas would have constrained land transport of bulk goods, a particularly important consideration in those areas where, as in the case of the Ecuadorian highlands, navigable rivers are absent. In contrast, llamas were already domesticated in the high Peruvian grasslands of

Junin by 6000 BP (Wheeler 2000), and by the end of the Initial Period they seemed to have been in wide use for transport even to the coast. By the beginning of the Early Horizon in Peru, domesticated camelids were being raised throughout the highland area, and llama caravans increased in scale and scope. Llama meat and camelid wool gained in popularity and became major features in the highland economy and were key items of exchange with the coast during the Chavín Horizon. The absence of camelids and camelid products from the Ecuadorian highlands during the Formative could only have made the *páramo* zone and the highlands in general less attractive to potential settlers and further constrained the growth of populations who chose to live there.

CULTURAL CONTACTS AND CULTURAL CONTRASTS

The foregoing remarks suggest that we can identify separable Ecuadorian and Peruvian cultural areas during the Formative and that the cultures in these two areas differed from each other in a host of fundamental ways. Many of these differences can be traced to differing conditions and resources and resulting adaptive strategies, but there also is a cultural dimension to these differences.

In delineating differing areas, we are not denying or minimizing the existence and importance of contact between the Ecuadorian and Peruvian areas. Several of the contributions in this volume touch upon the contact that existed between the Formative cultures of what is now southern Ecuador and northern Peru. These can be traced back into the mid-Holocene when the climate of the Peruvian north coast may have resembled that of modern Ecuador (Sandweiss 1996; Stothert and Quilter 1991), but they continued during the Formative after climatic conditions had achieved their modern configuration. During the Formative, the relations between northern Peru and southern Ecuador varied in character and in intensity, but the prehistory of these regions were unambiguously linked. As Betty Meggers (Meggers, Evans, and Estrada 1965: 169) first observed and Ed Lanning (1967: 76–77) and Lathrap (1974: 119–124) subsequently expanded upon, two pyroengraved gourds from Huaca Prieta were decorated with exotic designs of the Valdivia style. Their presence strongly suggests that the peoples of this Late Preceramic site in northern Peru were connected by some exchange mechanism to the Early Formative culture of Ecuador's south coast (see Bischof 2000 for an alternative interpretation).

No less ambiguous and far more common is the presence of spondylus and strombus shell at Late Preceramic, Initial Period, and Early Horizon sites on the Peruvian coast and adjacent highlands. Easy to recognize even by malacologically challenged archaeologists, few fragments of spondylus shell fragments in Peruvian sites remain unreported in the archaeological literature (Paulsen 1974). In addition to imported exotic raw or manufactured items, contact between the two areas during the Formative is also attested to by the transmission of ideas that served to inspire the production of local copies of alien artifactual forms. A well-known example of this is the adoption of Machililla- and Chorrera-style flat and cylindrical ceramic stamps, probably used for skin decoration, by the Cupisnique culture of Peru's Initial Period (Lathrap et al. 1975: 51). An even better known example was the late adoption of the stirrup-spouted bottle by the Cupisnique and other Peruvian cultures; according to John Staller's (2000) work in El Oro, such vessels were already being produced in southern Ecuador by late Valdivia times. Other evidence of contact between the Formative cultures of Peru and Ecuador can be seen in the roughly coeval representation of iconographic themes too idiosyncratic to have appeared independently. For example, the roughly coeval depiction of sculpted contortionists on both Chorrera and classic Cupisnique ceramics is hard to dismiss as a coincidence (Elera 1994: 239; Lathrap Collier, and Chandra 1975: 60).

While the evidence for these connections is difficult to dismiss, it is unclear how profound the influence of these contacts proved to be. It may be significant, for example, that while the ceramic stamps of the Ecuadorian Formative were emulated, the iconography on the Cupisnique versions of the stamps was distinctively local. While the anachronistic stirrup-spouted bottle of late Valdivia and Machililla inspired a long tradition of such vessels in Peru, their popularity in Peru did not occur until after 800 B.C. by which time they had fallen out of fashion among Ecuadorian cultures and had been replaced by single-necked bottles with strap handles.

Much has been made of the spondylus trade, whether by sea, as Marcos has proposed, or by land, as Hocquenghem has suggested, or both, yet the exchange of an easily identifiable exotic does not necessarily link cultures in any but the most superficial way. If intermediaries from the intervening frontier region served as mediators, the contact may have only limited impact beyond the transitional zone. For example, throughout the Middle Ages substantial quantities of ivory and gold from West Africa were supplied to Western Europe by Muslim trading groups centered in North Africa. These exotic materials were commonly used to adorn religious art and the clothing of the European elite; nevertheless, the impact of sub-Saharan culture on Europe, or even European awareness of the peoples producing these materials, was meager.

In the case of the highly valued spondylus shell, a reasonable analog to ivory in the Old World, there is ample evidence that during most of the Ecuadorian Formative small quantities of spondylus was transported southward to groups on the Peruvian coast and highlands, but the available evidence does not suggest that the symbolic meanings associated with the spiny oyster transferred crossculturally. In fact, there is some evidence to the contrary. The dyadic relationship of the spondylus with the strombus, representing female–male opposition, appears prominently in both the Chavín and Cupisnique cultures of Peru, whereas it is unknown among the Formative cultures of Ecuador (Stothert this volume). One of the most common ceremonial uses of the spondylus in Formative Ecuador was for the fabrication of shell masks; but these objects, presumably utilized in religious rituals in the highlands and on the coast, have never been recovered at Peruvian archaeological sites, and they appear to have been absent among the cultures of the Peruvian Formative.

The strombus shell, another mollusk from Ecuadorian waters sought after in Formative Peru, was especially valued in Chavín times as a shell trumpet, and strombus shell trumpets elaborately engraved with Chavín religious imagery have been recovered in situ on the summit of the temple at Kuntur Wasi (Kato 1994: 215). Yet while the strombus is native to Ecuador, trumpets made from this material do not appear to have held a comparably important place in ritual life among the cultures of the Ecuadorian Formative. The apparent failure to export the original symbolic associations of the spondylus, like the failure of the Chavín religious ideology to spread to the Ecuadorian cultures, suggests that the differences between the cultures of the Ecuadorian Formative and the coeval cultures within Peru were not significantly diminished by the contacts between them, nor were these differences solely based on subsistence, demography, and other aspects of human adaptation.

From an archaeological perspective, perhaps the most conspicuous difference between the formative cultures of Ecuador and their contemporaries in Peru is the general absence of large-scale public architecture. As was illustrated in the 1983 Dumbarton Oaks conference on monumental architecture in the Andes (Donnan 1985), massive constructions were featured at Peruvian sites beginning in the Late Preceramic, and this trend continued through the Initial Period and into the Early Horizon. While some of the Formative cultures of Ecuador may have had ceremonial centers featuring public architecture, little is known of these constructions. We do know that some late Valdivia sites such as La Emerenciana have gained attention partly because of the documentation of its platform constructions (Staller 1994). Yet the largest of these is a mere 1.5 m in height. Even the still undocumented public complexes Stothert discusses in this volume represent a rather small investment of labor when compared with its Initial Period Peruvian counterparts, which often rise between 15 to 30 m above the surrounding landscape. In coastal valleys such as Rimac, Chancay, Lurín, and Casma, there are several coeval massive pyramid complexes within a single valley. Public constructions of comparable scale have been documented in the highlands for the Early Horizon (Burger 1992). Measured in millions of person-days, the labor investment in these constructions bespeaks a culture in which communal labor for public purposes lies at the heart of societal concerns. Judging from the available evidence, the prominence of communal labor in the Central Andes was the result of the basic organization and ideology of quotidian life.

As recently confirmed at Caral in the Supe valley, this Central Andean pattern of massive public constructions appears by 2600 B. C. (calibrated) along the Peruvian coast and is consequently coeval with Valdivia (Shady, Haas, and Creamer 2001). Monumental architecture and the implicit reliance on corporate labor consequently predates the establishment of states with coercive authority or even stratified polities in the Central Andes. At roughly the same time, the characteristic Tropical Forest village pattern of large multifamily houses surrounding a central plaza had appeared at Real Alto in the Guayas drainage (Raymond this volume). The contrast between these two long-standing patterns suggests fundamentally different ideologies of social relations and the relationship between the individual family and the community, just as it reflects different notions of the appropriate way in which societies communicate with the supernatural.

When I first began to prepare this text, I kept remembering one of Don Lathrap's revisionist statements in his review of Kent Flannery's *Early Mesoamerican Village*. Flannery (1976) argued that with the appearance of "primary village farming communities," Mesoamerica first became definable as a culture area, distinct from the desert food gatherers to the north and the tropical forest peoples to the south. Lathrap (1977: 1321) disagreed and argued that with the appearance of Mesoamerican farming communities, there was an "essentially uniform culture" that extended all the way from Mesoamerica to northern Peru; the uniform agricultural basis for this entire area was Tropical Forest Culture. In this view, the Formative cultures of the fourth, third, and second millennium B.C. in northern Peru and Ecuador had yet to be distinguished in a fundamental way, and it was only with the rise of Chavín after 1000 B.C. that the Central Andes started to differentiate from this uniform agricultural substratum and finally embarked on its individual path toward civilization.

Over two decades have passed since Lathrap offered this statement, and I do not believe that the emerging pattern of evidence has supported his claim, at least in regard to Ecuador and Peru. While Formative peoples of Ecuador and Peru were in contact with each other and shared some characteristics, including their cultigens, there were considerable differences between the cultures of these areas from the beginning of the Ecuadorian Formative, if not earlier, in terms of economic systems, agricultural technology, religious patterns and sociopolitical organization. After reviewing the chapters in this volume and considering the existing literature, I must argue that with the appearance of "primary village farming communities," the Central Andes and Northern Andes, which includes Ecuador, embarked on different and distinctive pathways.

Nonetheless, Lathrap's identification of Chavín as a crucial watershed dividing the pathways taken by those of the Central Andes and those of the Northern Andes, including Ecuador, remains a valuable insight, since subsequent research has confirmed that it was during this time (i.e., the first millennium B.C.) that political hierarchies and highly stratified societies emerged in northern and central Peru. Meanwhile, the existing evidence on the coeval Late Formative cultures of Ecuador has led Stothert (this volume) to conclude that the Formative peoples of Ecuador lacked a political hierarchy focused on a dominant group of elites. Instead power was more widely and evenly distributed.

Given this fundamental contrast in sociopolitical organization, it is not surprising that the coeval Chorrera and Chavín art style appear to have moved in diametrically opposed directions. Chavín iconography, drawing upon the fierce and forbidding imagery of the Cupisnique and Manchay styles, features ever more complex composites of human and other predatory animals, most notably unnatural combinations of jaguars, caymans, serpents, hawks, and crested eagles. As the Chavín style evolves, it becomes more esoteric and involuted, while still reproducing the monstrous combinations of carnivorous animals that was its hallmark. Chavín iconography suggests a set of beliefs and practices linked to a sphere outside the realm of daily experience that is both dangerous and powerful. The Chorrera art style, in contrast, eschews hybrid and fantastic shapes. Instead it offers depictions of creatures or plants that exist in nature and does so with a degree of accuracy that allows the viewer to recognize the species as well as the genus of the representation (Cummins this volume). The visual representation of natural forms in Chorrera art suggest a cosmology that focuses on the set of relations observable in this world as a key to understanding the cosmos and the human role within it.

By the end of the Formative, the peoples of pre-Hispanic Ecuador and Peru shared many basic features, such as a sedentary life that was based on a stable system of intensive agriculture, and both were physically linked through long-standing exchange networks across the permeable frontier that separated them. Despite these similarities and linkages, the world of the Ecuadorian Formative appears to have been profoundly different from that of Central Andes in terms of its economic organization, its sociopolitical structure, and the ideological frameworks that made life comprehensible and meaningful.

BIBLIOGRAPHY

ARELLANO, A. JORGE
    2000   Primeras evidencias del Formativo Tardío en la sierra central del Ecuador. In *Formativo sudamericano* (Paulina Ledergerber-Crespo, ed.). Abya-Yala, Quito.

BISCHOF, HENNING
    2000   Los mates tallados de Huaca Prieta ¿Evidencias de arte Valdivia en el Arcaico centroandino? *Boletín Arqueología Pontificia Universidad Católica* 3: 85–119.

BRUHNS, KAREN OLSEN
    1994   *Ancient South America.* Cambridge University Press, Cambridge.

BURGER, RICHARD L.
    1984   Archaeological Areas and Prehistoric Frontiers: The Case of Formative Peru and Ecuador. In *Social and Economic Organization in the Pre-Hispanic Andes* (D. Browman, R. Burger, and M. Rivera, eds.), BAR International Series 194: 33–7. British Archaeological Reports, Oxford.
    1992   *Chavín and the Origins of Andean Civilization.* Thames and Hudson, London.

BURGER, RICHARD L. , FRANK ASARO, HELEN V. MICHEL, FRED H. STROSS, AND ERNESTO SALAZAR
    1994   An Initial Consideration of Obsidian Procurement and Exchange in Pre-hispanic Ecuador. *Latin American Antiquity* 5: 228–255.

BURGER, RICHARD L. , AND MICHAEL D. GLASCOCK
    2000   Locating the Quispisisa Obsidian Source in the Department of Ayacucho, Peru. *Latin American Antiquity* 11(3): 258–268.

BUYS, JOZEF, AND MICHAEL MUSE
    1987   Arqueología de asentamientos asociados a los campos elevados de Peñon del Río, Guayas, Ecuador. In *Pre-Hispanic Agricultural Fields in the Andean Region*, pt. 1 (William Denevan, Kent Mathewson, and Gregory Knapp, eds.): 225–248. BAR International Series 359 (i), British Archaeological Reports, Oxford.

CHAVEZ, JOSÉ ANTONIO
    1993   *La Erupción del Volcán Misti.* Impressions Zenit, Arequipa, Peru.

CHURCH, WARREN B.
    n. d.   *Prehistoric Cultural Development and Interregional Interaction in the Tropical Montane Forests of Peru.* Ph. D. dissertation. Department of Anthropology, Yale University. University Microfilms International, Ann Arbor, Mich.

DONNAN, CHRISTOPHER B. (ED.)
    1985   *Early Ceremonial Architecture in the Andes.* Dumbarton Oaks, Washington, D.C.

DULL, ROBERT A., JOHN R. SOUTHON, AND PAYSON SHEETS
    2001   Volcanism, Ecology and Culture. A Reassessment of the Volcán Ilopango TBJ Eruption in the Southern Maya Realm. *Latin American Antiquity* 12: 25–44.

ELERA, CARLOS
    1994   El Complejo Cupisnique. Antecedentes y desarrollo de su ideología religiosa. In *El Mundo ceremonial andino* (Luis Millones and Yoshio Onuki, eds.): 225–252. Editorial Horizonte, Lima.

FLANNERY, KENT
1976   *The Early Mesoamerican Village.* Academic Press, New York.

GRIEDER, TERENCE, ALBERTO BUENO, C. EARLE SMITH JR., AND ROBERT MALINA
1988   *La Galgada, Peru: A Preceramic Culture in Transition.* University of Texas Press, Austin.

GUFFROY, JEAN
1994   *Cerro Ñañanique: Un Etablissement Monumental de la Période Formative en Limite de Désert (Haut Piura, Perou).* ORSTOM Editions, Paris.

GUFFROY, J.N., N. ALMEIDA, P. LECOQ, C. CAILLARET, F. DUVERNEUIL, L. EMPERAIRE AND B. ARNAUD
1987   *Loja prehispanique.* Editions Recherches sur les Civilisations, Paris.

HEYERDAHL, THOR
1981   *The Tigris Expedition.* Doubleday, Garden City, N.Y.

HOCQUENGHEM, ANNE MARIE
1991   Frontera entre "areas culturales" nor y centroandinas en los valles y la costa del extremo norte peruano. *Bulletin de l'Institut Français d'Etudes Andines* 23(1): 309-348.

1995   Rutas de entrada del mullu en el extremo norte del Perú. *Bulletin de l'Institut Français d'Etudes Andines* 22(3): 701–719.

HOCQUENGHEM, ANNE MARIE, JAIME IDROVO, PETER KAULICKE, AND DOMINIQUE GOMIS
1993   Bases del intercambio entre sociedades norperuanas y surecuatorianas: Una zona de transición entre 1500 aC y 600 dC. *Bulletin de l'Institut Français d'Etudes Andines* 22(2): 443–466.

KATO, YASUTAKE
1994   Resultados de las excavaciones en Kuntur Wasi, Cajamarca. In *El Mundo ceremonial andino* (Luis Millones and Yoshio Onuki, eds.): 199–224. Editorial Horizonte, Lima.

KAULICKE, PETER
1998   El Período Formativo de Piura. Boletín de Arqueología Pontificia Universidad Católica del Perú 2: 19–36. Lima.

KUBLER, GEORGE
1948   Towards Absolute Time: Guano Archaeology. In *Reappraisal of Peruvian Archaeology* (Wendell Bennett, ed.). *American Antiquity* 12(4), pt. 2: 29–50.

LANNING, EDWARD P.
1967   Peru Before the Incas. Prentice Hall, Englewood Cliffs, N.J.

LATHRAP, DONALD
1973   The Antiquity and Importance of Long-Distance Trade Relationships in the Moist Tropics of Pre-Columbian South America. *World Archaeology* 5(2): 170–186.

1974   The Moist Tropics, the Arid Lands, and the Appearance of Great Art Styles in the New World. In Mary Elizabeth King and Idris R. Taylor, eds., *Special Publications of the Museum, Texas Tech University* 7: 155–158.

1977   Review of *The Early Mesoamerican Village* by Kent Flannery. *Science* 195: 1319–1321.

Richard L. Burger

LATHRAP, DONALD, DONALD COLLIER, AND HELEN CHANDRA
    1975   *Culture, Clay and Creativity 3000–300 B. C.* Field Museum of Natural History, Chicago.

LUMBRERAS, LUIS G.
    1981   *Arqueología de la America andina.* Editorial Milla Batres, Lima.

LUMBRERAS, LUIS G. (ED.)
    1979a   *Comentarios sobre el conjunto de notas que constituyen el documento de trabajo,* Documento de Trabajo 2, Proyecto Regional de Patrimonio Cultural Andino. UNESCO/PNUD, Lima.
    1979b   *Críticas y perspectivas de la arqueología andina. Documentos de Trabajo* 1, Proyecto Regional de Patrimonio Cultural Andino UNESCO/PNUD, Lima.

LYNCH, THOMAS
    1989   Chobshi Cave in Retrospect. *Andean Past* 2: 1–32.

MARCOS, JORGE
    1978   Cruising to Acapulco and Back with the Thorny Oyster Set: Model for a Linear Exchange System. *Journal of the Steward Anthropological Society* 9 (1/2): 99–132.

MARCOS, JORGE, AND PRESLEY NORTON (EDS.)
    1982   Primer Simposio de Correlaciones Antropológicas Andino-Mesoamericano. Escuela Técnica de Arqueología, Guyaquil.

MEGGERS, BETTY J. , CLIFFORD EVANS, AND EMILIO ESTRADA
    1965   *Early Formative Period of Coastal Ecuador: The Valdivia and Machalilla Phases.* Smithsonian Institution Press, Washington, D. C.

MILLER, GEORGE R. , AND RICHARD L. BURGER
    1995   Our Father the Cayman, Our Dinner the Llama: Animal Utilization at Chavín de Huantar, Peru. *American Antiquity* 60: 421–458.

MILLER, GEORGE R. , AND ANNE L. GILL
    1990   Zooarchaeology at Pirincay, a Formative Period Site in Highland Ecuador. *Journal of Field Archaeology* 17(1): 49–68.

MORALES, DANIEL
    1992   Chambira: Alfareros tempranos en la amazonia peruana. In *Estudios de arqueología peruana* (Duccio Bonavia, ed.): 149–176, FOMCIENCIAS, Lima.

MURRA, JOHN V.
    1975   *Formaciones económicas y políticas del mundo andino.* Instituto de Estudios Peruanos, Lima.

MUSEO ARQUEOLÓGICO RAFAEL LARCO HERRERA
    1999   *Spondylus: Ofrenda sagrada y símbolo de paz.* Fundación Telefónica, Lima.

NETHERLY, PATRICIA, OLAF HOLM, JORGE MARCOS, AND R. MARCA
    n. d.   Survey of the Arenillas Valley, El Oro Province, Ecuador. Paper presented at the 45th Annual Meeting of the Society for American Archaeology, Philadelphia, 1980.

OLIVERA, QUIRINO
    1999   Evidencias arqueológicas del Período Formativo en la cuenca baja del Río Utcubamba y Chinchipe. *Boletín de Arqueología* Pontificia Universidad Católica del Perú 2: 105–112.

484

Conclusions

PAULSEN, ALISON
> 1974   The Thorny Oyster and the Voice of God: Spondylus and Strombus in Andean Prehistory. *American Antiquity* 39: 597–601.

POZORSKI, SHELIA, AND THOMAS POZORSKI
> 1996   Ventilated Hearth Structures in the Casma Valley. *Latin American Antiquity* 7: 341–353.
> 1998   La dinámica del valle de Casma durante el período Inicial. *Boletín de Arqueología* Pontificia Universidad Católica del Perú 2: 83–100.

QUILTER, JEFFREY, BERNADINO OJEDA, DEBORAH PEARSALL, JOHN JONES, AND ELIZABETH WING
> 1991   Subsistence Economy of El Paraíso, Peru. *Science* 251: 277–283.

RAVINES, ROGGER
> 1982   *Panorama de la arqueología andina.* Instituto de Estudios Peruanos, Lima.

SANDWEISS, DANIEL
> 1996   Mid-Holocene Cultural Interaction between the North Coast of Peru and Ecuador. *Latin American Antiquity* 7(1): 41–50

SANDWEISS, DANIEL, JAMES B. RICHARDSON III, ELIZABETH J. REITZ, H. B. ROLLINS, AND K. A. MAASCH
> 1996   Geoarchaeological Evidence from Peru for a 5,000 Years B. P. Onset of El Niño. *Science* 273: 1531–1533.

SHADY, RUTH
> 1987   Tradición y cambio en las sociedades formativas de Bagua, Amazonas, Perú. *Revista Andina* 10: 457–487.
> 1998   *La Ciudad sagrada de Caral, Supe en los Albores de la civilización en el Perú.* Universidad Nacional Mayor de San Marcos, Lima.

SHADY, RUTH, JONATHAN HAAS, AND WINIFRED CREAMER
> 2001   Dating Caral, a Preceramic Site in the Supe Valley on the Central Coast of Peru. *Science* 292: 723–726.

SHEETS, PAYSON
> 1983   *Archaeology and Volcanism in Central America.* University of Texas Press, Austin.

STALLER, JOHN
> 1994   *Late Valdivia Occupation in El Oro Province Ecuador: Excavations at the Early Formative Period (3500–1500 B. C.). Site of La Emerenciana.* Ph. D. dissertation, Southern Methodist University. University Microfilms International, Ann Arbor, Mich.
> 2000   The Jeli Phase Complex at La Emerenciana, a Late Valdivia site in Southern El Oro Province, Ecuador. *Andean Past* 6: 117–174.

STEWARD, JULIAN, AND LOUIS FARON
> 1959   *Native Peoples of South America.* McGraw Hill, New York.

STOTHERT, KAREN
> 1995   Las albarradas tradicionales y el manejo de aguas en la península de Santa Elena. *Miscelanea Antropológica Ecuatoriana* 8: 131–160.

STOTHERT, KAREN, AND JEFFREY QUILTER
> 1991   Archaic Adaptations of the Andean Region, 9000–5000 BP. *Revista de Arqueología Americana* 4: 25–53.

Richard L. Burger

WHEELER, JANE
    2000   Patrones prehistóricos de la utilización de los camélidos sudamericanos. *Boletín Arqueología Pontificia Universidad Católica del Perú* 3: 297–305.

WILLEY, GORDON
    1971   *An Introduction to American Archaeology,* vol. 2. *South America.* Prentice Hall, Englewood Cliffs, N. J.

WILLEY, GORDON, AND PHILLIP PHILLIPS
    1958   *Method and Theory in American Archaeology.* University of Chicago Press, Chicago.

WILSON, DAVID J.
    1999   *Indigenous South Americans of the Past and Present: An Ecological Perspective.* Westview Press, Boulder, Colo.

Formative Period Chronology for the Coast and Western Lowlands of Ecuador

JAMES A. ZEIDLER

COLORADO STATE UNIVERSITY

INTRODUCTION

Appendix A summarizes the Formative period chronology for both the coast and interior western lowlands of Ecuador and encompasses the following six modern provinces from south to north: El Oro, Guayas, Los Ríos, Manabí, western Pichincha, and Esmeraldas. The chronological information amassed from this extensive area is more voluminous than for the highlands or the Oriente for a number of reasons. First, the land area encompassed by the coast and interior lowlands is larger. Secondly, the coastal lowlands have received a disproportionate amount of archaeological attention over the last century. Finally, it is believed there was a much higher density of Formative period populations inhabiting the coastal lowlands throughout the entire period, and especially in the Early Formative period. In chronological order, the three Formative period cultural complexes found in the coastal lowlands are the well-known Valdivia, Machalilla, and Chorrera complexes. Each of these is treated separately below.

The Formative period chronology of this extensive area is based on five dating methods. Absolute dating is based on *radiocarbon assays, thermoluminescence (TL)* assays, and to a lesser extent, *obsidian hydration*. Relative dating is based on *tephrostratigraphy* and *ceramic cross-dating*. Radiocarbon dating is by far the most important of these methods for our understanding of Formative chronology in the coastal lowlands, and primarily emphasis is given here to this method. This review is not intended as an exhaustive discussion of Formative period prehistory in the western Ecuadorian lowlands. It is focused on absolute chronology; therefore, specific archaeological contexts and ceramic complexes are discussed only insofar as they shed light on our understanding of absolute chronology. For supplementary information on the archaeological data discussed herein, see Marcos (1998).

Table A1 contains a compilation of 161 Formative period radiocarbon assays and their calibrated calendrical ranges in years B.C. They are arranged by province, beginning with Guayas province, and the assays are listed in descending chronological order within each province. Each listing includes the site name, cultural and phase affiliation, laboratory name and number, the uncalibrated age in radiocarbon years before present (RCYBP) along with the standard error, the calibrated calendrical age range (in years B.C.) at a 68.2% probability, the calibrated calendrical age range (in years B.C.) at a 95.4% probability, and bibliographic references for the published assays (or information on their archaeological context). Calibration of all radiocarbon determinations was carried out with the OxCal program, version 3.4 (see Bronk Ramsey 1994, 1995) on the basis of Stuiver and Reimer (1986) and extensions in Stuiver, Long, and Kra (1993). For additional information on some of the radiocarbon determinations in Table A1, see Ziólkowski et al. (n.d.: 95–195). For a comparison of the ^{14}C and TL chronology for Formative Ecuador, see Marcos and Obelic (1998).

VALDIVIA CHRONOLOGY

By far the best known and most investigated of the three Formative period cultures from the coastal lowlands of Ecuador is Valdivia, named after a fishing village on the north coast of Guayas province. It was initially defined by Ecuadorian archaeologist Emilio Estrada (1956, 1958) and subsequently studied in greater detail by Meggers, Evans, and Estrada (1965; Evans and Meggers 1957). Much has been written and debated about Valdivia chronology because of its status as one of the earliest pottery-producing cultures in the New World exhibiting a sedentary settlement pattern and a broad subsistence base dependent on marine resources and horticultural production. The Valdivia relative chronology is based on ceramic seriations developed by Meggers et al. (1965) derived from their pioneering excavations at the type-site (G-31) and elsewhere along the Guayas coast, and by Hill (1972–74) from ceramic material collected by Lanning (n.d.) on the Santa Elena peninsula. The former subdivides the Valdivia sequence into four broad phases (A, B, C, and D), while that of Hill provides a more refined breakdown of the Valdivia ceramic sequence into eight phases of varying duration (1–8). Subsequent research at large Valdivia village sites such as Real Alto and Loma Alta has confirmed the validity of the Hill sequence, as well as its greater utility for chronological analysis.

As Table A1 shows, some 95 radiocarbon determinations now exist for Valdivia: in Guayas, El Oro, and Manabí provinces. Terminal Valdivia (Phase 8) pottery has also been found in Los Ríos province, but no radiocarbon determinations are as yet available. Of these four provinces, only Guayas province exhibits the entire 3,000-year sequence, whereas Manabí contains all but the earliest phase, and the other two provinces contain only its terminal phases.

The most recent evaluation of the Valdivia chronology is that of Marcos and Michczynski (1996), who combined radiocarbon determinations with recent thermoluminescence assays of Valdivia pottery to form a revised absolute chronology for the eight phases of the Valdivia sequence. Three of these ceramic phases (1, 2, and 8) are divided into two subphases (a and b) yielding a sequence of 11 temporal periods. Phases 1, 2, 3, and 8 are dated with radiocarbon determinations, whereas Phases 4, 5, 6, and 7 are dated with TL assays. In some cases, both methods are employed. Table A2 reproduces their absolute chronology, which spans from 4400 to 1450 B.C.

First, they examined 80 radiocarbon determinations spanning the entire Valdivia sequence and provided calibrated calendrical age ranges at 95% probability for each (Marcos and Michczynski 1996: table 1). Noting that many of these determinations were derived from excavations that employed arbitrary levels and were thus dating "periods" rather than "events," they selected suites of 33 reliable radiocarbon determinations derived from controlled stratigraphic excavations pertaining to phases 1a,b, 2a,b, 3, and 8 at the sites of Ayalán, Colimes (Perinao site), Loma Alta, San Isidro, Real Alto, and Valdivia excavations by Bischof and Viteri Gamboa (1972; Marcos and Michczynski 1996: table 2). Even in these cases some feature contexts associated with building activity, such as wall trenches, were eliminated from consideration because of the higher likelihood of mixing. Examples include radiocarbon assays from Real Alto wall trench features dating to phases 4, 5, and 6. Likewise, charcoal samples derived from long-lived species of wood used for wall posts or roof timbers were avoided where possible, as radiocarbon analysis would result in "cutting" dates that may be a century or more older than the actual burning event (see Schiffer 1986). The 33 selected radiocarbon determinations were then used to calculate a composite probability distribution of calibrated radiocarbon dates for the six phases and sub-phases. The 68% confidence interval (CI) was then selected to represent the calibrated calendrical age ranges for each of the phases and subphases (see Table A2).

Next, the TL chronology was developed with assays from the sites of Real Alto, Punta La Tintina, Loma de Los Villones, and San Lorenzo del Mate. Selected pottery samples were stylistically affiliated with Valdivia Phases 1b, 2b, 3,

4, 5, 6, 7, and 8 (Alvarez, Marcos, and Spinolo 1995; Marcos and Michczynski 1996: app. 2; Martini et al. n.d) and served to augment the radiocarbon analysis by filling in gaps where reliable radiocarbon determinations were not available. The resulting TL chronology for these phases and subphases is provided in Table A2. By combining these two independent dating methods, Marcos and Michczynski (1996) then derived the new absolute chronology for Valdivia provided in the rightmost column of Table A2. Note that Table A2 contains a reference to Phase 8b for which no radiocarbon determinations nor TL assays are given. Jorge Marcos (personal communication; Marcos and Michczynski 1996) proposes this as a provisional subphase dating from 1600 to 1450 B.C. because of a distinct post-Phase 8 ceramic assemblage from the site of San Lorenzo del Mate. He argues that it may eventually warrant designation as Valdivia Phase 9 and should include a similar ceramic assemblage from the Emerenciana site in El Oro (Staller 1994). One caveat regarding this new chronology is that Marcos and Michczynski (1996) contains typographical errors in the transcription of several radiocarbon determinations and standard errors. For the most part, these are minor and even if inadvertently used to calculate the composite probability distributions, their effect would be minimal. One exception, however, is their use of one of the earliest determinations from Real Alto: ISGS-448, 5620 ± 250 (Liu, Riley, and Coleman 1986: 106), pertaining to Valdivia Phase 1a. It is listed incorrectly in two different tables as 5260 ± 256 (Marcos and Michczynski 1996: tables 1, 2), creating an error of 360 radiocarbon years. Calculating the composite probability distribution for Phase 1a with their figure, then their suggested beginning date of 4400 B.C. for Phase 1a would actually be earlier.

A second caveat concerns the use of TL assays as sole determinants of the age ranges of Phases 4 through 7. Since the samples used are not as geographically diverse as the radiocarbon determinations employed in the analysis, they may be biasing the results toward TL dates that apply to only restricted area(s) (i.e., the Chanduy valley and San Lorenzo del Mate in Guayas province). As a result, I argue that they may be systematically placing the age ranges of phases 5, 6, and 7 (as well as Phase 8) slightly later in time (i.e., younger) than may be warranted (see Table A2). This has important implications for the absolute dating of Phase 8. When radiocarbon determinations are utilized for deriving the Phase 8 B.C. chronology, all three of the CIs used (50%, 68.2%, and 95.4%) show that Phase 8 began *at least* by 2000 B.C. (Marcos and Michczynski 1996: table 3). This earlier start date also agrees perfectly with the results of a Bayesian statistical analysis conducted on radiocarbon determinations from the San Isidro site in the Jama River valley of northern Manabí (Zeidler, Buck, and Litton

1998: table 4). Yet when combining the radiocarbon results with the TL results, Marcos and Michczynski (1996) arrived at a questionable age range of 1800 to 1600 B.C. for Valdivia Phase 8. In the Jama valley case, the modal values of the 95% HPD (highest posterior density) regions for the start and end of Phase 8 in northern Manabí ranged from 2030 to 1880 B.C.. These figures correspond very closely to the 50% confidence interval provided by Marcos and Michczynski (1996: table 3) for Phase 8: 2030–1830 B.C., from the five San Isidro determinations and two determinations from the Ayalán site in Guayas province. They also agree well with the radiocarbon data from other Phase 8 sites such as La Emerenciana in El Oro province (Staller 1994) and the Anllula shell mound in Guayas province. Thus, several geographically dispersed radiocarbon determinations from El Oro, Guayas, and Manabí provinces are all in agreement that 2000 to 1800 B.C. is a highly likely age range for Valdivia Phase 8 throughout coastal Ecuador. The subsequent phase of the Valdivia sequence, termed Phase 8b or possibly Valdivia Phase 9, discussed by Marcos and Michczynski (1996), has been tentatively identified at San Lorenzo del Mate in Guayas province and by Staller (1994) at La Emerenciana in El Oro province. It represents a transitional phase between Terminal Valdivia and Early Machalilla ceramics and is suggested here to date between 1800 and possibly 1500 B.C. If Valdivia Phase 8 proper dates from 2000 to 1800 B.C., then the rather late age ranges suggested by Marcos and Michczynski (1996) for Phases 6 and 7 should be adjusted accordingly. In spite of these caveats, the Marcos and Michczynski absolute chronology represents a significant advance in Valdivia archaeology that will be of great heuristic utility for years to come.

MACHALILLA CHRONOLOGY

Neither the Machalilla nor the Chorrera cultural sequence has received the same amount of statistical scrutiny as Valdivia, nor are their internal phase designations as widely agreed upon as those of the Valdivia sequence Hill (1972–74) developed. The Machalilla complex, named after a coastal fishing village in southern Manabí province, was initially defined by Estrada (1958). Evans and Meggers (1961; Meggers and Evans 1962) and Meggers et al. (1965) made the earliest attempts to place Machalilla culture in a chronological context. They consistently regarded it as largely coeval with the final half of Valdivia Phase C and all of Phase D (roughly corresponding to Phases 4–8 in the Hill sequence), but their absolute chronology for Machalilla has varied over the years. As recently as 1977, however, they dated it from 2300 to 1500 B.C. because of their belief that Machalilla "trade sherds" and "deformed skulls" occurred in their excavations of certain Late Valdivia sites (Meggers and Evans 1977).

Most archaeologists working on the coast of Ecuador after the mid-1960s, however, have followed Estrada's (1958: 55) initial supposition that Machalilla culture succeeded Valdivia. Indeed, as mentioned above, clear evidence for a transitional ceramic phase linking Valdivia Phase 8 with Early Machalilla has been found at two sites (San Lorenzo del Mate and La Emerenciana) far removed geographically from the southern coast of Manabí province where Machalilla culture was initially defined. Interestingly, Machalilla does *not* follow Terminal Valdivia in at least one area of the coast: northern Manabi province (Zeidler et al. 1998). Here the Valdivia Phase 8 occupation ended at about 1880 B.C. due to ashfall from a major volcanic eruption (Tephra I) emanating from highland Ecuador (see Zeidler and Isaacson this volume). A 500-year hiatus followed, and the Jama valley was abandoned until the onset of the Late Formative Chorrera culture (Tabuchila variant) at 1300 B.C. in calibrated calendrical years (Zeidler et al. 1998).

With respect to relative dating, the internal delineation of ceramic phases within Machalilla culture has not met with the same amount of scholarly agreement as the Valdivia sequence. The earliest attempt at defining an internal ceramic sequence for Machalilla was that of Meggers et al. (1965), who proposed a sequence of three phases (A, B, and C) from Fordian seriation of excavated ceramic materials derived from arbitrary, horizontal, 20-cm levels. The shortcomings of their analytical method have been thoroughly reviewed by Lippi (1983: 226–230), and their three-phase sequence has not received widespread usage. Subsequent attempts at a seriation for Machalilla ceramics were those of Bischof (1975b) and Paulsen and McDougle (n.d.a; see also Paulsen and McDougle n.d.b), both of which proposed five-phase sequences that were based on limited ceramic data. Bischof's (1975b) scheme, from research in the vicinity of Valdivia, is convincing only for his Machalilla phases 2 and 5. The sequence proposed by Paulsen and McDougle (n.d.a), which was based on the La Libertad site on the Santa Elena peninsula, relies on a few ceramic attributes and is therefore of limited utility for comparisons outside the Santa Elena peninsula.

The most current and comprehensive Machalilla ceramic seriation is the seven-phase sequence Lippi (1983) proposed from his excavations at the La Ponga site. Here a broad range of Machalilla ceramic attributes associated with bowl forms were analyzed, forming a logical progression from Late Valdivia attributes to early Chorrera attributes. Unfortunately, none of these internal phase designations has been dated either through radiocarbon methods or through TL analysis. Consequently, they cannot be placed with certainty on an absolute time scale. Two of the radiocarbon determinations from Lippi's work at La Ponga (WIS 1140 and WIS 1141) are attributed to his Machalilla Phases 1 through 5 (Lippi 1983: 348), whereas three determinations from Paulsen and McDougle's (n.d.a) work at on the Santa Elena peninsula (I 7006, I 7008, and I 7013) are attributed to Machalilla phases 3 through 7 (Lippi 1983: 348; see Table A1). It is clear that a considerable amount of new field research will have to be conducted on the Machalilla occupation of coastal Ecuador before significant advancement can be made toward establishing an absolute chronology for these ceramic phases.

Absolute dating of Machalilla has thus been limited to a general bracketing of the entire cultural complex, and estimates have varied over the years as more radiocarbon determinations have been made available. Initial estimates by Lanning (n.d.), Lathrap, Collier, and Chandra (1975), and Lathrap, Marcos, and Zeidler (1977) placed the beginning date at 1500 B.C. and an end date at approximately 1000 B.C. In a subsequent estimate based on excavations in coastal Guayas province, Bischof (1975b) argued for a beginning date between 1750 and 1550 B.C. and an end date of 950 B.C. The earlier start date proposed by Bischof was based on his belief that his five-phase ceramic sequence (beginning with Machalilla 2 or Early Machalilla) required sufficient time depth to have developed out of Terminal Valdivia. Machalilla 1 was proposed as an undefined hypothetical phase. From their research at La Libertad on the Santa Elena peninsula, also in coastal Guayas province, Paulsen and McDougle (n.d.b) estimated a time span of 1300 to 900 B.C. This is slightly earlier that the estimate of 1200 to 800 B.C. suggested by Lippi based on his excavations at the La Ponga site in the Valdivia valley (Lippi 1983: 35).

Although several Machalilla radiocarbon determinations predating Lippi's 1200 B.C. start date exist for coastal Guayas province, Lippi (1983) has rejected these as unreliable. First, the early determination obtained by Meggers at al. (1965) from the Buena Vista site (SI 69, 3450 ± 50 RCYBP) is based on a shell sample from *mixed* Valdivia and Machalilla deposits (Lippi 1983: 351). Likewise, SI 107 (3320 ± 170 RCYBP) from the La Cabuya site was a *split sample* from a single charcoal specimen that provided the determination for SI 108 (2980 ± 160 RCYBP) and cannot be reliably used alone. Finally, the two radiocarbon determinations obtained by Norton at the Buena Vista site (SI 1050, 3250 ± 90 RCYBP; SI 1051, 2945 ± 115 RCYBP) are ambiguous because it is unclear, according to Lippi (1983: 351), whether they pertain to the Late Valdivia or the Machalilla components of the site. Thus, Lippi's (1983) estimated Machalilla time range of 1200 to 800 B.C. is based on a total of seven radiocarbon determinations: three from La Ponga (WIS 1125, 1140, and 1141), three from La Libertad (I 7006, I 7008, and I 7013), and one combined determination from the Buena Vista site (SI 107/108) in which the two assays are averaged.

A more recent estimate from current calibrated radiocarbon data places Machalilla culture from 1300 to 800 B.C. (Lippi 1996: 61). However, if we use the radiocarbon determinations from La Ponga and La Libertad as a guide, the calibrated 68.2% age ranges given in Table A1 span from about 1430 to 830 B.C. This start date coincides well with Marcos and Michczynski's (1996) absolute chronology for Valdivia, in which their provisional Valdivia Phase 8b ends at 1450 B.C. This date might serve as a better starting point for Machalilla culture at inland localities in Guayas and El Oro provinces and may actually mark the beginning of Early Machalilla occupations on the northern Guayas and southern Manabí coast for which reliable radiocarbon determinations have not yet been obtained.

Curiously, the end date of ca. 800 B.C. extends Machalilla culture well into Late Formative times because of absolute dating of Chorrera manifestations elsewhere in the coastal lowlands. Thus the end of a given cultural manifestation in one region may overlap considerably with the early florescence of a different but related manifestation in another region, until the former becomes totally eclipsed by the latter. Such may be the case with the Machalilla/Chorrera "transition" in certain parts of the coastal lowlands.

CHORRERA CHRONOLOGY

As for Valdivia Phase 8 and Machalilla culture, it is important to clarify the geographical limits of the radiocarbon determinations and TL assays used to make broad time range estimates for specific cultural occupations. We should not assume that a single time range applies equally to all areas of the coastal strip and western lowlands because of the well-known lag time or Doppler effect (Deetz and Dethlefsen 1965) in ceramic decorative traits when traced over large geographical areas (see also Zeidler et al. 1998). As David Braun (1985: 137) observes

> Different parts of . . . (a) region (may) in fact differ in the relative frequencies, and even in the presence vs. absence, of different decorative techniques among contemporaneous sites . . . As a result, we can never assume that a decorative technique or type will convey the same chronological information regardless of location, even controlling for so-called Doppler effects. (Deetz and Dethfelsen 1965)

Beginning and ending dates for a single cultural manifestation or ceramic phase may vary considerably from locality to locality, and this appears to be the case with Chorrera culture.

Chorrera culture was first defined somewhat independently in the Guayas basin at the type-site of La Chorrera on the Babahoyo River (Evans and Meggers 1954) and on the Guayas coast at the site of La Carolina (OGSE 46D or Engoroy cemetery) on the Santa Elena peninsula (Bushnell 1951). Some debate still exists over the extent to which Chorrera represents a true "cultural horizon" characterized by stylistic unity in ceramic manufacture (albeit encompassing some regional variation), or whether the numerous Late Formative regional variants such as Engoroy and Tabuchila, are better understood as *independent* regional archaeological cultures. Recent summaries of Chorrera archaeology can be found in Beckwith (n.d.) and Engwall (n.d.), and Cummins (1992; this volume) and Scott (1998) provide overviews of Chorrera ceramic art. Here a certain degree of stylistic unity in ceramic manufacture is acknowledged as a generalized Chorrera cultural manifestation extending from the Guayas basin and Guayas coast northward to include Manabí, Los Ríos, western Pichincha, and Esmeraldas provinces. Yet both the nature of this stylistic unity and the regional variation apparent in other ceramic traits are in need of further explanation. Correct chronological placement of these regional variants may help shed light on this issue.

Initial attempts at placing Chorrera in an absolute chronological context were made by Evans and Meggers (1960; 1961; Meggers 1966: fig. 4) in collaboration with Emilio Estrada (1962: cuadros 3, 4, and 5). These efforts included the use of a few radiocarbon determinations together with experimental results from the newly developing field of obsidian hydration dating (Evans and Meggers 1960; Friedman and Smith 1960). The radiocarbon evidence included a single Chorrera radiocarbon determination (HO 1307, 2800 ± 115 RCYBP) from the Véliz site (M 42) in northern Manabí province, and two determinations dating an apparent Chorrera/Bahía transition at the La Sequita site (M 55) in central Manabí (SI 43, 2540 ± 125 RCYBP; SI 35: 2525 ± 105 RCYBP) (see Meggers 1966: fig. 4). The obsidian hydration evidence, on the other hand, was more voluminous, although somewhat less reliable. Of the 122 thin sections from Ecuador measured for hydration layer thickness, 31 obsidian samples from four different archaeological sites were assigned a Chorrera affiliation (Evans and Meggers 1960: fig. 19; Friedman and Smith 1960: table 1). The four sites are the Chorrera type-site (R-B-1/Cut 1) on the Babahoyo River (9), the Naupe site (G-D-8/Cuts 3 and 4) on the Daule River (16), the Libertad site (G-76/Cut A) on the Santa Elena peninsula (5), and the Machalilla site (M-28) on the southern Manabí coast (1). Although Meggers and Evans considered the specimen from the Machalilla site to be of Chorrera age (Friedman and Smith 1960: table 1), Estrada (1962: cuadro 4) apparently disagreed, dating it prior to the Chorrera time range (pre-1500 B.C.); as a result, Evans and Meggers (1960: fig. 19) do not include it in their final evaluation of the obsidian hydration analysis. The other three sites yielded the following time ranges for the Late Formative Chorrera culture: the Chorrera type-site, 1840-540 B.C.; the Naupe site (Cut 3), 1640 to ca. 500 B.C.; the Naupe site (Cut 4), 1640 to ca. 500 B.C.; and the Libertad site, 1740 to 1240 B.C. (Evans and Meggers 1960: fig. 19). Subsequently, Estrada (1962: cuadro 4) reproduced these results and added an additional obsidian hydration date of 750 B.C. for the Véliz site in northern Manabí, although no provenance or specimen quantities were indicated.

At both the Chorrera type-site and the two cuts from the Naupe site, Chorrera ceramic traits appear to be replaced by Regional Developmental ceramic traits in the 550 to 500 B.C. time range, as estimated by hydration analysis. The somewhat early start date for Chorrera in the 1840 to 1640 B.C. time range appears to be consistent across the three sites. These results led Meggers (1966: fig. 4) to conclude that Chorrera culture dated from 1840 to 540 B.C.; yet, elsewhere in this influential volume the time range is rounded upward, extending from 1500 to 500 B.C. (Meggers 1966: 55, 66). Although the latter figures came to be widely accepted in both the academic and popular archaeological literature as a pan-Chorrera time range, it is now clear that the *actual* beginning and ending dates of Chorrera may vary from region to region. The 1500 to 500 B.C. time range derived from obsidian hydration analysis, even if considered reliable, may only apply to the Babahoyo and the lower Daule river areas where the Chorrera type site and the Naupe site are found. But even there, it must be considered a provisional dating because there is no correlative evidence from radiocarbon dating.

Subsequent investigators who believed, contrary to Meggers that the Machalilla culture succeeded Valdivia, have argued that Meggers's (1966) start date of 1500 B.C. for Chorrera was far too early and that her proposed end date of 500 B.C. may be too early as well. By the mid-1970s, for example, Lathrap proposed a 1000 to 300 B.C. time range for Chorrera (Lathrap et al. 1975) because of new data from the Engoroy variant in the greater Santa Elena peninsula and northern Guayas coast areas (Bischof 1975a; Paulsen and McDougle n.d.b).

With respect to relative chronology, the internal delineation of ceramic phases for Chorrera/Engoroy culture has been based largely on the Santa Elena peninsula and northern Guayas coast. Simmons (1970) proposed the first ceramic sequence for Engoroy materials recovered in archaeological excavations by Ferdon (1941a,b) at the La Carolina (OGSE-46D) site in the 1940s. Using a type-variety approach to ceramic analysis, Simmons subdivided Engoroy into a series of three phases: Early, Middle, and Late Engoroy. He also argued for clear transitions from Machalilla into Early Engoroy and from Late Engoroy into Guangala. From comparisons with Estrada's Bahía I material from the central Manabí coast (Estrada 1957, 1962; see also Meggers 1966: fig. 4), Early Engoroy was tentatively placed at around 850 B.C., whereas Middle Engoroy was thought to date from 500 to 100 B.C.

Parallel efforts to refine the Engoroy ceramic sequence were subsequently carried out by Bischof (1975a, 1982) and Paulsen and McDougle (n.d.a,b), with the added benefit of radiocarbon determinations. Bischof conducted research at two sites near the modern town of Palmar in the Javita valley, north of the Santa Elena peninsula. On the basis of stratigraphic excavations and a type-variety analysis of ceramic materials, Bischof proposed a series of six ceramic phases for Engoroy (Engoroy 1–6), which he then collapsed into three larger groupings: Early Engoroy (Phases 1–3); Middle Engoroy (Phase 4); and Late Engoroy (Phase 6). Phase 5 is suggested as a hypothetical transitional phase that was not documented stratigraphically (Bischof 1982: 141). The three larger groupings are then placed in a chronological context on the basis of available radiocarbon determinations (Bischof 1982: 162–165). Early Engoroy has a start date of 900 B.C., because of slighter earlier radiocarbon determinations (SI 67, SI 107, and SI 108) for Late Machalilla (see Table A1) and an end date of 600 B.C. Middle Engoroy has a range of 600 to 300 B.C. because of two radiocarbon determinations from Bischof's Palmar excavations (Hv 1293, 2385 ± 80 RCYBP; Hv 2978, 2295 ± 75 RCYBP), both of which directly date his Engoroy Phase 4. As Table A1 demonstrates, the calibrated calendrical range for these two determinations at 68.2% probability is 760 to 380 B.C. and 410 to 200 B.C., respectively. Late Engoroy has a range of 300 to 100 B.C., which is largely based on bracketing by radiocarbon determinations for the succeeding Guangala Phase 1 (HV 1294 and HV 2976; not in Table A1).

Paulsen and McDougle (n.d.a,b) have presented successive refinements of their ceramic seriation efforts from materials excavated at La Carolina (OGSE-46D) by McDougle. Their analysis was based on a limited number of ceramic attributes found on open bowl forms (collar nicking, interior and exterior tiers, and notched fillets); consequently, doubt clouds its overall utility for comparative purposes (Lippi 1983). Like Bischof, they proposed a six-phase ceramic sequence (Engoroy 1–6), but added a seventh transitional phase between 3 and 4. Two larger temporal groupings are also proposed: Early Engoroy, encompassing Phases 1 through 3 and the transitional Phase 3/4; and Late Engoroy, encompassing Engoroy phases 4 through 6. Of the 11 available radiocarbon determinations derived from these excavations, only four—all from Cut AA—

are considered reliable and in correct stratigraphic position by the excavators (Paulsen and McDougle n.d.a: 20). The uncalibrated determinations in question were transformed by the excavators into calendar years B.C. by simply subtracting 1,950 years from the determinations (Paulsen and McDougle n.d.c: fig. 2). The four resulting dates are as follows, in descending order: 1110 B.C. (Level SS), 870 B.C. (Cut RR), 625 B.C. (Cut MM), and 425 B.C. (Cut JJ). A fifth determination, 750 B.C. (Cut KK), was slightly out of stratigraphic order. These and other radiocarbon determinations from Paulsen and McDougle's Engoroy seriation are not included in Table A1, as they have no associated information (i.e., laboratory number, age in radiocarbon years before present, standard error) and hence cannot be calibrated with current analytical methods.

Another important piece of the Late Formative dating puzzle in Guayas province comes from the lower Guayas basin site of San Pedro de Guayaquil on the outskirts of modern Guayaquil. In the late 1960s Resfa and Ibrahim Parducci (Parducci and Parducci 1970, 1975) encountered a ceramic assemblage considered transitional between the Late Formative and Regional Developmental periods designated the Fase Guayaquil. Both ceramic cross-dating and a series of three radiocarbon determinations (Table A1) suggested it was roughly contemporaneous with the later part of the Engoroy sequences proposed by Bischof (1975a, 1982) and Paulsen and McDougle (n.d.a,b); that is, Engoroy 6 to Guangala 1 (Parducci and Parducci 1975). The three determinations are in descending chronological order: UW-125, 2290 ± 100 RCYBP; UW-124, 2185 ± 80 RCYBP; and UW-123, 2175 ± 60 RCYBP. When calibrated at the 68.2% confidence level, the latter determination ranges in age from 360 to 120 B.C., clearly marking the terminal portion of the Late Formative in the lower Guayas basin and demonstrating the continuity of Chorreroid ceramic traits.

While little new research has been devoted to the internal sequencing of Chorrera ceramics since 1981 through 1982 when the Bischoff and Paulsen and McDougle seriations appeared, considerable headway has been made with respect to absolute chronology. As Table A1 demonstrates, some 46 radiocarbon determinations now exist for Chorrera representing five provinces. Much of this new information comes from Guayas province and southern and northern Manabí province, but Los Ríos, Esmeraldas, and western Pichincha provinces are now represented as well.

Beginning with the Guayas basin, dissertation research carried out in the 1980s by Aleto (1988) on Puná Island and by Stemper (1989, 1993) in the Daule River basin each yielded a new radiocarbon determination marking terminal Chorrera occupations in their respective areas. Aleto's Bella Vista occupation on Puná Island yielded a determination of 2460 ± 110 RCYBP (ISGS

1347), which he equates with the Fase Guayaquil (Aleto 1988; see also Beckwith n.d.). When calibrated at the 68.2% CI this yields a calendrical time range of 760–410 B.C. (see Table A1), which overlaps with the calibrated range of the earliest Fase Guayaquil determination (UW 125) at the 68.2% CI (see Table A1). Stemper's excavations at site PL 18 along the Daule River near the town of Yumes yielded a single radiocarbon determination corresponding to Late Formative times and marking the end of his Silencio Phase 1 (Stemper 1989, 1993). The determination (AA-1763) was 2280 ± 110 RCYBP, which after calibration yielded a calendrical time range of 520 to 160 B.C. at the 68.2% CI (see Table A1). Stemper (1989: 334) considers the associated context (Deposit 8) and ceramic materials to be derived "from an earlier Chorrera-like style," rather than a pure Chorrera component.

In southern Manabí province, archaeological excavations by Marcos and Norton (1981, 1984) at La Plata Island yielded a series of nine new radiocarbon determinations for Late Machalilla and Chorrera components (see Table A1). Unfortunately, the radiocarbon evidence was unavailable at that time, and neither Marcos nor Norton has since published these results nor discussed their implications for Chorrera archaeology. They do, however, appear in Lippi's (1983: table c) discussion of the La Ponga site but unfortunately lack information on provenance associations. Although included in a list of radiocarbon determinations under the caption Machalilla Radiocarbon Dates, Lippi (1983: 351, 352) is careful to note that collectively the nine dates "must be used only as a rough bracket for Late Machalilla" and one of the excavators, Norton, indicated that their affiliation is "Late Machalilla and/or early Chorreroid." Therefore, Lippi (1983: 351–355) does not incorporate them into his absolute dating of Machalilla culture. All but one of these nine dates are assigned a Chorrera cultural affiliation in Table A1, whereas the earliest (GX 7821, 3065 ± 135 RCYBP) is listed as Late Machalilla/Chorrera. The rationale for this Chorrera designation is based on (a) the presence of Chorrera culture at the Salango site in southern Manabí, directly southeast of La Plata Island, at about the same time (GX 13027 3045 ± 150 RCYBP) (Lunniss and Mudd n.d.); and (b) the simultaneous beginning of Chorrera culture in northern Manabí province, where it has been termed the Tabuchila variant after Estrada (1957, 1962; Engwall n.d.; Zeidler et al. 1998; see also Zeidler and Sutliff 1994). Bayesian statistical analysis of the Tabuchila radiocarbon determinations suggest a calibrated calendrical date of 1300 B.C. for the onset of Chorrera in northern Manabí (Zeidler et al. 1998: table 4). This accords well with the calibrated age range (at 68.2% probability) given in Table A1 for the earliest La Plata date (GX 7821): 1500–1120 B.C. The approximate midpoint of this range falls close to 1300 B.C. The eight subsequent determinations from La Plata would fall squarely within the Chorrera time period, assuming they are derived from valid uncontaminated charcoal samples in correct stratigraphic context.

The radiocarbon determination mentioned above from the site of Salango (OMJPLP-141) has unfortunately never been published, but it represents one of three charcoal samples from a unique Chorrera ceremonial structure (Structure 1) carefully excavated by Lunnis and associates in Area 141-B of the site (Lunnis and Mudd n.d.; Norton et al. 1983). These excavations, initiated in 1982, were described in preliminary form in 1983 (Norton et al. 1983: 21–41). Excavations continued in succeeding years, yet by 1987 it was still only partially excavated (Lunniss and Mudd n.d.). Lunniss and Mudd (n.d.) have defined a four-phase multicomponent sequence of use, abandonment, and reconstruction of this ceremonial locality beginning in Chorrera times and extending through a Bahía 1/Engoroy occupation, a Bahía 2 occupation, and a Guangala occupation. Components included elite burials with grave goods as well as dedicatory ritual caches. Whereas the three latter phases involved the construction of a rectangular precinct measuring some 10 m X 10 m defined by thick adobe walls and posts, the initial Chorrera ceremonial center involved construction of a low mound or foundation layer with a clay cap (Context 7300) measuring 8.2 m X 4.2 m, supporting a simple wooden post structure (Lunniss and Mudd n.d.: Fig. 8).

The earliest radiocarbon determination (GX 13027, 3045 ± 150 RCYBP) apparently came from an ash layer (Context 6653-C) covering a portion of this occupation. The precise stratigraphic location of the second radiocarbon determination (GX 13028, 2540 + 85 RCYBP) is unclear but was extracted from posthole fill associated with the Chorrera foundation layer, thus *underlying* the previous determination. In spite of this, the authors assigned a greater contextual reliability to the earlier of the two determinations because the GX 13027 charcoal specimen was associated with in situ burning, while the other specimen was extracted from posthole fill that showed no evidence of *in situ* burning (Lunniss and Mudd n.d.). Finally, the third radiocarbon determination (GX 13026, 2340 ± 485 RCYBP) was extracted from an occupation layer found at the end of the four-phase multicomponent sequence and probably dates the final Guangala occupation of the ceremonial precinct. Its rather large standard error renders it useless for present purposes, however. What is most intriguing about the investigation of this ceremonial precinct is the clear stratigraphic separation between what the excavators identified as Chorrera proper in Construction Phase 1 and an overlying Engoroy/Bahía I occupation in Construction Phase 2 (Lunniss and Mudd n.d.).

Deep stratigraphic excavations in other areas of the Salango site (Area 141-C) have yielded additional radiocarbon determinations for the Chorrera component that accord well with the previous two determinations from Area 141-B and those from La Plata Island mentioned above. Although this radiocarbon information was never published (see Kurc n.d.), fortunately it recently appeared in Beckwith (n.d.: table 2.1), who researched the Chorrera ceramic material excavated from Levels 4, 5, and 6/7 in Area 141-C. These excavations yielded five new radiocarbon determinations, all of which fall in between the two determinations from Area 141-B (see Table A1). These five assays are in descending order of radiocarbon years before present: GX 9990, GX 9994, GX 9992, GX 9991, and GX 9995. The earliest of these (GX 9990, 2765 ± 175 RCYBP) yields a calibrated calendrical age range of 1260 to 780 B.C. (at 68.2% probability). The most recent one (GX 9995: 2590 ± 170 RCYBP) yields a calibrated calendrical age range of 900 to 410 B.C. (at 68.2% probability). Beckwith (n.d.: 234) has interpreted these ceramics as possibly representing two separate periods within the Late Formative. The early part, represented by Level 6/7, is equated with an early Chorrera phase derived in part from late Machalilla ceramic traits. Levels 4 and 5, on the other hand, are equated with Early Engoroy. The radiocarbon evidence seems to bear this out, as even the most recent date from Area 141-C (GX 9995) precedes Bischof's two determinations for his Engoroy Phase 4 (Hv 1293 and Hv 2978) by 200 to 300 radiocarbon years (see Table A1). This and the stratigraphic evidence of the Structure 1 ceremonial context discussed above suggest that for southern Manabí, Engoroy represents a later phase within the broader Late Formative cultural complex (see also Norton 1992: 28–32).

An early start date for the Chorrera ceramic complex is also found in the Jama valley of northern Manabí province, where it is apparently not preceded by the Machalilla culture (Zeidler and Sutliff 1994). Rather, it begins abruptly ca. 1300 B.C. following a lengthy occupational hiatus caused by a volcanic ashfall (Tephra 1) that fell during the Valdivia 8 period (Zeidler et al. 1998; Zeidler and Isaacson this volume). The northern Manabí variant of Chorrera was termed *Tabuchila* by Estrada (1957) based on his surface collections and purchases of Chorrera pottery from the Hacienda *Tabuchilla* (note different spelling) in the Río Muchacho drainage south of Jama and north of Canoa. Its chronological placement in the Late Formative period was later confirmed with what would become the first radiocarbon determination for Chorrera culture at the Véliz site (M-42) located just west of Bahía de Caráquez on the left bank of the Río Chone (Estrada 1962). Excavations in Cut B, in clear stratigraphic association with Chorrera ceramics, yielded a charcoal specimen (HO 1307) with an age of 2800 ± 115 RCYBP and a calibrated calendrical age range of 1130 to 820 B.C. at the 68.2% probability (see Table A1). Estrada also notes (1962: 24; cuadro 4) that obsidian hydration analysis on material from this same cut yielded an age estimate of 750 B.C.

In subsequent archaeological investigations in the Jama River valley, Zeidler and associates adopted Estrada's term *Tabuchila* to designate the extensive Chorrera occupation of the valley (Engwall n.d.; Zeidler et al. 1998; Zeidler and Sutliff 1994). A total of five radiocarbon determinations from the Jama valley absolute chronology pertain to the Tabuchila complex and are derived from four different archaeological sites (see Table A1). Four of the five determinations (from sites at La Mina, Dos Caminos, and San Isidro) fall toward the early part of the Chorrera time period; the fifth was derived from a charcoal specimen extracted from a tephra layer (Tephra 2) immediately overlying terminal Chorrera deposits at the Mocoral site (Engwall n.d.; see Zeidler and Isaacson this volume). Bayesian calibration of these determinations for purposes of phasing the Chorrera occupation of the Jama valley suggested a beginning date of 1300 B.C. and an end date of 750 B.C. (Zeidler et al. 1998). Since four of the five determination fell at the early end of this sequence, the proposed start date is probably more secure than the end date of 750 B.C. The latter should probably be considered provisional, pending the availability of new radiocarbon determinations for late Chorrera contexts. Even the Mocorral determination itself (ISGS 2377), with a calibrated age range of 800 to 410 B.C. (68.2% CI) seems a bit early when compared with the dating of the Pululahua eruption. Pyroclastic deposits close to the Pululahua source eruption yielded a radiocarbon determination of 2305 ± 65 RCYBP (SI 2128) (Hall 1977). Although not in Table A1, this determination yields a calibrated age range of 404 to 207 B.C. at the 68.2% CI. The approximate midpoint, 300 B.C., might serve as a reasonable estimate for the Pululahua eruption that blanketed much of the western Ecuadorian lowlands and caused a major perturbation in Chorrera culture wherever it fell. Samples of these dated tephras have been chemically correlated (Zeidler and Isaacson this volume); therefore, the discrepancy in the two radiocarbon age estimates are due to the vagaries of the dating method itself rather than a misidentification of eruptive events. This discrepancy could possibly be due to the "old wood problem" (Schiffer 1986) with the El Mocorral sample actually dating wood that was significantly older than the stratigraphic (depositional) context from which it was extracted.

Moving inland from the Manabí coast to Los Ríos province, three radiocarbon determinations are now available for the Late Formative period. The recent excavations by Reindel and Guillaume-Gentil at the La Cadena locality near Quevedo provide the earliest determination (Guillaume-Gentil 1996, 1998; Reindel 1995). Deep stratigraphic excavations in the base of Tola 5 at that site yielded a determination of 2430 ± 80 RCYBP (B 5560) and was associated with ceramic materials of clear Chorrera affiliation. When calibrated at the 68.2% CI, this assay yields a calendrical time range of 760 to 400 B.C. (see Table A1), which places it in the late portion of the Late Formative, more or less contemporaneous with the calibrated time range for the Mocorral assay from the Jama valley (800–410 B.C.). Two thermoluminescence dates were also obtained for Chorrera ceramic materials from these contexts as well as Chorrera contexts in Tola 1 (Guillaume-Gentil 1998; Wagner 1995). Two TL age estimates were 2789 ± 290 BP and 2611 ± 430 BP, and although they have rather large error terms, they both fall squarely within the known time range of classic Chorrera culture at the Salango site and La Plata Island in neighboring Manabí province (cf. Table A1).

The other two Late Formative radiocarbon determinations from Los Ríos province were both provided by Porras and derive from his excavations at the Palenque site between the modern towns of Quevedo and Santo Domingo de Los Colorados (Porras 1983). Both determinations occur rather late within the Late Formative period and the associated ceramic assemblage is interpreted by Porras (1983) as relating to the Fase Guayaquil material from the lower Guayas basin. The two determinations are 2220 ± 75 RCYBP (RK 4206) and 2170 ± 65 RCYBP (RK 2207). When calibrated at the 68.2% CI, they yield overlapping calendrical time ranges of 380 to 200 B.C. and 360 to 110 B.C., respectively (see Table A1).

Moving northward to western Pichincha province, Chorrera-related materials have been found at three sites: Nambillo in the Mindo valley (Lippi 1998); Nueva Era in the Tulipe valley (Isaacson 1987); and Santa Marta in the Toachi valley west of Santo Domingo de Los Colorados (Lubensky n.d.a,b). At Nambillo, Lippi (1998) has reported a series of five radiocarbon determinations, the two earliest of which (GX 12471 and GX 12470) apparently predate human occupation at the site (see Table A1). The remaining three determinations (GX 12473, GX 12469, and GX 12472) date the Nambillo phase, a Late Formative period complex that Lippi (1998: table 8.4) places between 1600 and 400 B.C. Two of these determinations (GX 12469 and GX 12472), however, have very large standard errors (260 years) and do not provide accurate age estimates, although they fall squarely within the Chorrera time range. The remaining determination (GX 12473) yielded an age estimate of 3330 ± 80 RCYBP, which in turn yields a calibrated age range of 1740 to 1510 B.C. (at the 68.2% CI). The somewhat early start date for Early Nambillo at 1600 B.C. is based upon this single determination coupled with the nature of the associated pottery. The ceramic assemblage of this complex appears to be a mix of highland Cotocollao (and La Chimba) ceramic traits, with a blend of several coastal Formative ceramic traits derived from Terminal Valdivia, Machalilla, and Chorrera cultures (Lippi 1998). The end date of ca. 400 B.C. is marked by the eruption of Pululahua. While Early Nambillo might be loosely considered Chorrera-like or Chorreroid in nature, it is important to note the strong highland influences as well as the earlier coastal influences (especially Machalilla) in the ceramic complex.

At the Nueva Era site, just 18 km to the north in the Tulipe valley, Isaacson (1987) reported a series of four radiocarbon determinations associated with his Late Formative Nueva Era phase. The earliest and latest of these (ISGS 1182 and ISGS 1187) were rejected by Isaacson (1987) as too early and too late, respectively (see Table A1). The ISGS-1182 determination was 3070 ± 250 RCYBP, which corresponds to the earliest Late Formative determinations from La Plata Island and the Jama valley in Manabí province, as well as the single determination from the Santa Marta site farther south. However, its rather large standard error reduces it utility. The remaining two Late Formative determinations from the Nueva Era site (ISGS 1176 and ISGS 1175) fall within 100 radiocarbon years of one another. The former is 2710 ± 100 RCYBP and the latter is 2620 ± 80 RCYBP (see Table A1). At the 68.2% CI, their respective calibrated age ranges are 1000 to 790 B.C. and 900 to 560 B.C., placing them well within the suite of calibrated determinations from Chorrera contexts on La Plata Island and at Salango in southern Manabí. They are also contemporaneous with the later portion of the Early Nambillo phase in the nearby Mindo valley. Stylistically, the Nueva Era ceramic assemblage shows a variable mix of highland (Cotocollao) and coastal lowland (primarily Chorrera) ceramic traits (Isaacson 1987), as does the Nambillo site. In spite of its partial contemporaneity and close proximity to Nambillo, however, Lippi (1998) sees notable differences in their respective ceramic assemblages. While their histories may have been different, both sites functioned as major gateway communities on trade routes between the Quito basin and the coastal lowlands, and both Late Formative communities were obliterated by the Pululahua eruption. Since both sites are not pure Chorrera manifestations, their associated radiocarbon determinations are referred to in Table A1 only by their local phase names.

The final Late Formative radiocarbon determination from western Pichincha is the single assay from the Santa Marta site, located on the Hacienda La Florida in the Toachi valley west of Santo Domingo de Los Colorados. Excavations by Earl Lubensky and Allison Paulsen (Lubensky n.d.a,b) at the base of a mound at the Santa Marta site yielded a charcoal specimen with an estimated age of

2950 ± 80 RCYBP.When calibrated at the 68.2% CI, it yields a calendrical age range from 1290 to 1020 B.C., placing it coeval with the early Tabuchila occupation of the Jama valley (e.g., the Dos Caminos site near San Isidro), the Nueva Era occupation of the Tulipe valley, and the later portion of the Early Nambillo phase in the Mindo valley. Stylistically, the associated Late Formative ceramics seem to share stronger similarities with other Chorrera manifestations from the coastal lowlands and somewhat less influence from the highlands than is the case with the Nueva Era and Nambillo assemblages.

In summary, the combined radiocarbon determinations for the Late Formative period in western Pichincha province are consistent with those from Manabí province in suggesting a relatively early start date of ca.1200 to 1300 B.C. for Chorrera culture and an end date of ca. 300 to 350 B.C., the latter marking the eruption of Pululahua.

In Esmeraldas province, Chorrera and Chorrera-like manifestations have been documented in several different regions: the Chévele complex on the Atacames coast (Guinea 1986), the Tachina complex at the mouth of the Esmeraldas River (López y Sebastián 1986; López y Sebastián and Caillavet 1979), the Mafa and Early Selva Alegre complexes in the interior Santiago–Cayapas River region (DeBoer 1996), and the Early La Tolita complex at the mouth of the Santiago River on the far northern coast (Bouchard 1996; Valdez 1987). Of these, only Early La Tolita and Early Selva Alegre have yielded radiocarbon determinations (see Table A1). Valdez's excavations at Tola Pajarito within the La Tolita site yielded a series of four radiocarbon determinations assigned to the Early La Tolita phase (Valdez 1987), characterized by a ceramic assemblage having marked Chorreroid features (Bouchard 1996; Valdez 1987). These determinations are in descending radiocarbon age: 2540 ± 75 RCYBP (GX 12374); 2502 ± 70 RCYBP (GX 12373); 2450 ± 80 RCYBP (GX 12380); and 2265 ± 80 RCYBP (GX 12379). As their corresponding calibrated age ranges demonstrate (see Table A1), these determinations all fall toward the late end of the Chorrera time range.

Farther inland, in the Santiago–Cayapas river basins, DeBoer (1996) has defined a Late Formative ceramic complex, the Mafa phase, at the beginning of his long cultural sequence. While he does not equate it with the Late Formative complexes farther south along the Ecuadorian coast and falls short of proclaiming it "Chorrera-like," DeBoer does point out similarities in ceramic traits that it shares with Early La Tolita: "Tentatively then, Temprano (Early La Tolita) and Mafa can be viewed as contemporary phases or even manifestations of the same phase" (DeBoer 1996: 104; parentheses added). Unfortunately, no reliable radiocarbon determinations exist for the Mafa phase. However, since it is known to precede the Selva Alegre phase, a radiocarbon determination for the beginning of the cultural complex serves as an appropriate *terminus ante quem* to date the end of the Mafa phase. The determination in question is B 33782 from the site of Colón Eloy (R36) in the Santiago drainage, which yielded an age estimate of 2390 ± 80 RCYBP. When calibrated at the 68.2% CI, it yields a calendrical age estimate of 760 to 390 B.C., almost identical to the calibrated age range of determination GX 12380 from La Tolita (see Table A1).

Although far beyond the present scope, it is important to note that "Chorreroid" manifestations also extend northward along the coast to the adjacent Tumaco region of Colombia, with progressively less Chorrera-like ceramic traits continuing as far as the Chocó coast and the Cauca valley (Bouchard 1996). However, these complexes are not discussed in this Appendix.

Regarding the so-called *Doppler effect* in the spread of ceramic traits over large geographical areas, the archaeological result is a mosaic of regional ceramic complexes that share many broad similarities, yet may vary considerably in their relative contemporaneity or coevalness. Such is the case with the Late Formative Chorrera manifestations of western Ecuador. Indeed, relative start dates may vary by several centuries and end dates vary depending on the extent to which they were affected by the major eruption of Pululahua.

From radiocarbon evidence, it appears that Chorrera culture had an earlier start in southern and northern Manabi province, as well as western Pichincha province, than elsewhere, perhaps as early as 1300 to 1200 B.C. It would have been coeval with a flourishing Machalilla culture on the coast of Guayas province. On the other hand, we cannot discount the possibility that early radiocarbon determinations in this same time range will eventually be found in the lower Guayas basin in the general area of the Chorrera type site (Evans and Meggers 1954, 1957) and Peñón del Río (Zedeño n.d.). Precise dating of these Chorrera manifestations represents one of the critical gaps in our current knowledge of the Ecuadorian Formative.

I argue for 300 B.C. as the best ending date for the Late Formative, at least in Manabí and western Pichincha, where Chorrera occupations were abruptly terminated by the eruption of Pululahua (Engwall n.d.; Isaacson 1987, 1994; Lippi 1998; Lubensky n.d.a; Zeidler 1994a,b; Zeidler and Isaacson this volume). The same eruptive event probably affected the La Cadena–Quevedo area of Los Ríos province as well. Along the coastal strip, the southernmost "footprint" of this eruption has been traced to the Agua Blanca valley in southern Manabí, while the northernmost footprint extends from the Quito basin westward to Cojimíes in northern Manabí (Zeidler and Isaacson this volume). Therefore, we should expect to find truncated Chorrera sequences with hiatuses of varying lengths immediately following the ashfall of the Pululahua eruption. Obviously, this would be an attenuating effect so that regions at the distal end of ashfall in far southern Manabí may not have been affected as dramatically (see Zeidler and Isaacson this volume).

Jama–Coaque I (Muchique Phase 1) from the Jama valley as well as Bahia I from the Esteros (M8) and Tarqui (M7) sites at Manta (Estrada 1962; Meggers et al. 1965; Stirling and Stirling 1963) are posteruptive phenomena and should be considered early Regional Developmental in age, as originally suggested by Estrada (1962: cuadro 4) and Meggers et al. (1965). Whether one agrees with that stage-based nomenclature (see Zeidler et al. 1998 for a detailed discussion), both ceramic complexes mark a major cultural break in their respective cultural sequences. Some continuity in Chorrera ceramic traits exists (Cummins 1992; Zeidler and Sutliff 1994), but overall, they represent new ceramic complexes.

Some nine radiocarbon determinations are available from the Manta excavations (Meggers et al. 1965: table H), eight from Los Esteros, and one from Tarqui. Seven of these nine determinations, when calibrated at the 68.2% CI would likely fall after the 350 to 300 B.C. estimate for the eruption of Pululahua. It should also be noted that the two determinations that might predate the eruption are not in stratigraphic order (i.e., they do not derive from the lowest part of the excavation units). The two determinations from the deepest levels of the Los Esteros site (M1316 and M734) yielded age estimates of 2120 ± 120 RCYBP and 2170 ± 200 RCYBP, respectively, which when calibrated at the 68.2% CI, would fall well after the Pululahua eruption. They are quite consistent with radiocarbon determinations for the early portion of the Regional Developmental period elsewhere in Manabí, such as the Muchique I phase from the Jama valley (see Zeidler et al. 1998: table 2).

In Esmeraldas province, a somewhat different pattern emerges. Chorrera manifestations appear to begin somewhat later than in Manabí and Guayas provinces, yet they continue without the truncation caused by the Pululahua eruption. Thus the Late Formative manifestations such as Chévele, Early La Tolita, Mafa, and Tachina appear to have more gradual transitions into the succeeding Regional Developmental cultures represented by Early Atacames for Chévele, Tiaone for Tachina, Classic La Tolita for Early La Tolita, and Selva Alegre for Mafa. Even here, however, these transitions appear to occur in the 350 to 300 B.C. time range (Bouchard 1996).

In Guayas province, the situation is also different. In this area, the Chorrera/ Engoroy occupation of the Santa Elena peninsula and southern Manabí coast from Salango southward was unaffected by the Pululahua eruption. In these regions, a more gradual transition to the succeeding Guangala and Bahía cultures appears to have occurred. Engoroy on the Santa Elena peninsula (Paulsen and McDougle n.d.a,b) and northern Guayas coast (Bischof 1975a; 1982) appears to evolve out of Machalilla, while at Salango in southern Manabí (Lunniss and Mudd n.d.; Norton et al. 1983), it appears to overlie classic Chorrera deposits. Fase Guayaquil in the lower Guayas basin (Parducci and Parducci 1975), and Bella Vista on Puná Island (Aleto 1988) probably represent uninterrupted continuities out of classic Chorrera extending up until the time of Christ. In these cases, then, the Late Formative may very well persist up to 100 B.C., as argued by Aleto (1988), but it would be a mistake to uncritically apply that scheme to the entire coastal lowlands.

Table A1

Formative Period Radiocarbon Chronology for the Coast and Western Lowlands of Ecuador, by Province and Site, from Earliest Uncalibrated Date to Most Recent Radiocarbon Year before Present (RCYBP)

Site, culture, and phase	Lab and lab no.	Uncalibrated date RCYBP	Probability calibrated range 68.2% (year B.C.)	95.4% (year B.C.)	Reference
			Guayas		
Real Alto	Geochron Labs and Ill. State Geological Survey				
Valdivia 1a	GX 5269	6195 ± 215	5400-4850	5650-4600	Damp n.d.
	ISGS 448	5620 ± 250	4800-4100	5200-3800	Damp n.d.; Liu, Riley, and Coleman 1986
	GX 5267	5495 ± 200	4540-4040	4800-3800	Damp n.d.
Loma Alta	Geochron Labs				
Valdivia 1a	GX 7704	5275 ± 175	4340-3940	4500-3700	Stahl 1984
Valdivia 1	GX 9457	5240 ± 420	4600-3500	5000-2900	Stahl 1984
Valdivia	Univ. Michigan				
Valdivia A*	M 1320	5150 ± 150	4200-3760	4350-3650	Meggers, Evans, and Estrada 1965
Loma Alta	Geochron Labs				
Valdivia 1	GX 9459	5050 ± 240	4250-3500	4500-3100	Stahl 1984
Valdivia 1a	Teledyne Isotopes and Ill. State Geo. Survey				
	I 7076	5010 ± 120	3950-3700	4050-3500	Norton n.d.a,b
	ISGS 142	5000 ± 190	4040-3530	4250-3350	Norton n.d.a,b
Valdivia 1	Geochron Labs and Simon Fraser Univ.				
	GX 9458	4960 ± 210	3990-3510	4440-3100	Stahl 1984
	SFU 123	4920 ± 200	4000-3350	4300-3100	Stahl 1984
Valdivia 1a	Teledyne Isotopes				
	I 7075	4920 ± 120	3940-3530	4000-3350	Norton n.d.a,b
Real Alto	Geochron Labs				
Valdivia 1b	GX 5268	4900 ± 170	3940-3510	4300-3100	Damp n.d.
Loma Alta	Simon Fraser Univ.				
Valdivia 1	SFU 110	4790 ± 160	3760-3360	4000-3100	Stahl 1984

(cont.)

Table A1 (cont.)
Formative Period Radiocarbon Chronology for the Coast and Western Lowlands of Ecuador, by Province and Site, from Earliest Uncalibrated Date to Most Recent Radiocarbon Year before Present (RCYBP)

Site, culture, and phase	Lab and lab no.	Uncalibrated date RCYBP	Probability calibrated range		Reference
			68.2% (year B.C.)	95.4% (year B.C.)	
Guayas (cont.)					
Real Alto	Ill. State Geo. Survey				
Valdivia 1b/2a?	ISGS 468	4760 ± 120	3650–3370	3800–3100	Damp n.d.; Liu et al. 1986
Loma Alta	Ill. State Geo. Survey				
Valdivia 2a	ISGS 146	4750 ± 120	3650–3370	3800–3100	Norton n.d.a,b
Punta Concepción	Lamont-Doherty				
Valdivia 1	L 1042D	4700 ± 100	3640–3360	3700–3100	Hill 1972/74; Stothert 1976
Loma Alta	Ill. State Geo. Survey				
Valdivia 1	GX 9460	4700 ± 270	3800–3000	4100–2600	Stahl 1984
Real Alto	Ill. State Geo. Survey				
Valdivia 1b/2a?	ISGS 452	4700 ± 300	3800–3000	4300–2500	Liu et al. 1986
Valdivia	Ill. State Geo. Survey				
Valdivia aceramic	ISGS 275	4700 ± 80	3630–3370	3700–3100	Bischof and Viteri Gamboa 1972; Liu et al. 1986
OGSE-63	Teledyne Isotopes				
Valdivia 1	I 7069	4685 ± 95	3630–3360	3700–3100	Hill 1972/74; Stothert 1976
Loma Alta	Geochron Labs				
Valdivia 2a	GX 7699	4630 ± 160	3650–3100	3700–2900	Stahl 1984
Valdivia	Univ. Michigan				
Valdivia A★	M 1322	4620 ± 140	3650–3100	3650–2900	Meggers et al. 1965
Loma Alta	Ill. State Geo. Survey				
Valdivia 1b/2a?	ISGS 192	4590 ± 120	3520–3090	3650–2900	Norton n.d.a,b
Valdivia	Hannover, Ill. State Geo. Survey, and Smithsonian Inst.				
Valdivia aceramic	ISGS 274	4580 ± 80	3500–3100	3650–3000	Bischof and Viteri Gamboa 1972; Liu et al. 1986
Valdivia A★	SI 84	4540 ± 150	3510–3020	3650–2850	Meggers et al. 1965
Valdivia aceramic	Hv 4839	4535 ± 55	3360–3100	3500–3030	Bischof and Viteri Gamboa 1972
Valdivia A★	SI 83	4530 ± 55	3360–3100	3490–3020	Meggers et al. 1965
Colimes	Ill. State Geo. Survey				
Valdivia 2a	ISGS 477	4525 ± 75	3360–3090	3500–2900	Raymond, Marcos, and Lathrap 1980

Site / Phase	Laboratory / Sample	Date ±	Range	Range	Reference
Colimes (Perinao) / Valdivia 2a	Ill. State Geo. Survey ISGS 478a	4510 ± 100	3360–3030	3550–2900	Liu et al. 1986
Valdivia / Valdivia aceramic	Hannover Hv 4674	4510 ± 95	3360–3030	3500–2900	Bischof and Viteri Gamboa 1972
	Hv 4840	4495 ± 100	3360–3030	3500–2900	Bischof and Viteri Gamboa 1972
Real Alto / Valdivia 2a	Geochron Labs GX 5266	4495 ± 160	3370–2920	3650–2700	Damp n.d.
Valdivia / Valdivia A★	Univ. Michigan M 1317	4480 ± 140	3360–2920	3650–2850	Meggers et al. 1965
Loma Alta / Valdivia 2	Simon Fraser Univ. SFU 122	4460 ± 130	3350–2920	3550–2750	Stahl 1984
Colimes (Perinao) / Valdivia 2a	Ill. State Geo. Survey ISGS 478b	4460 ± 100	3340–2940	3500–2850	Liu et al. 1986
Punta Concepción / Valdivia 1	Teledyne Isotopes I 7167	4460 ± 90	3340–3010	3370–2900	Hill 1972/74
Loma Alta / Valdivia 2	Simon Fraser Univ. SFU 105	4450 ± 120	3340–2920	3550–2850	Stahl 1984
Punta Concepción / Valdivia 1	Lamont-Doherty L 1042C	4450 ± 100	3340–2920	3400–2850	Hill 1972/74; Stothert 1976
Valdivia / Valdivia A★	Smithsonian Inst. and Nat. Ctr. of the U.S. Geo. Survey SI 22	4450 ± 90	3340–2920	3360–2900	Meggers et al. 1965
	W 631	4450 ± 200	3500–2850	3700–2500	Meggers et al. 1965
El Encanto / Valdivia A★	Smithsonian Inst. SI 1311	4405 ± 90	3310–2910	3350–2880	Porras 1973
Real Alto / Valdivia 2b	Ill. State Geo. Survey ISGS 466	4390 ± 80	3270–2900	3340–2880	Liu et al. 1986
Loma Alta / Valdivia 2	Geochron Labs GX 7703	4375 ± 135	3330–2880	3400–2600	Stahl 1984
El Encanto / Valdivia B★	Smithsonian Inst. SI 1184	4370 ± 85	3260–2880	3350–2850	Porras 1973
Loma Alta / Valdivia 2b	Smithsonian Inst. SI 1055	4370 ± 65	3090–2900	3330–2880	Norton n.d.a,b
Colimes / Valdivia 2b	Geochron Labs GX 5271	4365 ± 245	3400–2600	3700–2300	Raymond et al. 1980
Loma Alta	Simon Fraser Univ. and Hannover SFU 120	4360 ± 160	3350–2750	3500–2500	Stahl 1984
	Hv 4673	4335 ± 100	3350–2750	3350–2650	Norton n.d.a,b
Valdivia / Valdivia A★	Smithsonian Inst. SI 81	4270 ± 60	3010–2700	3030–2560	Meggers et al. 1965

(cont.)

Table A1 (cont.)
Formative Period Radiocarbon Chronology for the Coast and Western Lowlands of Ecuador, by Province and Site, from Earliest Uncalibrated Date to Most Recent Radiocarbon Year before Present (RCYBP)

Site, culture, and phase	Lab and lab no.	Uncalibrated date RCYBP	Probability calibrated range 68.2% (year B.C.)	95.4% (year B.C.)	Reference
Guayas (cont.)					
Real Alto Valdivia 2b/3?	Ill. State Geo. Survey ISGS 446	4270 ± 80	3020–2690	3100–2590	Liu et al. 1986
Loma Alta Valdivia 2	Geochron Labs GX 7701	4260 ± 145	3090–2590	3350–2450	Stahl 1984
Valdivia Valdivia 2	Hannover Hv 4838	4260 ± 100	3020–2660	3350–2450	Bischof and Viteri Gamboa 1972
Punta Concepción Valdivia 2	Lamont-Doherty L 1232	4250 ± 100	3020–2620	3350–2450	Hill 1972/74; Stothert 1976
Loma Alta Valdivia 2	Geochron Labs GX 7700	4245 ± 145	3030–2580	3350–2450	Stahl 1984
Real Alto Valdivia/Valdivia 6?	Geochron Labs GX 7439	4240 ± 180	3100–2500	3400–2300	Marcos and Michczynski 1996
Valdivia Valdivia B★	Smithsonian Inst. SI 18	4230 ± 100	2920–2620	3100–2450	Meggers et al. 1965
	SI 16	4220 ± 100	2920–2620	3100–2450	Meggers et al. 1965
Real Alto Valdivia 6?	Geochron Labs GX 7438	4205 ± 160	3050–2450	3350–2300	Marcos and Michczynski 1996
Valdivia Valdivia B★	Nat. Ctr., U.S. Geo. Survey W 632	4190 ± 200	3050–2450	3400–2200	Meggers et al. 1965
Real Alto Valdivia 5?	Geochron Labs GX 7437	4175 ± 165	2920–2470	3400–2200	Marcos and Michczynski 1996
Valdivia Valdivia B★	Smithsonian Inst. SI 85	4170 ± 90	2880–2620	2920–2490	Meggers et al. 1965
Valdivia Valdivia B★	Univ. Michigan M 1318	4170 ± 140	2910–2490	3100–2300	Meggers et al. 1965
Real Alto Valdivia 5?	Geochron Labs GX 7436	4145 ± 170	2910–2470	3400–2200	Marcos and Michczynski 1996
Valdivia 2	Ill. State Geo. Survey ISGS–467	4140 ± 190	3050–2350	3400–2100	Liu et al. 1986

Site / Phase	Lab / Lab No.	Date ±	Range 1	Range 2	Reference
Valdivia / Valdivia B*	Smithsonian Inst. SI 80	4140 ± 60	2870–2600	2890–2500	Meggers et al. 1965
Valdivia / Valdivia B*	Smithsonian Inst. SI 82	4120 ± 65	2870–2570	2880–2490	Meggers et al. 1965
Real Alto / Valdivia 2b/3?	Ill. State Geo. Survey ISGS 439	4110 ± 80	2870–2500	2880–2470	Liu et al. 1986
Valdivia / Valdivia B*	Univ. Michigan M 1321	4100 ± 140	2880–2490	3050–2200	Meggers et al. 1965
Valdivia / Valdivia San Pedro	Hannover Hv 4675	4075 ± 110	2870–2470	2900–2300	Bischof and Viteri Gamboa 1972
Real Alto / Valdivia 3	Geochron Labs GX 7429	4050 ± 185	2900–2350	3100–1900	Zeidler 1984
Valdivia / Valdivia C*	Nat. Ctr., U.S. Geo. Survey W 630	4050 ± 200	2900–2300	3100–1900	Meggers et al. 1965
Buena Vista / Valdivia C*	Smithsonian Inst. SI 71	4040 ± 55	2630–2470	2870–2450	Meggers et al. 1965
Anllula / Valdivia 7	Univ. Pa. P 2761	4020 ± 220	2900–2200	3300–1800	Lubensky 1974, n.d.a
Real Alto / Valdivia 6	Geochron Labs GX 7434	4015 ± 170	2900–2300	3100–1900	Marcos and Michczynski 1996
Loma Alta / Valdivia 2?	Geochron Labs GX 7702	3985 ± 140	2900–2200	2900–2050	Stahl 1984
Valdivia / Valdivia C*	Smithsonian Inst. SI 78	3970 ± 65	2580–2350	2700–2200	Meggers et al. 1965
Punta Concepción / Valdivia 7	Lamont-Doherty L 1232H	3900 ± 150	2580–2140	2900–1950	Hill 1972/74
Real Alto / Valdivia 3?	Geochron Labs GX 7430	3845 ± 240	2650–1900	3000–1600	Zeidler 1984
Loma Alta / Valdivia 2?	Ill. State Geo. Survey ISGS 190	3765 ± 85	2310–2030	2500–1950	Norton n.d.
Ayalán / Valdivia 8	Nishina Memorial N 2908	3665 ± 95	2200–1910	2350–1700	Marcos and Michczynski 1996
	N 2909	3630 ± 105	2190–1780	2300–1650	Marcos and Michczynski 1996
Buena Vista / Machalilla	Smithsonian Inst. SI 69	3450 ± 50	1880–1680	1890–1620	Meggers et al. 1965
La Cabuya / Machalilla	Smithsonian Inst. SI 107	3320 ± 170	1880–1410	2050–1100	Meggers et al. 1965
Buena Vista / Machalilla	Smithsonian Inst. SI 1050	3250 ± 90	1680–1420	1750–1310	Norton n.d.

(cont.)

Table A1 (*cont.*)
Formative Period Radiocarbon Chronology for the Coast and Western Lowlands of Ecuador, by Province and Site, from Earliest Uncalibrated Date to Most Recent Radiocarbon Year before Present (RCYBP)

Site, culture, and phase	Lab and lab no.	Uncalibrated date RCYBP	Probability calibrated range		Reference
			68.2% (year B.C.)	95.4% (year B.C.)	
		Guayas (*cont.*)			
La Libertad Machalilla	Teledyne Isotopes I 7013	3060 ± 90	1430–1130	1520–1040	Paulsen and McDougle n.d.a
	I 7008	3015 ± 90	1400–1120	1500–950	Paulsen and McDougle n.d.a
La Libertad Machalilla	Teledyne Isotopes I 7006	2990 ± 90	1380–1050	1430–970	Paulsen and McDougle n.d.a
La Cabuya Machalilla	Smithsonian Inst. SI 108	2980 ± 160	1400–1000	1600–800	Meggers et al. 1965
Buena Vista Machalilla	Smithsonian Inst. SI 1051	2945 ± 115	1370–1000	1450–800	Norton n.d.a,b
La Ponga Machalilla	Wisconsin WIS 1125	2925 ± 65	1260–1010	1320–920	Lippi n.d.
	WIS 1141	2880 ± 75	1210–930	1300–830	Lippi n.d.
Los Cerritos Machalilla/Chorrera	Wisconsin WIS 115	2840 ± 90	1190–890	1270–820	Bischof 1982; Zevallos Menéndez 1965/66
La Cabuya Machalilla	Smithsonian Inst. SI 67	2830 ± 45	1050–910	1130–840	Meggers et al. 1965
La Ponga Machalilla	Wisconsin WIS 1140	2790 ± 75	1010–830	1130–800	Lippi n.d.
La Libertad Chorrera	Beta Analytic Beta 15656	2720 ± 70	920–800	1050–780	Stothert 1995
Loma Alta Chorrera	Simon Fraser Univ. SFU 109	2540 ± 80	810–520	820–400	Stahl 1984
Los Cerritos Chorrera (Engoroy)	Wisconsin WIS 125	2540 ± 80	810–520	820–400	Bischof 1982; Zevallos Menéndez 1965/66
Bella Vista (Puná Island) Chorrera (Fase Guayaquil)	Ill. State Geo. Survey ISGS-1347	2460 ± 110	760–410	850–350	Aleto 1988
Palmar 3 Chorrera (Engoroy 4)	Hannover Hv 1293	2385 ± 80	760–380	800–200	Bischof 1982
Palmar 2 Chorrera (Engoroy 4)	Hannover Hv 2978	2295 ± 75	410–200	800–100	Bischof 1982

Site / Phase	Lab / Sample No.	Date (B.P.)	Calibrated range	Calibrated range	Reference
San Pedro de Guayaquil Chorrera (Fase Guayaquil)	Univ. Washington UW 125	2290 ± 100	520–170	800–50	Parducci and Parducci 1970, 1975
PL 18 (Daule River) Chorreroid	Univ. Arizona AA 1763	2280 ± 110	520–160	800–50	Stemper 1989
San Pedro de Guayaquil Chorrera (Fase Guayaquil)	Univ. Washington UW 124	2185 ± 80	380–120	400–40	Parducci and Parducci 1970, 1975
	UW 123	2175 ± 60	360–120	390–50	Parducci and Parducci 1970, 1975
El Oro					
La Emerenciana	Southern Methodist Univ.				
Valdivia 7	SMU 4259	4109 ± 215	2950–2300	3400–2000	Marcos and Michczynski 1996
Valdivia 8	SMU 2263	3775 ± 165	2460–1970	2700–1600	Staller 1994
	SMU 2225	3707 ± 148	2310–1880	2600–1650	Staller 1994
	SMU 4549	3629 ± 303	2500–1600	2900–1200	Marcos and Michczynski 1996
	SMU 2226	3400 ± 220	2050–1400	2400–1100	Staller 1994
	SMU 2241	3361 ± 246	2050–1300	2400–1000	Staller 1994
Manabí					
Salango	Geochron Labs				
Valdivia 2	GX 8964	4670 ± 195	3650–3100	4000–2800	Norton, Lunniss, and Nayling 1983
	GX 8962	4510 ± 210	3550–2900	3700–2600	Norton et al. 1983
San Isidro	Ill. State Geo. Survey and Univ. Pittsburgh				
Valdivia 8	ISGS 1221	3630 ± 70	2130–1880	2200–1770	Zeidler, Buck, and Litton 1998
	ISGS 1222	3620 ± 70	2130–1880	2200–1750	Zeidler et al. 1998
	ISGS 1223	3560 ± 70	2020–1770	2140–1690	Zeidler et al. 1998
	PITT 426	3545 ± 135	2120–1680	2300–1500	Zeidler et al. 1998
	ISGS 1220	3500 ± 70	1920–1690	2030–1630	Zeidler et al. 1998
La Plata Island	Geochron Labs				
Late Machalilla/Chorrera	GX 7821	3065 ± 135	1500–1120	1650–900	Lippi 1983; Marcos and Norton 1981
Salango	Geochron Labs				
Chorrera	GX 13027	3045 ± 150	1440–1050	1700–850	Lunnis and Mudd n.d.; Norton et al. 1983
La Mina	Ill. State Geo. Survey				
Chorrera (Tabuchila)	ISGS 2366	3030 ± 80	1400–1130	1440–1010	Engwall 2000; Zeidler et al. 1998
Dos Caminos	Ill. State Geo. Survey				
Chorrera (Tabuchila)	ISGS 3309	2930 ± 80	1260–1000	1380–910	Engwall 2000; Zeidler et al. 1998
La Plata Island	Geochron Labs				
Chorrera	GX 7823	2915 ± 140	1300–920	1450–800	Lippi 1983; Marcos and Norton 1981

(*cont.*)

Table A1 (*cont.*)
Formative Period Radiocarbon Chronology for the Coast and Western Lowlands of Ecuador, by Province and Site, from Earliest Uncalibrated Date to Most Recent Radiocarbon Year before Present (RCYBP)

Site, culture, and phase	Lab and lab no.	Uncalibrated date RCYBP	Probability calibrated range		Reference
			68.2% (year B.C.)	95.4% (year B.C.)	
Manabí (*cont.*)					
Dos Caminos Chorrera (Tabuchila)	Ill. State Geo. Survey ISGS 3310	2880 ± 70	1210–930	1290–840	Engwall 2000; Zeidler et al. 1998
San Isidro Chorrera (Tabuchila)	Univ. of Arizona AA 4140	2845 ± 95	1190–890	1300–810	Engwall 2000; Zeidler et al. 1998
La Plata Island Chorrera	Geochron Labs GX 7816	2830 ± 245	1400–750	1700–300	Lippi 1983; Marcos and Norton 1981
Veliz (M–42) Chorrera (Tabuchila)	Humble Oil HO 1307	2800 ± 115	1130–820	1400–750	Estrada 1962; Zeidler et al. 1998
Salango Chorrera	Geochron Labs GX 9990 GX 9994	2765 ± 175 2750 ± 190	1260–780 1300–750	1400–400 1400–400	Beckwith 1996; Kurc n.d. Beckwith 1996; Kurc n.d.
La Plata Island Chorrera	Geochron Labs GX 7818 GX 7820	2745 ± 150 2745 ± 140	1190–780 1130–790	1400–400 1400–500	Lippi 1983; Marcos and Norton 1981 Lippi 1983; Marcos and Norton 1981
Salango Chorrera	Geochron Labs GX 9992 GX 9991	2705 ± 150 2650 ± 165	1150–550 1010–520	1300–400 1300–350	Beckwith 1996; Kurc n.d. Beckwith 1996; Kurc n.d.
La Plata Island Chorrera	Geochron Labs GX 7817 GX 7822 GX 7824	2640 ± 220 2600 ± 130 2595 ± 130	1050–400 900–520 900–510	1400–200 1050–350 1050–350	Lippi 1983; Marcos and Norton 1981 Lippi 1983; Marcos and Norton 1981 Lippi 1983; Marcos and Norton 1981
Salango Chorrera	Geochron Labs GX 9995 GX 13028	2590 ± 170 2540 ± 85	900–410 810–520	1250–200 820–400	Beckwith 1996; Kurc n.d. Norton et al. 1983
La Sequita (M-55) Chorrera–Bahía	Smithsonian Inst. SI 43 SI 35	2540 ± 125 2525 ± 105	810–410 800–510	1000–350 840–390	Meggers et al. 1965 Meggers et al. 1965
El Mocoral Chorrera (Tabuchila)	Ill. State Geo. Survey ISGS 2377	2500 ± 160	800–410	1000–200	Engwall 2000; Zeidler et al. 1998

Site / Phase	Lab	Sample no.				Reference
			Los Ríos			
Salango Chorrera	Geochron Labs	GX 13026	2340 ± 485	1000– A.D. 300	1600– A.D. 700	Lunniss and Mudd n.d.; Norton et al. 1983
La Cadena Chorrera	Bern	B 5560	2430 ± 80	760–400	790–390	Reindel 1995
Palenque Chorrera (Fase Guayaquil)	Inst. of Physical and Chemical Research of Japan					Porras 1983
		RK 4206	2220 ± 75	380–200	410–60	
		RK 2207	2170 ± 65	360–110	400 – A.D. 1	
			Pichincha (western)			
Nambillo nonapplicable	Geochron Labs	GX 12471	5325 ± 110	4320–4000	4450–3900	Lippi 1996
nonapplicable		GX 12470	4540 ± 80	3370–3090	3550–2900	Lippi 1996
Early Nambillo		GX 12473	3330 ± 80	1740–1510	1870–1430	Lippi 1996
Early Nambillo		GX 12469	3225 ± 260	1900–1100	2200–800	Lippi 1996
Nueva Era Nueva Era	Ill. State Geo. Survey	ISGS 1182	3070 ± 250	1650–900	2000–700	Isaacson n.d.
Santa Marta Chorrera	Bern	B 43348	2950 ± 80	1290–1020	1390–930	Lubensky n.d.a
Nueva Era Nueva Era	Ill. State Geo. Survey	ISGS 1176	2710 ± 100	1000–790	1250–500	Isaacson n.d.
		ISGS 1175	2620 ± 70	900–560	1000–450	Isaacson n.d.
Nambillo Early Nambillo	Geochron Labs	GX 12472	2315 ± 260	800–100	1000– A.D. 300	Lippi 1996
Nueva Era Nueva Era	Geochron Labs	ISGS 1187	2010 ± 160	350–A.D. 250	400–A.D. 400	Isaacson n.d.
			Esmeraldas			
La Tolita:Tola Pajarito Chorrera/Early La Tolita	Geochron Labs	GX 12374	2540 ± 75	800–520	810–400	Bouchard 1996; Valdez 1987
		GX 12373	2505 ± 70	790–520	800–410	Bouchard 1996; Valdez 1987
		GX 12380	2450 ± 80	760–400	790–400	Bouchard 1996; Valdez 1987

(cont.)

Table A1 (*cont.*)
Formative Period Radiocarbon Chronology for the Coast and Western Lowlands of Ecuador, by Province and Site, from Earliest Uncalibrated Date to Most Recent Radiocarbon Year before Present (RCYBP)

Site, culture, and phase	Lab and lab no.	Uncalibrated date RCYBP	Probability calibrated range		Reference
			68.2% (year B.C.)	95.4% (year B.C.)	
Esmeraldas (cont.)					
Colon Eloy (R–36)	Bern				
Early Selva Alegre	B 33782	2390 ± 80	760–390	800–250	DeBoer 1996
La Tolita: Tola Pajarito	Geochron Labs				
Chorrera/Early La Tolita	GX 12379	2265 ± 80	400–200	550–50	Bouchard 1996; Valdez 1987

Notes: Data compiled by J. Zeidler. ★ = phase designation of Meggers, Evans, and Estrada 1965.

Table A2

Absolute Chronology for Valdivia Culture according to Phase

Phase	Chronology (years B.C.) Radiocarbon (68.2% probability)	TL	Phase duration (years B.C.)
8b			1600–1450
8	2090–1790	1700–1500	1800–1600
7		1900–1700	1950–1800
6		2100–1900	2100–1950
5		2400–2100	2250–2100
4		2600–2400	2400–2250
3	2870–2360	2900–2400	2800–2400
2b	3090–2695	3200–2900	3000–2800
2a	3555–3065		3300–3000
1b	3860–3340	3600–3200	3800–3300
1a	4460–3755		4400–3800

Notes: TL = thermoluminescence. After Marcos and Michczynski (1996: table 4).

BIBLIOGRAPHY

ALETO, THOMAS
 1988   *The Guayaquil Phase Ceramic Complex: The Late Formative Period in the Gulf of Guayaquil, Ecuador.* Ph.D. dissertation, Department of Anthropology, University of Illinois at Urbana-Champaign. University Microfilms International, Ann Arbor, Mich.

ALVAREZ, A., J. G. MARCOS, AND G. SPINOLO
 1995   The Early Formative Pottery from the Santa Elena Peninsula in Southwest Ecuador. In *Studies on Ancient Ceramics: Proceedings of the European Meetings on Ancient Ceramics* (M. Vendrell-Saz, T. Pradell, J. Molera, and M. Garcia, eds.): 95–107. Generalitat de Catalunya, Department de Cultura, Barcelona.

BECKWITH, LAURIE A.
 n.d.   Late Formative Ceramics from Southwestern Ecuador. Unpublished Ph.D. dissertation, Department of Archaeology, University of Calgary, Calgary, Alberta, 1996.

BISCHOF, HENNING
 1975a   La Fase Engoroy: Períodos, cronología, y relaciones. *Bonner Amerikenistischen Studien* 3 (U. Oberem, ed.): 41–62. Bonn.
 1975b   El Machalilla Temprano y algunos sitios cercanos a Valdivia. *Bonner Amerikenistischen Studien* 3 (U. Oberem, ed.): 13–38.
 1982   La Fase Engoroy: Períodos, cronología, y relaciones. In *Primer Simposio de Correlaciones Antropológicas Andino–Mesoamericano* (J. G. Marcos and P. Norton, eds.): 135–176. Escuela Superior Politécnica del Litoral, Guayaquil.

BISCHOF, HENNING, AND JULIO VITERI GAMBOA
 1972   Pre-Valdivia Occupations on the Southwest Coast of Ecuador. *American Antiquity* 37(4): 548–551.

BOUCHARD, JEAN-FRANÇOIS
 1996   Los datos de cronología cultural para el litoral del Pacífico nor-ecuatorial: Período Formativo Tardío y período de Desarrollo Regional, sur de Colombia, norte del Ecuador. In *Andes: Boletín de la Misión Arqueológica Andina* 1: 137–152. Warsaw.

BRAUN, DAVID P.
 1985   Ceramic Decorative Diversity and Illinois Woodland Regional Integration. In *Decoding Prehistoric Ceramics* (B. A. Nelson, ed.): 128–153. Southern Illinois University Press, Carbondale.

BRONK RAMSEY, CHRISTOPHER
 1994   Analysis of Chronological Information and Radiocarbon Calibration: The OxCal Program. *Archaeological Computing Newsletter* 41 (December): 11–16.
 1995   Radiocarbon Calibration and Analysis of Stratigraphy: The Program OxCal. *Radiocarbon* 37(2): 425–430.

BUCK, CAITLIN E., WILLIAM G. CAVANAGH, AND CLIFFORD D. LITTON
 1996   *Bayesian Approach to Interpreting Archaeological Data.* Wiley, Chicester.

Bushnell, Geoffrey H. S.

1951   *The Archaeology of the Santa Elena Peninsula in Southwestern Ecuador.* Cambridge University Press, Cambridge.

Cummins, Tom

1992   Tradition in Ecuadorian Pre-Hispanic Art: The Ceramics of Chorrera and Jama-Coaque. In *Amerindian Signs: 5,000 Years of Precolumbian Art in Ecuador* (Francisco Valdez and Diego Veintimilla, eds.): 63–81. Dinediciones, Quito.

Damp, Jonathan E.

n.d.   Better Homes and Gardens: The Life and Death of the Early Valdivia Community. Unpublished Ph.D. dissertation, Department of Archaeology, University of Calgary, Calgary, Alberta, 1979.

DeBoer, Warren R.

1996   *Traces behind the Esmeraldas Shore: Prehistory of the Santiago–Cayapas Region, Ecuador.* University of Alabama Press, Tuscaloosa.

Deetz, James, and Edwin Dethlefsen

1965   The Doppler Effect and Archaeology: A Consideration of the Spatial Aspects of Seriation. *Southwestern Journal of Anthropology* 21: 196–206.

Engwall, Evan

n.d.   History, Style, and Agency: An Archaeology of Late Formative Ecuador. Unpublished Ph.D. dissertation, Department of Anthropology, University of Illinois at Urbana–Champaign, in preparation.

Estrada, Emilio

1956   *Valdivia: Un sitio arqueológico formativo en la costa de la provincia del Guayas, Ecuador.* Museo Victor Emilio Estrada Publicación 1. Guayaquil.

1957   *Prehistoria de Manabí.* Museo Victor Emilio Estrada Publicación 4. Guayaquil.

1958   *Las culturas pre-clásicas, formativas, o arcaicos del Ecuador.* Museo Victor Emilio Estrada Publicación 5. Guayaquil.

1962   *Arqueología de Manabí central.* Museo Victor Emilio Estrada Publicación 7. Guayaquil.

Evans, Clifford, and Betty J. Meggers

1954   Informe preliminar sobre la investigaciones arqueológicas realizadas en la cuenca del Guayas, Ecuador. *Cuadernos de Historia y Arqueología* 7: 243–246. Guayaquil.

1957   Formative Period Cultures of the Guayas Basin, Coastal Ecuador. *American Antiquity* 22: 235–247.

1960   A New Dating Method Using Obsidian: pt. 2. An Archaeological Evaluation of the Method. *American Antiquity* 25: 253–257.

1961   Cronología relativa y absoluta de la costa del Ecuador. *Cuadernos de Historia Arqueología* 10(27): 147–152. Guayaquil.

Ferdon, Edwin N. Jr.

1941a   The Excavations at La Libertad. *El Palacio* 48: 38–42.

1941b   Preliminary Notes on Artifacts from La Libertad. *El Palacio* 48: 204–210.

Friedman, Irving, and Robert L. Smith

1960   A New Dating Method Using Obsidian: pt. 1. The Development of the Method. *American Antiquity* 25: 476–521.

GUILLAUME-GENTIL, NICOLAS

1996   El fenómeno de la tolas en la cuenca norte del Guayas Ecuador: Nuevas perspectivas. In *Andes: Boletín de la Misión Arqueológica Andina* 1: 153–172. Warsaw.

1998   Patrones de asentamiento en el piedemonte andino, en la alta cuenca del río Guayas. In *El área septentrional andina: Arqueología y etnohistoria* (M. Guinea, J. Marcos, and J. F. Bouchard, eds.): 149–196. Ediciones Abya-Yala, Quito.

GUINEA BUENO, MERCEDES

1986   El Formativo de la región sur de Esmeraldas. In *Arqueología y etnohistoria del sur de Colombia y norte del Ecuador* (J. Alcina-Franch and S. Moreno Yánez, eds.): 19–46. *Miscelánea Antropológica Ecuatoriana* 6. Guayaquil.

HALL, MINARD

1977   *El volcanismo en el Ecuador*. Instituto Panamericano de Geografía e Historia, Quito.

HILL, BETSY D.

1972/74   A New Chronology of the Valdivia Ceramic Complex from the Coastal Zone of Guayas Province, Ecuador. *Ñawpa Pacha* 10/12: 1–32.

ISAACSON, JOHN S.

1987   *Volcanic Activity and Human Occupation of the Northern Andes: The Application of Tephrostratigraphic Techniques to the Problem of Human Settlement in the Western Montaña during the Ecuadorian Formative*. Ph.D. dissertation, Department of Anthropology, University of Illinois at Urbana–Champaign. University Microfilms International, Ann Arbor, Mich.

1994   Volcanic Sediments in Archaeological Contexts from Western Ecuador. In *Regional Archaeology in Northern Manabí, Ecuador*, vol. 1: *Environment, Cultural Chronology, and Prehistoric Subsistence in the Jama River Valley* (J. A. Zeidler and D. M. Pearsall, eds.): 131–140. Memoirs in Latin American Archaeology 8. University of Pittsburgh, Pittsburgh Pa.

KURC, ALICIA

n.d.   Informe acerca de las excavaciones en el Sitio OMJPLP-141C. Manuscript on file, Fundación Presley Norton, Quito, 1984.

LANNING, EDWARD P.

n.d.   Archaeological Investigations on the Santa Elena Peninsula, Ecuador. Report submitted to the National Science Foundation, Grant GS-2-402. Washington, D.C., 1967.

LATHRAP, DONALD W., DONALD COLLIER, AND HELEN CHANDRA

1975   *Ancient Ecuador: Culture, Clay, and Creativity, 3000–300 B.C.* Field Museum of Natural History, Chicago.

LATHRAP, DONALD W., JORGE G. MARCOS, AND JAMES A. ZEIDLER

1977   Real Alto: An Ancient Ceremonial Center. *Archaeology* 30(1): 2–13.

LIPPI, RONALD D.

1983   *La Ponga and the Machalilla Phase of Coastal Ecuador*. Ph.D. dissertation, Department of Anthropology, University of Wisconsin–Madison. University Microfilms International, Ann Arbor, Mich.

1996   *La primera revolución ecuatoriana: El desarrollo de la vida agrícola en el antiguo Ecuador.* MARKA, Instituto de Historic y Antropología Andinas, Quito.

1998   *Una exploración arqueológica del Pichincha occidental, Ecuador.* Museo Jacinto Jijón y Caamaño, Pontificia Universidad Católica del Ecuador, Quito.

LIU, CHAO LI, KERRY M. RILEY, AND DENNIS D. COLEMAN

1986   Illinois State Geological Survey Dates 8. *Radiocarbon* 28(1): 78–109.

LÓPEZ Y SEBASTIÁN, LORENZO E.

1986   Contribución al estudio de las culturas formatívas en la costa norte del Ecuador. In *Arqueología y etnohistoria del sur de Colombia y norte del Ecuador* (J. Alcina-Franch and S. Moreno Yánez, eds.): 47–60. *Miscelánea Antropológica Ecuatoriana* 6. Guayaquil.

LÓPEZ Y SEBASTIÁN, LORENZO E., AND CHANTAL CAILLAVET

1979   La Fase Tachina en el contexto cultural del Horizonte Chorrera. *Actes du XLII Congrés International des Americanistes*, 9A: 199–215. Paris.

LUBENSKY, EARL H.

1974   Los cementerios de Anllulla. *Boletín de la Academia Nacional de Historia* 57(123): 16–23. Quito.

n.d.a   The Anllulla Cemetery. Paper presented at the 9th Annual Midwest Conference on Andean and Amazonian Archaeology and Ethnohistory, Columbia, Mo., 1981.

n.d.b   Excavación arqueológica en la Hacienda La Florida, enero 1979: Informe preliminar. Manuscript on file, Instituto Nacional del Patrimonio Cultural, Quito, 1979.

n.d.c   Prospección arqueológica, Hacienda La Florida, Santo Domingo de Los Colorados, enero 1979. Paper presented at the Conference 1977–1987 : Diez Años de Arqueología Ecuatoriana, Cuenca, August 15-19, 1988.

LUNNISS, RICHARD, AND ANDREW MUDD

n.d.   Analysis of Part of Structure 1, OMJPLP-141B: A Late Formative Structure Excavated at Salango, Manabí. Programa de Antropología para el Ecuador, Quito. Unpublished manuscript in possession of the author.

MARCOS, JORGE G.

1998   A Reassessment of the Chronology of the Ecuadorian Formative. In *El área septentrional andina: Arqueología y etnohistoria* (M. Guinea, J. Marcos, and J.-F. Bouchard, eds.): 277–324. Ediciones Abya-Yala, Quito.

MARCOS, JORGE G., AND ADAM MICHCZYNSKI

1996   Good Dates and Bad Dates in Ecuador: Radiocarbon Samples and Archaeological Excavation: A Commentary Based on the "Valdivia Absoulte Chronology." In *Andes: Boletín de la Misión Arqueológica Andina* 1: 93–114. Warsaw.

MARCOS, JORGE G., AND PRESLEY NORTON

1981   Interpretación sobre la arqueología de la Isla de La Plata. *Miscelánea Antropológica Ecuatoriana* 1: 136–154. Guayaquil.

1984   From the Yungas of Chinchay Suyo to Cuzco: The Role of La Plata Island in Spondylus Trade. In *Social and Economic Organization in the Prehispanic Andes* (D. L. Browman, R. L. Burger, and M. A. Rivera, eds.): 7–20. *Proceedings of the*

44th International Congress of Americanists, Manchester, 1982. BAR International Series 194, British Archaeological Reports, Oxford.

MARCOS, JORGE, G., AND BOGOMIL OBELIC

1998 ^{14}C and TL Chronology for the Ecuadorian Formative. In *El área septentrional andina: Arqueología y etnohistoria* (M. Guinea, J. Marcos, and J.-F. Bouchard, eds.): 325–337. Ediciones Abya-Yala, Quito.

MARTINI, M., E. SIBILIA, G. SPINOLO, C. ZELASCHI, A. ALVAREZ, AND J. G. MARCOS

n.d. The Early Formative Period Pottery from the Santa Elena Peninsula in Southwest Ecuador: Absolute TL Chronology. Unpublished manuscript in possession of the author.

MEGGERS, BETTY J.

1966 *Ecuador.* Praeger, New York.

MEGGERS, BETTY J., AND CLIFFORD EVANS

1962 The Machalilla Culture: An Early Formative Complex on the Ecuadorian Coast. *American Antiquity* 28: 86–192.

1977 Early Formative Period Chronology of the Ecuadorian Coast: A Correction. *American Antiquity* 42: 226.

MEGGERS, BETTY J., CLIFFORD EVANS, AND EMILIO ESTRADA

1965 *Early Formative Period of Coastal Ecuador: The Valdivia and Machalilla Phases.* Smithsonian Contributions to Anthropology 1. Smithsonian Institution. U.S. Government Printing Office, Washington, D.C.

NORTON, PRESLEY

1982 Preliminary Observations on Loma Alta, an Early Valdivia Midden in Guayas Province, Ecuador. In *Primer Simposio de Correlaciones Antropológicas Andino-Mesoamericano* (J. G. Marcos and P. Norton, eds.): 101–119. Escuela Superior Politécnica del Litoral, Guayaquil.

1992 Las culturas cerámicas prehispánicas del sur de Manabí. In *5000 años de ocupación: Parque Nacional Machalilla* (P. Norton, ed.): 9–40. Ediciones Abya-Yala and Centro Cultural Artes, Quito.

n.d.a Early Valdivia Middens at Loma Alta, Ecuador. Paper presented at the 37th Annual Meeting of the Society for American Archaeoology, Bal Harbor, Fla., 1972.

n.d.b The Loma Alta Connection. Paper presented at the 42nd Annual Meeting of the Society for American Archaeology, New Orleans, 1977.

NORTON, PRESLEY, RICHARD LUNNISS, AND NIGEL NAYLING

1983 Excavaciones en Salango, provincia de Manabí, Ecuador. *Miscelánea Antropológica Ecuatoriana* 3: 9–72. Guayaquil.

PARDUCCI, RESFRA, AND IBRAHIM PARDUCCI

1970 Un sitio arqueologico al norte de la ciudad: Fase Guayaquil. *Cuadernos de Historia y Arqueología* 37: 57–153. Guayaquil.

1975 Vasijas y elementos diagnósticos: Fase Guayaquil. *Cuadernos de Historia y Arqueología* 42: 155–284. Guayaquil.

PAULSEN, ALLISON C., AND EUGENE J. MCDOUGLE

n.d.a A Chronology of Machalilla and Engoroy Ceramics of the South Coast of Ecuador. Paper presented at the 9th Annual Midwest Conference on Andean and Amazonian Archaeology and Ethnohistory, Columbia, Mo., 1981.

n.d.b   The Machalilla and Engoroy Occupations of the Santa Elena Peninsula in South Coastal Ecuador. Paper presented at the 39th Annual Meeting of the Society for American Archaeology, Washington, D.C., 1974.

PORRAS, PEDRO

1973   *El Encanto–La Puná: Un sitio insular de la fase Valdivia asociado a un conchero anular.* Ediciones Huancavilca, Guayaquil.

1983   *Arqueología: Palenque, Los Ríos y La Ponga, Guayas.* Pontificia Universidad Católica del Ecuador, Centro de Investigaciones Arqueológicas, Quito.

RAYMOND, J. SCOTT, JORGE G. MARCOS, AND DONALD W. LATHRAP

1980   Evidence of Early Formative Settlement in the Guayas Basin, Ecuador. *Current Anthropology* 21: 700–701.

REINDEL, MARKUS

1995   *Das archäologische Projekt La Cadena, Ecuador.* Sonderdruck aus Beiträge zur Allgemeinen und Vergleichenden Archäologie Band 15. Verlag Phillip Von Zabern, Mainz am Rhein.

SCHIFFER, MICHAEL B.

1986   Radiocarbon Dates and the "Old Wood" Problem: The Case of the Hohokam Chronology. *Journal of Archaeological Science* 13: 13–30.

SCOTT, JOHN F.

1998   El estilo Chorrera y su influencia en los Andes septentrionales. In *El área septentrional andina: Arqueología y etnohistoria* (M. Guinea, J. Marcos, and J.-F. Bouchard, eds.): 261–276. Ediciones Abya-Yala, Quito.

SIMMONS, MICHAEL P.

1970   *The Ceramic Sequence from La Carolina, Santa Elena Peninsula, Ecuador.* Ph.D. dissertation, Department of Anthropology, University of Arizona. University Microfilms International, Ann Arbor, Mich.

STAHL, PETER W.

1984   *Tropical Forest Cosmology: The Cultural Context of the Early Valdivia Occupations at Loma Alta.* Ph.D. dissertation, Department of Anthropology, University of Illinois at Urbana-Champaign. University Microfilms International, Ann Arbor, Mich.

STALLER, JOHN

1994   *Late Valdivia Occupation in Southern Coastal El Oro Province, Ecuador: Excavations at the Early Formative Period (3500–1500 B.C.) Site of La Emerenciana.* Ph.D. dissertation, Department of Anthropology, Southern Methodist University, Dallas. University Microfilms International, Ann Arbor, Mich.

STEMPER, DAVID M.

1989   *The Persistence of Pre-Hispanic Chiefdom Formations, Río Daule, Coastal Ecuador.* Ph.D. dissertation, Department of Anthropology, University of Wisconsin–Madison. University Microfilms International, Ann Arbor, Mich.

1993   *The Persistence of Prehispanic Chiefdom Formations on the Río Daule, Coastal Ecuador.* Memoirs in Latin American Archaeology 7. University of Pittsburgh, Pittsburgh, Pa.

STIRLING, MATTHEW W., AND MARION STIRLING
  1963   Tarqui, an Early Site in Manabí Province, Ecuador. Smithsonian Institution,
            Bureau of American Ethnology Bulletin 186, Anthropological Papers 63.
            Washington, D.C.

STOTHERT, KAREN E.
  1976   The Early Prehistory of the Santa Elena Peninsula, Ecuador: Continuities
            between the Preceramic and Ceramic Cultures (88-98). *Actas Americanas del
            XLI Congreso Internacional de Americanistas.*
  1995   Las albarradas tradicionales y el manejo de aguas en la peninsula de Santa
            Elena. In *Miscelánea Antropológica Ecuatoriana* 8: 131–160.

STUIVER, MINZE, AUSTIN LONG, AND RENEE KRA (eds.)
  1993   Calibration 1993. *Radiocarbon* 35(1): 1–224.

STUIVER, MINZE, AND P. J. REIMER
  1986   A Computer Program for Radiocarbon Age Calculation. In *Calibration Issue,
            Proceedings of the 12th International ^{14}C Conference* (M. Stuiver and R. S. Kra,
            eds.) *Radiocarbon* 28(2B): 1022–1030.

VALDEZ, FRANCISCO
  1987   *Proyecto Arqueológico La Tolita.* Museos del Banco Central del Ecuador, Quito,
            Ecuador.

WAGNER, GÜNTHER A.
  1995   *Thermolumineszenz-Datierung an Gefäßkeramik des Fundplatzes La Cadena/
            Ecuador.* Zwischenbericht 12. Heidelberg.

ZEDEÑO, MARÍA NIEVES
  n.d.   Análisis de cerámica Chorrera del sitio Peñón del Río. Tésis de licenciatura,
            Centro de Estudios Arqueológicas y Antropológicos, Escuela Superior
            Politécnica del Litoral, Guayaquil, 1985.

ZEIDLER, JAMES A.
  1984   *Social Space in Valdivia Society: Community Patterning and Domestic Structure at
            Real Alto, 3000–2000 B.C.* Ph.D. dissertation, Department of Anthropology,
            University of Illinois at Urbana–Champaign. University Microfilms
            International, Ann Arbor, Mich.
  1994a   Archaeological Testing in the Middle Jama Valley. In *Regional Archaeology in
            Northern Manabí, Ecuador,* vol. 1: *Environment, Cultural Chronology, and Prehistoric
            Subsistence in the Jama River Valley* (J. A. Zeidler and D. M. Pearsall, eds.): 71–
            98. Memoirs in Latin American Archaeology 8. University of Pittsburgh,
            Pittsburgh, Pa.
  1994b   Archaeological Testing in the Lower Jama Valley. In *Regional Archaeology in
            Northern Manabí, Ecuador,* vol. 1: *Environment, Cultural Chronology, and Prehistoric
            Subsistence in the Jama River Valley* (J. A. Zeidler and D. M. Pearsall, eds.): 99–
            109. Memoirs in Latin American Archaeology 8. University of Pittsburgh,
            Pittsburgh, Pa.

ZEIDLER, JAMES A., CAITLIN E. BUCK, AND CLIVE D. LITTON
  1998   Integration of Archaeological Phase Information and Radiocarbon Results
            from the Jama River Valley, Ecuador: A Bayesian Approach. *Latin American
            Antiquity* 9(2): 160–179.

Appendixes

ZEIDLER, JAMES A., AND MARIE J. SUTLIFF
    1994   Definition of Ceramic Complexes and Cultural Occupation in the Jama
            Valley. In *Regional Archaeology in Northern Manabí, Ecuador,* vol. 1: *Environment,*
            Cultural Chronology, and Prehistoric Subsistence in the Jama River Valley (J. A.
            Zeidler and D. M. Pearsall, eds.): 111–130. Memoirs in Latin American
            Archaeology 8. University of Pittsburgh, Pittsburgh, Pa.

ZEVALLOS MENÉNDEZ, CARLOS
    1965/66   Informe preliminar sobre el cementerio Chorrera, bahía de Santa Elena,
               Ecuador. *Revista del Museo Nacional* 34: 20–27. Lima.

ZIÓLKOWSKI, M. S., M. F. PADZUR, A. KRZANOWSKI, AND A. MICHCZYNSKI (EDS.)
    n.d.   Andes: Radiocarbon Database for Bolivia, Ecuador, and Peru. Andean
            Archaeological Mission of the Institute of Archaeology, Warsaw University,
            Warsaw, and Gliwice Radiocarbon Laboratory, Institute of Physics, Silesian
            Technical University, Gliwice, 1994.

Appendix B

Formative Period Chronology for the Northern and Central Highlands of Ecuador

RONALD D. LIPPI

UNIVERSITY OF WISCONSIN–MARATHON COUNTY

Although this Appendix should include both the northern highlands (Carchi, Imbabura, and Pichincha provinces) and the central highlands (Bolívar, Chimborazo, Cotopaxi, and Tungurahua provinces), no Formative period material is yet known from the little studied central highlands. In fact, the known material comes from Pichincha and Imbabura provinces. These materials are mostly from inter-Andean sites, which are true sierra sites, and also include materials recently discovered on the western flank of Pichincha province in a subtropical and tropical forest area (the western *montaña*).

The chronology of Formative complexes in this region is based on three dating methods: radiocarbon assays, tephrostratigraphy, and cross-dating. Below brief mention is made of each of the known complexes, their possible affiliations, and—most importantly for our purposes—their chronology. Radiocarbon dates are in Table B1.

Certainly the best known Formative complex of the region is Cotocollao, named after the type-site in the former village of Cotocollao, now a barrio on the north end of the capital city of Quito. Limited work at the site by Padre Pedro Porras (1982) and much more extensive salvage work by a large team led by Marcelo Villalba (1988) has resulted in abundant information on the ceramics and chronology, as well as some understanding of the settlement plan, burial practices, and agriculture. Porras's four radiocarbon dates and stratigraphic analysis of the site were of somewhat dubious provenance and, as was his custom, he published only those three dates that seemed relevant. These are included in

Table B1, as are the five earliest and five latest dates of a total of 55 radiocarbon assays from Villalba.

Villalba defined 34 classes of pottery vessels on the basis of form, decoration, and surface treatment. These classes were arranged into a four-phase sequence (Cotocollao 1a, 1b, 2a, and 2b) according to their stratigraphic relationships, carbon dates, and a seriation that was a hybrid of the Fordian type-frequency method of seriating pottery classes and a type-frequency seriation of individual attributes. Since the site is quite large, the stratigraphy complicated, and the type-frequency seriation method problematic, questions remain regarding details of the ceramic sequence. Nonetheless, the overall chronological record seems fairly well-established on stratigraphic grounds. The multitude of radiocarbon dates suggests a calibrated time span for the Cotocollao site from approximately 1800 to 400 B.C.

The end of the Cotocollao occupation seems to coincide more or less with a major volcanic event in the northern highlands. This is presumed to be the eruption of Pululagua, situated 17 km north of the type-site. The date of that eruption is based on a single radiocarbon assay of a carbonized twig pulled from an ash deposit near the volcano (Hall 1977: 93). Minard Hall mistakenly reported the date in calendar years as 335 B.C. However, the Smithsonian Institution lab, which ran the date, recorded it as 2305 BP, which converts to 355 B.C. (uncalibrated). A second date for Pululagua (GP88-135, 2650 ± 150) may predate the eruption but is not considered reliable (Isaacson and Zeidler 1999: 45–46). Hall's solitary date, also in Table B1, probably falls within the range (calibrated) of 530 to 180 B.C. Porras (1982: 62) believed the site was briefly reoccupied by Cotocollao peoples following the eruption. Villalba (1988) does not address the possibility of recolonization directly, leaving the impression that the eruption was the definitive termination of site occupation. Pululagua's eruption was also a significant cutoff for other sites in the region and may serve as a nonarbitrary temporal boundary for the end of the Formative period in at least part of the northern highlands.

Villalba conducted surveys in the Quito valley and in the Tumbaco and Los Chillos valleys immediately east of Quito, cataloguing some 70 Cotocollao sites in the Pichincha highlands. My extensive but unsystematic 1988 regional survey of much of the western *montaña* of Pichincha, an area of subtropical cloud forest and tropical rainforest on the western flank of the Andes, has identified a handful of sites with a narrow sample of Cotocollao pottery. Test excavations were carried out at one of those sites, Nambillo, resulting in five radiocarbon dates from the earliest paleosol of three. It is this early stratum that contains the Cotocollao material and is separated from later occupations by deep tephravolcanic sediments. It is possible that the two earliest dates from that series represent preoccupational charcoal, since they are inexplicably earlier than the Cotocollao dates.

While the Cotocollao ceramics bear some generic Formative period characteristics found in other parts of Ecuador, the Cotocollao complex itself has not yet been identified in either adjacent or more remote areas with the exception of the western *montaña*.

Aside from the Cotocollao culture, the Pichincha and Imbabura highlands may harbor other Late Formative period complexes, though these proposals so far are controversial. The first such candidate was the Espejo complex from the shores of Lake San Pablo in southern Imbabura province. Thomas Myers (1976) defined this complex principally on the basis of a small surface collection. The Early Espejo phase he cross-dated with Valdivia and Late Espejo with Machalilla, both on the Ecuadorian coast. Myers suggested stylistic similarities between this highland complex and the well-known coastal phases, which have been largely rejected. Subsequently, Myers (1978) proposed that some of the Espejo pottery is related to La Chimba.

The large site of La Chimba, covering several hectares in Pichincha province 55 km northeast of Quito, was first studied by Stephen Athens and Alan Osborn (1974), who found superimposed occupations, named Early, Middle, and Late La Chimba. The Early and Middle phases are separated by a volcanic ash stratum. One late radiocarbon assay was discounted (Athens 1978: 493), leaving the site with an uncalibrated date around 150 B.C. for Middle La Chimba. The La Chimba materials were touted by Athens and others as Late Formative, contemporary in part with Cotocollao, and Early Regional Developmental period since the 1970s, but research on La Chimba was suspended for many years. Myers (1978) argued that La Chimba deposits were mixed together, not stratigraphically separate. But Athens (1978) countered this comparison of Espejo with the coastal Formative and charged that there was no basis for distinguishing Early and Late Espejo.

José Berenguer and José Echeverría (1988) shed light on this murkiness by excavating at the Tababuela site, in the far north of Imbabura province, where they found ceramics similar both to Espejo and La Chimba. From their stratigraphic excavation, they drew three important conclusons: (a) Early and Late Espejo are mixed stratigraphically and do not represent separate phases; (b) Middle La Chimba is a valid phase that occurs in isolation at Tababuela; and (c) Middle La Chimba is not contemporary with Cotocollao, but later.

Villalba and Santiago Ontaneda have collected ceramics from the site of Los Soles in San Antonio de Ibarra, Imbabura province. They believe it is Late

Formative, closely related to La Chimba, and somewhat influenced by Cotocollao (S. Ontaneda Luciano, personal communication, February 1999). With a few known complexes now in northeastern Pichincha and Imbabura provinces that are somewhat similar to La Chimba, the primary objective had to be the secure dating of La Chimba.

Athens resumed work on La Chimba in 1989, and the dating problem may now be resolved with a series of 15 radiocarbon assays from one stratified excavation unit at the site. The dates are generally internally consistent and they cluster around 900 B.C. to A.D. 200 (calibrated), which puts the earlier part of the La Chimba sequence into the Late Formative period prior to the catastrophic volcanic eruption.

Whether La Chimba, Tababuela, Espejo, Los Soles, and similar complexes in Imbabura province and northeastern Pichincha province have some affinity with Cotocollao is unclear. There is no obvious stylistic or morphological connection. Nonetheless, the abandonment of the Cotocollao type-site, and presumably of many other Cotocollao sites in the Quito area with the eruption of Pululagua, could have led to a migration of Formative peoples eastward and northward.

The only other present candidate for Formative "honors" in the region is the Nueva Era phase at the site of Tulipe in Pichincha's western *montaña*. Discovered by Holguer Jara on a hill overlooking the Tulipe pool complex and excavated by John Isaacson (n.d.), Nueva Era is a new and previously unknown Formative ceramic complex. Though the site is only 18 km north of Nambillo and 35 km northwest of Cotocollao, it appears unrelated to them. Isaacson (n.d.: 331) suggested a link to Momil and Tierra Adentro in Colombia, which I find unconvincing. Lathrap and Isaacson related Nueva Era to brown-incised ware and Quimbaya gold of Colombia (*The New Mexican* 1984). Further analysis has shown that the brown-incised ware from Colombia is not comparable to Nueva Era. A range of radiocarbon dates, however, places Nueva Era firmly in the Formative (see Table B1).

I (1998) have identified a few other sites in the western *montaña* of Pichincha with some sherds generally reminiscent of Formative pottery: thin walled, polished exterior, carinated bowls with nicking or punctation. However, these cannot yet be positively identified or dated. As I moved farther westward and downward in western Pichincha, I encountered a few sherds similar to Chorrera. This was not surprising, given that the westernmost part of the province, ecologically speaking, is coastal lowlands.

The published and unpublished radiocarbon dates from these various projects along with their calibrations and additional data are presented in Table B1. The only known dates that are excluded are 45 of the 55 dates from Cotocollao, since they are repetitive, but complete dates from the Cotocollao site are in Villalba (1988: fig. 136).

A general absence of serious archaeological research on the Formative period in the provinces of Bolívar, Chimborazo, and Tungurahua leaves the central highlands of Ecuador unknown for this time period. Bolívar province, in particular, should contain interesting Formative complexes given its strategic location along trade routes from the Santa Elena peninsula and the Gulf of Guayaquil region to the highlands. A recent reevaluation by Dennis Davies (n.d.) of Chimbo ceramics excavated by Jijón y Camaaño around 1920 failed to produce any indication of Formative period pottery in that large curated collection.

Table B1

Formative Period Radiocarbon Chronology for the Northern and Central Highlands of Ecuador, by Site, from the Earliest to Most Recent according to Radiocarbon Year before Present (RCYBP)

Site, culture, and phase	Lab and lab. no.	Uncalibrated date RCYBP	Probability calibrated range		Reference
			68.2% (year B.C.)	95.4% (year B.C.)	
			Pichincha		
Cotocollao					
Cotocollao 1a	Geochron Labs				
	GX 4768	3495 ± 210	2150–1500	2500–1300	Villalba 1988
	GX 7210	3340 ± 135	1880–1460	2050–1300	Villalba 1988
	GX 8323[a]	3310 ± 150	1870–1430	2050–1250	Villalba 1988
Cotocollao 1a or 1b	Geochron Labs				
GX 4766		3135 ± 165	1620–1160	1700–900	Villalba 1988
	GX 7207	3100 ± 140	1530–1130	1900–900	Villalba 1988
Cotocollao 2b	Geochron Labs				
	GX 8340-A	2355 ± 250	800–150	1100–A.D. 200	Villalba 1988
	GX 8326	2325 ± 125	800–200	800–100	Villalba 1988
	GX 8323[a]	2310 ± 185	800–150	850–A.D. 100	Villalba 1988
	GX 5064	2305 ± 135	800–150	800–50	Villalba 1988
	GX 8339-0	2200 ± 250	800–A.D. 100	900–A.D. 400	Villalba 1988
Cotocollao A	Nishina Memorial				
	N 2783	3960 ± 115	2900–2300	2900–2100	Porras 1982
	N 2784	3320 ± 115	1750–1450	1950–1300	Porras 1982
Cotocollao B	N 2785	2880 ± 70	1210–940	1310–900	Porras 1982
Pululagua volcano end of Formative?	Smithsonian Inst.				
	SI 2128	2305 ± 65[b]	480–200	800–150	Hall 1977[b]
Atacazo volcano end of Formative?	Ill. State Geo. Survey				
	ISGS 1228	2290 ± 70	410–200	800–150	Isaacson n.d.
Nambillo					
Early Nambillo?	Geochron Labs				
	GX 12471	5325 ± 110	4330–4040	4450–3950	Lippi 1998
	GX 12470	4540 ± 80	3370–3100	3550–2900	Lippi 1998
Early Nambillo	Geochron Labs				
	GX 12473	3330 ± 80	1740–1520	1880–1440	Lippi 1998
	GX 12469	3225 ± 260	1900–1150	2200–800	Lippi 1998
	GX 12472	2315 ± 260	800–100	1100–A.D. 300	Lippi 1998

Site / Phase	Lab	Lab No.	BP date	Calibration	Calibration	Reference
La Chimba Middle La Chimba?	Dicar and Dicarb Isotope; Case Western Reserve	DIC 388 CWR 72	2100 ± 100 1220 ± 140	360-B.C./A.D. A.D. 670-950	390-A.D. 70 A.D. 500-1200	Athens and Osborn 1974 Athens and Osborn 1974
			Imbabura			
Im-11 Middle La Chimba?	Dicar and Dicarb Isotope; Case Western Reserve	DIC 195 CWR 62	2770 ± 130 2670 ± 560	1100-800 1600-100	1400-550 2300-A.D. 600	Athens and Osborn 1974 Athens and Osborn 1974
			Pichincha			
La Chimba, Unit TP-7 La Chimba, beginning La Chimba	Beta Analytic	Beta 34805	2320 ± 70	550-200	800-150	Athens 1990, n.d.
		Beta 43191	1890 ± 60	A.D. 50-220	40-A.D. 250	Athens n.d.
		Beta 43192	2340 ± 50	520-370	800-200	Athens n.d.
		Beta 45747	2640 ± 70	910-780	990-540	Athens n.d.
		Beta 45748	2530 ± 50	800-540	810-410	Athens n.d.
		Beta 50487	1910 ± 70	A.D. 1-200	100-A.D. 250	Athens n.d.
		Beta 50488	2130 ± 70	360-90	380-10	Athens n.d.
		Beta 50489	2290 ± 70	410-200	800-150	Athens n.d.
		Beta 50490	2490 ± 60	790-520	800-410	Athens n.d.
		Beta 50491	2530 ± 70	810-530	810-410	Athens n.d.
		Beta 50492	2560 ± 90	830-530	900-400	Athens n.d.
		Beta 51690	2100 ± 50	200-50	360-A.D. 10	Athens n.d.
		Beta 51691	2100 ± 60	340-40	360-A.D. 20	Athens n.d.
		Beta 53022	2010 ± 70	110-A.D. 60	200-A.D. 130	Athens n.d.
		Beta 53023	2140 ± 60	360-100	380-40	Athens n.d.
Nueva Era Nueva Era	Ill. State Geo. Survey	ISGS 1182	3070 ± 250	1650-1000	2000-700	Isaacson n.d.
		ISGS 1176	2710 ± 100	990-800	1250-500	Isaacson n.d.
		ISGS 1175	2620 ± 70	910-600	930-520	Isaacson n.d.
		ISGS 1187	2010 ± 160	350-A.D. 200	400-A.D. 350	Isaacson n.d.

Notes: All data were compiled by R. Lippi. All calibrations were computed with the Oxcal program (Ramsey 1995). [a] Two different dates were erroneously given the same lab number in Villalba (1988). [b] Hall erroneously reported this date as 335 B.C.; Smithsonian notes give the date as 2305 BP (355 B.C.).

BIBLIOGRAPHY

ATHENS, J. STEPHEN

1978   Formative Period Occupations in the Highlands of Northern Ecuador: A Comment on Myers. *American Antiquity* 43: 493–496.

1990   Prehistoric Agricultural Expansion and Population Growth in Northern Highland Ecuador: Interim Report for 1989 Fieldwork. International Archaeological Research Institute, Honolulu.

n.d.   Cronología cultural y agricultura prehistórica: Investigaciones arqueológicas en la sierra norte del Ecuador, 1989, 1994, y 1997. Quito, Frontreras, in press.

ATHENS, J. STEPHEN, AND ALAN J. OSBORN

1974   Archaeological Investigations at Two Ceramic Period Sites in the Highlands of Northern Ecuador: Two Preliminary Reports. Instituto Otavaleño de Antropología, Otavalo, Ecuador.

BERENGUER, JOSÉ, AND JOSÉ ECHEVERRÍA

1988   Ocupaciones del período Formativo en la sierra norte del Ecuador. Un comentario a Myers y Athens. *Sarance* 12: 65–108. Instituto Otavaleño de Antropología, Otavalo, Ecuador.

DAVIES, DENNIS P. D.

n.d.   Integration Period Chimbo Culture in Bolívar, Ecuador: The Ceramic Evidence. Master's thesis, Trent University, Peterborough, Ontario, 1996.

HALL, MINARD

1977   *El volcanismo en el Ecuador*. Instituto Panamericano de Geografía e Historia, Quito.

ISAACSON, JOHN S.

n.d.   Volcanic Activity and Human Occupation of the Northern Andes: The Application of Tephrostratigraphic Techniques to the Problem of Human Settlement in the Western *Montaña* during the Ecuadorian Formative. Ph.D. dissertation, Department of Anthropology, University of Illinois at Urbana–Champaign, 1987.

ISAACSON, JOHN S., AND JAMES A. ZEIDLER

1999   Accidental History: Volcanic Activity and the End of the Formative in Northwestern Ecuador." In *Actividad volcánica y pueblos precolombinos en el Ecuador* (Patricia Mothes, ed.): 41–72. Ediciones Abya-Yala, Quito.

LIPPI, RONALD D.

1998   *Una exploración arqueológica del Pichincha occidental, Ecuador*. Museo Jacinto Jijón y Caamaño, Pontificia Universidad Católica del Ecuador, Banco Interamericano de Desarrollo, H. Consejo Provincial de Pichincha, Quito.

MYERS, THOMAS

1976   Formative Period Occupations in the Highlands of Northern Ecuador. *American Antiquity* 41: 353–360.

1978   Formative Period Occupations in the Highlands of Northern Ecuador: Rejoinder to Athens. *American Antiquity* 43: 497–500.

Appendixes

THE NEW MEXICAN
 1984 Pottery Shards Help Unravel Ancient Mystery. 14 June: A11.

PORRAS, PEDRO
 1982 *Arqueología de Quito I: Fase Cotocollao.* Centro de Investigaciones Arqueológicas, Pontificia Universidad Católica del Ecuador, Quito.

VILLALBA, MARCELO
 1988 *Cotocollao: Una aldea formativa del valle de Quito.* Serie Monográfica 2, Miscelánea Antropológica Ecuatoriana. Museos del Banco Central del Ecuador, Quito.

537

APPENDIX C

Formative Period Chronology for Eastern Ecuador

ARTHUR ROSTOKER
PH. D. PROGRAM IN ANTHROPOLOGY
CITY UNIVERSITY OF NEW YORK
GRADUATE CENTER

Largely on the basis of assertions by Padre Pedro Porras (1975, 1980, 1987, 1989), with qualified support from Donald Lathrap (see Marcos 1998: 312), unquestionable evidence of Formative period human settlement in at least some parts of the Ecuadorian Oriente has long been assumed. As Stephen Athens (1990) amply demonstrated in reviewing all published dates for the Fase Pastaza (Porras 1975), the stratigraphic integrity of the deposits and cultural associations of those carbon samples determined to be of Formative age from the Huasaga site are far less than certain. A proposed, lengthy, four-period chronological sequence remains unsupported by concrete evidence.

The so-called Pre-Upano phase, as described from seriation and analysis of material excavated at Huapula is also unclear. Specification of this putative early chronological period ultimately rests on two isolated radiocarbon dates for samples drawn from inadequately and inconsistently specified cultural contexts (see Athens 1990: 111–112). For the Fase Los Tayos (Porras 1980: 119–121), direct radiocarbon determinations on shell supposedly accord with thermoluminescence dates from pot sherds. These dates were used to suggest an occupation around 1500 B.C., consonant with apparent stylistic similarities of the recovered pottery to Machalilla wares (see Marcos 1998: 312–313).

The efficacy of more recent Formative dates for the Upano Tradition, on the basis of radiocarbon determinations for samples also submitted for operations at or around Huapula (Porras 1987: 296–297, 299; see Table C1), is difficult to evaluate. In short, the respective laboratory numbers, reported ages, and/or proveniences given in several sources are incomplete or inconsistent (Salazar 1998: 215–216, 228, 230; cf. Porras 1987: 296–297 with 299 and with Porras 1989: table 1; Marcos and Obelic 1998: 359; or Ziólkowski et al. n.d.: 156–157).

Temporal placement of other ceramic complexes from eastern Ecuador that Porras (1980) reported as having Formative components, including Chiguaza (1980: 123–127) and Cotundo (1980: 129–133), is founded largely on stylistic and other nonobjective criteria.

An oft-cited radiocarbon age determination of 2750 ± 440 BP from a site in the middle Upano valley that Michael Harner denominated as Ipíamais (1972: 13) is probably not meaningful. This assay had an extraordinarily large standard deviation. The sample itself may have been confused with another taken from the nearby Yaunchu site, which was under laboratory analysis at the same time (Rostoker 1996: 22). [An additional radiocarbon sample Harner collected from Yaunchu was clearly associated with Upano pottery (i.e., Red Banded Incised ware). Upon subsequent assay, it yielded a date well within the Regional Development period (Rostoker 1996: 22).]

Even a cursory review of the limited, scattered radiocarbon evidence of the Oriente available through 1990 reveals an obvious pattern. Despite recovery of carbon of probable Formative age at several places identified as prehistoric sites on other grounds—mainly the presence of fragmented ancient pottery—solid evidence of Formative human settlement in the Oriente is still elusive or equivocal at best.

Farther south, in Morona Santiago, a more recent inquiry has been carried out at Huapula (Rostain 1999; Salazar 1998), better known as the Sangay Complex (Porras 1987, 1989). That study gave rise to a smaller project at Yaunchu, one of the sites in the middle Upano valley first recognized by Harner (1972: 13) in 1957.

If the end of the Formative was 2300 BP, roughly 200 to 500 B.C., 3 of the 17 published radiocarbon dates from the Sangay–Upano project (Rostain 1999: 89) can be construed as probable indicators of Formative period human activity at Huapula. As calibrated at the two-sigma range, one of the dated samples might easily stem from the subsequent Regional Development period instead (see Table C1).

The ranges of other two-sigma calibrated dates determined for samples from the same site straddle the chronological boundary between the Formative and Regional Development periods (see Rostain 1999: 89). Given that five samples were from somewhere near the bottom—or at least within the basal strata—of artificial mounds, it can provisionally be expected that platform construction at Huapula might have begun at around that same time (Salazar 1998: 230).

Stratigraphic excavation both on- and off-mound at Yaunchu produced only one sample determined by radiocarbon assay to be of probable Formative age. Drawn from a nonmound context, the pertinent charcoal was well-associated with Upano Tradition pottery in situ. Unfortunately, this resultant early chronological age range could not be replicated by testing other samples from the same unit drawn at approximately the same level within a single discrete cultural layer. Two such samples were both dated to well within the Regional Development period.

A few other carbon samples from the Oriente, firmly associated with prehistoric cultural material and apparently of Formative age, have been reported to the Instituto Nacional de Patrimonio Cultural del Ecuador by investigators working in the "petroleum zone," including Florencio Delgado (n.d.), José Echeverria (n.d.), and Amelia Sanchez Mosquera (n.d.). Their results need to be further substantiated with confirming objective age determinations on samples having specifiable cultural associations. If that can be accomplished, these findings will constitute the best evidence of Formative period human settlement in eastern Ecuador.

Preceramic and aceramic settlements, as well as later pottery-using societies, likely were already established at some places in the Oriente well before 500 B.C. Nevertheless, proof of their existence is almost completely lacking. Material traces of these earlier groups seem to have been thoroughly obscured by a veritable explosion of human settlement that apparently took place beginning in the first few hundred years of the Regional Development period, especially along the base of the eastern escarpment of the Andes.

It is these later societies that evidence the pattern known throughout the western hemisphere as technologically Formative: more-or-less permanent nucleated settlements; widespread production and use of ceramic containers and other objects of fired clay; and significant reliance on food production, with a concomitant de-emphasis on gathering or hunting and other forms of wild food exploitation. The Ecuadorian Oriente is rich with evidence of the probable autochthonous development of complex society within tropically forested and other lowland settings. On the basis of the radiocarbon evidence now available, most—if not necessarily all—of these human groups appear to have been latecomers in relation to the Formative period societies of the coast and sierra, with which they have been so often and so enthusiastically compared.

Table C1

Formative Period Radiocarbon Chronology for Eastern (the Oriente of) Ecuador, by Site, according to Radiocarbon Year before Present (RCYBP)

Site, culture, and phase	Lab and lab no.	Uncalibrated date RCYBP	Probability calibrated range		Reference
			68.2% (year B.C.)	95.4% (year B.C.)	
Bicundo Chico	Comisión Ecuatoriana de Energía Atómica				
unknown	CEEA 161	3140 ± 70	1500–1310	1600–1210	Bolaños et al. n.d.
Borja-Minda BO-1	Smithsonian Inst.				
Cosanga?	SI 690	2390 ± 165	800–250	850–50	Ziółkowski et al. n.d.
Chiguaza?a	Nishina Memorial				
Chiguaza?	N 4158	2510 ± 95	800–510	810–400	Porras 1987
Curiurcu	Comisión Ecuatoriana de Energía Atómica				
unknown	CEEA 12	2620 ± 100	910–540	1000–400	Delgado n.d.
El Avispal	Comisión Ecuatoriana de Energía Atómica				
Cosanga?	CEEA 02	3360 ± 220	1950–1400	2300–1000	Delgado n.d.
El Guayabo	Comisión Ecuatoriana de Energía Atómica				
unknown	CEEA 162	2520 ± 70	800–520	800–410	Bolaños et al. n.d.
Huapula					
Pre-Upano	Nishina Memorial				
	N 4491	4700 ± 70	3630–3370	3640–3350	Porras 1987
	N 4201	4470 ± 35	3330–3030	3350–3020	Porras 1987
Upano	Beta Analytic and Nishina Memorial				
	N 4203	3050 ± 85	1410–1130	1500–1040	Porras 1987
	N 3869	2860 ± 135	1260–860	1400–750	Marcos and Obelic 1998
	Beta 89271	2780 ± 90	1020–820	1220–790	Rostain 1999
	N 3870	2750 ± 150	1190–780	1400–400	Marcos and Obelic 1998
	Beta 106086	2360 ± 60	760–370	800–200	Rostain 1999
	Beta 89270	2310 ± 70	490–200	800–150	Rostain 1999

(cont.)

Table C1 (*cont.*)
Formative Period Radiocarbon Chronology for Eastern (the Oriente of) Ecuador, by Site, according to Radiocarbon Year before Present (RCYBP)

Site, culture, and phase	Lab and lab no.	Uncalibrated date RCYBP	Probability calibrated range 68.2% (year B.C.)	Probability calibrated range 95.4% (year B.C.)	Reference
Huasaga					
Pastaza	Ill. State Geological Survey and Teledyne Isotopes				
	ISGS 385	4155 ± 75	2880–2620	2900–2490	Porras 1975
	I 9159	4000 ± 100	2840–2340	2900–2200	Porras 1975
Ipiamais[a]	Yale Univ. Geochronological Labs				
unknown	Y 617	2750 ± 440	1500–300	2100–A.D. 200	Harner 1972
Mamallacta BA-7	Smithsonian Inst.				
Cosanga?	SI 685	3445 ± 140	1930–1530	2150–1400	Ziólkowski et al. 1994
	SI 686	2615 ± 100	900–540	1000–400	Ziólkowski et al. 1994
Pata 1	Smithsonian Inst.				
unknown	Not available	2830 ± 140	1210–830	1450–750	Echeverria n.d.

Notes: Data compiled by A. Rostoker and Marco Vargas A. All calibrations were performed with OxCal software version 3.5 (Ramsey 2000). In some cases, resulting dates may differ from those published elsewhere.
[a] See Porras 1987: 299 (table note). [b] Date may pertain to the Upano Tradition at Yaunchu instead (see Rostoker 1996: 22).

BIBLIOGRAPHY

ATHENS, J. STEPHEN
    1990   The Site of Pumpuentsa and the Pastaza Phase in Southeastern Lowland Ecuador. *Ñawpa Pacha* 24 (1986): 111–124.

BOLAÑOS, M., MARIA MOREIRA, ROCÍO MURILLO, AND ALFREDO SANTAMARÍA
    n.d.   Rescate arqueológico en la nueva vía interoceánica: Presentado a constructora Norberto Odebrecht y Andrade Gutiérrez. INPC, Departamento de Arqueología, 1999.

DELGADO, FLORENCIO
    n.d.   Prospección sistemática, rescate monitoreo arqueológico del Proyecto de Desarollo Campo Villano: Bloque 10. Report submitted to the Instituto Nacional de Patrimonio Cultural del Ecuador, Quito, 1999.

ECHEVERRIA, JOSÉ
    n.d.   Informe final del proyecto de investigación arqueológica realizada en la Plataforma Pata 1, en el derecho de vía de la carretera (8 km) y en la Plataforma Palo Azul del Bloque 18 de Cayman International Company, región Amazónica ecuatoriana. Report submitted to the Instituto Nacional de Patrimonio Cultural del Ecuador, Quito, 1999.

HARNER, MICHAEL J.
    1972   *The Jívaro: People of the Sacred Waterfalls.* Natural History Press, New York.

MARCOS, JORGE G.
    1998   A Reassessment of the Chronology of the Ecuadorian Formative. In *El area septentrional andina: Arqueología y etnohistoria* (Mercedes Guinea, ed.). Biblioteca Abya-Yala/IFEA, Quito.

MARCOS, JORGE G., AND BOGOMIL OBELIC
    1998 ^{14}C and TL Chronology for the Ecuadorian Formative. In *El Area septentrional andina: Arqueologia y etnohistoria* (Mercedes Guinea, ed.). Biblioteca Abya-Yala/IFEA, Quito.

PORRAS, PEDRO
    1975   El Formativo en el valle Amazónico del Ecuador: Fase Pastaza. *Revista de la Universidad Católica* (Quito) 10: 75–136.
    1980   *Arqueología del Ecuador* (2d ed.). Artes Gráficas Señal, Quito.
    1987   *Investigaciones arqueologicas a las faldas del Sangay: Tradición Upano.* Centro de Investigaciones Arqueológicas, Universidad Católica, Quito.
    1989   Investigations at the Sangay Mound Complex. *National Geographic Research* 5(3): 374–381.

ROSTAIN, STÉPHEN
    1999   Secuencia arqueólogica en montículos del valle del Upano en la Amazonia ecuatoriana. *Bulletin de l'Institut Français d'Études Andines* 28(1): 53–89.

ROSTOKER, ARTHUR G.
    1996   *An Archaeological Collection from Eastern Ecuador.* Treganza Anthropology Museum Papers 18, San Francisco State University, San Francisco.

n.d.a   A New Look at Spatial Organization of a Prehistoric Mound Site in Eastern Ecuador (Yaunchu, Middle Upano Valley). Paper presented at the 17th Annual Northeast Conference on Andean and Amazonian Archaeology and Ethnohistory, Binghamton, N.Y., October 17–18, 1998.

n.d.b   Preliminary Results and Implications of Recent Investigations and Analysis of Prehistoric Spatial Organization at Yaunchu, Eastern Ecuador. Paper presented at the 39th Annual Meeting of the Institute of Andean Studies, Berkeley, Calif., January 8–9, 1999.

n.d.c   Recent Investigation and Analysis at Yaunchu, Eastern Ecuador. Paper presented at the 64th Annual Meeting of the Society for American Archaeology, Chicago, March 24–28, 1999.

SALAZAR, ERNESTO

1998   De vuelta al Sangay: Investigaciones arqueológicas en el Alto Upano, Amazonia ecuatoriana. *Bulletin de l'Institut Français de Études Andines* 27(2): 213–240.

SANCHEZ MOSQUERA, AMELIA M.

n.d.   Adenda al Informe de las excavaciones en el Sitio Grefa, Sectores 1, 2, y 3, Comuna Sumac Sacha, provincia de Napo, Ecuador. Report submitted to the Instituto Nacional de Patrimonio Cultural del Ecuador, Quito, March 1999.

ZIÓLKOWSKI, MARIUSZ S., MIECZYSLAW F. PAZDUR, ANDRZEJ KRZANOWSKI, AND ADAM MICHCZYNSKI

n.d.   Andes: Radiocarbon Database for Bolivia, Ecuador, and Peru. Andean Archaeological Mission of the Institute for Archaeology, Warsaw University, Warsaw, and Gliwice Radiocarbon Laboratory, Institute of Physics, Silesian Technical University, Gliwice, Poland, 1994.

APPENDIX D

Formative Period Chronology for the Southern Highlands of Ecuador

J. SCOTT RAYMOND
UNIVERSITY OF CALGARY

This Appendix presents the radiocarbon dates for the Formative period in the southern highlands of Ecuador, specifically for sites in the provinces of Azuay, Cañar, and Loja. Twenty-nine radiocarbon assays and their calibrated calendrical ranges are provided in Table D1, divided into two groups, the first with sites in Cañar and Azuay and the second in Loja. Within each of the groupings the radiocarbon assays are listed from earliest to latest. For each listing the radiocarbon date is given in radiocarbon years before present together with the standard error (RYBP ± SE). Each date was calibrated with the OxCal program, version 3.5, and the calendrical dates are given as age ranges at 68.2% probability and 95.4% probability.

As James Zeidler notes in Appendix A, there are far more Formative period radiocarbon assays from the coastal region than from the highlands or the Oriente. For the southern highlands the dates come from just seven sites. There is as yet no refined relative ceramic chronology for the region comparable to that of the coastal region, a further indication of the disproportionate attention the various regions of Ecuador have received from archaeologists.

The range of radiocarbon dates from the southern highlands falls mostly within the Late Formative period, as defined for the coastal chronology (see Appendix A; Marcos 1998), which fits with Bruhns's (this volume; 1989; Bruhns, Burton, and Miller, 1990) comparative study of ceramic styles. An exception is the early date of 3928 ± 60 BP (BM 896) from Cerro Narrío, which is suggestive of an occupation toward the end of the Early Formative. Robert Braun (1982) argued that Cerro Narrío was occupied from the beginning of the Early Formative, on the basis of his seriation of ceramics from Cerro Narrío and comparisons with coastal sequences. Karen Bruhns (this volume) argues cogently that ceramic styles from Cerro Narrío are no earlier than the Late Formative, from comparisons with the ceramic sequence at Pirincay, and she correctly points out that the deviant radiocarbon date came from a disturbed context.

Uncertainty about the age range of the occupations at Cerro Narrío is likely to continue, since the site has been badly disturbed by *huaqueros.* The onus seems to be on those who argue for an earlier occupation to find convincing evidence. The early radiocarbon date, however, may well be indicative of an occupation, but the question is *what kind of occupation.* In Appendix A Zeidler suggests that there may have been a lighter occupation in the highlands than on the coast during the Formative, especially the Early Formative, which might account for lesser amount of evidence. Additionally, we need to take into account the differential probability that evidence of occupation will survive. On the coast, if we compare the coastal valleys, such as the Valdivia valley, with the huge floodplain of the Guayas, the bias of preservation is overwhelmingly on the side of the smaller, drier valleys. From Bruhns's account of flooding, erosion, and sedimentation in the Paute valley, the probability seems low that evidence would survive of small Formative villages situated along the floodplains of the highland valleys. We clearly need a great deal more research in the southern highlands before we can know with a high degree of confidence just how early sedentary village life began there.

Table D1

Formative Period Radiocarbon Chronology for the Southern Highlands of Ecuador, by Site, according to Province, from Earliest to Most Recent Radiocarbon Year before Present (RCYBP)

Site by province	Lab and lab. no.	Uncalibrated date RCYBP	Probability calibrated range		Reference
			68.2% (year B.C.)	95.4% (year B.C.)	
Cañar and Azuay					
Cerro Narrío	British Museum BM 896	3928 ± 60	2550–2300	2580–2200	Burleigh, Hewson, and Meeks 1977
Pirincay	Cambridge Q 3191	3170 ± 120	1610–1260	1750–1050	Bruhns, Burton, and Miller 1990
	Oxford Radiocarbon Accelerator Unit OxA 1376	3000 ± 120	1400–1050	1550–900	Bruhns et al. 1990
Chaullabamba	British Museum BM 907	2964 ± 50	1290–1050	1380–1010	Burleigh and Hewson 1979
	BM 897	2909 ± 55	1220–1000	1270–920	Burleigh et al. 1977
	BM 906	2800 ± 48	1020–890	1130–830	Burleigh and Hewson 1979
Pirincay	British Museum BM 901	2697 ± 49	900–805	970–790	Burleigh et al. 1977
	BM 903	2635 ± 77	910–590	100–450	Burleigh et al. 1977
	BM 900	2581 ± 66	830–540	900–410	Burleigh et al. 1977
	Cambridge Q 3195	2525 ± 40	800–540	800–510	Bruhns et al. 1990
El Carmen (Bajo)	British Museum BM 905	2446 ± 50	760–400	770–400	Burleigh and Hewson 1979
Pirincay	Oxford Radiocarbon Accelerator Unit OxA 948	2440 ± 70	760–400	770–390	Marcos and Obelic 1998
El Carmen	British Museum BM 904	2334 ± 61	520–230	800–200	Burleigh et al. 1977
Pirincay	Cambridge Q 3161	2160 ± 60	360–110	380–50	Bruhns et al. 1990
	Q 3190	2250 ± 70	400–200	410–90	Bruhns et al. 1990
	Q 3196	2260 ± 75	400–200	520–90	Bruhns et al. 1990
Uchukay	British Museum BM 899	2242 ± 48	390–200	400–180	Burleigh et al. 1977

(cont.)

Table D1 *(cont.)*
Formative Period Radiocarbon Chronology for the Southern Highlands of Ecuador, by Site, according to Province, from Earliest to Most Recent Radiocarbon Year before Present (RCYBP)

Site by province	Lab and lab. no.	Uncalibrated date RCYBP	Probability calibrated range		Reference
			68.2% (year B.C.)	95.4% (year B.C.)	
			Loja		
Trapichillo	Centre de Recherches Geodynamiques[a] CRG 301	3480 ± 90	1920–1680	2050–1500	Guffroy 1987
Putushío	Hannover Hv 16798	3420 ± 255	2150–1400	2500–1000	Ziółkowski et al. n.d.
	Hv 16799	3210 ± 180	1740–1260	1950–1000	Marcos and Obelic 1998
La Vega	Centre de Recherches Geodynamiques[a] CRG 295	2900 ± 60	1220–990	1290–910	Guffroy 1987
	CRG 287	2870 ± 80	1210–920	1290–830	Guffroy 1987
Putushío	Hannover Hv 16797	2815 ± 95	1120–830	1260–800	Marcos and Obelic 1998
La Vega	Centre de Recherches Geodynamiques[a] CRG 211	2787 ± 94	1050–820	1220–790	Guffroy 1987
Putushío	Hannover Hv 15831	2780 ± 120	1110–800	1400–750	Ziółkowski et al. n.d.
	Hv 15835	2705 ± 155	1150–550	1300–400	Ziółkowski et al. n.d.
	Hv 14707	2560 ± 85	820–520	840–400	Marcos and Obelic 1998
	Hv 15832	2535 ± 120	810–430	950–350	Marcos and Obelic 1998
	Hv 14706	2450 ± 65	760–400	770–400	Marcos and Obelic 1998
	Hv 14704	2360 ± 130	800–200	800–100	Marcos and Obelic 1998

Notes: Data compiled by J. S. Raymond. All calibrations made with the OxCal software program version 3.5 (Ramsey 1995). Culture and phase information has been omitted because of unresolved issues of standardization.
[a] The Centre de Recherches Geodynamiques is located at the Université Pierre et Marie Curie.

BIBLIOGRAPHY

BRAUN, ROBERT
  1982   The Formative as Seen from the Southern Ecuadorian Highlands. In *Primer Simposio de Correlaciones Antropologicas Andino–Mesoamerica* (J. G. Marcos and P. Norton, eds.): 41–100. Escuela Superior Politécnica del Litoral, Guayaquil.

BRUHNS, KAREN O.
  1989   Intercambio entre la sierra y la costa en el Formativo Tardio, nuevas evidencias del Azuay. In *Relaciones interculturales en el area ecuatorial del pácifico durante la epoca precolombina* (J. F. Bouchard and M. Guinea, eds.): 57–74. BAR International Series 503. British Archaeological Reports, Oxford.

BRUHNS, KAREN O., JAMES H. BURTON, AND GEORGE R. MILLER
  1990   Excavations at Pirincay in the Paute Valley of Southern Ecuador, 1985-1988. *Antiquity* 64: 221–233.

BURLEIGH, RICHARD, AND ANDREW HEWSON
  1979   British Museum Natural Radiocarbon Measurements XI. *Radiocarbon* 21(3): 339–352.

BURLEIGH, RICHARD, ANDREW HEWSON, AND NIGEL MEEKS
  1977   British Museum Natural Radiocarbon Measurements IX. *Radiocarbon* 19(2): 144–160.

GUFFROY, JEAN
  1987   La Periode Formative. In *Loja préhispanique, recherches archéologiques dans les Andes méridionales de l'equateur* (J. Guffroy, ed.): 61–139. Editions Recherches sur les Civilisations, Paris.

MARCOS, JORGE G.
  1998   A Reassessment of the Chronology of the Ecuadorian Formative. In *El area septentrional andina, arqueología y etnohistoria* (Mercedes Guinea, ed.): 295–346.

MARCOS, JORGE G., AND BOGOMIL OBELIC
  1998 ^{14}C and TL Chronology for the Ecuadorian Formative. In *El area septentrional andina, arqueología y etnohistoria* (Mercedes Guinea, ed.): 247–259.

ZIÓLKOWSKI, MARIUSZ S., MIECZYSLAW F. PAZDUR, ANDRZEJ KRZANOWSKI, AND ADAM MICHCZYNSKI
  n.d.   Andes: Radiocarbon Database for Bolivia, Equador and Peru. Andean Archaeological Mission of the Institute of Archaeology, Warsaw University, Warsaw, and Gliwice Radiocarbon Laboratory, Institute of Physics, Silesian Technical University, Gliwice, Poland, 2001.

Index

Note: Page references followed by f indicate a figure; n, a footnote; and t, a table. These elements are not singled out in inclusive page references.